# FREQUENTLY USED SYMBOLS (CONTINUED)

| | |
|---|---|
| MACRS | Modified Accelerated Cost Recovery System |
| $M_e$ | Market Value of the Stock Trading Ex Rights |
| MNC | Multinational Company |
| MPR | Market Price Ratio of Exchange |
| MRP | Materials Requirement Planning |
| $M_w$ | Market Value of the Stock With Rights |
| $n$ | - Number of Periods—Typically Years |
| | - Number of Outcomes Considered |
| | - Years to Maturity |
| $N$ | - Number of Rights Needed to Purchase One Share of Stock |
| | - Number of Shares of Common Stock Obtainable with One Warrant |
| | - Number of Days Payment can be Delayed by Giving up the Cash Discount |
| $N_d$ | Net Proceeds from the Sale of Debt (Bond) |
| $NE$ | Number of Shares Needed to Elect a Certain Number of Directors |
| $N_n$ | Net Proceeds from the Sale of New Common Stock |
| $N_p$ | Net Proceeds from the Sale of the Preferred Stock |
| NPV | Net Present Value |
| $O$ | - Total Number of Shares of Common Stock Outstanding |
| | - Order Cost per Order |
| OC | Operating Cycle |
| $P_o$ | Value of Common Stock |
| PAC | Preauthorized Check |
| PD | Preferred Stock Dividend |
| P/E | Price/Earnings Ratio |
| PMT | Amount of Payment |
| Pr | Probability |

| | |
|---|---|
| PV | Present Value |
| $PVA_n$ | Present-Value of an $n$-Year Annuity |
| $PVIF_{k,n}$ | Present-Value Interest Factor for a Single Amount Discounted at $k$ Percent for $n$ Periods |
| $PVIFA_{k,n}$ | Present-Value Interest Factor for an Annuity When Interest Is Discounted Annually at $k$ Percent for $n$ Periods |
| $Q$ | - Order Quantity in Units |
| | - Sales Quantity in Units |
| RADR | Risk-Adjusted Discount Rate |
| $R_e$ | Theoretical Value of a Right When Stock Is Trading Ex Rights |
| RE | Ratio of Exchange |
| $R_F$ | Risk-Free Rate of Interest |
| ROA | Return on Total Assets |
| ROE | Return on Equity |
| $R_w$ | Theoretical Value of a Right When Stock Is Selling With Rights |
| $S$ | - Subscription Price of the Stock |
| | - Usage in Units per Period |
| SML | Security Market Line |
| $T$ | Firm's Marginal Tax Rate |
| $t$ | Time |
| TN | Total Number of Directors to Be Elected |
| TVW | Theoretical Value of a Warrant |
| V | Value of an Asset or Firm |
| VC | Variable Operating Cost per Unit |
| WACC | Weighted Average Cost of Capital |
| $w_j$ | Proportion of a Specific Source of Financing $j$ in the Firm's Capital Structure |
| WMCC | Weighted Marginal Cost of Capital |
| $\sigma$ | Standard Deviation |
| $\Sigma$ | Summation Sign |

# FOUNDATIONS

## OF

## MANAGERIAL

## FINANCE

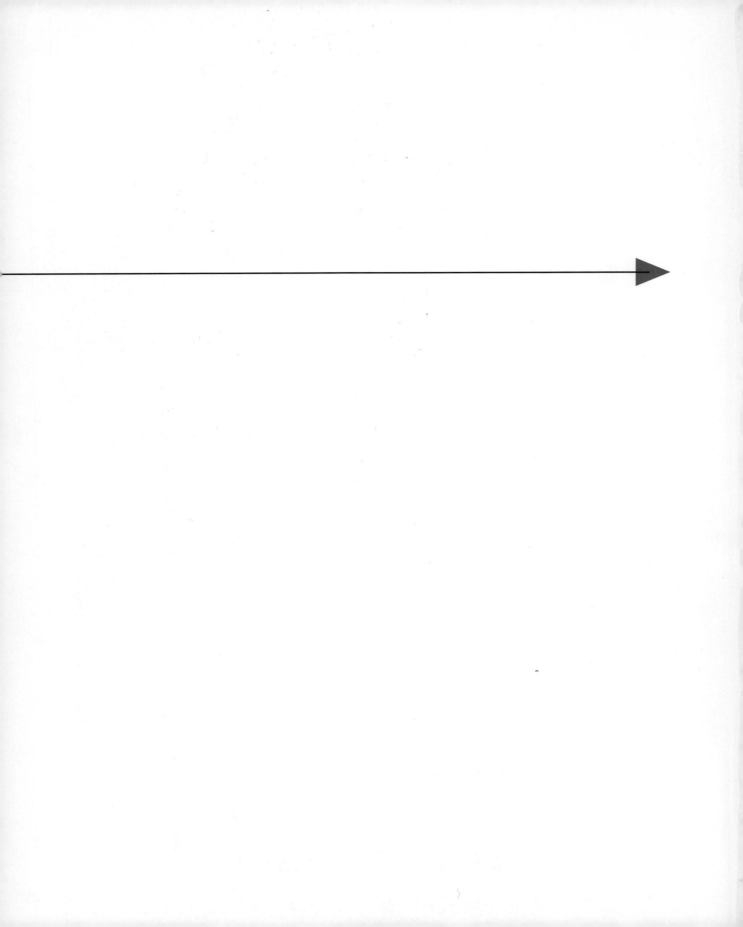

FOURTH EDITION

# FOUNDATIONS
# OF
# MANAGERIAL
# FINANCE

**Lawrence J. Gitman**
*San Diego State University*

 *HarperCollinsCollegePublishers*

Acquisitions Editor: *Kirsten D. Sandberg*
Developmental Editor: *Joan-Marie Cannon*
Project Coordination and Text Design: *York Production Services*
Cover Designer: *Kay Petronio*
Electronic Production Manager: *Christine Pearson*
Electronic Page Makeup: *York Graphic Services, Inc.*
Printer and Binder: *R.R. Donnelley*

**Foundations of Managerial Finance, Fourth Edition**

Library of Congress Cataloging-in-Publication Data

Gitman, Lawrence J.
    Foundations of managerial finance / Lawrence J. Gitman.—4th ed.
       p.     cm.
    Revised edition of: Basic managerial finance. 3rd ed. 1992.
    Includes index.
    ISBN 0-673-99567-4
    1. Business enterprises—Finance. 2. Corporations—Finance.
I. Gitman, Lawrence J. Basic managerial finance. II. Title.
HG4026.G59 1995
658.15—dc20                                                94-37810
                                                              CIP

95 96 97  9 8 7 6 5 4 3

To all teachers of finance,
with the hope that this text will enhance
their ability to communicate effectively an understanding
of managerial finance to their students, our future
business leaders

# BRIEF CONTENTS

# DETAILED CONTENTS

# ▶ P A R T I
## Introduction to Managerial Finance 1

# C H A P T E R 1
## Finance and the Financial Manager 2

# C H A P T E R 2
## The Firm's Environment 28

# ▶ P A R T   I I
# Financial Analysis
# and Planning   55

# C H A P T E R   3
## Financial Statements,
## Depreciation, and Cash Flow   56

# C H A P T E R   4
## Analysis of Financial
## Statements   84

### ▶ P A R T V
### Long-Term Investment Decisions 377

### C H A P T E R 14
### Capital Budgeting and Cash Flow Principles 378

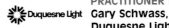

▶ **P A R T   V I I**
## Special Managerial Finance Topics  579

● **C H A P T E R   21**
### Mergers, LBOs, Divestitures, and Failure  580

● **C H A P T E R   20**
### Convertibles, Warrants, and Options  558

C H A P T E R    22

## International Managerial Finance   618

# ▶ A P P E N D I X E S

# LIST OF COMPANIES

Page numbers followed by B indicate boxed material; page numbers followed by N indicate notes; page numbers followed by T indicate tables.

# TO THE INSTRUCTOR

Under its former title of *Basic Managerial Finance*, this book has consistently met the needs of the introductory finance course in undergraduate business degree programs. It has also worked quite well in executive training programs and seminars, as well as in technical and continuing education. The fourth edition not only continues to satisfy market needs, but anticipates change.

Users asked that the title more accurately reflect how the streamlined, straightforward, and easily understandable approach blends the traditional accounting orientation with modern valuation techniques. Many recommended the new title, *Foundations of Managerial Finance (FMF)*, as the best alternative. Also, *Foundations* features an enhanced learning system that integrates pedagogy and color with concepts and practical applications. This system equips instructors to concentrate on the more difficult theories, concepts, and techniques needed to make keen financial decisions in an ever-changing and increasingly competitive global business environment. The improved pedagogy and generous use of examples also make the fourth edition an easily accessible resource for long-distance learning and self-study programs, as well as for large lecture-driven courses open to non-finance majors.

Since the previous edition, however, much has changed in both boardroom and classroom. Instructors and students alike have access to a seemingly infinite supply of data, and must somehow make sense of it all. The format of *Foundations* strives to help users do just that: To organize and use information in new and exciting ways. The book comes in two parts: a hardcover, four-color textbook; and a paperback, two-color book, subtitled *Applications*. This format allows students and professors to take only what they need, where they need it. For example, students can read the text outside the classroom, and bring the *Applications* book to each class, where instructors work through problems and cases. And instructors can tote the *Applications* with solutions and lecture notes into class. Each component now fits easily into briefcase or book bag, along with course notes, study guides, and business calculators. From computer lab to library or from office to lecture hall, the fourth edition of *Foundations of Managerial Finance* can go wherever users need to be.

# Major Changes in the Fourth Edition

## Reengineered Teaching/Learning System

**The *FMF* Teaching/Learning System** ties the two books together by building on proven learning goals (LGs). The LGs, marked by a special icon in the margin, are listed at the start of each chapter, tied to first-level heads, reviewed point by point at the chapter's end, reviewed and marked as well in the *Applications* book and *Study Guide,* and referenced in the Instuctor's Manual, Lecture Notes, and Test Bank. Now more than ever, students will know what to learn, where to find it in the chapter, and whether they've mastered it. Moreover, instructors can build lectures and assignments around the LGs. Following this preface is an eight-page Visual Guide to the *FMF* text package that walks users through all of the components of the *FMF* Teaching/Learning System.

**The *FMF* Toolbox** is a key visual aid in the Teaching/Learning System. The Toolbox is a cluster of icons used throughout *Foundations* in a number of ways. Inside the Toolbox, students find the learning tools and resources—learning goals, software tutorials, problem-solving disk routines, and spreadsheet templates—available to them as they attempt to master each learning goal. Documentation for the software tools appear in Appendix C, "Instructions for Using the *FMF* Disk," in *Applications,* and in Appendix B, "Using Computers and Spreadsheets in Managerial Finance" in *Foundations.*

**The *FMF* Example Method** is also a key part of the Teaching/Learning System because it infuses practical presentations into the learning process. Where applicable in this new edition, the solution of each realistic example demonstrates the use of time lines, tables, and business/financial calculators. Students can easily spot the calculator keystrokes of inputs, functions, and outputs in discussions and examples of time-value techniques in Chapter 11 and subsequent applications of those techniques. Financial tables are available in both Appendix A of the text and as a handy laminated card inserted into the *Applications* book.

**Chapter Cases** in the *Applications* book enable students to strengthen their practical understanding of financial techniques. Without the added expense of a separate case book, students can apply what they have learned in realistic settings. For example, in Chapter 12, students try their hand at assessing the effect of a proposed risky investment on a firm's bond and stock values.

## Improved Organization

The text's flexible organizational structure was carefully designed to ensure a smooth transition from accounting to managerial finance topics. It is structured around the corporate balance sheet, with linkages to share price. Various financial decisions are examined as they relate to the balance sheet and in terms of their influence on return, risk, and share price. Although the text is sequential, instructors can assign almost any chapter as a self-contained unit, thereby customizing the text to various course lengths and various teaching strategies. Because each instructor has particular topic preferences, the book's coverage is intentionally both extensive and flexible.

Specific improvements include the following: The chapter on financial statements, depreciation, and cash flow now begins Part II on financial analysis and planning so that students can review key accounting and basic cash flow concepts just prior to learning important analytical and planning techniques. To serve as a motivational device, the material on career opportunities in the field of managerial finance appears in Chapter 1 rather than in an end-of-text appendix. Part V, Chapters 14 and 15, now focuses solely on long-term investment decisions, and Part VI, Chapters 16 to 20, which focuses on long-term financing decisions, now begins with the chapter on capital structure and dividend policy. The restructuring of Parts V and VI distinguishes more clearly between the firm's investment and financing decisions to help students better understand these two key activities of the financial manager.

Part VII has been added to this edition to cover two important special topics in managerial finance—mergers, LBOs, divestitures, and failure in Chapter 21 and international managerial finance in a completely new chapter, Chapter 22. Note that *in addition to* being covered in the separate chapter, the international material continues to be integrated throughout the text using brief discussions of chapter topics. For example, the discussion of the consolidation of international financial statements in Chapter 3 is integrated into the chapter learning goals and end-of-chapter summaries in the text and problem material in the *Applications* book. Inclusion of the two special topic chapters allows interested instructors and students to expand coverage beyond the more fundamental topics covered in the first twenty chapters.

The first three parts are devoted to the firm's environment and short-term operations, and the next three parts are concerned with long-term financial topics. Finally, the new seventh part, "Special Managerial Finance Topics," includes the two chapters discussed above.

## Stronger Ties Between Theory and Practice

Practitioner Previews open each chapter with intriguing insights into the financial management of actual companies. These chapter launchers introduce students to industry leaders who explain in their own words the relevance of forthcoming material from a practical point of view. For example, in Chapter 11, Leo Vannoni, assistant treasurer of Reebok International Ltd., discusses how his firm uses time value of money concepts.

For their contributions to the Practitioner Previews special thanks go to the following:

**Carter Barrett**
*System Vice-President*
*Wachovia Bank of Georgia*
**Glynis Bryan**
*Assistant Treasurer*
*Ryder System Inc.*
**Mark R. Collman**
*Senior Financial Manager*
*Syncordia Corporation*

**Virginia Dennett**
*Director and Team Leader*
*Bank of Boston*
**William Dordelman**
*Assistant Treasurer*
*Comcast, Inc.*
**Sherrlyn J. Dunn**
*Vice-President, Finance*
*Hunter Industries*

**Karen Edlund**
*Assistant Treasurer*
*M/A-COM*
**William Flaherty**
*Director of Mergers and*
*Acquisitions*
*Blockbuster Entertainment*
**William C. Goings**
*Senior Business Analyst*
*Amoco Production Co.*
**Charles F. Kane**
*Director, Finance and*
*Administration*
*Stratus Computer, Inc.*
**Christopher Knight**
*Controller*
*Wilson N. Jones Memorial Hospital*
**Scott McNelis**
*Manager, Corporate Financial*
*Analysis*
*Hershey Foods Corporation*
**Martin Malk**
*Chief Financial Officer*
*Hotel Del Coronado*
**George V. Novello**
*Managing Director and Head of*
*Equity Mutual Funds*
*Greenwich Street Advisors*

**Christopher H. Savage**
*Assistant Controller and Director*
*The Gillette Company*
**Stewart A. Schoder**
*Director, International Treasury*
*Sara Lee Corporation*
**Gary Schwass**
*Chief Financial Officer*
*Duquesne Light*
**Irena Simmons**
*Manager of Treasury Services*
*Lotus Development*
**Woodrow A. Sutton**
*Treasurer*
*Encyclopaedia Britannica, Inc.*
**Samme Thompson**
*Senior Vice President*
*Kidder, Peabody & Co.*
**Steven R. Wasserman**
*Director of Investments and*
*Financial Analysis*
*EG&G Inc.*
**Leo Vannoni**
*Assistant Treasurer*
*Reebok International Ltd.*

All new Finance in Action boxed examples offer insights into important topics through real company experiences, both large and small. Chapter 11, for example, illustrates the concept of effective rates of return by taking a closer look at annual rates of return of mutual funds over a ten-year period. Each Finance in Action box is classified with regard to one of five themes: Careers, Ethics, In the News, International, and Small Business.

The *Applications* book includes new *Lotus 1-2-3* spreadsheet problems, keyed to the more complex problems in various chapters. The *FMF Disk,* shrinkwrapped with new copies of the *Applications* book at no additional cost, now includes *Lotus* preprogrammed templates so as to familiarize students with a popular commercial spreadsheet program, not to make them experts on *Lotus.* For quick reference a spreadsheet icon appears next to applicable problems with documentation in Appendix C. Appendix B in the text, "Using Computers and Spreadsheets in Managerial Finance," provides insight into the use of computers and spreadsheets in managerial finance today.

## More Contemporary Coverage, Including Key Tax Provisions of the *Omnibus Budget Reconciliation Act of 1993*

To keep course content current, my colleagues have come to expect and rely on updated coverage of important current and emerging issues, instruments, and techniques affecting the practice of financial management. Consistent exposure to current practical applications enables students to walk away from the book and onto the job with forward-looking, practical insight, rather than a merely static conceptual grasp of the challenges ahead. In addition to the many current Finance in Action items, contemporary topics include the following:

- Current thinking on agency costs relating to incentive and performance plans, the associated issue of executive compensation, and the financial manager's role in total quality management (TQM) (Chapter 1)
- The key tax provisions of the recently passed *Omnibus Budget Reconciliation Act of 1993* and the changing role of financial institutions (Chapter 2)
- Data on recent yields of popular marketable securities (Chapter 8)
- The problem faced by small businesses in managing their accounts receivable (Chapter 9)
- Efficient methods for using business/financial calculators to streamline various time value of money calculations (Chapter 11)
- Insights into the stock valuation activities of professional securities analysts (Chapter 12)
- The linkage between the optimal capital budget (financing and investment equilibrium) and the common presence of a management-imposed budget constraint (Chapter 13)
- Recognition of removal and cleanup costs in the analysis of replacing old assets (Chapter 14)
- Practical insight into determination of the optimal capital structure and dividend reinvestment plans (Chapter 16)
- Recent trends in the investment banking industry (Chapter 17)
- The use of preferred stock and the latest treatment of common stock voting rights (Chapter 19)
- The effects of contingent securities on earnings and the cause of market premiums on convertibles (Chapter 20)
- NAFTA and the European Open Market (Chapter 22)

## Key Content Improvements in the Fourth Edition

Because users often like to know where new material appears, here are the significant but less sweeping changes made in the fourth edition:

**Chapter 1**  on the role of finance and the financial manager now includes summary tables on career opportunities in both financial services and managerial finance, describes the basic forms of business organization (formerly covered in Chapter 2), introduces the concept of stakeholder wealth preservation, provides timely insights into the agency issue, including descriptions of incentive and performance plans and discussion of the current thinking with regard to executive compensation, and discusses the financial manager's role in total quality management (TQM).

**Chapter 2**  on the firm's environment now begins with discussion of business taxation, including comparison of average and marginal tax rates, contains updated coverage of the changing role of financial institutions, and describes securities offerings and trading—the role of the investment banker and interpretation of bond and stock quotes.

**Chapter 3** on financial statements, depreciation, and cash flow now uses the modified accelerated cost recovery system (MACRS) depreciation reference rather than ACRS and includes a streamlined step-by-step presentation of procedures for preparing the statement of cash flows.

**Chapter 4** on the analysis of financial statements includes an evaluation of common-size income statements, introduces the return on total assets (ROA) in place of the ROI, and streamlines discussion of the modified DuPont formula.

**Chapter 5** on breakeven analysis and leverage now includes a brief discussion of the ability to control leverage.

**Chapter 6** on financial planning has an updated look at the overall planning process, includes added practical insights, and explains more effectively the interpretation of the "plug" figure used in applying the judgmental approach to preparation of the pro forma balance sheet.

**Chapter 7** on working capital fundamentals stresses even more the importance of short-term financial management.

**Chapter 8** on cash and marketable securities now includes more practical insights on cash management and recent yield data on the popular marketable securities.

**Chapter 9** on accounts receivable and inventory briefly discusses the rationale for extending credit, describes the small-business problem associated with managing accounts receivable, and contains a summary table describing each of the basic collection techniques.

**Chapter 10** on sources of short-term financing describes the general formula for use in finding the effective interest rate on a loan and adds practical insights to the discussions of various short-term financing techniques and vehicles.

**Chapter 11** on the time value of money now opens with a brief section on the role of time value in finance, with a conceptual comparison of future and present values using time lines, and an explanation of how to use financial tables and business/financial calculators as important computational tools. Keystrokes are shown for all calculator routines. As a result, discussion of specific financial tables is no longer necessary. The present value of a perpetuity is now included in the discussion of the present value of cash flow streams.

**Chapter 12**  on risk, return, and valuation has been tightened up and now includes an improved discussion of the role of sensitivity analysis in assessing an asset's risk, contains an added caveat under coverage of common stock valuation models, and concludes with a look at the valuation activities of professional securities analysts.

**Chapter 13**  on the cost of capital is now consistent in its ongoing example, and ties the process of making financing and investment decisions to the common presence of a management-imposed budget constraint.

**Chapter 14**  on capital budgeting and cash flow principles now includes a clarified comparison of expansion and replacement decisions, presents a new streamlined and accessible format for finding a project's initial investment, and refers to both removal and cleanup costs associated with replacing old assets.

**Chapter 15**  on capital budgeting techniques now includes the formulas for finding NPV and IRR, and contains a brief discussion of why capital rationing should not exist.

**Chapter 16**  on capital structure and dividend policy includes a brief discussion of the practical reality of finding a firm's optimal capital structure and enhanced coverage of dividend reinvestment plans.

**Chapter 17**  on investment banking's role in raising long-term funds includes discussions of each of the most common roles played by investment bankers in security offerings, contains a figure depicting the breakdown of gross commissions, and compares public offerings to private placements.

**Chapter 18**  on long-term debt and leasing includes improved discussions of bond call features and financial (or capital) leases.

**Chapter 19**  on preferred and common stock now includes a new discussion on the use of preferred stock, and includes enhanced discussions of both the voting and preemptive rights of common stockholders.

**Chapter 20**  on convertibles, warrants, and options provides a new accounting-oriented description of the effects on earnings of contingent securities as well as a brief explanation of why market premiums often exist on convertibles.

**Chapter 21**  on mergers, LBOs, divestitures, and failure has been refined and updated to include more recent examples and practical wisdom with respect to corporate restructuring and business failure.

**Chapter 22**  on international managerial finance is a completely new chapter that augments the international material integrated throughout the text with cohesive coverage of all important aspects of international managerial finance. Rather than merely repeat and summarize the integrated international discussions, this chapter offers a fresh perspective that is consistent in content and order of presentation with the chapter discussions. Coverage includes an introduction to emerging trading blocs—both NAFTA and the European Open Market—along with current statistics and insights.

## Other Pedagogical Features

Progress Review Questions appear at the end of each section of the chapter (positioned before the next first-level head) and are marked with a special design element. As students progress through the chapter, they can test their understanding of each key theory, concept, and technique before moving on to the next section within the chapter.

End-of-chapter summaries are now keyed to learning goals and the *FMF Disk* using icons from the Toolbox. A vibrant, contemporary design, with pedagogical use of four colors in most charts, tables, and graphs, draws reader attention to features of the learning system. Marginal material includes running lists of key terms and definitions and equations references. Key terms are boldfaced in the index for easy access to the glossary entry. All figures have brief captions that highlight their content.

A list of companies discussed in the text appears just before this preface on pages xix and xx, in case professors want to assign specific companies for further or ongoing analysis. The endpapers now display frequently used symbols, since many students initially find the notation challenging.

# Supplements to the Learning System

## Teaching Tools for Instructors

**Instructor's Manual**[1]    *Compiled by Hadi Salavitabar, State University of New York at New Paltz, and Lawrence J. Gitman.* This comprehensive resource really pulls the teaching tools together so that professors can use the text easily and effectively in the classroom. Each chapter provides an overview of key topics, references to the *FMF Disk,* and detailed answers and solutions to Progress Review Questions from the text and problems and chapter cases found in the *Applications* book, all of which Hadi and I worked out carefully to ensure accuracy and consistency.

**Testing Materials**    *Created by Hadi Salavitabar, SUNY-New Paltz.* Thoroughly revised to accommodate changes in the text and significantly expanded to increase user flexibility, this test bank contains nearly 2,500 items, including all-new true/false questions, significantly improved multiple-choice items, and

---

[1]The *Instructor's Manual* includes the answers to all of the Progress Review Questions from the text as well as the answers to all (both the odd- and even-numbered) problems in the *Applications* book.

rejuvenated problems and essay questions. For quick test selection and con-struction, each chapter features a handy chart for identifying type of ques-tion, skill tested by learning goal, and level of difficulty. Because the test bank is available in both printed and electronic formats—ASCII files, WordPerfect word processing IBM-compatible files, and DOS or Macintosh TestMaster files—instructors should contact their HarperCollins representative to deter-mine which format best meets their testing needs.

Instructors can also download the TestMaster version of the test bank into *QuizMaster,* an on-line testing program for IBM and Mac that enables users to conduct timed or untimed exams at computer workstations. On completing tests, students can see their scores and view or print a diagnostic report of those topics or objectives requiring more attention. When installed on a lo-cal area network, *QuizMaster* allows instructors to save the scores on disk, print study diagnoses, and monitor progress of students individually or by class sec-tion and by all sections of the course.

**Presentation Tools** *Designed by Thomas J. Liesz, Western State College in Colorado.* Developed from my lecture notes, the *Lecture Outline Transparency System* includes approximately 20 pages per chapter, all formatted so that an instructor can copy them to acetates or integrate them into his or her own notes. To support the more quantitative and challenging course material, each chapter comprises a lecture outline and broad overview of chapter themes; points to introduce transparency acetates; key terms and equations with def-initions, plenty of examples and demonstrations, and worked-out table and time-line solutions; a section of teaching tips; and discussion problems, again with worked-out table and time-line solutions where appropriate. Finally, the *Electronic Transparency System* combines a collection of lecture notes, problems, and figures in a powerful software presentation kit.

**Video Lecture Launchers** These lecture launchers consist of videos from Fox television combined with a *Video Guide by Cecilia L. Wagner, Seton Hall University.* Adopters should ask their local HarperCollins representative about the media supplements to the teaching system, including video segments from *Fox Business News,* selected on the basis of timeliness, relevance to core topics in finance, and high production quality. Topics covered by the videos include ethics, financial markets, financial statements, ratio analysis, leverage, fi-nancial planning, cash management, inventory management, short-term financing, the time value of money, risk, return, and valuation, cost of capital, capital budgeting, capital structure, long-term financing, and issues in international managerial finance.

## Learning Tools for Students

Beyond the book itself students have access to several resources for success in this course.

**FMF Disk** Packaged with new copies of the *Applications* book at no addi-tional cost, your disk contains three useful tools: the *FMF Tutor,* the *FMF Problem-Solver,* and the *FMF Lotus Templates.* Appendix B in the text, "Using Computers and Spreadsheets in Managerial Finance," provides insight into the use of computers and spreadsheets in managerial finance. Documentation and practical advice for using the *FMF Disk* appears in the back of the *Applications* book in Appendix C, "Instructions for using the *FMF Disk*," and in Appendix D, "Key Equations and Disk Routines."

**The FMF Tutor**    written by John Hansen, George Flowers, and Robert Bush, all of *Houston Baptist University*, extends self-testing opportunities beyond those on the printed page. The *Tutor* helps students to identify and solve various types of managerial finance problems. The *Tutor* icon flags all *Tutor* applications in both the *Applications* book and *Study Guide*. Through user-friendly menus, they can access over fifty-five different problem types, constructed by random number generation for an inexhaustible supply of problems with little chance of repetition. Routines include financial ratios, time value of money, valuation, cost of capital, and capital budgeting.

**The FMF Problem Solver**    Programmed by Frederick Rexroad of Yellow Springs, Ohio, this software contains seven short menu-driven programs to accelerate learning by providing an efficient way to perform financial computations. The *Problem-Solver* icon points out all related applications throughout the text, the *Applications* book and *Study Guide*. Referenced to specific text pages for quick review of technique, the routines include financial ratios, breakeven analysis, cash budgets, pro forma statements, time value of money, bond and stock valuation, cost of capital, capital budgeting cash flows, capital budgeting techniques, bond refunding, and lease versus purchase.

**The FMF Lotus Templates**    Developed by Enrique Roberto Lunski, *State University of New York at New Paltz*, provide users with programmed Lotus templates, for inputting data and solving problems using perhaps the most popular and widely accepted practical software application. The template files correspond to selected end-of-chapter problems, and the template file names follow the chapter number and the problem number.

**Study Guide**    (ISBN 0067399032X) Created by Thomas M. Krueger, *University of Wisconsin-LaCrosse*, and D. Anthony Plath, *University of North Carolina-Charlotte*. An integral component of the *FMF* Learning System, this new edition offers many tools for studying finance: an introductory section called "And Now a Word From Our Sponsor" on overcoming the fear of finance, getting the most from the guide, and preparing thoroughly for tests and a unique section titled "Want to Win Friends, Fame, and Fortune?" on effective methods for setting up and solving finance problems, with a step-by-step example. Each chapter includes the following features: chapter review enumerated by learning goals; topical chapter outline, also broken down by learning goals for quick review; applications section including definition, objective items, a sample problem with a detailed solution, and then a full set of problems, some of which allow for use of software on the *FMF Disk*. Answers to definition and multiple-choice items appear in an appendix; however, solutions to problems remain at the end of each chapter. New FMF text packages include, free of charge, Chapter 11 (Time Value of Money) of the *Study Guide* so students can preview this superior learning tool before making a purchase decision, and five pages from the *Study Guide* are shown here on pages xxx to xxxiv.

**This exhibit is a sample page from the *Study Guide* to accompany the fourth edition of Gitman, *Foundations of Managerial Finance*. Please contact your bookstore for ordering information on this effective study tool.**

# Chapter 1

# Finance and the Financial Manager

## CHAPTER SUMMARY

**LG 1** Like most textbooks, the first chapter of *Foundations of Managerial Finance* provides an overview of the discipline, coverage, and textbook structure. Careful reading will provide a base that will enhance comprehension of concepts presented in subsequent chapters. Understanding these concepts will also improve personal financial decisions.

Chapter 1 acquaints the reader with the financial activities and decisions of business. Finance is defined as the art and science of managing money. The "science" aspect corresponds to the process, institutions, markets, and instruments involved in financing business assets, maximizing revenues, and minimizing expenses. The "art" aspect corresponds to the efficient coordination of personnel, processes, and procedures.

Many popular career opportunities exist in finance. Financial services industries such as banking, personal financial planning, investments, and real estate allow individuals to design and deliver financial services and products. Budgeting, cash management, credit administration, and funds procurement are important duties of the financial manager or treasurer. Career opportunities are rapidly arising in international finance for those able to manage the political and exchange rate risks arising from conducting businesses in multiple currencies.

Financial management should be understood by all business executives. Financial management effectiveness and efficiency will dictate the success of every organization, private or public, large or small, profit-seeking or not-for-profit, manufacturing, service, retail, or financial. All managers need a basic understanding of managerial finance, because forecasts and results are measured in financial terms. The objective of maximizing the value of the organization applies to all organizations. Several career opportunities are described in the text.

**LG 2** The three basic forms of business organization are the sole proprietorship, the partnership, and the corporation. A sole proprietorship is a business owned by one person who operates it for his or her own profit. A partnership involves two or more owners doing

**This exhibit is a sample page from the *Study Guide* to accompany the fourth edition of Gitman, *Foundations of Managerial Finance*. Please contact your bookstore for ordering information on this effective study tool.**

relationship between compensation and share price, evidence indicates that maximizing share price is normally the primary goal.

**LG 6** Ethical concerns may reduce the flexibility of financial managers seeking to maximize firm value. Yet, over time, ethical behavior is considered to be necessary for share price maximization. Employment of total quality management (TQM) techniques are consistent with the minimization of agency problems and ethical behavior of the business. Furthermore, productivity appears to increase quality in all financial manager activities.

Chapter 1 concludes with an overview of the text, which was developed around a set of learning objectives. The *toolbox* facilitating mastery of these objectives includes an Applications Workbook and a diskette with three sets of routines. The FMF Tutor includes additional questions for extended practice. Many routine financial calculations and procedures presented in the text can be solved with the FMF Problem-Solver. More complex problems can be solved using the FMF Lotus Template.

This exhibit is a sample page from the *Study Guide* to accompany the fourth edition of Gitman, *Foundations of Managerial Finance*. Please contact your bookstore for ordering information on this effective study tool.

## EXAMPLE PROBLEM

Amy Chen, who we met in Chapter 1, is considering an alternate computer. The alternative would require a lower cash outlay of $50,000, but the total benefits from the new computer (measured in today's dollars) would be a lesser $55,000. Other data from the text problem includes:

| | |
|---|---|
| Benefit of old computer: | $ 35,000 |
| Proceeds of sale of old computer: | 28,000 |
| Net benefit of $80,000 computer: | $ 13,000 |

Should Amy select the $80,000 computer described in the text or the $55,000 computer?

## EXAMPLE SOLUTION

1. *State the Problem.*

   Amy is attempting to maximize her firm's value by selecting the computer that will provide the highest rate of return without being too risky a venture. Finding information concerning the costs and benefits of the old and new computer is the "art" of finance, while applying marginal analysis is the "science" of finance. Excluding tax considerations, her analysis would be similar in a proprietorship, partnership, or corporation.

2. *Locate the relevant data.*

   Amy needs to get information on the costs of each computer and the revenues expected to be generated with each.

3. *Select the proper tool/equation to evaluate the problem:*

   Amy will subtract the financial costs of each computer from their financial benefits and then select the option that will provide the highest net benefit.

This exhibit is a sample page from the *Study Guide* to accompany the fourth edition of Gitman, *Foundations of Managerial Finance*. Please contact your bookstore for ordering information on this effective study tool.

4.    *Organize the data:*

The data should be organized into the following sequence

Benefits with new computer
- Benefits with old computer
Marginal (Added) Benefits (1)

Cost of new computer
- Proceeds from sale of old
Marginal (Added) Costs (2)

Net benefit = Marginal benefits - marginal costs = (1) - (2)

5.    *Manipulate the data:*

Marginal analysis is illustrated below using the computer project data.

| | | |
|---|---:|---:|
| Benefits with $50,000 computer | $55,000 | |
| Less: Benefits with old computer | 35,000 | |
| (1) Marginal (Added) Benefits | | $ 20,000 |
| Cost of $50,000 computer | $50,000 | |
| Less: Proceeds from sale of old | 28,000 | |
| (2) Marginal (Added) Costs | | $ 22,000 |
| Net benefit     [(1) - (2)] | | -$ 2,000 |

6.    *Explain the solution.*

Since the net benefit is negative, the $50,000 computer should not be selected. The marginal benefits of $20,000 are less than the marginal costs of $22,000. Comparing all three computers, Amy should select the $80,000 computer discussed in the text.

This exhibit is a sample page from the *Study Guide* to accompany the fourth edition of Gitman, *Foundations of Managerial Finance*. Please contact your bookstore for ordering information on this effective study tool.

## SOLUTIONS FOR CHAPTER PROBLEMS

1.  Cash outflows are subtracted from cash inflows to measure net cash flow.

Thomas Yachts
Statement of Cash Flows

| | |
|---|---|
| Cash inflow | $100,000 |
| Cash outflow | 80,000 |
| Net Cash flow | $ 20,000 |

The net cash flow from the sale can be used to pay the cost of doing business.

2.  Investment B should be chosen, if the decision is based solely upon total earnings per share, because it offers are return of $6.00 versus $5.10 for investment A.

Investment A:  $1.80 + $1.80 + $1.80 = $5.40
Investment B:  $2.50 + $2.00 + $1.50 = $6.00

3.  Investment B is probably more risky.  This observation is based upon two factors.  One, Investment A offers a stable earnings per share return, while Investment B's is variable. Two, Investment B's anticipated earnings per share are decreasing.  Alternative B would be priced higher because of its higher gross earnings.  However, risk-adverse investors would reduce the price of Investment B so that their higher rate of return compensates them for the additional risk involved.

4.  Investment B is preferable on the basis of cash flow timing, since its return exceeds that of Investment A in Year 1.  This is true despite the greater total cash flow from Investment A.

5.  The lower risk project is preferred when projects offer the same level of cash flow.  In this case, Midwestern Distillers will prefer the low alcohol brew.  Competitors also may see this advantage and provide competition, reducing the expected annual cash inflow.

# To My Colleagues, Friends, and Family

No textbook can consistently meet market needs without continual feedback from colleagues, students, practitioners, and members of the publishing team. Once again, I invite all my colleagues to relate their classroom experiences using my book and its package to me at San Diego State University or in care of my acquisitions editor in finance, HarperCollins College Publishers, 10 East 53rd Street, New York, New York 10022-5299. Any constructive criticism will undoubtedly help enhance the Teaching/Learning System further.

HarperCollins sought the advice of a great many excellent reviewers, all of whom strongly influenced various aspects of this volume. My special thanks go to the following individuals who analyzed all or part of the manuscript of previous editions:

Allen S. Anderson
Dwight Anderson
Stephen L. Avard
Brian Belt
Robert A. Benson
Holland Blades
Louis E. Bonanni
Paul J. Corr
Maurice P. Corrigan
Thomas P. Czubiak
Samir P. Dagher
Alberto Davila
Anthony N. Duruh
David R. Durst
Fred J. Ebeid
Stephen Elliott
Keith Wm. Fairchild
George W. Gallinger
Raj Guttha
Linda C. Hittle
Jim Hopkins
Brigitte Lea Jacob
Alvin Kelly
Theodore T. Latz
John L. Lohret

Martin I. Lowy
Ilhan Meric
Clifford D. Mpare
Dimitrios Pachis
Douglas M. Patterson
Janice L. Pitera
Eugene O. Poindexter
Ralph A. Pope
Howard L. Puckett
J. J. Quinn
Mary Ann Rafa
Daniel H. Raver
David K. Risley
Abu Selimuddin
Edwin C. Sims
Jean L. Souther
Alice Steljes
Bev S. Stevenson
George W. Trivoli
A. M. Tuberose
Dean R. Vickstrom
John Washecka
Richard Wiedemann
Loren Weishaar
Richard H. Yanow

The following individuals provided extremely useful commentary on the fourth edition and its package:

Steve Adkins, *Western Illinois University*
Mehdi Afait, *Chadron State College*
Vickie Bajtelsmit, *Colorado State University*
Omar Benkato, *Ball State University*

Dennis Debrecht, *Carroll College*
Zane Dennick-Ream, *Robert Morris College*
William L. Ferguson, *Marshall University*
Martin Gonzalez, *Pensacola Junior College*

Henry Guithues, *St. Louis University*

John Hael, *Lewis-Clark State College*

Martin Laurence, *The William Patterson College of New Jersey*

Ileen Malitz, *Fairleigh Dickinson University*

Iqbal Mansur, *Widener University*

Tim Manuel, *University of Montana*

Cynthia Miglietti, *Bowling Green State University*

Beverly Piper, *Ashland University*

Shafiqur Rahman, *Portland State University*

Randy Tatroe, *Community College of Aurora*

George W. Trivoli, *Jacksonville State University*

Charles Wellens, *Fitchburg State College*

In addition, a word of thanks is due the HarperCollins sales force for their questionnaire responses and outstanding efforts.

My special thanks go to all members of my book team whose vision, creativity, and ongoing support helped me to reengineer all elements of the Teaching/Learning System: to Thomas M. Krueger and D. Anthony Plath for once again preparing the Finance in Action inserts and for strengthening the *Study Guide;* to Marlene Bellamy for securing the well-received and highly motivating Practitioner Previews; to Tony Plath for his help in preparing the original draft of Chapter 17; to William L. Megginson of the University of Georgia for enriching the international dimension of managerial finance throughout the book and revising the final chapter, which was originally prepared by Mehdi Salehizadeh of San Diego State University; to Hadi Salavitabar for instituting and cultivating the now-huge and reliable database of test items for updating the *Instructor's Manual,* and for formatting the *Applications* component of the book; to Enrique Roberto Lunski for developing the *FMF Lotus Templates;* to John Hansen, George Flowers, and Robert Bush for upgrading the *FMF Tutor;* to Fred Rexroad for expanding the *FMF Problem-Solver;* to Tom Liesz and his associate Lorna Dotts for creatively cranking through the presentation package; to Cecilia Wagner for screening video segments and preparing the final video teaching guides; to Vickie Bajtelsmit for checking the final draft for accuracy, and to Angela Segalla for her excellent keyboarding and clerical assistance. I'm pleased by and proud of all their efforts, and I'm confident that our colleagues will appreciate everything they've done to ensure accuracy, consistency, and accessibility throughout the package.

The staff of HarperCollins—particularly Kirsten Sandberg, Joan Cannon, Kate Steinbacher, and Mike Roche—deserve thanks for their professional expertise, creativity, enthusiasm, and commitment to this text. Special thanks are due both to Kirsten Sandberg and Joan Cannon whose vision, customer focus, and very hard work resulted in raising *FMF* to new standards of pedagogical effectiveness and excellence. Thanks is also due project editor Susan Bogle, of York Production Services, for efficiently and effectively managing the text's design and production. And to the sales team of Bob Carlton, his excellent managers, and the highly professional and effective sales force, thanks for your hard work, enthusiasm, and support.

Finally, my wife, Robin, and our children, Zachary and Jessica, have played most important parts in patiently providing the support and understanding I needed during the writing of this book. To them I will be forever grateful.

Lawrence J. Gitman

A Visual Guide To:

# FOUNDATIONS OF
# MANAGERIAL FINANCE

## Fourth Edition

**Lawrence J. Gitman**
San Diego State University

ISBN 0-673-99031-1

*Foundations of Managerial Finance* provides a stimulating introduction to the basic concepts and practices of managerial finance. The fourth edition, retitled to reflect the market's perception of the text, has been completely reengineered to meet the changing needs of students and professors alike. Gitman now offers a **split package with a text and accompanying applications book** that offers students and professors maximum flexibility. The text puts the details of various financial decisions into a real-world context, while the applications component gets students into problems and cases so that they can practice their skills and test their mastery of concepts. Both text and applications incorporate the successful Gitman Learning System built upon Learning Goals for each major section in the text, captured in the chapter summaries, Progress Review questions, exercises, and problems.

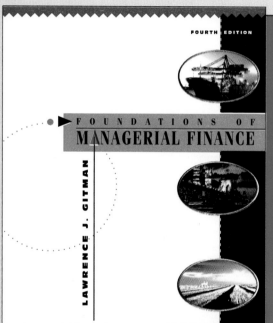

**TEXT
AND
APPLICATIONS BOOK**

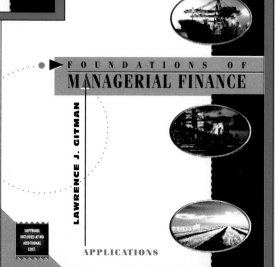

### TWO TEXT PACKAGE

For maximum teaching and learning flexibility, the package features two main parts—a hard cover TEXT with core concepts cast into realistic examples with progress reviews, and a companion APPLICATIONS paperback of exercises and problem sets, course notes, a financial tables card, and software—all at *no additional cost* to the buyer.

## LEARNING SYSTEM

*NEW!* The popular *Learning System,* integrated throughout both the TEXT and the APPLICATIONS book (as well as the supplements) sets achievable Learning Goals at the start of each chapter, points out which major section of the text covers the goal, and ties Progress Review questions and end-of-chapter applications to goals.

### LEARNING GOALS

After studying this chapter, you should be able to

LG **1** Discuss the role of time value in finance, particularly the two common views—future value and present value—and the use of financial tables and business/financial calculators to find them.

LG **2** Understand the concept of future value, its calculation for a single amount, and the procedures and effects on future value of compounding interest more frequently than annually, specifically, semiannually or quarterly.

LG **3** Find the future value of an annuity using either financial tables or a hand-held business/financial calculator to simplify the calculations.

LG **4** Review the concept of present value, its calculation for a single amount, and the relationship of present to future value.

LG **5** Determine the present value of a mixed stream of cash flows, an annuity, and a perpetuity.

LG **6** Describe the procedures involved in (1) determining deposits to accumulate a future sum, (2) loan amortization, and (3) finding interest or growth rates.

# 11 Time Value of Money

---

Most organizations make decisions involving the investment of resources for long periods of time. Typically, corporations have limited resources at their disposal, and they have to choose the best investments from among various alternatives. Many different methods can be used to deploy investment capital that take into consideration the time to re-

> **Understanding time value concepts helps managers . . . ask the right questions and work effectively . . . to make informed decisions.**

cover the project cost, rates of return, and risk.

The time value of money serves as a common denominator for making investment decisions. With knowledge of such time value concepts as present value, managers can analyze a project's future earnings and cash flow in terms of today's dollars. This allows them to make good investment decisions that increase shareholder value.

Businesses apply time value of money concepts in many

ways. Knowing how to apply time value techniques to investments, whether in tangible assets or securities, is a valuable skill. Reebok uses time value calculations in acquisition analysis as one way of determining how much to pay to acquire a firm. By looking at projected earnings and cash flow streams and applying present value techniques, we can determine what the company is worth to us today. The purchase price of an income-earning entity today has to reflect the present value of future earnings.

Calculating the return on investments, both short and long term, requires application of time value techniques. For example, companies that issue debt use time value techniques to determine the offering price based on the stated coupon versus the market interest rate.

Companies also purchase securities in the secondary market, where prices and yields change frequently. Financial managers have to make sure that the price they are quoted is correct. Although sophisticated computers and calculators perform the calculations, the quotes are sometimes wrong. You can't always rely on what someone else tells you or assume that the computer program is always right. I was involved in just this situation. The quoted price for some municipal securities seemed wrong, so I did the return calculations by hand. There were errors in the equipment providing the price quotes. Because I understood present-value concepts, I discovered the errors and avoided overpaying.

Understanding time value concepts helps managers in all departments ask the right questions and work effectively with financial managers to make informed decisions. Operations managers make decisions to build a new factory, buy new equipment, increase research and development spending, or hire more employees. This requires financial analysis that includes the application of time value techniques. Human resources managers use time value techniques to calculate the cost of offering long-term benefit plans and to advise employees on retirement plans. In addition, time value concepts apply to personal financial decisions—for example, calculations of loan and mortgage payments, analyzing whether to buy or lease a car, and estimating the values of security investment alternatives. Learning about time value pays off in many ways.

*Leo S. Vannoni joined Reebok International Ltd. as treasurer in 1993. From 1980 to 1993, he held financial management positions in the computer industry, serving as assistant treasurer of Stratus Computer; manager, international finance at Computervision Corp.; and senior treasury consultant for Digital Equipment Corporation. He received his B.A. in economics from Harvard College and his M.B.A. in finance from the Columbia University Graduate School of Business.*

279

## PRACTITIONER PREVIEWS

*NEW! Practitioner Previews* at the start of every chapter introduce readers financial decision-makers, who are on the job daily dealing with financial issues. The interviewees represent large and small companies at all levels of financial management within the firm.

▼▼▼▼▼▼▼▼▼▼▼▼▼▼▼▼▼▼▼▼▼▼▼▼▼▼▼▼

## Progress Review Questions

**11-1.** Why does the timing of cash flows have important economic consequences? What is a *time line*, and how is it used to depict cash flows?

**11-2.** What is the difference between *future value* and *present value*? Which approach is preferred by financial managers? Why?

**11-3.** What computational aids are available for streamlining future- and present-value calculations? How are financial tables laid out and accessed?

▲▲▲▲▲▲▲▲▲▲▲▲▲▲▲▲▲▲▲▲▲▲▲▲▲▲▲▲

## Future Value of a Single Amount

LG  2

The **future value** of a single amount is found by applying compound interest over a specified period. Savings institutions advertise compound interest returns at a rate of *x* percent or *x* percent compounded annually, semiannually, quarterly, monthly, weekly, daily, or even continuously. The principles of future value are quite simple, whatever the period of time involved.

**future value**
The value of a present amount at a future date, found by applying compound interest over a specified period.

### The Concept of Future Value

We speak of **compounded interest** when we wish to indicate that the amount earned on a given deposit has become part of the principal at the end of a specified period. The term **principal** refers to the amount of money on which the interest is paid. Annual compounding is the most common type used in managerial finance calculations. The concept of future value with annual compounding can be illustrated by a simple example.

**compounded interest**
Interest earned on a given deposit that has become part of the principal at the end of a specified period.

**principal**
The amount of money on which interest is paid.

▶ **E X A M P L E**

If Rich Saver places $100 in a savings account paying 8 percent interest compounded annually, at the end of one year he will have $108 in the account. This $108 represents the initial principal of $100 plus 8 percent ($8) in interest. The future value at the end of the first year is calculated by using Equation 11.1.

$$\text{Future value at end of year } 1 = \$100 \times (1 + .08) = \$108 \qquad (11.1)$$

Equation 11.1

If Rich leaves this money in the account for another year, he would be paid interest at the rate of 8 percent on the new principal of $108. At the end of this second year $116.64 would be in the account. This amount represents the principal at the beginning of year 2 ($108) plus 8 percent of the $108 ($8.64) in interest. The future value at the end of the second year is calculated by using Equation 11.2.

$$\text{end of year } 2 = \$108 \times (1 + .08) = \$116.64 \qquad (11.2)$$

Equation 11.2

---

Substituting the expression between the equal signs in Equation 11.1 for the $108 figure in Equation 11.2 gives us Equation 11.3.

Equation 11.3

$$\begin{aligned}\text{Future value at end of year } 2 &= \$100 \times (1 + .08) \times (1 + .08) \qquad (11.3)\\ &= \$100 \times (1.08)^2 \\ &= \$116.64\end{aligned}$$

◀

---

### The Calculation of Future Value

The basic relationship in Equation 11.3 can be generalized to find the future value after any number of periods. Let

$FV_n$ = the future value at the end of period $n$
$PV$ = the initial principal, or present value
$k$ = the annual rate of interest paid
      (*Note:* On business/financial calculators,
      $i$ is typically used to represent this rate.)
$n$ = the number of periods—typically
      years—the money is left on deposit

By using this notation a general equation for the future value at the end of period $n$ can be formulated.

Equation 11.4 **General formula for future value**

$$FV_n = PV \times (1 + k)^n \qquad (11.4)$$

Equation 11.4 can be used to find the future value, $FV_n$, in an account paying $k$ percent interest compounded annually for $n$ periods if $PV$ dollars is deposited initially. A simple example will illustrate.

**E X A M P L E**

Jane Frugal has placed $800 in a savings account paying 6 percent interest compounded annually. She wishes to determine how much money will be in the account at the end of five years. Substituting $PV = \$800$, $k = .06$, and $n = 5$ into Equation 11.4 gives the amount at the end of year 5.

$$FV_5 = \$800 \times (1 + .06)^5 = \$800 \times (1.338) = \$1,070.40$$

Jane will have $1,070.40 in the account at the end of the fifth year. This analysis can be depicted diagrammatically on a time line as shown in Figure 11.5. ◀

**FIGURE 11.5   Time Line for Future Value of a Single Amount ($800 Initial Principal, Earning 6 Percent Annual Interest, at End of Five Years)**

An initial principal, *PV*, of $800 deposited into an account paying 6 percent annual interest, *k*, will have a future value at the end of 5 years, *FV₅*, of $1,070.40.

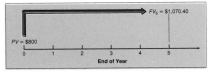

---

**GITMAN EXAMPLE METHOD**

The proven *Example Method* infuses practical presentations into the learning process by applying time lines, tables, and business/financial calculator keystrokes where appropriate in the TEXT, to walk students through potentially troublesome concepts.

Accommodating the AACSB guidelines, the fourth edition not only integrates international material throughout the TEXT, but also devotes a new chapter to global finance concepts, applications, and implications.

Part III  Short-Term Financial Management

tain local currency deposit balances in banks in every country in which the firm operates and to retain centralized control over cash balances and cash flows that, in total, can reach several billion dollars. The largest multinational corporations have honed their treasury operations to such an extent that they can balance these conflicting objectives efficiently and even profitably. To do so, they rely on the cash collection, disbursement, and foreign-exchange trading expertise of large international banks, all of which operate very sophisticated computerized treasury services.

Multinational firms can also minimize their cash requirements by using an **intracompany netting technique.** For example, when two subsidiaries in different countries trade with each other—thereby generating payment obligations to each other—only the net amount of payment owed is transferred across national boundaries. In fact, it may be possible to handle many of these transactions strictly internally (on the books of the parent company) without having to resort to the international payments system at all.

When it becomes necessary to make large international cash payments, these are almost invariably handled by one of the wire transfer services operated by international banking consortia. The most important of these networks is the **Clearing House Interbank Payment System (CHIPS).** It has been estimated that over $600 billion worth of payments are settled *every day* using wire transfer and settlement services. Although the bulk of these transactions result from foreign exchange trading, many are also due to settlement of international payment obligations.

Multinational companies with excess funds to invest benefit from having access to a wide variety of government and corporate investment vehicles. Companies naturally have access to all of the marketable securities offered to U.S. investors (described in the following section). Multinational companies can also invest funds in foreign government securities, or they can invest directly in the *Eurocurrency market* either in dollars or in other convertible currencies. This financial flexibility often provides multinational corporations with a key competitive advantage, particularly if they need to transfer funds into or out of countries experiencing political or financial difficulties.

**intracompany netting technique**
A technique used by multinational firms to minimize their cash requirements by transferring across national boundaries, at maximum, the net amount of payments owed between them. Sometimes bookkeeping entries are substituted for international payments.

**Clearing House Interbank Payment System (CHIPS)**
The most important wire transfer service; it is operated by international banking consortia.

▼▼▼▼▼▼▼▼▼▼▼▼▼▼▼▼▼▼▼▼▼▼▼▼▼▼▼

## Progress Review Questions

**8-6.** Define *float* and describe its three basic components. Compare and contrast collection and disbursement float, and state the financial manager's goal with respect to each of these types of float.

**8-7.** Briefly describe the key features of each of the following techniques for speeding up collections:
  **a.** Concentration banking
  **b.** Lockboxes
  **c.** Direct sends
  **d.** Preauthorized checks (PACs)
  **e.** Depository transfer checks (DTCs)

...se (ACH) debits

Chapter 8  Cash and Marketable Securities

**Differences in Banking Systems**  Banking systems outside the United States differ fundamentally from the U.S. model in several key aspects. First, foreign banks are generally far less restricted either geographically or in the services they are allowed to offer. Second, retail transactions are typically routed through a **Giro system** that is usually operated by, or in association with, the national postal system. Because of this direct payment system, checks are used much less frequently than in the United States. Third, banks in other countries are allowed to pay interest on corporate demand deposits, and they also routinely provide overdraft protection. To recoup the cost of these services, however, non-U.S. banks generally charge more and higher fees for services and also engage in the practice of **value dating.** This involves delaying, often for days or even weeks, the availability of funds deposited with the bank. This lag between when the date funds are deposited and when they are usable obviously complicates cash management procedures, and if a transaction involves collecting on a foreign-currency-denominated check drawn on a bank outside of the host country, the delay in availability of good funds can be very long indeed.

**Cash Management Practices**  The cash management practices of multinational corporations are made more complicated by the need both to main-

**Giro system**
System through which retail transactions are handled in association with a foreign country's national postal system.

**value dating**
A procedure used by non-U.S. banks to delay, often for days or even weeks, the availability of funds deposited within them.

F I N A N C E  I N

# A C T I O N

International

## Citibank Helps Old World Industries Expedite Collection and Transfer of Funds from China

Old World Industries, a Northbrook, Illinois, automotive products manufacturer, experienced problems collecting foreign funds from Chinese customers and transferring them to the U.S. Sometimes this process took as long as 18 months. Given the risks of operating in a foreign country, Old World Industries needed to expedite collection and transfer of funds to the United States. Consequently, in 1993, Old World Industries sought to replace the Bank of China as its banker.

The problem arose when Old World Industries' credit manager simply assumed that the Bank of China could handle funds transfers to the U.S. Much to Old World's chagrin, the Bank of China is a network of provincial banks and some do not have foreign-exchange capabilities. Old World Industries' solution was to work with a bank headquartered in the United States that had the following capabilities.

1. **Strong international presence:**
   Although Citicorp was chosen because of its massive overseas network, other banks often can provide sufficient services.
2. **Technical expertise:**
   Citibank was able to recommend collection and transfer strategies that were acceptable in different cultures.
3. **Services:**
   Citibank's offerings were reviewed with a local international accounting firm to verify the appropriateness of services offered.

Source: Jill Andrewsky Fraser, "Rushing Your Cash Home," *Inc.,* November 1993, p. 137.

*Finance in Action boxes* throughout the TEXT take readers to the front line of real firm finance as they relates to careers, ethics, small business, and large international companies, all in terms of the concepts at hand.

aggressive strategy but more risky than the conservative strategy. Under the trade-off strategy, if the total funds requirement is actually at the level represented by dashed line B in Figure 7.5, the likelihood that the firm will be able to obtain additional short-term financing is good, because a portion of its short-term financing requirements is actually being financed with long-term funds. Under this strategy the risk of having to refinance frequently at possibly higher interest rates falls between that of the aggressive and conservative strategies.

## Progress Review Questions

**7-11.** If a firm has a constant funds requirement throughout the year, which, if any, of the three financing strategies—aggressive, conservative, or trade-off—is preferable? Why?

**7-12.** As the difference between the cost of short-term and long-term financing becomes smaller, which financing strategy—aggressive or conservative—becomes more attractive? Is the aggressive or the conservative strategy preferable if the costs are equal? Why?

**TABLE 7.7  A Financing Strategy Based on a Trade-Off Between Profitability and Risk for Berenson Company**

| Month | Total Assetsª (1) | Long-Term Fundsᵇ (2) | Short-Term Funds (3) |
|---|---|---|---|
| January | $17,000 | $15,900 | $1,100 |
| February | 16,000 | 15,900 | 100 |
| March | 15,000 | 15,900 | 0 |
| April | 14,000 | 15,900 | 0 |
| May | 13,800 | 15,900 | 0 |
| June | 14,500 | 15,900 | 0 |
| July | 16,000 | 15,900 | 100 |
| August | 16,700 | 15,900 | 800 |
| September | 17,000 | 15,900 | 1,100 |
| October | 18,000 | 15,900 | 2,100 |
| November | 16,000 | 15,900 | 100 |
| December | 15,000 | 15,900 | 0 |
| Monthly Averageᶜ | | $15,900 | $ 450 |

ªThis represents the firm's total funds requirement from column 3 of Table 7.6.
ᵇFound by taking the average of the minimum monthly funds requirement of $13,800 (in May) and the maximum monthly funds requirement of $18,000 (in October)—[($13,800 + $18,000) ÷ 2 = $15,900].
ᶜ... nthly amounts for the 12 months and dividing the resulting to-

# SUMMARY OF LEARNING GOALS

**Understand the role of long-term financing, including internal and external sources, the need for external funds, and the methods used by both established and emerging small corporations to raise external funds.**  Businesses routinely need long-term funds to finance corporate growth and the replacement of worn-out equipment and to pay off debts and other obligations as they come due. The internal source of funds is funds generated within the firm from retained earnings. External sources of funds are raised outside of the firm through negotiated loans or the sale of bonds, preferred stock, or common stock. Firms use external funds to finance growth when their internally generated funds are inadequate to meet their long-term financing need. Firms typically raise external funds through either a public offering or a private placement of new debt or equity securities. Emerging small corporations frequently seek financing in the form of venture capital. Venture capital is financing invested in an emerging business firm by specialized financial intermediaries known as venture capitalists. Although they sometimes provide debt financing, in most cases they obtain common stock ownership in the businesses they finance.

**Explain the role of investment banking in long-term business financing: the bankers' role as underwriter, agent, adviser, and market maker, the use of shelf registration, and the formation of syndicates by underwriters.**  Investment bankers act as financial intermediaries between the issuers and buyers of new securities. Their most common roles in security offerings are as underwriter, agent, adviser, and market maker. The investment banker's primary function is underwriting, which involves buying a security issue from the issuing firm at a lower price than the investment banker plans to sell it for, thereby guaranteeing the issuer a specified amount from the issue and assuming the risk of price changes between the points of purchase and sale. Investment bankers also assist in private placement and can be hired to serve as the issuer's agent and sell its securities on a best efforts basis. A secondary, but important, function performed by investment bankers involves providing advice to issuers on appropriate financing, mergers, acquisitions, and refinancing decisions. Investment bankers also use their industry contacts with other investment banking firms to create the widest possible distribution for new issues and make a market in them. Shelf registration of new securities has become extremely popular because, in most cases, it minimizes the paperwork necessary to initiate security sales, thus reducing the transactions cost of bringing new securities to market. Investment bankers may form an underwriting syndicate—a group of investment banking firms that collectively participate in buying and selling a portion of the new issues—to reduce the price risk.

**Discuss investment banker compensation: the underwriting spread, the cost of public offerings, and the cost of private placements.**  Investment bankers are compensated with a gross commission (or gross underwriting spread)—the difference between the price at which an investment banker sells a se-

## PROBLEM SETS WITH WORK SPACE

At the end of each APPLICATIONS chapter, the extensive Problem Sets provide students with a generous margin of work space for quick hand-calculations, problem formatting and solutions, and other notes jotted from chalkboard, overhead, or business calculator.

---

▼▼▼▼▼▼▼▼▼▼▼▼▼▼▼▼▼▼▼▼▼▼▼▼▼▼▼▼▼▼▼

## PROBLEMS

LG 4  **11-1 Present Values** For each of the cases shown in the table, calculate the present value of the cash flow, discounting at the rate given and assuming that the cash flow is received at the end of the period noted.

| Case | Single Cash Flow ($) | Discount Rate (%) | End of Period (Years) |
|---|---|---|---|
| A | 7,000 | 12 | 4 |
| B | 28,000 | 8 | 20 |
| C | 10,000 | 14 | 12 |
| D | 150,000 | 11 | 6 |
| E | 45,000 | 20 | 8 |

LG 4  **11-2 Present Value** Terry Murphy has been offered a future payment of $500 three years from today. If his opportunity cost is 7 percent compounded annually, what value should he place on this opportunity?

LG 4  **11-3 Present Value** An Ohio state savings bond can be converted to $100 at maturity six years from purchase. If the state bonds are to be competitive with U.S. Savings Bonds, which pay 8 percent annual interest (compounded annually), at what price must the state sell its bonds? Assume no cash payments on savings bonds prior to redemption.

---

▼▼▼▼▼▼▼▼▼▼▼▼▼▼▼▼▼▼▼▼▼▼▼▼▼▼▼▼▼▼▼

## SELF-TEST PROBLEMS
### (Solutions in Appendix A)

LG 2   **ST 11-1 Future Values** Delia Martin has $10,000 that she can deposit in any of three savings accounts for a three-year period. Bank A compounds interest on an annual basis; Bank B compounds interest twice each year; and Bank C compounds interest each quarter. All three banks have a stated annual interest rate of 4 percent.

  **a.** What amount would Ms. Martin have at the end of the third year, leaving all interest paid on deposit, in each bank?

  **b.** On the basis of your findings in **a,** which bank should Ms. Martin deal with? Why?

LG 4  LG 5  **ST 11-2  Present Values** You have a choice of accepting either of two 5-year cash flow streams or lump-sum amounts. One cash flow stream is an annuity, and the other is a mixed stream. You may accept alternative A or B—either as a cash flow stream or as a lump sum. Given the cash flow and lump-sum amounts associated with each, and

---

## CHAPTER SELF-TESTS AND PROBLEMS

*NEW! Chapter Self-Tests* in every chapter of the APPLICATIONS book enable students to test their knowledge of financial concepts when preparing for exams and practicing their test-taking skills. The problems tied to the APPLICATIONS software accelerate the learning process through realistic scenario analyses. For example, the TUTOR program randomly generates an unlimited number of problems with worked-out solutions for students to analyze.

## CHAPTER CASES

*Cases* appear toward the end of each chapter in the APPLICATIONS book so that students can apply what they have learned in the chapter in realistic contexts and strengthen their practical understanding of the techniques presented—*without the added expense of a separate case book*. Select items are keyed to the APPLICATIONS software for developing the electronic problem-solving skills needed on the job.

## CHAPTER 11 CASE
## JMR's Retirement Program

JMR Corporation wishes to accumulate funds to provide a retirement annuity for its vice-president of research—Andrea McNutt. Ms. McNutt by contract will retire at the end of exactly 12 years. On retirement she is entitled to receive an annual end-of-year payment of $42,000 for exactly 20 years. If she dies prior to the end of the 20-year period, the annual payments will pass to her heirs. During the 12-year "accumulation period," JMR Corporation wishes to fund the annuity by making equal annual end-of-year deposits into an account earning 9 percent interest. Once the 20-year "distribution period" begins, JMR plans to move the accumulated monies into an account earning a guaranteed 12 percent per year. At the end of the distribution period, the account balance will equal zero. Note that the first deposit will be made at the end of year 1, and the first distribution payment will be received at the end of year 13. (*Hint:* It may be helpful to draw a time line of cash flows before solving this problem.)

**a.** How large a sum must JMR Corporation accumulate by the end of year 12 to provide the 20-year $42,000 annuity?

**b.** How large must JMR's equal annual end-of-year deposits into the account be over the 12-year accumulation period to fund fully Ms. McNutt's retirement annuity?

## CHAPTER OUTLINE FOR REVIEW

THE ROLE OF TIME VALUE IN FINANCE

Future Versus Present Value

Computational Aids

FUTURE VALUE OF A SINGLE AMOUNT

## STUDENT LECTURE NOTES

*NEW! Student Notes* at the end of each chapter in the APPLICATIONS book outline the chapter according to the presentation tools available for instructor use. This parallel in lecture materials allows students to listen carefully to what the instructor is saying, rather than to copy frantically what the instructor is showing.

# P A R T  I

## Introduction to Managerial Finance

1

L E A R N I N G   G O A L S

After studying this chapter, you should be able to

 **LG 1** Define finance and describe its major areas and opportunities.

 **LG 2** Review the basic forms of business organization and their respective strengths and weaknesses.

**LG 3** Describe the managerial finance function and differentiate managerial finance from the closely related disciplines of economics and accounting.

**LG 4** Justify the financial manager's focus on the goal of maximizing shareholder wealth rather than maximizing profit and on preservation of stakeholder wealth.

**LG 5** Discuss the agency issue—its resolution and current view—as it relates to owner wealth maximization and the role of ethics in achieving this goal.

**LG 6** Identify the key activities of the financial manager within the firm and his or her role in total quality management (TQM).

# 1 Finance and the Financial Manager

Most basic business decisions require some understanding of finance. All students, whatever their field of interest—accounting, manufacturing, human resources, marketing, or information systems—should have a working knowledge of finance to evaluate the financial implications of their decisions. Students considering a career in finance must understand the other functional areas of finance because financial decisions are not made in a vacuum.

At Amoco Corporation, a worldwide integrated petro-

## Financial decisions are critical to maximizing the firm's long-term value.

leum and chemical company, our financial managers have a wide range of responsibilities. They prepare budgets and financial statements, manage the company's liquidity position and financial risk, analyze investment opportunities, and arrange financing to support the company's operations. The financial manager also serves as a consultant to the operating divisions by providing financial advice covering a wide range of issues that assist the operating managers in making more effective business decisions.

Like other corporations, Amoco has a centralized finance department that manages and coordinates all financial affairs. It looks at individual projects and financial decisions in the context of the whole corporation and its strategies; sources all financing; manages risk and liquidity; and is responsible for accounting, taxes, mergers and acquisitions, and pension fund management functions. It works closely with our three operating companies (production, oil, and chemical) to provide assistance in managing their financial affairs.

Financial decisions are critical to maximizing the firm's long-term value. Financial managers can increase a firm's value in two ways: by improving cash flow or lowering the firm's cost of financing. However, of all the corporate decisions, investment decisions have the potential to add the greatest value. If management fails to make investment decisions that return profits in excess of the cost of funding these projects, shareholder value is not being created. Eventually, there will be nothing left to manage because the firm is in essence self-liquidating. Financing and day-to-day financial management decisions complement capital investment decisions.

Risk plays an important role in financial management as well. Most finance decisions require an analysis of the trade-off between risk and return. The financial manager must minimize the chance of loss and maximize the profit on any investment transaction, whether it's building a plant, drilling a well, or investing temporary cash surpluses. For example, a project to replace refining

equipment has a lower risk than one to build a new overseas refinery, and the analysis must take that into account.

Increasingly, companies are becoming more global. When you leave the United States, you enter a world of different currencies, tax regulations, business procedures, and cultures, which creates greater challenges for a firm to compete successfully. In addition to the financial risks, you must consider economic and political conditions in overseas markets.

To succeed in today's more complex and competitive environment, financial managers need a thorough grounding in financial tools and techniques, an understanding of the broader business environment, and good communication and decision-making skills.

*After receiving a B. A. in business administration from Morehouse College, Atlanta, **William Goings** spent 12 years as a corporate lender for Philadelphia National Bank, Continental Bank, and Citibank. He moved to Amoco in 1991 as a financial manager, raising financing worldwide for company projects. He is now a senior business consultant for strategic planning, advising management at Amoco Production Company. He is also studying for a master's degree in management at Northwestern University's Executive Masters Program.*

The financial manager plays an extremely important role in the operation and success of a business. All key employees of any business organization, however large or small, should understand the duties and activities of its financial manager. Developing such an understanding begins with some basic questions: What is finance? What career opportunities exist in the field of finance? What are the basic forms of legal organization? What is the managerial finance function, and what are the goals and activities of the financial manager? Answering these basic questions sets the stage for discussion of the basic concepts, tools, and techniques of managerial finance.

## Finance as an Area of Study

LG 1

The field of finance is broad and dynamic. It directly affects the lives of every person and every organization, financial or nonfinancial, private or public, large or small, profit-seeking or not-for-profit. Many areas of finance can therefore be studied, and a large number of career opportunities are available.

### What Is Finance?

**Finance** can be defined as the art and science of managing money. Virtually all individuals and organizations earn or raise money and spend or invest it. Finance is concerned with the process, institutions, markets, and instruments involved in the transfer of money among and between individuals, businesses, and governments. An understanding of finance benefits most adults by allowing them to make better personal financial decisions. Those who work in nonfinancial jobs benefit from an understanding of finance because it enables them to interact effectively with the firm's financial personnel, processes, and procedures.

**finance**
The art and science of managing money.

### Major Areas and Opportunities in Finance

The major areas of finance can be summarized by reviewing the career opportunities in finance. These opportunities can, for convenience, be divided into two broad parts: financial services and managerial finance.

**Financial Services**   **Financial services** is the area of finance concerned with the design and delivery of advice and financial products to individuals, business, and government. It involves a variety of interesting career opportunities within the areas of banking and related institutions, personal financial planning, investments, real estate, and insurance. Career opportunities available in each of these areas are described briefly in Table 1.1.

**financial services**
The part of finance concerned with design and delivery of advice and financial products.

**Managerial Finance**   **Managerial finance** is concerned with the duties of the financial manager in the business firm. **Financial managers** actively man-

**managerial finance**
Concerns the duties of the financial manager in the business firm.

**financial manager**
Actively manages the financial affairs of any type of business.

**TABLE 1.1   Career Opportunities in Financial Services**

| Area | Career Opportunities |
| --- | --- |
| Banking and related institutions | *Loan officers* evaluate and make recommendations with regard to installment, commercial, real estate, and consumer loans. *Retail bank managers* run bank offices and supervise the programs offered by the bank to customers. *Trust officers* administer trust funds for estates, foundations, and business firms. Others offer financial services in personal financial planning, investments, real estate, and insurance. |
| Personal financial planning | *Financial planners,* working independently or as employees, advise individuals with regard to the management of all aspects—budgeting, taxes, investments, real estate, insurance, and retirement and estate planning—of their personal finances and help them to develop a comprehensive financial plan that meets their objectives. |
| Investments | *Stockbrokers,* or account executives, assist clients in choosing, buying, and selling securities. *Securities analysts* study stocks and bonds, usually in specific industries, and advise securities firms and their customers, fund managers, and insurance companies with regard to them. *Portfolio managers* build and manage portfolios of securities for firms and individuals. *Investment bankers* provide advice to security issuers and act as liaisons between issuers and purchasers of newly issued stocks and bonds. |
| Real estate | *Real estate agents/brokers* list residential and commercial property for sale or lease, find buyers and lessees for listed property, show property, and negotiate the sale or lease of property. *Appraisers* estimate the market values of all types of property. *Real estate lenders* analyze and make recommendations or decisions with regard to loan applications. *Mortgage bankers* find and arrange financing for real estate projects. *Property managers* handle the day-to-day operations of properties to achieve maximum returns for their owners. |
| Insurance | *Insurance agents/brokers* interview prospects, develop insurance programs to meet their needs, sell them policies, collect premiums, and assist in claims processing and settlement. *Underwriters* appraise and select the risks that their company chooses to insure and set the associated premiums. |

age the financial affairs of many types of business—financial and nonfinancial, private and public, large and small, profit-seeking and not-for-profit. They perform such varied tasks as budgeting, financial forecasting, cash management, credit administration, investment analysis, and funds procurement. In recent years the changing economic and regulatory environments have increased the importance and complexity of the financial manager's duties. As a result many top executives in industry and government have come from the finance area.

Another important recent trend has been the globalization of business activity. U.S. corporations have dramatically increased their sales and investments in other countries, and foreign corporations have increased their sales and direct investments in the United States. These changes have created a need for financial managers who can help a firm to manage cash flows denominated in different currencies and protect against the political and foreign exchange risks that naturally arise from international transactions.

Although this need makes the managerial finance function more demanding and complex, it can also lead to a more rewarding and fulfilling career.

## The Study of Managerial Finance

An understanding of the concepts, tools, and techniques presented throughout this text will fully acquaint you with the financial manager's activities and decisions. Because most business decisions are measured in financial terms, the financial manager plays a key role in the operation of the firm. People in all areas of responsibility—accounting, manufacturing, human resources, marketing, or information systems—need a basic understanding of the managerial finance function. As you study, you will learn about the career opportunities in managerial finance that are briefly described in Table 1.2. Although this text focuses on profit-seeking firms, the principles presented here are equally applicable to public and nonprofit organizations. It is important to note that the same decision-making principles developed in this text can be applied in personal financial decisions. I hope that this first exposure to the exciting field of finance will provide the foundation and initiative for further study and possibly even a future career.

### TABLE 1.2   Career Opportunities in Managerial Finance

| Position | Description |
|---|---|
| Financial analyst | Primarily responsible for preparing and analyzing the firm's financial plans and budgets. Other duties include financial forecasting, performing financial ratio analysis, and working closely with accounting. |
| Capital budgeting analyst/manager | Responsible for the evaluation and recommendation of proposed asset investments. May be involved in the financial aspects of implementation of approved investments. |
| Project finance manager | In large firms, arranges financing for approved asset investments. Coordinates consultants, investment bankers, and legal counsel. |
| Cash manager | Responsible for maintaining and controlling the firm's daily cash balances. Frequently manages the firm's cash collection, short-term investment, transfer, and disbursement activities and coordinates short-term borrowing and banking relationships. |
| Credit analyst/manager | Administers the firm's credit policy by analyzing or managing the evaluation of credit applications, extending credit, and monitoring and collecting accounts receivable. |
| Pension fund manager | In large companies, responsible for coordinating the assets and liabilities of the employees' pension fund. Either performs investment management activities or hires and oversees the performance of these activities by a third party. |

## Progress Review Questions

**1-1.** What is *finance?* Explain how this field affects the lives of everyone and every organization.

**1-2.** What is the *financial services* area of finance? Briefly describe each of the following areas of career opportunity:
  **a.** Banking and related institutions
  **b.** Personal financial planning
  **c.** Investments
  **d.** Real estate
  **e.** Insurance

**1-3.** Describe the field of *managerial finance.* Compare and contrast this field with financial services. List and discuss three career positions in managerial finance.

---

LG  2

# Basic Forms of Business Organization

The three basic legal forms of business organization are the *sole proprietorship,* the *partnership,* and the *corporation.* The sole proprietorship is the most common form of organization. However, the corporation is by far the dominant form with respect to receipts and net profits. Corporations are given primary emphasis in this textbook.

## Sole Proprietorships

**sole proprietorship**
A business owned by one person and operated for his or her own profit.

A **sole proprietorship** is a business owned by one person who operates it for his or her own profit. About 75 percent of all business firms are sole proprietorships. The typical sole proprietorship is a small business, such as a neighborhood grocery, auto repair shop, or dry cleaner. Typically the proprietor, along with a few employees, operates the business. He or she normally raises capital from personal resources or by borrowing and is responsible for all business decisions. The sole proprietor has **unlimited liability,** which means that his or her total wealth, not merely the amount originally invested, can be taken to satisfy creditors. The majority of sole proprietorships are found in the wholesale, retail, service, and construction industries. The key strengths and weaknesses of sole proprietorships are summarized in Table 1.3.

**unlimited liability**
The condition of a sole proprietorship (or general partnership) allowing the owner's total wealth to be taken to satisfy creditors.

## Partnerships

**partnership**
A business owned by two or more persons and operated for profit.

A **partnership** consists of two or more owners doing business together for profit. Partnerships, which account for about 10 percent of all businesses, are

**TABLE 1.3   Strengths and Weaknesses of the Basic Forms of Business Organization**

| | Legal Form | | |
| --- | --- | --- | --- |
| | Sole Proprietorship | Partnership | Corporation |
| **Strengths** | • Owner receives all profits (as well as losses)<br>• Low organizational costs<br>• Income taxed as personal income of proprietor<br>• Secrecy<br>• Ease of dissolution | • Can raise more funds than sole proprietorships<br>• Borrowing power enhanced by more owners<br>• More available brain power and managerial skill<br>• Can retain good employees<br>• Income taxed as personal income of partners | • Owners have *limited liability*, which guarantees they cannot lose more than invested<br>• Can achieve large size due to marketability of stock (ownership)<br>• Ownership is readily transferable<br>• Long life of firm—not dissolved by death of owners<br>• Can hire professional managers<br>• Can expand more easily due to access to financial markets<br>• Receives certain tax advantages |
| **Weaknesses** | • Owner has *unlimited liability*—total wealth can be taken to satisfy debts<br>• Limited fund-raising power tends to inhibit growth<br>• Proprietor must be jack-of-all-trades<br>• Difficult to give employees long-term career opportunities<br>• Lacks continuity when proprietor dies | • Owners have *unlimited liability* and may have to cover debts of other less financially sound partners<br>• When a partner dies, partnership is dissolved<br>• Difficult to liquidate or transfer partnership<br>• Difficult to achieve large-scale operations | • Taxes generally higher because corporate income is taxed and dividends paid to owners are again taxed<br>• More expensive to organize than other business forms<br>• Subject to greater government regulation<br>• Employees often lack personal interest in firm<br>• Lacks secrecy because stockholders must receive financial reports |

typically larger than sole proprietorships. Finance, insurance, and real estate firms are the most common types of partnership. Public accounting and stock brokerage partnerships often have large numbers of partners.

Most partnerships are established by a written contract known as the **articles of partnership.** In a *general* (or *regular*) *partnership,* all the partners have unlimited liability. In a **limited partnership,** one or more partners can be designated as having limited liability as long as at least *one* partner has unlimited liability. A *limited partner* is normally prohibited from being active in the management of the firm. Strengths and weaknesses of partnerships are summarized in Table 1.3.

**articles of partnership**
The written contract used to formally establish a business partnership.

**limited partnership**
A partnership in which one or more partners has limited liability as long as at least one partner has unlimited liability.

## Corporations

**corporation**
An intangible business entity created by law.

A **corporation** is an artificial being created by law. Often called a "legal entity," a corporation has the powers of an individual in that it can sue and be sued, make and be party to contracts, and acquire property in its own name. Although only about 15 percent of all businesses are incorporated, the corporation is the dominant form of business organization. It accounts for nearly 90 percent of business receipts and 80 percent of net profits. Because corporations employ millions of people and have many thousands of shareholders, their activities affect the lives of everyone. Although corporations are involved in all types of business, manufacturing corporations account for the largest portion of corporate business receipts and net profits. The key strengths and weaknesses of large corporations are summarized in Table 1.3. It is important to recognize that there are many small private corporations in addition to the large corporations emphasized throughout this text. Many small corporations have no access to financial markets, and the requirement that the owner co-sign a loan moderates limited liability.

**stockholders**
The true owners of the firm by virtue of their equity in the form of preferred and common stock.

**board of directors**
Group elected by the firm's stockholders and having ultimate authority to guide corporate affairs and make general policy.

**president** or **chief executive officer (CEO)**
Corporate official responsible for managing the firm's day-to-day operations.

The major parties in a corporation are the stockholders, the board of directors, and the president. The top portion of Figure 1.1 depicts the relationship among these parties. The **stockholders** are the true owners of the firm by virtue of their equity in preferred and common stock.[1] They vote periodically to elect the members of the board of directors and to amend the firm's corporate charter. The **board of directors** has the ultimate authority in guiding corporate affairs and in making general policy. The directors include key corporate personnel as well as outside individuals who typically are successful business persons and executives of other major organizations. Outside directors for major corporations are typically paid an annual fee of $10,000 to $20,000 or more and, in addition, are frequently granted options to buy a specified number of shares of the firm's stock at a stated—and often attractive—price. The **president** or **chief executive officer (CEO)** is responsible for managing day-to-day operations and carrying out the policies established by the board. The CEO is required to report periodically to the firm's directors. It is important to note the division between owners and managers in a large corporation, as shown by the dashed line in Figure 1.1. This separation and some of the issues surrounding it are addressed in the discussion of the *agency issue* later in this chapter.

## Progress Review Questions

**1-4.** What are the three basic forms of business organization? Which form is most common? Which form is dominant in terms of business receipts and net profits? Why?

**1-5.** Describe the role and basic relationship between the major parties in a corporation—stockholders, board of directors, and president. What typically is the relationship between owners and managers in a large corporation?

---

[1]Some corporations have "members" rather than stockholders. These members, similarly to stockholders, are entitled to vote and receive dividends. Examples of member-owned businesses include mutual savings banks, credit unions, mutual insurance companies, and a whole host of charitable organizations.

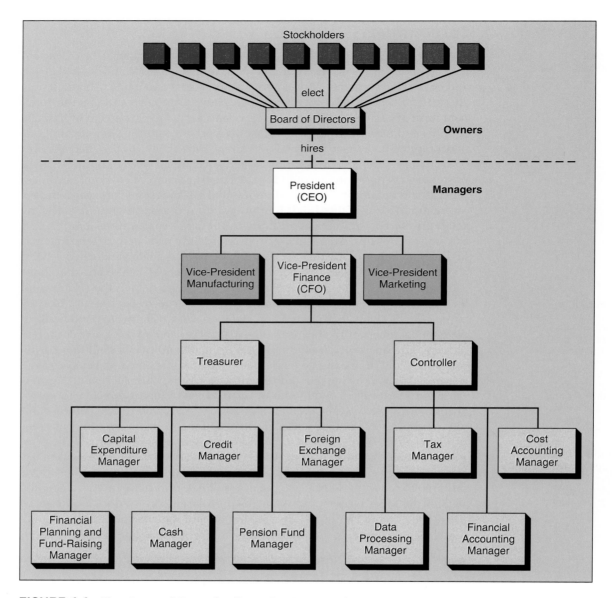

**FIGURE 1.1** **The General Organization of a Corporation and the Finance Function.**

The finance function is shown in gold. The stockholders are the owners of the firm. They elect the board of directors who establish policies and hire the president, or chief executive officer (CEO), to manage the firm and implement their policies. An agency issue results from the separation of owners and managers in the large corporation. The treasurer and controller typically report to the vice-president of finance, or chief financial officer (CFO), who reports to the company president or CEO. The treasurer commonly handles financial activities, and the controller handles accounting activities.

LG  3

# The Managerial Finance Function

As noted earlier, people in all areas of responsibility within the firm have to interact with finance personnel, processes, and procedures to get their jobs done. Everyone has to justify personnel requirements, negotiate operating budgets, worry about financial performance appraisals, and sell proposals at least partially on financial merits to get resources from upper management. Of course, financial personnel, to make useful forecasts and decisions, must be willing and able to talk to everybody else in the firm. The managerial finance function can be broadly described by considering its role within the organization and its relationship to economics and accounting. Here we look at these important aspects of the managerial finance function.

## Organization of the Finance Function

**treasurer**
The officer responsible for the firm's financial activities.

**controller**
The officer responsible for the firm's accounting activities.

The size and importance of the managerial finance function depend on the size of the firm. In small firms the finance function is generally performed by the accounting department. As a firm grows, the importance of the finance function typically results in the evolution of a separate department. It is usually linked directly to the company president or chief executive officer (CEO) through a vice-president of finance, commonly called the chief financial officer (CFO). The lower portion of the organizational chart in Figure 1.1 shows the structure of the finance activity in a typical medium-to-large-size firm. Reporting to the vice-president of finance are the treasurer and the controller. The **treasurer,** or financial manager, is commonly responsible for handling financial activities. These include financial planning and fund raising, making capital expenditure decisions, managing cash, managing credit activities, and managing the pension fund. The **controller** typically handles the accounting activities, such as tax management, data processing, and cost and financial accounting. The treasurer's focus tends to be more external, whereas the controller's focus is more internal. The activities of the treasurer, or financial manager, are the primary concern of this text.

If international sales or purchases are important to a firm, it may well employ one or more finance professionals whose job is to monitor and manage the firm's exposure to loss from currency fluctuations. This exposure arises if, for example, a company has booked a sale to a British customer for which delivery and payment will be made, in British pounds, in three months. If the dollar value of the British pound were to decline during the next three months (the pound depreciates), the dollar value of the firm's account receivable would also decline, and the firm would experience a foreign exchange loss, because it would be able to exchange the pounds received for fewer dollars than planned three months earlier. A trained financial manager can "hedge," or protect against, this and similar risks, at reasonable cost, using a variety of financial instruments. These **foreign exchange managers** (or traders) typically report to the firm's treasurer.

**foreign exchange manager**
The manager responsible for monitoring and managing the firm's exposure to loss from currency fluctuations.

## Relationship to Economics

The field of finance is closely related to economics. Because every business firm operates within the general economy, financial managers must under-

# F I N A N C E   I N

## A C T I O N

### "Float Like a Butterfly, Sting Like a Bee"
### Chrysler Again Avoids Bankruptcy

The rhyme, attributed to heavyweight boxing champion Mohammed Ali, is a slogan Chrysler's CEO Robert Eaton lives by. Nor do the similarities stop there. Like the heavyweight champion, Chrysler has been "on the ropes" several times, including as recently as 1991. Although Chrysler was out for the count in the 1970s, special government assistance helped put this competitor back in the ring.

In fact, entering 1994, Chrysler was the world's most successful automaker. From a business strategy perspective, Chrysler certainly does not follow the crowd. Whereas Ford and Mazda collaborate and General Motors and Toyota are in alliance, Chrysler prefers to go it alone. Instead, Chrysler integrated design, engineering, manufacturing, and finance divisions on spacious floors to facilitate continuous, informal discussions. One result is the Chrysler Neon, which *Automobile Magazine* named automobile of the year in 1994.

Chrysler, however, was following the lead of Japanese automakers by focusing on market share instead of profitability. For instance, Chrysler was planning on producing a roofed version of the Viper Roadster, a project which analysts figured would have a negative net present value. Consequently, while General Motors cut costs, Chrysler's innovations resulted in a financially weak position. With sales of $42 billion, Chrysler lost $3 billion. Stated another way, Chrysler lost $1 for every $14 in sales, resulting in a negative return on equity of 50 percent. Accounts payable to suppliers equalled cash in the bank, and unfunded pension liabilities stood at $2 billion. Nonetheless, investors were expecting a strong economy in 1994 and 1995 to boost Chrysler's overall volume past the breakeven level and had bid up the price of Chrysler stock fivefold.

Source: Alex Taylor III, "Will Success Spoil Chrysler?," *Fortune*, January 10, 1994, pp. 88–92.

stand the economic framework. They must be alert to the consequences of varying levels of economic activity and changes in economic policy. They must also be able to use economic theories as guidelines for efficient business operation. The primary economic principle used in managerial finance is **marginal analysis,** the principle that financial decisions should be made and actions taken only when the added benefits exceed the added costs. Nearly all financial decisions ultimately come down to an assessment of their marginal benefits and marginal costs. A basic knowledge of economics is therefore necessary to understand both the environment and the decision techniques of managerial finance.

**marginal analysis**
States that financial decisions should be made and actions taken only when added benefits exceed added costs.

## ▶ E X A M P L E

Amy Chen is a financial manager for Strom Department Stores—a large chain of upscale department stores operating primarily in the western United States. She is currently trying to decide whether to replace one of the firm's computers with a new, more sophisticated one that would both speed processing time and handle a larger volume of transactions. The new computer requires a cash outlay of $80,000. The old computer could be sold to net $28,000. The total benefit from the new computer (measured in today's dollars) is $100,000. The benefit over a similar time period from the old computer (measured in today's dollars) is $35,000. Applying marginal analysis to this data we get:

| | | |
|---|---|---|
| Benefits with new computer | $100,000 | |
| Less: Benefits with old computer | 35,000 | |
| (1) Marginal (Added) benefits | | $65,000 |
| Cost of new computer | $80,000 | |
| Less: Proceeds from sale of old computer | 28,000 | |
| (2) Marginal (Added) costs | | 52,000 |
| Net benefit [(1) − (2)] | | $13,000 |

Because the marginal (added) benefits of $65,000 exceed the marginal (added) costs of $52,000, the purchase of the new computer to replace the old one is recommended. The firm experiences a net gain of $13,000 as a result of this action.

## Relationship to Accounting

The firm's finance (treasurer) and accounting (controller) activities are typically within the control of the financial vice president (CFO), as shown in the lower portion of Figure 1.1. These functions are closely related and generally overlap. Indeed, managerial finance and accounting are not often easily distinguishable. In small firms the controller often carries out the finance function; in large firms many accountants are intimately involved in various finance activities. However, there are two basic differences between finance and accounting. One difference relates to the emphasis on cash flows and the other to decision making.

**Emphasis on Cash Flows**   The accountant's primary function is to develop and provide data for measuring the performance of the firm, assessing its financial position, and paying taxes. Using certain standardized and generally accepted principles, the accountant prepares financial statements that recognize revenue at the point of sale and expenses when incurred. This approach is commonly referred to as the **accrual method.**

**accrual method**
Recognizes revenue at the point of sale and recognizes expenses when incurred.

The financial manager, on the other hand, places primary emphasis on *cash flows,* the intake and outgo of cash. He or she maintains the firm's solvency by analyzing and planning its cash flows. The firm's cash flows must allow it to satisfy its obligations and acquire the assets needed to achieve its goals. The financial manager uses this **cash method** to recognize revenues and expenses only with respect to actual inflows and outflows of cash.

**cash method**
Recognizes revenues and expenses only with respect to actual inflows and outflows of cash.

A simple analogy may help to clarify the basic difference in viewpoint between the accountant and the financial manager. If we consider the human body as a business firm in which each beat of the heart represents a transaction, the accountant's primary concern is *recording* each of these beats as sales revenues, expenses, and profits. The financial manager is primarily concerned with whether the resulting flow of blood through the arteries reaches the cells and keeps the various organs of the whole body functioning. It is possible for a body to have a strong heart but cease to function due to the development of blockages or clots in its circulatory system. Similarly, a firm may be profitable but still may fail due to an insufficient flow of cash to meet its obligations as they come due.

▶ **E X A M P L E**

Thomas Yachts, a small yacht dealer, in the calendar year just ended sold one yacht for $100,000; the yacht was purchased during the year at a total cost of $80,000. Although the firm paid in full for the yacht during the year, at year end it has yet to collect the $100,000 from the customer. The accrual-based accounting view and the cash-flow-oriented financial view of the firm's performance during the year are given by the following income and cash flow statements, respectively.

| Accounting View | | Financial View | |
|---|---|---|---|
| **Income Statement**<br>**Thomas Yachts**<br>**for the Year Ended 12/31** | | **Cash Flow Statement**<br>**Thomas Yachts**<br>**for the Year Ended 12/31** | |
| Sales revenue | $100,000 | Cash inflow | $        0 |
| Less: Costs | 80,000 | Less: Cash outflow | 80,000 |
| Net profit | $20,000 | Net cash flow | ($80,000) |

Whereas in an accounting sense the firm is quite profitable, it is a financial failure in terms of actual cash flow. Thomas Yachts' lack of cash flow resulted from the uncollected account receivable of $100,000. Without adequate cash inflows to meet its obligations the firm will not survive, regardless of its level of profits.

The example above shows that accrual accounting data do not fully describe the circumstances of a firm. Thus the financial manager must look beyond financial statements to obtain insight into developing or existing problems. The financial manager, by concentrating on cash flow, should be able to avoid insolvency and achieve the firm's financial goals. Of course, although both accountants and financial managers are aware of each others' concerns and methods, the primary emphasis of accountants is on accrual methods and the primary emphasis of financial managers is on cash flow methods.

**Decision Making**   We come now to the second major difference between finance and accounting: decision making. The accountant devotes the most attention to the collection and presentation of financial data. The financial manager evaluates the accountant's statements, develops additional data, and makes decisions based on his or her assessment of the associated returns and risks. The accountant's role is to provide consistently developed and easily interpreted data about the firm's past, present, and future operations. The financial manager uses these data, either in raw form or after certain adjustments and analyses, as an important input to the decision-making process. Of course, this does not mean that accountants never make decisions or that financial managers never gather data; but the primary focuses of accounting and finance are distinctly different.

## Progress Review Questions

**1-6.** How does the finance function evolve within the business firm? What financial activities does the treasurer, or financial manager, perform in the mature firm?

**1-7.** Describe the close relationship between finance and economics, and explain why the financial manager should possess a basic knowledge of economics. What is the primary economic principle used in managerial finance?

**1-8.** What are the major differences between accounting and finance with respect to
   **a.** Emphasis on cash flows?
   **b.** Decision making?

# The Goal of the Financial Manager

As noted earlier in Figure 1.1, the owners of a corporation are normally distinct from its managers. The goal of the financial manager should be to achieve the objectives of the firm's owners, its stockholders. In most cases, if the managers are successful in this endeavor, they also achieve their own financial and professional objectives. In the sections that follow we first evaluate profit maximization, then describe the relationship of profit and risk to wealth maximization, and consider the preservation of stakeholder wealth. We also discuss the *agency issue* related to potential conflicts between the goals of stockholders and the actions of management, and finally we consider the role of ethics.

## Maximize Profit?

Some people believe that the owner's objective is always to maximize profits. To achieve the goal of profit maximization the financial manager takes only those actions that are expected to make a major contribution to the firm's overall profits. Thus, for each alternative being considered, the financial manager would select the one expected to result in the highest monetary return. For corporations, profits are commonly measured in terms of **earnings per share (EPS).** These represent the amount earned during the period—typically a quarter (three months) or a year—on each outstanding share of common stock. EPS are calculated by dividing the period's total earnings available for the firm's common stockholders—the firm's owners—by the number of shares of common stock outstanding.

**earnings per share (EPS)**
The amount earned during the period on each outstanding share of common stock.

# E X A M P L E

Nick Bono, the financial manager of Harper's Inc., a major manufacturer of fishing gear, is attempting to choose between two alternative investments: X and Y. Each is expected to have the following earnings-per-share effects over its three-year life.

| | Earnings per Share (EPS) | | | |
| --- | --- | --- | --- | --- |
| Investment | Year 1 | Year 2 | Year 3 | Total for Years 1, 2, and 3 |
| X | $1.40 | $1.00 | $ .40 | $2.80 |
| Y | .60 | 1.00 | 1.40 | 3.00 |

Based on the profit-maximization goal, investment Y is preferred over investment X. It results in higher earnings per share over the three-year period ($3.00 EPS for Y is greater than $2.80 EPS for X).

Profit maximization fails for a number of reasons: It ignores (1) the timing of returns, (2) cash flows available to stockholders, and (3) risk.

**Timing**   Because the firm can earn a return on funds it receives, the *receipt of funds sooner as opposed to later is preferred.* In our example, investment X may be preferred due to the greater EPS it provides in the first year. This is true in spite of the fact that the total earnings from investment X are smaller than those from Y. The greater returns in Year 1 could be reinvested to provide greater future earnings.

**Cash Flows**   A firm's earnings do *not* represent cash flows available to the stockholders. Owners receive returns either through cash dividends paid them or by selling their shares for a higher price than they initially paid. A greater EPS does not necessarily mean that dividend payments increase, because the payment of dividends results solely from the action of the firm's board of directors. Furthermore, a higher EPS does not necessarily translate into a higher stock price. Firms sometimes experience earnings increases without any correspondingly favorable change in stock price. Only when earnings increases are accompanied by increased current or expected cash flows or both is a higher stock price expected.

**Risk**   Profit maximization also disregards **risk**—the chance that actual outcomes may differ from those expected. A basic premise in managerial finance is that a trade-off exists between return (cash flow) and risk. *Return and risk are in fact the key determinants of share price, which represents the wealth of the owners in the firm.* Cash flow and risk affect share price differently: Higher cash flow is generally associated with a higher share price. Higher risk tends to result in a lower share price because the stockholder must be compensated for the greater risk. In general, stockholders are **risk-averse**—that is, they want to avoid risk. Where risk is involved, stockholders expect to earn higher rates of return on investments of higher risk and vice versa.

**risk**
The chance that actual outcomes may differ from those expected.

**risk-averse**
Seeking to avoid risk.

## ▶ E X A M P L E

Midwestern Distillers, a manufacturer of bourbon and blended whiskeys, is interested in expanding into one of two new product lines: gin or vodka. Because competition and availability of vodka is significantly affected by political events

(Russia is a major producer of vodka), it is viewed as a higher risk line of business than is gin. Today's cost of entering either of these markets is $45 million. The annual cash inflows from each product line are expected to average $9 million per year over the next 10 years, as shown in column 2 of the table below. To be compensated for taking risk, the firm must earn a higher rate of return on the higher risk vodka than on the lower risk gin line. The firm's required rate of return for each line is shown in column 3 of the table. Applying present-value techniques (quantitative financial techniques presented in Chapter 11), we can find the present value (today's value) of the average annual cash inflows over the 10 years for each product line as shown in column 4 of the table.

| Product Line | Risk (1) | Average Annual Cash Inflows ($ million) (2) | Required Rate of Return (%) (3) | Present Value of Cash Inflows[a] ($ million) (4) |
|---|---|---|---|---|
| Gin | Lower | 9 | 12 | 50.9 |
| Vodka | Higher | 9 | 15 | 45.2 |

[a]These values were found using present-value techniques, which are fully explained and demonstrated in Chapter 11.

Three important observations can be made: (1) Because the firm's stockholders are *risk-averse,* they must earn a higher rate of return on the higher risk vodka line than on the lower risk gin line. (2) Although the vodka line and the gin line have the same expected annual cash inflows, the vodka line's *greater risk causes its cash flows to be worth less* today than the gin line's cash flows ($45.2 million for vodka versus $50.9 million for gin). And (3) although both product lines appear attractive because their benefits (present value of cash inflows) exceed the $45 million cost, the gin alternative is preferred ($50.9 million for gin and only $45.2 million for vodka). It should be clear from this example that differences in risk can significantly affect the value of an investment and therefore the wealth of an owner.

## Maximize Shareholder Wealth

*The goal of the firm, and therefore all managers and employees, is to maximize the wealth of the owners for whom it is being operated.* The wealth of corporate owners is measured by the share price of the stock. The share price, in turn, is based on the timing of returns (cash flows), their magnitude, and their risk. When considering each financial decision alternative or possible action in terms of its effect on the share price of the firm's stock, *financial managers should accept only those actions that are expected to increase share price.* (Figure 1.2 depicts this process.) Because share price represents the owners' wealth in the firm, share price maximization is consistent with owner wealth maximization. Note that *return (cash flows) and risk are the key decision variables in the wealth maximization process.* It is also important to recognize that earnings per share (EPS), because they are an important component of the firm's return (cash flows), affect share price.

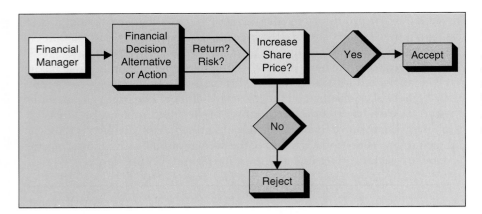

**FIGURE 1.2  Financial Decisions and Share Price**

The financial manager, when evaluating decision alternatives or potential actions, must consider both return and risk and their expected effect on share price. Actions expected to increase share price should be accepted.

## Preserve Stakeholder Wealth

Although shareholder wealth maximization is the primary goal, in recent years many firms have broadened their focus to include the interests of *stakeholders* as well as shareholders. **Stakeholders** are groups, such as employees, customers, suppliers, creditors, and others, who have a direct economic link to the firm. Employees are paid for their labor, customers purchase the firm's products or services, suppliers are paid for the materials and services they provide, and creditors provide financing that is to be repaid subject to specified terms. A firm with a stakeholder focus consciously avoids actions that would prove detrimental to stakeholders by damaging their wealth positions through the transfer of stakeholder wealth to the firm. The goal is not to maximize stakeholder well-being but to preserve it.

The stakeholder view, although not altering the shareholder wealth maximization goal, tends to limit the firm's actions to preserve the wealth of stakeholders. Such a view is often considered part of the firm's "social responsibility" and is expected to provide maximum long-term benefit to shareholders by maintaining positive stakeholder relationships. Such relationships should minimize stakeholder turnover, conflicts, and litigation. Clearly, the firm can better achieve its goal of shareholder wealth maximization with the cooperation of, rather than conflict with, its stakeholders.

**stakeholders**
Groups, such as employees, customers, suppliers, creditors, and others, who have a direct economic link to the firm.

## The Agency Issue

The control of the modern corporation is frequently placed in the hands of professional nonowner managers. (This separation of owners and managers is shown by the dashed horizontal line in Figure 1.1.) We have seen that the goal of the financial manager should be to maximize the wealth of the owners of the firm. Management can thus be viewed as *agents* of the owners who have hired them and given them decision-making authority to manage the firm for the owners' benefit. Technically, any manager owning less than 100 percent of the firm is to some degree an agent of the other owners.

In theory, most financial managers agree with the goal of owner wealth maximization. In practice, however, managers are also concerned with their personal wealth, job security, lifestyle, and fringe benefits, such as country club memberships, limousines, and posh offices, all provided at company expense. Such concerns may make managers reluctant or unwilling to take more than moderate risk if they perceive that too much risk might result in a loss of job and damage to personal wealth. The result of such a "satisficing" approach (a compromise between satisfaction and maximization) is a less than maximum return and a potential loss of wealth for the owners.

### Resolving the Agency Problem

**agency problem**
The likelihood that managers may place personal goals ahead of corporate goals.

From this conflict of owner and personal goals arises what has been called the **agency problem**—the likelihood that managers may place personal goals ahead of corporate goals. Two factors, market forces and *agency costs,* act to prevent or minimize agency problems.

**Market Forces.** One market force is *major shareholders,* particularly large institutional investors, such as mutual funds, life insurance companies, and pension funds. These holders of large blocks of a firm's stock have begun, during recent years, to communicate with and exert pressure on management to perform. When necessary they actively exercise their voting rights to oust underperforming management and replace it with more competent management. Another market force is the *threat of takeover* by another firm or group that believes that it can enhance the firm's value by restructuring its management (by firing and replacing them), operations, and financing. The constant threat of takeover tends to motivate management to act in the best interest of the firm's owners by attempting to maximize share price.

**agency costs**
The costs borne by stockholders to prevent or minimize agency problems.

**Agency Costs.** To respond to potential market forces by preventing or minimizing agency problems and contributing to the maximization of owners' wealth, stockholders incur **agency costs.** These are the costs of monitoring management behavior, ensuring against dishonest acts of management, and giving managers the financial incentive to act in a fashion consistent with share price maximization. The most popular, powerful, and expensive approach is to *structure management compensation* to correspond with share price maximization. The objective is to give management incentives to act in the best interests of the owners and to compensate managers for such actions. In addition, the resulting compensation packages allow firms to compete for and hire the best managers available. Today more firms are tying management compensation to the firm's performance. This incentive appears to motivate managers to operate in a manner reasonably consistent with stock price maximization.

### The Current View

Although experts agree that an effective way to motivate management is to tie compensation to performance, the execution of many compensation plans has been closely scrutinized in recent years. Stockholders—both individuals and institutions—as well as the Securities and Exchange Commission (SEC) have publicly questioned the appropriateness of the multimillion-dollar compensation packages (including salary, bonus, and long-term compensation) that many corporate executives receive. For example, the three highest paid CEOs in 1993, were (1) Michael D. Eisner of Walt Disney, who earned $203,011,000; (2) Sanford I. Weill of Travelers, who earned $52,810,000; and (3) Joseph R. Hyde III of Autozone, who earned $32,220,000. Tenth on the same list was Thomas M. Hahn, Jr., of Georgia-Pacific, who earned $13,680,000. During 1993, the compensation of the average CEO of a major U.S. corporation remained unchanged from 1992.

CEOs of 361 large and medium-sized U.S. industrial companies surveyed by *Business Week* using data from Standard & Poor's Compustat Services Inc., earned an average of $3.8 million in total compensation; the average for the 20 largest companies was $26.0 million.

Although sizable compensation packages may be justified by significant increases in shareholder wealth, recent studies have failed to find a strong relationship between CEO compensation and share price. The publicity surrounding these large compensation packages (without corresponding share price performance) is expected to continue to drive down executive compensation in the future. Contributing to this publicity is the relatively recent SEC requirement that publicly traded companies disclose to shareholders and others both the amount of and method used to determine compensation paid to their highest paid executives. At the same time, new compensation plans that more closely tie management's earnings to its success in enhancing shareholder wealth are expected to be developed and implemented. Unconstrained, managers may have other goals in addition to share price maximization, but much of the evidence suggests that share price maximization—the focus of this book—is the primary goal of most firms.

## The Role of Ethics

In recent years the legitimacy of actions taken by certain businesses has received major public attention. Examples include the Big Six public accounting firm Ernst & Young's agreement to pay $400 million to settle federal charges that it inadequately audited four large thrifts that failed at a cost to the government of $6.6 billion; Salomon Brothers' attempts to rig U.S. Treasury bill auctions through the use of fake bids; Michael Milken's conviction for racketeering, insider trading, and fraud; and Charles Keating Jr.'s conviction for racketeering and other charges related to self-dealing with depositor funds that resulted in the failure of Lincoln Savings and Loan of California. Clearly, these and other similar actions have raised the question of **ethics**—standards of conduct or moral judgment. Today, society in general and the financial community in particular, primarily because of such notorious financial offenders as Milken and Keating, are developing and enforcing ethical standards. The goal of these standards is to motivate business and market participants to adhere to both the letter and the spirit of laws and regulations concerned with all aspects of business and professional practice.

**ethics**
Standards of conduct or moral judgment.

**Opinions**   An opinion survey of business leaders, business school deans, and members of Congress showed that 94 percent of the more than 1,000 respondents felt that the business community is troubled by ethical problems.[2] In addition, only 32 percent of the respondents felt that this issue had been overblown by the news media and political leaders. Most striking was the survey's finding that 63 percent of respondents felt that a business firm actually strengthens its competitive position by maintaining high ethical standards. Respondents to the survey believed that the best way to encourage ethical business behavior is for firms to adopt a business code of ethics. They rated legislation as the least effective way.

---

[2]*Ethics in American Business* (New York: Touche Ross), December 1987.

**Considering Ethics**   Robert A. Cooke, a noted ethicist, suggests the following questions be used to assess the ethical viability of a proposed action:[3]

1. Is the action . . . arbitrary or capricious? Does it unfairly single out an individual or group?
2. Does the action . . . violate the moral or legal rights of any individual or group?
3. Does the action . . . conform to accepted moral standards?
4. Are there alternative courses of action that are less likely to cause actual or potential harm?

Clearly, considering such questions prior to taking an action can help to ensure its ethical viability.

Today more and more firms are directly addressing the issue of ethics by establishing corporate ethics policies and guidelines and by requiring employee compliance with them. Frequently employees are required to sign a formal pledge to uphold the firm's ethics policies. Such policies typically apply to employee actions in dealing with all corporate constituents, including other employees, customers, vendors, creditors, owners, regulators, and the public at large. Many companies require employees to participate in ethics seminars and training programs that convey and demonstrate corporate ethics policy. Role playing and case exercises are sometimes used to give employees hands-on experience in effectively dealing with potential ethical dilemmas.

**Ethics and Share Price**   The implementation of a pro-active ethics program is believed to enhance corporate value. An ethics program can produce a number of positive benefits: reduce potential litigation and judgment costs; maintain a positive corporate image; build shareholder confidence; and gain the loyalty, commitment, and respect of all the firm's constituents. Such actions, by maintaining and enhancing cash flow and reducing perceived risk (as a result of greater investor confidence), are expected to affect positively the firm's share price. *Ethical behavior is therefore viewed as necessary for achievement of the firm's goal of owner wealth maximization.*

▼▼▼▼▼▼▼▼▼▼▼▼▼▼▼▼▼▼▼▼▼▼▼▼▼▼▼▼▼

## Progress Review Questions

**1-9.**  Briefly describe three basic reasons why profit maximization fails to be consistent with wealth maximization.

**1-10.**  What is *risk?* Why must risk as well as return be considered by the financial manager when evaluating a decision alternative or action?

**1-11.**  What is the goal of the firm and therefore of all managers and employees? Discuss how one measures achievement of this goal.

**1-12.**  Who are a firm's *stakeholders,* and what consideration is often given them in pursuing the firm's goal? Why?

---

[3]"Business Ethics: A Perspective," *Arthur Anderson Cases on Business Ethics,* September 1988, p. 2.

**1-13.** What is the *agency problem?* How do market forces, both major share-holders and the threat of takeover, act to prevent or minimize this problem?

**1-14.** Define *agency costs,* and explain why firms incur them. How do firms attempt to structure management compensation to prevent or minimize agency problems? What is the current view on the execution of many compensation plans?

**1-15.** Why has corporate ethics become so important in recent years? Describe the role of corporate ethics policies and guidelines, and discuss the relationship that is believed to exist between ethics and share price.

▲▲▲▲▲▲▲▲▲▲▲▲▲▲▲▲▲▲▲▲▲▲▲▲▲▲▲▲▲▲▲▲▲▲▲▲

# Key Activities of the Financial Manager

LG 6

The financial manager's activities, all of which are aimed at achieving the goal of owner wealth maximization, can be related to the firm's basic financial statements. The primary activities are (1) performing financial analysis and planning; (2) making investment decisions; and (3) making financing decisions. Figure 1.3 relates each of these financial activities to the firm's **balance sheet,** which shows the firm's financial position at a given point in time. Today, many financial managers employ *total quality management* (*TQM*) principles when performing each of these important activities. Note that although investment and financing decisions can be conveniently viewed in terms of the balance sheet, these decisions are made on the basis of their cash flow effects. This emphasis on cash flow becomes clearer in Chapter 3 as well as in later chapters.

**balance sheet**
Record that shows the firm's financial position at a given point in time.

## Performing Financial Analysis and Planning

Financial analysis and planning is concerned with (1) transforming financial data into a form that can be used to monitor the firm's financial condition; (2) evaluating the need for increased (or reduced) productive capacity; and

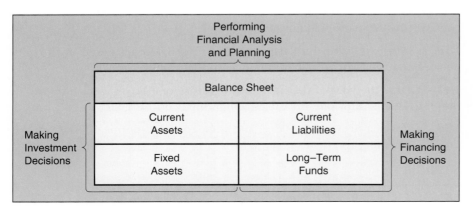

**FIGURE 1.3  Key Activities of the Financial Manager**

The financial manager's key activities—(1) performing financial analysis and planning, (2) making investment decisions, and (3) making financing decisions—can be related to the firm's balance sheet.

## F I N A N C E  I N

## A C T I O N

**Careers**

### Ampro Computers Debugs Its Program for Selecting Financial Managers

Ampro Computers' CEO David Feldman learned about the importance of picking the right financial officer the hard way Lacking a financial background, Feldman chose an individual using inappropriate qualifications and gave a misleading description of job responsibilities. After the Sunnyvale, California, firm terminated its unsuccessful hire, Ampro was charged with wrongful termination. The suit cost Ampro more than $400,000 in settlement and legal fees and Feldman 1,200 hours on related legal matters in 1991 and 1992.

Subsequently, Feldman has identified four criteria for selecting a financial officer. They are

1. **Shared values:**
   The individual should have the same goals, ethics, and even chemistry as the current management team.
2. **Hands-on experience:**
   The individual should have experience meeting a payroll or interest payment.
3. **Potential to grow:**
   The individual should be willing to explore new projects, such as the value of entering international markets.
4. **Technical expertise:**
   The individual should understand accounts payable and receivable, inventory control, and cash management.

Feldman now relies on recruiting specialists, who receive this list, augmented by advice from Ampro's accountant, banker, and corporate lawyer, and enhanced by his own personal experiences.

Source: Jill Andresky Fraser, "Checking out the Best CFO," *Inc.*, July 1993, p. 35.

(3) determining what additional (or reduced) financing is required. These functions encompass the entire balance sheet as well as the firm's income statement and other financial statements. Although this activity relies heavily on accrual-based financial statements, its underlying objective is to assess the firm's cash flows and develop plans that ensure adequate cash flow is available to support achievement of its goals.

## Making Investment Decisions

Investment decisions determine both the mix and the type of assets found on the firm's balance sheet. This activity is concerned with the left-hand side of the balance sheet. *Mix* refers to the number of dollars of current and fixed assets. Once the mix is established, the financial manager must attempt to maintain certain optimal levels of each type of current asset. The financial manager must also decide which are the best fixed assets to acquire and know when existing fixed assets need to be modified, replaced, or liquidated. These decisions are important because they affect the firm's success in achieving its goals.

## Making Financing Decisions

Financing decisions deal with the right-hand side of the firm's balance sheet and involve two major areas. First, the most appropriate mix of short-term and long-term financing must be established. A second and equally important concern is which individual short-term or long-term sources of financing are best at a given time. Many of these decisions are dictated by necessity. However some require an in-depth analysis of the available financing alternatives, their costs, and their long-term implications. Again, it is the effect of these decisions on the firm's goal achievement that is most important.

## The Financial Manager's Role in Total Quality Management (TQM)

**Total quality management** (**TQM**), the application of quality principles to all aspects of a company's operations, is an important concept for today's financial manager. Quality control was once considered primarily a production responsibility. By contrast, TQM is now a companywide goal affecting *all* departments. TQM principles include continual efforts to improve operations by streamlining processes to achieve greater efficiency and satisfaction of the needs of all customers—both internal and external. (Departments are *internal customers* of each other. For example, the finance department, a user of accounting data, is a customer of the accounting department; the facilities planning group is a customer for the capital budgeting group's project analyses.)

**total quality management (TQM)**
The application of quality principles to all aspects of a company's operations.

**Benefits and Costs of TQM**    A commitment to TQM directly relates to profitability. In the past, managers considered quality and productivity to be mutually exclusive; one increased only at the expense of the other. More recent experience shows that as quality increases, so does productivity. And improved quality also lowers costs by reducing the time, materials, and service required to correct errors. This obviously should have a positive effect on operating profits. If, by applying TQM, the time to design, develop, and market a new product is shortened, the company will receive sales revenues from this product sooner. The finance department can contribute to the firm's overall quality effort by streamlining its operations so that budgets are available on a timely basis, the level of analysis is appropriate for the size and type of project, and decisions are made more quickly.

The cost of quality includes not only the cost to implement TQM programs that get the job done correctly the first time, but also the cost to correct bad quality when work is *not* performed correctly the first time. The cost of bad quality can be considerable: reprocessing orders, excess demands for service, customer complaints, lost business, and so on.

**TQM in Action**    Two notable examples of TQM in action at U.S. companies are at Ford Motor Company and Du Pont. Ford, whose motto is "Quality is Job #1," achieved significant cost reductions in labor, overhead, and materials required to produce its cars by adopting TQM. It needs one-third fewer labor hours to build its cars than rival General Motors, a savings of about $800 per car. Du Pont enjoyed an 80 percent market share for its Kalrez plastic until Japanese competition with better customer service began making inroads.

The company quickly responded by shortening the production cycle by more than 75 percent, reducing the time to fill orders by more than 50 percent, and increasing on-time deliveries from 70 percent to 100 percent. As a result, sales increased 22 percent.

▼▼▼▼▼▼▼▼▼▼▼▼▼▼▼▼▼▼▼▼▼▼▼▼▼▼▼▼▼▼▼▼▼▼▼

## Progress Review Questions

**1-16.** What are the three key activities of the financial manager? Relate them to the firm's balance sheet.

**1-17.** What is *total quality management* (TQM)? Discuss the benefits (and costs) of TQM.

▲▲▲▲▲▲▲▲▲▲▲▲▲▲▲▲▲▲▲▲▲▲▲▲▲▲▲▲▲▲▲▲▲▲▲

## An Overview of the Text

This text's organization is structured around the corporate balance sheet, with linkages to share price. The activities of the financial manager are described in seven separate but related parts:

>    Part I: Introduction to Managerial Finance
>    Part II: Financial Analysis and Planning
>    Part III: Short-Term Financial Management
>    Part IV: Long-Term Financial Concepts
>    Part V: Long-Term Investment Decisions
>    Part VI: Long-Term Financing Decisions
>    Part VII: Special Managerial Finance Topics

The activities of the financial manager in each of the areas in the above list are presented in relation to the firm's balance sheet. The book gives primary attention to both return and risk factors and their potential impact on the owner's wealth as reflected by share value. Coverage of international events and topics is integrated into the chapter discussions. A separate international managerial finance chapter is also included.

This text was developed using a group of about 130 learning goals, typically six per chapter. Mastery of these goals results in a broad understanding of the concepts, tools, and techniques of managerial finance. These goals have been carefully integrated into a learning system. Each chapter begins with a numbered list of its learning goals. Next to each major text heading is a *toolbox*, which (in addition to the computer software icons described later) notes by number the specific learning goal addressed in that section. In the *Applications* book, the chapter summaries, self-tests, and problem sets are also keyed by number to each chapter's learning goals. The integrated learning system, by linking all elements to the learning goals, facilitates their mastery.

Keyed to various parts of the text is the *FMF Disk,* a menu-driven computer disk for use with IBM PCs and compatible microcomputers. The disk contains three different sets of routines: The *FMF Tutor,* the *FMF Problem-Solver,* and the *FMF Lotus Templates.* The *FMF Tutor* is a user-friendly program that extends self-testing opportunities in the more quantitative chapters beyond those included in the *Applications* book. It gives immediate feedback with detailed solutions, provides tutorial assistance, and for convenience includes text page references. Text discussions and workbook problems with which the *FMF Tutor* can be used are marked with a 🖳. The *FMF Problem-Solver* can be used as an aid in performing many of the routine financial calculations and procedures presented in both the text and *Applications* book. For convenience, a disk symbol, 🖳, is used to identify those text discussions and *Applications* problems that can be solved with the *FMF Problem-Solver.* The *FMF Lotus Templates* can be used with Lotus 1-2-3 to input data and solve more complex problems for selected chapters. These problems are clearly marked in the *Applications* book with a spreadsheet symbol, 🖳, to enable you to carry out "what if" types of analyses. A detailed discussion of how to use the *FMF Disk*—the *Tutor,* the *Problem-Solver,* and the *Lotus Templates*—is included in the *Applications* book.

# SUMMARY OF LEARNING GOALS

**Define finance and describe its major areas and opportunities.** Finance, the art and science of managing money, affects the lives of every person and every organization. Major opportunities in financial services are included within the areas of banking and related institutions, personal financial planning, investments, real estate, and insurance. Managerial finance, which is concerned with the duties of the financial manager in the business firm, offers numerous career opportunities, such as financial analyst, capital budgeting analyst/manager, and pension fund manager. In addition, the recent trend toward globalization of business activity has created new demands and opportunities in managerial finance.

LG  **1**

**Review the basic forms of business organization and their respective strengths and weaknesses.** The basic forms of business organization are the sole proprietorship, the partnership, and the corporation. Although there are more sole proprietorships than any other form of business organization, the corporation is dominant in terms of business receipts and net profits. Limited liability and the resulting ability to market its ownership are major strengths of the corporation that differentiate it from sole proprietorships and partnerships.

LG  **2**

**Describe the managerial finance function and differentiate managerial finance from the closely related disciplines of economics and accounting.** In large firms the managerial finance function might be handled by a separate department headed by the vice-president of finance (CFO), to whom the treasurer and controller report. In small firms the finance function is generally performed by the accounting department. Managerial finance is closely related to the disciplines of economics and accounting. The finan-

LG  **3**

cial manager must understand the economic environment and relies heavily on the economic principle of marginal analysis when making decisions. Financial managers use accounting data but differ from accountants, who devote primary attention to accrual methods and to gathering and presenting data, by concentrating on cash flows and decision making.

LG 4

**Justify the financial manager's focus on the goal of maximizing shareholder wealth rather than maximizing profit and on preservation of stakeholder wealth.** The goal of the financial manager is to maximize the owners' wealth (dependent on stock price) rather than profits, because profit maximization ignores the timing of returns, does not directly consider cash flows, and ignores risk. Because risk and return are the key determinants of share price, both must be assessed by the financial manager when evaluating alternative decisions or actions. The stakeholder view, while not altering the shareholder wealth maximization goal, tends to limit the firm's actions to preserve the wealth of stakeholders. Such a view is often considered part of the firm's "social responsibility" and is expected to provide maximum long-term benefit to shareholders by maintaining positive stakeholder relationships.

LG 5

**Discuss the agency issue—its resolution and current view—as it relates to owner wealth maximization and the role of ethics in achieving this goal.** Agency problems resulting from managers placing personal goals ahead of corporate goals can be minimized by two forces: market forces and agency costs. In addition, positive ethical practices by the firm and its managers are believed necessary for achieving the firm's goal of owner wealth maximization.

LG 6

**Identify the key activities of the financial manager within the firm and his or her role in total quality management (TQM).** The three key activities of the financial manager are (1) performing financial analysis and planning, (2) making investment decisions, and (3) making financing decisions. Today, many financial managers employ total quality management (TQM) principles when performing each of these important activities. TQM principles include continual efforts to improve operations by streamlining processes to achieve greater efficiency and satisfaction of the needs of all customers—both internal and external.

# 2 The Firm's Environment

The business environment can either open up doors to new capital or practically shut down access to financing. This fact is currently relevant for communications companies like Comcast Corporation, which operates in several areas of this growing industry. Comcast is the third largest cable television system operator in the country. It also operates cellular telephone franchises on the East Coast and has ownership interests in companies that produce cable programming, such as Turner

## Marketplace changes can significantly change a company's . . . ability to obtain financing.

Broadcasting and QVC Network.

Marketplace changes can significantly change a company's business prospects and, therefore, its ability to obtain financing. Financial managers must continuously monitor economic, regulatory, tax, and political developments at the federal, state, and local level, to adapt to new situations. For example, after six years as an unregulated industry, Congress passed the Cable Act in April 1993 which re-regulated the cable industry and effec-

tively froze the rates at which we bill our customer base. For a short time cable firms had difficulty obtaining new funds because investors and lenders were uncertain about the industry's future earnings potential. Several cable companies saw their share price drop about 50 percent in just one month! Once the financial community analyzed the situation and realized it wasn't the end of the world, the debt and equity markets again opened up, and bond and stock prices rose accordingly.

Financial managers must understand the financial institutions and money and capital markets, which bridge the gap between suppliers and demanders of funds, to raise and manage financing efficiently. Because cable companies are capital intensive, financing activities are critical to their success. Comcast borrows from financial institutions, such as banks and insurance companies, and sells bonds and stocks in the public markets to individual and institutional investors. Our borrowing strategy depends on interest rate forecasts. If we expect future rates to be stable or lower, we prefer a floating rate of interest—just like you would on a home mortgage. If we think interest rates are going to rise, we want to lock in current rates for a longer term—as we did in 1993, when rates were at 20-year lows.

Currently our business is 95 percent domestic. Much of our future growth, however, will be international. We already have three joint ventures for combined phone and cable systems in the United Kingdom, with partners from the Far East and Europe. In ad-

dition, we are pursuing cable and cellular telephone franchises with local firms in countries around the world. Entering the international arena also brings new risks. For the first time, Comcast is generating revenue in a currency other than dollars. If the British pound loses value against the dollar, it affects our bottom line. We can't just think about U.S. operations; we now have to look at other economies and operating environments, as well as how other currencies move in relation to the dollar.

Communications technology is changing rapidly, and we have to respond quickly to changes in market conditions. Billions of dollars can be made or lost based on which technology a company chooses. Therefore, financial managers must work closely with operating managers to coordinate a cohesive strategy for the future.

*Comcast Corporation's Assistant Treasurer and Director of Finance* **William E. Dordelman** *received his B.A. in economics and French from St. Lawrence University. Before joining Comcast in 1993, he managed MontWest Capital Partners, a private equity partnership, for three years and from 1985 to 1990 was employed by Lazard Fréres & Co. and Morgan Stanley & Co.'s communications and media groups.*

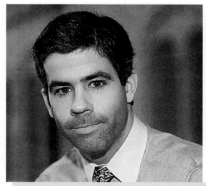

$A$ firm operates not as an isolated entity but in a close and dynamic interrelationship with the government and various financial intermediaries and markets. Business taxation, financial institutions, financial markets, securities offerings and trading, and interest rates and required returns are all key aspects of the firm's environment. In this chapter we study these important aspects of finance to understand both how they limit and create opportunities for the financial manager.

# Business Taxation

LG 1

Businesses, like individuals, must pay taxes on their income. The actual rates of taxation differ depending on the forms of business organization. Income can be subject to either individual or corporate income taxes. The income of sole proprietorships and partnerships is taxed as the income of the individual owners. Corporate income is subject to corporate taxes. Whatever their legal form, all businesses can earn two types of income: ordinary and capital gains. Both types of income are treated the same for tax purposes under current law. Frequent amendments in the tax code, such as the *Omnibus Budget Reconciliation Act of 1993,* which is reflected in the following discussions, make it likely that the 1993 tax rates given below will change before the next edition of this text is published. Because the corporation is financially dominant in our economy, *emphasis is given here to corporate taxation.* A special type of corporate tax-reporting entity is the S corporation, which we also discuss.

## Ordinary Income

The **ordinary income** of a corporation is income earned through the sale of its goods or services. Ordinary income is currently taxed subject to the rates depicted in the corporate tax rate schedule given in Table 2.1.

**ordinary income**
Income earned through the sale of a firm's goods or services.

## ▶ E X A M P L E

Western Manufacturing, Inc., a small producer of kitchen utensils, has before-tax earnings of $250,000. The tax on these earnings can be found using the tax rate schedule given in Table 2.1

$$\text{Total taxes due} = \$22,250 + [.39 \times (\$250,000 - \$100,000)]$$
$$= \$22,250 + (.39 \times \$150,000)$$
$$= \$22,250 + \$58,500 = \underline{\$80,750}$$

The firm's total taxes on its before-tax earnings are therefore $80,750. If the firm had earned only $20,000 before taxes, its total tax liability would have been $3,000 [$0 + (.15 × $20,000)].

From a financial point of view it is important to understand the difference between average and marginal tax rates, the treatment of interest and dividend income, and the effect of tax-deductibility on the after-tax cost of expenses.

**average tax rate**
A firm's taxes divided by its taxable income.

**Average Versus Marginal Tax Rates**   The **average tax rate** paid on the firm's ordinary income can be calculated by dividing its taxes by its taxable income. For firms with taxable income of $10,000,000 or less, the average tax rate ranges from 15 to 34 percent, reaching 34 percent when taxable income equals or exceeds $335,000. For firms with taxable income in excess of $10,000,000, the average tax rate ranges between 34 and 35 percent. The average tax rate paid by Western Manufacturing, Inc., in our preceding example, was 32.3 percent ($80,750 ÷ $250,000). Table 2.2 presents the firm's tax liability and average tax rate for various levels of pretax income; as income increases, the rate approaches and finally reaches 34 percent. It remains at that level up to $10,000,000 of taxable income, beyond which it rises toward but never reaches an average tax rate of 35 percent.

**marginal tax rate**
The rate at which additional income is taxed.

The **marginal tax rate** represents the rate at which additional income is taxed. In the current corporate tax structure, the marginal tax rate on income up to $50,000 is 15 percent; from $50,000 to $75,000 it is 25 percent; from $75,000 to $100,000 it is 34 percent; for income between $100,000 and $335,000 it is 39 percent; for income between $335,000 and $10,000,000 it is 34 percent; and for income in excess of $10,000,000 it is 35 percent. To simplify calculations in the text, *a fixed 40-percent tax rate is assumed to be applicable to ordinary corporate income.*

## E X A M P L E

If Western Manufacturing's earnings go up to $300,000, the marginal tax rate on the additional $50,000 of income will be 39 percent. The company will therefore have to pay additional taxes of $19,500 (.39 × $50,000). Total taxes on the $300,000, then, will be $100,250 ($80,750 + $19,500). Checking this

**TABLE 2.1   Corporate Tax Rate Schedule**

| Range of Taxable Income | | Base Tax | + | (Rate | × | Amount over Base Bracket) |
|---|---|---|---|---|---|---|
| $      0–$ | 50,000 | $        0 | + | (15% | × | Amount over $          0) |
| 50,000– | 75,000 | 7,500 | + | (25 | × | Amount over     50,000) |
| 75,000– | 100,000 | 13,750 | + | (34 | × | Amount over     75,000) |
| 100,000– | 335,000[a] | 22,250 | + | (39 | × | Amount over    100,000) |
| 335,000– | 10,000,000 | 113,900 | + | (34 | × | Amount over    335,000) |
| Over $10,000,000[b] | | 3,400,000 | + | (35 | × | Amount over  10,000,000) |

[a]Because corporations with taxable income in excess of $100,000 must increase their tax by the lesser of $11,750 or 5% of the taxable income in excess of $100,000, they will end up paying a 39% surtax on taxable income between $100,000 and $335,000. The 5% surtax that raises the tax rate from 34% to 39% causes all corporations with taxable income between $335,000 and $10,000,000 to have an *average tax rate* of 34%, as can be seen in Table 2.2.

[b]This bracket and its associated 35% tax rate was created with passage of the *Omnibus Budget Reconciliation Act of 1993,* which was signed into law on August 10, 1993 and is retroactive to its effective date of January 1, 1993.

**TABLE 2.2   Pretax Income, Tax Liabilities, and Average Tax Rates**

| Pretax Income (1) | Tax Liability (2) | Average Tax Rate [(2) ÷ (1)] (3) |
|---|---|---|
| $   50,000 | $    7,500 | 15.00% |
| 75,000 | 13,750 | 18.33 |
| 100,000 | 22,250 | 22.25 |
| 200,000 | 61,250 | 30.63 |
| 335,000 | 113.900 | 34.00 |
| 500,000 | 170,000 | 34.00 |
| 1,000,000 | 340,000 | 34.00 |
| 2,500,000 | 850,000 | 34.00 |
| 10,000,000 | 3,400,000 | 34.00 |
| 12,000,000 | 4,100,000 | 34.17 |
| 25,000,000 | 8,650,000 | 34.60 |

figure using the tax rate schedule in Table 2.1, we get a total tax liability of $22,250 + [.39 × ($300,000 − $100,000)] = $22,250 + $78,000 = $100,250. This is the same value obtained by applying the marginal tax rate to the added income and adjusting the known tax liability.

The *average tax rate* tends to be most useful in evaluating taxes historically, and the *marginal tax rate* is more frequently used in financial decision making. For example, it is often helpful to know the average tax rate at which taxes were paid over a given period. But in making decisions the important concern is the rate at which the earnings from alternative proposals will *actually* be taxed, that is, the marginal tax rate. With *progressive tax rates*—higher rates for higher levels of taxable income—the average tax rate is always less than or equal to the marginal tax rate. Given our focus on financial decision making, the *tax rates used throughout this text are assumed to represent marginal tax rates.*

**Interest and Dividend Income**   In the process of determining taxable income, any *interest received* by the corporation is included as ordinary income and therefore taxed at the firm's applicable tax rates. *Dividends received* on common and preferred stock held in other corporations, and representing less than 20 percent ownership in them, on the other hand, are subject to a 70 percent exclusion for tax purposes.[1] Because of the dividend exclusion, only 30 percent of these **intercorporate dividends** are included as ordinary

**intercorporate dividends**
Dividends received by one corporation on common and preferred stock held in other corporations.

----

[1]The exclusion is 80 percent if the corporation owns between 20 and 80 percent of the stock in the corporation paying it dividends; 100 percent of the dividends received are excluded if it owns more than 80 percent of the corporation paying it dividends. For convenience, here we are assuming the ownership interest in the dividend-paying corporation is less than 20 percent.

income. The tax law provides this exclusion to avoid *triple taxation*—the first and second corporations are taxed on income prior to paying the dividend, and the dividend recipient must include the dividend in his or her taxable income. This feature in effect provides some relief by eliminating most of the potential tax liability from the dividend received by the second (and any subsequent) corporations.

# EXAMPLE

Checker Industries, a major manufacturer of molds for the plastics industry, during the year just ended received $100,000 in interest on bonds it held and $100,000 in dividends on common stock it owned in other corporations. The firm is subject to a 40 percent marginal tax rate and is eligible for a 70 percent exclusion on its intercorporate dividend receipts. The after-tax income realized by Checker from each of these sources of investment income is found as shown in the table.

|  | Interest Income | Dividend Income |
|---|---|---|
| (1) Before-tax amount | $100,000 | $100,000 |
| Less: Applicable exclusion | 0 | (.70 × $100,000) = 70,000 |
| Taxable amount | $100,000 | $ 30,000 |
| (2) Tax (40%) | 40,000 | 12,000 |
| After-tax amount [(1) − (2)] | $ 60,000 | $ 88,000 |

As a result of the 70 percent dividend exclusion, the after-tax amount is greater for the dividend income than for the interest income. Clearly the dividend exclusion enhances the attractiveness of stock investments relative to bond investments made by one corporation in another corporation.

**Tax-Deductible Expenses** When calculating their taxes, corporations are allowed to deduct operating expenses, such as advertising, sales commissions, and bad debts as well as *interest expense,* which is the "rent" paid lenders for the use of their funds. The tax-deductibility of these expenses reduces their after-tax cost, making them less costly than they might at first appear. The following example illustrates the benefit of tax-deductibility.

# EXAMPLE

Companies X and Y each expect in the coming year to have earnings before interest and taxes of $200,000. Company X during the year has to pay $30,000 in interest. Company Y has no debt and therefore has no interest expense. Calculation of the earnings after taxes for these two firms, which pay a 40 percent tax on ordinary income, are shown in the table.

|                                        | Company X  | Company Y  |
|----------------------------------------|------------|------------|
| Earnings before interest and taxes     | $200,000   | $200,000   |
| Less: Interest expense                 | 30,000     | 0          |
| Earnings before taxes                  | $170,000   | $200,000   |
| Less: Taxes (40%)                      | 68,000     | 80,000     |
| Earnings after taxes                   | $102,000   | $120,000   |
| Difference in earnings after taxes     | $18,000    |            |

The data demonstrate that although Company X had $30,000 more interest expense than Company Y, Company X's earnings after taxes are only $18,000 less than those of Company Y ($102,000 for Company X versus $120,000 for Company Y). This difference is attributable to the fact that Company X's $30,000 interest expense deduction provided a tax savings of $12,000 ($68,000 for Company X versus $80,000 for Company Y). This amount can be calculated directly by multiplying the tax rate by the amount of interest expense (.40 × $30,000 = $12,000). Similarly, the $18,000 *after-tax cost* of the interest expense can be calculated directly by multiplying one minus the tax rate times the amount of interest expense [(1 − .40) × $30,000 = $18,000].

The tax-deductibility of certain expenses can be seen to reduce their actual (after-tax) cost to the profitable firm. Note that both for accounting and tax purposes *interest is a tax-deductible expense, whereas dividends, which are earnings distributions to owners (stockholders), are not.* Because dividends are not tax-deductible, their after-tax cost is equal to the amount of the dividend. Thus a $30,000 cash dividend has an after-tax cost of $30,000.

## Capital Gains

If a firm sells a capital asset[2] such as stock held as an investment for more than its initial purchase price, the difference between the sale price and the purchase price is called a **capital gain.** For corporations, capital gains are added to ordinary corporate income and taxed at the regular corporate rates, with a maximum marginal tax rate of 39 percent.[3] To simplify the computations presented in later chapters of the text, as for ordinary income, a *40 percent tax rate is assumed to be applicable to corporate capital gains.*

**capital gain**
The amount by which the sale price of an asset exceeds the asset's initial purchase price.

## ▶ E X A M P L E

The Loos Company, a manufacturer of pharmaceuticals, has operating earnings of $500,000. It has just sold for $40,000 a capital asset initially purchased two years ago for $36,000. Because the asset was sold for more than its initial

---

[2]To simplify the discussion, only capital assets are considered here. The full tax treatment of gains and losses on depreciable assets is presented as part of the discussion of capital-budgeting cash flows in Chapter 14.

[3]The *Omnibus Budget Reconciliation Act of 1993* included a provision that allows the capital gains tax to be halved on gains resulting from investments made after January 1, 1993 in startup firms with a value of less than $50 million that have been held for at least five years. This special provision, which is intended to help startup firms, is ignored throughout this text.

purchase price, there is a capital gain of $4,000 ($40,000 sale price − $36,000 initial purchase price). The corporation's taxable income totals $504,000 ($500,000 ordinary income + $4,000 capital gain). Because this total is above $335,000, the capital gain is taxed at the 34 percent rate, resulting in a tax of $1,360 (.34 × $4,000).

## S Corporations

**S corporation**
A tax-reporting entity whose earnings are taxed not as a corporation but as the incomes of its stockholders, thus avoiding *double taxation*.

**double taxation**
Occurs when the once-taxed earnings of a corporation are distributed as cash dividends to its stockholders, who are then taxed on these dividends.

Subchapter S of the Internal Revenue Code permits corporations meeting specified requirements, and having 35 or fewer stockholders, to elect to be taxed like partnerships. That is, income is normally taxed as direct personal income of the shareholders, whether it is actually distributed to them or not. The **S corporation** is a tax-reporting entity rather than a tax-paying entity. The key advantage of this form of organization is that the stockholders receive all the organizational benefits of a corporation while escaping the *double taxation* normally associated with the distribution of corporate earnings. (**Double taxation** results when the already once-taxed earnings of a corporation are distributed as cash dividends to stockholders, who must pay taxes on these dividends.) S corporations do not receive the other tax advantages accorded regular corporations.

## FINANCE IN ACTION

### Ethics

### Reading the Prospectus Might Not Be Enough

The Permanent Portfolio Treasury Bill Fund marketed by the Permanent Portfolio Family of Funds, Inc. offered mutual fund investors a really great deal. Investing in Treasury securities, the fund planned to convert interest income into capital gains by retaining income, rather than paying daily dividends like most mutual funds. In the process, investors could save a bundle in taxes, because the tax rate on individuals' income in 1993 could run as high as 39.6 percent, whereas the tax on individuals' long-term capital gains was only 28 percent.

Unfortunately, the 1993 tax code probably made this investment strategy, known as a conversion transaction, illegal. Most mutual funds selling similar investment products recognized the problem in mid-1993 and adjusted the contents of their prospectus documents to advise fund buyers of the higher potential tax liability.

Permanent Portfolio Family of Funds, however, went right on promoting the fund's capital gains tax treatment through early 1994, arguing that the 1993 tax code section concerning conversion transactions was irrelevant.

Until the matter is resolved by IRS auditors examining 1993 tax returns, it's not certain precisely *how* the new tax law will affect the Permanent Portfolio Treasury Bill Fund. But given the uncertainty of the 1993 tax treatment associated with this fund, do you think that Permanent Portfolio Family of Funds had an obligation to inform potential investors in the fund's prospectus? After all, isn't the purpose of the prospectus to describe clearly the investment strategy and potential risks of a particular investment?

Source: J. Laderman, "Ill-Gotten Capital Gains?," *Business Week*, January 24, 1994, p. 84.

▼▼▼▼▼▼▼▼▼▼▼▼▼▼▼▼▼▼▼▼▼▼▼▼▼▼▼▼▼▼▼▼

## Progress Review Questions

**2-1.** Briefly define ordinary corporate income and capital gains, and describe the tax treatments of each. What is the *average tax rate?* What is the *marginal tax rate?*

**2-2.** Describe the *intercorporate dividend exclusion.* Why might this feature make corporate stock investments by one corporation in another more attractive than bond investments?

**2-3.** What benefit results from the tax-deductibility of certain corporate expenses? Compare and contrast the tax treatment of corporate interest and dividend payments.

▲▲▲▲▲▲▲▲▲▲▲▲▲▲▲▲▲▲▲▲▲▲▲▲▲▲▲▲▲▲▲▲

# Financial Institutions

**Financial institutions** are intermediaries that channel the savings of individuals, businesses, and governments into loans or investments. Many financial institutions directly or indirectly pay savers interest on deposited funds. Others provide services for which they charge depositors (for example, the service charges levied on checking accounts). Some financial institutions accept customers' savings deposits and lend this money to other customers; others invest customers' savings in earning assets, such as real estate or stocks and bonds; and still others both lend money and invest savings. *Financial institutions are required by the government to operate within established regulatory guidelines.*

**financial institution**
An intermediary that channels the savings of individuals, businesses, and governments into loans or investments.

## Key Participants in Financial Transactions

The key suppliers and demanders of funds are individuals, businesses, and governments. The savings of individual consumers placed in certain financial institutions provide these institutions with a large portion of their funds. Individuals not only supply funds to financial institutions but also demand funds from them in the form of loans. However, the important point here is that individuals as a group are the *net suppliers* for financial institutions: They save more money than they borrow.

Business firms also deposit some of their funds in financial institutions, primarily in checking accounts with various commercial banks. Firms, like individuals, also borrow funds from these institutions. As a group, business firms, unlike individuals, are *net demanders* of funds: They borrow more money than they save.

Governments maintain deposits of temporarily idle funds, certain tax payments, and social security payments in commercial banks. They do not borrow funds directly from financial institutions. However, by selling their securities to various institutions, governments indirectly borrow from them. The government, like business firms, is typically a *net demander* of money: it borrows more than it saves. This attribute of government contributes to the budget deficits occurring at federal, state, and local levels of government.

The major financial institutions in the U.S. economy are commercial banks, savings banks, savings and loans, credit unions, life insurance companies, pension funds, and mutual funds. These institutions attract funds from individuals, businesses, and governments, combine them, and perform certain services to make attractive loans available to individuals and businesses. They may also make some of these funds available to fulfill various government demands. A brief description of the major financial institutions is found in Table 2.3.

## The Changing Role of Financial Institutions

*Depository Institutions Deregulation and Monetary Control Act of 1980 (DIDMCA)*
Eliminated interest-rate ceilings on all accounts and permitted certain institutions to offer new types of accounts and services.

Passage of the ***Depository Institutions Deregulation and Monetary Control Act of 1980*** (**DIDMCA**) signaled the beginning of the "financial services revolution" that continues to change the nature of financial institutions. This act eliminated interest rate ceilings on all accounts and permitted certain institutions to offer new types of accounts and services. It thus intensified competition and blurred traditional distinctions among these institutions. The acquisition by Prudential Insurance of Bache & Co. and by American Express of Shearson Lehman Brothers and E. F. Hutton, both brokerage firms, is testimony to this revolution. Until late 1992, what appeared to be evolving was the **financial supermarket,** in which a customer could obtain a full array of financial services such as checking, savings, loans, credit cards, securities brokerage, insurance, and retirement and estate planning. Sears, Roebuck and Company's "Sears Financial Network" offered a broad range of financial services and was widely touted as a model financial supermarket. But in late 1992, Sears began to dismantle its supermarket by selling its Dean Witter Financial Services unit, which included both stock brokerage and Discover card operations, most of its Coldwell Banker real estate holdings, and 20 percent of its Allstate insurance unit. At the same time a number of other emerging financial supermarkets, such as American Express, began to dismantle their operations. Apparently, the breakup of the one-stop financial supermarket was the result of an inability to achieve the expected benefits of combining a number of financial service firms. At this time it appears that the financial supermarket may be on its way to extinction.

**financial supermarket**
An institution at which the customer can obtain a full array of financial services.

The role of financial institutions is undergoing further change as a result of the "savings & loan (S&L) crisis" of the late 1980s which was caused by a number of factors, including (1) enhanced competition stimulated by DIDMCA, (2) plummeting oil and real estate prices in the "oil patch" (oil-producing areas of the country), (3) defaults on high-risk, high-yield "junk bond" investments, (4) generally poor management, (5) poor regulation by S&L authorities, and (6) the illegal and unethical acts of officers of some major S&Ls. The failures of numerous S&Ls resulted in the Bush administration's thrift bailout plan. This plan—the cost of which is of course being borne by taxpayers—was aimed at resolving the S&L crisis by providing needed financing and more restrictive regulation and enforcement of the nation's S&Ls. It resulted in the creation of two new agencies to bail out the S&L industry. The Office of Thrift Supervision (OTS) regulates the industry. The Resolution Trust Corporation (RTC), a unit of the FDIC, takes over insolvent

**TABLE 2.3   Major Financial Institutions**

| Institution | Brief Description |
|---|---|
| Commercial bank | Accepts both demand (checking) and time (savings) deposits. Also offers negotiable order of withdrawal (NOW) accounts, which are interest-earning savings accounts against which checks can be written. In addition, currently offers money market deposit accounts, which pay interest at rates competitive with other short-term investment vehicles. Makes loans directly to borrowers or through the financial markets. |
| Savings bank | Similar to commercial banks except that it may not hold demand (checking) deposits. Obtains funds from savings, NOW, and money market deposit accounts. Generally lends or invests funds through financial markets, although some residential real estate loans are made to individuals. Located primarily in New York, New Jersey, and the New England states. |
| Savings and loan | Similar to a savings bank in that it holds savings deposits, NOW accounts, and money market deposit accounts. Also raises capital through the sale of securities in the financial markets. Lends funds primarily to individuals and businesses for real estate mortgage loans. Some funds are channeled into investments in the financial markets. |
| Credit union | A financial intermediary that deals primarily in transfer of funds between consumers. Membership is generally based on some common bond, such as working for a given employer. Accepts members' savings deposits, NOW account deposits, and money market deposit accounts. Lends the majority of these funds to other members, typically to finance automobile or appliance purchases or home improvements. |
| Life insurance company | The largest type of financial intermediary handling individual savings. Receives premium payments that are placed in loans or investments to accumulate funds to cover future benefit payments. Lends funds to individuals, businesses, and governments or channels them through the financial markets to those who demand them. |
| Pension fund | Set up so that employees of various corporations or government units can receive income after retirement. Often employers match the contributions of their employees. Money is sometimes transferred directly to borrowers, but the majority is lent or invested via the financial markets. |
| Mutual fund | Pools funds of savers and makes them available to business and government demanders. Obtains funds through sale of shares and uses proceeds to acquire bonds and stocks issued by various business and governmental units. Creates a diversified and professionally managed portfolio of securities to achieve a specified investment objective, such as liquidity with a high return. Hundreds of funds, with a variety of investment objectives, exist. Money market mutual funds, which provide competitive returns with very high liquidity, are popular, particularly when short-term interest rates are high. |

thrifts, safeguards their deposits, and sells the assets—real estate and loans—of these failed institutions. Through mid-1992 the RTC had taken over more than 700 insolvent institutions, and many more were in danger of insolvency. The cost to taxpayers of the massive S&L bailout has been estimated to be about $500 billion. As a result of government actions, not only should future crises be avoided, but a further blurring of the lines of distinction between banks, S&Ls, and other financial institutions is also expected.

## Progress Review Questions

**2-4.** What role do financial institutions play in our economy? Who are the key participants in these transactions? Indicate who are net suppliers and who are net demanders.

**2-5.** Briefly describe each of the following financial institutions:
  **a.** Commercial bank
  **b.** Savings and loan
  **c.** Life insurance company
  **d.** Mutual fund

**2-6.** What did the *Depository Institutions Deregulation and Monetary Control Act of 1980* (DIDMCA) do to begin the "financial services revolution"? Describe the "financial supermarket" and its future. What is the "savings and loan (S&L) crisis," and what effect has it had on financial institutions?

# Financial Markets

**financial markets**
Provide a forum in which suppliers of funds and demanders of loans and investments can transact business directly.

**Financial markets** provide a forum in which suppliers of funds and demanders of loans and investments can transact business directly. Whereas the loans and investments of institutions are made without the direct knowledge of the suppliers of funds (savers), suppliers in the financial markets know where their funds are being lent or invested.

## The Relationship Between Institutions and Markets

Financial institutions actively participate in the financial markets as both suppliers and demanders of funds. Figure 2.1 depicts the general flow of funds through and between financial institutions and financial markets; private placement transactions are also shown. The suppliers and demanders of funds may be domestic or foreign. Because of the importance to the firm of the two key financial markets—the money market and the capital market—the next two sections of this chapter are devoted to these topics.

## The Money Market

**money market**
A financial relationship created between suppliers and demanders of *short-term funds*.

**marketable securities**
Short-term debt instruments issued by government, business, and financial institutions.

The **money market** is created by a financial relationship between suppliers and demanders of *short-term funds,* which have maturities of one year or less. The money market is not an actual organization housed in some central location, although the majority of money market transactions culminate in New York City. Most money market transactions are made in the form of **marketable securities**—short-term debt instruments, such as U.S. Treasury bills, commercial paper, and negotiable certificates of deposit issued by government, business, and financial institutions, respectively. (Marketable securities are described in Chapter 8.)

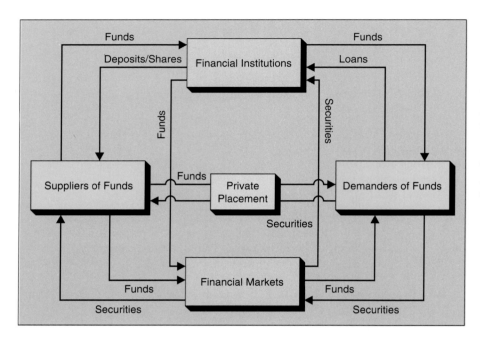

**FIGURE 2.1  Flow of Funds for Financial Institutions and Markets**
Financial institutions and financial markets as well as private placements are the mechanisms used to transfer funds between individuals, business, and government suppliers and demanders. These mechanisms allow savings to be converted into investment.

The money market exists because certain individuals, businesses, governments, and financial institutions have temporarily idle funds. Rather than leave the funds idle, they wish to place them in some type of liquid asset or short-term, interest-earning instrument. At the same time, other individuals, businesses, governments, and financial institutions find themselves in need of seasonal or temporary financing. The money market thus brings together these suppliers and demanders of short-term liquid funds.

## The Eurocurrency Market

The international equivalent of the domestic money market is called the **Eurocurrency market.** This is a market for short-term bank deposits denominated in U.S. dollars or other easily convertible currencies. Historically, the Eurocurrency market has been centered in London, but it has evolved into a truly global market. Eurocurrency deposits arise when a corporation or individual makes a deposit in a bank in a currency other than the local currency of the country where the bank is located. If, for example, a multinational corporation deposits U.S. dollars in the London branch of a European or an American bank, it creates a Eurodollar deposit (a dollar deposit at a bank in Europe). Almost all Eurodollar deposits are time deposits, meaning that the bank promises to repay the deposit, with interest, at a fixed date in the future—say, six months. During the interim the bank is free to lend this dollar deposit to creditworthy corporate or government borrowers, and the bank makes a profit on the "spread" or difference between the interest rate that it pays for the deposit and the rate that it collects on the loan. The Eurocurrency market has grown rapidly since its creation in the 1950s, primarily because it is an unregulated, wholesale market that capably fills the needs of both borrowers and lenders.

**Eurocurrency market**
International equivalent of the domestic money market.

## The Capital Market

**capital market**
A financial relationship created by institutions and arrangements, allowing suppliers and demanders of *long-term funds* to make transactions.

The **capital market** is a financial relationship created by a number of institutions and arrangements that allows the suppliers and demanders of *long-term funds*—funds with maturities of more than one year—to make transactions. Included among long-term funds are securities issues of business and government. The backbone of the capital market is formed by the various *securities exchanges* that provide a forum for debt and equity transactions. The smooth functioning of the capital market is important to the long-run growth of business.

**bond**
Long-term debt instrument used by businesses and government to raise large sums of money.

**Key Securities**   Major securities traded in the capital market include bonds (long-term debt) and both common and preferred stock (equity, or ownership). **Bonds** are long-term debt instruments used by business and government to raise large sums of money, generally from a diverse group of lenders. *Corporate bonds* typically pay interest *semiannually* (every six months) at a stated *coupon interest rate,* have an initial *maturity* of from 10 to 30 years, and have a *par,* or *face, value* of $1,000 that must be repaid at maturity. Bonds are described in detail in Chapter 18.

## E X A M P L E

Lakeview Industries, a television picture tube manufacturer, has just issued a 12-percent coupon interest rate, 20-year bond with a $1,000 par value that pays interest semiannually. Investors who buy this bond receive the contractual right to (1) $120 annual interest (12% coupon interest rate × $1,000 par value) distributed as $60 at the end of each six months ($\frac{1}{2}$ × $120) for 20 years and (2) the $1,000 par value at the end of year 20.

**common stock**
Collectively, units of ownership interest, or equity, in a corporation.

Shares of **common stock** are units of ownership interest, or equity, in a corporation. Common stockholders expect to earn a return by receiving **dividends**—periodic distributions of earnings—or by realizing gains through increases in share price. **Preferred stock** is a special form of ownership that has features of both a bond and common stock. Preferred stockholders are promised a fixed periodic dividend that must be paid prior to payment of any dividends to the owners of common stock. In other words, preferred stock has "preference" over common stock. Preferred and common stock are described in detail in Chapter 19.

**dividends**
Periodic distributions of earnings to the owners of stock in a firm.

**preferred stock**
A special form of ownership having a fixed periodic dividend that must be paid prior to payment of any common stock dividends.

**primary market**
Financial market in which securities are initially issued.

**Primary and Secondary Markets**   All securities, whether in the money or capital markets, are initially issued in the **primary market.** This is the only market in which the corporate or government issuer is directly involved in the transaction and receives direct benefit from the issue—that is, the company actually receives the proceeds from the sale of securities. Once the securities begin to trade among individual, business, government, or financial institution savers and investors, they become part of the **secondary market.** The primary market is the one in which "new" securities are sold; the secondary market can be viewed as a "used" or "preowned" securities market.

**secondary market**
Financial market in which preowned securities are traded.

**securities exchanges**
The marketplace in which firms can raise funds through the sale of new securities and in which purchasers can resell securities.

## Major Securities Exchanges

As we noted earlier, **securities exchanges** provide the marketplace in which firms can raise funds through the sale of new securities. They also enable purchasers of securities to maintain liquidity by being able to easily resell them when necessary. In addition they create **efficient markets,** which allocate funds to the most productive uses. This is especially true for securities that are actively traded on major exchanges where the competition among wealth-maximizing investors determines and publicizes prices that are believed to be close to their true value.

> **efficient market**
> Market that allocates funds to their most productive uses as a result of competition among wealth-maximizing investors.

Many people call securities exchanges "stock markets," but this label is somewhat misleading because bonds, common stock, preferred stock, and a variety of other investment vehicles are all traded on these exchanges. The two key types of securities exchange are the organized exchange and the over-the-counter exchange. In addition, important markets exist outside of the United States.

### Organized Securities Exchanges

**Organized securities exchanges** are tangible organizations that act as *secondary markets* where outstanding securities are resold. Organized exchanges account for over 72 percent of the *total dollar volume* of domestic shares traded. The dominant organized exchanges are the New York Stock Exchange (NYSE) and the American Stock Exchange (AMEX), both headquartered in New York City. There are also regional exchanges, such as the Midwest Stock Exchange (in Chicago) and the Pacific Stock Exchange (in San Francisco).

> **organized securities exchanges**
> Tangible organizations on whose premises outstanding securities are resold.

Most exchanges are modeled after the New York Stock Exchange, which accounts for over 85 percent of the total annual dollar volume of shares traded on organized exchanges. To make transactions on the "floor" of the New York Stock Exchange, an individual or firm must own a "seat" on the exchange. There are a total of 1,366 seats on the NYSE. Most are owned by brokerage firms. To be listed for trading on an organized stock exchange, a firm must file an application for listing and meet a number of requirements. Trading is carried out on the floor of the exchange through an *auction process*. The goal of trading is to fill *buy orders* (orders to purchase securities) at the lowest price and to fill *sell orders* (orders to sell securities) at the highest price, thereby giving both purchasers and sellers the best possible deal. Once placed, an order to either buy or sell can be executed in minutes, thanks to sophisticated telecommunication devices. Information on the daily trading of securities is reported in various media, including financial publications such as *The Wall Street Journal*. (The interpretation of such information is briefly discussed in a later section.)

### The Over-the-Counter Exchange

The **over-the-counter (OTC) exchange** is not an organization but an intangible market for the purchase and sale of securities not listed by the organized exchanges. Active traders in this market are linked by a sophisticated telecommunications network. Unlike the auction process on the organized securities exchanges, the prices at which securities are traded in the OTC market result from both competitive bids and negotiation. The OTC, in addition to creating a *secondary* (resale) *market* for outstanding securities, is a *primary market* in which new public issues are sold. The OTC accounts for nearly 28 percent of the *total dollar volume* of domestic shares traded.

> **over-the-counter (OTC) exchange**
> Not an organization, but an intangible market for the purchase and sale of securities not listed by the organized exchanges.

### International Capital Markets

Although U.S. capital markets are by far the world's largest, important debt and equity markets exist outside the United

**Small Business**

## The American Stock Exchange Has Much in Common with Rodney Dangerfield

In recent promotional campaigns, the New York Stock Exchange has started calling itself "the capital of capital," whereas the NASDAQ likes to refer to itself as "the stock market for the next 100 years." Lost in the recent wave of marketing wars, however, is the lowly American Stock Exchange. In terms of equity listings and trading volume, the AMEX runs a distant third to the NYSE and NASDAQ exchanges.

But the AMEX has a great deal to offer smaller firms with relatively limited trading volume. For starters, many financial managers believe there's less price movement on the AMEX. As Peter Heath, CFO at Editek, Inc. in Burlington, North Carolina observes, "Sometimes you get trading for the wrong reasons; brokers trading not on the fundamentals of a company, but on the movement of the stock price."

According to Heath, more price-movement trades occur on the NASDAQ. In addition, the AMEX recently inaugurated an Emerging Company Marketplace, offering small growth companies an efficient and orderly trading environment and broader corporate visibility. In spite of these benefits, trading volume on the AMEX plunged from 5.9 percent of total shares traded on the big three stock exchanges in 1981 to 3.5 percent in 1992. Like Rodney Danger-field, the AMEX just doesn't get the respect that many people feel it deserves.

Source: B. Graham, "Should the AMEX Get More Respect?," *CFO Magazine*, January 1994, p. 53.

**Eurobond market**
The oldest and largest international bond market.

**bearer bonds**
Bonds for which payments are made to the bearer.

**foreign bond**
Bond issued by a foreign corporation or government that is denominated in the investor's home currency and sold in the investor's home market.

States. The oldest and largest international bond market, the **Eurobond market,** is in many ways the long-term equivalent of the Eurocurrency markets discussed earlier. In this market, corporations and governments issue bonds denominated in dollars or other currencies that can be converted into dollars and sell them to investors located outside the United States or the country in whose currency the bonds are denominated. A U.S. corporation might, for example, issue dollar-denominated bonds that are purchased by investors in Belgium, Germany, Switzerland, or other countries. Investors find Eurobonds attractive because they provide currency diversification and because, as **bearer bonds** (for which payments are made to the bearer), they provide anonymity to the investor wishing to avoid payment of taxes. Issuing firms and governments appreciate the Eurobond market because it allows them to tap a much larger pool of investors than is generally available in the local market and because competition keeps their fees attractively low.

The foreign bond market is another market for long-term debt securities involving international issuers and investors. A **foreign bond** is a bond issued by a foreign corporation or government that is denominated in the investor's home currency and sold in the investor's home market. A bond issued by a U.S. company that is denominated in Swiss francs and sold in Switzerland is an example of a foreign bond. Although the foreign bond market is much smaller than the Eurobond market, many issuers have found this to be an attractive way of tapping debt markets in Switzerland, Germany, the United States, and Japan, as well as other countries.

Finally, a vibrant **international equity market** has emerged during the past decade. Many corporations have discovered that they can sell large blocks of shares to investors in several different countries simultaneously. This has not only allowed corporations to diversify their investor base, but has also allowed them to raise far larger amounts of capital than they could have raised in any single national market.

**international equity market**
A vibrant equity market that emerged during the past decade to allow corporations to sell large blocks of shares in several different countries simultaneously.

## Progress Review Questions

**2-7.** Where are *financial markets,* and what role do they play in our economy? What relationship exists between financial institutions and financial markets?

**2-8.** What is the *money market?* How does it differ from the capital market? What is the *Eurocurrency market?* How does it work?

**2-9.** What is the *capital market?* What are *primary* and *secondary* markets? What role do securities exchanges play in the capital market?

**2-10.** How does the over-the-counter exchange operate? How does it differ from the organized securities exchanges?

**2-11.** Briefly describe the international capital markets, particularly the *Eurobond market* and the *international equity market.*

## Securities Offerings and Trading

LG 5

Firms raise needed funds through the sale of securities in the money and capital markets. Short-term funds can be obtained through the public sale of debt (IOUs) in the *money market.* Investors with temporary surpluses of funds buy these securities in order to earn interest on those funds. The use of the money market to raise short-term funds is discussed in Chapter 10 and the purchase of money market securities (i.e., marketable securities) as short-term investments is discussed in Chapter 8. The focus here is on long-term funds raised in the *capital market.*

Long-term funds can be raised publicly by selling either bonds (long-term debt) or preferred or common stock (ownership). As noted earlier, the initial sale of bonds or stock occurs in the *primary market,* typically the *over-the-counter (OTC) exchange.* Once issued these securities trade on one of the securities exchanges. Although the subsequent trading of a firm's bonds or stock in the capital market does not provide it with additional cash flow, it is important in that it brings together the forces of supply and demand to determine the bond's or stock's market value, that is, its price. Here we take a brief look at the role of the *investment banker* in the initial sale of securities by the issuer and the basics of interpreting bond and stock price quotations.

## The Role of the Investment Banker

**private placement**
The sale of a new security issue, typically debt or preferred stock, directly to an investor or group of investors.

**public offering**
The nonexclusive sale of either bonds or stock to the general public.

**investment banker**
A financial intermediary who purchases securities from corporate and government issuers and resells them to the general public in the primary market.

To raise money in the capital market, firms can use either private placements or public offerings. **Private placement** involves the sale of a new security issue, typically debt or preferred stock, directly to an investor or group of investors, such as an insurance company or pension fund. However, most firms raise money through a **public offering** of securities, which is the nonexclusive sale of either bonds or stock to the general public. In making a securities offering, whether private or public, most firms hire an investment banker to find buyers for new security issues.

The term *investment banker* is somewhat misleading because an investment banker is neither an investor nor a banker; furthermore, he or she neither makes long-term investments nor guards the savings of others. Instead, acting as an intermediary between the issuer and the buyers of new security issues, the **investment banker** purchases securities from corporate and government issuers and resells them to the general public in the *primary market*. In addition to bearing the risk of selling a security issue, investment bankers provide a variety of additional services to their clients. In the United States, for example, during the first 6 months of 1994 Merrill Lynch, Lehman Brothers, and CS First Boston were the top three investment banking firms. (Detailed discussion of the role of investment banking in raising long-term funds is included in Chapter 17.)

## Interpreting Bond and Stock Price Quotations

**quotations**
Price information on bonds, stocks, and other securities, including current price data and statistics on recent price behavior.

The financial manager needs to stay abreast of the market values of the firm's outstanding bonds and stocks. Similarly, existing and prospective bondholders and stockholders need to monitor the prices of bonds and stocks, respectively. These prices are important because they represent the current value of the securities—the amounts (before brokerage fees and taxes) an investor could recover from selling (or pay to purchase) the bond or stock today. Information on bonds, stocks, and other securities is contained in their **quotations,** which include current price data along with statistics on recent price behavior. Security price quotations are readily available for actively traded bonds and stocks. The most up-to-date "quotes" can be obtained, typically from a stockbroker, by using a personal computer to access electronically the given security exchange's data base. Price information is widely available in published news media—both financial and nonfinancial. Popular sources of security price quotations are financial newspapers, such as *The Wall Street Journal* and *Investor's Business Daily,* or the business sections of daily general newspapers published in most major cities. The interpretation of bond and stock quotations, which use a compact format and abbreviations, are described separately later on.

**Bond Quotations**    Part **A** of Figure 2.2 includes an excerpt from the New York Stock Exchange (NYSE) bond quotations reported in the August 18, 1993, *The Wall Street Journal* for transactions through the close of trading on Tuesday, August 17, 1993. Let's use the corporate bond quotation for IBM, which is highlighted in Figure 2.2, to demonstrate interpretation of its quotation. The numbers following the company name—IBM—represent the bond's coupon interest rate and the year it matures; "$8\frac{3}{8}$ 19" means that the

## A. Bond Quotations (August 17, 1993)

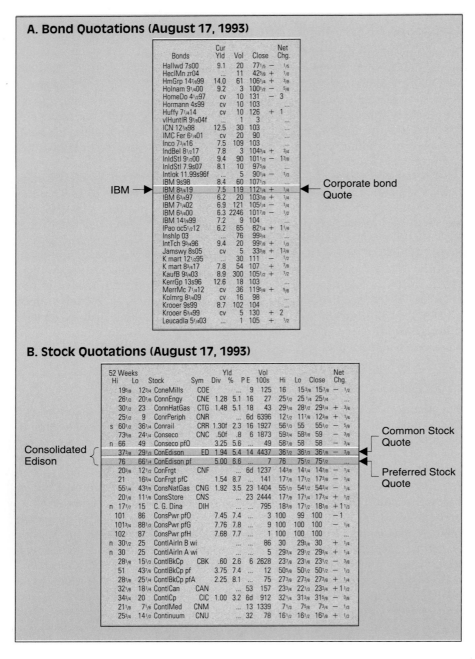

| Bonds | Cur Yld | Vol | Close | Net Chg. |
|---|---|---|---|---|
| Hallwd 7s00 | 9.1 | 20 | 77¹⁄₅ | − ¹⁄₅ |
| HeclMn zr04 | ... | 11 | 42⁵⁄₈ | + ¹⁄₈ |
| HmGrp 14⁷⁄₈99 | 14.0 | 61 | 106¹⁄₄ | + ³⁄₈ |
| Holnam 9¹⁄₄00 | 9.2 | 3 | 100¹⁄₂ | − ⁵⁄₈ |
| HomeDo 4¹⁄₂97 | cv | 10 | 131 | − 3 |
| Hormann 4s99 | cv | 10 | 103 | ... |
| Huffy 7¹⁄₄14 | cv | 10 | 126 | + 1 |
| vlHuntlR 9⁷⁄₈04f | ... | 1 | 3 | ... |
| ICN 12⁷⁄₈98 | 12.5 | 30 | 103 | ... |
| IMC Fer 6¹⁄₄01 | cv | 20 | 90 | ... |
| Inco 7³⁄₄16 | 7.5 | 109 | 103 | ... |
| IndBel 8¹⁄₂17 | 7.8 | 3 | 104³⁄₄ | + ³⁄₄ |
| InldStl 9¹⁄₂00 | 9.4 | 90 | 101¹⁄₂ | − 1³⁄₈ |
| InldStl 7.9s07 | 8.1 | 10 | 97⁵⁄₈ | ... |
| Intlok 11.99s96f | ... | 5 | 90¹⁄₄ | − ¹⁄₃ |
| IBM 9s98 | 8.4 | 60 | 107¹⁄₃ | ... |
| IBM 8³⁄₈19 | 7.5 | 119 | 112¹⁄₄ | + ¹⁄₄ |
| IBM 6³⁄₈97 | 6.2 | 20 | 103³⁄₈ | + ¹⁄₄ |
| IBM 7¹⁄₂02 | 6.9 | 121 | 105¹⁄₄ | − ¹⁄₄ |
| IBM 6³⁄₈00 | 6.3 | 2246 | 101⁷⁄₈ | − ¹⁄₂ |
| IBM 14⁷⁄₈99 | 7.2 | 9 | 104 | ... |
| IPao oc5¹⁄₂12 | 6.2 | 65 | 82¹⁄₄ | + 1¹⁄₄ |
| Inshlp 03 | ... | 76 | 99³⁄₄ | ... |
| IntTch 9³⁄₄96 | 9.4 | 20 | 99⁷⁄₈ | + ¹⁄₃ |
| Jamswy 8s05 | cv | 5 | 33³⁄₈ | + 1³⁄₈ |
| K mart 12¹⁄₂95 | ... | 30 | 111 | − ¹⁄₂ |
| K mart 8³⁄₄17 | 7.8 | 54 | 107 | + ⁷⁄₈ |
| KaufB 9³⁄₄03 | 8.9 | 300 | 105¹⁄₂ | + ¹⁄₂ |
| KerrGp 13s96 | 12.6 | 18 | 103 | ... |
| MerrMc 7¹⁄₄12 | cv | 36 | 119⁵⁄₈ | + ⁵⁄₈ |
| Kolmrg 8³⁄₄09 | cv | 16 | 98 | ... |
| Krooer 9s99 | 8.7 | 102 | 104 | ... |
| Krooer 6³⁄₄99 | cv | 5 | 130 | + 2 |
| Leucadla 5¹⁄₄03 | ... | 1 | 105 | + ¹⁄₂ |

IBM → (IBM 8³⁄₈19 row)    ← Corporate bond Quote

## B. Stock Quotations (August 17, 1993)

| 52 Weeks Hi | Lo | Stock | Sym | Div | Yld % | P E | Vol 100s | Hi | Lo | Close | Net Chg. |
|---|---|---|---|---|---|---|---|---|---|---|---|
| 19⁵⁄₈ | 12³⁄₄ | ConeMills | COE | ... | ... | 9 | 125 | 16 | 15³⁄₈ | 15⁷⁄₈ | − ¹⁄₂ |
| 26¹⁄₂ | 20¹⁄₈ | ConnEngy | CNE | 1.28 | 5.1 | 16 | 27 | 25¹⁄₄ | 25 ¹⁄₄ | 25¹⁄₄ | ... |
| 30¹⁄₂ | 23 | ConnHatGas | CTG | 1.48 | 5.1 | 18 | 43 | 29¹⁄₄ | 28¹⁄₂ | 29¹⁄₄ | + ³⁄₄ |
| 25¹⁄₂ | 9 | ConrPeriph | CNR | ... | ... | 6d | 6396 | 12¹⁄₂ | 11⁷⁄₈ | 12³⁄₈ | + ¹⁄₄ |
| s 60¹⁄₂ | 36¹⁄₄ | Conrail | CRR | 1.30f | 2.3 | 16 | 1927 | 56¹⁄₃ | 55 | 55¹⁄₂ | − ⁵⁄₈ |
| 73⁵⁄₈ | 24¹⁄₄ | Conseco | CNC | .50f | .8 | 6 | 1873 | 59³⁄₄ | 58³⁄₈ | 59 | − ³⁄₈ |
| n 66 | 49 | Conseco pfO | | 3.25 | 5.6 | ... | 49 | 58⁷⁄₈ | 58 | 58 | − ³⁄₄ |
| 37³⁄₈ | 29³⁄₈ | ConEdison | ED | 1.94 | 5.4 | 14 | 4437 | 36¹⁄₂ | 36¹⁄₃ | 36³⁄₈ | − ³⁄₈ |
| 76 | 66¹⁄₄ | ConEdison pf | | 5.00 | 6.6 | ... | 7 | 76 | 75¹⁄₂ | 75¹⁄₂ | ... |
| 20³⁄₈ | 12¹⁄₂ | ConFrgt | CNF | ... | ... | 6d | 1237 | 14³⁄₈ | 14¹⁄₄ | 14³⁄₈ | − ¹⁄₄ |
| 21 | 16³⁄₄ | ConFrgt pfC | | 1.54 | 8.7 | ... | 141 | 17⁷⁄₈ | 17¹⁄₂ | 17³⁄₈ | − ¹⁄₄ |
| 55¹⁄₄ | 43³⁄₈ | ConsNatGas | CNG | 1.92 | 3.5 | 23 | 1404 | 55¹⁄₂ | 54¹⁄₂ | 54³⁄₄ | − ¹⁄₄ |
| 20¹⁄₈ | 11³⁄₄ | ConsStore | CNS | ... | ... | 23 | 2444 | 17⁷⁄₈ | 17¹⁄₄ | 17³⁄₄ | + ¹⁄₂ |
| n 17¹⁄₇ | 15 | C. G. Dina | DIH | ... | ... | ... | 795 | 18³⁄₈ | 17¹⁄₂ | 18³⁄₈ | +1¹⁄₃ |
| 101 | 86 | ConsPwr pfO | | 7.45 | 7.4 | ... | 3 | 100 | 99 | 100 | − 1 |
| 101³⁄₄ | 88¹⁄₂ | ConsPwr pfG | | 7.76 | 7.8 | ... | 9 | 100 | 100 | 100 | − ¹⁄₄ |
| 102 | 87 | ConsPwr pfH | | 7.68 | 7.7 | ... | 1 | 100 | 100 | 100 | ... |
| n 30¹⁄₂ | 25 | ContlAirln B wi | | ... | ... | ... | 86 | 30 | 29³⁄₄ | 30 | + ¹⁄₄ |
| n 30 | 25 | ContlAirln A wi | | ... | ... | ... | 5 | 29³⁄₄ | 29¹⁄₂ | 29³⁄₄ | + ¹⁄₄ |
| 28¹⁄₈ | 15¹⁄₄ | ContlBkCp | CBK | .60 | 2.6 | 6 | 2628 | 23⁷⁄₈ | 23¹⁄₈ | 23¹⁄₂ | − ³⁄₈ |
| 51 | 43⁷⁄₈ | ContlBkCp pf | | 3.75 | 7.4 | ... | 12 | 50⁵⁄₈ | 50¹⁄₂ | 50¹⁄₂ | − ¹⁄₃ |
| 28¹⁄₈ | 25¹⁄₄ | ContlBkCp pfA | | 2.25 | 8.1 | ... | 75 | 27³⁄₈ | 27³⁄₈ | 27³⁄₄ | + ¹⁄₄ |
| 32¹⁄₈ | 18¹⁄₄ | ContlCan | CAN | ... | ... | 53 | 157 | 23³⁄₄ | 22¹⁄₈ | 23³⁄₄ | +1¹⁄₂ |
| 34³⁄₄ | 20 | ContlCp | CIC | 1.00 | 3.2 | 6d | 912 | 32¹⁄₄ | 31³⁄₈ | 31⁵⁄₈ | − ¹⁄₄ |
| 21¹⁄₈ | 7¹⁄₈ | ContlMed | CNM | ... | ... | 13 | 1339 | 7¹⁄₃ | 7⁵⁄₈ | 7³⁄₄ | − ¹⁄₃ |
| 25³⁄₄ | 14¹⁄₂ | Continuum | CNU | ... | ... | 32 | 78 | 16¹⁄₂ | 16¹⁄₂ | 16⁷⁄₈ | + ¹⁄₂ |

Consolidated Edison (ConEdison and ConEdison pf rows)    Common Stock Quote / Preferred Stock Quote

**FIGURE 2.2  Bond and Stock Quotations**

A. This bond quotation gives the bond's coupon interest rate, maturity date, current yield, trading volume, closing price, and price change from the previous day. B. Common stock quotes include the 52-week high and low price; trading symbol; expected annual cash dividend; dividend yield; price/earnings ratio; volume; high, low, and closing price; and the net change in the closing price from the previous day. Preferred stock quotes are similar to those for common stock.
Source: *Wall Street Journal*, August 18, 1993, pp. C20, C4.

bond has a stated coupon interest rate of $8\frac{3}{8}$ percent and matures sometime in the year 2019. This information is important because it allows investors to differentiate between the various bonds issued by the corporation. Note that IBM has six bonds listed on the day of this quote. The next column, labeled "Cur Yld," gives the bond's *current yield*, which is found by dividing its annual coupon ($8\frac{3}{8}$%, or 8.375%) by its closing price ($112\frac{1}{4}$), which in this case rounds to 7.5 percent ($8.375 \div 112.25 = .0746 \approx 7.5\%$).

The "Vol." column indicates the actual number of bonds that traded on the given day; 119 IBM bonds traded on Tuesday, August 17, 1993. The final two columns include price information—the closing price and the net change in closing price from the prior trading day. It is important to recognize that although most corporate bonds are issued with a *par, or face, value* of $1,000, *all bonds are quoted as a percentage of par.* This means that a $1,000-par-value bond, quoted at 92, is priced at $920 (92% × $1,000). Corporate bonds trade and are quoted in fractions of $\frac{1}{8}$, which for $1,000-par-value bonds represents 1.25 *dollars.* Note that fractions are reduced to their lowest common denominator—$\frac{2}{8}$, $\frac{4}{8}$, and $\frac{6}{8}$—and are expressed as $\frac{1}{4}$, $\frac{1}{2}$, and $\frac{3}{4}$, respectively. Thus IBM's closing price of $112\frac{1}{4}$ for the day was $1,122.50, that is, 112.25 percent × $1,000. Because a "Net Chg." of $\frac{1}{4}$ is given in the final column, the bond must have closed at 112 or $1,120 (112% × $1,000) on the prior day, Monday, August 16. Its price increased by $\frac{1}{4}$, or $2.50 ($\frac{1}{4}$% × $1,000), on Tuesday, August 17. Note that although additional information may be included in a bond quotation, discussion of it is beyond the scope of this text.

**Stock Quotations**    Part **B** of Figure 2.2 includes an excerpt from the NYSE stock quotations, also reported in the August 18, 1993, *The Wall Street Journal* for transactions through the close of trading on Tuesday, August 17, 1993. We use both the common stock and preferred stock quotations for Consolidated Edison, highlighted in Figure 2.2, to demonstrate interpretation of both types of quotation. A review of the quotations shows that stock prices are quoted in eighths of a dollar, with the fractions reduced to their lowest common denominator ($\frac{2}{8}$, $\frac{4}{8}$, and $\frac{6}{8}$ are expressed as $\frac{1}{4}$, $\frac{1}{2}$, and $\frac{3}{4}$, respectively). The first two columns, labeled "Hi" and "Lo," contain the highest and lowest price at which the stock sold during the preceding 52 weeks. Consolidated Edison, abbreviated "ConEdison," common stock, for example, traded between $29\frac{7}{8}$ and $37\frac{3}{8}$ during the 52-week period ending August 17, 1993. Listed to the right of the company's abbreviated name is its *stock symbol*—Consolidated Edison goes by "ED." Stock symbols are used by securities industry professionals and traders to identify specific companies. The figure listed right after the stock symbol under "Div" is the annual cash dividend paid on each share of stock. The dividend for Consolidated Edison was $1.94 per share. The next item, labeled "Yld%," is the dividend yield, which is found by dividing the stated dividend by the closing share price. The dividend yield for Consolidated Edison is 5.4 percent ($1.94 \div 36\frac{1}{8} = 1.94 \div 36.125 = .0537 \approx 5.4\%$).

The price/earnings (P/E) ratio, labeled "PE," follows the dividend yield. It is calculated by dividing the closing market price by the firm's most recent annual earnings per share (EPS). The P/E ratio is believed to reflect investor expectations concerning the firm's future prospects—higher P/E ratios reflect investor optimism and confidence; lower P/E ratios reflect investor pessimism and concern. Consolidated Edison's P/E ratio was 14, which means that the stock was trading at 14 times it earnings. The daily volume, labeled "Vol 100s," follows the P/E ratio. Here the day's sales are quoted in lots of 100 shares. On August 17, 1993, the value 4437 for Consolidated Edison indicates that 443,700 shares of its common stock were traded on that day. The "Hi," "Lo," and "Close" columns, contain the highest, lowest, and closing (last) price, respectively, at which the stock sold on the given day. These values for

Consolidated Edison were a high of $36.50, a low of $36.125, and a closing price of $36.125. The final column, "Net Chg," indicates the change in the closing price from that on the prior trading day. For Consolidated Edison, it closed down $\frac{3}{8}$ ($.375) from August 16, 1993, which means the closing price on that day must have been $36.50 ($36\frac{1}{2}$).

Note that preferred stocks are listed with common stocks. For example, following Consolidated Edison's common stock in the quotes in part **B** of Figure 2.2 is its preferred stock, which is identified by the letters "pf" following its name. The quotation for preferred stock, is nearly identical to that of common stock except that the value for the P/E ratio is left blank because it is irrelevant in the case of preferred stock. It is also important to note that similar quotation systems are used for common and preferred stocks that trade on other exchanges such as the American Stock Exchange (AMEX) and the over-the-counter (OTC) exchange's National Association of Securities Dealers Automated Quotation (NASDAQ) national market issues. Also note that when a bond or stock issue is not traded on a given day it generally is not quoted in the financial and business press.

## Progress Review Questions

**2-12.** What is an *investment banker?* What role does he or she play in private placements and public offerings?

**2-13.** What information is found in a bond quotation? What unit of measurement is used to quote bond price data?

**2-14.** Describe the key items of information included in a stock quotation. What information does the stock's price/earnings (P/E) ratio provide? How are preferred stock quotations differentiated from those of common stock?

# Interest Rates and Required Returns

Financial institutions and markets create the mechanism through which funds flow between savers (funds suppliers) and investors (funds demanders). When funds are lent, the cost of borrowing the funds is the **interest rate.** When funds are obtained by selling an ownership (or equity) interest—as in the sale of stock—the cost to the issuer (demander) is commonly called the **required return.** In both cases the supplier is compensated for providing funds. Generally, the lower the interest rate or required return, the greater the flow of funds from savers to investors, and therefore the greater the economic growth, and the higher the interest rate or required return, the lesser the flow of funds from savers to investors, and therefore the lesser the economic growth. Of course, because they represent the firm's cost of financing, the levels of interest rates and required returns are important concerns of the financial manager.

**interest rate**
When funds are lent, the cost of borrowing funds.

**required return**
The cost of funds obtained by selling an equity interest in a firm.

## The Term Structure of Interest Rates

**term structure of interest rates**
The relationship between the time to maturity and the interest rate or rate of return on similar-risk securities.

**yield**
The annual rate of interest earned on a security purchased on a given day and held to maturity.

**yield curve**
A graph that shows the term structure of interest rates.

For any class of similar-risk securities, the **term structure of interest rates** relates the interest rate or rate of return to the time to maturity. The annual rate of interest earned on a security purchased on a given day and held to maturity is called its **yield.** At any point in time the relationship between the yield and the remaining time to maturity can be represented by a **yield curve.** In other words, the yield curve shows the pattern of interest rates on securities of equal quality and different maturity; it is a graphic depiction of the term structure of interest rates.

Figure 2.3 shows three yield curves for all U.S. Treasury securities—one at May 22, 1981, a second at September 29, 1989, and a third at May 29, 1992. It can be seen that both the position and the shape of the yield curves change over time. The May 22, 1981, curve was *downward-sloping*, reflecting expected lower future interest rates. On May 29, 1992, the yield curve was *upward-sloping*, reflecting the expectation of higher future rates. And on September 29, 1989, the curve was *flat*, indicating a stable expectation—future interest rates similar to current interest rates.

The position and shape of the yield curve affect the firm's financing decisions. For example, a financial manager who faces a downward-sloping yield curve is likely to rely more heavily on cheaper long-term financing, whereas when the yield curve is upward-sloping, the manager is more likely to use cheaper short-term financing. Although, as explained in subsequent chapters, a variety of other factors and considerations influence the choice of loan maturity, the shape of the yield curve provides useful insight into future interest rate expectations.

**FIGURE 2.3  Yield Curves for U.S. Treasury Securities at Three Points in Time**

The May 22, 1981, yield curve was downward-sloping, reflecting an expected long-run decline in interest rates. On May 29, 1992, the upward-sloping yield curve reflected an expected increase in interest rates. On September 29, 1989, the flat yield curve reflected an expectation of stable interest rates. Source: Data from *Federal Reserve Bulletin*, June 1981, p. A25, December 1989, p. A24, and August 1992, p. A24.

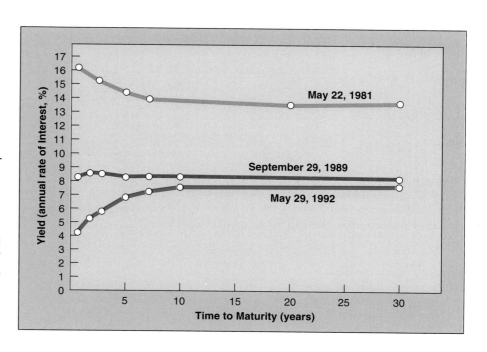

## Risk and Return[4]

A positive relationship exists between risk and return. After assessing the risk embodied in a given asset, investors tend to make those investments that are expected to provide a return commensurate with the risk involved. The actual return earned on an investment affects investors' subsequent actions—whether they sell, hold, or buy additional assets. In addition, most investors look to certain types of assets to provide a given range of risk-return behaviors.

**Actual and Expected Return**   The **actual return** on an investment is measured as a percentage return on the initial price or amount invested. Equation 2.1 presents the basic expression for calculating actual return.

$$\text{Return} = \frac{\text{ending value} - \text{initial value} + \text{cash received}}{\text{initial value}} \qquad (2.1)$$

**actual return**
The percentage return on the initial price or amount invested.

**Equation 2.1** Formula for calculating actual return

Basically the equation expresses the change in value plus any cash received as a percentage of the initial value. This method of calculating investment return is commonly applied over annual periods or expressed as an annual rate of return.[5]

## ▶ E X A M P L E

Roberta's Gameroom, a high-traffic video arcade, wishes to determine the actual rate of return on two of its video machines: Starman and Avenger. Starman was purchased exactly one year ago for $20,000 and currently has a market value of $21,500. During the year it generated $800 of after-tax cash receipts. Avenger was purchased four years ago, and its value at the beginning and end of the year just completed declined from $12,000 to $11,800. During the year it generated $1,700 of after-tax cash receipts. Substituting into Equation 2.1, the annual rate of return for each video machine is calculated.

STARMAN

$$\text{Return} = \frac{\$21,500 - \$20,000 + \$800}{\$20,000} = \frac{\$2,300}{\$20,000} = \underline{\underline{11.5\%}}$$

AVENGER

$$\text{Return} = \frac{\$11,800 - \$12,000 + \$1,700}{\$12,000} = \frac{\$1,500}{\$12,000} = \underline{\underline{12.5\%}}$$

Although the value of Avenger declined during the year, its relatively high cash flow caused it to earn a higher rate of return than that earned by Starman during the same period. Clearly, the combined effect of changes in value and cash flow measured by the rate of return is important.

---

[4]Detailed discussions of risk and return and their linkage to value are included in Chapter 12.

[5]The measurement of return over longer periods of time using present-value techniques is presented in Chapters 13 and 15. For now this single time period measure is assumed.

**FIGURE 2.4  Risk-Return Profile for Popular Securities**

The greater the risk of a given security, the higher the expected return (cost to the issuer). Low-risk securities include U.S. Treasury bills and prime-grade commercial paper; high-risk securities include all types of common stocks.

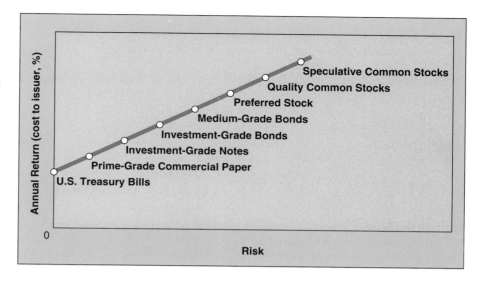

**expected return**
The sum of the forecast change in an investment's value and any expected cash receipts expressed as a percentage of the initial amount invested.

**risk-return trade-off**
The expectation that for accepting greater risk, investors must be compensated with greater returns.

The return calculated using Equation 2.1 is typically an actual rather than an expected return. When estimating **expected return,** the decision maker must forecast the ending value and cash receipts, thus introducing an element of risk or uncertainty as to the actual outcome.

**The Basic Trade-Off**   A **risk-return trade-off** exists such that investors must be compensated for accepting greater risk with the expectation of greater returns.[6] Figure 2.4 illustrates the typical relationship between risk and return for several popular securities. Clearly, higher returns (costs to the issuer) are expected with greater risk. Financial managers must attempt to keep revenues up and costs down, but they must also consider the risks associated with each investment and financing alternative. Decisions ultimately rest on an analysis of the effect of risk and return on share price.

▼▼▼▼▼▼▼▼▼▼▼▼▼▼▼▼▼▼▼▼▼▼▼▼▼▼▼▼▼▼▼▼

# Progress Review Questions

**2-15.** What does the *term structure of interest rates* mean and how does it relate to the *yield curve?* For a given class of similar-risk securities, what does each of the following yield curves reflect about interest rates? Which form has been historically dominant?
 **a.** Downward-sloping
 **b.** Upward-sloping
 **c.** Flat

---

[6]The risk-return trade-off is discussed in detail in Chapter 12, where certain refinements are introduced to explain why investors are actually rewarded with higher returns for taking only certain types of "nondiversifiable" or inescapable risks.

**2-16.** How are actual and expected returns measured, and what is the difference between them? What is meant by the *risk-return trade-off*? How should this relationship affect the actions of financial managers?

▲▲▲▲▲▲▲▲▲▲▲▲▲▲▲▲▲▲▲▲▲▲▲▲▲▲▲▲▲▲

▼                    ▼                    ▼

# SUMMARY OF LEARNING GOALS

**Explain the fundamentals of business taxation of ordinary income and capital gains, and the role of S corporations.** Corporations are subject to corporate tax rates applicable to both ordinary income (after deducting allowable expenses) and capital gains, which are sales proceeds received in excess of an asset's initial purchase price. The average tax rate paid by a corporation ranges from 15 to 35 percent. (For convenience, we assume a 40 percent marginal tax rate in this book.) Certain provisions in the tax code, such as intercorporate dividend exclusions and tax-deductible expenses, provide corporate taxpayers with opportunities to reduce their taxes. In addition, S corporations—small corporations meeting specified IRS requirements—can elect to be taxed as partnerships.

**LG  1**

**Identify the key participants in financial transactions and the basic activities and changing role of financial institutions.** Financial institutions, such as banks, savings and loans, and mutual funds, channel the savings of various individuals, businesses, and governments into the hands of demanders of these funds. Both the *Depository Institutions Deregulation and Monetary Control Act of 1980* (DIDMCA) and the S&L crisis of the late 1980s have resulted in increased competition and a blurring of the lines of distinction between various institutions. Although DIDMCA seemed to usher in the one-stop financial supermarket, in late 1992 Sears and other large financial services companies began to dismantle such operations as a result of their inability to achieve the expected profits.

**LG  2**

**Understand the relationship between institutions and markets, and the basic function and operation of the money market.** The financial markets—the money and capital markets—provide a forum in which suppliers and demanders of loans and investments can transact business directly. Financial institutions actively participate in the financial markets as both suppliers and demanders of funds. In the money market, short-term debt instruments are traded. The Eurocurrency market is the international equivalent of the domestic money market.

**LG  3**

**Describe the capital market and the two key types of securities exchanges— organized and over the counter—that serve as its backbone.** In the capital market, long-term debt (bonds) and equity (common and preferred stock) transactions are made. The backbone of the capital market is the securities exchanges. The organized exchanges are the dominant exchanges providing secondary (resale) markets for securities. The over-the-counter (OTC)

**LG  4**

exchange is both a primary market in which new public issues are sold and a secondary market for outstanding securities. Important debt and equity markets—the Eurobond market and the international equity market—exist outside of the United States. The securities exchanges, in addition to creating continuous liquid markets in which firms can obtain needed financing, create efficient markets that determine and publicize security prices and allocate funds to their most productive uses.

LG 5  **Review the role of the investment banker in securities offerings and the interpretation of bond and stock price quotations.** Acting as an intermediary between the issuer and the buyers of new security issues, the investment banker purchases securities from corporate and government issuers and resells them to the general public in the primary market. Information on bonds, stocks, and other securities is contained in their quotations, which include current price along with statistics on recent price behavior.

LG 6  **Discuss the fundamentals of interest rates and required returns: their role, the term structure, and risk and rates of return.** The flow of funds between savers (suppliers) and investors (demanders) is regulated by the interest rate, or required return. The term structure of interest rates reflects the relationship between the interest rate, or rate of return, and the time to maturity. Yield curves can be downward-sloping, upward-sloping, or flat, reflecting lower, higher, or stable future interest rate expectations, respectively. Because investors must be compensated for taking risk, they expect higher returns for greater risk. Each type of security offers a range of risk-return trade-offs.

# P A R T   II

## Financial Analysis and Planning

# 3 Financial Statements, Depreciation, and Cash Flow

Financial statements give lenders, investors, and corporate management the financial information necessary to evaluate a company's performance. There are four major financial statements: the income statement (operating results), the balance sheet (financial position), statement of retained earnings (owner's equity), and statement of cash flows (changes in financial position). They must conform to a set of standards—in the United States, generally accepted accounting principles, or GAAP—that make it possible to compare different compa-

---

**Financial statements provide a foundation for making informed decisions.**

---

nies. Although each statement is individually important, they should be interpreted collectively, along with their accounting notes, to understand a company's total performance. Accounting notes are important because they explain accounting policies and changes, methods of depreciation, and any adjustments from prior reporting periods.

Financial statements provide a foundation for making informed decisions. For example, bankers analyze financial statements to evaluate the

risks of lending. They focus primarily on the balance sheet, to evaluate existing obligations, and the cash flow statement to determine the company's ability to repay the loan. Investors look primarily at the income statement and statement of retained earnings to predict future earnings expectations for their investments. Management focuses on the "internal" income statement, which emphasizes internal control issues inherent to running the business.

Perhaps the most overlooked statement is the statement of cash flows. It shows the company's sources and uses of cash, identifying changes between the beginning and ending balance sheets. It is important to recognize that profits do not equal cash. For example, a profitable company may require new machinery to keep up with increased demand, yet be unable to meet the heavier financial obligations from the additional debt used to finance this equipment. The statement of cash flows helps managers identify potential cash shortages and track them back to the balance sheet.

At Syncordia, a subsidiary of British Telecommunications (BT) formed in 1991 to provide global telecommunications solutions to multinational companies, financial statement preparation is highly complex. The 11 legal operating entities of Syncordia, which are located in the United States, France, Japan, Italy, and the United Kingdom consolidate their financial results in the United States. Financial statements are prepared in U.S. dollars for management control purposes and then sent to

the United Kingdom, where they are restated in British pounds. Therefore, Syncordia must comply with UK GAAP terminology and standards, which often differ from those in the United States. For example, U.S. GAAP allow for depreciation of furniture and software, but in the United Kingdom, such items are expensed. Syncordia's 1993 statement of cash flows shows that our primary use of cash was to purchase fixed assets, such as network equipment and communications lines. This fits our current objective, which is to gain a leadership position in the global telecommunications market. Because Syncordia is completely funded, it does not have to secure external sources of capital—not the usual situation for a start-up company. Typically, a new company is concerned with having enough cash flow to operate the business. Once established, its focus can shift more toward strategic goals.

*After receiving a B.A. in finance from the University of Georgia in 1987, **Mark Collman** joined Equifax Inc. as a financial systems manager. He moved to Syncordia in 1993, where as senior financial manager he has responsibility for budget preparation, financial reporting, and analysis.*

$E$very corporation has many and varied uses for the standardized records and reports of its financial activities. Periodically, reports must be prepared for regulators, creditors (lenders), owners, and management. Regulators, such as federal and state securities commissions, enforce the proper and accurate disclosure of corporate financial data. Creditors uses financial data to evaluate the firm's ability to meet scheduled debt payments. Owners use corporate financial data in assessing the firm's financial condition and in deciding whether to buy, sell, or hold its stock. Management is concerned with regulatory compliance, satisfying creditors and owners, and monitoring the firm's performance.

The guidelines used to prepare and maintain financial records and reports are known as **generally accepted accounting principles (GAAP).** These accounting practices and procedures are authorized by the accounting profession's rule-setting body, the **Financial Accounting Standards Board (FASB).** In the sections that follow we examine the most important of the various corporate documents that depend on the application and interpretation of these fundamental accounting principles.

**generally accepted accounting principles (GAAP)**
The practice and procedure guidelines used to prepare and maintain financial records and reports.

**Financial Accounting Standards Board (FASB)**
The accounting profession's rule-setting body.

# The Stockholders' Report

**Publicly held corporations** are those whose stock is traded on either an organized securities exchange or the over-the-counter exchange or those with more than $5 million in assets and 500 or more stockholders.[1] These corporations are required by the **Securities and Exchange Commission (SEC)**—the federal regulatory body that governs the sale and listing of securities—and by state securities commissions to provide their stockholders with an annual **stockholders' report.** This report summarizes and documents the firm's financial activities during the past year. It begins with a letter to the stockholders from the firm's president or chairman of the board of directors (or both) and is followed by the key financial statements. In addition, other information about the firm is often included.

**publicly held corporations**
Corporations whose stock is traded on either an organized securities exchange or the over-the-counter exchange or those with more than $5 million in assets and 500 or more stockholders.

**Securities and Exchange Commission (SEC)**
The federal regulatory body that governs the sale and listing of securities.

**stockholders' report**
Annual report that summarizes and documents for stockholders the firm's financial activities during the past year.

## The Letter to Stockholders

The **letter to stockholders** is the primary communication from management to the firm's owners. Typically the first element of the annual stockholders' report, it describes the events considered to have had the greatest impact on the firm during the year. In addition, the letter generally discusses management philosophy, strategies, and actions as well as plans for the coming year and their anticipated effects on the firm's financial condition. Figure 3.1 includes excerpts from the president's letter from the 1993 stockholders' report of U.S. Robotics, Inc., a leading designer, manufacturer, and seller of

**letter to stockholders**
Typically the first element of the annual stockholders' report and the primary communication from management to the firm's owners.

[1] Although the Securities and Exchange Commission (SEC) does not have an official definition of "publicly held," these financial measures mark the cutoff point it uses to require informational reporting, regardless of whether the firm publicly sells its securities. Firms that do not meet these requirements are commonly called "closely held" firms.

Fiscal 1993 was our eighth consecutive year of record sales and net earnings and a year of tremendous expansion of our business and product offerings. Performance such as this is a direct result of the accomplishments of the talented and dedicated people who work at U.S. Robotics worldwide. During fiscal 1993, our work force grew to 755, while we continued to expand revenue per employee to $315,000, an increase of 20% from the prior year. I want to extend my thanks to all of our employees for their contributions to this fantastic year.

During 1993, our Company made great strides toward its mission to become the best data communications company worldwide.

First, we launched our Total Control line of digital and analog wide area network (WAN) hubs. These products connect local area networks to wide area networks in both analog and digital communications environments. Based on a flexible high-speed architecture, the Total Control hubs are ideal for transaction processing and enterprise connectivity. These products lay the foundation for our growth in the high-speed analog and digital dial-up "backbone" networks such as the proposed "Information Highway."

Second, we became a dominant player in the market for personal and home office data communications products, with our Sportster brand of high-speed modems. Using an aggressive policy of cost reduction, attractive pricing and broad distribution, U.S. Robotics reached the number one position in high-speed modem sales during the fourth quarter at Ingram Micro and TechData, two of the world's largest computer and peripheral distributors, as well as CompUSA and many other retailers. To complement our value pricing in 1993, we greatly expanded the number of retail outlets that carry U.S. Robotics personal communications products. We concluded resale deals with Best Buy, Software Etc., Egghead, Price Club and many other electronics and computer resellers.

In 1993, we greatly enhanced our ability to provide worldwide communications solutions through our rapid international expansion. This was due, in part, to our acquisition of P.N.B., s.a., (PNB) the largest European manufacturer of modems for laptop computers. The PNB acquisition gives us a strong position in the French market for branded products, the original equipment manufacturer (OEM) laptop market and a European-based research and development team.

In addition to the PNB acquisition, international growth was driven by our launch of the Sportster product line in Europe, emulating our successful North American Strategy. We also received approvals to sell Courier products in 10 additional countries during 1993. I am confident that as the economic environment improves, we will see strong growth in the international data communications markets.

**Continued Strong Finacial Performance**   Your management believes it is critical to deliver superior financial performance to you, our stockholders, while we continue to build the strategic foundation of the business.   As you review the financial information, you will see why 1993 was an outstanding year. Net sales increased 68% over fiscal 1992 to $189.2 million. Over the past five years, we have grown sales by 46% compounded annually. During the same period, net earnings increased at a compound annual rate of 75%, growing to $17.0 million in 1993. The $1.42 primary earnings per share in 1993 represents an increase of 42% over the $1.00 per share of fiscal 1992, and 74% compounded annually over the last five years.

This impressive growth required additional funding obtained through a follow-on offering in which the company sold one million shares of common stock. The proceeds of the offering, $20.7 million, were used to provide working capital and expand manufacturing capacity. Continued investment in our Skokie, Illinois, manufacturing facilities has resulted in improvements in manufacturing cost efficiency, flexibility and increased productivity.

**Positioning for the Future**   As we build on the accomplishments of 1993, and continue to effectively execute our stategy in 1994, I believe we are well-positioned to capitalize on growth opportunities forecast for our markets. Some of the key areas include:

- **The growth of hybrid analog/digital network environments ...**

- **The explosive growth of home office computing, ...**

- **The growth in Local Area Networks (LANs) ...**

- **The new V.34 modulation standard, ...**

- **Expansion of our product lines ...**

All of us at U.S. Robotics are extremely proud of our accomplishments during the past year and feel we are well-positioned for continued growth. Our success is directly attributable to the diligent efforts of our people. They provide the foundation for our continuous drive to make U.S. Robotics the best data communications company worldwide. In recognition of their competitive spirit and dedication, we present this 1993 annual report.

Sincerely,

*Casey Cowell*

President and Chief Executive Officer

**FIGURE 3.1   Excerpt from U.S. Robotics Inc.'s 1993 President's Letter to Stockholders**
The letter to stockholders is the first element of a stockholders' report. It describes the key events—both positive and negative—considered to have had the greatest impact on the firm during the year. This excerpt from U.S. Robotics's letter describes its major business activities and financial results for its fiscal year and briefly discusses the firm's growth opportunities. Source: U.S. Robotics, Inc., *1993 Annual Report*, pp. 4–5.

# F I N A N C E   I N
# C T I O N

## In the News

## Psst . . . Want Some Help with Your Finance Homework?

Just when you thought it was safe to go back in the computer lab, here comes the latest and greatest innovation in financial software. But this is one product you're really gonna like. Offered by Stage 1 Development of Lake Forest, CA, CFO Advisor represents a cross between a spreadsheet and a financial analysis package. The software comes with a built-in model for analyzing financial statements and general ledger data, and it understands the relationship between different financial statement accounts, like sales revenue and profit. The program also computes a slew of financial ratios automatically, with no need for any programming instructions. Once you get the ratios, the program even lets you change values and perform "what-if" analyses.

All this, without ever having to enter a cell reference, an @-function, or a range name. Just think, fifteen minutes in the computer lab and your finance homework is history. Your balance sheets balance, your income statements add up, and you have a full set of financial ratios instantly computed to amaze your classmates and professors. Oh, um, there is one catch. Since CFO Advisor is aimed at the corporate software market, rather than college students, it costs $1,995 a copy. Maybe you could ask your finance professor to obtain a copy for you. . . .

Source: J. Zenakis, "Your Personal Consultant," *CFO Magazine*, December 1993, p. 18.

data communications products with dominant brands in both the personal communications and data center/network product markets. Products include high-speed modems in the personal communications market and desktop modems, shared access LAN communication and fax servers, and analog and digital WAN hubs. The letter discusses U.S. Robotics's financial results ($189.2 million in sales, net earnings of $17.0 million, and $1.42 of earnings per share) for the fiscal year ended October 1, 1993, and its operations, products, and growth opportunities.

## Financial Statements

Following the letter to stockholders are, at minimum, the four key financial statements required by the Securities and Exchange Commission (SEC). Those statements are (1) the income statement, (2) the balance sheet, (3) the statement of retained earnings, and (4) the statement of cash flows.[2] The annual corporate report must contain these statements for at least the three most recent years of operation (two years for balance sheets). Following the

---

[2] Although these statement titles are consistently used throughout this text, it is important to recognize that in practice, companies frequently use different statement titles. For example, General Electric uses "Statement of Earnings" rather than "Income Statement" and "Statement of Financial Position" rather than "Balance Sheet"; Bristol Myers Squibb uses "Statement of Earnings and Retained Earnings" rather than "Income Statement"; and Pfizer uses "Statement of Shareholders' Equity" rather than "Statement of Retained Earnings."

financial statements are *Notes to Financial Statements*—an important source of information on the accounting policies, procedures, calculations, and transactions underlying entries in the financial statements. Historical summaries of key operating statistics and ratios for the past 5 to 10 years are also commonly included with the financial statements. (Financial ratios are discussed in Chapter 4.)

## Other Features

The stockholders' reports of most widely held corporations also include discussions of the firm's activities, new products, research and development, and the like. Most companies view the annual report not only as a requirement, but also as an important vehicle for influencing owners' perceptions of the company and its future outlook. Because of the information it contains, the stockholders' report may affect expected risk, return, stock price, and ultimately the viability of the firm.

## Progress Review Questions

**3-1.** What are *generally accepted accounting principles (GAAP)*? Who authorizes GAAP? What role does the *Securities and Exchange Commission (SEC)* play in the financial reporting activities of corporations?

**3-2.** Describe the basic contents, including the key financial statements, of the stockholders' reports of publicly held corporations.

# The Four Key Financial Statements

Our chief concern in this section is to understand the factual information presented in the four required corporate financial statements. The financial statements from the 1995 stockholders' report of a hypothetical firm, the Elton Corporation, are presented and briefly discussed. In addition, the procedures for consolidating international financial statements are briefly described.

## Income Statement

**income statement**
Provides a financial summary of the firm's operating results during a specified period.

The **income statement** provides a financial summary of the firm's operating results during a specified period. Most common are income statements covering a one-year period ending at a specified date, ordinarily December 31 of the calendar year. (Many large firms, however, operate on a 12-month financial cycle, or *fiscal year,* that ends at a time other than December 31.) Monthly statements are typically prepared for use by management, and quarterly statements must be made available to the stockholders of publicly held corporations.

Table 3.1 presents Elton Corporation's income statement for the year ended December 31, 1995. The statement begins with *sales revenue*—the total dollar amount of sales during the period—from which the *cost of goods sold* is

**TABLE 3.1   Elton Corporation Income Statement ($000) for the Year Ended December 31, 1995**

| | | |
|---|---:|---:|
| Sales revenue | | $1,700 |
| Less: Cost of goods sold | | 1,000 |
| Gross profits | | $ 700 |
| Less: Operating expenses | | |
| Selling expense | $ 80 | |
| General and administrative expense | 150 | |
| Depreciation expense | 100 | |
| Total operating expense | | 330 |
| Operating profits | | $ 370 |
| Less: Interest expense[a] | | 70 |
| Net profits before taxes | | $ 300 |
| Less: Taxes (rate = 40%) | | 120 |
| Net profits after taxes | | $ 180 |
| Less: Preferred stock dividends | | 10 |
| Earnings available for common stockholders | | $ 170 |
| Earnings per share (EPS)[b] | | $ 1.70 |

[a] Interest expense includes the interest component of the annual financial lease payment as specified by the Financial Accounting Standards Board (FASB).
[b] Calculated by dividing the earnings available for common stockholders by the number of shares of common stock outstanding ($170,000 ÷ 100,000 shares = $1.70 per share).

deducted. The resulting *gross profits* of $700,000 represents the amount remaining to satisfy operating, financial, and tax costs after meeting the costs of producing or purchasing the products sold. Next, *operating expenses,* which include sales expense, general and administrative expense, and depreciation expense, is deducted from gross profits.[3] The resulting *operating profits* of $370,000 represents the profit earned from producing and selling products; it does not take into account financial and tax costs. (Operating profit is often called *earnings before interest and taxes,* or *EBIT.*) Next, the financial cost—interest expense—is subtracted from operating profits to find *net profits* (or *earnings*) *before taxes.* After subtracting $70,000 in 1995 interest, Elton Corporation had $300,000 of net profits before taxes.

After the appropriate tax rates have been applied to before-tax profits, taxes are calculated and deducted to determine *net profits* (or *earnings*) *after taxes.* Elton Corporation's net profits after taxes for 1995 were $180,000. Next, any preferred stock dividends must be subtracted from net profits after taxes to arrive at *earnings available for common stockholders.* This is the amount earned by the firm on behalf of the common stockholders during the period. Dividing earnings available for common stockholders by the number of shares of com-

---

[3] Depreciation expense can be, and frequently is, included in manufacturing costs—cost of goods sold—in order to calculate gross profits. Depreciation is shown as an expense in this text in order to isolate its effect on cash flows.

mon stock outstanding results in *earnings per share* (*EPS*). EPS represents the amount earned during the period on each outstanding share of common stock. In 1995 Elton Corporation earned $170,000 for its common stockholders, which represents $1.70 for each outstanding share. (The earnings per share amount rarely equals the amount, if any, of common stock dividends paid to shareholders.)

## Balance Sheet

**balance sheet**
Summary statement of the firm's financial position at a given time.

The **balance sheet** presents a summary statement of the firm's financial position at a given time. The statement balances the firm's *assets* (what it owns) against its financing, which can be either *debt* (what it owes) or *equity* (what was provided by owners). Elton Corporation's balance sheets on December 31 of 1995 and 1994, respectively, are presented in Table 3.2. They show a variety of asset, liability, and equity accounts. An important distinction is made between short-term and long-term assets and liabilities. The **current assets** and **current liabilities** are *short-term* assets and liabilities, which means they are expected to be converted into cash within one year or less. All other assets and liabilities, along with stockholders' equity, which is assumed to have an infinite life, are considered *long-term,* or *fixed,* because they are expected to remain on the firm's books for one year or more.

**current assets**
Short-term assets, expected to be converted into cash within one year or less.

**current liabilities**
Short-term liabilities, expected to be converted into cash within one year or less.

A few points about Elton Corporation's balance sheets need to be highlighted. As is customary, the assets are listed beginning with the most liquid down to the least liquid. Current assets therefore precede fixed assets. *Marketable securities* represent very liquid short-term investments, such as U.S. Treasury bills or certificates of deposit, held by the firm. Because of their highly liquid nature, marketable securities are frequently viewed as a form of cash. *Accounts receivable* represent the total monies owed the firm by its customers on credit sales made to them. *Inventories* include raw materials, work-in-process (partially finished goods), and finished goods held by the firm. The entry for *gross fixed assets* is the original cost of all fixed (long-term) assets owned by the firm.[4] The term *net fixed assets* represents the difference between gross fixed assets and *accumulated depreciation*—the total expense recorded for the depreciation of fixed assets. (The net value of fixed assets is called their *book value.*)

Like assets, the liabilities and equity accounts are listed on the balance sheet from short-term to long-term. Current liabilities include: *accounts payable,* amounts owed for credit purchases by the firm; *notes payable,* outstanding short-term loans, typically from commercial banks; and *accruals,* amounts owed for services for which a bill may not or will not be received. (Examples of accruals include taxes due the government and wages due employees.) *Long-term debt* represents debt for which payment is not due in the current year.

*Stockholders' equity* represents the owners' claims on the firm. The *preferred stock* entry shows the historic proceeds from the sale of preferred stock ($100,000 for Elton Corporation). Next, the amount paid in by the original purchasers of common stock is shown by two entries—common stock and

---

[4] For convenience the term *fixed assets* is used throughout this text to refer to what, in a strict accounting sense, is captioned "property, plant, and equipment." This simplification of terminology permits us to develop certain financial concepts more easily.

**TABLE 3.2   Elton Corporation Balance Sheets ($000)**

| | December 31 | |
| --- | --- | --- |
| **Assets** | **1995** | **1994** |
| Current assets | | |
| Cash | $  400 | $  300 |
| Marketable securities | 600 | 200 |
| Accounts receivable | 400 | 500 |
| Inventories | 600 | 900 |
| Total current assets | $2,000 | $1,900 |
| Gross fixed assets (at cost) | | |
| Land and buildings | $1,200 | $1,050 |
| Machinery and equipment | 850 | 800 |
| Furniture and fixtures | 300 | 220 |
| Vehicles | 100 | 80 |
| Other (includes certain leases) | 50 | 50 |
| Total gross fixed assets (at cost) | $2,500 | $2,200 |
| Less: Accumulated depreciation | 1,300 | 1,200 |
| Net fixed assets | $1,200 | $1,000 |
| Total assets | $3,200 | $2,900 |

| **Liabilities and Stockholders' Equity** | | |
| --- | --- | --- |
| Current liabilities | | |
| Accounts payable | $  700 | $  500 |
| Notes payable | 600 | 700 |
| Accruals | 100 | 200 |
| Total current liabilities | $1,400 | $1,400 |
| Long-term debt | $  600 | $  400 |
| Total liabilities | $2,000 | $1,800 |
| Stockholders' equity | | |
| Preferred stock | $  100 | $  100 |
| Common stock—$1.20 par, 100,000 shares outstanding in 1995 and 1994 | 120 | 120 |
| Paid-in capital in excess of par on common stock | 380 | 380 |
| Retained earnings | 600 | 500 |
| Total stockholders' equity | $1,200 | $1,100 |
| Total liabilities and stockholders' equity | $3,200 | $2,900 |

**par value**
Per share value arbitrarily assigned to an issue of common stock.

**paid-in capital in excess of par**
The amount of proceeds in excess of the par value received from the original sale of common stock.

**retained earnings**
The cumulative total of all earnings, net of dividends, that have been retained and reinvested in the firm since its inception.

paid-in capital in excess of par on common stock. The *common stock* entry is the **par value** of common stock, an arbitrarily assigned per-share value used primarily for accounting purposes. **Paid-in capital in excess of par** represents the amount of proceeds in excess of the par value received from the original sale of common stock. The sum of the common stock and paid-in capital accounts divided by the number of shares outstanding represents the original price per share received by the firm on a single issue of common stock. Elton Corporation therefore received $5.00 per share [($120,000 par + $380,000 paid-in capital in excess of par) ÷ 100,000 shares] from the sale of its common stock. Finally, **retained earnings** represent the cumulative total of all earnings, net of dividends, that have been retained and reinvested in the firm since its inception. It is important to recognize that retained earnings *are not cash,* but rather have been utilized to finance the firm's assets.

Elton Corporation's balance sheets in Table 3.2 show that the firm's total assets increased from $2,900,000 in 1994 to $3,200,000 in 1995. The $300,000 increase was due primarily to the $200,000 increase in net fixed assets. The asset increase in turn appears to have been financed primarily by an increase of $200,000 in long-term debt. Better insight into these changes can be derived from the statement of cash flows, which we discuss shortly.

## Statement of Retained Earnings

**statement of retained earnings**
Reconciles the net income earned and any cash dividends paid with the change in retained earnings between the start and end of a given year.

The **statement of retained earnings** reconciles the net income earned during a given year, and any cash dividends paid, with the change in retained earnings between the start and end of that year. Table 3.3 presents this statement for Elton Corporation for the year ended December 31, 1995. A review of the statement shows that the company began the year with $500,000 in retained earnings and had net profits after taxes of $180,000. From this amount it paid a total of $80,000 in dividends, resulting in year-end earnings of $600,000. Thus the net increase for Elton Corporation was $100,000 ($180,000 net profits after taxes minus $80,000 in dividends) during 1995.

## Statement of Cash Flows

**statement of cash flows**
Provides a summary of the firm's operating, investment, and financing cash flows, over a certain period.

The **statement of cash flows** provides a summary of the cash flows over the period of concern, typically the year just ended. The statement, which is sometimes called a "source and use statement," provides insight into the firm's op-

---

**TABLE 3.3   Elton Corporation Statement of Retained Earnings ($000) for the Year Ended December 31, 1995**

| | | |
|---|---:|---:|
| Retained earnings balance (January 1, 1995) | | $500 |
| Plus: Net profits after taxes (for 1995) | | 180 |
| Less: Cash dividends (paid during 1995) | | |
| Preferred stock | ($10) | |
| Common stock | (70) | (80) |
| Retained earnings balance (December 31, 1995) | | $600 |

erating, investment, and financing cash flows. It reconciles them with changes in its cash and marketable securities during the period of concern. Elton Corporation's statement of cash flows for the year ended December 31, 1995, is presented in Table 3.10 on page 79. However, before we look at the preparation of this statement, it is helpful to understand various aspects of depreciation.

## Consolidating International Financial Statements

So far, this chapter has discussed financial statements involving only one currency, the U.S. dollar. How do we interpret the financial statements of companies that have significant operations in other countries and cash flows denominated in one or more foreign currencies? As it happens, the issue of how to handle consolidation of a company's foreign and domestic financial statements has bedeviled the accounting profession for many years, and the current policy is described in **Financial Accounting Standards Board (FASB) Standard No. 52.** This ruling by the policy-setting body of the accounting profession mandates that U.S.-based companies must translate their foreign-currency-denominated assets and liabilities into dollars (for consolidation with the parent company's financial statements) using a technique called the current rate method.

Under the **current rate (translation) method,** all of a U.S. parent company's foreign currency assets and liabilities are converted into dollar values using the exchange rate prevailing at the fiscal year ending date (the current rate). Income statement items are treated similarly, although they can also be translated by using an average exchange rate for the accounting period in question. Equity accounts, on the other hand, are translated into dollars by using the exchange rate that prevailed when the parent's equity investment was made (the historical rate). Retained earnings are adjusted to reflect each year's operating profits or losses, but this account does not reflect gains or losses resulting from currency movements. Instead, translation gains and losses are accumulated in an equity reserve account on the parent company's books labeled **cumulative translation adjustment.** Translation gains increase this account balance, and translation losses decrease it and can even result in a negative balance. However, the gains and losses are not "realized" (run through the income statement and consolidated to retained earnings) until the parent company sells or shuts down its foreign subsidiary or its assets. International accounting rules and managerial issues are discussed in more detail in Chapter 22, but an example can be used now to describe briefly how translation gains and losses occur.

**FASB Standard No. 52**
Ruling by FASB—the policy-setting body of the U.S. accounting profession—that mandates that U.S.-based companies must translate their foreign-currency-denominated assets and liabilities into dollars using the *current rate (translation) method.*

**current rate (translation) method**
Technique used by U.S.-based companies to translate their foreign-currency-denominated assets and liabilities into dollars (for consolidation with the parent company's financial statements).

**cumulative translation adjustment**
Equity reserve account on parent company's books in which translation gains and losses are accumulated.

▶ E X A M P L E

Suppose that an American company owns a subsidiary operating in Germany. (The unit of German currency is the deutsche mark, denoted DM.) Suppose the subsidiary has total assets worth DM 10,000,000, total liabilities of DM 5,000,000, and DM 5,000,000 in equity. Suppose further that the exchange rate at the beginning of the fiscal year was DM 2.00/US$, which also equals the reciprocal of this, US$.50/DM. Therefore at the beginning of the period the dollar value of the subsidiary's assets, liabilities, and equity is $5,000,000, $2,500,000, and $2,500,000, respectively.

Now suppose that by the end of the fiscal year the deutsche mark had depreciated to a value of DM 2.50/US$, or US$.40/DM. When the subsidiary's accounts are then translated into dollars, the assets have declined in value by $1,000,000 to $4,000,000 (DM 10,000,000 × US$.40/DM). The subsidiary's liabilities have also declined in dollar value, but only by $500,000 to $2,000,000 (DM 5,000,000 × US$.40/DM), and the dollar value of the equity accounts remains unchanged at $2,500,000. The parent company experienced a decline in the dollar value of its foreign assets that exceeded the decline in the dollar value of its liabilities. It has therefore experienced a translation loss of $500,000 ($1,000,000 decline in asset value minus $500,000 decline in the value of liabilities). This $500,000 translation loss is recorded as a deficit in the parent company's cumulative translation adjustment account.

## Progress Review Questions

**3-3.** What basic information is contained in each of the following financial statements? Briefly describe each.
   **a.** Income statement
   **b.** Balance sheet
   **c.** Statement of retained earnings

**3-4.** What role does *Financial Accounting Standards Board* (*FASB*) *Standard No. 52* play in the consolidation of a company's foreign and domestic financial statements? What is the *current rate* (*translation*) *method* and the *cumulative translation adjustment?*

# Depreciation

**depreciation**
The systematic charging of a portion of the costs of fixed assets against annual revenues over time.

Business firms are permitted systematically to charge a portion of the costs of fixed assets against annual revenues. This allocation of historic cost over time is called **depreciation.** For tax purposes, the depreciation of business assets is regulated by the Internal Revenue Code, which experienced major changes under the *Tax Reform Act of 1986.* Because the objectives of financial reporting are sometimes different from those of tax legislation, a firm often uses different depreciation methods for financial reporting than those required for tax purposes. (An observer should thus not jump to the conclusion that a company is attempting to "cook the books" simply because it keeps two different sets of records.) Tax laws are used to accomplish economic goals such as providing incentives for business investment in certain types of assets, whereas the objectives of financial reporting are of course quite different.

**modified accelerated cost recovery system (MACRS)**
System used to determine the depreciation of assets for tax purposes.

Depreciation for tax purposes is determined using the **modified accelerated cost recovery system** (**MACRS**).[5] For financial reporting purposes a variety of

---

[5] The MACRS system, which was first established in 1981 with passage of the *Economic Recovery Tax Act,* was initially called the "accelerated cost recovery system (ACRS)." As a result of modifications to this system in the *Tax Reform Act of 1986,* it is now commonly called the "modified accelerated cost recovery system (MACRS)." Although some people continue to refer to this system as "ACRS," we correctly call it "MACRS" throughout this text.

depreciation methods are available. Before discussing the methods of depreciating an asset, we must understand the relationship between depreciation and cash flows, the depreciable value of an asset, and the depreciable life of an asset.

## Depreciation and Cash Flows

The financial manager is concerned with cash flows rather than net profits as reported on the income statement. To adjust the income statement to show *cash flow from operations,* all noncash charges must be *added back* to the firm's *net profits after taxes.* **Noncash charges** are expenses that are deducted on the income statement but do not involve an actual outlay of cash during the period. Depreciation, amortization, and depletion allowances are examples. Because depreciation expenses are the most common noncash charges, we shall focus on their treatment; amortization and depletion charges are treated in a similar fashion.

**noncash charges** Expenses deducted on the income statement that do not involve an actual outlay of cash during the period.

The general rule for adjusting net profits after taxes by adding back all noncash charges is expressed as follows:

$$\text{Cash flow from operations} = \text{net profits after taxes} + \text{noncash charges} \quad (3.1)$$

**Equation 3.1** Formula for determining cash flow from operations

Applying Equation 3.1 to the 1995 income statement for Elton Corporation presented earlier in Table 3.1 yields a cash flow from operations of $280,000 due to the noncash nature of depreciation:

| | |
|---|---|
| Net profits after taxes | $180,000 |
| Plus: Depreciation expense | 100,000 |
| Cash flow from operations | $280,000 |

(This value is only approximate because not all sales are made for cash and not all expenses are paid when they are incurred.)

Depreciation and other noncash charges shield the firm from taxes by lowering taxable income. Some people do not define depreciation as a source of funds. However, it is a source of funds in the sense that it represents a "nonuse" of funds. Table 3.4 shows the Elton Corporation's income statement prepared on a cash basis as an illustration of how depreciation shields income and acts as a nonuse of funds. Ignoring depreciation, except in determining the firm's taxes, results in cash flow from operations of $280,000—the value obtained in the previous cash flow calculation. Adjustment of the firm's net profits after taxes by adding back noncash charges such as depreciation is used on many occasions in this text to estimate cash flow.

## Depreciable Value of an Asset

Under the basic MACRS procedures, the depreciable value of an asset (the amount to be depreciated) is its *full* cost including outlays for installation.[6] No adjustment is required for expected salvage value.

---

[6] Land values are *not* depreciable. Therefore to determine the depreciable value of real estate, the value of the land is subtracted from the cost of the real estate. In other words, only buildings and other improvements are depreciable.

**TABLE 3.4    Elton Corporation Income Statement Calculated on a Cash Basis ($000) for the Year Ended December 31, 1995**

| | | |
|---|---:|---:|
| Sales revenue | | $1,700 |
| Less: Cost of goods sold | | 1,000 |
| Gross profits | | $ 700 |
| Less: Operating expenses | | |
|   Selling expense | $ 80 | |
|   General and administrative expense | 150 | |
|   Depreciation expense (noncash charge) | 0 | |
|     Total operating expense | | 230 |
| Operating profits | | $ 470 |
| Less: Interest expense | | 70 |
| Net profits before taxes | | $ 400 |
| Less: Taxes (from Table 3.1) | | 120 |
| Cash flow from operations | | $ 280 |

# EXAMPLE ◄

Elton Corporation acquired a new machine at a cost of $38,000, with installation costs of $2,000. Whatever its expected salvage value, the depreciable value of the machine is $40,000: ($38,000 cost + $2,000 installation cost). ◄

## Depreciable Life of an Asset

**depreciable life**
Time period over which an asset is depreciated.

The period over which an asset is depreciated—its **depreciable life**—can significantly affect the pattern of cash flows. The shorter the depreciable life, the quicker the cash flow created by the depreciation write-off is received. Given the financial manager's preference for faster receipt of cash flows, a shorter depreciable life is preferred to a longer one. However, the firm must abide by certain Internal Revenue Service (IRS) requirements for determining depreciable life. These MACRS standards, which apply to both new and used assets, require the taxpayer to use as an asset's depreciable life the appropriate MACRS **recovery period,** except in the case of certain assets depreciated under the *alternative depreciation system.*[7] There are six MACRS recovery periods: 3, 5, 7, 10, 15, and 20 years, excluding real estate. As is customary, the property classes (excluding real estate) are referred to in accordance with their recovery periods, as 3-year, 5-year, 7-year, 10-year, 15-year, and 20-year property. The first four property classes—those routinely used by business—are defined in Table 3.5.

**recovery period**
The appropriate depreciable life of a particular asset as determined by MACRS.

---

[7] For convenience, the depreciation of assets under the *alternative depreciation system* is ignored in this text.

**TABLE 3.5   First Four Property Classes under MACRS**

| Property Class (Recovery Period) | Definition |
|---|---|
| 3-year | Research and experiment equipment and certain special tools. |
| 5-year | Computers, typewriters, copiers, duplicating equipment, cars, light-duty trucks, qualified technological equipment, and similar assets. |
| 7-year | Office furniture, fixtures, most manufacturing equipment, railroad track, and single-purpose agricultural and horticultural structures. |
| 10-year | Equipment used in petroleum refining or in the manufacture of tobacco products and certain food products |

## Depreciation Methods

For *tax purposes,* using MACRS recovery periods, assets in the first four property classes are depreciated by the double-declining balance (200%) method using the half-year convention and switching to straight-line depreciation when advantageous. Although tables of depreciation percentages are not provided by law, the *approximate percentages* (i.e., rounded to nearest whole percent) written off each year for the first four property classes are given in Table 3.6 on page 74. Rather than using the percentages in the table, the firm can either use straight-line depreciation over the asset's recovery period with the half-year convention or use the alternative depreciation system. For purposes of this text, we use the MACRS depreciation percentages given in Table 3.6 because they generally provide for the fastest write-off and therefore the best cash flow effects for the profitable firm.

Because MACRS requires use of the half-year convention, assets are assumed to be acquired in the middle of the year. Therefore only one-half of the first year's depreciation is recovered in the first year. As a result, the final half year of depreciation is recovered in the year immediately following the asset's stated recovery period. In Table 3.6 the depreciation percentages for an *n*-year class asset are given for $n + 1$ years. For example, a 5-year asset is depreciated over 6 recovery years. (*Note:* The percentages in Table 3.6 have been rounded to the nearest whole percentage to simplify calculations while retaining realism.)

For *financial reporting purposes* a variety of depreciation methods—straight-line, double-declining balance, and sum-of-the-years'-digits—can be used.[8] Because primary concern in managerial finance centers on cash flows, *only tax depreciation methods are used throughout this textbook.* The application of the tax depreciation percentages given in Table 3.6 can be demonstrated by a simple example.

---

[8] For a review of these depreciation methods as well as other aspects of financial reporting, see any recently published financial accounting text.

# E X A M P L E

Elton Corporation acquired, for an installed cost of $40,000, a machine having a recovery period of five years. Using the applicable percentages from Table 3.6, the firm calculated the depreciation in each year as shown in the following table:

| Year | Cost (1) | Percentages (from Table 3.6) (2) | Depreciation [(1) × (2)] (3) |
|------|----------|----------------------------------|------------------------------|
| 1 | $40,000 | 20% | $ 8,000 |
| 2 | 40,000 | 32 | 12,800 |
| 3 | 40,000 | 19 | 7,600 |
| 4 | 40,000 | 12 | 4,800 |
| 5 | 40,000 | 12 | 4,800 |
| 6 | 40,000 | 5 | 2,000 |
| Totals | | 100% | $40,000 |

Column 3 shows that the full cost of the asset is written off over six recovery years.

**TABLE 3.6   Rounded Depreciation Percentages by Recovery Year Using MACRS for First Four Property Classes**

| | Percentage by Recovery Year[a] | | | |
|---|---|---|---|---|
| Recovery Year | 3-Year | 5-Year | 7-Year | 10-Year |
| 1 | 33% | 20% | 14% | 10% |
| 2 | 45 | 32 | 25 | 18 |
| 3 | 15 | 19 | 18 | 14 |
| 4 | 7 | 12 | 12 | 12 |
| 5 | | 12 | 9 | 9 |
| 6 | | 5 | 9 | 8 |
| 7 | | | 9 | 7 |
| 8 | | | 4 | 6 |
| 9 | | | | 6 |
| 10 | | | | 6 |
| 11 | | | | 4 |
| Totals | 100% | 100% | 100% | 100% |

[a] These percentages have been rounded to the nearest whole percent to simplify calculations while retaining realism. To calculate the *actual* depreciation for tax purposes, be sure to apply the actual unrounded percentages or directly apply double-declining balance (200%) depreciation using the half-year convention.

# F I N A N C E   I N
# C T I O N

## Depreciation Expenses on Trial at Liquid Paper

Although most businesses would like to depreciate all of the assets they own, the IRS can be very picky when it comes to allowable depreciation deductions. Depreciation reduces tax revenue, because noncash depreciation expenses reduce taxable income reported by businesses to the IRS.

So what does it take to claim a legal depreciation deduction for a particular asset? The asset in question must have (1) an identifiable market value, and (2) a finite useful life that can be measured accurately. These requirements sound simple enough—at least until you start to apply them to actual business assets.

Take the case of Liquid Paper Corporation's quest to depreciate the white goop it manufactures to cover up typing mistakes. Liquid Paper claimed that the unpatented, "secret formula" in its correction fluid had a known

useful life, but the IRS argued that the life of unpatented technology was unknowable. Accordingly, the IRS used a little white-out of its own to remove this depreciation deduction on Liquid Paper's tax return.

The case went to tax court, where Liquid Paper officials were able to demonstrate that the life of their trade secret was easy to define. The firm showed that technological advances in typewriter technology, such as the introduction of the microcomputer and word processing software in the business world, would destroy 95 percent of the market for correction fluid by 1995. The court agreed, and Liquid Paper won back from the IRS its depreciation deduction for the secret formula contained in its correction fluid.

Source: *Taxation for Accountants*, August 1990, p. 110.

## Progress Review Questions

**3-5.** In what sense does depreciation act as cash inflow? How can a firm's after-tax profits be adjusted to determine cash flow from operations?

**3-6.** Briefly describe the first four modified accelerated cost recovery system (MACRS) property classes and recovery periods. Explain how the depreciation percentages are determined by using the MACRS recovery periods.

## Analyzing the Firm's Cash Flow          LG  6

The *statement of cash flows*, briefly described earlier, summarizes the firm's cash flow over a given period of time. Because it can be used to capture historic cash flow, the statement is developed in this section. First, however, we need to discuss cash flow through the firm and the classification of sources and uses.

## The Firm's Cash Flows

**operating flows**
Cash flows directly related to
production and sale of the
firm's products and services.

Figure 3.2 illustrates the firm's cash flows. Note that both cash and marketable securities, which because of their highly liquid nature are considered the same as cash, represent a reservoir of liquidity that is increased by cash inflows and decreased by cash outflows. Also note that the firm's cash flows have been divided into (1) operating flows, (2) investment flows, and (3) financing flows. The **operating flows** are cash flows—inflows and outflows—directly related to production and sale of the firm's products and services. These flows capture

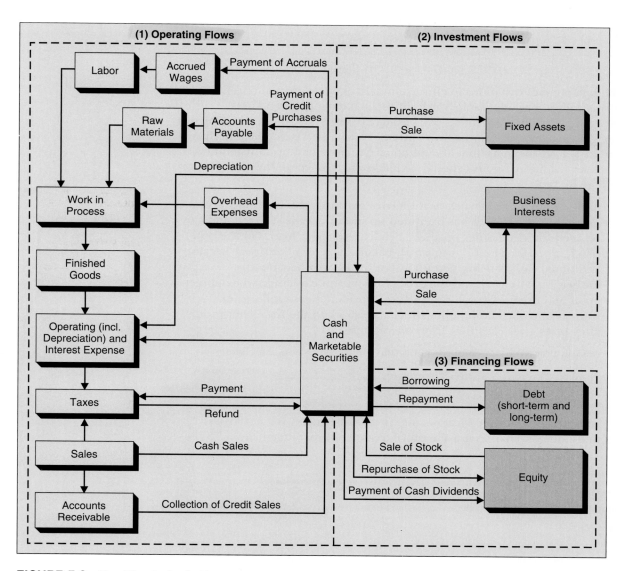

**FIGURE 3.2  The Firm's Cash Flows**
The firm's cash flows can be broken into (1) operating flows, (2) investment flows, and (3) financing flows. Operating flows are directly related to production and sale of the firm's products and services. Investment flows are associated with purchase and sale of both fixed assets and business interests. Financing flows result from debt and equity financing transactions.

the income statement and current account transactions (excluding notes payable) occurring during the period. **Investment flows** are cash flows associated with purchase and sale of both fixed assets and business interests. Clearly, purchase transactions result in cash outflows, whereas sales transactions generate cash inflows. The **financing flows** result from debt and equity financing transactions. Borrowing and repaying either short-term debt (notes payable) or long-term debt result in a corresponding cash inflow or outflow. Similarly the sale of stock results in a cash inflow, whereas the repurchase of stock or payment of cash dividends results in a financing outflow. In combination, the firm's operating, investment, and financing cash flows during a given period increase, decrease, or leave unchanged the firm's cash and marketable securities balances.

**investment flows**
Cash flows associated with purchase and sale of both fixed assets and business interests.

**financing flows**
Cash flows that result from debt and equity financing transactions.

## Classifying Sources and Uses of Cash

The statement of cash flows in effect summarizes the sources and uses of cash during a given period. (Table 3.7 classifies the basic sources and uses of cash.) For example, if a firm's accounts payable increases by $1,000 during the year, this change is a *source of cash*. If the firm's inventory increased by $2,500, the change is a *use of cash,* meaning that an additional $2,500 is tied up in inventory.

A few additional points should be made with respect to the classification scheme in Table 3.7:

1. A *decrease* in an asset, such as the firm's cash balance, is a *source of cash flow* because cash that has been tied up in the asset is released and can be used for some other purpose such as repaying a loan. On the other hand, an *increase* in the firm's cash balance is a *use of cash flow,* because additional cash is being tied up in the firm's cash balance.

2. Earlier, Equation 3.1 and the related discussion explained why depreciation and other noncash charges are considered cash inflows, or sources of cash. Adding noncash charges back to the firm's net profits after taxes gives cash flow from operations:

    Cash flow from operations = net profits after taxes + noncash charges

    Note that a firm can have a *net loss* (negative net profits after taxes) and still have positive cash flow from operations when noncash charges (typically depreciation) during the period are greater than the net loss. In the statement of cash flows, net profits after taxes (or net losses) and noncash charges are therefore treated as separate entries.

*[handwritten margin note: distinction between cash flow and cash balance]*

**TABLE 3.7    The Sources and Uses of Cash**

| Sources | Uses |
|---|---|
| Decrease in any asset | Increase in any asset |
| Increase in any liability | Decrease in any liability |
| Net profits after taxes | Net loss |
| Depreciation and other noncash charges | Dividends paid |
| Sale of stock | Repurchase or retirement of stock |

3. Because depreciation is treated as a separate source of cash, only *gross* rather than *net* changes in fixed assets appear on the statement of cash flows. This treatment avoids the potential double counting of depreciation.

4. Direct entries of changes in retained earnings are not included on the statement of cash flows. Instead, entries for items that affect retained earnings appear as "net profits (or losses) after taxes" and "dividends paid."

## Developing the Statement of Cash Flows

The statement of cash flows can be developed in five steps: (1, 2, and 3) prepare a statement of sources and uses of cash, (4) obtain needed income statement data, and (5) properly classify and present relevant data from steps 1 through 4. With this five-step procedure, we can use the financial statements for Elton Corporation presented in Tables 3.1 and 3.2 to demonstrate the preparation of its December 31, 1995, statement of cash flows.

### Preparing a Statement of Sources and Uses of Cash (Steps 1, 2, 3)

The first three steps in developing the statement of cash flows guide the preparation of the statement of sources and uses of cash.

> **Step 1:** Calculate the balance sheet changes in assets, liabilities, and stockholders' equity over the period of concern. (*Note:* Calculate the *gross* fixed asset change for the fixed asset account along with any change in accumulated depreciation.)
>
> **Step 2:** Using the classification scheme in Table 3.7, classify each change calculated in step 1 as either a source (S) or a use (U). (*Note:* An increase in accumulated depreciation is classified as a source, whereas a decrease in accumulated depreciation is a use. Changes in stockholders' equity accounts are classified in the same way as changes in liabilities—increases are sources, and decreases are uses.)
>
> **Step 3:** Separately sum all sources and all uses found in steps 1 and 2. If this statement is prepared correctly, *total sources should equal total uses.*

## E X A M P L E ◀

Elton Corporation's balance sheets in Table 3.2 can be used to develop its statement of sources and uses of cash for the year ended December 31, 1995.

> **Step 1:** The key balance entries from Elton Corporation's balance sheets in Table 3.2 are listed in a stacked format in Table 3.8. Column 1 lists the account name, and columns 2 and 3 give the December 31, 1995 and 1994 values, respectively, for each account. In column 4 the change in the balance sheet account between December 31, 1994, and December 31, 1995, is calculated. Note that for fixed assets, both the gross fixed asset change of +$300,000 and the accumulated depreciation change of +$100,000 are calculated.
>
> **Step 2:** Based on the classification scheme from Table 3.7 and recognizing that changes in stockholders' equity are classified in the same way as changes in liabilities, each change in column 4 of Table 3.8 is listed as either a source in column 5 or a use in column 6.

**Step 3:** The sources and uses in columns 5 and 6, respectively, of Table 3.8 are totaled at the bottom. Because total sources of $1,000,000 equal total uses of $1,000,000, it appears that the statement has been correctly prepared.

**Obtaining Income Statement Data (Step 4)**   Step 4 involves obtaining three important inputs to the statement of cash flows from an income statement for the period of concern. These inputs are (1) net profits after taxes, (2) depreciation and any other noncash charges, and (3) cash dividends paid on both preferred and common stock.

**Step 4:** Net profits after taxes and depreciation typically can be taken directly from the income statement. Dividends may have to be calculated using the following equation:

**TABLE 3.8   Elton Corporation Statement of Sources and Uses of Cash ($000) for the Year Ended December 31, 1995**

| Account (1) | Account Balance December 31 (from Table 3.2) | | Change | Classification | |
|---|---|---|---|---|---|
| | 1995 (2) | 1994 (3) | [(2) − (3)] (4) | Source (5) | Use (6) |
| Assets | | | | | |
| Cash | $  400 | $  300 | +$100 | | $  100 |
| Marketable securities | 600 | 200 | +  400 | | 400 |
| Accounts receivable | 400 | 500 | −  100 | $  100 | |
| Inventories | 600 | 900 | −  300 | 300 | |
| Gross fixed assets | 2,500 | 2,200 | +  300 | | 300 |
| Accumulated depreciation[a] | 1,300 | 1,200 | +  100 | 100 | |
| Liabilities | | | | | |
| Accounts payable | 700 | 500 | +  200 | 200 | |
| Notes payable | 600 | 700 | −  100 | | 100 |
| Accruals | 100 | 200 | −  100 | | 100 |
| Long-term debt | 600 | 400 | +  200 | 200 | |
| Stockholders' equity | | | | | |
| Preferred stock | 100 | 100 | 0 | | |
| Common stock at par | 120 | 120 | 0 | | |
| Paid-in capital in excess of par | 380 | 380 | 0 | | |
| Retained earnings | 600 | 500 | +  100 | 100 | |
| | | | Totals | $1,000 | $1,000 |

[a]Because accumulated depreciation is treated as a deduction from gross fixed assets, an increase in it is classified as a source; any decrease is classified as a use.

**Equation 3.2 Formula for finding dividends paid**

$$\text{Dividends} = \text{net profits after taxes} - \text{change in retained earnings} \quad (3.2)$$

The value of net profits after taxes can be obtained from the income statement, and the change in retained earnings can be found in the statement of sources and uses of cash or can be calculated by using the beginning- and end-of-period balance sheets. The dividend value could be obtained directly from the statement of retained earnings, if available.

# E X A M P L E

Elton Corporation's net profits after taxes, depreciation, and dividends can be found in its financial statements.

> **Step 4:** Elton Corporation's net profits after taxes and depreciation for 1995 can be found on its income statement presented in Table 3.1.

| | |
|---|---|
| Net profits after taxes ($000) | $180 |
| Depreciation ($000) | $100 |

Substituting the net profits after taxes value of $180,000 and the increase in retained earnings of $100,000 from Elton Corporation's statement of sources and uses of cash for the year ended December 31, 1995, given in Table 3.8 into Equation 3.2, we find the 1995 cash dividends to be

$$\text{Dividends (\$000)} = \$180 - \$100 = \$80$$

Note that the $80,000 of dividends calculated here could have been drawn directly from Elton's statement of retained earnings, given in Table 3.3.

**Classifying and Presenting Relevant Data (Step 5)**   The relevant data from the statement of sources and uses of cash (prepared in steps 1, 2, and 3) along with the net profit, depreciation, and dividend data obtained (in step 4) from the income statement can be used to prepare the statement of cash flows.

> **Step 5:** Classify relevant data into one of three categories:
>
> 1.  Cash flow from operating activities
> 2.  Cash flow from investment activities
> 3.  Cash flow from financing activities

These three categories are consistent with the operating, investment, and financing cash flows depicted in Figure 3.2. Table 3.9 lists the items included in each category on the statement of cash flows. In addition, the source of each data item is noted.

Relevant data should be listed in a fashion consistent with the order of the categories and data items given in Table 3.9. All sources as well as net profits after taxes and depreciation are treated as positive values—cash inflows. All uses, any losses, and dividends paid are treated as negative values—cash outflows. The items in each category—operating, investment, and financing—should be totaled, and these three totals should be added to get the "net increase (decrease) in cash and marketable securities"

**TABLE 3.9   Categories and Sources of Data Included in the Statement of Cash Flows**

| Categories and Data Items | Data Source |
|---|---|
| | I/S = Income Statement<br>S/U = Statement of Sources<br>and Uses of Cash |
| **Cash Flow from Operating Activities** | |
| Net profits (losses) after taxes | I/S |
| Depreciation and other noncash charges | I/S |
| Changes in all current assets other than cash and marketable securities | S/U |
| Changes in all current liabilities other than notes payable | S/U |
| **Cash Flow from Investment Activities** | |
| Changes in gross fixed assets | S/U |
| Changes in business interests | S/U |
| **Cash Flow from Financing Activities** | |
| Changes in notes payable | S/U |
| Changes in long-term debt | S/U |
| Changes in stockholders' equity other than retained earnings | S/U |
| Dividends paid | I/S |

for the period. As a check, this value should reconcile with the actual change in cash and marketable securities for the year, which can be obtained from either the beginning- and end-of-period balance sheets or the statement of sources and uses of cash for the period.

► E X A M P L E

The relevant data developed for Elton Corporation for 1995 can be combined by using the procedure described above to create its statement of cash flows.

Step 5:   Classifying and listing the relevant data from earlier steps in a fashion consistent with Table 3.9 results in Elton Corporation's statement of cash flows, presented in Table 3.10. On the basis of this statement, the firm experienced a $500,000 increase in cash and marketable securities during 1995. Looking at Elton Corporation's December 31, 1994 and 1995 balance sheets in Table 3.2 or its statement of sources and uses of cash in Table 3.8, we can see that the firm's cash increased by $100,000 and its marketable securities increased by $400,000 between December 31, 1994, and December 31, 1995. The $500,000 net increase in cash and marketable securities from the statement of cash flows therefore reconciles with the total change of $500,000 in these accounts during 1995. The statement is therefore believed to have been correctly prepared.

## Interpreting the Statement

The statement of cash flows allows the financial manager and other interested parties to analyze the firm's past and possibly future cash flow. The manager should pay particular attention to both the major categories of cash flow and the individual items of cash inflow and outflow to assess whether any developments have occurred that are contrary to the company's financial policies. In addition, the statement can be used to evaluate the fulfillment of projected goals. Specific links between cash inflows and outflows cannot be made by using this statement, but it can be used to isolate inefficiencies. For example, increases in accounts receivable and inventories resulting in major cash outflows may signal credit or inventory problems, respectively.

**TABLE 3.10   Elton Corporation Statement of Cash Flows ($000) for the Year Ended December 31, 1995**

| | | |
|---|---:|---:|
| **Cash Flow from Operating Activities** | | |
| Net profit after taxes | $ 180 | |
| Depreciation | 100 | |
| Decrease in accounts receivable | 100 | |
| Decrease in inventories | 300 | |
| Increase in accounts payable | 200 | |
| Decrease in accruals | (100)[a] | |
|   Cash provided by operating activities | | $780 |
| **Cash Flow from Investment Activities** | | |
| Increase in gross fixed assets | ($300) | |
| Changes in business interests | 0 | |
|   Cash used for investment activities | | (300) |
| **Cash Flow from Financing Activities** | | |
| Decrease in notes payable | ($100) | |
| Increase in long-term debts | 200 | |
| Changes in stockholders' equity[b] | 0 | |
| Dividends paid | (80) | |
|   Cash provided by financing activities | | 20 |
|     Net increase in cash and marketable securities | | $500 |

[a] As is customary, parentheses are used to denote a negative number, which in this case is a cash outflow.

[b] Consistent with this data item in Table 3.9, retained earnings are excluded here because their change is actually reflected in the combination of the net profits after taxes and dividend entries.

In addition, the financial manager can prepare and analyze a statement of cash flows developed from projected, or pro forma, financial statements. This approach can be used to determine whether planned actions are desirable in view of the resulting cash flows.

# ► E X A M P L E

Analysis of Elton Corporation's statement of cash flows in Table 3.10 does not seem to indicate the existence of any major problems for the company. Its $780,000 of cash provided by operating activities plus the $20,000 provided by financing activities was used to invest an additional $300,000 in fixed assets and to increase cash and marketable securities by $500,000. The individual items of cash inflow and outflow seem to be distributed in a fashion consistent with prudent financial management. The firm seems to be growing, because (1) less than half of its earnings ($80,000 out of $180,000) was paid to owners as dividends and (2) gross fixed assets increased by three times the amount of historic cost written off through depreciation expense ($300,000 increase in gross fixed assets versus $100,000 in depreciation expense). Major cash inflows were realized by decreasing inventories and increasing accounts payable. The major outflow of cash was to increase cash and marketable securities by $500,000, thereby improving liquidity. Other inflows and outflows of Elton Corporation tend to support the fact that the firm was well managed financially during the period. *An understanding of the basic financial principles presented throughout this text is a prerequisite to the effective interpretation of the statement of cash flows.*

# Progress Review Questions

**3-7.** Describe the overall cash flow through the firm in terms of
  **a.** Operating flows
  **b.** Investment flows
  **c.** Financing flows

**3-8.** List and describe *sources of cash* and *uses of cash*. Discuss why a decrease in cash is a source and an increase in cash is a use.

**3-9.** Describe the procedure (the first three steps for developing the statement of cash flows) used to develop the statement of sources and uses of cash. How are changes in fixed assets and accumulated depreciation treated on this statement?

**3-10.** What three inputs to the statement of cash flows are typically obtained (in step 4) from an income statement for the period of concern? Explain how the income statement and statement of sources and uses of cash can be used to determine dividends for the period of concern. What other methods can be used to obtain the value of dividends?

**3-11.** Describe the general format of the statement of cash flows, and review the final step (step 5) involved in preparing the statement. How can the accuracy of the final statement balance, "net increase (decrease) in cash and marketable securities," be conveniently verified?

**3-12.** How is the statement of cash flows interpreted and used by the financial manager and other interested parties?

# SUMMARY OF LEARNING GOALS

**LG 1**   **Describe the purpose and basic components of the stockholders' report.** The annual stockholders' report, which publicly traded corporations are required to provide to their stockholders, summarizes and documents the firm's financial activities during the past year. It includes, in addition to the letter to stockholders and various subjective and factual information, four key financial statements: (1) the income statement, (2) the balance sheet, (3) the statement of retained earnings, and (4) the statement of cash flows.

**LG 2**   **Review the format and key components of the income statement and the balance sheet, and interpret these statements.** The income statement summarizes operating results during the period of concern by subtracting costs, expenses, and taxes from sales revenue to find the period's profits. The balance sheet summarizes the firm's financial position at a given point in time by balancing the firm's assets (what it owns) against its financing, which can be either debt (what it owes) or equity (what was provided by owners). The statement makes an important distinction between short-term (current) and long-term assets and liabilities.

**LG 3**   **Identify the purpose and basic content of the statement of retained earnings, the statement of cash flows, and the procedures for consolidating international financial statements.** The statement of retained earnings reconciles the net income earned during a given year and any cash dividends paid with the change in retained earnings between the start and end of that year. The statement of cash flows provides a summary of the cash flows over the period of concern, typically the year just ended. The statement provides insight into the firm's operating, investment, and financing cash flows, and reconciles them with changes in its cash and marketable securities during the period of concern. Financial statements of companies that have operations in other countries where their cash flows are denominated in one or more foreign currencies follow FASB Standard No. 52, which requires use of the current rate (translation) method to translate foreign-currency-denominated assets and liabilities into dollars.

**LG 4**   **Understand the effect of depreciation and other noncash charges on the firm's cash flows.** Depreciation, or the allocation of historic cost, is the most common type of corporate noncash expenditure. To estimate cash flow from operations, depreciation and any other noncash charges are added back to net profits after taxes. Because they shield the firm from taxes by lowering taxable income without an actual outflow of cash, noncash charges act as a source of funds to the firm.

**Determine the depreciable value of an asset, its depreciable life, and the amount of depreciation allowed each year for tax purposes using the modified accelerated cost recovery system (MACRS).** The depreciable value of an asset and its depreciable life are determined using the modified accelerated cost recovery system (MACRS) standards set out in the federal tax code. MACRS groups assets (excluding real estate) into six property classes based on length of recovery period—3, 5, 7, 10, 15, and 20 years—and can be applied over the appropriate period using a schedule of yearly depreciation percentages for each period.

LG 5

**Analyze the firm's cash flows, and develop and interpret the statement of cash flows.** The cash flow of a firm over a given period can be summarized in the statement of cash flows, which is broken into operating, investment, and financing flows. The statement can be developed in five steps. The first three steps guide the preparation of a statement of sources and uses of cash: the fourth step involves obtaining needed income statement data; and the fifth, and final, step is properly to classify and present relevant data from steps 1 through 4. The "net increase (decrease) in cash and marketable securities" found in the statement should reconcile with the actual change in cash and marketable securities during the period. Interpretation of the statement of cash flows requires an understanding of basic financial principles and involves evaluation of both the major categories of cash flow and the individual items of cash inflow and outflow.

LG 6

After studying this chapter, you should be able to

 **LG 1** Understand the parties interested in performing financial ratio analysis and the common types of ratio comparisons.

**LG 2** Describe some of the cautions that should be considered in performing financial ratio analysis.

**LG 3** Use popular ratios to analyze a firm's liquidity and the activity of inventory, accounts receivable, accounts payable, fixed assets, and total assets.

**LG 4** Assess the firm's debt position and its ability to meet the payments associated with debt.

**LG 5** Evaluate a firm's profitability relative to its sales, asset investment, owners' equity investment, and share value.

**LG 6** Use the DuPont system and a summary of a large number of ratios to perform a complete financial analysis of all aspects of a firm's financial condition, and make appropriate recommendations.

# 4 Analysis of Financial Statements

Financial statement analysis is a valuable skill that is used daily by financial managers. A solid understanding of financial analysis can open the door to job opportunities in banking, accounting, securities-related fields, and corporate finance. If you want to own your own business, whether starting one from scratch, taking over a family business, or buying an existing firm, knowledge of financial analysis greatly improves your chance for success. Even if you don't pursue a career that requires financial analysis, it is useful in personal financial planning.

# Ratio analysis provides an *objective* assessment of financial condition.

Most people, at some point, have to make investment decisions. The ability to analyze a company's financial statements is helpful in making informed choices about investments without having to rely on others for advice.

As a commercial banker, I use financial statement analysis every day to determine a company's ability to repay loans. Ratio analysis provides an *objective* assessment of financial condition. It helps to evaluate a company's past performance, diagnose its present financial condition, and anticipate future financial performance. Financial ratios are used extensively to identify trends. Is a company's current performance improving or deteriorating? In addition, ratio analysis is a way of comparing a company to others in its industry.

Balance sheet ratios that provide a quick picture of the company's overall financial health are a good place to start. For example, looking at the ratio of equity to debt over the past few years tells me if the company's financial situation is stable, improving, or declining. The more equity, the greater the "cushion" against adverse events. The ratio of current assets to current liabilities is another key measure. It reflects a company's liquidity, or ability to meet its current obligations. Typically, a ratio of greater than 1 is desirable.

Income statement ratios such as gross and net profit margins show operating performance and profitability trends. It is important to know if sales and profitability are stable or erratic. Ideally, we look for steady growth in sales and profitability. Ironically, dramatic sales growth can be a double-edged sword. A company may earn higher profits, but its cash flow could be extremely stretched because it has to finance a larger investment in accounts receivable, inventory, and equipment. Activity ratios tell you how a company is managing these items. For example, a slower average collection period reduces cash flow and may increase bank borrowing needs.

Corporate financial managers must find ways to improve profitability and cash flow, to provide appropriate funding, and to maintain adequate liquidity to ultimately increase shareholder value. Ratio analysis is a useful tool for pinpointing areas that may need improvement.

As useful as ratios are, it is dangerous to rely too heavily on them. Numbers can only reveal so much, and ratios can be misleading. The current ratio may be strong, but a closer look could show that many receivables are uncollectible and inventory is obsolete. The ratio alone could give a false impression of a company's ability to meet short-term obligations. Be careful when using the past to predict the future. Ratios are but one part of the analysis process. It must also include subjective considerations such as the quality, integrity, and experience of management, and the nature of the business and the industry.

*Carter Barrett is an assistant vice-president at Wachovia Bank of Georgia, N.A. He specializes in loans to companies with sales of $2 million to $50 million. He received a bachelor's degree in business administration, majoring in finance, from the University of Georgia in 1987.*

85

In the preceding chapter we studied the format, components, and primary purpose of each of the firm's four basic financial statements. The information contained in these statements is of major significance to shareholders, creditors, and managers, all of whom regularly need to have relative measures of the company's operating efficiency and condition. *Relative* is the key word here, because the analysis of financial statements is based on the knowledge and use of *ratios,* or *relative values.*

# The Use of Financial Ratios

LG 1    LG 2

**Ratio analysis** involves the methods of calculating and interpreting financial ratios to assess the firms' performance and status. The basic inputs to ratio analysis are the firm's income statement and balance sheet for the periods to be examined. However, before proceeding further, we need to describe the various interested parties and the types of ratio comparisons.

**ratio analysis**
Involves the methods of calculating and interpreting financial ratios to assess the firm's performance and status.

## Interested Parties

Ratio analysis of a firm's financial statements is of interest to shareholders, creditors, and the firm's own management. Both present and prospective shareholders are interested in the firm's current and future level of risk and return. These two dimensions directly affect share price. The firm's creditors are primarily interested in the short-term liquidity of the company and in its ability to make interest and principal payments. A secondary concern of creditors is the firm's profitability; they want assurance that the business is healthy and will continue to be successful. Management, like stockholders, must be concerned with all aspects of the firm's financial situation. Thus it attempts to operate in a manner that will result in financial ratios considered favorable by both owners and creditors. In addition, management uses ratios to monitor the firm's performance from period to period. Any unexpected changes are examined to isolate developing problems.

## Types of Ratio Comparisons

Ratio analysis is not merely the application of a formula to financial data to calculate a given ratio. More important is the *interpretation* of the ratio value. To answer such questions as, Is it too high or too low? Is it good or bad?, a meaningful standard or basis for comparison is needed. Two types of ratio comparisons can be made: cross-sectional and time-series.

**Cross-Sectional Analysis**    **Cross-sectional analysis** involves the comparison of different firms' financial ratios at the same point in time. The typical business is interested in how well it has performed in relation to its competitors. (If the competitors are also publicly held corporations, their reported financial statements should be available for analysis.) Often the firm's performance is compared with that of the industry leader, and the firm may uncover major

**cross-sectional analysis**
The comparison of different firm's financial ratios at the same point in time.

**TABLE 4.1   Industry Average Ratios for Selected Lines of Business[a]**

| Line of Business (Number of Concerns Reporting)[b] | Quick Ratio (X) | Current Ratio (X) | Current Liabilities to Net Worth (%) | Current Liabilities to Inventory (%) | Total Liabilities to Net Worth (%) | Fixed Assets to Net Worth (%) | Collection Period (Days) | Sales to Inventory (X) | Total Assets to Sales (%) | Sales to Net Working Capital (X) | Accounts Payable to Sales (%) | Return on Sales (%) | Return on Total Assets (%) | Return on Net Worth (%) |
|---|---|---|---|---|---|---|---|---|---|---|---|---|---|---|
| Department stores (663) | 2.5 **1.2** 0.4 | 7.5 **3.5** 2.1 | 13.3 **36.2** 72.8 | 29.7 **47.6** 78.8 | 18.0 **57.7** 138.3 | 7.3 **20.3** 53.2 | 4.4 **20.6** 50.5 | 5.9 **4.6** 3.2 | 35.4 **49.2** 70.8 | 6.7 **3.8** 2.5 | 2.8 **4.9** 7.6 | 3.7 **1.2** (0.8) | 6.5 **2.7** (0.8) | 14.1 **4.6** (6.7) |
| Electronic computers (224) | 1.9 **1.2** 0.8 | 3.3 **2.0** 1.3 | 28.8 **67.2** 187.3 | 79.1 **146.0** 225.2 | 39.4 **90.3** 226.7 | 10.9 **25.3** 47.6 | 27.7 **49.0** 81.1 | 19.2 **9.0** 5.6 | 23.2 **45.9** 76.3 | 13.0 **7.2** 3.2 | 3.0 **6.0** 10.6 | 6.9 **2.7** 0.2 | 11.1 **4.5** (2.5) | 26.6 **11.9** (3.7) |
| Grocery stores (1424) | 1.3 **0.6** 0.3 | 4.2 **2.1** 1.3 | 20.3 **51.7** 106.3 | 37.3 **73.8** 127.3 | 31.4 **82.5** 190.2 | 20.3 **52.5** 113.6 | 1.1 **2.6** 6.2 | 26.2 **18.2** 12.2 | 12.5 **18.1** 27.7 | 35.9 **18.3** 9.7 | 1.5 **2.5** 3.8 | 3.2 **1.4** 0.3 | 15.0 **6.0** 1.2 | 29.4 **13.8** 3.7 |
| Household audio/video equipment (101) | 1.5 **0.9** 0.6 | 3.9 **2.1** 1.4 | 33.4 **74.0** 198.0 | 51.1 **91.1** 153.7 | 39.9 **119.9** 273.1 | 14.3 **29.5** 65.2 | 22.3 **39.5** 56.4 | 9.7 **5.8** 4.1 | 30.5 **45.4** 58.9 | 8.7 **5.2** 3.8 | 3.4 **6.3** 8.9 | 8.8 **3.1** 0.6 | 13.7 **4.8** 0.9 | 30.1 **12.4** 2.9 |
| Motor vehicles (80) | 1.3 **0.7** 0.4 | 3.2 **1.8** 0.9 | 33.9 **72.5** 231.5 | 46.3 **113.8** 179.5 | 37.2 **89.6** 244.2 | 12.2 **46.5** 153.8 | 18.6 **30.3** 48.2 | 12.6 **6.7** 4.5 | 23.5 **35.9** 65.0 | 14.0 **7.9** 4.2 | 3.8 **6.6** 10.8 | 6.7 **2.2** (0.2) | 13.4 **3.0** (2.0) | 39.3 **10.0** (0.1) |
| Petroleum refining (98) | 1.0 **0.8** 0.5 | 1.9 **1.3** 1.0 | 38.3 **68.4** 116.4 | 122.5 **193.7** 374.6 | 77.2 **147.4** 274.2 | 82.0 **131.5** 178.5 | 17.2 **34.8** 44.2 | 21.1 **14.6** 10.3 | 38.7 **53.5** 93.4 | 30.4 **15.8** 9.9 | 5.6 **9.1** 12.4 | 4.2 **1.5** 0.3 | 6.5 **2.3** 0.3 | 18.0 **6.7** 1.1 |
| Specialized industrial machinery (311) | 2.2 **1.0** 0.7 | 3.6 **1.9** 1.3 | 125.9 **64.6** 161.6 | 76.4 **136.4** 239.3 | 38.2 **95.7** 201.1 | 14.1 **33.6** 69.2 | 30.7 **44.2** 57.4 | 18.4 **8.1** 5.1 | 32.5 **45.3** 66.5 | 13.1 **6.0** 3.4 | 3.0 **5.9** 8.8 | 8.5 **3.4** 0.8 | 16.7 **5.7** 0.8 | 36.7 **11.7** 2.4 |

[a] These 1992 values are given for each ratio for each line of business. The center value (in boldface) is the median, and the values immediately above and below it are the upper and lower quartiles, respectively.

[b] Standard Industrial Classification (SIC) codes for the lines of business shown are, respectively: SIC #5311, SIC #3571, SIC #5411, SIC #3651, SIC #3711, SIC #2911, SIC #3559.

Source: "Industry Norms and Key Business Ratios," Copyright © 1993, Dun & Bradstreet, Inc., reprinted with permission.

operating differences, which, if changed, may increase efficiency. Another popular type of comparison is to industry averages. These figures can be found in the *Almanac of Business and Industrial Financial Ratios, Dun & Bradstreet's Key Business Ratios, Business Month, FTC Quarterly Reports, Robert Morris Associates Statement Studies,* and other sources such as industry association publications.[1] A sample from one available source of industry averages is given in Table 4.1.

The comparison of a particular ratio to the standard is made to isolate any *deviations from the norm.* Many people mistakenly believe that in the case of ratios for which higher values are preferred, as long as the firm being analyzed has a value in excess of the industry average, it can be viewed favorably. However,

---

[1]Cross-sectional comparisons of firms operating in several lines of business are difficult to perform. The use of weighted-average industry average ratios based on the firm's product line or mix or, if data are available, analysis of the firm on a product-line basis can be performed to analyze a multiproduct firm.

this "bigger is better" viewpoint can be misleading. Quite often a ratio value that has a large but positive deviation from the norm can be indicative of problems. These may, on more careful analysis, be more severe than had the ratio been below the industry average.[2] It is therefore important for the analyst to investigate *significant deviations to either side* of the industry standard.

The analyst must also recognize that ratio comparisons resulting in large deviations from the norm reflect only the *symptoms* of a problem. Further analysis of the financial statements coupled with discussions with key managers is typically required to isolate the *causes* of the problem. Once this is accomplished, the financial manager must develop prescriptive actions for eliminating such causes. The fundamental point is that *ratio analysis merely directs the analyst to potential areas of concern; it does not provide conclusive evidence as to the existence of a problem.*

▶ E X A M P L E

In early 1996, Marie Sanchez, the chief financial analyst at Dwiggans Manufacturing, a producer of refrigeration equipment, gathered data on the firm's financial performance during 1995, the year just ended. She calculated a variety of ratios and obtained industry averages for use in making comparisons. One ratio she was especially interested in was inventory turnover, which reflects the speed with which the firm moves its inventory from raw materials through production into finished goods and to the customer as a completed sale. Generally, higher values of this ratio are preferred because they indicate a quicker turnover of inventory. Dwiggans Manufacturing's calculated inventory turnover for 1995 and the industry average inventory turnover were, respectively:

|  | Inventory Turnover, 1995 |
| --- | --- |
| Dwiggans Manufacturing | 14.8 |
| Industry average | 9.7 |

Marie's initial reaction to these data was that the firm had managed its inventory significantly better than the average firm in the industry. The turnover was in fact nearly 53 percent faster than the industry average. On reflection, however, she felt there could be a problem, because a very high inventory turnover could also mean very low levels of inventory. In turn, the consequence of low inventory could be excessive stockouts (insufficient inventory). Marie's review of other ratios and discussions with persons in the manufacturing and marketing departments did in fact uncover such a problem: The firm's inventories during the year were extremely low as a result of numerous production delays that hindered its ability to meet demand and resulted in lost sales. What had initially appeared to reflect extremely efficient inventory management was actually the symptom of a major problem.

---

[2]Similarly, in the case of ratios for which "smaller is better," one must be as concerned with calculated values that deviate significantly *below* the norm, or industry average, as with values that fall above it. Significant deviations on either side of the norm require further investigation by the analyst.

**time-series analysis**
Evaluation of the firm's financial performance over time using financial ratio analysis.

**Time-Series Analysis**   **Time-series analysis** is applied when a financial analyst evaluates performance over time. Comparison of current to past performance, using ratio analysis, allows the firm to determine whether it is progressing as planned. Developing trends can be seen by using multiyear comparisons, and knowledge of these trends should assist the firm in planning future operations. As in cross-sectional analysis, any significant year-to-year changes can be evaluated to assess whether they are symptomatic of a major problem. The theory behind time-series analysis is that the company must be evaluated in relation to its past performance, developing trends must be isolated, and appropriate action must be taken to direct the firm toward immediate and long-run goals. Time-series analysis is often helpful in checking the reasonableness of a firm's projected (pro forma) financial statements. A comparison of *current* and *past* ratios to those resulting from an analysis of *projected* statements may reveal discrepancies or overoptimism.

**Combined Analysis**   The most informative approach to ratio analysis is one that combines cross-sectional and time-series analyses. A combined view permits assessment of the trend in the behavior of the ratio in relation to the trend for the industry. Figure 4.1 depicts this type of approach using the average collection period ratio of Alcott Company, a small manufacturer of patio furniture, over the years 1992–1995. Generally, lower values of this ratio, which reflect the average amount of time it takes to collect bills, are preferred. A look at the figure quickly discloses that (1) Alcott's effectiveness in collecting its receivables is poor relative to the industry, and (2) the trend is toward longer collection periods. Clearly Alcott needs to shorten its collection period.

## Cautions for Doing Ratio Analysis

Before discussing specific ratios, we should consider the following cautions:

1. A single ratio does not generally provide sufficient information from which to judge the overall performance of the firm. Only when a

**FIGURE 4.1
Combined Cross-Sectional and Time-Series View of Alcott Company's Average Collection Period, 1992–1995**

Combining cross-sectional and time-series analysis permits assessment of the trend in the behavior of the ratio in relation to the trend for the industry. Alcott's collection of receivables is poor both in comparison to the industry and in its trend.

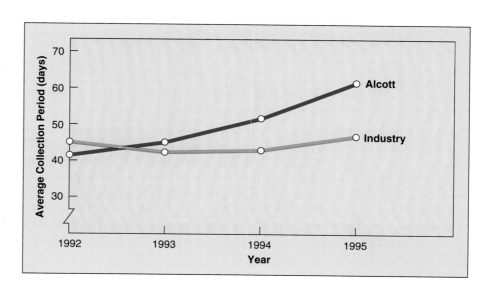

group of ratios is used can reasonable judgments be made. If an analysis is concerned only with certain specific aspects of a firm's financial position, one or two ratios may be sufficient.

2. The financial statements being compared should be dated at the same point in time during the year. If not, the effects of seasonality may produce erroneous conclusions and decisions. For example, comparisons of the inventory turnover of a toy manufacturer at the end of June with its end-of-December value can be misleading. The relatively high inventory at the end of June would result in low inventory turnover, whereas at year-end the low inventory balance would result in a very high inventory turnover. Clearly the seasonal effect of the December holiday selling season makes the firm's inventory management falsely appear to have greatly improved. Erroneous conclusions such as this can be avoided by comparing results for June of the current year to June of the prior year, December to December, and so forth, to eliminate the effects of seasonality.

3. It is preferable to use audited financial statements for ratio analysis. If the statements have not been audited, there may be no reason to believe that the data contained in them reflect the firm's true financial condition.

4. The financial data being compared should have been developed in the same way. The use of differing accounting treatments—especially relative to inventory and depreciation—can distort the results of ratio analysis, regardless of whether cross-sectional or time-series analysis is used.

5. When the ratios of one firm are compared with those of another or with those of the firm itself over time, results can be distorted due to inflation. Inflation can cause book values of inventory and depreciable assets to greatly differ from their true (replacement) values. Additionally, inventory costs and depreciation write-offs can differ from their true values, thereby distorting profits. These inflationary effects typically have greater influence the larger the differences in the ages of the assets of the firms being compared. Without adjustment, inflation tends to cause older firms (older assets) to appear more efficient and profitable than newer firms (newer assets). Clearly, care must be taken in comparing ratios of older to newer firms or a firm to itself over a long period.

## Groups of Financial Ratios

Financial ratios can for convenience be divided into four basic groups or categories: liquidity ratios, activity ratios, debt ratios, and profitability ratios. Liquidity, activity, and debt ratios primarily measure risk; profitability ratios measure return. In the near term the important elements are liquidity, activity, and profitability, because these provide the information that is critical to the short-run operation of the firm. (If a firm cannot survive in the short run, we need not be concerned with its longer term prospects.) Debt ratios are useful primarily when the analyst is sure the firm will successfully weather the short run.

# FINANCE IN ACTION

## Can Corporations Be Blinded by Profits?

If a leading financial services company offered you "Something new, one of the most widely discussed retirement plans in the investment world today . . . high money-market interest rates . . . access to the cash fund . . . [and] deposits that could be made monthly," what would you be getting? Actually, behind all the sales puffery is a simple whole life insurance policy. It might not *sound* like life insurance, but that's exactly what Metro-politan Life Insurance Company was selling in its 1993 letter to members of the nursing profession.

Why all the sales hype concerning whole life insurance products as savings plans? In part, because consumers respond better to these offers, but there's also a darker side to this story. MetLife's insurance agents can receive up to 55 percent, or $550 on a $1,000 premium, in com-

mission from selling a whole life policy. In contrast, selling a $1,000 retirement annuity produces a commission of just 2 percent, or $20. Given the significantly greater profit margin associated with whole life insurance, financial firms, such as MetLife, New York Life, and Prudential Insurance, established commission structures that encouraged and rewarded agents for exaggerating the benefits of these products. In the long run, however, is it worth it? Will the extra profits obtained from policyholders who believe they were deceived by these firms ever equal the lost sales and credibility the life insurers will suffer? Time will tell. . . .

Source: S. Woolley, "Policies of Deception," *Business Week*, January 17, 1994, p. 24.

As a rule, the necessary inputs to an effective financial analysis include, at minimum, the income statement and the balance sheet. The 1995 and 1994 income statements and balance sheets for Alcott Company are presented in Tables 4.2 and 4.3, respectively, to demonstrate ratio calculations. Note that the ratios presented in the remainder of this chapter are the standard ratios that can be applied to nearly any company. Of course, many companies in different industries use ratios that are particularly focused on aspects peculiar to their industry.

## Progress Review Questions

**4-1.** With regard to financial ratio analyses of a firm, how do the viewpoints held by the firm's present and prospective shareholders, creditors, and management differ? How can these viewpoints be related to the firm's fund-raising ability?

**4-2.** How can ratio analysis be used for *cross-sectional* and *time-series* comparisons? Which type of comparison is more common for internal analysis? Why?

**TABLE 4.2   Alcott Company Income Statements ($000)**

|  | For the Years Ended December 31 | |
|---|---|---|
|  | **1995** | **1994** |
| Sales revenue | $3,074 | $2,567 |
| Less: Cost of goods sold | 2,088 | 1,711 |
| Gross profits | $ 986 | $ 856 |
| Less: Operating expenses |  |  |
|   Selling expense | $ 100 | $ 108 |
|   General and administrative expenses | 194 | 187 |
|   Lease expense[a] | 35 | 35 |
|   Depreciation expense | 239 | 223 |
|    Total operating expense | $ 568 | $ 553 |
| Operating profits | $ 418 | $ 303 |
| Less: Interest expense | 93 | 91 |
| Net profits before taxes | $ 325 | $ 212 |
| Less: Taxes (rate = 29%)[b] | 94 | 64 |
| Net profits after taxes | $ 231 | $ 148 |
| Less: Preferred stock dividends | 10 | 10 |
| Earnings available for common stockholders | $ 221 | $ 138 |
| Earnings per share (EPS)[c] | $ 2.90 | $ 1.81 |

[a] Lease expense is shown here as a separate item rather than included as interest expense and amortization as specified by the FASB for financial reporting purposes. The approach used here is consistent with tax reporting rather than financial reporting procedures.

[b] The 29% tax rate for 1995 results from the fact that the firm has certain special tax write-offs that do not show up directly on its income statement.

[c] Calculated by dividing the earnings available for common stockholders by the number of shares of common stock outstanding: 76,262 in 1995 and 76,244 in 1994. Earnings per share in 1995: ($221,000 ÷ 76,262 = $2.90); in 1994: ($138,000 ÷ 76,244 = $1.81).

**4-3.** When performing cross-sectional ratio analysis, to what types of deviations from the norm should the analyst devote primary attention? Explain why.

**4-4.** Why is it preferable to compare financial statements that are dated at the same point in time during the year? What is the problem associated with the analysis of unaudited financial statements?

**4-5.** Financial ratio analysis is often divided into four areas: *liquidity, activity, debt,* and *profitability.* Describe and differentiate each of these areas of ratio analysis from the others. Which is of the greatest relative concern to present and prospective creditors?

## TABLE 4.3  Alcott Company Balance Sheets ($000)

| | December 31 | |
|---|---|---|
| **Assets** | 1995 | 1994 |
| Current assets | | |
| Cash | $ 363 | $ 288 |
| Marketable securities | 68 | 51 |
| Accounts receivable | 503 | 365 |
| Inventories | 289 | 300 |
| Total current assets | $1,223 | $1,004 |
| Gross fixed assets (at cost)[a] | | |
| Land and buildings | $2,072 | $1,903 |
| Machinery and equipment | 1,866 | 1,693 |
| Furniture and fixtures | 358 | 316 |
| Vehicles | 275 | 314 |
| Other (includes financial leases) | 98 | 96 |
| Total gross fixed assets (at cost) | $4,669 | $4,322 |
| Less: Accumulated depreciation | 2,295 | 2,056 |
| Net fixed assets | $2,374 | $2,266 |
| Total assets | $3,597 | $3,270 |

| **Liabilities and Stockholders' Equity** | | |
|---|---|---|
| Current liabilities | | |
| Accounts payable | $ 382 | $ 270 |
| Notes payable | 79 | 99 |
| Accruals | 159 | 114 |
| Total current liabilities | $ 620 | $ 483 |
| Long-term debts (includes financial leases)[b] | $1,023 | $ 967 |
| Total liabilities | $1,643 | $1,450 |
| Stockholders' equity | | |
| Preferred stock—cumulative 5%, $100 par, 2,000 shares authorized and issued[c] | $ 200 | $ 200 |
| Common stock—$2.50 par, 100,000 shares authorized, shares issued and outstanding in 1995: 76,262; in 1994: 76,244 | 191 | 190 |
| Paid-in capital in excess of par on common stock | 428 | 418 |
| Retained earnings | 1,135 | 1,012 |
| Total stockholders' equity | $1,954 | $1,820 |
| Total liabilities and stockholders' equity | $3,597 | $3,270 |

[a]In 1995, the firm has a six-year financial lease requiring annual beginning-of-year payments of $35,000. Four years of the lease have yet to run.

[b]Annual principal repayments on a portion of the firm's total outstanding debt amount to $71,000.

[c]The annual preferred stock dividend is $5 per share (5% × $100 par), or a total of $10,000 annually ($5 per share × 2,000 shares).

# Analyzing Liquidity

The **liquidity** of a business firm is measured by its ability to satisfy its short-term obligations *as they come due*. Liquidity refers to the solvency of the firm's *overall* financial position—the ease with which it can pay its bills. The three basic measures of liquidity are (1) net working capital, (2) the current ratio, and (3) the quick (acid-test) ratio.

**liquidity**
A firm's ability to satisfy its short-term obligations as they come due.

## Net Working Capital

**Net working capital,** although not actually a ratio, is commonly used to measure a firm's overall liquidity. It is calculated as follows:

$$\text{Net working capital} = \text{current assets} - \text{current liabilities}$$

The net working capital for Alcott Company in 1995 is

$$\text{Net working capital} = \$1,223,000 - \$620,000 = \$603,000$$

This figure is *not* useful for comparing the performance of different firms but is quite useful for internal control.[3] A time-series comparison of the firm's net working capital is often helpful in evaluating its operations.

**net working capital**
A measure of liquidity, calculated by subtracting current liabilities from current assets.

## Current Ratio

The **current ratio,** one of the most commonly cited financial ratios, measures the firm's ability to meet its short-term obligations. It is expressed as follows:

$$\text{Current ratio} = \frac{\text{current assets}}{\text{current liabilities}}$$

The current ratio for Alcott Company in 1995 is

$$\frac{\$1,223,000}{\$620,000} = 1.97$$

**current ratio**
A measure of liquidity, calculated by dividing the firm's current assets by its current liabilities.

A current ratio of 2.0 is occasionally cited as acceptable, but a value's acceptability depends on the industry in which the firm operates. For example, a current ratio of 1.0 is considered acceptable for a utility but might be unacceptable for a manufacturing firm. The more predictable a firm's cash flows, the lower the acceptable current ratio. Because Alcott Company is in a business with a relatively predictable annual cash flow, its current ratio of 1.97 should be quite acceptable.

It is useful to note that whenever a firm's current ratio is 1.0, its net working capital is zero. If a firm has a current ratio of less than 1.0, it has negative working capital. Net working capital is useful only in comparing the liquidity

---

[3]To make cross-sectional as well as better time-series comparisons, *net working capital as a percentage of sales* can be calculated. For Alcott Company in 1995 this ratio is 19.6 percent ($603,000 ÷ $3,074,000). In general, the larger this value, the greater the firm's liquidity, and the smaller this value, the lesser the firm's liquidity. Because of the relative nature of this measure, it is often used to make liquidity comparisons.

of the same firm over time. It should not be used to compare the liquidity of different firms; the current ratio should be used, instead, for that purpose.

## Quick (Acid-Test) Ratio

**quick ("acid-test") ratio**
A measure of liquidity, calculated by dividing the firm's current assets minus inventory by current liabilities.

The **quick ("acid-test") ratio** is similar to the current ratio except that it excludes inventory, which is generally the least liquid current asset. The quick ratio is calculated as follows:

$$\text{Quick ratio} = \frac{\text{current assets} - \text{inventory}}{\text{current liabilities}}$$

The quick ratio for Alcott Company in 1995 is

$$\frac{\$1,223,000 - \$289,000}{\$620,000} = \frac{\$934,000}{\$620,000} = 1.51$$

A quick ratio of 1.0 or greater is occasionally recommended, but, as with the current ratio, an acceptable value depends largely on the industry. The quick ratio provides a better measure of overall liquidity only when a firm's inventory cannot easily be converted into cash. If inventory is liquid, the current ratio is a preferred measure of overall liquidity.

## Progress Review Question

**4-6.** Why is net working capital useful only in time-series comparisons of overall liquidity, whereas the current and quick ratios can be used for both cross-sectional and time-series analysis?

# Analyzing Activity

**activity ratios**
Measure the speed with which various accounts are converted into sales or cash.

**Activity ratios** are used to measure the speed with which various accounts are converted into sales or cash. Measures of liquidity are generally inadequate because differences in the composition of a firm's current assets and liabilities can significantly affect the firm's "true" liquidity. For example, consider the current portion of the balance sheets for firms A and B in the table.

### Firm A

| | | | | |
|---|---|---|---|---|
| Cash | $ 0 | Accounts payable | $ 0 |
| Marketable securities | 0 | Notes payable | 10,000 |
| Accounts receivable | 0 | Accruals | 0 |
| Inventories | 20,000 | Total current liabilities | $10,000 |
| Total current assets | $20,000 | | |

**Firm B**

| | | | |
|---|---|---|---|
| Cash | $ 5,000 | Accounts payable | $ 5,000 |
| Marketable securities | 5,000 | Notes payable | 3,000 |
| Accounts receivable | 5,000 | Accruals | 2,000 |
| Inventories | 5,000 | Total current liabilities | $10,000 |
| Total current assets | $20,000 | | |

Both firms appear to be equally liquid because their current ratios are both 2.0 ($20,000 ÷ $10,000). However, a closer look at the differences in the composition of current assets and liabilities suggests that *firm B is more liquid than firm A*. This is true for two reasons: First, firm B has more liquid assets in the form of cash and marketable securities than firm A, which has only a single and relatively nonliquid asset in the form of inventories. Second, firm B's current liabilities are in general more flexible than the single current liability—notes payable—of firm A.

It is therefore important to look beyond measures of overall liquidity to assess the activity (liquidity) of specific current accounts. A number of ratios are available for measuring the activity of the most important current accounts, which include inventory, accounts receivable, and accounts payable. The activity (efficiency of utilization) of fixed and total assets can also be assessed.

## Inventory Turnover

**Inventory turnover** commonly measures the activity, or liquidity, of a firm's inventory. It is calculated as follows:

**inventory turnover**
Measures the activity, or liquidity, of a firm's inventory.

$$\text{Inventory turnover} = \frac{\text{cost of goods sold}}{\text{inventory}}$$

Note that because inventory is measured at cost, cost of goods sold rather than sales is used in the numerator for consistency. Applying this relationship to Alcott Company in 1995 yields

$$\text{Inventory turnover} = \frac{\$2,088,000}{\$289,000} = 7.2$$

The resulting turnover is meaningful only when it is compared with that of other firms in the same industry or to the firm's past inventory turnover. An inventory turnover of 20.0 is not unusual for a grocery store, whereas a common inventory turnover for an aircraft manufacturer is 4.0.

Inventory turnover can easily be converted into an **average age of inventory** by dividing it into 360—the number of days in a year.[4] For Alcott Company, the average age of inventory is 50.0 days (360 ÷ 7.2). This value can also be viewed as the average number of days' sales in inventory.

**average age of inventory**
The average length of time inventory is held by the firm.

---

[4]Unless otherwise specified, a 360-day year consisting of twelve 30-day months is assumed throughout this text. This assumption allows for some simplification of the calculations used to illustrate key concepts.

## Average Collection Period

average collection period
The average amount of time
needed to collect accounts
receivable.

The **average collection period,** or average age of accounts receivable, is useful in evaluating credit and collection policies.[5] It is arrived at by dividing the average daily sales[6] into the accounts receivable balance:

$$\text{Average collection period} = \frac{\text{accounts receivable}}{\text{average sales per day}}$$

$$= \frac{\text{accounts receivable}}{\frac{\text{annual sales}}{360}}$$

The average collection period for Alcott Company in 1995 is

$$\frac{\$503,000}{\frac{\$3,074,000}{360}} = \frac{\$503,000}{\$8,539} = 58.9 \text{ days}$$

On average it takes the firm 58.9 days to collect an accounts receivable.

The average collection period is meaningful only in relation to the firm's credit terms. If, for instance, Alcott Company extends 30-day credit terms to customers, an average collection period of 58.9 days may indicate a poorly managed credit or collect department, or both. Of course, the lengthened collection period could be the result of an intentional relaxation of credit-term enforcement by the firm in response to competitive pressures. If the firm had extended 60-day credit terms, the 58.9-day average collection period is acceptable. Clearly, additional information is required to draw definitive conclusions about the effectiveness of the firm's credit and collection policies.

## Average Payment Period

average payment period
The average amount of time
needed to pay accounts
payable.

The **average payment period,** or average age of accounts payable, is calculated in the same manner as the average collection period:

$$\text{Average payment period} = \frac{\text{accounts payable}}{\text{average purchases per day}}$$

$$= \frac{\text{accounts payable}}{\frac{\text{annual purchases}}{360}}$$

The difficulty in calculating this ratio stems from the need to find annual purchases—a value not available in published financial statements. Ordinarily, purchases are estimated as a given percentage of cost of goods sold. If we assume that Alcott Company's purchases equaled 70 percent of its cost of goods sold in 1995, its average payment period is

$$\frac{\$382,000}{\frac{0.70 \times \$2,088,000}{360}} = \frac{\$382,000}{\$4,060} = 94.1 \text{ days}$$

---

[5]A discussion of the evaluation and establishment of credit and collection policies is presented in Chapter 9.

[6]The formula as presented assumes, for simplicity, that all sales are made on a credit basis. If such is not the case, *average credit sales per day* should be substituted for average sales per day.

This figure is meaningful only in relation to the average credit terms extended to the firm. If Alcott Company's suppliers, on the average, have extended 30-day credit terms, an analyst would give it a low credit rating. If the firm has been generally extended 90-day credit terms, its credit would be acceptable. Prospective lenders and suppliers of trade credit are especially interested in the average payment period because it provides them with a sense of the bill-paying patterns of the firm.

## Fixed Asset Turnover

The **fixed asset turnover** measures the efficiency with which the firm has been using its *fixed,* or earning, assets to generate sales. It is calculated by dividing the firm's sales by its net fixed assets.

$$\text{Fixed asset turnover} = \frac{\text{sales}}{\text{net fixed assets}}$$

**fixed asset turnover**
Measures the efficiency with which the firm has been using its *fixed,* or earning, assets to generate sales.

The fixed asset turnover for Alcott Company in 1995 is

$$\frac{\$3,074,000}{\$2,374,000} = 1.29$$

This means that the company turns over its net fixed assets 1.29 times a year. Generally, higher fixed asset turnovers are preferred, because they reflect greater efficiency of fixed-asset utilization.

## Total Asset Turnover

The **total asset turnover** indicates the efficiency with which the firm uses *all* its assets to generate sales. Generally, the higher a firm's total asset turnover, the more efficiently its assets have been used. This measure is probably of greatest interest to management, because it indicates whether the firm's operations have been financially efficient. Total asset turnover is calculated as follows:

$$\text{Total asset turnover} = \frac{\text{sales}}{\text{total assets}}$$

**total asset turnover**
Indicates the efficiency with which the firm uses *all* its assets to generate sales.

The value of Alcott Company's total asset turnover in 1995 is

$$\frac{\$3,074,000}{\$3,597,000} = .85$$

The company therefore turns its assets over .85 times a year.

## Progress Review Question

**4-7.** To assess the reasonableness of the firm's average collection period and average payment period ratios, what additional information is needed in each instance? Explain.

LG 4

# Analyzing Debt

The *debt position* of the firm indicates the amount of other people's money being used in attempting to generate profits. In general, the financial analyst is most concerned with long-term debts; these commit the firm to paying interest over the long run as well as eventually repaying the principal borrowed. Because creditors' claims must be satisfied before the distribution of earnings to shareholders,[7] present and prospective shareholders pay close attention to degree of indebtedness and ability to repay debts. Lenders are also concerned about the firm's degree of indebtedness and ability to repay debts, because the more indebted the firm, the higher the probability that the firm will be unable to satisfy the claims of all its creditors. Management obviously must be concerned with indebtedness because of the attention paid to it by other parties and in the interest of keeping the firm solvent.

In general, the more debt a firm uses in relation to its total assets, the greater its *financial leverage*. **Financial leverage** is the magnification of risk and return introduced through the use of fixed-cost financing, such as debt and preferred stock. In other words, the more fixed-cost debt, or financial leverage, a firm uses, the greater its risk and expected return. The concept of financial leverage is developed in Chapter 5. Attention is given here to the use of financial debt ratios to assess externally the degree of corporate indebtedness and the ability to meet fixed payments associated with debt.

**financial leverage**
The magnification of risk and return introduced through the use of fixed-cost financing.

## Debt Ratio

The **debt ratio** measures the proportion of total assets financed by the firm's creditors. The higher this ratio, the greater the amount of other people's money being used in an attempt to generate profits. The ratio is calculated as follows:

**debt ratio**
Measures the proportion of total assets financed by the firm's creditors.

$$\text{Debt ratio} = \frac{\text{total liabilities}}{\text{total assets}}$$

The debt ratio for Alcott company in 1995 is

$$\frac{\$1,643,000}{\$3,597,000} = .457 = 45.7\%$$

This indicates that the company has financed 45.7 percent of its assets with debt. The higher the ratio, the more financial leverage the firm has.

## Times Interest Earned Ratio

The **times interest earned ratio** measures the ability to make contractual interest payments. The higher the value of this ratio, the better able the firm

**times interest earned ratio**
Measures the firm's ability to make contractual interest payments.

---

[7]The law requires that creditors' claims be satisfied before those of the firm's owners. This makes sense, because the creditor is providing a service to the owners and should not be expected to bear the risks of ownership.

## F I N A N C E   I N

# C T I O N

In the News

## Debt Drives Asset Sales at Sears and Roebuck

When you need to raise cash in a hurry, what assets do you think of selling first? If you're like most corporations you turn to your money-losers, shedding unprofitable operations while keeping your core money-making businesses intact. In 1993, retailing giant Sears surprised the investment community by doing just the opposite. The firm sold its profitable financial services businesses and retained its poorly performing retail business.

Why sell your most profitable assets? At Sears, the financial services businesses consumed too much of the firm's capital. By selling 20 percent of its Dean Witter brokerage business and spinning the rest of this business off to current shareholders, selling 20 percent of its Allstate Insurance subsidiary, and all of its

Coldwell Banker residential real estate business, Sears raised $4 billion in cold hard cash. These transactions, coupled with their cash proceeds, allowed Sears to reduce its debt load from $37 billion to $17 billion, and cut its ratio of long-term debt to equity from an alarming 3.4 to a comfortable 1.7. The stock market applauded Sears' return to its retailing roots—and its reduction in debt. Between 1990 and 1993, Sears' stock price per share advanced from a low of $25 to a high of $60. In the process, the total market value of the firm's stock rose by $12 billion.

Source: A. Monroe, "Sale of the Century," *CFO Magazine*, January 1994, p. 27.

is to fulfill its interest obligations. Times interest earned ratio is calculated as follows:

$$\text{Times interest earned} = \frac{\text{earnings before interest and taxes}}{\text{interest}}$$

Applying this ratio to Alcott Company yields the following 1995 value:

$$\text{Times interest earned} = \frac{\$418,000}{\$93,000} = 4.5$$

The value of earnings before interest and taxes is the same as the figure for operating profits shown in the income statement given in Table 4.2. The times interest earned ratio for Alcott Company seems acceptable. As a rule, a value of at least 3.0—and preferably closer to 5.0—is suggested.

## Fixed-Payment Coverage Ratio

The **fixed-payment coverage ratio** measures the firm's ability to meet all fixed-payment obligations, such as loan interest and principal, lease payments, and preferred stock dividends. Like the times interest earned ratio, the higher this value, the better. Principal payments on debt, scheduled lease payments,

**fixed-payment coverage ratio**
Measures the firm's ability to meet all fixed-payment obligations.

and preferred stock dividends[8] are commonly included in this ratio. The formula for the fixed-payment coverage ratio is as follows:

$$\text{Fixed-payment coverage ratio} = \frac{\text{earnings before interest and taxes} + \text{lease payments}}{\text{interest} + \text{lease payments} + [(\text{principal payments} + \text{preferred stock dividends}) \times [1/(1-T)]]}$$

where $T$ is the corporate tax rate applicable to the firm's income. The term $1/(1-T)$ is included to adjust the after-tax principal and preferred stock dividend payments back to a before-tax equivalent that is consistent with the before-tax values of all other terms. Applying the formula to Alcott Company's 1995 data yields the following value:

$$\text{Fixed-payment coverage ratio} = \frac{\$418,000 + \$35,000}{\$93,000 + \$35,000 + [(\$71,000 + \$10,000) \times [1/(1-.29)]]}$$

$$= \frac{\$453,000}{\$242,000} = 1.9$$

Because the earnings available are nearly twice as large as its fixed-payment obligations, the firm appears able to meet the latter safely.

Like the times interest earned ratio, the fixed-payment coverage ratio measures risk. The lower the ratio, the greater the risk to both lenders and owners, and the greater the ratio, the lower the risk. This risk results from the fact that if the firm were unable to meet scheduled fixed payments, it could be driven into bankruptcy. An examination of the ratio therefore allows owners, creditors, and managers to assess the firm's ability to handle additional fixed-payment obligations such as debt.

▼▼▼▼▼▼▼▼▼▼▼▼▼▼▼▼▼▼▼▼▼▼▼▼▼▼▼▼▼▼▼▼

## Progress Review Question

**4-8.** What is *financial leverage*? What ratio can be used to measure the degree of indebtedness? What ratios are used to assess the ability of the firm to meet fixed payments associated with debt?

▲▲▲▲▲▲▲▲▲▲▲▲▲▲▲▲▲▲▲▲▲▲▲▲▲▲▲▲▲▲▲▲

## Analyzing Profitability

There are many measures of profitability. Each relates the returns of the firm to its sales, assets, equity, or share value. As a group, these measures allow the analyst to evaluate the firm's earnings with respect to a given level of sales, a

---

[8]Although preferred stock dividends, which are stated at the time of issue, can be "passed" (not paid) at the option of the firm's directors, it is generally believed that the payment of such dividends is necessary. This text therefore treats the preferred stock dividend as a contractual obligation to be paid as a fixed amount as scheduled.

certain level of assets, the owner's investment, or share value. Without profits, a firm cannot attract outside capital. Moreover, present owners and creditors become concerned about the company's future and attempt to recover their funds. Owners, creditors, and management pay close attention to boosting profits due to the great importance placed on earnings in the marketplace.

## Common-Size Income Statements

A popular tool for evaluating profitability in relation to sales is the **common-size income statement**. On this statement, each item is expressed as a percentage of sales, thus enabling the relationship between sales and specific revenues and expenses to be easily evaluated. Common-size income statements are especially useful for comparing the performance for a particular year with that of another year. Two frequently cited ratios of profitability that can be read directly from the common-size income statement are (a) the gross profit margin and (b) the net profit margin. These are both discussed later on.

Common-size income statements for 1995 and 1994 for Alcott Company are presented and evaluated in Table 4.4. The evaluation of these statements reveals that the firm's cost of goods sold increased from 66.7 percent of sales in 1994 to 67.9 percent in 1995, resulting in a decrease in the gross profit margin from 33.3 to 32.1 percent. However, thanks to a decrease in operating expenses from 21.5 percent in 1994 to 18.5 percent in 1995, the firm's

**common-size income statement**
An income statement in which each item is expressed as a percentage of sales.

**TABLE 4.4    Alcott Company Common-Size Income Statements**

| | For the Years Ended December 31 | | Evaluation[a] |
|---|---|---|---|
| | 1995 | 1994 | 1994–1995 |
| Sales revenue | 100.0% | 100.0% | same |
| Less: Cost of goods sold | 67.9 | 66.7 | worse |
| (a) Gross profit margin | 32.1% | 33.3% | worse |
| Less: Operating expenses | | | |
| Selling expense | 3.3% | 4.2% | better |
| General and administrative expenses | 6.3 | 7.3 | better |
| Lease expense | 1.1 | 1.3 | better |
| Depreciation expense | 7.8 | 8.7 | better |
| Total operating expense | 18.5% | 21.5% | better |
| Operating profits | 13.6% | 11.8% | better |
| Less: Interest expense | 3.0 | 3.5 | better |
| Net profits before taxes | 10.6% | 8.3% | better |
| Less: Taxes | 3.1 | 2.5 | worse |
| (b) Net profit margin | 7.5% | 5.8% | better |

[a]Subjective assessments based on data provided.

net profit margin rose from 5.8 percent of sales in 1994 to 7.5 percent in 1995. The decrease in expenses in 1995 more than compensated for the increase in the cost of goods sold. A decrease in the firm's 1995 interest expense (3.0% of sales versus 3.5% in 1994) added to the increase in 1995 profits.

## Gross Profit Margin

**gross profit margin**
Measures the percentage of each sales dollar remaining after the firm has paid for its goods.

The **gross profit margin** measures the percentage of each sales dollar remaining after the firm has paid for its goods. The higher the gross profit margin the better, and the lower the relative cost of merchandise sold. Of course, the opposite case is also true, as the Alcott Company example shows. The gross profit margin is calculated as follows:

$$\text{Gross profit margin} = \frac{\text{sales} - \text{cost of goods sold}}{\text{sales}} = \frac{\text{gross profits}}{\text{sales}}$$

The value for Alcott Company's gross profit margin for 1995 is

$$\frac{\$3,074,000 - \$2,088,000}{\$3,074,000} = \frac{\$986,000}{\$3,074,000} = 32.1\%$$

This value is shown on line (a) of the common-size income statement in Table 4.4.

## Net Profit Margin

**net profit margin**
Measures the percentage of each sales dollar remaining after all expenses, including taxes, have been deducted.

The **net profit margin** measures the percentage of each sales dollar remaining after all expenses, including taxes, have been deducted. The higher the firm's net profit margin, the better. The net profit margin is a commonly cited measure of the firm's success with respect to earnings on sales. "Good" net profit margins differ considerably across industries. A net profit margin of 1 percent or less is not unusual for a grocery store, whereas a net profit margin of 10 percent is low for a retail jewelry store. The net profit margin is calculated as follows:

$$\text{Net profit margin} = \frac{\text{net profits after taxes}}{\text{sales}}$$

Alcott Company's net profit margin for 1995 is

$$\frac{\$231,000}{\$3,074,000} = 7.5\%$$

This value is shown on line (b) of the common-size income statement in Table 4.4.

## Return on Total Assets

**return on total assets (ROA)**
Measures the overall effectiveness of management in generating profits with its available assets; also called *return on investment.*

The **return on total assets (ROA)**, which is often called the firm's *return on investment,* measures the overall effectiveness of management in generating profits with its available assets. The higher the firm's return on total assets, the better. The return on total assets is calculated as follows:

$$\text{Return on total assets} = \frac{\text{net profit after taxes}}{\text{total assets}}$$

Alcott Company's return on total assets in 1995 is

$$\frac{\$231,000}{\$3,597,000} = 6.4\%$$

This value, which seems acceptable, can be derived by using the *DuPont system of analysis*, which is described in a subsequent section.

## Return on Equity

The **return on equity** (**ROE**) Measures the return earned on the owners' (both preferred and common stockholders') investment in the firm. Generally, the higher this return, the better for the owners. Return on equity is calculated as follows:

$$\text{Return on equity} = \frac{\text{net profits after taxes}}{\text{stockholders' equity}}$$

This ratio for Alcott Company in 1995 is

$$\frac{\$231,000}{\$1,954,000} = 11.8\%$$

The above value, which seems to be quite good, can also be derived by using the *DuPont system of analysis*, to be described later.

**return on equity (ROE)** Measures the return earned on the owners' (both preferred and common stockholders') investment in the firm.

## Earnings per Share

The firm's *earnings per share* (*EPS*) are generally of interest to present or prospective stockholders and management. The earnings per share represent the number of dollars earned on behalf of each outstanding share of common stock. They are closely watched by the investing public and are considered an important indicator of corporate success. Earnings per share, as noted in Chapter 1, are calculated as follows:

$$\text{Earnings per share} = \frac{\text{earnings available for common stockholders}}{\text{number of shares of common stock outstanding}}$$

The value of Alcott Company's earnings per share in 1995 is

$$\frac{\$221,000}{76,262} = \$2.90$$

The figure represents the dollar amount *earned* on behalf of each share outstanding. It does not represent the amount of earnings actually distributed to shareholders.

## Price/Earnings (P/E) Ratio

Though not a true measure of profitability, the **price/earnings (P/E) ratio** is commonly used to assess the owners' appraisal of share value.[9] The P/E ratio measures the amount investors are willing to pay for each dollar of the

**price/earnings (P/E) ratio** Measures the amount investors are willing to pay for each dollar of the firm's earnings.

---

[9]Use of the price/earnings ratio to estimate the value of the firm is part of the discussion of "Other Approaches to Common Stock Valuation" in Chapter 12.

firm's earnings. The level of the price/earnings ratio indicates the degree of confidence (or certainty) that investors have in the firm's future performance. The higher the P/E ratio, the greater the investor confidence in the firm's future. The P/E ratio is calculated as follows:

$$\text{Price/earnings (P/E) ratio} = \frac{\text{market price per share of common stock}}{\text{earnings per share}}$$

If Alcott Company's common stock at the end of 1995 was selling at $32\frac{1}{4}$ (i.e., $32.25), using the *earnings per share* (EPS) of $2.90 from the income statement in Table 4.2, the P/E ratio at year-end 1995 is

$$\frac{\$32.25}{\$2.90} = 11.1$$

This figure indicates that investors were paying $11.10 for each $1.00 of earnings.

## Progress Review Questions

**4-9.** What is a *common-size income statement?* Which two ratios of profitability are found on this statement? How is the statement used?

**4-10.** How can a firm's having a high *gross profit margin* and a low *net profit margin* be explained? To what must this situation be attributable?

**4-11.** Define and differentiate between *return on total assets* (ROA), *return on equity* (ROE), and *earnings per share* (EPS). Which measure is probably of greatest interest to owners? Why?

**4-12.** What is the *price/earnings* (P/E) *ratio?* How does its level relate to the degree of confidence (or certainty) of investors in the firm's future performance? Is the P/E ratio a true measure of profitability?

   LG **6**

# A Complete Ratio Analysis

As indicated in the chapter, no single ratio is adequate for assessing all aspects of the firm's financial condition. Two popular approaches to a complete ratio analysis are (1) the DuPont system of analysis and (2) the summary analysis of a large number of ratios. Each of these approaches has merit. The DuPont system acts as a *search technique* aimed at finding the key areas responsible for the firm's financial performance. The summary analysis approach tends to view *all aspects* of the firm's financial activities to isolate key areas of responsibility.

**DuPont system of analysis**
System used to dissect a firm's financial statements and assess its financial condition.

## DuPont System of Analysis

The **DuPont system of analysis** has for many years been used by financial managers as a structure for dissecting the firm's financial statements to assess its financial condition. The DuPont system merges the income statement and balance sheet into two summary measures of profitability: return on total assets (ROA) and return on equity (ROE). Figure 4.2 depicts the basic DuPont system with Alcott Company's 1995 monetary and ratio values. The upper portion of the chart summarizes the income statement activities; the lower portion summarizes the balance sheet activities.

The DuPont system first brings together the *net profit margin*, which measures the firm's profitability on sales, with its *total asset turnover*, which indicates how efficiently the firm has used its assets to generate sales. In the **DuPont formula**, the product of these two ratios results in the *return on total assets (ROA):*

**DuPont formula**
Relates the firm's net profit margin and total asset turnover to its return on total assets (ROA).

$$ROA = \text{net profit after margin} \times \text{total asset turnover}$$

Substituting the appropriate formulas into the equation and simplifying results in the formula given earlier,

$$ROA = \frac{\text{net profits after taxes}}{\text{sales}} \times \frac{\text{sales}}{\text{total assets}} = \frac{\text{net profits after taxes}}{\text{total assets}}$$

If the 1995 values of the net profit margin and total asset turnover for Alcott Company, calculated earlier, are substituted into the DuPont formula, the result is

$$ROA = 7.5\% \times .85 = 6.4\%$$

As expected, this value is the same as that calculated directly in an earlier section. The DuPont formula allows the firm to break down its return into a profit-on-sales and an efficiency-of-asset-use component. Typically, a firm with a low net profit margin has a high total asset turnover, which results in a reasonably good return on total assets. Often, the opposite situation exists.

The second step in the DuPont system employs the **modified DuPont formula**. This formula relates the firm's return on total assets (ROA) to the return on equity(ROE). The latter is calculated by multiplying the return on total assets (ROA) by the **financial leverage multiplier (FLM)**, which is the ratio of total assets to stockholders' equity:

**modified DuPont formula**
Relates the firm's return on total assets (ROA) to its return on equity (ROE) using the *financial leverage multiplier (FLM)*.

**financial leverage multiplier (FLM)**
The ratio of the firm's total assets to stockholders' equity.

$$ROE = ROA \times FLM$$

Substituting the appropriate formulas into the equation and simplifying results in the formula given earlier,

$$ROE = \frac{\text{net profits after taxes}}{\text{total assets}} \times \frac{\text{total assets}}{\text{stockholders' equity}}$$
$$= \frac{\text{net profits after taxes}}{\text{stockholders' equity}}$$

Use of the financial leverage multiplier (FLM) to convert the ROA to the ROE reflects the effect of leverage (use of debt) on owners' return. Substituting the values for Alcott Company's ROA of 6.4 percent, calculated earlier, and Alcott's financial leverage multiplier (FLM) of 1.84 ($3,597,000 total assets ÷ $1,954,000 stockholders' equity) into the modified DuPont formula yields

$$ROE = 6.4\% \times 1.84 = 11.8\%$$

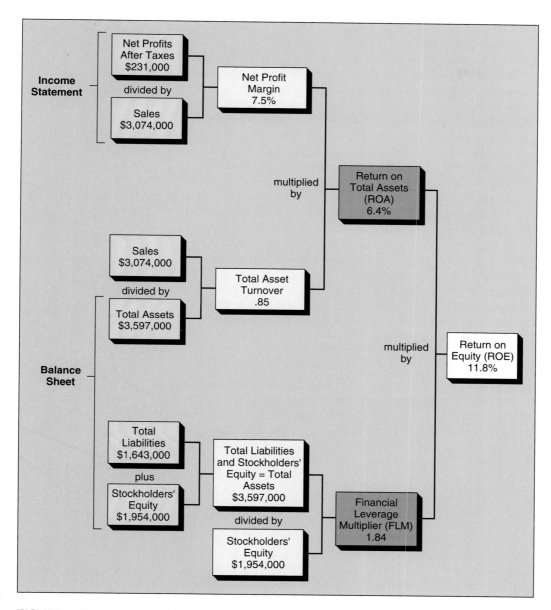

**FIGURE 4.2   The DuPont System of Analysis with Application to Alcott Company (1995)**

The DuPont system of analysis creates a structure used to dissect the firm's income statement and balance sheet to assess its financial condition. The system focuses on return on total assets (ROA) and return on equity (ROE). Alcott Company's return on equity (ROE) of 11.8% is considerably higher than its return on total assets (ROA) of 6.4% because of its use of leverage (debt) reflected in its financial leverage multiplier (FLM) of 1.84.

The 11.8 percent ROE calculated by using the modified DuPont formula is the same as that calculated directly.

The considerable advantage of the DuPont system is that it allows the firm to break its return on equity into a profit-on-sales component (net profit margin), an efficiency-of-asset-use component (total asset turnover), and a use-of-leverage component (financial leverage multiplier). The total return to the owners can therefore be analyzed in light of these important dimensions. As an illustration, let's look ahead to the ratio values summarized in Table 4.5 on pages 110–111. Alcott Company's net profit margin and total asset turnover increased between 1994 and 1995 to levels above the industry average. In combination, improved profit on sales and better asset utilization resulted in an improved return on total assets (ROA). Increased asset return coupled with the increase use of debt reflected in the increased financial leverage multiplier (not shown) caused the owners' return (ROE) to increase. Simply stated, it is clear from the DuPont system of analysis that the improvement in Alcott Company's 1995 ROE resulted from greater profit on sales, better asset utilization, and the increased use of leverage. Of course, it is important to recognize that the increased return reflected in the ROE may be attributable to the increased risk caused by the higher leverage reflected in the FLM. In other words, the use of more financial leverage increases *both* return and risk.

## Summarizing All Ratios

The 1995 ratio values calculated earlier and the ratio values calculated for 1993 and 1994 for Alcott Company, along with the industry average ratios for 1995, are summarized in Table 4.5. The table shows the formula used to calculate each ratio. Using these data, we can discuss the four key aspects of Alcott's performance—(1) liquidity, (2) activity, (3) debt, and (4) profitability—on a cross-sectional and time-series basis.

**Liquidity**    The overall liquidity of the firm seems to exhibit a reasonably stable trend. It has been maintained at a level that is relatively consistent with the industry average in 1995. The firm's liquidity seems to be good.

**Activity**    Alcott Company's inventory appears to be in good shape. Its inventory management seems to have improved, and in 1995 it performed at a level above that of the industry. The firm may be experiencing some problems with accounts receivable. The average collection period seems to have crept up to a level above that of the industry. Alcott also appears to be slow in paying its bills; it is paying nearly 30 days later than the industry average. Payment procedures should be examined to make sure that the company's credit standing is not adversely affected. Whereas overall liquidity appears to be good, some attention should be given to the management of accounts receivable and payable. Alcott's fixed asset turnover and total asset turnover reflect sizable declines in the efficiency of fixed and total asset utilization between 1993 and 1994. Although in 1995 the total asset turnover rose to a level considerably above the industry average, it appears that the pre-1994 level of efficiency has not yet been achieved.

**Debt**    Alcott Company's indebtedness increased over the 1993–1995 period and is currently at a level above the industry average. Although the increase in the debt ratio may be cause for alarm, the firm's ability to meet interest and fixed-payment obligations improved from 1994 to 1995 to a level that outperforms the industry. The firm's increased indebtedness in 1994 apparently caused a deterioration in its ability to pay debt adequately. However, Alcott has evidently improved its income in 1995 so that it is able to meet its interest and fixed-payment obligations in a fashion consistent with the average firm in the industry. In summary, it appears although 1994 was an off year, the company's ability to pay debts in 1995 adequately compensates for the increased degree of indebtedness.

**Profitability**   Alcott's profitability relative to sales in 1995 was better than that of the average company in the industry, although it did not match the firm's 1993 performance. Although the *gross* profit margin in 1994 and 1995 was better than in 1993, it appears that higher levels of operating and interest expenses in 1994 and 1995 caused the 1995 *net* profit margin to fall below that of 1993. However, Alcott Company's 1995 net profit margin is quite favorable when compared with the industry average. The firm's return on total assets, return on equity, and earnings per share behaved in a fashion similar to its net profit margin over the 1993–1995 period. Alcott appears to have experienced either a sizable drop in sales between 1993 and 1994 or a rapid expansion in assets during that period. The owners' return, as evidenced by the exceptionally high 1995 level of return on equity (ROE), seems to suggest that the firm is performing quite well. Of course, as we noted in the discussion of the application of the DuPont system of analysis to Alcott's 1995 results, the firm's increased ROE actually resulted from the increased returns from its improved ROA and the increased risk reflected in its increased degree of indebtedness. This can be seen in its increased debt ratio and financial leverage multiplier (FLM). In addition, although the firm's shares are selling at a price/earnings (P/E) multiple below that of the industry, some improvement occurred between 1994 and 1995. The firm's above-average returns—net profit margin, ROA, ROE, and EPS—may be attributable to its above-average risk as reflected in its below-industry-average P/E ratio.

In summary, it appears that the firm is growing and has recently undergone an expansion in assets, this expansion being financed primarily through the use of debt. The 1994–1995 period seems to reflect a phase of adjustment and recovery from the rapid growth in assets. Alcott's sales, profits, and other performance factors seem to be growing with the increase in the size of the operation. In short, the firm appears to have done quite well in 1995.

## Progress Review Questions

**4-13.** Three areas of analysis or concern are combined in using the *DuPont system of analysis*. What are these concerns, and how are they combined to explain the firm's return on equity (ROE)? How is risk associated with financial leverage captured using this system?

**4-14.** Describe how to approach a complete ratio analysis of the firm on both a cross-sectional and a time-series basis by summarizing a large number of ratios.

**TABLE 4.5 Summary of Alcott Company Ratios (1993–1995, Including 1995 Industry Averages)**

| Ratio | Formula | Year | | | Industry Average 1995[c] | Evaluation[d] | | |
|---|---|---|---|---|---|---|---|---|
| | | 1993[a] | 1994[b] | 1995[b] | | Cross-Sectional 1995 | Time-Series 1993–1995 | Overall |
| **Liquidity** | | | | | | | | |
| Net working capital | current assets − current liabilities | $583,000 | $521,000 | $603,000 | $427,000 | good | good | good |
| Current ratio | $\dfrac{\text{current assets}}{\text{current liabilities}}$ | 2.04 | 2.08 | 1.97 | 2.05 | OK | OK | OK |
| Quick (acid-test) ratio | $\dfrac{\text{current assets − inventory}}{\text{current liabilities}}$ | 1.32 | 1.46 | 1.51 | 1.43 | OK | good | good |
| **Activity** | | | | | | | | |
| Inventory turnover | $\dfrac{\text{cost of goods sold}}{\text{inventory}}$ | 5.1 | 5.7 | 7.2 | 6.6 | good | good | good |
| Average collection period | $\dfrac{\text{accounts receivable}}{\text{average sales per day}}$ | 43.9 days | 51.2 days | 58.9 days | 44.3 days | poor | poor | poor |
| Average payment period | $\dfrac{\text{accounts payable}}{\text{average purchases per day}}$ | 75.8 days | 81.2 days | 94.1 days | 66.5 days | poor | poor | poor |
| Fixed-asset turnover | $\dfrac{\text{sales}}{\text{net fixed assets}}$ | 1.50 | 1.13 | 1.29 | 1.35 | OK | OK | OK |
| Total asset turnover | $\dfrac{\text{sales}}{\text{total assets}}$ | 0.94 | 0.79 | 0.85 | 0.75 | OK | OK | OK |

| Ratio | Formula | Year | | | Industry Average 1995[c] | Evaluation[d] | | |
| --- | --- | --- | --- | --- | --- | --- | --- | --- |
| | | 1993[a] | 1994[b] | 1995[b] | | Cross-Sectional 1995 | Time-Series 1993–1995 | Overall |
| **Debt** | | | | | | | | |
| Debt ratio | $\dfrac{\text{total liabilities}}{\text{total assets}}$ | 36.8% | 44.3% | 45.7% | 40.0% | OK | OK | OK |
| Times interest earned ratio | $\dfrac{\text{earnings before interest and taxes}}{\text{interest}}$ | 5.6 | 3.3 | 4.5 | 4.3 | good | OK | OK |
| Fixed-payment coverage ratio | $\dfrac{\text{earnings before interest and taxes + lease payments}}{\text{int. + lease payments} + [(\text{prin. + pref. div.}) \times [1/(1-T)]]}$ | 2.4 | 1.4 | 1.9 | 1.5 | good | OK | good |
| **Profitability** | | | | | | | | |
| Gross profit margin | $\dfrac{\text{gross profits}}{\text{sales}}$ | 31.4% | 33.3% | 32.1% | 30.0% | OK | OK | OK |
| Net profit margin | $\dfrac{\text{net profits after taxes}}{\text{sales}}$ | 8.8% | 5.8% | 7.5% | 6.4% | good | OK | good |
| Return on total assets (ROA) | $\dfrac{\text{net profits after taxes}}{\text{total assets}}$ | 8.3% | 4.5% | 6.4% | 4.8% | good | OK | good |
| Return on equity (ROE) | $\dfrac{\text{net profits after taxes}}{\text{stockholders' equity}}$ | 13.1% | 8.1% | 11.8% | 8.0% | good | OK | good |
| Earnings per share (EPS) | $\dfrac{\text{earnings available for common stockholders}}{\text{number of shares of common stock outstanding}}$ | $3.26 | $1.81 | $2.90 | $2.26 | good | OK | good |
| Price/earnings (P/E) ratio | $\dfrac{\text{market price per share of common stock}}{\text{earnings per share}}$ | 10.5 | 10.0 | 11.1 | 12.5 | OK | OK | OK |

[a]Calculated from data not included in the chapter.
[b]Calculated using the financial statements presented in Tables 4.2 and 4.3.
[c]Obtained from sources not included in this chapter.
[d]Subjective assessments based on data provided.

▼            ▼            ▼

# SUMMARY OF LEARNING GOALS

**Understand the parties interested in performing financial ratio analysis and the common types of ratio comparisons.** Ratio analysis allows present and prospective stockholders and lenders and the firm's management to evaluate the firm's financial performance and status. It can be performed on a cross-sectional or a time-series basis. Cross-sectional analysis involves comparisons of different firms' financial ratios at the same point in time. Time-series analysis measures a firm's performance over time.

LG 1

**Describe some of the cautions that should be considered in performing financial ratio analysis.** Cautions in ratio analysis include: (1) A single ratio does not generally provide sufficient information; (2) Financial statements being compared should be dated at the same point in time during the year; (3) Audited financial statements should be used; (4) Data should be checked for consistency of accounting treatment; and (5) Inflation and different asset ages can distort ratio comparisons.

LG 2

**Use popular ratios to analyze a firm's liquidity and the activity of inventory, accounts receivable, accounts payable, fixed assets, and total assets.** The liquidity, or ability of the firm to pay its bills as they come due, can be measured by the firm's net working capital, its current ratio, or its quick (acid-test) ratio. Activity ratios measure the speed with which various accounts are converted into sales or cash. The activity of inventory can be measured by its turnover, that of accounts receivable by the average collection period, and that of accounts payable by the average payment period. Fixed and total asset turnovers can be used to measure the efficiency with which the firm has used its fixed and total assets to generate sales. Formulas for these liquidity and activity ratios are summarized in Table 4.5.

LG 3

**Assess the firm's debt position and its ability to meet the payments associated with debt.** The more debt a firm uses, the greater its financial leverage, which results in the magnification of both risk and return. Financial debt ratios measure both the degree of indebtedness and the ability to pay debts. A commonly used measure of debt position is the debt ratio. The ability to pay contractual obligations, such as interest, principal, lease payments, and preferred stock dividends, can be measured by times interest earned and fixed-payment coverage ratios. Formulas for these debt ratios are summarized in Table 4.5.

LG 4

**Evaluate a firm's profitability relative to its sales, asset investment, owners' equity investment, and share value.** Measures of profitability can be made in various ways. The common-size income statement, which shows all items as a percentage of sales, can be used to determine gross profit margin and net profit margin. Other measures of profitability include return on total assets, return on equity, earnings per share, and the price/earnings ratio. Formulas for these profitability ratios are summarized in Table 4.5.

LG 5

LG  6

**Use the DuPont system and a summary of a large number of ratios to perform a complete financial analysis of all aspects of a firm's financial condition, and make appropriate recommendations.** The DuPont system of analysis is a search technique aimed at finding key areas responsible for the firm's financial performance. It allows the firm to break the return on equity into a profit-on-sales component, an efficiency-of-asset-use component, and a use-of-leverage component. The structure of the DuPont system of analysis is summarized in Figure 4.2. By summarizing a large number of ratios, the financial analyst can assess all aspects of the firm's activities to isolate key areas of responsibility.

L E A R N I N G   G O A L S

After studying this chapter, you should be able to

 LG 1 Relate operating leverage, financial leverage, and total leverage to the firm's income statement.

 LG 2 Discuss the role of breakeven analysis and the calculation and graphic depiction of the operating breakeven point in terms of units, dollars, and cash.

LG 3 Describe the chief limitations inherent in the use of breakeven analysis.

 LG 4 Measure the degree of operating leverage and discuss its relationship to fixed costs and business risk.

LG 5 Calculate the degree of financial leverage, graphically compare financing plans, and discuss financial risk.

 LG 6 Discuss the degree of total leverage and describe its relationship to operating leverage, financial leverage, and total risk.

# 5 Breakeven Analysis and Leverage

The primary objective of managers, whatever the size of the business or their primary area of responsibility, is to increase their firm's value by increasing profitability. Understanding how the financial side of the business operates is therefore absolutely fundamental to accomplishing this goal. Breakeven analysis is a tool that helps managers

> Leverage, which is related to breakeven analysis, involves the use of fixed costs . . . to increase potential returns.

make decisions about a business unit's profitability. Leverage, which is related to breakeven analysis, involves the use of fixed costs, either operating or financial, to increase potential returns.

At the Hotel del Coronado, a San Diego resort hotel, we use breakeven analysis to determine whether to add a new restaurant, discontinue an existing one, or open a retail store. If you were making a presentation about a $500,000 restaurant project to management or potential lenders,

they would probably ask, "How much revenue do you need to break even on this project? And how likely are you to achieve the breakeven point?"

Breakeven analysis provides a practical and simple way to approach a project. Once you have revenue and expenses, divided into fixed and variable costs, you can calculate the breakeven point. This tells you the level of sales, in units or dollars, necessary to cover all costs. Above that level you earn a profit.

In the hotel industry, fixed expenses—those that exist whatever the level of business activity—include interest payments on debt, depreciation, insurance, advertising, maintenance costs, and supervisory staff salaries. Variable expenses change with the level of business activity. In our case, they depend on occupancy levels, salaries for employees, consumable supplies for rooms and food operations, and food. Labor is a hotel's biggest expense, accounting for one-third of total revenue, and the most critical to manage.

Breakeven analysis does, however, have certain limitations. Expense is fixed only up to a certain level of sales. For example, if sales volumes triple, you may need more space, supervisors, or equipment. Breakeven analysis doesn't consider qualitative factors, such as employee morale. Managers must use breakeven analysis together with sound business judgment to make appropriate decisions.

Leverage is related to breakeven analysis. The higher your fixed overhead, the more

highly leveraged you are and the greater your potential profits or losses. Operating leverage is created by fixed costs of day-to-day operations, whereas financial leverage is created by fixed-cost financing. As fixed costs increase, you need higher revenues to break even. This increases your risk. But on the incremental revenue, you make more profit. For example, consider the following two competing hotels, Hotel A and Hotel B.

Although both hotels break even at the same point, Hotel B has higher fixed costs, or leverage. Hotel B earns $.60 of each revenue dollar *above* breakeven, but Hotel A earns only $.40. However, for every revenue dollar *below* breakeven, Hotel B loses $.60 whereas Hotel A loses only $.40. Hotel B is a more highly leveraged hotel and has more risk than Hotel A. This clearly demonstrates the effect of leverage on profitability.

**Martin Malk** *received a bachelor's degree in finance from the University of Witwatersrand, Johannesburg, South Africa. He worked for 10 years in public accounting, as a chartered accountant in South Africa and as a certified public accountant after moving to California in 1978. In 1979 he joined the Hotel del Coronado as accounting manager, becoming controller in 1981 and chief financial officer in 1988.*

**B**reakeven analysis and leverage are two closely related concepts that can be used to evaluate various aspects of the firm's return and risk. *Breakeven analysis* is a popular technique used to measure the firm's returns (profits) against various cost structures and levels of sales. **Leverage** results from the use of fixed-cost assets or funds to magnify returns to the firm's owners. Generally, increases in leverage result in increased return and risk, whereas decreases in leverage result in decreased return and risk. Unlike some causes of risk, management has almost complete control over the risk introduced through the use of leverage. The level of fixed-cost assets or funds that management selects can therefore affect the firm's value by affecting return and risk. Because of its effect on value, the financial manager must understand how to measure and evaluate leverage.

**leverage**
Results from the use of fixed-cost assets or funds to magnify returns to the firm's owners.

# Types of Leverage

LG 1

The three basic types of leverage can best be defined with reference to the firm's income statement. In the general income statement format in Table 5.1, the portions related to the firm's operating leverage, financial leverage, and total leverage are clearly labeled. *Operating leverage* is concerned with the relationship between the firm's sales revenue and its earnings before interest and taxes, or EBIT. (EBIT is a descriptive label for *operating profits*.) *Financial leverage* is concerned with the relationship between the firm's earnings before interest and taxes (EBIT) and its common stock earnings per share (EPS). *Total leverage* is concerned with the relationship between the firm's sales revenue and the earnings per share (EPS). It is important to recognize that the demonstrations of these three forms of leverage that follow are *not* routinely

**TABLE 5.1   General Income Statement Format and Types of Leverage**

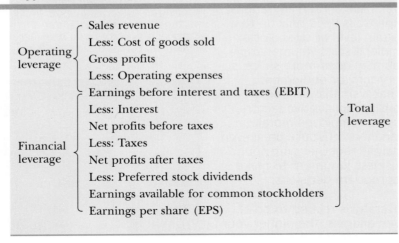

| | |
|---|---|
| Operating leverage { | Sales revenue |
| | Less: Cost of goods sold |
| | Gross profits |
| | Less: Operating expenses |
| | Earnings before interest and taxes (EBIT) |
| Financial leverage { | Less: Interest |
| | Net profits before taxes |
| | Less: Taxes |
| | Net profits after taxes |
| | Less: Preferred stock dividends |
| | Earnings available for common stockholders |
| | Earnings per share (EPS) |

Total leverage

used by financial managers for decision-making purposes. But first, before examining the three leverage concepts separately in detail, breakeven analysis is used to demonstrate the effects of fixed costs on the firm's operations.

## Progress Review Question

**5-1.** What is meant by the term *leverage?* How do operating leverage, financial leverage, and total leverage relate to the income statement?

# Breakeven Analysis

**breakeven analysis (cost-volume-profit) analysis**
Concept used (1) to determine the level of operations necessary to cover all operating costs and (2) to evaluate the profitability associated with various levels of sales.

**Breakeven analysis,** which is sometimes called **cost-volume-profit analysis,** is used by the firm (1) to determine the level of operations necessary to cover all operating costs and (2) to evaluate the profitability associated with various levels of sales. To understand breakeven analysis, we must analyze further the firm's costs.

## Types of Costs

**fixed costs**
Costs that are a function of time, not sales volume.

**variable costs**
Costs that change directly with sales and that are a function of volume rather than time.

**semivariable costs**
Costs that are partly fixed and partly variable; also called *semifixed costs.*

The three types of costs are depicted graphically in Figure 5.1. **Fixed costs** are a function of time, not sales volume, and are typically contractual. These costs require the payment of a specified amount in each accounting period. Rent, for example, is a fixed cost. **Variable costs** change directly with sales and are a function of volume rather than time. Shipping costs, for example, are variable costs. **Semivariable costs** (also called *semifixed costs*) are partly fixed and partly variable. One example of semivariable costs might be sales commissions, which may be fixed for a certain volume of sales and then increase to higher levels for higher volumes.

## Finding the Operating Breakeven Point

**operating breakeven point**
The level of sales necessary to cover all operating costs.

The firm's **operating breakeven point** is the level of sales necessary to cover all operating costs. At the operating breakeven point, earnings before interest and taxes, or EBIT, equals zero.[1] The first step in finding the operating breakeven point is to divide the cost of goods sold and operating expenses into fixed and variable operating costs. The top portion of Table 5.1 can then be recast as shown in the left-hand side of Table 5.2. Using this framework, the firm's operating breakeven point can be developed and evaluated.

---

[1]Quite often the breakeven point is calculated so that it represents the point where *all operating and financial costs* are covered. Our concern in this chapter is not with this overall breakeven point.

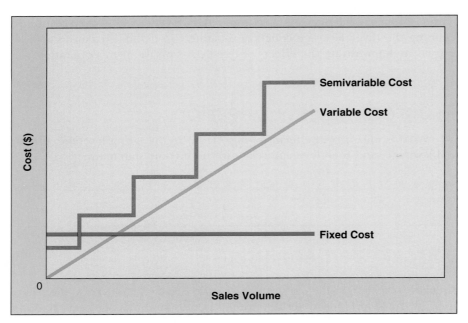

**FIGURE 5.1 Types of Costs**
Costs may be fixed, variable, or semivariable. Fixed costs are a function of time, not sales volume; variable costs change with sales; and semivariable costs are partly fixed and partly variable.

**The Algebraic Approach**    Using the following variables, we can represent the operating portion of the firm's income statement as shown in the right-hand portion of Table 5.2.

$$P = \text{sale price per unit}$$

$$Q = \text{sales quantity in units}$$

$$FC = \text{fixed operating cost per period}$$

$$VC = \text{variable operating cost per unit}$$

Rewriting the algebraic calculations in Table 5.2 as a formula for earnings before interest and taxes yields Equation 5.1.

$$\text{EBIT} = (P \times Q) - FC - (VC \times Q) \tag{5.1}$$

**Equation 5.1 Formula for EBIT**

Simplifying Equation 5.1 yields

$$\text{EBIT} = Q \times (P - VC) - FC \tag{5.2}$$

**Equation 5.2 Simplified formula for EBIT**

As already noted, the operating breakeven point is the level of sales at which all fixed and variable operating costs are covered—that is, the level at which EBIT equals zero. Setting EBIT equal to zero and solving Equation 5.2 for $Q$ yields

$$Q = \frac{FC}{P - VC} \tag{5.3}$$

**Equation 5.3 Formula for the operating breakeven point**

$Q$ is the firm's operating breakeven point. Let us look at an example.

▶ **E X A M P L E**

Assume that Omnibus Posters, a small poster retailer, has fixed operating costs of $2,500, its sale price per unit (poster) is $10, and its variable operating cost per unit is $5. Applying Equation 5.3 to these data yields

$$Q = \frac{\$2,500}{\$10 - \$5} = \frac{\$2,500}{\$5} = 500 \text{ units}$$

At sales of 500 units the firm's EBIT should just equal zero.

In the example, the firm has positive EBIT for sales greater than 500 units and negative EBIT, or a loss, for sales fewer than 500 units. We can confirm this by substituting values above and below 500 units, along with the other values given, into Equation 5.1.

**The Graphic Approach**   Figure 5.2 presents in graph form the breakeven analysis of the data in the example above. The firm's operating breakeven point is the point at which its *total operating cost,* or the sum of its fixed and variable operating costs, equals sales revenue. At this point EBIT equals zero. The figure shows that a loss occurs when the firm's sales are *below* the operating breakeven point. In other words, for sales of fewer than 500 units, total operating costs exceed sales revenue and EBIT is less than zero. For sales levels *greater than* the breakeven point of 500 units, sales revenue exceeds total operating costs and EBIT is greater than zero.

## Changing Costs and the Operating Breakeven Point

A firm's operating breakeven point is sensitive to a number of variables: fixed operating costs ($FC$), the sale price per unit ($P$), and the variable operating cost per unit ($VC$). The effects of increases or decreases in each of these variables can be readily assessed by referring to Equation 5.3. The sensitivity of the breakeven sales volume ($Q$) to an *increase* in each of these variables is summarized in Table 5.3. As might be expected, the table indicates that an increase in cost ($FC$ or $VC$) tends to increase the operating breakeven point, whereas an increase in the sale price per unit ($P$) decreases the operating breakeven point.

## E X A M P L E

Assume that Omnibus Posters wishes to evaluate the impact of (1) increasing fixed operating costs to $3,000, (2) increasing the sale price per unit to $12.50, (3) increasing the variable operating cost per unit to $7.50, and (4) simulta-

---

**TABLE 5.2   Operating Leverage, Costs, and Breakeven Analysis**

| Item | Algebraic Representation |
|---|---|
| Operating leverage — Sales revenue | $(P \times Q)$ |
| Operating leverage — Less: Fixed operating costs | $-\quad FC$ |
| Operating leverage — Less: Variable operating costs | $-(VC \times Q)$ |
| Earnings before interest and taxes | EBIT |

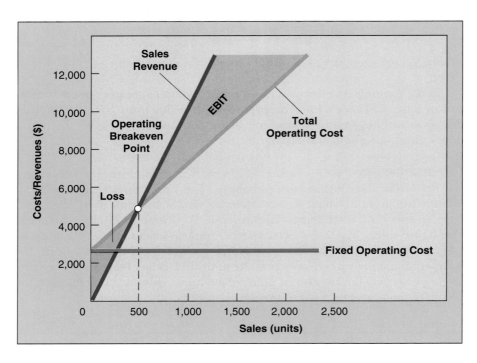

**FIGURE 5.2  Graphic Operating Breakeven Analysis**

The operating breakeven point of 500 units is the level of sales at which total operating cost, which is the sum of fixed and variable operating costs, equals sales revenue. EBIT is positive above the operating breakeven point, and a loss occurs below it.

neously implementing all three of these changes. Substituting the appropriate data into Equation 5.3 yields the following:

1. Operating breakeven point $= \dfrac{\$3,000}{\$10 - \$5} = 600$ units

2. Operating breakeven point $= \dfrac{\$2,500}{\$12.50 - \$5} = 333\frac{1}{3}$ units

3. Operating breakeven point $= \dfrac{\$2,500}{\$10 - \$7.50} = 1,000$ units

4. Operating breakeven point $= \dfrac{\$3,000}{\$12.50 - \$7.50} = 600$ units

Comparing the resulting operating breakeven points to the initial value of 500 units, we can see that, as noted in Table 5.3, the cost increases (actions 1 and 3) raise the breakeven point (600 units and 1,000 units, respectively), whereas the revenue increase (action 2) lowers the breakeven point to $333\frac{1}{3}$ units. The combined effect of increasing all three variables (action 4) results in an increased breakeven point of 600 units.

## Other Approaches to Breakeven Analysis

Two other popular approaches to breakeven analysis are (1) measuring the breakeven point in terms of dollars and (2) determining the cash breakeven point. Each of these approaches is briefly described below.

**Breakeven in Dollars**   When a firm has more than one product, it is useful to calculate the breakeven point in terms of dollars rather than units. The use of a dollar breakeven point is especially important for firms that have a variety of products, each selling at a different price. Assuming that the firm's product mix remains relatively constant, the breakeven point can be calculated in terms of dollars by using a contribution margin approach. The **contribution margin** in this case is defined as the percentage of each sales dollar that remains after satisfying variable operating costs. Using the following notation, we can define the firm's dollar operating breakeven point:

**contribution margin**
The percentage of each sales dollar that remains after satisfying variable operating costs.

$TR$ = total sales revenue in dollars

$TVC$ = total variable operating costs paid to achieve $TR$ dollars of sales

$FC$ = total fixed operating costs paid during the period in which $TR$ dollars of sales are achieved

In the case of a single-product firm, using the notation presented earlier, $TR = P \times Q$, and $TVC = VC \times Q$. The variable operating cost per dollar of sales can be represented as $TVC \div TR$. Subtracting $TVC \div TR$ from 1 yields the contribution margin, which reflects the per-dollar contribution toward fixed operating costs and profits provided by each dollar of sales:

**Equation 5.4** Formula for the contribution margin

$$\text{Contribution margin} = 1 - \frac{TVC}{TR} \tag{5.4}$$

Dividing the contribution margin into the fixed operating costs, $FC$, yields the dollar (of sales) breakeven point, $D$.

**Equation 5.5** Formula for the dollar breakeven point

$$D = \frac{FC}{\left(1 - \frac{TVC}{TR}\right)} \tag{5.5}$$

Let us look at the following example.

# EXAMPLE

Assume that during a period Stat Industries, a small producer of motor casings, has total fixed operating costs of $100,000, total sales of $800,000, and total variable operating costs of $600,000. Applying Equation 5.5 to these data yields

$$D = \frac{\$100,000}{\left(1 - \frac{\$600,000}{\$800,000}\right)} = \frac{\$100,000}{.25} = \$400,000$$

Assuming the firm's product mix does not change, at a $400,000 sales level the firm breaks even on its operation. At that point its EBIT equals zero.

**TABLE 5.3  Sensitivity of Operating Breakeven Point to Increases in Key Breakeven Variables**

| Increase in Variable | Effect on Operating Breakeven Point |
| --- | --- |
| Fixed operating cost ($FC$) | Increase |
| Sale price per unit ($P$) | Decrease |
| Variable operating cost per unit ($VC$) | Increase |

*Note:* Decreases in each of the variables shown have the opposite effect from that indicated on the breakeven point.

F I N A N C E   I N
C T I O N

## Oakwood Homes Snatches Victory from the Jaws of Defeat

After the collapse of the Texas oil economy in the 1980s, North Carolina-based Oakwood Homes Corporation looked like a dying company. To boost sales in the Texas market for manufactured homes, Oakwood had guaranteed mortgages at Texas banks that financed the sale of Oakwood's homes to Texas buyers. As the Texas economy plunged into recession, Oakwood was forced to repay the defaulted mortgages on thousands of repossessed homes.

To survive this crisis, Oakwood embarked on an aggressive expansion plan. The firm reconfigured itself as a vertically integrated home builder that included manufacturing, retailing, financing, and land development operations under a single roof. The firm's retail outlets grew from 71 offices in 9 states in 1990 to 121 offices in 13 states by 1994.

How could the firm afford such vigorous expansion while facing financial ruin in Texas? They used judicious cost containment, and hired other firms to deliver and assemble the houses they manufactured. At present, local contractors perform much of the work required to build an Oakwood home, and the firm's breakeven point has fallen by 33 percent—from 300 homes per month in 1990 to just 200 homes per month today. Creative hiring arrangements that minimized the firm's fixed operating expenses provided the financing Oakwood needed to recover from the Texas calamity and expand its operations in just four short years.

Source: S. Barr, "Oakwood Homes," *CFO Magazine*, January 1994, p. 21.

**Cash Breakeven Analysis**   Under certain conditions it is sometimes useful to perform a **cash breakeven analysis.** This technique is used to find the operating breakeven point when certain noncash charges such as depreciation constitute an important portion of the firm's fixed operating costs. Any charges of this type that are included as part of the firm's fixed costs must be deducted when preparing the cash analysis. If they are not, the presence of such charges tends to overstate the firm's breakeven point. Assuming that the firm has certain noncash charges, *NC,* included in its fixed operating costs, we can rewrite Equation 5.3 for the cash operating breakeven point as shown in Equation 5.6:

**cash breakeven analysis**
A technique used to find the operating breakeven point when certain noncash charges make up a portion of the firm's fixed operating costs.

$$\text{Cash operating breakeven point} = \frac{FC - NC}{P - VC}$$   (5.6)

**Equation 5.6** Formula for the cash operating breakeven point

## ▶ E X A M P L E

Assume that Omnibus Posters (see example on page 119) had included in its fixed operating costs of $2,500, $1,500 of depreciation. Substituting this information (*FC* = $2,500 and *NC* = $1,500) along with the firm's $10 per unit sale price (*P*) and $5 per unit variable operating cost (*VC*) into Equation 5.6 yields the following:

$$\text{Cash operating breakeven point} = \frac{\$2,500 - \$1,500}{\$10 - \$5}$$

$$= \frac{\$1,000}{\$5}$$

$$= 200 \text{ units}$$

The firm's cash operating breakeven point is therefore 200 units. This point is considerably below the 500-unit operating breakeven point calculated earlier using accounting data.

Although the cash breakeven analysis provides a convenient mechanism for assessing the level of sales necessary to meet cash operating costs, it is not a substitute for detailed cash plans. Chapter 6 provides a discussion of more formal techniques for analyzing and budgeting cash flows.

## Limitations of Breakeven Analysis

Although breakeven analysis is widely used by business, it has a number of inherent limitations. First it assumes that the firm faces linear, or nonvarying, sales revenue and total operating cost functions. Generally, however, this is not the case: neither the firm's sale price per unit nor its variable cost per unit is independent of sales volume. The sale price per unit generally decreases with increasing sales volume; the cost per unit generally increases with increasing sales volume, thereby resulting in *curved,* rather than straight (linear), revenue and cost functions. Figure 5.3 shows a graphic operating breakeven analysis using nonlinear sales revenue and total operating cost functions. Recognition of these curved functions may complicate the analysis and result in solutions different from those obtained using linear revenue and cost functions.

**FIGURE 5.3   A Nonlinear Operating Breakeven Analysis**

Nonlinear (curved) breakeven analysis reflects the fact that the firm faces varying sales revenue and total operating cost functions. This occurs because the sale price generally decreases with increasing sales volume, and cost per unit generally increases with increasing sales volume.

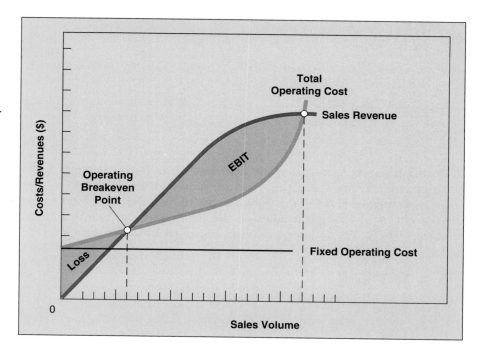

A second limitation of breakeven analysis is the difficulty of breaking semi-variable costs into fixed and variable components. Still another limitation occurs in the application of breakeven analysis to multiproduct firms. Due to the difficulty of allocating costs to products, special and more sophisticated multiproduct breakeven models must be used to determine breakeven points for each product line.

Finally, the short-term—typically one year—time horizon of breakeven analysis often limits its use. A large outlay in the current financial period can significantly raise the firm's breakeven point, whereas the benefits may occur over a period of years. Expenses for advertising and research and development (R and D) are examples of such outlays. Clearly, all of these potential limitations must be considered when applying breakeven analysis.

## Progress Review Questions

**5-2.** Define and differentiate between fixed costs, variable costs, and semi-variable costs. Which of these costs is the key element creating leverage?

**5-3.** Define and differentiate between each of the following operating breakeven points:
  **a.** Breakeven in *units*
  **b.** Breakeven in *dollars*
  **c.** *Cash* breakeven

**5-4.** How do changes in fixed operating costs, the sale price per unit, and the variable operating cost per unit affect the firm's *operating breakeven point?*

**5-5.** One of the key limitations of breakeven analysis is the assumption of linear sales revenue and total operating cost functions. Why might these functions actually be curved? What are some other limitations of breakeven analysis?

## Operating Leverage

LG 4

Operating leverage results from the existence of *fixed operating costs* in the firm's income stream. Using the structure presented in Table 5.2, we can define **operating leverage** as the potential use of *fixed operating costs* to magnify the effects of changes in sales on the firm's earnings before interest and taxes (EBIT). The following example illustrates how operating leverage works.

**operating leverage**
The potential use of *fixed operating costs* to magnify the effects of changes in sales on the firm's EBIT.

## ▶ E X A M P L E

Using the data presented earlier for Omnibus Posters (sale price, $P = \$10$ per unit; variable operating cost, $VC = \$5$ per unit; fixed operating cost, $FC = \$2,500$), Figure 5.4 presents the operating breakeven chart originally shown

## FIGURE 5.4
### Breakeven Analysis and Operating Leverage

The breakeven chart can be used to demonstrate operating leverage. As sales increase by 50 percent from 1,000 units ($Q_1$) to 1,500 units ($Q_2$), EBIT increases by 100 percent from $2,500 (EBIT$_1$) to $5,000 (EBIT$_2$).

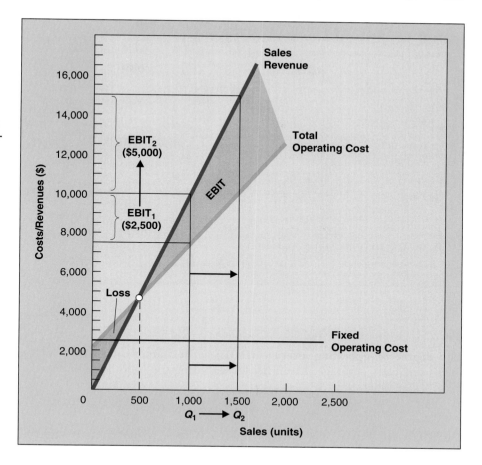

in Figure 5.2. The additional notations on the chart indicate that as the firm's sales increase from 1,000 to 1,500 units ($Q_1$ to $Q_2$), its EBIT increases from $2,500 to $5,000 (EBIT$_1$ to EBIT$_2$). In other words, a 50 percent increase in sales (1,000 to 1,500 units) results in a 100 percent increase in EBIT. Table 5.4 includes the data for Figure 5.4 as well as relevant data for a 500-unit sales level. We can illustrate two cases using the 1,000-unit sales level as a reference point.

**Case 1:** A 50 percent *increase* in sales (from 1,000 to 1,500 units) results in a 100 percent *increase* in earnings before interest and taxes (from $2,500 to $5,000).

**Case 2:** A 50 percent *decrease* in sales (from 1,000 to 500 units) results in a 100 percent *decrease* in earnings before interest and taxes (from $2,500 to $0).

From this example we see that operating leverage works in both directions. When a firm has fixed operating costs, operating leverage is present. An increase in sales results in an increase in earnings before interest and taxes that is more than proportional. A decrease in sales results in a decrease in earnings before interest and taxes that is more than proportional.

**TABLE 5.4   The EBIT for Various Sales Levels**

|  | Case 2 | | Case 1 |
|---|---|---|---|
|  | −50% | | +50% |
| Sales (in units) | 500 | 1,000 | 1,500 |
| Sales revenue[a] | $5,000 | $10,000 | $15,000 |
| Less: Variable operating costs[b] | 2,500 | 5,000 | 7,500 |
| Less: Fixed operating costs | 2,500 | 2,500 | 2,500 |
| Earnings before interest and taxes (EBIT) | $    0 | $ 2,500 | $ 5,000 |
|  | −100% | | +100% |

[a]Sales revenue = $10/unit × sales in units.
[b]Variable operating costs = $5/unit × sales in units.

## Measuring the Degree of Operating Leverage

The **degree of operating leverage (DOL)** is the numerical measure of the firm's operating leverage. It can be derived using the following equation:[2]

$$DOL = \frac{\text{percentage change in EBIT}}{\text{percentage change in sales}} \qquad (5.7)$$

Whenever the percentage change in EBIT resulting from a given percentage change in sales is greater than the percentage change in sales, operating leverage exists. This means that as long as DOL is greater than 1, operating leverage exists.

**degree of operating leverage (DOL)**
The numerical measure of the firm's operating leverage

**Equation 5.7 Formula for the degree of operating leverage (DOL)**

▶ E X A M P L E

Applying Equation 5.7 to cases 1 and 2 in Table 5.4 yields the following results.[3]

**Case 1:** $\dfrac{+100\%}{+50\%} = 2.0$

**Case 2:** $\dfrac{-100\%}{-50\%} = 2.0$

Because the result is greater than 1, operating leverage exists. For a given base level of sales, the higher the value resulting from applying Equation 5.7, the greater the degree of operating leverage.

---

[2]The degree of operating leverage also depends on the base level of sales used as a point of reference. The closer the base sales level used is to the operating breakeven point, the greater the operating leverage. *Comparison of the degree of operating leverage of two firms is valid only when the base level of sales used for each firm is the same.*

[3]Because the concept of leverage is *linear*, positive and negative changes of equal magnitude always result in equal degrees of leverage when the same base sales level is used as a point of reference. This relationship holds for all types of leverage discussed in this chapter.

A more direct formula for calculating the degree of operating leverage at a base sales level, $Q$, is shown in Equation 5.8, using the symbols given on page 118.

**Equation 5.8 Direct formula for the degree of operating leverage (DOL)**

$$\text{DOL at base sales level } Q = \frac{Q \times (P - VC)}{Q \times (P - VC) - FC} \qquad (5.8)$$

## E X A M P L E

Substituting $Q = 1,000$, $P = \$10$, $VC = \$5$, and $FC = \$2,500$ into Equation 5.8 yields the following result:

$$\text{DOL at 1,000 units} = \frac{1,000 \times (\$10 - \$5)}{1,000 \times (\$10 - \$5) - \$2,500}$$

$$= \frac{\$5,000}{\$2,500} = 2.0$$

The use of the formula results in the same value for DOL (2.0) as that found using Table 5.4 and Equation 5.7.[4]

## Fixed Costs and Operating Leverage

Changes in fixed operating costs affect operating leverage significantly. Firms can sometimes incur fixed operating costs rather than variable operating costs, and at other times may be able to substitute one type of cost for the other. For example, a firm can make fixed-dollar lease payments, rather than payments equal to a specified percentage of sales, or it can compensate sales representatives with a fixed salary and bonus rather than with a pure percentage-of-sales commission. The effects of changes in fixed operating costs on operating leverage can best be illustrated by continuing our example.

## E X A M P L E

Assume that Omnibus Posters is able to exchange a portion of its variable operating costs (by eliminating sales commissions) for fixed operating costs (by increasing sales salaries). This exchange results in a reduction in the variable operating cost per unit from $5 to $4.50 and an increase in the fixed operating costs from $2,500 to $3,000. Table 5.5 presents an analysis similar to that given in Table 5.4 using these new costs. Although the EBIT of $2,500 at the 1,000-unit sales level is the same as before the shift in operating cost

---

[4]When total sales in dollars—instead of unit sales—are available, the following equation in which $TR$ = dollar level of base sales and $TVC$ = total variable operating costs in dollars can be used:

$$\text{DOL at base dollar sales } TR = \frac{TR - TVC}{TR - TVC - FC}$$

This formula is especially useful for finding the DOL for multiproduct firms. It should be clear that because in the case of a single-product firm $TR = P \times Q$ and $TVC = VC \times Q$ substitution of these values into Equation 5.8 results in the equation given here.

structure, Table 5.5 shows that by shifting to greater fixed operating costs, the firm has increased its operating leverage.

With the substitution of the appropriate values into Equation 5.8, the degree of operating leverage at the 1,000-unit base level of sales becomes

$$\text{DOL at 1,000 units} = \frac{1,000 \times (\$10 - \$4.50)}{1,000 \times (\$10 - \$4.50) - \$3,000}$$

$$= \frac{\$5,500}{\$2,500} = 2.2$$

Comparing this value to the DOL of 2.0 before the shift to more fixed costs, we see that the higher the firm's fixed operating costs relative to variable operating costs, the greater the degree of operating leverage.

## Business Risk

Because leverage works in two ways, a shift toward more fixed costs increases business risk. Stated simply, **business risk** is the risk to the firm of being unable to cover operating costs. In the foregoing examples the increase in business risk can be demonstrated by comparing the operating breakeven points before and after the shift. Before the shift, the firm's operating breakeven point is 500 units [$2,500 ÷ ($10 − $5)]. After the shift the operating breakeven point is 545 units [$3,000 ÷ ($10 − $4.50)]. Clearly the firm must achieve a higher level of sales to meet increased fixed operating costs. On the positive side, however, higher operating leverage causes EBIT to increase more for a given increase in sales. When considering fixed operating cost increases, the financial manager must weigh the increased business risk associated with greater operating leverage against the expected increase in returns.

**business risk**
The risk to the firm of being unable to cover operating costs.

## TABLE 5.5  Operating Leverage and Increased Fixed Costs

|  |  | Case 2 | | Case 1 |
| --- | --- | --- | --- | --- |
|  |  | −50% | | +50% |
| Sales (in units) |  | 500 | 1,000 | 1,500 |
| Sales revenue[a] |  | $5,000 | $10,000 | $15,000 |
| Less: Variable operating costs[b] |  | 2,250 | 4,500 | 6,750 |
| Less: Fixed operating costs |  | 3,000 | 3,000 | 3,000 |
| Earnings before interest and taxes (EBIT) |  | −$250 | $ 2,500 | $ 5,250 |
|  |  | −110% | | +110% |

[a]Sales revenue was calculated as indicated in Table 5.4.
[b]Variable operating costs = $4.50/unit × sales in units.

▼▼▼▼▼▼▼▼▼▼▼▼▼▼▼▼▼▼▼▼▼▼▼▼▼▼▼▼▼▼▼▼▼▼

## Progress Review Questions

**5-6.** What is meant by *operating leverage?* What causes it? How is the *degree of operating leverage (DOL)* measured?

**5-7.** What is the relationship between operating leverage and business risk? How is each of these related to the operating breakeven point and risk-return trade-off?

▲▲▲▲▲▲▲▲▲▲▲▲▲▲▲▲▲▲▲▲▲▲▲▲▲▲▲▲▲▲▲▲▲

LG ⑤

# Financial Leverage

**financial leverage**
The potential use of *fixed financial costs* to magnify the effects of changes in EBIT on the firm's EPS.

Financial leverage results from the presence of *fixed financial costs* in the firm's income stream. Using the framework in Table 5.1, we can define **financial leverage** as the potential use of *fixed financial costs* to magnify the effects of changes in earnings before interest and taxes (EBIT) on the firm's earnings per share (EPS). The two fixed financial costs that may be found on the firm's income statement are (1) interest on debt and (2) preferred stock dividends. These charges must be paid regardless of the amount of EBIT available to pay them.[5] The following example illustrates how financial leverage works.

## E X A M P L E

◄

Pedros, a small Mexican food company, expects earnings before interest and taxes of $10,000 in the current year. It has a $20,000 bond with a 10 percent (annual) coupon rate of interest and an issue of 600 shares of $4 (annual dividend per share) preferred stock outstanding. It also has 1,000 shares of common stock outstanding. The annual interest on the bond issue is $2,000 (.10 × $20,000). The annual dividends on the preferred stock are $2,400 ($4.00/ share × 600 shares). Table 5.6 presents the earnings per share corresponding to levels of earnings before interest and taxes of $6,000, $10,000, and $14,000, assuming the firm is in the 40 percent tax bracket. Two situations are illustrated in the table.

> **Case 1:** A 40 percent *increase* in EBIT (from $10,000 to $14,000) results in a 100 percent *increase* in earnings per share (from $2.40 to $4.80).
>
> **Case 2:** A 40 percent *decrease* in EBIT (from $10,000 to $6,000) results in a 100 percent *decrease* in earnings per share (from $2.40 to $0).

◄

---

[5]As noted in Chapter 4, although preferred stock dividends can be "passed" (not paid) at the option of the firm's directors, it is generally believed that the payment of such dividends is necessary. *This text therefore treats the preferred stock dividend as if it were a contractual obligation, not only to be paid as a fixed amount, but also to be paid as scheduled.* Although failure to pay preferred dividends cannot force the firm into bankruptcy, it increases the common stockholders' risk because they cannot be paid dividends until the claims of preferred stockholders are satisfied.

**TABLE 5.6    The EPS for Various EBIT Levels**

|  | | Case 2 | | Case 1 |
|---|---|---|---|---|
|  | | −40% | | +40% |
| EBIT | $6,000 | $10,000 | | $14,000 |
| Less: Interest (*I*) | 2,000 | 2,000 | | 2,000 |
| Net profits before taxes (*NPBT*) | $4,000 | $ 8,000 | | $12,000 |
| Less: Taxes (*T* = .40) | 1,600 | 3,200 | | 4,800 |
| Net profits after taxes (*NPAT*) | $2,400 | $ 4,800 | | $ 7,200 |
| Less: Preferred stock dividends (*PD*) | 2,400 | 2,400 | | 2,400 |
| Earnings available for common (*EAC*) | $    0 | $ 2,400 | | $ 4,800 |
| Earnings per share (*EPS*) | $\dfrac{\$0}{1,000} = \$0$ | $\dfrac{\$2,400}{1,000} = \$2.40$ | | $\dfrac{\$4,800}{1,000} = \$4.80$ |
|  | | −100% | | +100% |

The effect of financial leverage is such that an increase in the firm's EBIT results in a more-than-proportional increase in the firm's earnings per share, whereas a decrease in the firm's EBIT results in a more-than-proportional decrease in EPS.

## Measuring the Degree of Financial Leverage

The **degree of financial leverage (DFL)** is the numerical measure of the firm's financial leverage. It can be computed in a fashion similar to that used to measure the degree of operating leverage. The following equation presents one approach for obtaining DFL.[6]

$$DFL = \frac{\text{percentage change in EPS}}{\text{percentage change in EBIT}} \qquad (5.9)$$

**degree of financial leverage (DFL)**
The numerical measure of the firm's financial leverage.

**Equation 5.9 Formula for the degree of financial leverage (DFL)**

Whenever the percentage change in EPS resulting from a given percentage change in EBIT is greater than the percentage change in EBIT, financial leverage exists. This means that whenever DFL is greater than 1, there is financial leverage.

▶ E X A M P L E

Applying Equation 5.9 to cases 1 and 2 in Table 5.6 yields

**Case 1:** $\dfrac{+100\%}{+40\%} = 2.5$

**Case 2:** $\dfrac{-100\%}{-40\%} = 2.5$

---

[6]This approach is valid only when the base level of EBIT used to calculate and compare these values is the same. In other words, *the base level of EBIT must be held constant to compare the financial leverage associated with different levels of fixed financial costs.*

In both cases, the quotient is greater than 1, and financial leverage exists. ■ The higher this value, the greater the degree of financial leverage. ◀

A more direct formula for calculating the degree of financial leverage at a base level of EBIT is given by Equation 5.10, using the notation from Table 5.6. Note that in the denominator the term, $1/(1 - T)$, converts the after-tax preferred stock dividend to a before-tax amount for consistency with the other terms in the equation.

**Equation 5.10** Direct formula for the degree of financial leverage (DFL)

$$\text{DFL at base level EBIT} = \frac{\text{EBIT}}{\text{EBIT} - I - \left(PD \times \dfrac{1}{1 - T}\right)} \qquad (5.10)$$

# E X A M P L E ◀

Substituting EBIT = $10,000, $I$ = $2,000, $PD$ = $2,400, and the tax rate ($T$ = .40) into Equation 5.10 yields the following result:

$$\text{DFL at \$10,000 EBIT} = \frac{\$10,000}{\$10,000 - \$2,000 - \left(\$2,400 \times \dfrac{1}{1 - .40}\right)}$$

$$= \frac{\$10,000}{\$4,000} = 2.5$$

Notice that the formula given in Equation 5.10 provides a more direct method for calculating the degree of financial leverage than the approach illustrated using Table 5.6 and Equation 5.9. ◀

## Graphic Comparison of Financing Plans

Financing plans can be compared graphically by plotting them on a set of EBIT-EPS axes. This approach can be illustrated with an example.

# E X A M P L E ◀

The key characteristics of the financing plan presented earlier, referred to as plan A, and a new financing plan, plan B, are summarized in the table.

| Type of Financing | Plan A | Plan B |
|---|---|---|
| Debt<br>  Annual interest | $20,000 of 10% interest<br>.10 × $20,000 = $2,000 | $10,000 of 10% interest<br>.10 × $10,000 = $1,000 |
| Preferred stock<br>  Annual dividend | 600 shares of $4 dividend<br>600 × $4 = $2,400 | 300 shares of $4 dividend<br>300 × $4 = $1,200 |
| Common stock<br>  Number of shares | 1,000 | 1,750 |

These two plans can be illustrated graphically. Like all plans of this type, they can be plotted as a *straight line* on a set of EBIT-EPS axes. Two EBIT-EPS coordinates, or plotting points, are needed for each plan. These coordinates can be drawn from Table 5.6 for plan A, but we need to calculate two coordinates for plan B. The EPS associated with EBIT values of $10,000 and $14,000, respectively, are calculated for plan B in Table 5.7. It can be seen that for plan B a 40 percent increase in the firm's EBIT results in a 57 percent increase in EPS. Applying Equation 5.10 to these values yields

$$\text{DFL at \$10,000 EBIT} = \frac{\$10,000}{\$10,000 - \$1,000 - \left(\$1,200 \times \frac{1}{1-.40}\right)}$$

$$= \frac{\$10,000}{\$7,000} = 1.4$$

Plan B's degree of financial leverage of 1.4, when compared with the DFL of 2.5 calculated earlier for plan A, indicates that plan B has a lower degree of financial leverage than plan A.

The three EBIT-EPS coordinates from Table 5.6 for plan A and the two coordinates derived in Table 5.7 for plan B are summarized in the table.

| | Coordinates | |
|---|---|---|
| Plan | EBIT | EPS |
| A | $ 6,000 | $0.00 |
| | 10,000 | 2.40 |
| | 14,000 | 4.80 |
| B | $10,000 | $2.40 |
| | 14,000 | 3.77 |

With these coordinates, the two financing plans are presented graphically in Figure 5.5.

As Figure 5.5 illustrates, the slope of plan A is steeper than that of plan B, indicating that plan A has more financial leverage than plan B. This result

**TABLE 5.7   Calculation of Plan B's EBIT-EPS Coordinates**

| | | +40% | |
|---|---|---|---|
| EBIT | $10,000 | | $14,000 |
| −I | 1,000 | | 1,000 |
| NPBT | $ 9,000 | | $13,000 |
| −Taxes (T = .40) | 3,600 | | 5,200 |
| NPAT | $ 5,400 | | $ 7,800 |
| −PD | 1,200 | | 1,200 |
| EAC | $ 4,200 | | $ 6,600 |
| EPS | $\frac{\$4,200}{1,750} = \$2.40$ | | $\frac{\$6,600}{1,750} = \$3.77$ |

+57%

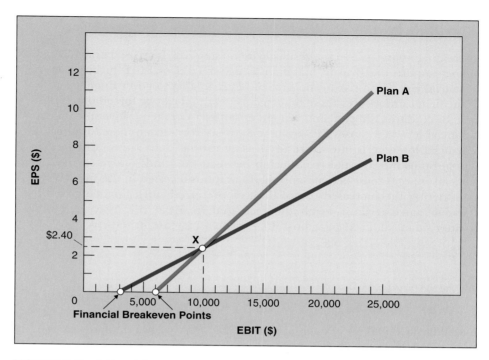

**FIGURE 5.5   A Graphic Presentation of Alternative Financing Plans**
Because the slope of plan A is steeper than that of plan B, plan A has more financial leverage. Plan A has a higher financial breakeven point ($6,000) than plan B
($3,000). At EBIT below the $10,000 indifference point plan B is preferred; above
$10,000 EBIT plan A is preferred.

is as expected, because the degree of financial leverage (DFL) is 2.5 for plan
A and 1.4 for plan B. The higher the DFL, the greater the leverage a plan
has, and the steeper its slope when plotted on EBIT-EPS axes.

**Financial Breakeven Point**   In our example, the point of intersection of
each plan with the EBIT axis represents the amount of earnings before interest and taxes necessary for the firm to just cover all fixed financial costs—
that is, the point at which EPS = $0. This point of intersection can be thought
of as a **financial breakeven point,** because it represents the level of EBIT necessary for the firm to just cover all fixed financial costs. The breakeven EBIT
for plan A is $6,000; for plan B it is $3,000. In other words, earnings before
interest and taxes of less than $6,000 with plan A or less than $3,000 with plan
B results in a loss, or negative EPS.

**financial breakeven point**
The level of EBIT necessary
for the firm to just cover all
fixed financial costs.

**indifference point**
On a graphed comparison of
two financing plans, the
point at which, for a given
EBIT, EPS is the same for both
plans.

**Indifference Point**   The point labeled X in Figure 5.5 represents the **indifference point** between plan A and plan B. It indicates that at a level of
EBIT of $10,000, EPS of $2.40 results under both plans. At levels of EBIT below $10,000, plan B results in higher levels of EPS. At levels of EBIT above
$10,000, plan A results in higher levels of EPS. The usefulness of this type of
analysis is discussed in Chapter 16.

## Financial Risk

Increasing financial leverage results in increasing risk. Increased financial payments require the firm to maintain a higher level of EBIT to break even. **Financial risk** is the risk to the firm of being unable to cover financial costs. If the firm cannot cover these financial payments, it can be forced out of business by creditors whose claims remain unsettled.[7] On the positive side, higher financial leverage causes EPS to increase more for a given increase in EBIT. Financial leverage is often measured using various debt ratios (Chapter 4). These ratios indicate the relationship between the funds on which fixed financial charges must be paid and the total funds invested in the firm. When considering the increased use of debt or preferred stock financing, the financial manager must weigh the increased financial risk associated with greater financial leverage against the expected increase in returns.

**financial risk**
The risk to the firm of being unable to cover financial costs.

▼▼▼▼▼▼▼▼▼▼▼▼▼▼▼▼▼▼▼▼▼▼▼▼▼▼▼▼▼▼▼▼

## Progress Review Questions

**5-8.** What is meant by *financial leverage?* What causes it?

**5-9.** What is the *degree of financial leverage (DFL)?* What two methods can be used to calculate the DFL?

**5-10.** Why must financial managers assess the firm's degree of financial leverage? Why is this measure important in evaluating various financing plans?

**5-11.** What is the relationship between financial leverage and financial risk? How is each of these related to the financial breakeven point and risk-return trade-off?

▲▲▲▲▲▲▲▲▲▲▲▲▲▲▲▲▲▲▲▲▲▲▲▲▲▲▲▲▲▲▲▲

## Total Leverage

The combined effect of operating and financial leverage on the firm's risk can be assessed using a framework similar to that used to develop the individual concepts of leverage. This combined effect, or **total leverage,** can be defined as the potential use of *fixed costs, both operating and financial,* to magnify the effect of changes in sales on the firm's earnings per share (EPS). Total leverage can therefore be viewed as the total effect of the fixed costs on the firm's operating and financial structure.

**total leverage**
The potential use of *fixed costs, both operating and financial,* to magnify the effect of changes in sales on the firm's EPS.

▶ **E X A M P L E**

Health Cereal, a small cereal company, expects sales of 20,000 units at $5 per unit in the coming year and must meet the following: variable operating costs

---

[7]Preferred stockholders do not have the power to force liquidation if their claims remain unpaid. The problem with not paying preferred stock dividends is that then the common stockholders can receive no dividends.

Chapter 5 Breakeven Analysis and Leverage 135

of $2 per unit; fixed operating costs of $10,000; interest of $20,000; and preferred stock dividends of $12,000. The firm is in the 40 percent tax bracket and has 5,000 shares of common stock outstanding. Table 5.8 presents the levels of earnings per share (EPS) associated with the expected sales of 20,000 units and with sales of 30,000 units.

The table illustrates that as a result of a 50 percent increase in sales (20,000 to 30,000 units), the firm would experience a 300 percent increase in earnings per share (from $1.20 to $4.80). Although not shown in the table, a 50 percent decrease in sales would, conversely, result in a 300 percent decrease in earnings per share. The linear nature of the leverage relationship accounts for the fact that sales changes of equal magnitude in opposite directions result in earnings-per-share changes of equal magnitude in the corresponding direction. At this point it should be clear that whenever a firm has fixed costs—operating or financial—in its structure, total leverage exists.

## Measuring the Degree of Total Leverage

**degree of total leverage (DTL)**
The numerical measure of the firm's total leverage.

The **degree of total leverage (DTL)** is the numerical measure of the firm's total leverage. It can be obtained in a fashion similar to that used to measure operating and financial leverage. The following equation presents one approach for measuring DTL.[8]

**Equation 5.11 Formula for the degree of total leverage (DTL)**

$$DTL = \frac{\text{percentage change in EPS}}{\text{percentage change in sales}} \tag{5.11}$$

Whenever the percentage change in EPS resulting from a given percentage change in sales is greater than the percentage change in sales, total leverage exists. This means that as long as the DTL is greater than 1, there is total leverage.

## EXAMPLE

Applying Equation 5.11 to the data in Table 5.8 yields

$$DTL = \frac{+300\%}{+50\%} = 6.0$$

Because this result is greater than 1, total leverage exists. The higher the value, the greater the degree of total leverage.

A more direct formula for calculating the degree of total leverage at a given base level of sales, $Q$, is given by Equation 5.12, which uses the same notation presented earlier:

**Equation 5.12 Direct formula for the degree of total leverage (DTL)**

$$DTL \text{ at base sales level } Q = \frac{Q \times (P - VC)}{Q \times (P - VC) - FC - I - \left(PD \times \frac{1}{1-T}\right)} \tag{5.12}$$

[8]This approach is valid only when the base level of sales used to calculate and compare these values is the same. In other words, *the base level of sales must be held constant to compare the total leverage associated with different levels of fixed costs.*

## TABLE 5.8   The Total Leverage Effect

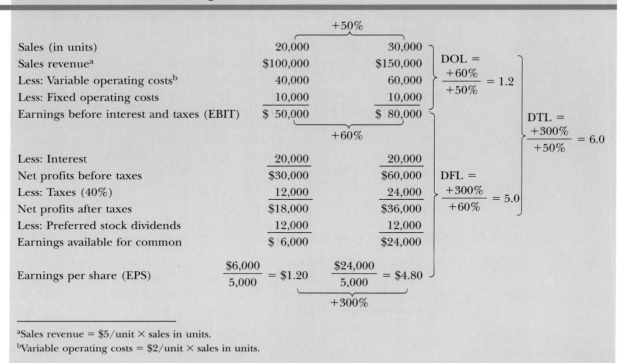

$$^a\text{Sales revenue} = \$5/\text{unit} \times \text{sales in units.}$$
$$^b\text{Variable operating costs} = \$2/\text{unit} \times \text{sales in units.}$$

## ▶ E X A M P L E

Substituting $Q = 20{,}000$, $P = \$5$, $VC = \$2$, $FC = \$10{,}000$, $I = \$20{,}000$, $PD = \$12{,}000$, and the tax rate ($T = .40$) into Equation 5.12 yields the following result:

$$\text{DTL at 20,000 units} = \frac{20{,}000 \times (\$5 - \$2)}{20{,}000 \times (\$5 - \$2) - \$10{,}000 - \$20{,}000 - \left(\$12{,}000 \times \dfrac{1}{1 - .40}\right)}$$

$$= \frac{\$60{,}000}{\$10{,}000} = 6.0$$

Clearly, the formula used in Equation 5.12 provides a more direct method for calculating the degree of total leverage than the approach illustrated using Table 5.8 and Equation 5.11.

## The Relationship of Operating, Financial, and Total Leverage

Total leverage reflects the combined effect of operating and financial leverage on the firm. High operating and high financial leverage cause total leverage to be high. The opposite is also true. The relationship between operating and financial leverage is *multiplicative* rather than *additive*. The relationship between the degree of total leverage (DTL) and the degrees of operating (DOL) and financial (DFL) leverage is given by Equation 5.13.

$$\text{DTL} = \text{DOL} \times \text{DFL} \tag{5.13}$$

Equation 5.13 Formula depicting the relationship between the degrees of total, operating, and financial leverage

## F I N A N C E  I N  A C T I O N

### These Firms Struggle to Make Crime Pay

It may be a grim statistic, but it is a fact. Drug arrests and tougher sentencing requirements have sent America's prison population soaring by 51 percent since 1986, while prison capacity increased just 30 percent during this period. By early 1994, the nation had 925,247 inmates in state and Federal prisons designed to accommodate only 770,000 individuals. For private security companies Wackenhut Corp. and Corrections Corporation of America, these grim statistics signal a golden business opportunity. Or do they?

Wackenhut and CCA are quietly becoming leaders in building, managing, and operating private prison facilities. With rising crime rates, overcrowding in public prisons, and new government mandates to fight crime and incarcerate repeat criminal offenders, these firms see private correctional facilities as the next growth industry in the United States. And at present, the market stands wide open. Private prisons house just 2 percent of the total prison population, divided among just three firms.

So what's the catch? Traditionally, private prisons generate plenty of sales growth, but very little income. Significant overhead expenses, such as marketing, training, and administrative labor costs, elevate breakeven points so that it becomes extremely difficult to earn profits in small and medium size prisons. In addition, building and operating private prisons require substantial capital investments as well as plenty of working capital.

So how do private prison operations make crime pay? At CCA the answer lies in slashing operating costs and expanding prison size to gain scale economies. After seven years of consecutive losses, CCA turned its first profit of $1.67 million in 1990. By 1993, the firm was earning $2.4 million annually, and profits are expected to reach $5.7 million in 1994. Using astute financial management, CCA is discovering the right revenue-operating cost mix to make crime pay.

Source: *Business Week,* December 17, 1990, p. 95. Updated 1994.

## E X A M P L E

Substituting the values calculated for DOL and DFL, shown on the right-hand side of Table 5.8, into Equation 5.13 yields

$$DTL = 1.2 \times 5.0 = 6.0$$

The resulting degree of total leverage (6.0) is the same value as was calculated directly in the preceding examples.

### Total Risk

**total risk**
The risk to the firm of being unable to cover both operating and financial costs.

In a relationship similar to those between operating leverage and business risk, and financial leverage and financial risk, total leverage reflects the total risk of the firm. The firm's **total risk** is therefore the firm's risk of being unable to cover both operating and financial costs. With increasing costs—especially fixed operating and financial costs—comes increasing risk, because the firm has to achieve a higher level of sales just to break even. If a firm is unable to meet these costs, it can be forced out of business by its creditors.

On the positive side, higher total leverage causes EPS to increase more for a given increase in sales. When considering fixed operating or financial cost increases, the financial manager must weigh the increased risk associated with greater leverage against the expected increase in returns.

▼▼▼▼▼▼▼▼▼▼▼▼▼▼▼▼▼▼▼▼▼▼▼▼▼▼▼▼▼▼▼

## Progress Review Question

**5-12.** What is the general relationship among operating leverage, financial leverage, and the total leverage of the firm? Do these types of leverage complement each other? Why, or why not?

▲▲▲▲▲▲▲▲▲▲▲▲▲▲▲▲▲▲▲▲▲▲▲▲▲▲▲▲▲▲▲

▼                    ▼                    ▼

# SUMMARY OF LEARNING GOALS

**Relate operating leverage, financial leverage, and total leverage to the firm's income statement.** Operating leverage is the relationship between a firm's sales and its earnings before interest and taxes (EBIT). Financial leverage is the relationship between the firm's EBIT and its earnings per share (EPS). Total leverage is the relationship between the firm's sales and its EPS.

**Discuss the role of breakeven analysis and the calculation and graphic depiction of the operating breakeven point in terms of units, dollars, and cash.** Breakeven analysis is used both to determine the level of sales necessary to cover all operating costs and to evaluate profitability. Below the operating breakeven point, the firm experiences a loss. Above the operating breakeven point, the firm's earnings before interest and taxes (EBIT) is positive. Cost increases raise the breakeven point, and sales price increases lower it, and vice versa. The operating breakeven point can be found in terms of units of sales, dollars of sales, or on a cash basis.

**Describe the chief limitations inherent in the use of breakeven analysis.** Breakeven analysis suffers from a number of limitations, chief among which are the assumption of linearity, the difficulty of classifying costs, problems caused by multiproduct situations, and the short-term nature of the typical time horizon.

**Measure the degree of operating leverage and discuss its relationship to fixed costs and business risk.** Operating leverage is the potential use of fixed operating costs by the firm to magnify the effects of changes in sales on earnings before interest and taxes (EBIT). The higher the fixed operating costs, the greater the operating leverage. The degree of operating leverage (DOL) at a specified level of sales can be calculated using a tabular approach or by formula. The firm's business risk is directly related to its degree of operating leverage.

LG **5**   **Calculate the degree of financial leverage, graphically compare financing plans, and discuss financial risk.** Financial leverage is the potential use of fixed financial costs by the firm to magnify the effects of changes in earning before interest and taxes (EBIT) on earnings per share (EPS). The higher the fixed financial costs—typically interest on debt and preferred stock dividends—the greater the financial leverage. The degree of financial leverage (DFL) at a specified level of earnings before interest and taxes can be calculated using a tabular approach or by formula. Financing plans can be graphed on a set of EBIT-EPS axes. The steeper the slope of the financing plan, the higher its degree of financial leverage. The level of EBIT at which EPS just equals zero is the financial breakeven point. The firm's financial risk is directly related to its degree of financial leverage.

LG **6**   **Discuss the degree of total leverage and describe its relationship to operating leverage, financial leverage, and total risk.** The total leverage of the firm is the potential use of fixed costs—both operating and financial—to magnify the effects of changes in sales on earnings per share. The higher these fixed costs, the greater the total leverage. The degree of total leverage (DTL) at a specified level of sales can be measured using a tabular approach or by formula. It can also be found by multiplying the degree of operating leverage (DOL) by the degree of financial leverage (DFL). The firm's total risk is directly related to its degree of total leverage.

# S U M M A R Y   O F   K E Y
# D E F I N I T I O N S   A N D
# E Q U A T I O N S

## Variable Definitions

$D$ = dollar breakeven point

DFL = degree of financial leverage

DOL = degree of operating leverage

DTL = degree of total leverage

EBIT = earnings before interest and taxes

EPS = earnings per share

$FC$ = fixed operating cost per period

$I$ = interest expense

$NC$ = noncash charges

$P$ = sale price per unit

$PD$ = preferred stock dividends

$Q$ = sales quantity in units

$T$ = tax rate

$TR$ = dollar level of base sales = $P \times Q$

$TVC$ = total variable operating costs in dollars = $VC \times Q$

$VC$ = variable operating cost per unit

## Equations

EBIT

$$EBIT = (P \times Q) - FC - (VC \times Q) \qquad \text{[Eq. 5.1]}$$

Simplified formula for EBIT

$$EBIT = Q \times (P - VC) - FC \qquad \text{[Eq. 5.2]}$$

Operating breakeven point

$$Q = \frac{FC}{P - VC} \qquad \text{[Eq. 5.3]}$$

$$\text{Contribution margin} = 1 - \frac{TVC}{TR} \qquad \text{[Eq. 5.4]}$$

Dollar breakeven point

$$D = \frac{FC}{\left(1 - \dfrac{TVC}{TR}\right)} \qquad \text{[Eq. 5.5]}$$

$$\text{Cash operating breakeven point} = \frac{FC - NC}{P - VC} \qquad \text{[Eq. 5.6]}$$

Degree of operating leverage

$$DOL = \frac{\text{percentage change in EBIT}}{\text{percentage change in sales}} \qquad \text{[Eq. 5.7]}$$

Direct formula for the degree of operating leverage at base sales level $Q$

$$DOL = \frac{Q \times (P - VC)}{Q \times (P - VC) - FC} \qquad \text{[Eq. 5.8]}$$

$$\text{DOL at base dollar sales } TR = \frac{TR - TVC}{TR - TVC - FC}$$

Degree of financial leverage

$$DFL = \frac{\text{percentage change in EPS}}{\text{percentage change in EBIT}} \qquad \text{[Eq. 5.9]}$$

Direct formula for the degree of financial leverage at base level EBIT

$$DFL = \frac{EBIT}{EBIT - I - \left(PD \times \dfrac{1}{1 - T}\right)} \qquad \text{[Eq. 5.10]}$$

Degree of total leverage

$$DTL = \frac{\text{percentage change in EPS}}{\text{percentage change in sales}} \qquad \text{[Eq. 5.11]}$$

Direct formula for the degree of total leverage at base sales level $Q$

$$DTL = \frac{Q \times (P - VC)}{Q \times (P - VC) - FC - I - \left(PD \times \dfrac{1}{1 - T}\right)} \qquad \text{[Eq. 5.12]}$$

Relationship between the degrees of total, operating, and financial leverage

$$DTL = DOL \times DFL \qquad \text{[Eq. 5.13]}$$

After studying this chapter, you should be able to

**LG 1** Understand the financial planning process, including the role of and interrelationship between long-term (strategic) financial plans and short-term (operating) plans.

**LG 2** Discuss the cash planning process, the role of sales forecasts, and the procedures for preparing the cash budget.

**LG 3** Describe the cash budget evaluation process and the procedure for coping with uncertainty in the cash budget.

**LG 4** Prepare a pro forma income statement using both the percentage-of-sales method and a breakdown of costs and expenses into their fixed and variable components.

**LG 5** Explain the procedures used to develop a pro forma balance sheet using the judgmental approach and the role and use of the plug figure—external financing required—in this process.

**LG 6** Describe the weaknesses of the simplified approaches to pro forma preparation and the common uses of pro forma financial statements.

# 6 Financial Planning

Financial planning plays a key role in the success of a company's strategic business plan. All managers should understand how to convert the business plan to a financial plan that shows the effect of the plan on the company's financial performance. Financial managers work closely with business managers to develop these plans and then provide

> **The financial manager who understands the company's characteristics, issues, and trends knows how to develop realistic financial plans.**

the resources to implement them.

Lotus Development Corporation's business—software products and support services—is not capital-intensive, so the planning process focuses more on operating plans than fixed-asset management plans. Our main financial planning documents are pro forma (projected) financial statements and the cash budget. First, the operating units prepare an annual pro forma income statement. The corporate finance analysts then

draft an annual pro forma balance sheet and cash flow statement. From that we develop more detailed, quarterly pro formas.

The other important financial planning statement is the cash budget, a rolling 12-week forecast of cash needs based on receipt and payment data from the various departments. The cash budget provides a good check against the pro forma statements.

Financial planning cannot be done in a vacuum. Writing good financial plans calls for a thorough understanding of the company and its industry. A good way to start is to talk directly to the people involved in day-to-day operations. Developing a good rapport with them pays off, because they provide the basic inputs for financial plans. It's important to show nonfinancial managers how their actions affect the company's financial performance, and how they can participate in the planning process.

For example, our business is not seasonal; revenue cycles are governed by new product releases, upgrades, and marketing programs. Unless we learn from marketing personnel when products or programs will be introduced, we can't forecast correctly. We also need to know the sales pattern over the year and within a quarter. Sales growth of 20 percent per year may show a very comfortable year-end profit, but the company might have to borrow to finance growth until cash starts flowing. Unless financial managers ask the sales staff the right questions, they won't be able to predict cash flow accurately.

External trends must also be factored into the financial plan. The business environment changes so quickly today that you can't assume any trend will continue in the future. Financial managers must be able to revise financial plans when external events change.

Even the best plans can encounter unforeseen difficulties. That's why it's critical to use sensitivity analysis and run several "what if" versions of business and financial plans, using different assumptions to better understand the plans' variability. If the base assumption is 20 percent per year sales growth, the analyst might look at cash flow if sales grow 10 or 30 percent per year. The financial manager who understands the company's characteristics, issues, and trends knows how to develop realistic financial plans.

**Irena Simmons** *received a B.A. in economics and French from Tufts University and an M.B.A. from Boston University. From 1983 to 1989 she held various positions in financial analysis and international treasury for Millipore Corporation and Computervision Corporation. She was assistant treasurer at Unitrode Corporation before joining Lotus Development Corporation in 1992 as manager, treasury services.*

Financial planning is an important aspect of the firm's operation and livelihood because it provides road maps for guiding, coordinating, and controlling the firm's actions to achieve its objectives. Two key aspects of the financial planning process are *cash planning* and *profit planning*. Cash planning involves the preparation of the firm's cash budget. Without adequate cash—whatever the level of profits—any firm can fail. Profit planning is usually done by means of pro forma financial statements, which show anticipated levels of profits, assets, liabilities, and equity. Cash budgets and pro forma statements not only are useful for internal financial planning but also are routinely required by present and prospective lenders. Before studying the preparation and use of these statements, we examine the relationship between long-term and short-term financial plans.

# The Financial Planning Process

The **financial planning process** begins with long-term, or strategic, financial plans that in turn guide the formulation of short-term, or operating, plans and budgets. Generally, the short-term plans and budgets implement the firm's long-term strategic objectives. Although the major emphasis in this chapter is on short-term financial plans and budgets, we begin with a few comments on long-term financial plans.

**financial planning process** Planning that begins with long-term financial plans that in turn guide short-term plans and budgets.

## Long-Term (Strategic) Financial Plans

**Long-term (strategic) financial plans** are planned long-term financial actions and the anticipated financial effect of those actions. Such plans tend to cover periods ranging from 2 to 10 years. The use of five-year strategic plans, which are periodically revised as significant new information becomes available, is common. Generally, firms that are subject to high degrees of operating uncertainty, relatively short production cycles, or both tend to use shorter planning horizons. Long-term financial plans are part of an integrated strategic plan that along with production, marketing, and other plans use a common set of assumptions and objectives to guide the firm toward achievement of its strategic goals. They consider proposed fixed-asset outlays, research and development activities, marketing and product development actions, and both the mix and major sources of financing. Also included are termination of existing projects, product lines, or lines of business; repayment or retirement of outstanding debts; and any planned acquisitions. Such plans tend to be supported by a series of annual budgets and profit plans.

**long-term (strategic) financial plans** Planned long-term financial actions and the anticipated financial effect of those actions.

## Short-Term (Operating) Financial Plans

**Short-term (operating) financial plans** are planned short-term financial actions and the anticipated financial effect of those actions. These plans most

**short-term (operating) financial plans** Planned short-term financial actions and the anticipated financial effect of those actions.

often cover a one- to two-year period. Key inputs include the sales forecast and various forms of operating and financial data. Key outputs include a number of operating budgets, the cash budget, and pro forma financial statements. The short-term financial planning process, from the initial sales forecast through the development of the cash budget and pro forma income statement and balance sheet, is presented in the flow diagram in Figure 6.1.

From the sales forecast are developed production plans that take into account lead (preparation) times and include estimates of the required types and quantities of raw materials. Using the production plans, the firm can estimate direct labor requirements, factory overhead outlays, and operating expenses. Once these estimates have been made, the firm's pro forma income statement and cash budget can be prepared. With the basic inputs—pro forma income statement, cash budget, fixed-asset outlay plan, long-term financing plan, and current-period balance sheet—the pro forma balance sheet can finally be developed. Throughout the remainder of this chapter we concentrate on the key outputs of the short-term financial planning process: the cash budget, the pro forma income statement, and the pro forma balance sheet. Although not specifically addressed in this chapter, it is important to recognize that electronic spreadsheets, such as Lotus 1-2-3, Excel, and Quattro Pro, are widely used to streamline the process of preparing and evaluating these short-term financial planning statements.

**FIGURE 6.1  The Short-Term (Operating) Financial Planning Process**

The sales forecast is used to develop production plans that take into account lead (preparation) times and include estimates of the required types and quantities of raw materials. These estimates are input to the pro forma income statement and cash budget, which with additional data are used to prepare the pro forma balance sheet.

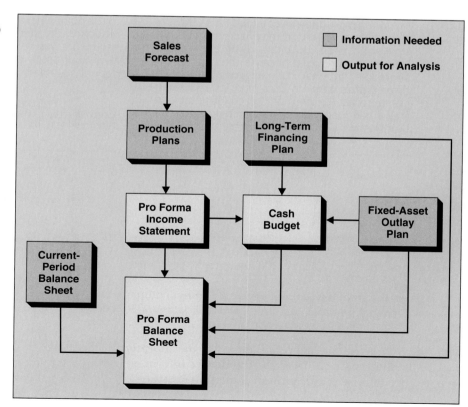

F  I  N  A  N  C  E  I  N

▲ C   T   I   O   N

## Careful Financial Planning Leads to American Healthcare Management's Recovery

When Steven Volla took over American Healthcare Management in 1989, the for-profit hospital chain was on the critical list. In fact, it had recently been resuscitated and avoided death in bankruptcy court through a reorganization. External complications included the federal government's reduction in Medicare reimbursements, managed-care insurance plans requesting payment at less than the listed rate, and a junk bond offering with an interest rate exceeding 13 percent.

Furthermore, the situation was akin to a new lead surgeon being brought in at the sudden death of the prior lead surgeon and having a team speaking different dialects. Volla could discern no real strategy behind the previous management's acquisitions. As far as he could tell, when management obtained funds through stock or bond offerings they had simply bought smaller hospitals. Hospitals losing money were frequently purchased because they were more affordable. Internal complications included a three-month delay in obtaining internal financial reports. Furthermore, each hospital controller had modified the general ledger to meet that hospital's own personal preferences.

Recognizing the importance of financial information in planning American Healthcare's recovery, Volla immediately prescribed an on-line reporting system, with daily reports of each hospital's revenues, patients, cash position, and expenses. Reports were then compared with forecast values and headquarters contacted hospitals when values for staffing, patient stays, accounts receivable collection, and other financial facets of the business deviated from expectations.

Furthermore, Volla defined the mission of the hospital chain as being urban primary care facilities. Capital budgets and financial statements were assessed on the basis of how they coincided with the firm's primary focus. By 1991, American Healthcare's condition had improved to the point where profit facilitated a 22 percent reduction in debt. And in 1993, American Healthcare was well enough to be relisted on the New York Stock Exchange and refinanced its debt at a 7.9 percent rate.

Source: Martha E. Mangelsdorf, "Higher Math," *Inc.*, December 1993, pp. 110–116.

## Progress Review Questions

**6-1.** What is the *financial planning process?* Define, compare, and contrast *long-term (strategic) financial plans* and *short-term (operating) financial plans.*

**6-2.** Which three statements result as part of the short-term (operating) financial planning process? Describe the flow of information from the sales forecast through the preparation of these statements.

## Cash Planning: Cash Budgets

**cash budget (cash forecast)**
A statement of the firm's planned inflows and outflows of cash used to estimate its short-term cash requirements.

The **cash budget,** or **cash forecast,** is a statement of the firm's planned inflows and outflows of cash used to estimate its short-term cash requirements. The firm gives particular attention to planning for surplus cash and for cash shortages. A firm expecting a cash surplus can plan short-term investments (marketable securities). A firm expecting shortages in cash must arrange for short-term financing (notes payable). The cash budget gives the financial manager a clear view of the timing of the firm's expected cash inflows and outflows over a given period.

Typically, the cash budget is designed to cover a one-year period, although any time period is acceptable. The period covered is normally divided into smaller time intervals. The number and type of intervals depend on the nature of the business. The more seasonal and uncertain a firm's cash flows, the greater the number of intervals. Because many firms are confronted with a seasonal cash flow pattern, the cash budget is quite often presented on a monthly basis. Firms with stable patterns of cash flow may use quarterly or annual time intervals. If a cash budget is developed for a period greater than one year, fewer time intervals may be warranted due to the difficulty and uncertainty of forecasting sales and other related cash items.

### The Sales Forecast

**sales forecast**
The prediction of the firm's sales over a given period, based on external or internal data.

The key input to the short-term financial planning process and therefore any cash budget is the firm's **sales forecast.** This is the prediction of the firm's sales over a given period and is ordinarily furnished to the financial manager by the marketing department. On the basis of this forecast, the financial manager estimates the monthly cash flows that will result from projected sales receipts and from production-related, inventory-related, and sales-related outlays. The manager also determines the level of fixed assets required and the amount of financing, if any, needed to support the forecast level of production and sales. In practice, obtaining good data is the most difficult aspect of forecasting; most forecasting techniques are relatively straightforward and easily automated. The sales forecast may be based on an analysis of external or internal data or on a combination of the two.

**external forecast**
A sales forecast based on the relationships between the firm's sales and certain key external economic indicators.

**External Forecasts**   An **external forecast** is based on the relationships that can be observed between the firm's sales and certain key external economic indicators, such as the gross domestic product (GDP), new housing starts, or disposable personal income. Forecasts containing these indicators are readily available. The rationale for this approach is that because the firm's sales are often closely related to some aspect of overall national economic activity, a forecast of economic activity should provide insight into future sales.

**internal forecast**
A sales forecast based on a consensus of forecasts through the firm's own sales channels.

**Internal Forecasts**   **Internal forecasts** are based on a buildup, or consensus, of sales forecasts through the firm's own sales channels. Typically, the firm's salespeople in the field are asked to estimate the number of units of each type of product they expect to sell in the coming year. These forecasts are collected and totaled by the sales manager, who may adjust the figures using his or her own knowledge of specific markets or of the salesperson's fore-casting ability. Finally, adjustments may be made for such additional internal factors as production capabilities.

**Combined Forecasts**   Firms generally use a combination of external and internal forecast data to make the final sales forecast. The internal data provide insight into sales expectations. The external data provide a means of adjusting these expectations to take into account general economic factors. The nature of the firm's product also often affects the mix and types of forecasting methods used.

## Preparing the Cash Budget

The general format of the cash budget is presented in Table 6.1. We discuss each of its components individually.

**Cash Receipts**   **Cash receipts** includes all items from which cash inflows result in any given financial period. The most common components of cash receipts are cash sales, collections of accounts receivable, and other cash receipts.

**cash receipts**
All cash inflows during a given financial period.

▶ E X A M P L E

Halley Company, a defense contractor, is developing a cash budget for October, November, and December. Halley's sales in August and September were $100,000 and $200,000, respectively. Sales of $400,000, $300,000, and $200,000 have been forecast for October, November, and December, respectively. Historically, 20 percent of the firm's sales have been for cash, 50 percent have generated accounts receivable collected after one month, and the remaining 30 percent have generated accounts receivable collected after two months. Bad-debt expenses (uncollectible accounts) have been negligible.[1]

**TABLE 6.1   The General Format of the Cash Budget**

|  | Jan. | Feb. | ... | Nov. | Dec. |
|---|---|---|---|---|---|
| Cash receipts |  |  |  |  |  |
| Less: Cash disbursements | ___ | ___ | ... | ___ | ___ |
| Net cash flow |  |  |  |  |  |
| Add: Beginning cash | ___ ↗ | ___ ↗ | ... ↗ | ___ ↗ | ___ |
| Ending cash |  |  |  |  |  |
| Less: Minimum cash balance | ___ | ___ | ... | ___ | ___ |
| Required total financing |  |  | ... |  |  |
| Excess cash balance |  |  | ... |  |  |

[1]Normally the collection percentages would be expected to total slightly less than 100 percent to reflect the fact that some of the accounts receivable are uncollectible. In this example the sum of the collection percentages is 100 percent (20% + 50% + 30%), which reflects the fact that all sales are assumed to be collected because bad debts are said to be negligible.

**TABLE 6.2   A Schedule of Projected Cash Receipts for Halley Company ($000)**

|  | Aug. | Sept. | Oct. | Nov. | Dec. |
|---|---|---|---|---|---|
| **Forecast Sales** | $100 | $200 | $400 | $300 | $200 |
| Cash sales (.20) | $ 20 | $ 40 | $ 80 | $ 60 | $ 40 |
| Collections of A/R: |  |  |  |  |  |
|   Lagged one month (.50) |  | 50 | 100 | 200 | 150 |
|   Lagged two months (.30) |  |  | 30 | 60 | 120 |
| Other cash receipts |  |  |  |  | 30 |
|   Total cash receipts |  |  | $210 | $320 | $340 |

In December, the firm will receive a $30,000 dividend from stock in a subsidiary. The schedule of expected cash receipts for the company is presented in Table 6.2. It contains the following items.

**Forecast Sales**   This initial entry is *merely informational*. It is provided as an aid in calculating other sales-related items.

**Cash Sales**   The cash sales shown for each month represent 20 percent of the total sales forecast for that month.

**Collections of A/R**   These entries represent the collection of accounts receivable (A/R) resulting from sales in earlier months.

***Lagged one month***   These figures represent sales made in the preceding month that generated accounts receivable collected in the current month. Because 50 percent of the current month's sales are collected one month later, the collections of accounts receivable with a one-month lag shown for September, October, November, and December represent 50 percent of the sales in August, September, October, and November, respectively.

***Lagged two months***   These figures represent sales made two months earlier that generated accounts receivable collected in the current month. Because 30 percent of sales are collected two months later, the collections with a two-month lag shown for October, November, and December represent 30 percent of the sales in August, September, and October, respectively.

**Other Cash Receipts**   These are cash receipts expected to result from sources other than sales. Items, such as interest received, dividends received, proceeds from the sale of equipment, stock and bond sale proceeds, and lease receipts, may show up here. For Halley Company, the only cash receipt is the $30,000 dividend due in December.

**Total Cash Receipts**   This figure represents the total of all the cash receipt items listed for each month in the cash receipt schedule. In the case of Halley Company, we are concerned only with October, November, and December; the total cash receipts for these months are shown in Table 6.2.

**Cash Disbursements**   **Cash disbursements** include all outflows of cash in the period covered. The most common cash disbursements are

> **cash disbursements**
> All cash outflows during a given financial period.

Cash purchases
Payments of accounts payable
Rent (and lease) payments
Wages and salaries
Tax payments
Fixed-asset outlays
Interest payments
Cash dividend payments
Principal payments (loans)
Repurchases or retirements of stock

It is important to recognize that *depreciation and other noncash charges are NOT included in the cash budget* because they merely represent a scheduled write-off of an earlier cash outflow. The effect of depreciation, as noted in Chapter 3, is reflected in the level of cash outflow represented by the tax payments.

▶ **E X A M P L E**

Halley Company has gathered the following data needed for the preparation of a cash disbursements schedule for the months of October, November, and December.

**Purchases**   The firm's purchases represent 70 percent of sales. Ten percent of this amount is paid in cash, 70 percent is paid in the month immediately following the month of purchase, and the remaining 20 percent is paid two months following the month of purchase.[2]

**Rent Payments**   Rent of $5,000 is paid each month.

**Wages and Salaries**   The firm's wages and salaries can be estimated by adding 10 percent of its monthly sales to the $8,000 fixed-cost figure.

**Tax Payments**   Taxes of $25,000 must be paid in December.

**Fixed-Asset Outlays**   New machinery costing $130,000 will be purchased and paid for in November.

**Interest Payments**   An interest payment of $10,000 is due in December.

---

[2]Unlike the collection percentages for sales, the total of the payment percentages should equal 100 percent because it is expected that the firm pays off all of its accounts payable. In line with this expectation, the percentages for Halley Company total 100 percent (10% + 70% + 20%).

**Cash Dividend Payments**    Cash dividends of $20,000 will be paid in October.

**Principal Payments (Loans)**    A $20,000 principal payment is due in December.

**Repurchases or Retirements of Stock**    No repurchase or retirement of stock is expected during the October–December period.

The firm's cash disbursements schedule, based on the data above, is presented in Table 6.3. Some items in Table 6.3 are explained in greater detail below.

**Purchases**    This entry is *merely informational*. The figures represent 70 percent of the forecast sales for each month. They have been included to facilitate the calculation of the cash purchases and related payments.

**Cash Purchases**    The cash purchases for each month represent 10 percent of the month's purchases.

**Payments of A/P**    These entries represent the payment of accounts payable (A/P) resulting from purchases in earlier months.

**Lagged one month**    These figures represent purchases made in the preceding month that are paid for in the current month. Because 70 percent of the firm's purchases are paid for one month later, the payments lagged one

**TABLE 6.3    A Schedule of Projected Cash Disbursements for Halley Company ($000)**

|  | Aug. | Sept. | Oct. | Nov. | Dec. |
|---|---|---|---|---|---|
| Purchases (.70 × sales) | $70 | $140 | $280 | $210 | $140 |
| Cash purchases (.10) | $ 7 | $ 14 | $ 28 | $ 21 | $ 14 |
| Payments of A/P: |  |  |  |  |  |
| Lagged one month (.70) |  | 49 | 98 | 196 | 147 |
| Lagged two months (.20) |  |  | 14 | 28 | 56 |
| Rent payments |  |  | 5 | 5 | 5 |
| Wages and salaries |  |  | 48 | 38 | 28 |
| Tax payments |  |  |  |  | 25 |
| Fixed-asset outlays |  |  |  | 130 |  |
| Interest payments |  |  |  |  | 10 |
| Cash dividend payments |  |  | 20 |  |  |
| Principal payments |  |  |  |  | 20 |
| Total cash disbursements |  |  | $213 | $418 | $305 |

month shown for September, October, November, and December represent 70 percent of the August, September, October, and November purchases, respectively.

***Lagged two months***   These figures represent purchases made two months earlier that are paid for in the current month. Because 20 percent of the firm's purchases are paid for two months later, the payments lagged two months for October, November, and December represent 20 percent of the August, September, and October purchases, respectively.

**Wages and Salaries**   These values were obtained by adding $8,000 to 10 percent of the *sales* in each month. The $8,000 represents the salary component; the rest represents wages.

The remaining items on the cash disbursements schedule are self-explanatory.

**Net Cash Flow, Ending Cash, Financing, and Excess Cash**   A firm's **net cash flow** is found by subtracting the cash disbursements from cash receipts in each period. By adding beginning cash to the firm's net cash flow, we can find the **ending cash** for each period. Finally, subtracting the desired minimum cash balance from ending cash yields the **required total financing** or the **excess cash balance.** If the ending cash is less than the minimum cash balance, *financing* is required. Such financing is typically viewed as short-term and therefore represented by notes payable. If the ending cash is greater than the minimum cash balance, *excess cash* exists. Any excess cash is assumed invested in a liquid, short-term, interest-paying vehicle and therefore included in marketable securities.

**net cash flow**
The mathematical difference between the firm's cash receipts and its cash disbursements in each period.

**ending cash**
The sum of the firm's beginning cash and its net cash flow for the period.

**required total financing**
Amount of funds needed by the firm if the ending cash for the period is less than the desired minimum cash balance.

**excess cash balance**
The amount available for investment by the firm if the period's ending cash is greater than the desired minimum cash balance.

▶ E X A M P L E

Table 6.4 presents Halley Company's cash budget, based on the cash receipt and cash disbursement data already developed for the firm. Halley's end-of-September cash balance was $50,000. The company wishes to maintain as a reserve for unexpected needs a minimum cash balance of $25,000.

For Halley Company to maintain its required $25,000 ending cash balance, it needs to have borrowed $76,000 in November and $41,000 in December. In the month of October the firm will have an excess cash balance of $22,000, which can be held in an interest-earning marketable security. The required total financing figures in the cash budget refer to *how much will be owed at the end of the month;* they do *not* represent the monthly changes in borrowing.

The monthly changes in borrowing as well as excess cash can be found by further analyzing the cash budget in Table 6.4. In October the $50,000 beginning cash, which becomes $47,000 after the $3,000 net cash outflow is deducted, results in a $22,000 excess cash balance once the $25,000 desired minimum cash is deducted. In November the $76,000 of required total financing results from the $98,000 net cash outflow less the $22,000 of excess cash from October. The $41,000 of required total financing in December results from reducing November's $76,000 of required total financing by the $35,000 of

**TABLE 6.4    A Cash Budget for Halley Company ($000)**

|  | Oct. | Nov. | Dec. |
|---|---|---|---|
| Total cash receipts[a] | $210 | $320 | $340 |
| Less: Total cash disbursements[b] | 213 | 418 | 305 |
| Net cash flow | $ (3) | $(98) | $ 35 |
| Add: Beginning cash | 50 | 47 | (51) |
| Ending cash | $ 47 | $(51) | $(16) |
| Less: Minimum cash balance | 25 | 25 | 25 |
| Required total financing (notes payable)[c] | — | $ 76 | $ 41 |
| Excess cash balance (marketable securities)[d] | $ 22 | — | — |

[a]From Table 6.2.

[b]From Table 6.3.

[c]Values are placed in this line when the ending cash is less than the desired minimum cash balance because in this instance financing is required. These amounts are typically financed short term and therefore are represented by notes payable.

[d]Values are placed in this line when the ending cash is greater than the desired minimum cash balance because in this instance an excess cash balance exists. These amounts are typically assumed invested short term and therefore are represented by marketable securities.

net cash inflow during December. Summarizing, the financial activities for each month result in the following:

October: Invest $22,000 of excess cash.

November: Liquidate $22,000 of excess cash and borrow $76,000.

December: Repay $35,000 of amount borrowed.

## Evaluating the Cash Budget

The cash budget provides the firm with figures indicating the expected ending cash balance. These can be analyzed to determine whether a cash shortage or surplus is expected to result in each of the months covered by the forecast. Halley Company can expect a surplus of $22,000 in October, a deficit of $76,000 in November, and a deficit of $41,000 in December. Each of these figures is based on the internally imposed requirement of a $25,000 minimum cash balance and *represents the total balance at the end of the month.*

The excess cash balance in October can be invested in marketable securities. The deficits in November and December have to be financed—typically, by short-term borrowing (notes payable). Because it may be necessary for the firm to borrow up to $76,000 for the three-month period evaluated, the financial manager should be sure that a line of credit is established or some other arrangement made to ensure the availability of these funds. The manager usually requests or arranges to borrow more than the maximum financing indicated in the cash budget. This is necessary due to the uncertainty of the ending cash values, which are based on the sales forecast and other forecast values.

## Coping with Uncertainty in the Cash Budget

In addition to carefully preparing sales forecasts and other estimates included in the cash budget, the financial manager frequently copes with the statement's uncertainty by preparing several cash budgets: one based on a pessimistic forecast, one based on the most likely forecast, and a third based on an optimistic forecast.[3] An evaluation of these cash flows allows the financial manager to determine the amount of financing necessary to cover the most adverse situation. The use of several cash budgets, each based on differing assumptions, should also give the financial manager a sense of the riskiness of alternatives so that more intelligent short-term financial decisions can be made. The sensitivity (or "what if") analysis approach is often used to analyze cash flows under a variety of possible circumstances. Computers and spreadsheet programs are commonly used to simplify greatly the process of performing sensitivity analysis.

▶ E X A M P L E

Table 6.5 presents the summary results of the Halley Company's cash budget prepared for each month of concern using a pessimistic, most likely, and optimistic estimate of cash receipts and cash disbursements. The most likely estimate is based on the expected outcomes presented earlier in Tables 6.2 through 6.4; the pessimistic and optimistic outcomes are based on the worst and best possible outcomes, respectively. During the month of October, Halley will need a maximum of $15,000 of financing; at best it will have a $62,000 excess cash balance available for short-term investment. During November, its financing requirement will be between $0 and $185,000. It could experience an excess cash balance of $5,000 during November. The December projections reflect maximum borrowing of $190,000 with a possible excess cash balance of $107,000. By considering the extreme values reflected in the pessimistic and optimistic outcomes, Halley Company should be better able to plan cash requirements. For the three-month period, the peak borrowing requirement under the worst circumstances is $190,000, an amount considerably greater than the most likely estimate of $76,000 for this period.

▶

▼▼▼▼▼▼▼▼▼▼▼▼▼▼▼▼▼▼▼▼▼▼▼▼▼▼▼▼▼▼▼

## Progress Review Questions

**6-3.** What is the purpose of the *cash budget*? The key input to the cash budget is the sales forecast. What is the difference between *external* and *internal* forecast data?

**6-4.** Briefly describe the basic format of the cash budget, beginning with forecast sales and ending with required total financing or excess cash balance.

---

[3]The term *uncertainty* is used here to refer to the variability of the cash flow outcomes that may actually occur. A thorough discussion of risk and uncertainty is presented in Chapter 12.

**TABLE 6.5 A Sensitivity Analysis of Halley Company's Cash Budget ($000)**

| | October | | | November | | | December | | |
|---|---|---|---|---|---|---|---|---|---|
| | Pessi-mistic | Most Likely | Opti-mistic | Pessi-mistic | Most Likely | Opti-mistic | Pessi-mistic | Most Likely | Opti-mistic |
| Total cash receipts | $160 | $210 | $285 | $ 210 | $320 | $410 | $ 275 | $ 340 | $422 |
| Less: Total cash disbursements | 200 | 213 | 248 | 380 | 418 | 467 | 280 | 305 | 320 |
| Net cash flow | $(40) | $ (3) | $ 37 | $(170) | $ (98) | $(57) | $ (5) | $ 35 | $102 |
| Add: Beginning cash | 50 | 50 | 50 | 10 | 47 | 87 | (160) | (51) | 30 |
| Ending cash | $ 10 | $ 47 | $ 87 | $(160) | $ (51) | $ 30 | $(165) | $ (16) | $132 |
| Less: Minimum cash balance | 25 | 25 | 25 | 25 | 25 | 25 | 25 | 25 | 25 |
| Required total financing | $ 15 | — | — | $ 185 | $ 76 | — | $ 190 | $ 41 | — |
| Excess cash balance | — | $ 22 | $ 62 | — | — | $ 5 | — | — | $107 |

**6-5.** How can the two bottom lines of the cash budget be used to determine the firm's short-term borrowing and investment requirements?

**6-6.** What is the cause of uncertainty in the cash budget? What technique can be used to cope with uncertainty?

## Profit Planning: Pro Forma Statement Fundamentals

**pro forma statements**
Projected financial statements—income statements and balance sheets.

The profit planning process centers on the preparation of **pro forma statements,** which are projected, or forecast, financial statements—income statements and balance sheets. The preparation of these statements requires a careful blending of a number of procedures to account for the revenues, costs, expenses, assets, liabilities, and equity resulting from the firm's anticipated level of operations. The basic steps in this process were shown in the flow diagram presented in Figure 6.1. The financial manager frequently uses one of a number of simplified approaches to estimate the pro forma statements. The most popular are based on the belief that the financial relationships reflected in the firm's historical (past) financial statements will not change in the coming period. The commonly used approaches are presented in subsequent discussions.

Two inputs are required for preparing pro forma statements using the simplified approaches: (1) financial statements for the preceding year and (2) the sales forecast for the coming year. A variety of assumptions must also be made when using simplified approaches. The company we use to illustrate the simplified approaches to pro forma preparation is Metcalfe Manufacturing Company, which manufactures and sells one product. It has two basic models:

model X and model Y. Although each model is produced by the same process, each requires different amounts of raw material and labor.

## Past Year's Financial Statements

The income statement for the firm's 1995 operations in Table 6.6 indicates that Metcalfe had sales of $100,000, total cost of goods sold of $80,000, net profits before taxes of $9,000, and net profits after taxes of $7,650. The firm paid $4,000 in cash dividends, leaving $3,650 to be transferred to retained earnings. The firm's balance sheet at the end of 1995 is given in Table 6.7.

## Sales Forecast

Like the cash budget, the key input for the development of pro forma statements is the sales forecast. The sales forecast by model for the coming year, 1996, for Metcalfe Company is given in Table 6.8. This forecast is based on both external and internal data. The unit sale prices of the products reflect an increase from $20 to $25 for model X and from $40 to $50 for model Y. These increases are required to cover the firm's anticipated increases in the cost of labor, material, overhead, and operating expenses.

**TABLE 6.6   An Income Statement for Metcalfe Manufacturing Company for the Year Ended December 31, 1995**

| | | |
|---|---:|---:|
| Sales revenue | | |
| Model X (1,000 units at $20/unit) | $20,000 | |
| Model Y (2,000 units at $40/unit) | 80,000 | |
| Total sales | | $100,000 |
| Less: Cost of goods sold | | |
| Labor | $28,500 | |
| Material A | 8,000 | |
| Material B | 5,500 | |
| Overhead | 38,000 | |
| Total cost of goods sold | | 80,000 |
| Gross profits | | $ 20,000 |
| Less: Operating expenses | | 10,000 |
| Operating profits | | $ 10,000 |
| Less: Interest expense | | 1,000 |
| Net profits before taxes | | $ 9,000 |
| Less: Taxes (.15 × $9,000) | | 1,350 |
| Net profits after taxes | | $ 7,650 |
| Less: Common stock dividends | | 4,000 |
| To retained earnings | | $ 3,650 |

**TABLE 6.7   A Balance Sheet for Metcalfe Manufacturing Company (December 31, 1995)**

| Assets | | Liabilities and Equities | |
|---|---|---|---|
| Cash | $ 6,000 | Accounts payable | $ 7,000 |
| Marketable securities | 4,000 | Taxes payable | 300 |
| Accounts receivable | 13,000 | Notes payable | 8,300 |
| Inventories | 16,000 | Other current liabilities | 3,400 |
| Total current assets | $39,000 | Total current liabilities | $19,000 |
| Net fixed assets | $51,000 | Long-term debts | $18,000 |
| Total assets | $90,000 | Stockholders' equity | |
| | | Common stock | $30,000 |
| | | Retained earnings | $23,000 |
| | | Total liabilities and stockholders' equity | $90,000 |

**TABLE 6.8   1996 Sales Forecast for Metcalfe Manufacturing Company**

| | |
|---|---|
| Unit sales | |
| Model X | 1,500 |
| Model Y | 1,950 |
| Dollar sales | |
| Model X ($25/unit) | $ 37,500 |
| Model Y ($50/unit) | 97,500 |
| Total | $135,000 |

# Progress Review Questions

**6-7.** What is the purpose of *pro forma financial statements?* Which of the pro forma statements must be developed first? Why?

**6-8.** What are the two key inputs required for preparing pro forma statements using the simplified approaches? What role do assumptions play in this process?

# Preparing the Pro Forma Income Statement

A simple method for developing a pro forma income statement is to use the **percentage-of-sales method.** It forecasts sales and then expresses the cost of goods sold, operating expenses, and interest expense as a percentage of projected sales. The percentages used are likely to be the percentage of sales for these items in the immediately preceding year. For Metcalfe Manufacturing Company, these percentages are

**percentage-of-sales method**
Method for developing the pro forma income statement that expresses the cost of goods sold, operating expenses, and interest expense as a percentage of projected sales.

$$\frac{\text{Cost of goods sold}}{\text{Sales}} = \frac{\$80,000}{\$100,000} = 80.0\%$$

$$\frac{\text{Operating expenses}}{\text{Sales}} = \frac{\$10,000}{\$100,000} = 10.0\%$$

$$\frac{\text{Interest expense}}{\text{Sales}} = \frac{\$1,000}{\$100,000} = 1.0\%$$

The dollar values are from the 1995 income statement (Table 6.6).

Applying these percentages to the firm's forecast sales of $135,000, developed in Table 6.8, and assuming the firm will pay $4,000 in common stock dividends in 1996, results in the pro forma income statement in Table 6.9. The expected contribution to retained earnings is $6,327, representing a considerable increase over $3,650 in the previous year (see Table 6.6).

## Considering Types of Costs and Expenses

The technique used to prepare the pro forma income statement in Table 6.9 assumes that all the firm's costs (or expenses) are *variable.* This means that the use of the historical (1995) ratios of cost of goods sold, operating expenses, and interest expense to sales assumes that for a given percentage increase in sales, the same percentage increase in each of these cost (or expense) components results. For example, as Metcalfe's sales increased by 35 percent (from $100,000 in 1995 to $135,000 projected for 1996), its cost of goods sold also increased by 35 percent (from $80,000 in 1995 to $108,000 projected for 1996). Based on this assumption, the firm's net profits before taxes also increased by 35 percent (from $9,000 in 1995 to $12,150 projected for 1996).

In the approach just illustrated, the broader implication is that because the firm has no fixed costs, it does not receive the benefits often resulting from them.[4] Therefore, the use of past cost and expense ratios generally tends to understate profits when sales are increasing and overstate profits when sales are decreasing. Clearly, if the firm has fixed operating and financial costs, when sales increase these costs do not change. The result is increased profits. When sales decline, these costs, by remaining unchanged, tend to lower profits. The best way to adjust for the presence of fixed costs when using a simplified approach for pro forma income statement preparation is to break

---

[4] The potential returns as well as risks resulting from use of fixed (operating and financial) costs to create "leverage" are discussed in Chapter 5. The key point to recognize here is that when the firm's revenue is *increasing,* fixed costs can magnify returns.

**TABLE 6.9   A Pro Forma Income Statement, Using the Percentage-of-Sales Method, for Metcalfe Manufacturing Company for the Year Ended December 31, 1996**

| | |
|---|---:|
| Sales revenue | $135,000 |
| Less: Cost of goods sold (.80) | 108,000 |
| Gross profits | $ 27,000 |
| Less: Operating expenses (.10) | 13,500 |
| Operating profits | $ 13,500 |
| Less: Interest expense (.01) | 1,350 |
| Net profits before taxes | $ 12,150 |
| Less: Taxes (.15 × $12,150) | 1,823 |
| Net profits after taxes | $ 10,327 |
| Less: Common stock dividends | 4,000 |
| To retained earnings | $  6,327 |

the firm's historical costs into *fixed* and *variable components* and make the forecast using this relationship.

# E X A M P L E

Metcalfe Manufacturing Company's last-year (1995) and pro forma (1996) income statements, which are broken into fixed- and variable-cost components, are given in the table.

### Metcalfe Manufacturing's Income Statements

| | Last Year (1995) | Pro Forma (1996) |
|---|---:|---:|
| Sales revenue | $100,000 | $135,000 |
| Less: Cost of goods sold | | |
| Fixed cost | 40,000 | 40,000 |
| Variable cost (.40 × sales) | 40,000 | 54,000 |
| Gross profits | $ 20,000 | $ 41,000 |
| Less: Operating expenses | | |
| Fixed expense | 5,000 | 5,000 |
| Variable expense (.05 × sales) | 5,000 | 6,750 |
| Operating profits | $ 10,000 | $ 29,250 |
| Less: Interest expense (all fixed) | 1,000 | 1,000 |
| Net profits before taxes | $  9,000 | $ 28,250 |
| Less: Taxes (.15 × net profits before taxes) | 1,350 | 4,238 |
| Net profits after taxes | $  7,650 | $ 24,012 |

**Ethics**

## Pledging to Improve S. C. Johnson's Corporate Statements Using an Environmental Agenda

Ideal pro forma statements are accurate and show the firm is financially strong and growing. The trick is to identify and implement policies that lead to these goals. In our present environment-conscious society, S. C. Johnson used environment-related concepts to define its strategy.

The maker of Pledge furniture polish and Raid insect spray developed a policy statement to focus on pollution prevention, pollution reduction, and education. The firm believes that, in addition to being a morally good objective, environmental consciousness also makes good business sense. For instance, producing less waste reduces the time S. C. Johnson spends reformulating its products. Replacing toxic chemicals where possible with water reduces liability and related costs. Recycled packaging is less costly than virgin packaging.

An environmental accounting system was developed. Revenue aspects include polls of consumer preferences and concern about environmental waste. Expense aspects include measures of air emissions, water effluent, and solid wastes. Simply put, S. C. Johnson attempted to create a business based on eco-efficiency. Although not as concrete as focusing directly on net income or stock value, one positive outcome was having *Fortune* magazine cite the firm for its clean environmetal record.

Source: Jane Hutterly, "How I Did It: Advancing an Environmental Agenda," *Working Woman*, January 1994, pp. 22–23.

By breaking Metcalfe's costs and expenses into fixed and variable components, we get a more accurate projection of the firm's pro forma profit. Treating all costs as variable, the pro forma (1996) net profits before taxes equal 9 percent of sales, just as was the case in 1995 ($9,000 net profits before taxes ÷ $100,000 sales). As shown in Table 6.9, by assuming *all* costs are variable, the net profits before taxes are $12,150 (.09 × $135,000 projected sales) instead of the $28,250 of net profits before taxes obtained by using the firm's fixed-cost/variable-cost breakdown.

▶ The preceding example should make it clear that strict application of the percentage-of-sales method is a naive approach that assumes all costs (or expenses) are variable—that is, there are *no* fixed costs. Because nearly all firms have fixed costs, ignoring them in the pro forma income statement preparation process typically results in misstatement of the firm's forecast profit. Therefore, when using a simplified approach to pro forma income statement preparation, it is advisable to consider first breaking down costs and expenses into fixed and variable components. For convenience, the pro forma income statement prepared for Metcalfe Manufacturing Company in Table 6.9 was based on the assumption that all costs were variable—which is *not* likely to be the case. Therefore, Metcalfe's projected profits were understated using the percentage-of-sales method.

## Progress Review Questions

**6-9.** Briefly describe the pro forma income statement preparation process using the *percentage-of-sales method*. What are the strengths and weaknesses of this simplified approach?

**6-10.** Comment on the following statement: "Because nearly all firms have fixed costs, ignoring them in the pro forma income statement preparation process typically results in misstatement of the firm's forecast profit." How can such a "misstatement" be avoided?

# Preparing the Pro Forma Balance Sheet

**judgmental approach**
Method for developing the pro forma balance sheet in which the values of certain accounts are estimated and others are calculated, using the firm's external financing as a "plug" figure.

A number of simplified approaches are available for preparing the pro forma balance sheet. Probably the best and most popular is the judgmental approach.[5] Under the **judgmental approach** for developing the pro forma balance sheet, the values of certain balance sheet accounts are estimated and others are calculated. When this approach is applied, the firm's external financing is used as a balancing, or "plug," figure. To apply the judgmental approach to prepare Metcalfe Manufacturing Company's 1996 pro forma balance sheet, a number of assumptions must be made.

1. A minimum cash balance of $6,000 is desired.
2. Marketable securities are assumed to remain unchanged from their current level of $4,000.
3. Accounts receivable on average represents 45 days of sales. Because Metcalfe's annual sales are projected to be $135,000, accounts receivable should average $16,875 ($\frac{1}{8} \times$ $135,000). (Forty-five days expressed fractionally is one-eighth of a year: $45/360 = \frac{1}{8}$).
4. The ending inventory should remain at a level of about $16,000, of which 25 percent (approximately $4,000) should be raw materials, and the remaining 75 percent (approximately $12,000) should consist of finished goods.
5. A new machine costing $20,000 will be purchased. Total depreciation for the year is $8,000. Adding the $20,000 acquisition to the existing net fixed assets of $51,000 and subtracting the depreciation of $8,000 yields net fixed assets of $63,000.
6. Purchases are expected to represent approximately 30 percent of annual sales, which in this case is approximately $40,500 (.30 ×

---

[5]The judgmental approach represents an improved version of the *percentage-of-sales approach* to pro forma balance sheet preparation. Because the judgmental approach requires only slightly more information and should yield better estimates than the somewhat naive percentage-of-sales approach, it is presented here.

$135,000). The firm estimates it can take 72 days on average to satisfy its accounts payable. Thus accounts payable should equal one-fifth (72 days ÷ 360 days) of the firm's purchases, or $8,100 ($\frac{1}{5}$ × $40,500).

7. Taxes payable are expected to equal one-fourth of the current year's tax liability, which equals $455 (one-fourth of the tax liability of $1,823 shown in the pro forma income statement presented in Table 6.9).

8. Notes payable are assumed to remain unchanged from their current level of $8,300.

9. No change in other current liabilities is expected. They remain at the level of the previous year: $3,400.

10. The firm's long-term debts and its common stock are expected to remain unchanged, at $18,000 and $30,000, respectively, because no issues, retirements, or repurchases of bonds or stocks are planned.

11. Retained earnings will increase from the beginning level of $23,000 (from the balance sheet dated December 31, 1995, in Table 6.7) to $29,327. The increase of $6,327 represents the amount of retained earnings calculated in the year-end 1996 pro forma income statement in Table 6.9.

A 1996 pro forma balance sheet for Metcalfe Manufacturing Company based on these assumptions is presented in Table 6.10. A **"plug" figure**—called the **external financing required**—of $8,293 is needed to bring the statement into balance. This means that the firm must obtain about $8,293 of additional external financing to support the increased sales level of $135,000 for 1996.

A *positive* value for "external financing required," like that shown in Table 6.10 for Metcalfe Manufacturing Company, means that to support the firm's forecast level of operations it must raise funds externally using debt or equity financing or both. Once the form of financing is determined, the pro forma

**external financing required ("plug" figure)** The amount of external financing needed to bring the pro forma balance sheet into balance under the judgmental approach.

---

**TABLE 6.10   A Pro Forma Balance Sheet, Using the Judgmental Approach, for Metcalfe Manufacturing Company (December 31, 1996)**

| Assets | | | Liabilities and Equities | |
|---|---|---|---|---|
| Cash | | $ 6,000 | Accounts payable | $ 8,100 |
| Marketable securities | | 4,000 | Taxes payable | 455 |
| Accounts receivable | | 16,875 | Notes payable | 8,300 |
| Inventories | | | Other current liabilities | 3,400 |
| Raw materials | $ 4,000 | | Total current liabilities | $ 20,255 |
| Finished goods | 12,000 | | Long-term debts | $ 18,000 |
| Total inventory | | 16,000 | Stockholders' equity | |
| Total current assets | | $ 42,875 | Common stock | $ 30,000 |
| Net fixed assets | | $ 63,000 | Retained earnings | $ 29,327 |
| Total assets | | $105,875 | Total | $ 97,582 |
| | | | External financing required[a] | $ 8,293 |
| | | | Total liabilities and stockholders' equity | $105,875 |

[a]The amount of external financing needed to force the firm's balance sheet to balance. Due to the nature of the judgmental approach, the balance sheet is not expected to balance without some type of adjustment.

balance sheet is modified to replace "external financing required" with the planned increases in the debt or equity accounts. When the value of "external financing required" is *negative*, it indicates that the firm's forecast financing is in excess of its needs. In this case funds are available for use in repaying debt, repurchasing stock, or increasing dividends. Once the specific actions are determined, the "external financing required" is replaced in the pro forma balance sheet with the planned reductions in the debt or equity accounts. Although the focus here is on the use of the judgmental approach to prepare the pro forma balance sheet, it is important to recognize that analysts frequently use this approach specifically to estimate the firm's financing requirements.

## Progress Review Questions

**6-11.** Describe the *judgmental approach* for simplified preparation of the pro forma balance sheet. Contrast this with the more detailed approach shown in Figure 6.1.

**6-12.** What is the significance of the balancing ("plug") figure, *external financing required,* used with the judgmental approach for preparing the pro forma balance sheet? Differentiate between the interpretation and strategy associated with positive and negative values for *external financing required.*

LG 6

# Evaluation of Pro Forma Statements

It is difficult to forecast the many variables involved in pro forma statement preparation. As a result, analysis—including investors, lenders, and managers—frequently use the techniques presented here to make rough estimates of pro forma financial statements. Although the growing use of personal computers and electronic spreadsheets is streamlining the financial planning process, simplified approaches to pro forma preparation are expected to remain popular. An understanding of the basic weaknesses of these simplified approaches is therefore important. Equally important is the ability to use pro forma statements effectively to make financial decisions.

## Weaknesses of Simplified Approaches

The basic weakness of the simplified pro forma approaches shown in this chapter lie in two assumptions: (1) that the firm's past financial condition is an accurate indicator of its future and (2) that certain variables, such as cash, accounts receivable, and inventories, can be forced to take on certain "desired" values. These assumptions cannot be justified solely on the basis of their ability to simplify the calculations involved. Good financial analysts do not generally assume that simplification of the forecasting model and assumptions enhances insight into what's going to happen. Because the quality of pro forma statements depends on the quality of the forecasting model and its assumptions, practicing analysts tend to spend time attempting to seek out the best model and assumptions for use in preparing these statements.

Other simplified approaches exist. Most are based on the assumption that certain relationships among revenues, costs, expenses, assets, liabilities, and equity will prevail in the future. For example, in preparing the pro forma balance sheet, all assets, liabilities, *and* equity are often increased by the percentage increase expected in sales. The financial analyst must know the techniques used in preparing pro forma statements to judge the quality of the estimated values and thus the degree of confidence he or she can have in them.

## Using Pro Forma Statements

In addition to estimating the amount, if any, of external financing required to support a given level of sales, pro forma statements also provide a basis for analyzing in advance the level of profitability and overall financial performance of the firm in the coming year. Using pro forma statements, the financial manager, as well as lenders, can analyze the firm's sources and uses of cash as well as various aspects of performance, such as liquidity, activity, debt, and profitability. Sources and uses can be evaluated by preparing a pro forma statement of cash flows. Various ratios can be calculated from the pro forma income statement and balance sheet to evaluate performance.

After analyzing the pro forma statements, the financial manager can take steps to adjust planned operations to achieve short-term financial goals. For example, if profits shown on the pro forma income statement are too low, a variety of pricing or cost-cutting actions, or both, might be initiated. If the projected level of accounts receivable shown on the pro forma balance sheet is too high, changes in credit or collection policy may avoid this outcome. Pro forma statements are therefore of key importance in solidifying the firm's financial plans for the coming year.

# Progress Review Questions

**6-13.** What are two key weaknesses of the simplified approaches to pro forma statement preparation? How do practicing financial analysts deal with these weaknesses?

**6-14.** How may the financial manager wish to evaluate pro forma statements? What is his or her objective in evaluating these statements?

# SUMMARY OF LEARNING GOALS

**LG 1** **Understand the financial planning process, including the role of and inter-relationship between long-term (strategic) financial plans and short-term (operating) plans.** The two key aspects of the financial planning process are cash planning and profit planning. Cash planning involves the cash budget or cash forecast. Profit planning relies on preparation of the pro forma income statement and balance sheet. Long-term (strategic) financial plans act as a guide for preparing short-term (operating) financial plans. Long-term plans tend to cover periods ranging from 2 to 10 years and are updated periodically. Short-term plans most often cover a one- to two-year period.

**LG 2** **Discuss the cash planning process, the role of sales forecasts, and the procedures for preparing the cash budget.** The cash planning process uses the cash budget, which is based on a sales forecast, to estimate short-term cash surpluses and shortages. The sales forecast may be based on an analysis of external or internal data or on a combination of the two. The cash budget is typically prepared for a one-year period divided into months. It lists cash receipts and disbursements for each period in order to calculate net cash flow. Ending cash is estimated by adding beginning cash to the net cash flow. By subtracting the desired minimum cash balance from the ending cash, the financial manager can determine required total financing (typically represented by notes payable) or the excess cash balance (typically included in marketable securities).

**LG 3** **Describe the cash budget evaluation process and the procedure for coping with uncertainty in the cash budget.** The cash budget allows the financial manager to plan investment of forecast cash surpluses in marketable securities and to arrange for adequate borrowing, typically through a line of credit to ensure the availability of funds to meet forecast cash shortages. To cope with uncertainty in the cash budget, sensitivity analysis (which involves preparation of several cash budgets) is frequently used.

**LG 4** **Prepare a pro forma income statement using both the percentage-of-sales method and a breakdown of costs and expenses into their fixed and variable components.** A pro forma income statement can be developed by calculating past percentage relationships between certain cost and expense items and the firm's sales and then applying these percentages to forecasts. Because this approach implies that all costs (or expenses) are variable, it tends to understate profits when sales are increasing and overstate profits when sales are decreasing. This problem can be avoided by breaking down costs and expenses into fixed and variable components and using them to prepare the statement. In this case the fixed components remain unchanged from the most recent year, and the variable costs and expenses are forecast on a percentage-of-sales basis.

**LG 5** **Explain the procedures used to develop a pro forma balance sheet using the judgmental approach and the role and use of the plug figure—external financing required—in this process.** Under the judgmental approach for developing a pro forma balance sheet, the values of certain balance sheet accounts are estimated and others are calculated, frequently on the basis of their relationship to sales. When this approach is applied, the firm's external financing is used as a balancing, or "plug" figure. A positive value for "external financing required" means that to support the firm's forecast level of operations, it must raise funds externally; a negative value indicates that funds are available for use in repaying debt, repurchasing stock, or increasing dividends.

**Describe the weaknesses of the simplified approaches to pro forma preparation and the common uses of pro forma financial statements.** The use of simplified approaches to pro forma statement preparation, although quite popular, can be criticized for assuming the firm's past condition is an accurate predictor of the future and for assuming that certain variables can be forced to take on desired values. Pro forma statements are commonly used by financial managers and lenders to analyze in advance the firm's level of profitability and overall financial performance. Based on their analysis, financial managers adjust planned operations to achieve short-term financial goals.

 LG 6

# P A R T  III

# Short-Term Financial Management

# CHAPTER

## LEARNING GOALS

After studying this chapter, you should be able to

**LG 1**   Define net working capital using both the common and alternative definitions and discuss its implications.

**LG 2**   Understand the trade-off between profitability and risk as it relates to changing levels of current assets and current liabilities.

**LG 3**   Explain how the firm's funds requirements, when viewed over time, can be broken into a permanent component and a seasonal component.

**LG 4**   Describe, in terms of profitability and risk, the aggressive strategy for determining the firm's financing mix.

**LG 5**   Describe, in terms of profitability and risk, the conservative strategy for determining the firm's financing mix and compare it with the aggressive strategy.

**LG 6**   Discuss the trade-off financing strategy that is a compromise between the high-profit, high-risk aggressive strategy and the low-profit, low-risk conservative strategy.

# 7 Working Capital Fundamentals

Management of the firm's working capital—its current assets—is critical for most companies. Working capital can be either a source or use of cash. Poor management of working capital can ruin a business. A company can run out of funds to sustain growth yet show an operating profit if working capital management is poor. On the other hand, good management of working capital gives a company more flexibility. A company that manages its working capital position well can produce cash in a downturn and keep its balance sheet strong and its borrowings low—even while sustaining accounting losses.

## . . . Good management of working capital gives a company more flexibility.

Not every company or industry has the same working capital concerns. For example, manufacturing and retail firms need working capital to support their trade cycles, so they devote considerable time to working capital management. A distributor buys and sells finished goods, so working capital represents most of its asset investment. At the other extreme, cable television companies have low accounts receivable and almost no inventory. For them, fixed asset investment and operating leverage are more important than working capital considerations.

From a lender's perspective, looking at working capital practices is an excellent way to learn about a company. What we are financing in the case of a manufacturer is the operating cycle, the period of time for a company to buy raw materials, turn them into finished goods, sell the product, and convert receivables into cash. Understanding how long that cycle is, and why, gives us insight into the company's operations and its cash, fixed assets, and financing needs. A company's seasonal sales cycle is also important. Unless managers know when cash needs peak, they can't plan ahead for necessary financing.

Sound working capital management practices depend on proper control systems. Without them, a company loses control of invoices, payments to suppliers, receivables, and similar documentation. Computer technology is helping in this area, but often management does not take full advantage of what's available. A company that's growing quickly and is very sales-oriented may focus too heavily on chasing new sales, measuring performance by the revenue line, and not enough on working capital management, which can affect both the top and bottom line.

For many small- and middle-market companies (those with sales under $150 million), the amount they can borrow is determined by a borrowing base formula such as 80 percent of receivables under 60 days and 50 percent of specified inventory. If the firm doesn't collect receivables in a timely manner and manage inventory well (turn it over at an appropriate rate), it may not have adequate borrowing capacity to finance its operations.

Even when loans are made on an unsecured basis, the bank wants to see that working capital is managed properly. For example, the borrower could be losing money because it offers such long payment terms that it is, in essence, financing its customers. As a result, cash is tied up in receivables and isn't available to invest in inventory or equipment to generate more sales.

Today, technology is reducing the amount of working capital companies need. It improves manufacturing processes so that less inventory is needed. Companies send invoices and purchase orders using electronic data interchange, speeding up payment time and shortening the trade cycle. The result is less cash tied up in working capital so that borrowing needs and interest expense are reduced and funds are available to invest in the company.

*Virginia Dennett, who joined Bank of Boston in 1979, is director and team leader of its Boston middle-market division and manages a team of 10 middle-market lenders. From 1989 to 1993, she was the bank's director of credit training, before which she spent eight years lending to large corporate customers in the Midwest. Ms. Dennett received a B.A. in Spanish and economics from Purdue University.*

An important responsibility of the financial manager is overseeing the firm's day-to-day financial activities. This area of finance, known as **short-term financial management,** is concerned with management of the firm's current assets and current liabilities. In U.S. manufacturing firms, current assets currently account for about 40 percent of total assets; current liabilities represent about 26 percent of total financing.  It is therefore not surprising that short-term financial management is one of the most important and time-consuming activities of the financial manager. The goal is to manage each of the firm's current assets (cash, marketable securities, accounts receivable, and inventory) and current liabilities (accounts payable, notes payable, and accruals) to achieve a balance between profitability and risk that contributes positively to the firm's value. In this chapter we give attention to the basic relationship between current assets and current liabilities. In following chapters we consider the individual current accounts.

**short-term financial management**
Management of current assets and current liabilities.

# Net Working Capital

 LG 1

The firm's current assets, commonly called **working capital,** represent the portion of investment that circulates from one form to another in the ordinary conduct of business. This idea embraces the recurring transition from *cash to inventories to receivables and back to cash* that forms the **operating cycle** of the firm. As a cash substitute, *marketable securities* are considered part of working capital.

**working capital**
Current assets, which represent the portion of investment that circulates from one form to another in the ordinary conduct of business.

Current liabilities represent the firm's short-term financing because they include all debts of the firm that come due (must be paid) in one year or less. These debts usually include amounts owed to suppliers (*accounts payable*), banks (*notes payable*), and employees and governments (*accruals*), among others.

**operating cycle**
The recurring transition of a firm's working capital from cash to inventories to receivables *and back to cash.*

## The Common Definition and Its Implications

As noted in Chapter 4, **net working capital** is commonly defined as the difference between the firm's current assets and its current liabilities. When the current assets exceed the current liabilities, the firm has *positive net working capital.* In the less common case, when current assets are less than current liabilities, the firm has *negative net working capital.* In general, the more a firm's current assets cover its short-term obligations (current liabilities), the better able it is to pay its bills as they come due. The conversion of current assets from inventory to receivables to cash provides the source of cash used to pay the current liabilities, which represent a use of cash.

**net working capital**
The difference between the firm's current assets and its current liabilities; alternatively, the portion of the firm's current assets financed with long-term funds.

The cash outlays for current liabilities are relatively predictable. When an obligation is incurred, the firm generally learns when the corresponding bill is due. For instance, when merchandise is purchased on credit, the terms extended by the seller require payment by a known point in time. What is difficult to predict are the cash inflows—that is, the conversion of the current assets to more liquid forms. The more predictable its cash inflows, the less net working capital a firm needs. Because they are unable to match cash inflows to outflows with certainty, most firms need current assets that more than cover outflows for current liabilities. Let us look at an example.

# E X A M P L E

Berenson Company, a sausage manufacturer, has the current position given in Table 7.1. All $600 of the firm's accounts payable, plus $200 of its notes payable and $100 of accruals, are due at the end of the current period. The $900 in outflows is certain; how the firm will cover these outflows is not certain. The firm can be sure that $700 is available since it has $500 in cash and $200 in marketable securities, which can easily be converted into cash. The remaining $200 must come from the collection of accounts receivable, the sale of inventory for cash, or both.[1] However, the firm cannot be sure when either the collection of an account receivable or a cash sale will occur. Generally, the more accounts receivable and inventories on hand, the greater the probability that some of these items will be converted into cash.[2] Thus a certain level of net working capital is often recommended to ensure the firm's ability to pay bills. Berenson Company has $1,100 of net working capital (current assets minus current liabilities, or $2,700 − $1,600), which will most likely be sufficient to cover its bills. Its current ratio of 1.69 (current assets divided by current liabilities, or $2,700 ÷ $1,600) should provide sufficient liquidity as long as its accounts receivable and inventories remain relatively active.

## An Alternative Definition of Net Working Capital

**net working capital**
The portion of the firm's current assets financed with long-term funds; alternatively, the difference between the firm's current assets and its current liabilities.

As an alternative to the earlier definition, **net working capital** can be defined as the portion of the firm's current assets financed with long-term funds. This definition can best be illustrated by a special type of balance sheet. Its vertical axis is a dollar scale on which all the major items on the firm's regular balance sheet are indicated. As the special balance sheet for Berenson Company presented in Figure 7.1 shows, the firm has current assets of $2,700, fixed assets of $4,300, total assets of $7,000, current liabilities of $1,600, long-term debts of $2,400 ($4,000 − $1,600), and stockholders' equity of $3,000 ($7,000 − $4,000). The firm's **long-term funds**—the sum of long-term debt and stockholders' equity—equal $5,400. The portion of Berenson's current

**long-term funds**
The sum of the firm's long-term debt and stockholders' equity.

### TABLE 7.1    The Current Position of Berenson Company

| Current Assets | | Current Liabilities | |
|---|---|---|---|
| Cash | $  500 | Accounts payable | $  600 |
| Marketable securities | 200 | Notes payable | 800 |
| Accounts receivable | 800 | Accruals | 200 |
| Inventories | 1,200 | Total | $1,600 |
| Total | $2,700 | | |

---

[1] A sale of inventory for credit shows up as a new account receivable, which cannot be easily converted into cash. Only a *cash sale* guarantees the firm that its bill-paying ability during the period of the sale has been enhanced.

[2] Note that levels of accounts receivable or inventory can be too high, reflecting certain management inefficiencies. Acceptable levels for any firm can be calculated. The efficient management of accounts receivable and inventory is discussed in Chapter 9.

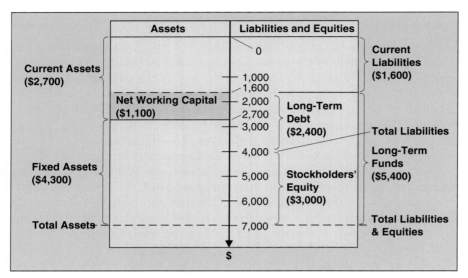

**FIGURE 7.1  A Special Balance Sheet for Berenson Company**

This special balance sheet with a dollar scale on the vertical axis demonstrates that Berenson Company's net working capital of $1,100 can be viewed as the portion of current assets financed with long-term funds (long-term debt plus stockholders' equity).

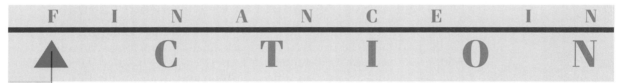

## Working Capital Guarantees Antenna Products' Loan Request Will Receive a Positive Reception

**Small Business**

Obtaining financing in rural sections of the United States is difficult. Major banks tend to concentrate activities in urban areas. With financing options being highly limited, Antenna Products, an antenna manufacturer in Mineral Wells, Texas, was doing everything possible to reduce risk and optimize its working capital position through efficient receivables and inventory management and limited short-term borrowing. Nonetheless, when Gary Skaggs went looking for money to finance a $1.2 million expansion of Antenna Products, the closest bank rejected his original loan request. Fortunately, the bank made Skaggs aware of the loan guarantee program administered by the Farmers Home Administration (FmHA), a division of the Department of Agriculture.

Though small, FmHA's programs are critical in rural America and almost any business can apply. The 1994 federal budget authorizes FmHA to guarantee $200 million in loans. For many trying to expand their companies in capital-scarce rural areas, a guarantee can make the difference between getting a loan and not. To be eligible for a FmHA guarantee, the primary criterion is that the business not be located too close to a community with over 25,000 residents. The bank still decides whether it will approve the loan and sets the interest rate, but the likelihood of getting a loan and obtaining a lower rate increases dramatically.

In this instance, Gary Skaggs obtained the financing using a loan against his working capital. Although the short-term note would normally have put Antenna Products in a high-risk bracket, the government guarantee allowed Skaggs to get the loan at a rate slightly below the prime rate.

Source: Bruce G. Posner, "Loans for Rural America," *Inc.*, November 1993, p. 135.

assets that have been financed with long-term funds equals $1,100. It is labeled "net working capital" in Figure 7.1. Because current liabilities represent the firm's sources of short-term funds, as long as current assets exceed current liabilities, the amount of the excess must be financed with longer term funds. The usefulness of this alternative definition of net working capital becomes more apparent later in the chapter.

▼▼▼▼▼▼▼▼▼▼▼▼▼▼▼▼▼▼▼▼▼▼▼▼▼▼▼▼▼▼▼

## Progress Review Questions

**7-1.** Why is *short-term financial management* one of the most important and time-consuming activities of the financial manager? What are the two most common definitions of *net working capital?*

**7-2.** What relationship do you expect between the predictability of a firm's cash inflows and its required level of net working capital?

▲▲▲▲▲▲▲▲▲▲▲▲▲▲▲▲▲▲▲▲▲▲▲▲▲▲▲▲▲▲▲

LG ② 

# The Trade-Off Between Profitability and Risk

**profitability**
The relationship between revenues and costs.

**risk (of technical insolvency)**
The probability that a firm will be unable to pay its bills as they come due.

**technically insolvent**
Describes a firm that is unable to pay its bills as they come due.

A trade-off exists between a firm's profitability and its risk. **Profitability,** in this context, is the relationship between revenues and costs. A firm's profits can be increased in two ways: (1) by increasing revenues or (2) by decreasing costs. **Risk,** in the context of short-term financial management, is the probability that the firm will be unable to pay its bills as they come due. A firm that cannot pay its bills as they come due is said to be **technically insolvent.** The risk of becoming technically insolvent is commonly measured using either the current ratio or the amount of net working capital. In this chapter the latter measure is used. It is generally assumed that *the greater the firm's net working capital, the lower its risk.* In other words, the more net working capital, the more liquid the firm, and therefore the *lower its risk of becoming technically insolvent.* We now discuss separately the effects of changes in current assets and in current liabilities on the firm's profitability-risk trade-off and then examine the combined effect.

## Changes in Current Assets

The effects of changing the level of the firm's current assets on its profitability-risk trade-off can be demonstrated using the ratio of current assets to total assets. This ratio indicates the *percentage of total assets* that is current. Assuming that the level of total assets remains unchanged,[3] the effects of an increase or decrease in this ratio on both profitability and risk are summarized in the upper portion of Table 7.2. When the ratio increases, profitability decreases. The rea-

---

[3]The level of total assets is assumed *constant* in this and the following discussion in order to isolate the effect of changing asset and financing mixes on the firm's profitability and risk.

**TABLE 7.2   Effects of Changing Ratios on Profits and Risk**

| Ratio | Change in Ratio | Effect on Profit | Effect on Risk |
|---|---|---|---|
| Current assets | Increase | Decrease | Decrease |
| Total assets | Decrease | Increase | Increase |
| Current liabilities | Increase | Increase | Increase |
| Total assets | Decrease | Decrease | Decrease |

son is that current assets are less profitable than fixed assets. Fixed assets are more profitable because they add more value to the product than that provided by current assets. Without the fixed assets, the firm could not produce the product.

The risk effect, however, decreases as the ratio of current assets to total assets increases. The increase in current assets increases net working capital, thereby reducing the risk of technical insolvency. In addition, as you go down the asset side of the balance sheet, the risk associated with the assets increases. Investment in cash and marketable securities is less risky than investment in accounts receivable, inventories, and fixed assets. Accounts receivable investment is less risky than investment in inventories and fixed assets. Investment in inventories is less risky than investment in fixed assets. The nearer an asset is to cash, the less risky it is. It is generally easier to turn receivables into the more liquid asset cash than it is to turn inventory into cash. As another example, fixed assets are long-term investments, and newer, more efficient machines and facilities can quickly make the firm's fixed assets relatively inefficient or obsolete. The opposite effects on profit and risk result from a decrease in the ratio of current assets to total assets.

▶ E X A M P L E

The balance sheet for Berenson Company presented in Figure 7.1 is shown in Table 7.3 with the initial as well as a second asset mix. Assume the firm earns 2 percent annually on its current assets and 15 percent annually on its fixed assets. As noted in the evaluation in Table 7.3, the initial asset mix results in a ratio of current to total assets of .386, an annual profit on total assets of $699, and net working capital of $1,100. If the firm shifts its asset mix by investing $300 more in fixed assets (and thus $300 less in current assets), current and fixed assets are as shown in Table 7.3. After the shift the ratio of current to total assets drops to .343, annual profits on total assets increase by $39 to $738, and net working capital drops by $300 to $800. Clearly, a decrease in the ratio resulted in higher profits ($39 increase) and higher risk (liquidity is reduced by $300 from net working capital of $1,100 to $800). These shifts support our earlier conclusions concerning the profitability-risk trade-off as related to changes in current assets.

## Changes in Current Liabilities

The effects of changing the level of the firm's current liabilities on its profitability-risk trade-off can be demonstrated using the ratio of current liabilities to total

---

**TABLE 7.3   Evaluation of a Shift in Berenson's Current Assets**

| | | | | |
|---|---|---|---|---|
| **Balance Sheet** | | | | |
| | **Assets** | | | |
| | **Initial** | **After Shift** | **Liabilities and Equity** | |
| Current assets | $2,700 | $2,400 | Current liabilities | $1,600 |
| Fixed assets | 4,300 | 4,600 | Long-term funds | 5,400 |
| Total | $7,000 | $7,000 | Total | $7,000 |

**Evaluation**

*Initial assets*

| | | |
|---|---|---|
| Ratio of current to total assets = $2,700 ÷ $7,000 | = | .386 |
| Profit on total assets = (2% × $2,700) + (15% × $4,300) | = | $699 |
| Net working capital = $2,700 − $1,600 | = | $1,100 |

*After shift in assets*

| | | |
|---|---|---|
| Ratio of current to total assets = $2,400 ÷ $7,000 | = | .343 |
| Profit on total assets = (2% × $2,400) ÷ (15% × $4,600) | = | $738 |
| Net working capital = $2,400 − $1,600 | = | $800 |

| | | |
|---|---|---|
| Effect of shift on profit = $738 − $699 | = | +$39 |
| Change in net working capital = $800 − $1,100 | = | −$300 |

---

assets. This ratio indicates the percentage of total assets that has been financed with current liabilities. Assuming that total assets remain unchanged, the effects on both profitability and risk of an increase or decrease in the ratio are summarized in the lower portion of Table 7.2. When the ratio increases, profitability increases; the firm uses more of the less expensive current-liability financing and less long-term financing. Current liabilities (accounts payable, notes payable, and accruals) are less expensive because only notes payable have a cost. (Notes payable represent only about 20 percent of the typical manufacturer's current liabilities.) The other current liabilities are basically debts on which the firm pays no charge or interest.

Risk also increases as the ratio of current liabilities to total assets increases. The increase in current liabilities decreases net working capital, thereby increasing the risk of technical insolvency. The opposite effects on profit and risk result from a decrease in the ratio.

# EXAMPLE

The balance sheet for Berenson Company is shown with the initial as well as a second financing mix in Table 7.4. Assume that the firm's current liabilities cost 3 percent annually to maintain and that the average cost of long-term funds is 11 percent. As noted in the evaluation in Table 7.4, the initial financing mix results in a ratio of current liabilities to total assets of .229, an annual cost of total financing of $642, and net working capital of $1,100. If the firm shifts its financing mix by using $300 more current-liability financing (and thus $300 less in long-term financing), current liabilities and long-term funds are as shown in Table 7.4. After the shift the ratio of current liabilities to total assets rises to .271, the annual cost of total financing decreases by $24 to $618, and net working capital drops to $800. Clearly, an increase in the ratio resulted in higher profits ($24 increase due to a decrease in financing cost) and higher risk (liquidity is reduced by $300 from net working capital of $1,100 to $800). This supports our earlier conclusions concerning the profitability-risk trade-off as related to changes in current liabilities.

## Combined Effects of Changes

In the preceding examples, the effects of a decrease in the ratio of current assets to total assets and the effects of an increase in the ratio of current liabilities to total assets were illustrated. Both changes were shown to increase the firm's profits and, correspondingly, its risk. Logically, then, the *combined effect* of these actions should also increase profits and increase risk (decrease net working capital).

---

**TABLE 7.4   Evaluation of a Shift in Berenson's Current Liabilities**

### Balance Sheet

| Assets | | Liabilities and Equity | | Initial | After Shift |
|---|---|---|---|---|---|
| Current assets | $2,700 | Current liabilities | | $1,600 | $1,900 |
| Fixed assets | 4,300 | Long-term funds | | 5,400 | 5,100 |
| Total | $7,000 | Total | | $7,000 | $7,000 |

### Evaluation

*Initial financing*

Ratio of current liabilities to total assets = $1,600 ÷ $7,000 =   .229

Cost of total financing = (3% × $1,600) + (11% × $5,400) =   $642

Net working capital = $2,700 − $1,600                        = $1,100

*After shift in financing*

Ratio of current liabilities to total assets = $1,900 ÷ $7,000 =   .271

Cost of total financing = (3% × $1,900) + (11% × $5,100) =   $618

Net working capital = $2,700 − $1,900                      =   $800

Effect of shift on profit[a] = −$618 − (−$642)            =  +$24

Change in net working capital = $800 − $1,100            = −$300

---

[a]The minus sign preceding the $618 and $642 values reflects the fact that they are costs.

**TABLE 7.5   The Combined Effects of Changes in Berenson's Current Assets and Current Liabilities**

| Change | Change in Profits | Change in Net Working Capital |
|---|---|---|
| Decrease in ratio of current to total assets | +$39 | −$300 |
| Increase in ratio of current liabilities to total assets | +$24 | −$300 |
|    Combined effect | +$63 | −$600 |

# E X A M P L E

Table 7.5 illustrates the results of combining the changes in current assets and current liabilities demonstrated in Tables 7.3 and 7.4. The values in Table 7.5 show that the combined effect of the two shifts illustrated earlier is an increase in annual profits of $63 and a decrease in net working capital (liquidity) of $600. The trade-off here is obvious; the firm has increased its profitability by increasing its risk.

## Progress Review Questions

**7-3.** How are net working capital, liquidity, and the risk of technical insolvency related?

**7-4.** Why is an increase in the ratio of current to total assets expected to decrease both profits and risk as measured by net working capital?

**7-5.** How can changes in the ratio of current liabilities to total assets affect profitability and risk?

**7-6.** How do you expect an increase in a firm's ratio of current assets to total assets and a decrease in its ratio of current liabilities to total assets to affect profit and risk? Why?

LG 3

# Determining the Firm's Financing Mix

One of the most important decisions that must be made with respect to current assets and liabilities is how current liabilities are used to finance current assets. The amount of current liabilities available is limited by the dollar amount of purchases in the case of accounts payable, by the dollar amount of accrued liabilities in the case of accruals, and by the amount of seasonal borrowing considered acceptable by lenders in the case of notes payable.

**TABLE 7.6   Estimated Funds Requirements for Berenson Company**

| Month | Current Assets (1) | Fixed Assets (2) | Total Assets[a] [(1) + (2)] (3) | Permanent Funds Requirement[b] (4) | Seasonal Funds Requirement [(3) − (4)] (5) |
|---|---|---|---|---|---|
| January | $4,000 | $13,000 | $17,000 | $13,800 | $3,200 |
| February | 3,000 | 13,000 | 16,000 | 13,800 | 2,200 |
| March | 2,000 | 13,000 | 15,000 | 13,800 | 1,200 |
| April | 1,000 | 13,000 | 14,000 | 13,800 | 200 |
| May | 800 | 13,000 | 13,800 | 13,800 | 0 |
| June | 1,500 | 13,000 | 14,500 | 13,800 | 700 |
| July | 3,000 | 13,000 | 16,000 | 13,800 | 2,200 |
| August | 3,700 | 13,000 | 16,700 | 13,800 | 2,900 |
| September | 4,000 | 13,000 | 17,000 | 13,800 | 3,200 |
| October | 5,000 | 13,000 | 18,000 | 13,800 | 4,200 |
| November | 3,000 | 13,000 | 16,000 | 13,800 | 2,200 |
| December | 2,000 | 13,000 | 15,000 | 13,800 | 1,200 |
| Monthly Average[c] | | | | $13,800 | $1,950 |

[a]This represents the firm's total funds requirement.
[b]This figure represents the minimum total asset requirement.
[c]Found by summing the monthly amounts for the 12 months and dividing the resulting totals by 12.

Lenders make short-term loans to allow a firm to finance seasonal buildups of accounts receivable or inventory. *They generally do not lend short-term money for long-term uses.*[4]

The firm's financing requirements can be separated into a permanent and a seasonal need. The **permanent need,** which consists of fixed assets plus the permanent portion of the firm's current assets, remains unchanged over the year. The **seasonal need,** which is attributable to certain temporary current assets, varies over the year. The relationship between current and fixed assets and permanent and seasonal funds requirements can be illustrated graphically with the aid of a simple example.

**permanent need**
Financing requirements for the firm's fixed assets plus the permanent portion of the firm's current assets, which remain unchanged over the year.

**seasonal need**
Financing requirements for temporary current assets, which vary over the year.

▶ E X A M P L E

Berenson Company's estimate of current, fixed, and total asset requirements on a monthly basis for the coming year is given in columns 1, 2, and 3 of Table 7.6. Note that the relatively stable level of total assets over the year reflects,

---

[4]The rationale for, techniques of, and parties to short-term business loans are discussed in detail in Chapter 10. The primary sources of short-term loans to businesses—commercial banks—make these loans *only for seasonal or self-liquidating purposes,* such as temporary buildups of accounts receivable or inventory.

for convenience, an absence of growth by the firm. Columns 4 and 5 present a breakdown of the total requirement into its permanent and seasonal components. The permanent component (column 4) is the lowest level of total assets during the period; the seasonal portion is the difference between the total funds requirement (i.e., total assets) for each month and the permanent funds requirement.

By comparing the firm's fixed assets (column 2) to its permanent funds requirement (column 4), we can see that the permanent funds requirement exceeds the firm's level of fixed assets. This result occurs because *a portion of the firm's current assets is permanent,* because they are apparently always being replaced. The size of the permanent component of current assets is $800 for Berenson Company. This value represents the basic level of current assets that remains on the firm's books throughout the entire year. This value can also be found by subtracting the level of fixed assets from the permanent funds requirement ($13,800 − $13,000 = $800). The relationships presented in Table 7.6 are depicted graphically in Figure 7.2.

There are a number of strategies for determining the appropriate mix of short-term (current liability) and long-term financing. The three basic strategies—(1) the aggressive strategy, (2) the conservative strategy, and (3) a trade-off between the two—are discussed below in terms of both cost and risk considerations. In these discussions the alternative definition that defines *net working capital* as *the portion of current assets financed with long-term funds* is applied.

**FIGURE 7.2 Berenson Company's Estimated Funds Requirements**

Berenson Company's total funds requirement varies over the year. It consists of a permanent component, which includes fixed assets and the permanent portion of current assets, and a seasonal component attributable to temporary current assets.

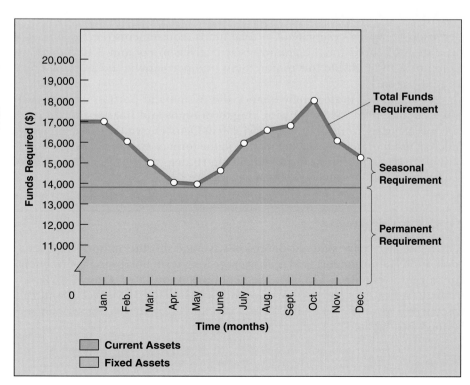

▼▼▼▼▼▼▼▼▼▼▼▼▼▼▼▼▼▼▼▼▼▼▼▼▼▼▼▼▼▼▼▼▼▼

## Progress Review Questions

**7-7.** For each of the following current liabilities indicate what limits the amount of the financing available.
  **a.** Accounts payable
  **b.** Accruals
  **c.** Notes payable

**7-8.** With regard to a firm's financing over time differentiate between the *permanent need* and the *seasonal need*. How can these values be determined from a series of monthly balance sheets covering a time period of one year or more?

▲▲▲▲▲▲▲▲▲▲▲▲▲▲▲▲▲▲▲▲▲▲▲▲▲▲▲▲▲▲▲▲▲▲

# An Aggressive Financing Strategy

An **aggressive financing strategy** results in the firm financing at least its seasonal needs, and possibly some of its permanent needs, with short-term funds. The balance is financed with long-term funds. This strategy can be illustrated graphically.

▶ E X A M P L E

Berenson Company's estimate of its total funds requirements (i.e., total assets) on a monthly basis for the coming year is given in column 3 of Table 7.6. Columns 4 and 5 divide this requirement into permanent and seasonal components.

An aggressive strategy may finance the permanent portion of the firm's funds requirement ($13,800) with long-term funds and finance the seasonal portion (ranging from $0 in May to $4,200 in October) with short-term funds. Much of the short-term financing may be in the form of *trade credit* (i.e., accounts payable). The application of this financing strategy to the firm's total funds requirement is illustrated graphically in Figure 7.3.

**aggressive financing strategy**
Strategy by which the firm finances at least its seasonal needs, and possibly some of its permanent needs, with short-term funds and the majority of its permanent needs with long-term funds.

## Cost Considerations

Under the aggressive strategy, Berenson's average short-term borrowing (seasonal funds requirement) is $1,950; average long-term borrowing (permanent funds requirement) is $13,800. (See columns 4 and 5 of Table 7.6) If the annual cost of short-term funds needed by Berenson is 3 percent and the annual cost of long-term financing is 11 percent, the total cost of the financing strategy is estimated as follows:

$$\text{Cost of short-term financing} = 3\% \times \$\ 1,950 = \$\ \ \ 58.50$$
$$\text{Cost of long-term financing} = 11\% \times \ \ 13,800 = \underline{\ \ 1,518.00}$$
$$\text{Total cost} \qquad\qquad\qquad\qquad\qquad \underline{\underline{\$1,576.50}}$$

**FIGURE 7.3   Applying the Aggressive Strategy to Berenson Company's Funds Requirements**

Under the aggressive financing strategy Berenson Company finances its permanent need of $13,800 with long-term funds and its seasonal needs with short-term funds. This strategy results in $800 of net working capital ($13,800 long-term financing − $13,000 fixed assets).

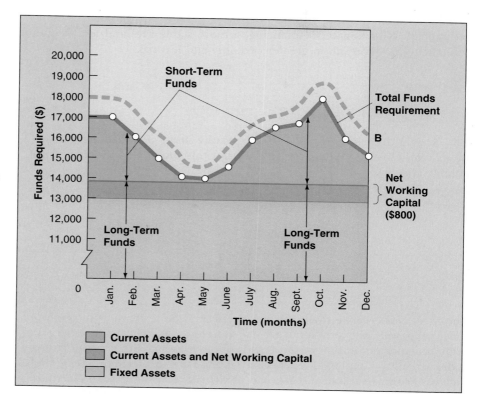

The total annual cost of $1,576.50 becomes more meaningful when compared with the cost of various other financing strategies. The relatively low cost of short-term financing results from using a high amount of free trade credit (a topic discussed in Chapter 10).

## Risk Considerations

The aggressive strategy operates with minimum net working capital because only the permanent portion of the firm's current assets is being financed with long-term funds. For Berenson Company, as shown in Figure 7.3, the level of net working capital is $800, which is the amount of permanent current assets ($13,800 permanent funds requirement − $13,000 fixed assets = $800).

The aggressive financing strategy is risky. Not only is the net working capital at a minimum, but also the firm must draw as heavily as possible on its short-term sources of funds to meet seasonal fluctuations in its requirements. If its total requirement turns out to be, say, the level represented by dashed curve B in Figure 7.3, the firm may find it difficult to obtain longer term funds quickly enough to satisfy short-term needs. This aspect of risk associated with the aggressive strategy results from the fact that a firm has only a limited amount of short-term borrowing capacity. If it draws too heavily on this capacity, unexpected needs for funds may become difficult to satisfy.

A final aspect of risk associated with the aggressive strategy's maximum use of short-term financing is the fact that changing short-term interest rates can result in significantly higher borrowing costs as the short-term debt is refinanced. With long-term financing, a more stable rate and less frequent refinancing needs result in greater certainty and less risk.

## Progress Review Question

**7-9.** What is the basic premise of the *aggressive strategy* for meeting a firm's funds requirements? What are the effects of this strategy on the firm's profitability and risk?

## A Conservative Financing Strategy

The most **conservative financing strategy** should be to finance all projected funds needs with long-term funds and use short-term financing for an emergency or an unexpected outflow of funds. It is difficult to imagine how this strategy could actually be implemented, because the use of short-term financing tools, such as accounts payable and accruals, is virtually unavoidable. In illustrating this strategy, the spontaneous short-term financing provided by payables and accruals is ignored.

**conservative financing strategy**
Strategy by which the firm finances all projected funds needs with long-term funds and uses short-term financing only for emergencies or unexpected outflows.

▶ E X A M P L E

Figure 7.4 shows graphically the application of the conservative strategy to the total funds requirement for Berenson Company given in Table 7.6. Long-term financing of $18,000, which equals the firm's peak need (during October), is used under this strategy. Therefore all the funds required over the one-year period, including the entire $18,000 forecast for October, are financed with long-term funds.

### Cost Considerations

In the preceding example the annual cost of long-term funds was 11 percent per year. Because the average long-term financing balance under the conservative financing strategy is $18,000, the total cost of this strategy is $1,980 or (11% × $18,000). Comparing this figure to the total cost of $1,576.50 using the aggressive strategy indicates the greater expense of the conservative strategy. The reason for this higher expense is apparent if we examine Figure 7.4. The area above the total funds requirement curve and below the long-term funds, or borrowing, line represents the level of funds not actually needed but for which the firm is paying interest. In spite of the fact that the financial manager invests these excess funds in some type of marketable security so as partially to offset their borrowing cost, it is highly unlikely that the firm can earn a return on such funds in excess of their interest cost.

**FIGURE 7.4** Applying the Conservative Strategy to Berenson Company's Funds Requirements

Under the conservative financing strategy Berenson Company finances all projected funds requirements, including the entire $18,000 forecast for October, with long-term funds. This strategy results in $5,000 of net working capital ($18,000 long-term financing − $13,000 fixed assets).

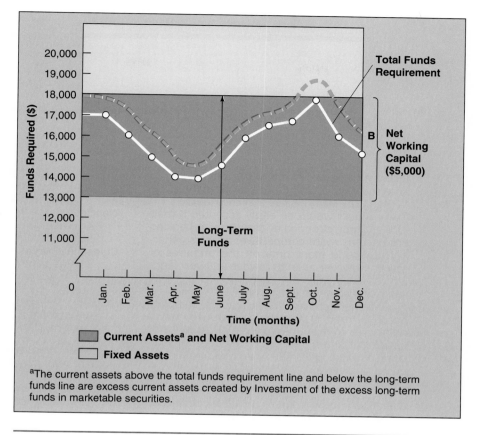

aThe current assets above the total funds requirement line and below the long-term funds line are excess current assets created by Investment of the excess long-term funds in marketable securities.

## Risk Considerations

The $5,000 of net working capital ($18,000 long-term financing − $13,000 fixed assets) associated with the conservative strategy should mean a very low level of risk for the firm.[5] The firm's risk should also be lowered by the fact that the strategy does not require the firm to use any of its limited short-term borrowing capacity. In other words, if total required financing actually turns out to be the level represented by the dashed line B in Figure 7.4, sufficient short-term borrowing capacity should be available to cover the unexpected needs and avoid technical insolvency. In addition, the need to frequently refinance high levels of short-term financing, possibly at high rates, is avoided, thereby further lowering risk.

## Conservative Versus Aggressive Strategy

Unlike the aggressive strategy, the conservative strategy requires the firm to pay interest on unneeded funds. The lower cost of the aggressive strategy therefore makes it more profitable than the conservative strategy. However,

---

[5]The level of net working capital is constant throughout the year because the firm has $5,000 in current assets that are fully financed with long-term funds. Because the portion of the $5,000 in excess of the scheduled level of current assets is assumed to be held as marketable securities, the firm's current asset balance increases to this level.

# FINANCE IN ACTION

## Aggressive or Conservative?—In the Eyes of Wachovia

Business managers often believe that balance sheets give an unflattering summary of their firm. Many believe that their next loan request would be easily accepted if their banker simply dropped by their firm. As banking has become more competitive, bankers generally do spend more time on the premises of clients. However, as Keith Lawder, a 20-year lending veteran at Wachovia points out, "a visit may indicate that a loan is too risky."

Wachovia, a large bank holding company headquartered in Atlanta, uses the following guidelines to examine the creditworthiness of its current and potential clients. Questions related to each guideline are those frequently posed by Lawder.

**Guideline 1: Knowledge of financial conditions.**
What is your business worth in a pinch?
What is the net working capital position of the firm?
**Guideline 2: Anticipation of safety and environmental concerns.**

How neat are the facilities? Are hard hats offered, if needed?
**Guideline 3: Ready explanation of inefficiencies.**
Are there any idle machines or large quantities of goods in progress sitting idle?
**Guideline 4: Backup plans.**
What is done if a critical machine breaks or a major customer quits ordering products?
**Guideline 5: Employee quality.**
Are capable individuals taking pride in what they are doing?

When managers understand their financial position, are concerned about safety and the environment, run efficient firms, have backup plans, and allow unrestricted access to employees, Lawder's report notes that assisting them with financing is a relatively more conservative venture than financing data alone would indicate.

Source: Bruce G. Posner, "Sprucing up for the Banker," *Inc.*, July 1993, p. 31.

the aggressive strategy involves much more risk. For most firms a trade-off between the extremes represented by these two strategies should result in an acceptable financing strategy.

## Progress Review Question

**7-10.** What is the *conservative strategy* for financing funds requirements? What kind of profitability-risk trade-off is involved?

LG  6

## A Trade-Off Financing Strategy

**trade-off financing strategy**
A compromise financing strategy between the aggressive financing strategy and the conservative financing strategy.

Most firms employ a **trade-off financing strategy,** a compromise between the high-profit, high-risk aggressive strategy and the low-profit, low-risk conservative strategy. One of the many possible trade-offs in Berenson Company's case is described in the following example.

### E X A M P L E

After careful analysis, Berenson Company has decided on a financing plan based on an amount of permanent financing equal to the midpoint of the minimum and maximum monthly funds requirements for the period. An examination of column 3 of Table 7.6 reveals that the minimum monthly funds requirement is $13,800 (in May) and the maximum monthly funds requirement is $18,000 (in October). The midpoint between these two values is $15,900 [($13,800 + $18,000) ÷ 2]. Thus the firm uses $15,900 in long-term funds each month and raises any additional funds required from short-term sources. The breakdown of long- and short-term funds under this plan is given in Table 7.7.

Column 3 in Table 7.7 shows the amount of short-term funds required each month. These values were found by subtracting $15,900 from the total funds required each month, given in column 1. For March, April, May, June, and December, the level of total funds required is less than the level of long-term funds available; therefore, no short-term funds are needed. Figure 7.5 presents graphically the trade-off strategy (line 3) described in Table 7.7 along with the plans based on the aggressive (line 1) and the conservative (line 2) strategies, respectively. Line 3 represents the $15,900 financed with long-term funds; the seasonal needs above that amount are financed with short-term funds.

### Cost Considerations

Under the trade-off strategy Berenson's average short-term borrowing is $450 and average long-term borrowing is $15,900. (See columns 2 and 3 of Table 7.7.) With the cost of short-term financing at 3 percent and the cost of long-term financing at 11 percent, the total cost of this financing strategy is estimated as follows:

$$\text{Cost of short-term financing} = 3\% \times \$\quad 450 = \$\quad 13.50$$
$$\text{Cost of long-term financing} = 11\% \times \quad 15,900 = \quad \underline{1,749.00}$$
$$\text{Total cost} \qquad\qquad\qquad\qquad\qquad\qquad \underline{\$1,762.50}$$

The total financing cost under the trade-off strategy is therefore $1,762.50

### Risk Considerations

As Figure 7.5 shows, the trade-off strategy results in $2,900 of net working capital ($15,900 long-term financing − $13,000 fixed assets). This is less risky than the aggressive strategy but more risky than the conservative strategy. Under the trade-off strategy, if the total funds requirement is actually at the level represented by dashed line B in Figure 7.5, the likelihood that the firm will be able to obtain additional short-term financing is good, because a portion of its short-term financing requirements is actually being financed with long-term funds. Under this strategy the risk of having to refinance frequently at possibly higher interest rates falls between that of the aggressive and conservative strategies.

▼▼▼▼▼▼▼▼▼▼▼▼▼▼▼▼▼▼▼▼▼▼▼▼▼▼▼▼▼▼▼▼▼▼

## Progress Review Questions

**7-11.** If a firm has a constant funds requirement throughout the year, which, if any, of the three financing strategies—aggressive, conservative, or trade-off—is preferable? Why?

**7-12.** As the difference between the cost of short-term and long-term financing becomes smaller, which financing strategy—aggressive or conservative—becomes more attractive? Is the aggressive or the conservative strategy preferable if the costs are equal? Why?

▲▲▲▲▲▲▲▲▲▲▲▲▲▲▲▲▲▲▲▲▲▲▲▲▲▲▲▲▲▲▲▲▲▲

**TABLE 7.7    A Financing Strategy Based on a Trade-Off Between Profitability and Risk for Berenson Company**

| Month | Total Assets[a] (1) | Long-Term Funds[b] (2) | Short-Term Funds (3) |
|---|---|---|---|
| January | $17,000 | $15,900 | $1,100 |
| February | 16,000 | 15,900 | 100 |
| March | 15,000 | 15,900 | 0 |
| April | 14,000 | 15,900 | 0 |
| May | 13,800 | 15,900 | 0 |
| June | 14,500 | 15,900 | 0 |
| July | 16,000 | 15,900 | 100 |
| August | 16,700 | 15,900 | 800 |
| September | 17,000 | 15,900 | 1,100 |
| October | 18,000 | 15,900 | 2,100 |
| November | 16,000 | 15,900 | 100 |
| December | 15,000 | 15,900 | 0 |
| Monthly Average[c] | | $15,900 | $  450 |

[a]This represents the firm's total funds requirement from column 3 of Table 7.6.

[b]Found by taking the average of the minimum monthly funds requirement of $13,800 (in May) and the maximum monthly funds requirement of $18,000 (in October)—
[($13,800 + $18,000) ÷ 2 = $15,900].

[c]Found by summing the monthly amounts for the 12 months and dividing the resulting totals by 12.

**FIGURE 7.5   Three Alternative Financing Strategies for Berenson Company**

Under the trade-off financing strategy, represented by line 3, Berenson finances $15,900 of its funds need with long-term funds and the remaining seasonal needs with short-term funds. This strategy results in $2,900 of net working capital ($15,900 long-term financing − $13,000 fixed assets).

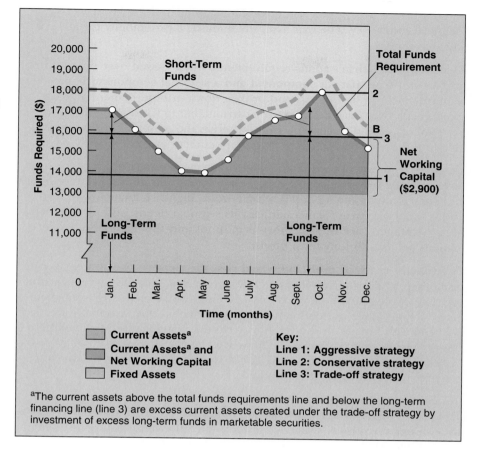

Key:
Current Assets[a]
Current Assets[a] and Net Working Capital
Fixed Assets
Line 1: Aggressive strategy
Line 2: Conservative strategy
Line 3: Trade-off strategy

[a]The current assets above the total funds requirements line and below the long-term financing line (line 3) are excess current assets created under the trade-off strategy by investment of excess long-term funds in marketable securities.

# SUMMARY OF LEARNING GOALS

**LG 1** **Define net working capital using both the common and alternative definitions and discuss its implications.** Net working capital is defined as the difference between current assets and current liabilities, or, alternatively, as the portion of a firm's current assets financed with long-term funds. Firms maintain net working capital to provide a cushion between cash outflows and inflows. Generally the higher the firm's net working capital, the better able it is to pay its bills as they come due.

**LG 2** **Understand the trade-off between profitability and risk as it relates to changing levels of current assets and current liabilities.** Profitability, in this context, is the relationship between revenues and costs. Risk, in the context of short-term financial management, is the probability that a firm will become technically insolvent, that is, unable to pay its bills as they come due. Net working capital is often used to measure this risk. In general, the more liquid a firm is, the higher its net working capital and the lower its risk of technical insolvency. The firm typically trades less profitability for less risk, and vice versa.

**Explain how the firm's funds requirements, when viewed over time, can be broken into a permanent component and a seasonal component.** Financing requirements can be forecast and broken down into permanent and seasonal needs. The permanent need is attributable to fixed assets and the permanent portion of current assets, whereas the seasonal need is attributable to the existence of certain temporary current assets.

LG 3

**Describe, in terms of profitability and risk, the aggressive strategy for determining the firm's financing mix.** The aggressive strategy for determining an appropriate financing mix is a high-profit, high-risk financing strategy under which the firm finances at least its seasonal needs, and possibly some of its permanent needs, with short-term funds and the majority of its permanent needs with long-term funds.

LG 4

**Describe, in terms of profitability and risk, the conservative strategy for determining the firm's financing mix and compare it with the aggressive strategy.** The conservative strategy is a low-profit, low-risk financing strategy under which all funds requirements—both permanent and seasonal—are financed with long-term funds. Short-term financing is saved for emergencies or unexpected outflows. The lower cost of the aggressive strategy makes it more profitable than the conservative strategy. However, the aggressive strategy involves much more risk.

LG 5

**Discuss the trade-off financing strategy that is a compromise between the high-profit, high-risk aggressive strategy and the low-profit, low-risk conservative strategy.** Trade-off strategies result in a compromise between the high-profit, high-risk aggressive strategy and the low-profit, low-risk conservative strategy. As a result, some seasonal needs are financed with long-term funds. The more seasonal needs financed with long-term funds, the lower the profit and risk, and vice versa.

LG 6

After studying this chapter, you should be able to

 **Discuss** the motives for holding cash and marketable securities, estimation of cash balances, and the level of marketable securities investment.

 **Demonstrate,** using the firm's operating and cash conversion cycles, the three basic strategies for the efficient management of cash to minimize financing needs.

 **Explain** float, including its three basic components, and the firm's major objective with respect to the levels of collection float and disbursement float.

 **Review** popular techniques for speeding up collections and slowing down disbursements, the role of strong banking relationships in cash management, and international cash management.

 **Understand** the basic characteristics of marketable securities and the key government issues: Treasury bills, Treasury notes, and federal agency issues.

 **List** and briefly describe the key features of the popular non-government marketable securities: negotiable certificates of deposit, commercial paper, banker's acceptances, Eurodollar deposits, money market mutual funds, and repurchase agreements.

**8**

# Cash and
# Marketable
# Securities

A company requires cash to meet its daily expenses, invest in working capital or fixed assets, and pay a return to its stockholders in the form of dividends. Without adequate cash, you can't operate. Financial managers have the responsibility of maximizing the company's cash flow to efficiently utilize cash to add to the firm's value.

Encyclopaedia Britannica, Inc. is a privately owned, international reference book publisher with revenues of about $540 million. We sell directly to the consumer on an installment sale basis, which creates a significant investment in accounts receivable. The company uses bank and insurance

## Without adequate cash, you can't operate.

company funds to finance that investment. We therefore keep as little idle cash as possible, managing cash very tightly to reduce financing costs.

Forecasting our cash receipts is as uncertain as any other type of forecasting. We receive cash primarily from collections from our installment customers. Our expenses, on the other hand, are relatively easy to determine. The largest items are salaries and commissions, paper purchases, and manufacturing, with the latter two done on a contractual basis.

Britannica processes 150,000 to 400,000 payments each month through our retail lockbox. We convert them into usable funds as quickly as possible. Using bar-coded return envelopes that can be machine-sorted at the post office helps reduce mail float. Our bank picks up mail several times during the night from a post office box to which payments are mailed. Making deposits early is critical; missing a deadline means losing a day of funds availability.

Because paper and printing are Britannica's biggest accounts payable, we want to negotiate favorable payment terms on those contracts. We look at the trade-off. Do we have to pay a higher price to delay payment? The accounts payable department analyzes payment terms offered by other suppliers to decide whether it makes sense to take cash discounts. To manage accounts payable, we use a controlled disbursement system. By 10 AM, the bank tells us the dollar total of checks presented against our account that day. We then transfer funds from our collection account and use financing if a cash deficit occurs. At one time companies stretched out their payables by writing checks on banks in remote locations. Today the Federal Reserve requires most banks to clear checks in one day and clears major checks electronically, minimizing any advantage to that system.

Being an international company adds two more dimensions to our cash management. Within a foreign country, the company must operate its cash system according to local practices.

Britannica has few cross-border transactions. However in countries where we sell encyclopedias we do need systems to receive payments from our many customers. Those systems vary from France's highly sophisticated electronic debit system to the Philippines, where we send representatives on motorcycles to collect some payments. Banking systems vary, too. Italian banks give credit for cash deposits the day *after* they're made and debit an account the date the check was written, not when presented. We also have to understand local customs to forecast overseas cash collections. For example, in Japan worker bonuses are paid at the end of December and June, making January and July big collection months.

**Woodrow Sutton** *joined Encyclopaedia Britannica in 1976 as director of cash management. He was promoted to assistant treasurer in 1979 and treasurer in 1985. From 1971 to 1976 he was an international lender at Central National Bank in Chicago. He received a B.S. in chemistry from Rose Hulman Institute, Terre Haute, Indiana, and his M.B.A. from the University of Chicago. He also studied international finance at the Université de Louvain, Belgium.*

Cash and marketable securities are the most liquid of the firm's assets. **Cash** is the ready currency to which all liquid assets can be reduced. **Marketable securities** are short-term interest-earning money market instruments used by the firm to obtain a return on temporarily idle funds. Together cash and marketable securities act as a pool of funds that can be used to pay bills as they come due and to meet any unexpected outlays.

**cash**
The ready currency to which all liquid assets can be reduced.

**marketable securities**
Short-term interest-earning money market instruments used to obtain a return on temporarily idle funds.

# Cash and Marketable Security Balances

LG 1

Because the rate of interest applied by banks to checking accounts is relatively low, firms tend to use excess bank balances to purchase marketable securities. The firm must therefore determine the appropriate balances for both cash and marketable securities in order to reduce the risk of technical insolvency to an acceptable level. The desired balances are determined by carefully considering the motives for holding them. The higher they are, the lower the risk of technical insolvency, and vice versa.

## Motives for Holding Cash and Near-Cash Balances

There are three motives for holding cash and **near-cash (marketable security)** balances. Each motive is based on two underlying questions: (1) What is the appropriate degree of liquidity to maintain? and (2) What is the appropriate distribution of liquidity between cash and marketable securities?

**near-cash**
Marketable securities viewed the same as cash because of their high liquidity.

**Transactions Motive**   A firm maintains cash balances to satisfy the **transactions motive,** which is to make planned payments for such items as materials and wages. If cash inflows and cash outflows are closely matched, transaction cash balances can be smaller. Although firms *must* achieve this motive, they typically *try to* achieve the following two motives as well.

**transactions motive**
A motive for holding cash or near-cash—to make planned payments for such items as materials and wages.

**Safety Motive**   Balances held to satisfy the **safety motive** are invested in highly liquid marketable securities that can be immediately transferred from securities to cash. Such securities protect the firm against being unable to satisfy unexpected demands for cash.

**safety motive**
A motive for holding cash or near-cash—to protect the firm against being unable to satisfy unexpected demands for cash.

**Speculative Motive**   At times, firms invest in marketable securities in excess of needs, as well as in long-term instruments, to satisfy the safety motive. A firm may do so because it currently has no other use for certain funds, or because it wants to be able to take advantage quickly of unexpected opportunities that may arise. These funds satisfy the **speculative motive,** which is the least common of the three motives.

**speculative motive**
A motive for holding cash or near-cash—to put unneeded funds to work or to be able to take advantage quickly of unexpected opportunities.

## Estimating Cash Balances

Management's goal should be to *maintain levels of transactional cash balances and marketable securities investments that contribute to improving the value of the firm.*

If levels of cash or marketable securities are too high, the profitability of the firm is lower than if more optimal balances were maintained. This concept was examined in the previous chapter in the profitability-risk trade-off discussion. Firms can use either quantitative models or subjective approaches to determine appropriate transactional cash balances. Quantitative cash balance models are beyond the scope of this text. A subjective approach might be to maintain a transactional balance equal to 10 percent of the following month's forecast sales. If the forecast amount of sales for the following month is $500,000, the firm maintains a $50,000 (.10 × $500,000) transactional cash balance.

## The Level of Marketable Securities Investment

In addition to earning a positive return on temporarily idle funds, the marketable securities portfolio serves as a safety stock of cash that can be used to satisfy unexpected demands for funds. The level of the safety stock is the difference between management's desired liquidity level and the level of transactional cash balances determined by the firm. For example, if management wishes to maintain $70,000 of liquid funds and a transactional balance of $50,000 is desired, a $20,000 ($70,000 − $50,000) safety stock of cash is held as marketable securities. The firm may use as safety stocks its prearranged

## FINANCE IN ACTION

### In the News

## Centrex Underwriters and General Reinsurance Offer Security for Bank Deposits

Under the current banking system in the United States, the Federal Deposit Insurance Corporation (FDIC) insures the first $100,000 invested in a given bank regardless of how many accounts a firm might have there. Beyond that sum, the business would be out of luck in all but a few instances. Given the likelihood that some banking institutions will fail this year, businesses may be inclined to look to Centrex Underwriters and General Reinsurance for further security.

Centrex Underwriters is one of the independent property and liability insurers offering coverage on excess marketable securities held at a single bank. The Memphis, Tennessee, insurance company is prepared to write policies on deposits at about eighty percent of the nation's banks. While Centrex has coined the term "depositure" for this type of coverage, other carriers nationwide offer similar products. All policies are reinsured through General Reinsurance, the nation's largest reinsurance group.

With depositure, all bank deposits, including certificates of deposit and mutual fund holdings, are insured up to $5 million per bank. The price of the coverage is .25 percent of the amount covered, or $250 per $100,000. Although seemingly steep given the fewer instances of bank failures in recent years, the coverage eliminates worry about the safety of marketable securities.

Source: Bruce G. Posner, "Security for Bank Deposits," *Inc.*, July 1993, p. 32.

short-term borrowing power (known as a *line of credit,* which is discussed in Chapter 10) instead of a portfolio of marketable securities or a combination of such borrowing power and marketable securities.

## Progress Review Questions

**8-1.** List and describe the three motives for holding cash and near-cash (marketable securities). Which are the most common motives?

**8-2.** What is management's goal with respect to the management of cash and marketable securities?

## The Efficient Management of Cash

LG **2**

Cash balances and safety stocks of cash are significantly influenced by the firm's production and sales techniques and by its procedures for collecting sales receipts and paying for purchases. These influences can be understood better through analysis of the firm's operating and cash conversion cycles.[1] By efficiently managing these cycles, the financial manager can maintain a low level of cash investment and thereby contribute toward maximization of share value.

### The Operating Cycle

The **operating cycle (OC)** of a firm is defined as the amount of time that elapses from the point when the firm inputs material and labor into the production process (i.e., begins to build inventory) to the point when cash is collected from the sale of the finished product that contains these production inputs. The cycle is made up of two components: the average age of inventory and the average collection period of sales. The firm's operating cycle (OC) is simply the sum of the *average age of inventory (AAI)* and the *average collection period (ACP):*

$$OC = AAI + ACP \qquad (8.1)$$

The concept of the operating cycle can be illustrated using a simple example.

**operating cycle (OC)**
The amount of time that elapses from when the firm begins to build inventory to when cash is collected from sale of the resulting finished product.

**Equation 8.1 Expression for calculating the operating cycle**

▶ E X A M P L E

RIF Company, a producer of paper dinnerware, sells all its merchandise on credit. The credit terms require customers to pay within 60 days of a sale. The

[1]The conceptual model used in this part to demonstrate basic cash management strategies was developed by Lawrence J. Gitman in "Estimating Corporate Liquidity Requirements: A Simplified Approach," *The Financial Review,* 1974, pp. 79–88, and refined and operationalized by Lawrence J. Gitman and Kanwal S. Sachdeva in "A Framework for Estimating and Analyzing the Required Working Capital Investment," *Review of Business and Economic Research,* Spring 1982, pp. 35–44.

firm's calculations reveal that, on average, it takes 85 days to manufacture, warehouse, and ultimately sell a finished good. In other words, the firm's average age of inventory (AAI) is 85 days. Calculation of the average collection period (ACP) indicates that it is taking the firm, on average, 70 days to collect its accounts receivable. Substituting AAI = 85 days and ACP = 70 days into Equation 8.1, we find RIF's operating cycle to be 155 days (85 days + 70 days). It is graphically depicted above the time line in Figure 8.1.

## The Cash Conversion Cycle

**cash conversion cycle (CCC)**
The amount of time the firm's cash is tied up between the payment for production inputs and receipt of payment from the sale of the resulting finished product.

A company is usually able to purchase many of its production inputs (i.e., raw materials and labor) on credit. The time it takes the firm to pay for these inputs is called the *average payment period (APP)*. The ability to purchase production inputs on credit allows the firm partially to (or maybe even totally) offset the length of time resources are tied up in the operating cycle. The total number of days in the operating cycle less the average payment period for inputs to production represents the **cash conversion cycle (CCC):**

**Equation 8.2 Expression for calculating the cash conversion cycle**

$$CCC = OC - APP \qquad (8.2)$$
$$= AAI + ACP - APP$$

A continuation of the RIF Company example illustrate this concept.

## EXAMPLE

The credit terms extended the firm for raw material purchases currently require payment within 40 days of a purchase, and employees are paid every 15 days. The firm's calculated weighted average payment period for raw materials and

**FIGURE 8.1  RIF Company's Operating and Cash Conversion Cycles**

The RIF Company's operating cycle of 155 days results from the fact that items are in inventory for an average of 85 days and it takes an average of 70 days to collect accounts receivable. The firm's cash conversion cycle of 120 days results from the fact that cash inflow occurs on day 155 at the end of the operating cycle and cash outflow occurs on day 35, which is the end of the average payment period.

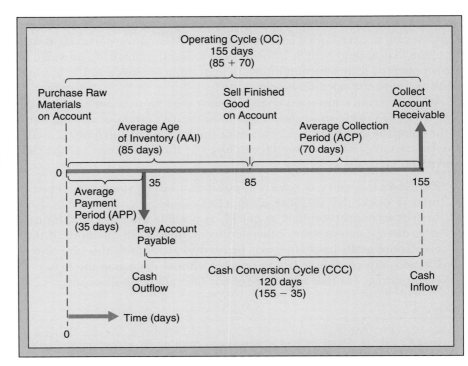

labor is 35 days, which represents the average payment period (APP). Substituting RIF Company's 155-day operating cycle (OC), found in the preceding example, and its 35-day average payment period (APP) into Equation 8.2 results in its cash conversion cycle (CCC):

$$CCC = OC - APP$$
$$= 155 - 35 = 120 \text{ days}$$

RIF Company's cash conversion cycle is graphically depicted below the time line in Figure 8.1. There are 120 days between the *cash outflow* to pay the accounts payable (on day 35) and the *cash inflow* from the collection of the account receivable (on day 155). During this period—the cash conversion cycle—the firm's money is tied up.

## Managing the Cash Conversion Cycle

A *positive* cash conversion cycle, as in the case of RIF Company in the above example, means that the firm must obtain financing (i.e., borrow) to support the cash conversion cycle. This should be obvious from the previous discussion because the cash conversion cycle is the difference between the number of days resources are tied up in the operating cycle and the average number of days the firm can delay making payment on the production inputs purchased on credit.

Ideally, a firm likes to have a *negative* cash conversion cycle. A negative CCC means the average payment period (APP) exceeds the operating cycle (OC) (see Equation 8.2). Manufacturing firms usually do not have negative cash conversion cycles unless they extend their average payment periods an unreasonable length of time, a topic further discussed later. Nonmanufacturing firms are more likely to have negative cash conversion cycles; they generally carry smaller, faster moving inventories and often sell their products for cash. As a result, these firms have shorter operating cycles. These operating cycles may be shorter than the firm's average payment periods, thereby resulting in negative cash conversion cycles. When a firm's cash conversion cycle is negative, the firm should benefit by being able to use the financing provided by the suppliers of its production inputs to help support aspects of the business other than just the operating cycle.

When the cash conversion cycle is positive (the more common case), the firm needs to pursue strategies to minimize the CCC without causing harm to the company in the form of lost sales or the inability to purchase on credit. The basic strategies that should be employed by the firm to manage the cash conversion cycle are as follows:

1. Turn over inventory as quickly as possible, avoiding stockouts (depletions of stock) that might result in a loss of sales.
2. Collect accounts receivable as quickly as possible without losing future sales due to high-pressure collection techniques. Cash discounts, if they are economically justifiable, may be used to accomplish this objective.
3. Pay accounts payable as late as possible without damaging the firm's credit rating, but take advantage of any favorable cash discounts.[2]

---

[2]A discussion of the variables to consider when determining whether to take cash discounts appears in Chapter 10. A cash discount is often an enticement to pay accounts payable early to effectively reduce the purchase price of goods. Strategies for the use of accruals as a free source of short-term financing are also discussed in Chapter 10.

The effects of each of these strategies are described in the following paragraphs using the RIF Company data. The costs of implementing each proposed strategy are ignored; in practice these costs are measured against the calculated savings to make the appropriate strategic decision.

**Efficient Inventory-Production Management**   One strategy available to RIF is to increase inventory turnover. To do so, the firm can increase raw materials turnover, shorten the production cycle, or increase finished goods turnover. Regardless of which of these approaches is used, the result is a reduction in the amount of financing required—that is, the cash conversion cycle is shortened.

## E X A M P L E

If RIF Company manages to increase inventory turnover by reducing the average age of inventory from the current level of 85 days to 70 days—a reduction of 15 days—the effect on the firm can be estimated as follows. Suppose RIF currently spends $12 million annually on operating cycle investments. The daily expenditure is $33,333 (i.e., $12 million ÷ 360 days). Because the cash conversion cycle is reduced 15 days, $500,000 (i.e., $33,333 × 15) of financing can be repaid. If RIF pays 10 percent for its financing, the firm reduces financing costs and thereby increases profit by $50,000 (.10 × $500,000) as a result of managing inventory more efficiently.

**Accelerating the Collection of Accounts Receivable**   Another means of reducing the cash conversion cycle (and the financing need) is to speed up, or accelerate, the collection of accounts receivable. Accounts receivable, like inventory, tie up dollars that could otherwise be used to reduce financing or be invested in earning assets. Let us consider the following example.

## E X A M P L E

If RIF Company, by changing its credit terms, is able to reduce the average collection period from the current level of 70 days to 50 days, it reduces its cash conversion cycle by 20 days (70 days − 50 days) to 100 days (CCC = 120 days − 20 days = 100 days). Again, assume that $12 million is spent annually—$33,333 daily—to support the operating cycle. By improving the management of accounts receivable by 20 days, the firm requires $666,666 (i.e., $33,333 × 20) less in financing. With an interest rate of 10 percent, the firm is able to reduce financing costs and thereby increase profits by $66,666 (.10 × $666,666).

**stretching accounts payable**
Paying the firm's bills as late as possible without damaging its credit rating.

**Stretching Accounts Payable**   A third strategy is **stretching accounts payable**—that is, paying its bills as late as possible without damaging its credit rating. Although this approach is financially attractive, it raises an important ethical issue: clearly, a supplier does not look favorably on a customer who purposely postpones payment.[3]

---

[3]The resolution of this ethical issue is not further addressed in this text. Suffice it to say that although the use of various techniques to slow down payments is widespread due to its financial appeal, it may not be justifiable on purely ethical grounds.

▶ E X A M P L E

If RIF Company can stretch the payment period from the current average of 35 days to an average of 45 days, its cash conversion cycle will be reduced to 110 days (CCC = 85 days + 70 days − 45 days = 110 days). Once more, if operating cycle expenditures total $12 million annually, stretching accounts payable 10 additional days reduces the firm's financing need by $333,333 [($12 million ÷ 360) × 10 days]. With an interest rate of 10 percent, the firm can reduce its financing costs and thereby increase profits by $33,333 (.10 × $333,333).

## Combining Cash Management Strategies

Firms typically do not attempt to implement just one cash management strategy; they attempt to use them all to reduce their financing needs. Of course, when implementing these policies, firms should take care to avoid having a large number of inventory stockouts, to avoid losing sales due to the use of high-pressure collection techniques, and to not damage the firm's credit rating by overstretching accounts payable. Using a combination of these strategies has the following effects on RIF Company.

▶ E X A M P L E

If RIF simultaneously decreased the average age of inventory by 15 days, sped the collection of accounts receivable by 20 days, and increased the average payment period by 10 days, its cash conversion cycle would be reduced to 75 days, as shown here.

| | | |
|---|---|---|
| Initial cash conversion cycle | | 120 days |
| Reduction due to: | | |
| 1. Decreased inventory age 85 days to 70 days = | 15 days | |
| 2. Decreased collection period 70 days to 50 days = | 20 days | |
| 3. Increased payment period 35 days to 45 days = | 10 days | |
| Less: Total reduction in cash conversion cycle | | 45 days |
| New cash conversion cycle | | 75 days |

The 45-day reduction in RIF Company's cash conversion cycle means that it can reduce its financing needs. If annual expenditures for operations are $12 million, then financing can be reduced by $1.5 million [($12 million ÷ 360 days) × 45 days]. If the company pays 10 percent interest on its financing, then it is able to save $150,000 (i.e., .10 × $1,500,000) through improved management of the cash conversion cycle.

▼▼▼▼▼▼▼▼▼▼▼▼▼▼▼▼▼▼▼▼▼▼▼▼▼▼▼▼▼▼▼▼▼

## Progress Review Questions

**8-3.** What is the firm's *operating cycle?* What is the *cash conversion cycle?* Compare and contrast them. What is the firm's objective with respect to each of them?

**8-4.** What are the *key strategies* with respect to inventory, accounts receivable, and accounts payable for the firm that wants to manage its cash conversion cycle efficiently?

**8-5.** If a firm reduces the average age of its inventory, what effect might this action have on the cash conversion cycle? On the firm's total sales? Is there a trade-off between average inventory and sales? Give reasons for your answer.

▲▲▲▲▲▲▲▲▲▲▲▲▲▲▲▲▲▲▲▲▲▲▲▲▲▲▲▲▲▲▲▲▲

# Cash Management Techniques

Financial managers have at their disposal a variety of cash management techniques that can provide additional savings. These techniques are aimed at minimizing the firm's financing requirements by taking advantage of certain imperfections in the collection and payment systems. Assuming that the firm has done all it can to stimulate customers to pay promptly and has selected vendors offering the most attractive and flexible credit terms, certain techniques can further speed collections and slow disbursements. These procedures take advantage of the "float" existing in the collection and payment systems.

## Float

**float**
Funds dispatched by a payer that are not yet in a form that can be spent by the payee.

In the broadest sense, **float** refers to funds that have been dispatched by a payer (the firm or individual *making* payment) but are not yet in a form that can be spent by the payee (the firm or individual *receiving* payment). Float also exists when a payee has received funds in a spendable form but these funds have not been withdrawn from the account of the payer. Delays in the collection-payment system resulting from the transportation and processing of checks are responsible for float. With electronic payment systems as well as deliberate action by the Federal Reserve system, it seems clear that in the foreseeable future float will virtually disappear. Until that time, however, financial managers must continue to understand and take advantage of float.

**collection float**
The delay between the time a payer deducts a payment from its checking account ledger and the time the payee actually receives the funds in a spendable form.

**disbursement float**
The lapse between the time a firm deducts a payment from its checking account ledger (disburses it) and the time funds are actually withdrawn from its account.

**Types of Float**   Currently business firms and individuals can experience both collection and disbursement float as part of the process of making financial transactions. **Collection float** results from the delay between the time that a payer or customer deducts a payment from its checking account ledger and the time that the payee or vendor actually receives these funds in a spendable form. Thus collection float is experienced by the payee and is a delay in the receipt of funds. **Disbursement float** results from the lapse between the time that a firm deducts a payment from its checking account ledger (disburses it) and the time that funds are actually withdrawn from its account. Disbursement float is experienced by the payer and is a delay in the actual withdrawal of funds.

**mail float**
The delay between the time a payer mails a payment and the time the payee receives it.

**Components of Float**   Both collection float and disbursement float have the same three basic components:

1. **Mail float:** The delay between the time that a payer places payment in the mail and the time that it is received by the payee.

2. **Processing float:** The delay between the receipt of a check by the payee and the deposit of it in the firm's account.

3. **Clearing float:** The delay between the deposit of a check by the payee and the actual availability of the funds. This component of float is attributable to the time required for a check to clear the banking system. It is important to note that the use of new electronic methods to process checks within the banking system continues to reduce clearing float.

Figure 8.2 illustrates the key components of float resulting from a check issued and mailed by the payer company to the payee company on day zero. The entire process required a total of nine days: three days' mail float; two days' processing float; and four days' clearing float. To the payer company, the delay is disbursement float; to the payee company, the delay is collection float.

## Speeding Up Collections

The firm's objective is not only to stimulate customers to pay their accounts as promptly as possible but also to convert their payments into a spendable form as quickly as possible—in other words, to *minimize collection float.* A variety of techniques aimed at *speeding up collections,* and thereby reducing collection float, are available.

**Concentration Banking**    Firms with sales outlets throughout the country often designate certain offices as collection centers for given geographic areas. Customers in these areas send their payments to these sales offices, which in turn deposit the receipts in local banks. At certain times, or on a when-needed basis, funds are transferred by wire from these regional banks to a concentration, or disbursing, bank. Bill payments are dispatched from there.

**Concentration banking** is used to reduce collection float by shortening the mail and clearing float components. Mail float is reduced because regionally dispersed collection centers bring the collection point closer to the point from which the check is sent. Clearing float should also be reduced because the payee's regional bank is likely to be in the same Federal Reserve district or the same city as the bank on which the check is drawn; it may even be the same bank. A reduction in clearing float, of course, makes funds available to the firm more quickly.

▶ E X A M P L E

Suppose Style, Inc., a hair products manufacturer, can go to concentration banking and reduce its collection period by three days. If the company normally carried $10 million in receivables and that level represented 30 days of sales, cutting 3 days from the collection process results in a $1 million decline in receivables [$(3 \div 30) \times \$10,000,000$]. Given a 10 percent opportunity cost, the gross annual benefits (profits) of concentration banking amount to $100,000 ($.10 \times \$1,000,000$). Clearly, assuming no change in risk, so long as total annual costs (*incremental* administrative costs and bank service fees, and the opportunity cost of holding specified minimum bank balances) are less than the expected annual benefits of $100,000, Style, Inc.'s proposed program of concentration banking should be implemented.

**processing float**
The delay between the receipt of a check by the payee and its deposit in the firm's account.

**clearing float**
The delay between the deposit of a check by the payee and the actual availability of the funds.

**concentration banking**
A collection procedure in which payments are made to regionally disbursed collection centers, then deposited in local banks for quick clearing.

**FIGURE 8.2   Float Resulting from a Check Issued and Mailed by the Payer Company to the Payee Company**

On a check issued by the payer company to the payee company it takes three days (mail float) to reach the payee. The payee then takes two days (processing float) to process the check and deposit it in its account where it takes four days (clearing float) to clear the banking system and become spendable funds. A total of nine days (total float) therefore results from this transaction.

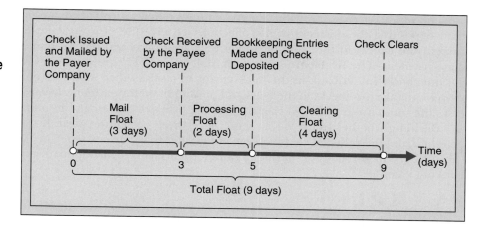

**lockbox system**
A collection procedure in which payers send payments to a nearby post office box from which the firm's bank empties and deposits payment checks in its account several times daily.

**Lockboxes**   Another method used to reduce collection float is the **lockbox system,** which differs from concentration banking in several important ways. Instead of mailing payment to a collection center, the payer sends it to a post office box that is emptied by the firm's bank one or more times each business day. The bank opens the payment envelopes, deposits the checks in the firm's account, and sends a deposit slip (or, under certain arrangements, a computer file) indicating the payments received, along with any enclosures, to the collecting firm. Lockboxes normally are geographically dispersed, and the funds, when collected, are wired from each lockbox bank to the firm's disbursing bank.

The lockbox system is superior to concentration banking because it reduces processing float as well as mail and clearing float. The receipts are immediately deposited in the firm's account by the bank so that processing occurs after, rather than before, funds are deposited in the firm's account. This allows the firm to use the funds almost immediately for disbursing payments. Additional reductions in mail float may also result because payments do not have to be delivered but are picked up by the bank at the post office.

## E X A M P L E

Davidson Products, a manufacturer of disposable razors, has annual credit sales of $6 million, which are billed at a constant rate each day. It takes about four days to receive customers' payments at corporate headquarters. It takes another day for the credit department to process receipts and deposit them in the bank. A cash management consultant has told Davidson that a lockbox system would shorten the mail float from four days to a day and a half and completely eliminate the processing float. The lockbox system would cost the firm $8,000 per year. Davidson currently earns 12 percent on investments of comparable risk. The lockbox system would free $58,333 of cash [(($6 million ÷ 360 days) × (4 days mail float + 1 day processing float − 1½ days mail float)] that is currently tied up in mail and processing float. The gross annual benefit would be $7,000 (.12 × $58,333). Because the $7,000 gross annual benefit is less than the $8,000 annual cost, Davidson should *not* use the lockbox.

**Direct Sends**   To reduce clearing float, firms that have received large checks drawn on distant banks, or a large number of checks drawn on banks in a given city, may arrange to present these checks directly for payment to the bank on which they are drawn. Such a procedure is called a **direct send.** Rather than depositing these checks in its collection account, the firm arranges to present the checks to the bank on which they are drawn and receive immediate payment. The firm can use Express Mail or private express services to get the checks into a bank in the same city or to a sales office where an employee can take the checks to the bank and present them for payment. In most cases the funds are transferred via wire into the firm's disbursement account.

Deciding whether to use direct sends is relatively straightforward. If the benefits from the reduced clearing time are greater than the cost, the checks should be sent directly for payment rather than cleared through normal banking channels.

**direct send**
A collection procedure in which the payee presents payment checks directly to the banks on which they are drawn.

▶ E X A M P L E

If a firm with an opportunity to earn 10 percent on its idle balances can, through a direct send, make available $1.2 million three days earlier than otherwise is the case, the benefit of this direct send is $1,000 [.10 × (3 days ÷ 360 days) × $1,200,000]. If the cost of achieving this three-day reduction in float is less than $1,000, the direct send is recommended.

**Other Techniques**    A number of other techniques can be used to reduce collection float. One method commonly used by firms that collect a fixed amount from customers on a regular basis, such as insurance companies, is the preauthorized check. A **preauthorized check (PAC)** is a check written against a customer's checking account for a previously agreed-on amount by the firm to which it is payable. Because the check has been legally authorized by the customer, it does not require the customer's signature. The payee merely issues and then deposits the PAC in its account. The check clears through the banking system just as if it were written by the customer and received and deposited by the firm.

A method used by firms with multiple collection points to speed up the transfer of funds is the depository transfer check. A **depository transfer check (DTC)** is an unsigned check drawn on one of the firm's bank accounts and deposited into its account at another bank—typically a concentration or major disbursing bank. Once the DTC has cleared the bank on which it is drawn, the actual transfer of funds is completed. Most firms currently transmit deposit information via telephone rather than by mail to their concentration banks, which then prepare and deposit DTCs into the firm's accounts.

Firms frequently use wire transfers to reduce collection float by quickly transferring funds from one bank account to another. **Wire transfers** are telegraphic communications that, via bookkeeping entries, remove funds from the payer's bank and deposit them into the payee's bank. Wire transfers can eliminate mail and clearing float and may provide processing float reductions as well. They are sometimes used instead of DTCs to move funds into key disbursing accounts, although a wire transfer is more expensive than a DTC.

Another popular method of accelerating cash inflows involves the use of **automated clearinghouse (ACH) debits.** These are preauthorized electronic withdrawals from the payer's account. A computerized clearing facility (called an automated clearinghouse, or ACH) makes a paperless transfer of funds between the payer and payee banks. An ACH settles accounts among participating banks. Individual depositor accounts are settled by respective bank balance adjustments. ACH transfers clear in one day, in most cases reducing mail, processing, and clearing float.

**preauthorized check (PAC)**
A check written by the payee against a customer's checking account for a previously agreed-upon amount.

**depository transfer check (DTC)**
An unsigned check drawn on one of the firm's bank accounts and deposited into its account at a concentration or major disbursement bank.

**wire transfers**
Telegraphic communications that, via bookkeeping entries, remove funds from the payer's bank and deposit them into the payee's bank.

**automated clearinghouse (ACH) debits**
Preauthorized electronic withdrawals from the payer's account, which are then transferred to the payee's account via a settlement among banks by the automated clearinghouse.

# Slowing Down Disbursements

The firm's objective relative to accounts payable is not only to pay its accounts as late as possible but also to slow down the availability of funds to suppliers and employees once the payment has been dispatched—in other words, to *maximize disbursement float.* A variety of techniques aimed at *slowing down disbursements,* and thereby increasing disbursement float, are available.

### Controlled Disbursing

**controlled disbursing**
The strategic use of mailing points and bank accounts to lengthen mail float and clearing float, respectively.

**Controlled disbursing** involves the strategic use of mailing points and bank accounts to lengthen mail float and clearing float, respectively. When the date of postmark is considered the effective date of payment by the supplier, the firm may be able to lengthen the mail time associated with disbursements. It can place payments in the mail at locations from which it is known they take a considerable time to reach the supplier. Typically, small towns not close to major highways and cities provide excellent opportunities to increase mail float. Of course, the benefits of using selected mailing points may not justify the costs of this strategy, particularly in light of the fact that the U.S. Postal Service gives rate reductions on mail that is presorted by ZIP code and sent from designated major post offices.

The widespread availability of computers and data on check clearing times allows firms to develop disbursement schemes that maximize clearing float on their payments. These methods involve assigning payments going to vendors in certain geographic areas to be drawn on specific banks from which maximum clearing float results.

### Playing the Float

**playing the float**
A method of consciously anticipating the resulting delay associated with the payment process and using it to keep funds in an interest-earning form for as long as possible.

**Playing the float** is a method of consciously anticipating the resulting float, or delay, associated with the payment process. Firms often play the float by writing checks against funds not currently in their checking accounts. They are able to do this because they know a delay occurs between issuing checks to suppliers and the actual withdrawal of funds from their checking accounts. It is likely that the firm's bank account will not be drawn down by the amount of the payments for a number of days. Although the ineffective use of this practice can result in problems associated with "bounced" checks, many firms use float to stretch out their accounts payable.

**staggered funding**
Depositing a certain proportion of a payroll or payment into the firm's checking account on several successive days *following* the actual issuance of checks.

Firms play the float in a variety of ways—all of which are aimed at keeping funds in an interest-earning form for as long as possible. For example, one way of playing the float is to deposit a certain proportion of a payroll or payment into the firm's checking account on several successive days *following* the actual issuance of a group of checks. This technique is commonly referred to as **staggered funding.** If the firm can determine from historic data that only 25 percent of its payroll checks are cashed on the day immediately following the issuance of the checks, then only 25 percent of the value of the payroll needs to be in its checking account one day later. The amount of checks cashed on each of several succeeding days can also be estimated, until the entire payroll is accounted for. Normally, however, to protect itself against any irregularities a firm places slightly more money in its account than is needed to cover the expected withdrawals.

### Overdraft Systems, Zero-Balance Accounts, and ACH Credits

**overdraft system**
Automatic coverage by the bank of all checks presented against the firm's account, regardless of the account balance.

Firms that aggressively manage cash disbursements often arrange for some type of overdraft system or a zero-balance account. In an **overdraft system,** if the firm's checking account balance is insufficient to cover all checks presented against the account, the bank automatically lends the firm enough money to cover the amount of the overdraft. The bank, of course, charges the firm interest on the funds lent and limits the amount of overdraft coverage. Such an arrangement is important for a business that actively plays the float.

Firms can also establish **zero-balance accounts**—checking accounts in which zero balances are maintained. Under this arrangement, each day the bank notifies the firm of the total amount of checks presented against the account. The firm then transfers only that amount—typically from a master account or through liquidation of a portion of its marketable securities—into the account. Once the corresponding checks have been paid, the account balance reverts to zero. The bank, of course, is paid for this service.

**Automated clearinghouse (ACH) credits** are frequently used by corporations for making direct bank deposits of payroll into the payees' (employees') accounts. Disbursement float is sacrificed with this technique because ACH transactions immediately draw down the company's payroll account on payday. The benefit of ACH credits is that employees enjoy convenience, which the firm hopes generates enough goodwill to justify its loss of float.

**zero-balance account**
A checking account in which a zero balance is maintained and the firm is required to deposit funds to cover checks drawn on the account only as they are presented for payment.

**automated clearinghouse (ACH) credits**
Deposits of payroll directly into the payees' (employees') accounts.

## The Role of Strong Banking Relationships

Establishing and maintaining strong banking relations is one of the most important elements in an effective cash management system. Banks have become keenly aware of the profitability of corporate accounts. In recent years banks have developed a number of innovative services and packages designed to attract various types of businesses. No longer are banks simply a place to establish checking accounts and secure loans; instead, they have become the source of a wide variety of cash management services. For example, banks are selling sophisticated information-processing packages to commercial clients. These packages are designed to help financial managers maximize day-to-day cash availability and facilitate short-term investing.

Today most bank services are offered to corporations on a direct-fee basis, but some of the depository functions are still paid for with deposit balances rather than direct charges. Banks prefer the "compensating balance" approach—giving credit against bank service charges for amounts maintained in the customer's checking account. This approach fosters deposit growth and provides a foundation for the future growth of bank earnings. Of course, bank services should be used only when the benefits to be derived from them are greater than their costs.

## International Cash Management

Although the motivations for holding cash balances and the basic concepts underlying optimal cash management are the same worldwide, dramatic differences exist in practical cash management techniques for international versus strictly domestic business transactions. In fact, the differences between U.S. and international banking and payment systems are so great that only an elementary comparison can be made here. More detailed information about payments and cash management systems abroad can be found in textbooks on international finance or short-term financial (working capital) management.

### Differences in Banking Systems

**Giro system**
System through which retail transactions are handled in association with a foreign country's national postal system.

**value dating**
A procedure used by non-U.S. banks to delay, often for days or even weeks, the availability of funds deposited within them.

**Differences in Banking Systems**    Banking systems outside the United States differ fundamentally from the U.S. model in several key aspects. First, foreign banks are generally far less restricted either geographically or in the services they are allowed to offer. Second, retail transactions are typically routed through a **Giro system** that is usually operated by, or in association with, the national postal system. Because of this direct payment system, checks are used much less frequently than in the United States. Third, banks in other countries are allowed to pay interest on corporate demand deposits, and they also routinely provide overdraft protection. To recoup the cost of these services, however, non-U.S. banks generally charge more and higher fees for services and also engage in the practice of **value dating.** This involves delaying, often for days or even weeks, the availability of funds deposited with the bank. This lag between the date funds are deposited and when they are usable obviously complicates cash management procedures, and if a transaction involves collecting on a foreign-currency-denominated check drawn on a bank outside of the host country, the delay in availability of good funds can be very long indeed.

**Cash Management Practices**    The cash management practices of multinational corporations are made more complicated by the need both to main-

## FINANCE IN ACTION

**International**

### Citibank Helps Old World Industries Expedite Collection and Transfer of Funds from China

Old World Industries, a Northbrook, Illinois, automotive products manufacturer, experienced problems collecting foreign funds from Chinese customers and transferring them to the U.S. Sometimes this process took as long as 18 months. Given the risks of operating in a foreign country, Old World Industries needed to expedite collection and transfer of funds to the United States. Consequently, in 1993, Old World Industries sought to replace the Bank of China as its banker.

The problem arose when Old World Industries' credit manager simply assumed that the Bank of China could handle funds transfers to the U.S. Much to Old World's chagrin, the Bank of China is a network of provincial banks and some do not have foreign-exchange capabilities. Old World Industries' solution was to work with a bank headquartered in the United States that had the following capabilities.

1. **Strong international presence**: Although Citicorp was chosen because of its massive overseas network, other banks often can provide sufficient services.
2. **Technical expertise**: Citibank was able to recommend collection and transfer strategies that were acceptable in different cultures.
3. **Services**: Citibank's offerings were reviewed with a local international accounting firm to verify the appropriateness of services offered.

Source: Jill Andrewsky Fraser, "Rushing Your Cash Home," *Inc.,* November 1993, p. 137.

tain local currency deposit balances in banks in every country in which the firm operates and to retain centralized control over cash balances and cash flows that, in total, can reach several billion dollars. The largest multinational corporations have honed their treasury operations to such an extent that they can balance these conflicting objectives efficiently and even profitably. To do so, they rely on the cash collection, disbursement, and foreign-exchange trading expertise of large international banks, all of which operate very sophisticated computerized treasury services.

Multinational firms can also minimize their cash requirements by using an **intracompany netting technique.** For example, when two subsidiaries in different countries trade with each other—thereby generating payment obligations to each other—only the net amount of payment owed is transferred across national boundaries. In fact, it may be possible to handle many of these transactions strictly internally (on the books of the parent company) without having to resort to the international payments system at all.

When it becomes necessary to make large international cash payments, these are almost invariably handled by one of the wire transfer services operated by international banking consortia. The most important of these networks is the **Clearing House Interbank Payment System (CHIPS).** It has been estimated that over $600 billion worth of payments are settled *every day* using wire transfer and settlement services. Although the bulk of these transactions result from foreign exchange trading, many are also due to settlement of international payment obligations.

Multinational companies with excess funds to invest benefit from having access to a wide variety of government and corporate investment vehicles. Companies naturally have access to all of the marketable securities offered to U.S. investors (described in the following section). Multinational companies can also invest funds in foreign government securities, or they can invest directly in the *Eurocurrency market* either in dollars or in other convertible currencies. This financial flexibility often provides multinational corporations with a key competitive advantage, particularly if they need to transfer funds into or out of countries experiencing political or financial difficulties.

**intracompany netting technique**
A technique used by multinational firms to minimize their cash requirements by transferring across national boundaries, at maximum, the net amount of payments owed between them. Sometimes bookkeeping entries are substituted for international payments.

**Clearing House Interbank Payment System (CHIPS)**
The most important wire transfer service; it is operated by international banking consortia.

▼▼▼▼▼▼▼▼▼▼▼▼▼▼▼▼▼▼▼▼▼▼▼▼▼▼▼▼▼▼▼▼▼

# Progress Review Questions

**8-6.** Define *float* and describe its three basic components. Compare and contrast collection and disbursement float, and state the financial manager's goal with respect to each of these types of float.

**8-7.** Briefly describe the key features of each of the following techniques for speeding up collections:
  **a.** Concentration banking
  **b.** Lockboxes
  **c.** Direct sends
  **d.** Preauthorized checks (PACs)
  **e.** Depository transfer checks (DTCs)
  **f.** Wire transfers
  **g.** Automated clearinghouse (ACH) debits

**8-8.** Briefly describe the key features of each of the following techniques for slowing down disbursements:
   **a.** Controlled disbursing
   **b.** Playing the float
   **c.** Overdraft systems
   **d.** Zero-balance accounts
   **e.** Automated clearinghouse (ACH) credits

**8-9.** Describe the role of strong banking relationships in the cash management process. How should available bank services be evaluated?

**8-10.** Describe the key differences between banking systems outside of the United States and the U.S. model. What is *value dating*, and how does it affect international cash management?

**8-11.** What is an *intracompany netting technique*, and what is its purpose? What is *CHIPS*, and what role does it play in the international payment system?

# Marketable Securities

*Marketable securities* are short-term, interest-earning, money market instruments that can easily be converted into cash.[4] Marketable securities are classified as part of the firm's liquid assets. The securities most commonly held as part of the firm's marketable securities portfolio are divided into two groups: (1) government issues and (2) nongovernment issues. Before describing the popular government and nongovernment marketable securities, we discuss the basic characteristics of marketable securities and making purchase decisions. Table 8.1 summarizes the key features and recent (July 27, 1994) yields for the marketable securities described in the following sections.

## Characteristics of Marketable Securities

**breadth of a market**
A characteristic of a ready market, determined by the number of participants (buyers) in the market.

**depth of a market**
A characteristic of a ready market, determined by its ability to absorb the purchase or sale of a large dollar amount of a particular security.

The characteristics of marketable securities affect the degree of their salability. To be truly marketable, a security must have two basic characteristics: (1) a ready market and (2) safety of principal (no likelihood of loss in value).

**A Ready Market**   The market for a security should have both breadth and depth to minimize the amount of time required to convert it into cash. The **breadth of a market** is determined by the number of participants (buyers). A broad market is one that has many participants. The **depth of a market** is determined by its ability to absorb the purchase or sale of a large dollar amount of a particular security. It is therefore possible to have a broad market

---

[4]As explained in Chapter 2, the *money market* results from a financial relationship between the suppliers and demanders of short-term funds, that is, marketable securities.

## TABLE 8.1   Features and Recent Yields on Popular Marketable Securities[a]

| Security | Issuer | Description | Initial Maturity | Risk and Return | Yield on July 27, 1994[b] |
|---|---|---|---|---|---|
| **Government Issues** | | | | | |
| Treasury bills | U.S. Treasury | Issued weekly at auction. Sold at a discount. Strong secondary market. | 91 days, 182 days, occasionally 1 year | Lowest, virtually risk free | 4.43% |
| Treasury notes | U.S. Treasury | Stated interest rate. Interest paid semiannually. Strong secondary market. | 1–10 years | Low, but slightly higher than U.S. Treasury bills. | 4.45 |
| Federal agency issues | Agencies of federal government | Not an obligation of U.S. Treasury. Strong secondary market. | 9 months– 30 years | Slightly higher than U.S. Treasury issues | 4.63[c] |
| **Nongovernment Issues** | | | | | |
| Negotiable certificates of deposit (CDs) | Commercial banks | Represent specific cash deposit in commercial banks. Amounts and maturities tailored to-investor needs. Large denominations. Good secondary market. | 1 month– 3 years | Higher than U.S. Treasury issues and comparable to commercial paper | 4.68 |
| Commercial paper | Corporation with a high credit standing | Unsecured note of issuer. Large denominations | 3–270 days | Higher than U.S Treasury issues and comparable to negotiable CDs | 4.74 |
| Banker's acceptances | Banks | Results from a bank guarantee of a business transaction. Sold at discount from maturity value. | 30–180 days | Slightly lower than negotiable CDs and commercial paper but higher than U.S. Treasury issues | 4.62 |
| Eurodollar deposits | Foreign banks | Deposits of currency not native to the country in which the bank is located. Large denominations. Active secondary market. | 1 day–3 years | Highest, due to less regulation of depository banks and some foreign exchange risk | 4.81 |
| Money market mutual funds | Professional portfolio management companies | Professionally managed portfolios of marketable securities. Provide instant liquidity. | None— depends on wishes of investor | Vary, but generally higher than U.S. Treasury issues and comparable to negotiable CDs and commercial paper | 3.76[d] |
| Repurchase agreements | Bank or security dealer | Bank or security dealer sells specific securities to firm and agrees to repurchase them at a specific price and time. | Customized to purchaser's needs | Generally slightly below that associated with the outright purchase of the security | |

[a]The prime rate of interest at this time was 7.25%.

[b]Yields obtained for three-month maturities of each security.

[c]A Federal Home Loan Bank (FHLB) issue maturing in October 1994 is used here in the absence of any average-yield data.

[d]The Paine Webber Cash Fund with an average maturity of 36 days is used here in the absence of any average-yield data.

Source: *The Wall Street Journal*, July 28, 1994, pp. C16, C18, C20.

that has no depth. Thus 100,000 participants each willing to purchase 1 share of a security is less desirable than 1,000 participants each willing to purchase 2,000 shares. Although both breadth and depth are desirable, for a security to be salable it is much more important for a market to have depth.

**Safety of Principal (No Likelihood of Loss in Value)**   There should be little or no loss in the value of a marketable security over time. Consider a security recently purchased for $1,000. If it can be sold quickly for $500, does that make it marketable? No. According to the definition of marketability, the security not only must be salable quickly, but also must be salable for close to the $1,000 initially invested. This aspect of marketability is referred to as **safety of principal.** Only securities that can be easily converted into cash without any appreciable reduction in principal are candidates for short-term investment.

> **safety of principal**
> The ease of salability of a security for close to its initial value.

## Making Purchase Decisions

A major decision confronting the business firm is when to purchase marketable securities. This decision is difficult because it involves a trade-off between the opportunity to earn a return on idle funds during the holding period and the brokerage costs associated with the purchase and sale of marketable securities.

## E X A M P L E

◀

Assume that a firm must pay $35 in brokerage costs to purchase and sell $4,500 worth of marketable securities yielding an annual return of 8 percent that will be held for one month. Because the securities are to be held for $\frac{1}{12}$ of a year, the firm earns interest of .67 percent ($\frac{1}{12} \times 8\%$) or $30 (.0067 $\times$ $4,500). Because the interest return is less than the $35 cost of the transaction, the firm should *not* make the investment. This trade-off between interest returns and brokerage costs is a key factor in determining when and whether to purchase marketable securities.

◀

## Government Issues

The short-term obligations issued by the federal government and available as marketable security investments are Treasury bills, Treasury notes, and federal agency issues. These securities have relatively low yields due to their low risk and the fact that the interest income on all Treasury issues and most federal agency issues, although taxable at the federal level, is exempt from state and local taxes.

> **Treasury bills**
> U.S. Treasury obligations issued weekly on an auction basis, having varying maturities, generally under one year, and virtually no-risk.

**Treasury Bills**   **Treasury bills** are obligations of the U.S. Treasury that are issued weekly on an auction basis. The most common maturities are 91 and 182 days, although bills with one-year maturities are occasionally sold. Treasury bills are sold by competitive bidding. Because they are issued in bearer form, there is a strong *secondary (resale) market*. The bills are sold at a discount from their face value (the face value being received at maturity). The smallest denomination of a Treasury bill currently available is $10,000. Because Treasury bills are issues of the U.S. government, they are considered to be virtually risk-free. For this reason, and because of the strong secondary market for them, Treasury bills are one of the most popular marketable securities. The yields on Treasury bills are generally lower than those on any other marketable securities due to their virtually risk-free nature and favorable tax status.

**Treasury Notes**    **Treasury notes** have initial maturities of between 1 and 10 years. Due to the existence of a strong secondary market, they are quite attractive marketable security investments. They are generally issued in minimum denominations of either $1,000 or $5,000, carry a coupon interest rate, and pay interest semiannually. A firm that purchases a Treasury note that has less than one year left to maturity is in the same position as if it had purchased a marketable security with an initial maturity of less than one year. Due to their virtually risk-free nature and favorable tax status, Treasury notes generally have a low yield relative to other securities with similar maturities.

**treasury notes**
U.S. Treasury obligations with initial maturities of between 1 and 10 years, paying interest at a stated rate semiannually, and having virtually no risk.

**Federal Agency Issues**    Certain agencies of the federal government issue their own debt. These **federal agency issues** are not part of the public debt, are not a legal obligation of the U.S. Treasury, and are not guaranteed by the U.S. Treasury. Regardless of their lack of direct government backing, the issues of government agencies are readily accepted as low-risk securities because most purchasers feel they are implicitly guaranteed by the federal government. Agency issues generally have minimum denominations of $1,000 or more and are issued either with a stated interest rate or at a discount. Agencies commonly issuing short-term instruments include the Farm Credit Banks (FCB), the Federal Home Loan Banks (FHLB), and the Federal National Mortgage Association (FNMA). Of course, rather than buying agency issues with short initial maturities, other longer term agency issues with less than one year to maturity can be purchased. Most agency issues offer slightly higher yields than U.S. Treasury issues having similar maturities. Agency issues have a strong secondary market, which is most easily reached through government security dealers.

**federal agency issues**
Low-risk securities issued by government agencies but not guaranteed by the U.S. Treasury, having short maturities, and offering slightly higher yields than comparable U.S. Treasury issues.

## Nongovernment Issues

A number of additional marketable securities are issued by banks or businesses. These nongovernment issues typically have slightly higher yields than government issues with similar maturities due to the slightly higher risks associated with them and the fact that their interest income is taxable at all levels—federal, state, and local. The principal nongovernment marketable securities are negotiable certificates of deposit, commercial paper, banker's acceptances, Eurodollar deposits, money market mutual funds, and repurchase agreements.

**Negotiable Certificates of Deposit**    **Negotiable certificates of deposit (CDs)** are negotiable instruments representing the deposit of a certain number of dollars in a commercial bank. The amounts and maturities are normally tailored to the investor's needs. Average maturities of 30 days are quite common. A good secondary market for CDs exists. Normally the smallest denomination for a negotiable CD is $100,000. (Nonnegotiable CDs can be purchased for smaller amounts.) The yields on CDs are initially set on the basis of size, maturity, and prevailing money market conditions. They are typically above those on U.S. Treasury issues and comparable to the yields on commercial paper with similar maturities.

**negotiable certificates of deposit (CDs)**
Negotiable instruments representing specific cash deposits in commercial banks, having varying maturities and yields based on size, maturity, and prevailing money market conditions.

**commercial paper**
Short-term, unsecured promissory note issued by a corporation with a very high credit standing.

**Commercial Paper**  **Commercial paper** is a short-term, unsecured promissory note issued by a corporation with a very high credit standing.[5] These notes are issued, generally in multiples of $100,000, by all types of firms and have initial maturities of anywhere from 3 to 270 days. They can be sold directly by the issuer or through dealers. The yield on commercial paper typically is above that paid on U.S. Treasury issues and is comparable to that available on negotiable CDs with similar maturities.

**banker's acceptances**
Short-term, low-risk marketable securities arising from bank guarantees of business transactions.

**Banker's Acceptances**  **Banker's acceptances** arise from a short-term credit arrangement used by businesses to finance transactions, especially those involving firms in foreign countries or firms with unknown credit capacities. The purchaser, to ensure payment to the seller, requests its bank to issue a *letter of credit* on its behalf, authorizing the seller to draw a *time draft*—an order to pay a specified amount at a specified time—on the bank in payment for the goods. Once the goods are shipped, the seller presents a time draft along with proof of shipment to its bank. The seller's bank then forwards the draft with appropriate shipping documents to the buyer's bank for acceptance and receives payment for the transaction. The buyer's bank may either hold the acceptance to maturity or sell it at a discount in the money market. If sold, the size of the discount from the acceptance's maturity value and the amount of time until the acceptance is paid determine the purchaser's yield.

As a result of its sale, the banker's acceptance becomes a marketable security that can be traded in the marketplace. The initial maturities of banker's acceptances are typically between 30 and 180 days; 90 days is most common. A banker's acceptance is a low-risk security because at least two, and sometimes three, parties may be liable for its payment at maturity. The yields on banker's acceptances are generally slightly below those on negotiable CDs and commercial paper, but generally higher than those on U.S. Treasury issues with similar maturities.

**Eurodollar deposits**
Negotiable deposits of currency not native to the country in which the bank is located.

**Eurodollar Deposits**  **Eurodollar deposits** are deposits of currency that are not native to the country in which the bank is located. London is the center of the Eurodollar market. Other important centers are Paris, Frankfurt, Zurich, Nassau (Bahamas), Singapore, and Hong Kong. Nearly 75 percent of these deposits are in the form of U.S. dollars. The deposits are negotiable, usually pay interest at maturity, and are typically denominated in units of $1 million. Maturities range from overnight to several years, with most of the money in the one-week to six-month maturity range. Eurodollar deposits tend to provide yields above nearly all other marketable securities, government or nongovernment, with similar maturities. These higher yields are attributable to (1) the fact that the depository banks are generally less closely regulated than U.S. banks and are therefore more risky, and (2) some foreign-exchange risk may be present. An active secondary market allows Eurodollar deposits to be used to meet all three motives for holding cash and near-cash balances.

**money market mutual funds**
Professionally managed portfolios of various popular marketable securities.

**Money Market Mutual Funds**  **Money market mutual funds,** often called *money funds,* are professionally managed portfolios of marketable securities such as those described earlier. Shares or interests in these funds can be easily

---

[5]The role of commercial paper from the point of view of the issuer is included in the discussion of the various sources of short-term financing available to business in Chapter 10.

acquired—often without paying any brokerage commissions. A minimum initial investment of as low as $500, but generally $1,000 or more, is required. Money funds provide instant liquidity, much like a checking or savings account. In exchange for investing in these funds, investors earn returns that are typically comparable to or above those obtainable from negotiable CDs and commercial paper. Note that during recent years the generally low interest rates have caused many fund returns to fall below those on most other marketable securities. Due to the high liquidity, competitive yields, and often low transaction costs, these funds have achieved significant growth in size and popularity in recent years.

**Repurchase Agreements**   A **repurchase agreement** is not a specific security. It is an arrangement whereby a bank or security dealer sells specific marketable securities to a firm and agrees to buy them back at a specific price at a specified future time. In exchange for the tailor-made maturity date provided by this arrangement, the bank or security dealer provides a return slightly below that obtainable through outright purchase of similar marketable securities. The benefit to the purchaser is the guaranteed repurchase, and the tailor-made maturity date ensures that the purchaser will have cash at a specified future time. The actual securities involved may be government or nongovernment issues. Repurchase agreements are ideal for marketable securities investments made to satisfy the transactions motive.

**repurchase agreement**
An agreement whereby a bank or security dealer sells a firm specific securities and agrees to buy them back at a specific price and time.

# Progress Review Questions

**8-12.** What two characteristics are deemed essential for a security to be marketable? Which aspect of a market for a security is more important—breadth or depth? Why?

**8-13.** Discuss the two reasons why government issues of marketable securities have generally lower yields than nongovernment issues with similar maturities.

**8-14.** For each of the following government-backed marketable securities, give a brief description emphasizing issuer, initial maturity, liquidity, risk, and return.
 **a.** Treasury bill
 **b.** Treasury note
 **c.** Federal agency issue

**8-15.** Describe the basic features, including issuer, initial maturity, liquidity, risk, and return, of each of the following nongovernment marketable securities:
 **a.** Negotiable certificate of deposit (CD)
 **b.** Commercial paper
 **c.** Banker's acceptance
 **d.** Eurodollar deposit

**8-16.** Briefly describe the basic features of the following marketable securities and explain how they both involve other marketable securities:
 **a.** Money market mutual fund
 **b.** Repurchase agreement.

# SUMMARY OF LEARNING GOALS

 **1** **Discuss the motives for holding cash and marketable securities, estimation of cash balances, and the level of marketable securities investment.** The three motives for holding cash and near-cash (marketable security) balances are: (1) the transactions motive, (2) the safety motive, and (3) the speculative motive. Management's goal should be to maintain levels of transactional cash balances and marketable securities investments that contribute to improving the value of the firm.

**2** **Demonstrate, using the firm's operating and cash conversion cycles, the three basic strategies for the efficient management of cash to minimize financing needs.** The efficient management of cash is affected by the firm's operating and cash conversion cycles. Ideally, management wants to minimize the length of these cycles without jeopardizing profitability. The three basic strategies for managing the cash conversion cycle to achieve this objective are (1) turning over inventory as quickly as possible, (2) collecting accounts receivable as quickly as possible, and (3) paying accounts payable as late as possible without damaging the firm's credit rating. Employment of these strategies should reduce the firm's cash conversion cycle and financing need, thereby improving its profitability.

**3** **Explain float, including its three basic components, and the firm's major objective with respect to the levels of collection float and disbursement float.** Float refers to funds that have been dispatched by a payer (the firm or individual *making* payment) but are not yet in a form that can be spent by the payee (the firm or individual *receiving* payment). Both collection and disbursement float have the same three basic components: (1) mail float, (2) processing float, and (3) clearing float. The firm's major objective with respect to float is to minimize collection float and maximize disbursement float within reasonable limits.

**4** **Review popular techniques for speeding up collections and slowing down disbursements, the role of strong banking relationships in cash management, and international cash management.** Popular collection techniques include concentration banking, lockboxes, direct sends, preauthorized checks (PACs), depository transfer checks (DTCs), wire transfers, and automated clearinghouse (ACH) debits. Disbursement techniques include controlled disbursing, playing the float, overdraft systems, zero-balance accounts, and automated clearinghouse (ACH) credits. Establishing and maintaining strong banking relationships is crucial for effective cash management. Dramatic differences between foreign and domestic banking systems exist and result in more complex cash management practices for international firms than for purely domestic firms.

**5** **Understand the basic characteristics of marketable securities and the key government issues: Treasury bills, Treasury notes, and federal agency issues.** Marketable securities allow the firm to earn a return on temporarily idle funds. For a security to be considered marketable, it must have a ready market that has both breadth and depth. Furthermore, the risk associated with the safety of principal must be quite low. The decision to purchase marketable securities depends on the trade-off between the return earned during the holding period and the brokerage costs associated with purchasing and selling the securities. Government issue marketable securities are Treasury bills, Treasury notes, and federal agency issues. Table 8.1 summarizes the key features and recent yields for each of these marketable securities. These securities have relatively low yields due to their low risk and the fact that interest income on all Treasury issues and most federal agency issues, although taxable at the federal level, is exempt from state and local taxes.

**List and briefly describe the key features of the popular nongovernment marketable securities: negotiable certificates of deposit, commercial paper, banker's acceptances, Eurodollar deposits, money market mutual funds, and repurchase agreements.** Nongovernment issues include negotiable certificates of deposit (CDs), commercial paper, banker's acceptances, Eurodollar deposits, money market mutual funds, and repurchase agreements. Table 8.1 summarizes the key features and recent yields for each of these marketable securities. These securities have slightly higher yields than government issues with similar maturities due to the slightly higher risks associated with them and the fact that their interest income is taxable at all levels—federal, state, and local.

# SUMMARY OF KEY DEFINITIONS AND EQUATIONS

## Variable Definitions

AAI = average age of inventory
ACP = average collection period
APP = average payment period
CCC = cash conversion cycle
OC = operating cycle

## Equations

Operating cycle

$$OC = AAI + ACP$$   [Eq. 8.1]

Cash conversion cycle

$$CCC = OC - APP$$   [Eq. 8.2]

$$= AAI + ACP - APP$$

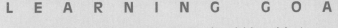

**C H A P T E R**

**L E A R N I N G   G O A L S**

After studying this chapter, you should be able to

 **LG 1** Discuss the key aspects of credit selection, including the five C's of credit, obtaining credit information, analyzing credit information, credit scoring, and managing international credit.

 **LG 2** Understand how to isolate and measure the key variables and use them to evaluate quantitatively the effects of either relaxing or tightening a firm's credit standards.

 **LG 3** Review the three components of a firm's credit terms, the effects of changes in each of them on key variables and profits, and the procedure for evaluating the quantitative effects of proposed cash discount changes.

 **LG 4** Explain the key features of collection policy, including aging accounts receivable, the basic trade-offs, and the types of collection techniques.

 **LG 5** Understand the types of inventory, differing viewpoints about inventory level, inventory as an investment, the relationship between inventory and accounts receivable, and international inventory management.

 **LG 6** Describe the common techniques for managing inventory, including the ABC system, the basic economic order quantity (EOQ) model, the reorder point, the materials requirement planning (MRP) system, and the just-in-time (JIT) system.

# Accounts Receivable and Inventory

Accounts receivable and inventory represent a significant investment for a company. With careful management, these accounts can improve a company's profits, cash flow, and value. Hunter Industries, a 10-year old manufacturer of irrigation products, has about 95 percent of current assets and 26 percent of total assets tied up in these two accounts.

> ... Careful management [of accounts receivable and inventory] can improve a company's profits, cash flow, and value.

Hunter sells its products through an established network of distributors with whom we have an ongoing relationship. The way we manage receivables and inventory is therefore very important to the firm's long-term success.

Receivables arise when a company sells on credit to its customers. In essence, the customer gets a short-term loan. Until recently, Hunter offered a 10 percent discount for payment within 15 days. Encouraging prompt payment improved our cash flow.

Currently our customers get a 5 percent discount for payment within 30 days. These longer terms were due in part to the economic downturn, but they still offer a strong incentive to pay early.

Although the sales, marketing, and finance departments share the same strategic goals—improving profits, cash flow, and value—a natural conflict arises among their objectives. Sales and marketing want to offer liberal credit terms to help build sales volume. Finance wants low accounts receivable and inventories and policies that result in a quick conversion to cash. Sales wants to ship products; finance wants outstanding bills paid first. To minimize problems, we educate the sales and marketing staff on financial issues so they understand the financial side of the business and see how proposed programs affect financial performance. Over time, they have become more conservative, developing programs that also help meet financial objectives.

On the inventory side, three departments work together to determine Hunter's investment in inventory. The finance department uses the sales forecast and production plans to project inventory levels, factoring in the seasonality of the irrigation industry. Inventory peaks in December and January as we get ready for the major selling season— May through August. Hunter has annual sales promotions to encourage customers to order and take shipment early. These promotions help to even out the production cycle and get our products on the shelves first.

About 20 percent of Hunter's sales are international. Selling abroad requires awareness of different business customs and potential communication problems from dealing across time zones and in other languages. International accounts tend to pay more slowly, and monitoring their receivables is harder. Hunter offers longer terms for international sales. Because we sell in dollars to non-U.S. distributors, we avoid foreign exchange risk. Export versions of our products differ from domestic ones, so we have separate international inventories. Despite the complexities of doing business worldwide, in today's increasingly global economy a company can't afford to ignore international markets.

*Sherry Dunn joined Hunter Industries in 1990 as controller and was promoted to vice-president, finance in January 1994. Her previous experience includes two years as controller for Artecon, a computer peripherals manufacturer, and three years in public accounting at Arthur Andersen. She is a CPA and has a B.A. in finance and accounting from San Diego State University.*

*A*ccounts *receivable* represent the extension of credit by the firm to its customers. *Inventory,* or goods on hand, is a necessary current asset that permits the production-sale process to operate with a minimum of disturbance. Accounts receivable and inventory are the dominant current assets held by most firms. For the average manufacturer, together they account for about 79 percent of *current assets* and about 34 percent of *total assets.* The firm's financial manager generally has direct control over accounts receivable; he or she must act as a "watchdog" and adviser in matters concerning inventory, which is generally under the direct control of the firm's manufacturing department. In the following sections we examine the important aspects of accounts receivable followed by a brief discussion of inventory.

# Credit Selection

LG    1

The accounts receivable of the average manufacturer account for over 37 percent of *current assets* and nearly 16 percent of *total assets.* The extension of credit by most manufacturers is a cost of doing business. The firm, by keeping its money tied up in accounts receivable, loses the use of that money and runs the risk of non-payment by its customers. In return for incurring these costs, however, the firm can be competitive, attract and retain customers, and improve and maintain sales and profits.

Accounts receivable are most often directly controlled by the firm's financial manager through involvement in the establishment and management of (1) **credit policy,** which includes determining credit selection, credit standards, and credit terms, and (2) **collection policy,** which is the set of procedures for collecting accounts receivable when they are due. The firm's approach to managing each of these aspects of accounts receivable is heavily influenced by competitive conditions—typically greater leniency enhances competition, and vice versa. Here we discuss credit selection; in the following sections we look at credit standards, credit terms, and collection policy.

A firm's **credit selection** activity involves deciding whether to extend credit to a customer and how much credit to extend. Appropriate *sources of credit information* and *methods of credit analysis* must be developed. Each of these aspects of credit policy is important to the successful management of accounts receivable. First we look at the five C's of credit, which are the traditional focus of credit investigation.

**credit policy**
The determination of credit selection, credit standards, and credit terms.

**collection policy**
The procedures for collecting a firm's accounts receivable when they are due.

**credit selection**
The decision whether to extend credit to a customer and how much credit to extend.

## The Five C's of Credit

A firm's credit analysts often use the **five C's of credit** to determine an applicant's creditworthiness. They analyze these five dimensions—character, capacity, capital, collateral, and conditions—as follows:

**five C's of credit**
The five key dimensions—character, capacity, capital, collateral, and conditions—used by credit analysts to determine an applicant's creditworthiness.

1. *Character:* The applicant's record of meeting past obligations: financial, contractual, and moral. Past payment history as well as any pending or resolved legal judgments against the applicant are used to evaluate its character.

2. *Capacity:* The applicant's ability to repay the requested credit. Financial statement analysis (see Chapter 4) with particular emphasis on liquidity and debt ratios is typically used to assess the applicant's capacity.

3. *Capital:* The financial strength of the applicant as reflected by its ownership position. Analysis of the applicant's debt relative to equity and its profitability ratios are frequently used to assess its capital.

4. *Collateral:* The amount of assets the applicant has available for use in securing the credit. The larger the amount of available assets, the greater the chance a lender will recover its funds if the applicant defaults. A review of the applicant's balance sheet, asset value appraisals, and any legal claims filed against the applicant's assets can be used to evaluate its collateral.

5. *Conditions:* The current economic and business climate as well as any unique circumstances affecting either party to the credit transaction. For example, if the lender has excess inventory of the item the applicant wishes to purchase on credit, it may be willing to sell on more favorable terms or to less creditworthy applicants. The effect of general economic and business conditions, as well as special circumstances on the applicant or firm, are analyzed to assess conditions.

The credit analyst typically gives primary attention to the first two C's—character and capacity—because they represent the most basic requirements for extending credit to an applicant. Consideration of the last three C's—capital, collateral, and conditions—is important in structuring the credit arrangement and making the final credit decision, which is affected by the credit analyst's experience and judgment.

## Obtaining Credit Information

When a business is approached by a customer desiring credit terms, the credit department typically begins the evaluation process by requiring the applicant to fill out various forms requesting financial and credit information and references. Working from the application, the firm obtains additional information from other sources. If the firm has previously extended credit to the applicant, it has its own information on the applicant's payment history. The major external sources of credit information are as follows:

**Financial Statements**   With the credit applicant's financial statements for the past few years, the firm can analyze the applicant firm's liquidity, activity, debt, and profitability positions.

**Dun & Bradstreet (D&B)**
The largest mercantile credit-reporting agency in the United States.

**Dun & Bradstreet**   **Dun & Bradstreet (D&B)** is the largest mercantile credit-reporting agency in the United States. It provides subscribers with a copy of its *Reference Book,* which contains credit ratings and keyed estimates of overall financial strength for virtually millions of U.S. and international companies. The key to the D&B ratings is shown in Figure 9.1. For example, a firm rated 2A3 has an estimated financial strength (net worth) in the range of $750,000 to $999,999 and has a *fair* credit appraisal. D&B subscribers can also purchase detailed reports on specific companies and electronic access to D&B's database of business information through its *Electronic Access Systems.*

| Key to Ratings | | | | | | |
|---|---|---|---|---|---|---|
| Estimated Financial Strength | | | Composite Credit Appraisal | | | |
| | | | High | Good | Fair | Limited |
| 5A | $50,000,000 | and over | 1 | 2 | 3 | 4 |
| 4A | $10,000,000 to | 49,999,999 | 1 | 2 | 3 | 4 |
| 3A | 1,000,000 to | 9,999,999 | 1 | 2 | 3 | 4 |
| 2A | 750,000 to | 999,999 | 1 | 2 | 3 | 4 |
| 1A | 500,000 to | 749,999 | 1 | 2 | 3 | 4 |
| BA | 300,000 to | 499,999 | 1 | 2 | 3 | 4 |
| BB | 200,000 to | 299,999 | 1 | 2 | 3 | 4 |
| CB | 125,000 to | 199,999 | 1 | 2 | 3 | 4 |
| CC | 75,000 to | 124,999 | 1 | 2 | 3 | 4 |
| DC | 50,000 to | 74,999 | 1 | 2 | 3 | 4 |
| DD | 35,000 to | 49,999 | 1 | 2 | 3 | 4 |
| EE | 20,000 to | 34,999 | 1 | 2 | 3 | 4 |
| FF | 10,000 to | 19,999 | 1 | 2 | 3 | 4 |
| GG | 5,000 to | 9,999 | 1 | 2 | 3 | 4 |
| HH | Up to | 4,999 | 1 | 2 | 3 | 4 |

**DUN & BRADSTREET**
**Information Services**
DB a company of
The Dun & Bradstreet Corporation

**FIGURE 9.1  The Key to Dun & Bradstreet's Ratings**
The rating key used in the *Dun & Bradstreet Reference Book* indicates both the estimated financial strength and a composite credit appraisal for each rated firm. A rating of 2A3 indicates an estimated financial strength (net worth) between $750,000 and $999,999 and a *fair* credit appraisal.

**Credit Interchange Bureaus**    The National Credit Interchange System is a national network of local credit bureaus that exchange information. The reports obtained through these exchanges contain factual data rather than analyses. A fee is usually levied for each inquiry.

**Direct Credit Information Exchanges**    Often, local, regional, or national trade associations serve as clearinghouses for credit information that is supplied by and made available to their member companies. Another approach is to contact other suppliers selling to the applicant and obtain information on the applicant's payment history.

**Bank Checking**    It may be possible for the firm's bank to obtain credit information from the applicant's bank. However, the type of information obtained will most likely be vague, unless the applicant helps the firm obtain it. Typically, an estimate of the firm's cash balance is provided. For instance, the bank may indicate that the applicant normally maintains a "high five-figure" balance in its checking account.

## Analyzing Credit Information

Firms typically establish set procedures for use in **credit analysis**—the evaluation of credit applicants. Often the firm not only must determine the creditworthiness of a customer but also must estimate the maximum amount of

**credit analysis**
The evaluation of credit applicants.

# FINANCE IN ACTION

## Insuring Accounts Receivable with Dun & Bradstreet

What can be done if a client cannot or will not pay its bill? A technique that is gaining acceptance in the United States is credit insurance. In Europe, the technique is almost as common as property and liability insurance. Carriers of accounts receivable insurance have found it sells well to businesses seeking ways to preserve their capital from the ravages of uncollectible accounts.

New in the United States, accounts receivable insurance is rapidly becoming a means of obtaining a bank loan backed by receivables. Credit insurance increases the quality of accounts receivable, making it possible to borrow as much as 90 percent of the accounts receivable balance. Bankers especially like clients to have credit insurance when the business relies on only a few accounts.

Dun & Bradstreet's American Credit Indemnity (ACI) division is the biggest carrier of credit insurance. ACI targets firms with revenues ranging from $5 to $150 million and insures both domestic and foreign receivables. Continental Insurance and Fidelity and Deposit insure businesses with sales as low as $1 million. Whereas Continental Insurance services firms in food, electronic, and retail industries, Fidelity and Deposit focuses on firms in the food, lumber, and paper industries. Premiums run from 0.1 to 0.5 percent of the amount covered and are tax-deductible.

Source: Bruce G. Posner, "How to Impress a Banker," *Inc.*, November 1993, p. 135.

---

**line of credit**
The maximum amount a credit customer can owe the lending firm at any one time.

credit the customer is capable of supporting. Once this is done, the firm can establish a **line of credit,** the maximum amount the customer can owe the firm at any given time. Lines of credit are established to eliminate the necessity of checking a major customer's credit each time a large purchase is made. We now consider procedures for analyzing credit information, the economic considerations involved in such analyses, and the small business problem.

**Procedures**   A credit applicant's financial statements and accounts payable ledger can be used to calculate its "average payment period." This value can be compared with the credit terms currently extended to the firm. For customers requesting large amounts of credit or lines of credit, a thorough ratio analysis of the firm's liquidity, activity, debt, and profitability should be performed using the relevant financial statements. A time-series comparison (discussed in Chapter 4) of similar ratios for various years should uncover any developing trends. The *Dun & Bradstreet Reference Book* can be used for estimating the maximum line of credit to extend. Dun & Bradstreet suggests no more than 10 percent of a customer's "estimated financial strength" (see Figure 9.1).

One of the key inputs to the final credit decision is the credit analyst's *subjective judgment* of a firm's creditworthiness. Experience provides a "feel" for the nonquantifiable aspects of the quality of a firm's operations. The analyst adds his or her knowledge of the character of the applicant's management, references from other suppliers, and the firm's historic payment patterns to any quantitative figures developed to determine creditworthiness. The analyst then makes the final decision as to whether to extend credit to the applicant and possibly what amount of credit to extend. Often these decisions are made not by one individual but by a credit review committee.

**Economic Considerations**   Whereas a firm would be unwise to spend $100 to investigate the creditworthiness of a customer making a one-time $40 purchase, $100 for a credit investigation may be a good investment in the case of a customer expected to make credit purchases of $60,000 annually. Clearly, the firm's credit selection procedures must be established on a sound economic basis that considers the costs and benefits of obtaining and analyzing credit information.

**The Small Business Problem**   Management of accounts receivable is one of the biggest financial problems facing small businesses. These firms typically lack the appropriate personnel and processes needed to make informed credit decisions. In addition they are eager to increase sales volumes through the extension of credit, sometimes at the expense of bad debts. Frequently for small firms, their credit customers are other local businesses managed by personal friends, which makes denying credit particularly difficult. However, the credit decision must be made on the basis of sound financial and business principles. Clearly, it is better to have a potential credit customer get upset than for excessive uncollectible receivables to bankrupt the firm.

## Credit Scoring

Consumer credit decisions, because they involve a large group of similar applicants, each representing a small part of the firm's total business, can be handled using impersonal, computer-based credit decision techniques. One popular technique is **credit scoring.** This procedure results in a score that measures an applicant's overall credit strength, derived as a weighted average of the scores obtained on a variety of key financial and credit characteristics. Credit scoring is often used by large credit card operations, such as oil companies and department stores.

**credit scoring**
A measure of an applicant's overall credit strength, derived as a weighted average of scores on key financial and credit characteristics.

▶ E X A M P L E

Paula's Stores, a major regional department store chain, uses a credit scoring model to make its consumer credit decisions. Each credit application is reviewed and scored by one of the company's credit analysts, and then the relevant information is entered into the computer. The rest of the process, including making the credit decision, generating a letter of acceptance or rejection to the applicant, and dispatching the preparation and mailing of a credit card, is automated.

Table 9.1 demonstrates the calculation of Herb Conseca's credit score. The firm's predetermined credit standards are summarized in Table 9.2. The cutoff credit scores were developed to accept the group of credit applicants

**TABLE 9.1   Credit Scoring of Herb Conseca by Paula's Stores**

| Financial and Credit Characteristics | Score (0–100) (1) | Predetermined Weight (2) | Weighted Score [(1) × (2)] (3) |
|---|---|---|---|
| Credit references | 80 | .15 | 12.00 |
| Home ownership | 100 | .15 | 15.00 |
| Income range | 70 | .25 | 17.50 |
| Payment history | 75 | .25 | 18.75 |
| Years at address | 90 | .10 | 9.00 |
| Years on job | 80 | .10 | 8.00 |
| | Total | 1.00 | Credit score  80.25 |

*Key:* Column 1: Scores assigned by analyst or computer using company guidelines on the basis of data presented in credit application. Scores range from 0 (lowest) to 100 (highest). Column 2: Weights based on the company's analysis of the relative importance of each financial and credit characteristic in predicting whether or not a customer will pay an account. The sum of these weights must be 1.00.

that will result in a positive contribution to the firm's share value. In evaluating Herb Conseca's credit score of 80.25 in light of the firm's credit standards, Paula's decides to *extend standard credit terms* to him (80.25 > 75).

The attractiveness of credit scoring should be clear from the previous example. Unfortunately, most manufacturers sell to a diversified group of different-sized businesses, not to individuals. The statistical characteristics necessary for applying credit scoring to decisions regarding *mercantile credit*— credit extended by business firms to other business firms—rarely exist. After the discussion of international credit management concerns, we concentrate on the basic concepts of mercantile credit decisions, which cannot easily be expressed in quantifiable terms.

## Managing International Credit

Credit management is difficult enough for managers of purely domestic companies, but these tasks become much more complex for companies that

**TABLE 9.2   Credit Standards for Paula's Stores**

| Credit Score | Action |
|---|---|
| Greater than 75 | Extend standard credit terms. |
| 65 to 75 | Extend limited credit; if account is properly maintained, convert to standard credit terms after one year. |
| Less than 65 | Reject application. |

operate internationally. This is partly because international operations typically expose a firm to **exchange rate risk**—the chance that an unfavorable change occurs in the *exchange rate* between the dollar and a specified foreign currency. International operations also expose the firm to risk due to the dangers and delays involved in shipping goods long distances and having to cross at least two international borders.

**exchange rate risk**
The chance that an unfavorable change occurs in the *exchange rate* between the dollar and a specified foreign currency.

Exports of finished goods are usually denominated in the currency of the importer's local market; most commodities, on the other hand, are denominated in dollars. Therefore, a company that sells a product in, for example, France has to price that product in French francs and extend credit to a French wholesaler in the local currency (francs). If the franc *depreciates* against the dollar before the U.S. exporter collected on its account receivable, the U.S. company experiences an exchange rate loss because the francs collected are worth fewer dollars than expected at the time the sale was made. Of course, the dollar could just as easily depreciate against the franc, yielding an exchange rate gain to the U.S. exporter, but most companies fear the loss more than they welcome the gain.

For a major currency like the French franc, the exporter can protect against this risk, but it is costly to do so, particularly for relatively small amounts. If the exporter is selling to a customer in a developing country—where 40 percent of U.S. exports are now sold—there is probably no effective instrument available for protecting against exchange rate risk, at any price. This risk may be further magnified because credit standards (and acceptable collection techniques) may be much lower in developing countries than in the United States. Although it may seem tempting to just "not bother" with exporting, U.S. companies no longer have the luxury of conceding foreign markets to international rivals. These export sales, if carefully monitored and, where possible, effectively protected against exchange rate risk, often prove to be very profitable. Novice or infrequent exporters may choose to rely on third parties, known as *factors* (see Chapter 10), to manage their international export (credit) sales. Although expensive, these firms are typically much better at evaluating the creditworthiness of foreign customers and are better able to bear credit risk than are most small exporters.

▼▼▼▼▼▼▼▼▼▼▼▼▼▼▼▼▼▼▼▼▼▼▼▼▼▼▼▼▼▼▼

# Progress Review Questions

**9-1.** What do the *accounts receivable* of a firm typically represent? What is meant by a firm's *credit policy*? What is meant by a firm's *collection policy*?

**9-2.** What does the *credit selection* activity include? Briefly list, define, and discuss the role of the *five C's of credit* in this process.

**9-3.** Summarize the basic sources of credit information? What procedures are commonly used to analyze credit information?

**9-4.** How do economic considerations affect the depth of credit analysis performed by a firm on a potential credit customer? Explain why the management of accounts receivable is one of the biggest financial problems facing small business.

**9-5.** Describe *credit scoring* and explain why this technique is typically applied to consumer credit decisions rather than to mercantile credit decisions.

**9-6.** Describe why the risks involved in international credit management are more complex than those associated with purely domestic credit sales.

▲▲▲▲▲▲▲▲▲▲▲▲▲▲▲▲▲▲▲▲▲▲▲▲▲▲▲▲▲▲▲▲▲▲

 LG 2

# Changing Credit Standards

**credit standards**
The minimum requirements for extending credit to a customer.

The firm's **credit standards** are the minimum requirements for extending credit to a customer. Understanding the key variables that must be considered when a firm is contemplating relaxing or tightening its credit standards gives a general idea of the kinds of decisions involved.

## Key Variables

The major variables that should be considered when evaluating proposed changes in credit standards are (1) sales volume, (2) the investment in accounts receivable, and (3) bad debt expenses. Let us examine each in more detail.

**Sales Volume**   Changing credit standards can be expected to change the volume of sales. If credit standards are relaxed, sales are expected to increase; if credit standards are tightened, sales are expected to decrease. Generally, increases in sales affect profits positively, whereas decreases in sales affect profits negatively.

**Investment in Accounts Receivable**   Carrying, or maintaining, accounts receivable involves a cost to the firm. This cost is the forgone earnings opportunities resulting from tying up funds in accounts receivable. Therefore, the higher the firm's investment in accounts receivable, the greater the carrying cost, and vice versa. If the firm relaxes its credit standards, the volume of accounts receivable increases and so does the firm's carrying cost (increased investment). This change results from increased sales and longer collection periods due to slower payment on average by credit customers. The opposite occurs if credit standards are tightened. Thus a relaxation of credit standards is expected to affect profits negatively due to higher carrying costs; tightening credit standards affects profits positively as a result of lower carrying costs.

**Bad Debt Expenses**   The probability, or risk, of acquiring a bad debt increases as credit standards are relaxed. The increase in bad debts associated with relaxation of credit standards raises bad debt expenses and has a negative effect on profits. Tightening credit standards reduces bad debt expenses and has a positive effect on profits.

The basic changes and effects on profits resulting from the *relaxation* of credit standards are shown in the table below. If credit standards are tightened, the opposite effects can be expected.

| Variable | Direction of Change | Effect on Profits |
|---|---|---|
| Sales volume | Increase | Positive |
| Investment in accounts receivable | Increase | Negative |
| Bad debt expenses | Increase | Negative |

## Determining Values of Key Variables

The way in which the key credit standard variables are determined can be illustrated by the following example.

▶ E X A M P L E

Binz Tool, a manufacturer of small tools, is currently selling a tool for $10. Sales (all on credit) for last year were 60,000 units. The variable cost per unit is $6. The firm's total fixed costs are $120,000.

The firm is currently contemplating a *relaxation of credit standards* that is expected to result in a 5 percent increase in unit sales to 63,000, an increase in the average collection period from its current level of 30 days to 45 days, and an increase in bad debt expenses from the current level of 1 percent of sales to 2 percent. The firm's required return on equal-risk investments, which is the opportunity cost of tying up funds in accounts receivable, is 15 percent.

To determine whether to implement the proposed relaxation of credit standards, Binz Tool must calculate the effect on the firm's additional profit contribution from sales, the cost of the marginal investment in accounts receivable, and the cost of marginal bad debts.

**Additional Profit Contribution from Sales**   The additional profit contribution from sales expected from the relaxation of credit standards can be calculated easily. Because fixed costs are unaffected by a change in the sales level, the only cost relevant to a change in sales is out-of-pocket, or variable costs. Sales are expected to increase by 5 percent, or 3,000 units. The profit contribution per unit equals the difference between the sale price per unit ($10) and the variable cost per unit ($6). The profit contribution per unit is therefore $4. Thus the total additional profit contribution from sales is $12,000 (3,000 units × $4 per unit).

**Cost of the Marginal Investment in Accounts Receivable**   The cost of the marginal investment in accounts receivable can be calculated by finding the difference between the cost of carrying receivables before and after the introduction of the relaxed credit standards. Because our concern is only with the out-of-pocket costs rather than fixed costs (which are unaffected by this decision), *the relevant cost in this analysis is the variable cost.* The average investment in accounts receivable $(A/R)$[1] can be calculated using the following formula:

**Equation 9.1 Expression for the average investment in accounts receivable**

$$\text{Average investment in accounts receivable} = \frac{\text{total variable cost of annual sales}}{\text{turnover of accounts receivable}} \quad (9.1)$$

where

$$\text{Turnover of accounts receivable} = \frac{360}{\text{average collection period}}$$

The total variable cost of annual sales under the proposed and present plans can be found as noted below.

*Total variable cost of annual sales:*

Under proposed plan: ($6 × 63,000 units) = $378,000

Under present plan: ($6 × 60,000 units) = $360,000

The calculation of the total variable cost for both plans involves the straightforward use of the variable cost per unit of $6. The total variable cost under the proposed plan is $378,000, and under the present plan it is $360,000. Therefore, implementation of the proposed plan causes the total variable cost of annual sales to increase from $360,000 to $378,000.

The turnover of accounts receivable refers to the number of times each year the firm's accounts receivable are actually turned into cash. In each case it is found by dividing the average collection period into 360—the number of days in a year.[2]

*Turnover of accounts receivable:*

$$\text{Under proposed plan: } \frac{360}{45} = 8$$

$$\text{Under present plan: } \frac{360}{30} = 12$$

With implementation of the proposed plan, the accounts receivable turnover slows from 12 to 8 times per year.

Substituting the cost and turnover data just calculated into Equation 9.1 for each case, the following average investments in accounts receivable result:

*Average investment in accounts receivable:*

$$\text{Under proposed plan: } \frac{\$378,000}{8} = \$47,250$$

$$\text{Under present plan: } \frac{\$360,000}{12} = \$30,000$$

---

[1]Throughout the text, A/R is often used interchangeably with *accounts receivable.*

[2]The turnover of accounts receivable can also be calculated by *dividing annual sales by accounts receivable.* For the purposes of this chapter, only the formula transforming the average collection period to a turnover of accounts receivable is emphasized.

The marginal investment in accounts receivable as well as its cost are calculated as follows:

*Cost of marginal investment in accounts receivable:*

| | |
|---|---:|
| Average investment under proposed plan | $47,250 |
| − Average investment under present plan | 30,000 |
| Marginal investment in accounts receivable | $17,250 |
| × Required return on investment | .15 |
| Cost of marginal investment in A/R | $ 2,588 |

The cost of investing an additional $17,250 in accounts receivable was found by multiplying this marginal investment by 15 percent (the firm's required return on investment). The resulting value of $2,588 is considered a cost because it represents the maximum amount that could have been earned on the $17,250 had it been placed in the best equal-risk investment alternative available.

**Cost of Marginal Bad Debts**   The cost of marginal bad debts is found by taking the difference between the level of bad debts before and after the relaxation of credit standards, as shown here.

*Cost of marginal bad debts:*

| | |
|---|---:|
| Under proposed plan: | |
| (.02 × $10/unit × 63,000 units) | $12,600 |
| Under present plan: | |
| (.01 × $10/unit × 60,000 units) | 6,000 |
| Cost of marginal bad debts | $ 6,600 |

Note that the bad debt costs are calculated using the sale price per unit ($10) to take into account not just the true loss of variable (or out-of-pocket) cost ($6) that results when a customer fails to pay its account, but also the profit contribution per unit—in this case $4 ($10 sale price − $6 variable cost)—that is included in the "additional profit contribution from sales." Thus the resulting cost of marginal bad debts is $6,600.

## Making the Credit Standard Decision

To decide whether the firm should relax its credit standards, the additional profit contribution from sales must be compared with the sum of the cost of the marginal investment in accounts receivable and the cost of marginal bad debts. If the additional profit contribution is greater than marginal costs, credit standards should be relaxed; otherwise, present standards should remain unchanged. Let us look at an example.

# ▶ E X A M P L E

The results and key calculations relative to Binz Tool's decision to relax its credit standards are summarized in Table 9.3. The additional profit contribution from the increased sales is $12,000. This amount exceeds the sum of the cost of the marginal investment in accounts receivable and the cost of

---

**TABLE 9.3 The Effects on Binz Tool of a Relaxation of Credit Standards**

Additional profit contribution from sales
 [3,000 units × ($10 − $6)] .......................................... $12,000

Cost of marginal investment in A/R[a]

 Average investment under proposed plan:
 $$\frac{(\$6 \times 63,000)}{8} = \frac{\$378,000}{8}$$ .......... $47,250

 Average investment under present plan:
 $$\frac{(\$6 \times 60,000)}{12} = \frac{\$360,000}{12}$$ .......... 30,000

  Marginal investment in A/R .......... $17,250

   Cost of marginal investment in A/R
   (.15 × $17,250) .......................................... ($ 2,588)

Cost of marginal bad debts

 Bad debts under proposed plan:
 (.02 × $10 × 63,000) .......... $12,600

 Bad debts under present plan:
 (.01 × $10 × 60,000) .......... 6,000

  Cost of marginal bad debts .......................................... ($ 6,600)

Net profit from implementation of proposed plan .......... $ 2,812

---

[a]The denominators 8 and 12 in the calculation of the average investment in accounts receivable under the proposed and present plans are the accounts receivable turnovers for each of these plans (360/45 = 8 and 360/30 = 12).

---

marginal bad debts; the firm *should* therefore relax its credit standards as proposed. The net addition to total profits resulting from such an action is $2,812 per year.

The technique described here for making a credit standard decision is commonly used for evaluating other types of changes in the management of accounts receivable as well. If the firm in the preceding example were contemplating tightening its credit standards, the cost would be a reduction in the profit contribution from sales, and the return would be from reductions in the cost of the marginal investment in accounts receivable and in bad debts. Another application of this analytical technique is demonstrated later in the chapter.

## Progress Review Question

**9-7.** What key variables should be considered when evaluating possible changes in a firm's *credit standards?* What are the basic trade-offs in a *tightening* of credit standards?

# Changing Credit Terms

**credit terms**
Specify the repayment terms required of a firm's credit customers.

A firm's **credit terms** specify the repayment terms required of all its credit customers.[3] Typically, a type of shorthand is used. For example, credit terms may be stated as *2/10 net 30*. This notation means that the purchaser receives a 2 percent cash discount if the bill is paid within 10 days after the beginning of the credit period; if the customer does not take the cash discount, the full amount must be paid within 30 days after the beginning of the credit period. Credit terms cover three things: (1) the cash discount, if any (in this case 2 percent); (2) the cash discount period (in this case 10 days); and (3) the credit period (in this case 30 days). Changes in any aspect of the firm's credit terms may have an effect on its overall profitability. The positive and negative factors associated with such changes, and quantitative procedures for evaluating them, are presented in this section.

## Cash Discount

When a firm initiates or *increases* a cash discount, the changes and effects on profits shown in the table can be expected.

| Variable | Direction of Change | Effect on Profits |
|---|---|---|
| Sales volume | Increase | Positive |
| Investment in accounts receivable due to nondiscount takers paying earlier | Decrease | Positive |
| Investment in accounts receivable due to new customers | Increase | Negative |
| Bad debt expenses | Decrease | Positive |
| Profit per unit | Decrease | Negative |

The sales volume should increase because if a firm is willing to pay by day 10, the unit price decreases. The net effect on the accounts receivable investment is difficult to determine because the nondiscount takers paying earlier reduce the accounts receivable investment, but the accounts receivable resulting from new customers increase this investment. The bad debt expenses should decline because, as customers on the average pay earlier, the probability of their not paying at all decreases.[4] Both the decrease in the receivables

---

[3]An in-depth discussion of credit terms as viewed by the *customer*—that is, *accounts payable,* is presented in Chapter 10. In this chapter our concern is with *accounts receivable*—credit terms from the point of view of the *seller.*

[4]This contention is based on the fact that the longer a person has to pay, the less likely it is that the person will pay. The more time that elapses, the more opportunities exist for a customer to become technically insolvent or fail. Therefore, the probability of a bad debt is expected to increase directly with increases in the credit period.

investment and the decrease in bad debt expenses should result in increased profits. The negative aspect of an increased cash discount is a decreased profit per unit as more customers take the discount and pay the reduced price.

Decreasing or eliminating a cash discount has opposite effects. The quantitative effects of changes in cash discounts can be evaluated by a method similar to that used earlier to evaluate changes in credit standards.

# E X A M P L E

Assume that Binz Tool is considering initiating a cash discount of 2 percent for payment prior to day 10 after a purchase. The firm's current average collection period is 30 days [turnover = (360/30) = 12], credit sales of 60,000 units are made, and the variable cost per unit is $6. The firm expects that if the cash discount is initiated, 60 percent of its sales will be on discount, and sales will increase by 5 percent to 63,000 units. The average collection period is expected to drop to 15 days [turnover = (360/15) = 24]. Bad debt expenses are expected to drop from the current level of 1 percent of sales to .5 percent of sales. The firm's required return on equal-risk investments remains at 15 percent.

The analysis of this decision is presented in Table 9.4. The calculations are similar to those presented for Binz's credit standard decision in Table 9.3

**TABLE 9.4   The Effects on Binz Tool of Initiating a Cash Discount**

| | | |
|---|---|---|
| Additional profit contribution from sales | | |
| [3,000 units × ($10 − $6)] | | $12,000 |
| Cost of marginal investment in A/R | | |
| Average investment under proposed plan: | | |
| $\dfrac{(\$6 \times 63{,}000)}{24} = \dfrac{\$378{,}000}{24}$ | $15,750 | |
| Average investment under present plan: | | |
| $\dfrac{(\$6 \times 60{,}000)}{12} = \dfrac{\$360{,}000}{12}$ | 30,000 | |
| Marginal investment in A/R | ($14,250) | |
| Cost of marginal investment in A/R | | |
| (.15 × $14,250) | | $ 2,138[a] |
| Cost of marginal bad debts | | |
| Bad debts under proposed plan: | | |
| (.005 × $10 × 63,000) | $ 3,150 | |
| Bad debts under present plan: | | |
| (.01 × $10 × 60,000) | 6,000 | |
| Cost of marginal bad debts | | $ 2,850[a] |
| Cost of cash discount[b] (.02 × .60 × $10 × 63,000) | | ($ 7,560) |
| Net profit from implementation of proposed plan | | $ 9,428 |

[a]This value is positive because it represents a savings rather than a cost.
[b]This calculation reflects the fact that a 2 percent cash discount is taken on 60 percent of the new level of sales—63,000 units at $10 each.

except for the final entry, "Cost of cash discount." This cost of $7,560 reflects the fact that *profits are reduced* as a result of a 2 percent cash discount being taken on 60 percent of the new level of sales. Binz Tool can increase profit by $9,428 by initiating the proposed cash discount. Such an action therefore seems advisable. This type of analysis can also be applied to decisions concerning the elimination or reduction of cash discounts.

## Cash Discount Period

The net effect of changes in the cash discount period is quite difficult to analyze due to the nature of the forces involved. For example, if the cash discount period *increases,* the changes shown in the table can be expected.

| Variable | Direction of Change | Effect on Profits |
|---|---|---|
| Sales volume | Increase | Positive |
| Investment in accounts receivable due to nondiscount takers paying earlier | Decrease | Positive |
| Investment in accounts receivable due to discount takers still getting cash discount but paying later | Increase | Negative |
| Investment in accounts receivable due to new customers | Increase | Negative |
| Bad debt expenses | Decrease | Positive |
| Profit per unit | Decrease | Negative |

The problems in determining the exact results of changes in the cash discount period are directly attributable to the three forces affecting the firm's *investment in accounts receivable.* If the firm shortens the cash discount period, the effects are the opposite of those described in the table.

## Credit Period

Changes in the credit period also affect the firm's profitability. The effects on profits shown in the table can be expected from an *increase* in the length of the credit period.

| Variable | Direction of Change | Effect on Profits |
|---|---|---|
| Sales volume | Increase | Positive |
| Investment in accounts receivable | Increase | Negative |
| Bad debt expenses | Increase | Negative |

Increasing the length of the credit period should increase sales, but both the investment in accounts receivable and bad debt expenses are likely to increase as well. Thus the net effect on profits of the sales increase is positive, whereas the increases in accounts receivable investment and bad debt expenses affect profits negatively. A decrease in the length of the credit period is likely to have the opposite effect. The credit period decision is analyzed in the same way as the credit standard decision illustrated in Table 9.3.

## Progress Review Questions

**9-8.** Discuss what is meant by *credit terms*. What are the three components of credit terms? How do credit terms affect the firm's accounts receivable?

**9-9.** What are the expected effects of a *decrease* in the firm's cash discount on sales volume, investment in accounts receivable, bad debt expenses, and per-unit profits, respectively?

**9-10.** What are the expected effects of a *decrease* in the firm's credit period? What is likely to happen to sales volume, investment in accounts receivable, and bad debt expenses, respectively?

LG 4

## Collection Policy

As noted earlier, the firm's *collection policy* is the set of procedures for collecting accounts receivable when they are due. The effectiveness of this policy can be partly evaluated by looking at the level of bad debt expenses. This level depends not only on collection policy but also on the policy on which the extension of credit is based. If one assumes that the level of bad debts attributable to *credit policy* is relatively constant, increasing collection expenditures can be expected to reduce bad debts. This relationship is depicted in Figure 9.2. As the figure indicates, beyond point A, additional collection expenditures do not reduce bad debt losses sufficiently to justify the outlay of funds. Popular approaches used to evaluate credit and collection policies include the *average collection period ratio* (presented in Chapter 4) and *aging accounts receivable*.

### Aging Accounts Receivable

**aging**
A technique used to evaluate credit or collection policies by indicating the proportion of the accounts receivable balance that has been outstanding for a specified period.

**Aging** is a technique that indicates the proportion of the accounts receivable balance that has been outstanding for a specified period. By highlighting irregularities, it allows the analyst to pinpoint the cause of credit or collection problems. Aging requires that the firm's accounts receivable be broken down into groups based on the time of origin. This breakdown is typically made on a month-by-month basis, going back three or four months. Let us look at an example.

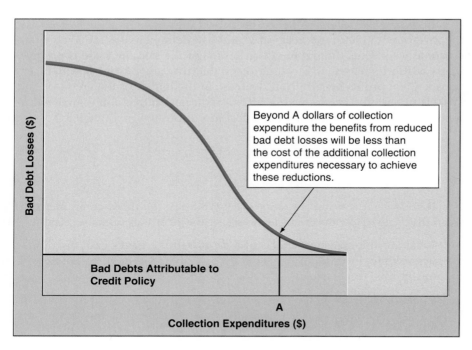

**FIGURE 9.2   Collection Expenditures and Bad Debt Losses**

By increasing collection expenditures, the firm can decrease bad debt losses up to a point (A), beyond which bad debts cannot be economically reduced. These inescapable bad debts are attributed to the firm's credit policy.

Beyond A dollars of collection expenditure the benefits from reduced bad debt losses will be less than the cost of the additional collection expenditures necessary to achieve these reductions.

Bad Debts Attributable to Credit Policy

A

Collection Expenditures ($)

Bad Debt Losses ($)

▶ E X A M P L E

Assume that Binz Tool extends 30-day credit terms to its customers. The firm's December 31, 1995, balance sheet shows $200,000 of accounts receivable. An evaluation of the $200,000 of accounts receivable results in the breakdown shown in the table.

| Days | Current | 0–30 | 31–60 | 61–90 | Over 90 | |
|---|---|---|---|---|---|---|
| Month | Dec. | Nov. | Oct. | Sept. | Aug. | Total |
| Accounts receivable | $60,000 | $40,000 | $66,000 | $26,000 | $8,000 | $200,000 |
| Percentage of total | 30 | 20 | 33 | 13 | 4 | 100 |

Because it is assumed that Binz Tool gives its customers 30 days after the end of the month in which the sale is made to pay off their accounts, any December receivables still on the firm's books are considered current. November receivables are between zero and 30 days overdue, October receivables still unpaid are 31 to 60 days overdue, and so on.

The table shows that 30 percent of the firm's receivables are current, 20 percent are one month late, 33 percent are two months late, 13 percent are three months late, and 4 percent are more than three months late. Payment seems generally slow, but a noticeable irregularity in these data is the high percentage represented by October receivables. This indicates that some problem may have occurred in October. Investigation may find that the problem can be attributed to the hiring of a new credit manager, the acceptance of a new account that has made a large credit purchase it has not yet paid for, or ineffective collection policy. When accounts are aged and such a discrepancy is found, the analyst should determine its cause.

## Results of Increased Collection Efforts

The basic trade-offs expected to result from an *increase* in collection efforts are as shown in the table.

| Variable | Direction of Change | Effect on Profits |
|---|---|---|
| Sales volume | None or decrease | None or negative |
| Investment in accounts receivable | Decrease | Positive |
| Bad debt expenses | Decrease | Positive |
| Collection expenditures | Increase | Negative |

Increased collection efforts should reduce the investment in accounts receivable and bad debt expenses, increasing profits. The costs of this strategy may include lost sales in addition to increased collection expenditures if the level of collection effort is too intense. In other words, if the firm pushes its customers too hard to pay their accounts, they may get angry and take their business elsewhere. The firm should therefore be careful not to be overly aggressive. The basic collection policy trade-offs can be evaluated quantitatively in a manner similar to that used to evaluate the trade-offs for credit standards and cash discounts.

## Types of Collection Techniques

A number of collection techniques are employed. As an account becomes more and more overdue, the collection effort becomes more personal and more intense. The basic techniques are briefly described in Table 9.5, listed in the order typically followed in the collection process.

▼▼▼▼▼▼▼▼▼▼▼▼▼▼▼▼▼▼▼▼▼▼▼▼▼▼▼▼▼▼

# Progress Review Questions

**9-11.** Why, regardless of its level of collection expenditures, can't a firm's collection policy typically reduce bad debt losses to zero? Explain how *aging accounts receivable* can be used to evaluate the effectiveness of both the credit policy and the collection policy.

**9-12.** Describe the basic trade-offs involved in collection policy decisions, and describe the popular types of collection techniques.

▲▲▲▲▲▲▲▲▲▲▲▲▲▲▲▲▲▲▲▲▲▲▲▲▲▲▲▲▲▲

## TABLE 9.5    Basic Collection Techniques

| Technique[a] | Brief Description |
| --- | --- |
| **Letters** | After an account receivable becomes overdue a certain number of days, the firm normally sends a polite letter reminding the customer of its obligation. If the account is not paid within a certain period after the letter has been sent, a second, more demanding letter is sent. This letter may be followed by yet another letter, if necessary. Collection letters are the first step in the collection process for overdue accounts. |
| **Telephone Calls** | If letters prove unsuccessful, a telephone call may be made to the customer to personally request immediate payment. Such a call is typically directed to the customer's accounts payable department where the responding employee acts on instructions of his or her boss. If the customer has a reasonable excuse, arrangements may be made to extend the payment period. A call from the seller's attorney may be used if all other discussions seem to fail. |
| **Personal Visits** | This technique is much more common at the consumer credit level, but it may also be effectively employed by industrial suppliers. Sending a local salesperson or a collection person to confront the customer can be a very effective collection procedure. Payment may be made on the spot. |
| **Using Collection Agencies** | A firm can turn uncollectible accounts over to a collection agency or an attorney for collection. The fees for this service are typically quite high; the firm may receive less than 50 cents on the dollar from accounts collected in this way. |
| **Legal Action** | Legal action is the most stringent step in the collection process. It is an alternative to the use of a collection agency. Not only is direct legal action expensive, but it may force the debtor into bankruptcy, thereby reducing the possibility of future business without guaranteeing the ultimate receipt of the overdue amount. |

[a]Techniques are listed in the order typically followed in the collection process.

LG **5**

# Inventory Management

*Inventory*, or goods on hand, is a necessary current asset. Like accounts receivable, inventory represents a significant monetary investment on the part of most firms. For the average manufacturer, it accounts for about 42 percent of *current assets* and about 18 percent of *total assets*. Chapter 8 illustrated the importance of turning over inventory quickly in order to reduce financing costs. The financial manager generally acts as a "watchdog" and advisor in matters concerning inventory; he or she does not have direct control over inventory but does provide input into the inventory management process.

## Inventory Fundamentals

Two aspects of inventory require some elaboration. One is the *types of inventory;* the other concerns differing viewpoints as to the *appropriate level of inventory.*

**raw materials inventory**
Items purchased by the firm for use in the manufacture of a finished product.

**Types of Inventory**   The three basic types of inventory are raw materials, work in process, and finished goods. **Raw materials inventory** consists of items purchased by the firm—usually basic materials, such as screws, plastic, raw steel, or rivets—for use in the manufacture of a finished product. If a firm manufactures complex products with numerous parts, its raw materials inventory may consist of manufactured items that have been purchased from another company or from another division of the same firm. **Work-in-process inventory** consists of all items currently in production. These are normally partially finished goods at some intermediate stage of completion. **Finished goods inventory** consists of items that have been produced but not yet sold.

**work-in-process inventory**
All items currently in production.

**finished goods inventory**
Items that have been produced but not yet sold.

**Differing Viewpoints About Inventory Level**   Differing viewpoints concerning appropriate inventory levels commonly exist among the finance, marketing, manufacturing, and purchasing managers of a company. Each sector views inventory levels in light of its own objectives. The *financial manager's* general disposition toward inventory levels is to keep them low. The financial manager must police the inventories, making sure that the firm's money is not being unwisely invested in excess resources. The *marketing manager,* on the other hand, prefers large inventories of each of the firm's finished products. This ensures that all orders can be filled quickly, eliminating the need for backorders due to stockouts.

The *manufacturing manager's* major responsibility is to make sure that the production plan is correctly implemented and that it results in the desired quantity of finished goods of acceptable quality at a low cost. In fulfilling this role, the manufacturing manager prefers to keep raw materials inventories high to avoid production delays and favors high finished goods inventories by making large production runs for the sake of lower unit production costs. The *purchasing manager* is concerned solely with the raw materials inventories. He or she is responsible for seeing that whatever raw materials are required by production are available in the correct quantities at the desired times and

### Outsourcing Inventory to Solectron Helps Big Blue Reboot

It took International Business Machines up to 18 months to get new computers from the design stage into customers' hands back in 1991. Consequently, Apple Computer and Compaq were consistently beating Big Blue to the marketplace. When Louis V. Gerstner took over IBM, in the midst of its stock price decline from over $100 to $42, he called on Solectron for help.

Solectron's specialty is making complex printed circuit boards that are at the heart of virtually every high-tech device. Gerstner arranged an outsourcing deal with Solectron, whereby Solectron supplied the boards with IBM's assistance. By outsourcing, IBM was able to avoid large capital investments in inventory.

In fact, Solectron purchased IBM's plant in Bordeaux, France, which freed additional funds for research and development. IBM was also able to have boards produced at Solectron's shop cost of $25 an hour, instead of IBM's $50 an hour cost.

Both firms benefitted from the outsourcing. Solectron's sales and earnings rose 200 percent. Meanwhile, IBM's reduced inventory investment helped Big Blue get new models off the drawing board in half its previous time.

Sources: Ira Sager, "IBM Reboots Bit-by-Bit," *Business Week*, January 17, 1994, pp. 82–83; Gene Marcial, "Solectron: Why This High-Tech Small Fry Sizzles," *Business Week*, January 17, 1994, p. 74.

at a favorable price. Without proper control, the purchasing manager may purchase larger quantities of resources than are actually needed in order to get quantity discounts or in anticipation of rising prices or a shortage of certain materials.

## Inventory as an Investment

Inventory is an investment in the sense that it requires that the firm tie up its money, thereby forgoing certain other earnings opportunities. In general, the higher a firm's average inventories, the larger the dollar investment and cost required, and vice versa. In evaluating planned changes in inventory levels, the financial manager should consider such changes from the standpoint of benefits versus costs.

▶ E X A M P L E

Excellent Manufacturing is contemplating making larger production runs in order to reduce the high setup costs associated with the production of its only product, industrial hoists. The total *annual* reduction in setup costs that can be obtained has been estimated at $20,000. As a result of the larger production runs, the average inventory investment is expected to increase from $200,000 to $300,000. If the firm can earn 25 percent per year on equal-risk investments, the *annual* cost of the additional $100,000 ($300,000 −

$200,000) inventory investment is $25,000 (.25 × $100,000). Comparing the annual $25,000 cost of the system with the annual savings of $20,000 shows that the proposal should be rejected because it results in a net annual *loss* of $5,000.

## The Relationship Between Inventory and Accounts Receivable

The level and the management of inventory and accounts receivable are closely related. Generally in the case of manufacturing firms, when an item is sold, it moves from inventory to accounts receivable and ultimately to cash. Because of the close relationship between inventory and accounts receivable, their management should not be viewed independently. For example, the decision to extend credit to a customer can result in an increased level of sales, which can be supported only by higher levels of inventory and accounts receivable. The credit terms extended also affect the investment in inventory and receivables, because longer credit terms may allow a firm to move items from inventory to accounts receivable. Generally the advantage to such a strategy is that the cost of carrying an item in inventory is greater than the cost of carrying an account receivable. This is true because the cost of carrying inventory includes, in addition to the required return on the invested funds, the costs of storing, insuring, and otherwise maintaining the physical inventory. This relationship can be shown using a simple example.

## E X A M P L E

Most Industries, a producer of PVC pipe, estimates that the annual cost of carrying $1 of merchandise in inventory for a one-year period is 25 cents, whereas the annual cost of carrying $1 of receivables is 15 cents. The firm currently maintains average inventories of $300,000 and an average *investment* in accounts receivable of $200,000. The firm believes that by altering its credit terms, it can encourage its customers to purchase in larger quantities on the average, thereby reducing its average inventories to $150,000 and increasing the average investment in accounts receivable to $350,000. The altered credit terms are not expected to generate new business but will result only in a shift in purchasing and payment patterns. The costs of the present and proposed inventory-accounts receivable systems are calculated in Table 9.6.

Table 9.6 shows that by shifting $150,000 of inventory to accounts receivable, Most Industries is able to lower the cost of carrying inventory and accounts receivable from $105,000 to $90,000—a $15,000 ($105,000 − $90,000) addition to profits. This profit is achieved without changing the level of average inventory and accounts receivable investment from its $500,000 total. Rather, the profit is attributed to a shift in the mix of these current assets so that a larger portion of them is held in the form of accounts receivable, which is less costly to hold than inventory.

The inventory-accounts receivable relationship is affected by decisions made in all areas of the firm: finance, marketing, manufacturing, and purchasing. The financial manager should consider the interactions between inventory and accounts receivable when developing strategies and making de-

**TABLE 9.6   Analysis of Inventory-Accounts Receivable Systems for Most Industries**

| Variable | Cost/ Return (1) | Present Average Investment (2) | Present Cost [(1) × (2)] (3) | Proposed Average Investment (4) | Proposed Cost [(1) × (4)] (5) |
|---|---|---|---|---|---|
| Average inventory | 25% | $300,000 | $ 75,000 | $150,000 | $37,500 |
| Average receivables | 15 | 200,000 | 30,000 | 350,000 | 52,500 |
| Totals | | $500,000 | $105,000 | $500,000 | $90,000 |

cisions related to the production-sale process. This interaction is especially important when making credit decisions, because the required as well as actual levels of inventory are directly affected.

## International Inventory Management

International inventory management is typically much more complicated for exporters in general, and for multinational companies in particular, than for purely domestic companies. The production and manufacturing economies of scale that would seem to come from selling products globally may prove elusive if products must be tailored for individual local markets, as very frequently happens, or if actual production of goods takes place in factories around the world. When raw materials, intermediate goods, or finished products have to be transported long distances—particularly via ocean shipping—there will inevitably be more delays, confusion, damage, theft, and other difficulties to overcome than occur in a one-country operation. The international inventory manager therefore puts a premium on flexibility, and he or she is usually less concerned about ordering the economically optimal level of inventory than about ensuring that sufficient quantities of materials are delivered where and when they are needed and in a condition to be used as planned.

## Progress Review Questions

9-13. What is the financial manager's role with respect to the management of inventory? What are likely to be the viewpoints of each of the following managers about the levels of the various types of inventory?
  **a.** Finance
  **b.** Marketing
  **c.** Manufacturing
  **d.** Purchasing

9-14. Explain the relationship between inventory and accounts receivable. Assuming the total investment in inventory and accounts receivable remains constant, what effect does lengthening the credit terms have on the firm's profits? Why?

---

**9-15.** What factors make managing inventory more difficult for exporters and multinational companies?

▲▲▲▲▲▲▲▲▲▲▲▲▲▲▲▲▲▲▲▲▲▲▲▲▲▲▲▲▲

LG 6

# Techniques for Managing Inventory

Techniques commonly used in managing inventory are (1) the ABC system, (2) the basic economic order quantity (EOQ) model, (3) the reorder point, (4) the materials requirement planning (MRP) system, and (5) the just-in-time (JIT) system. Although these techniques are not strictly financial, it is helpful for the financial manager to understand them.

## The ABC System

**ABC system**
Inventory management technique that divides inventory into three categories of descending importance based on the dollar investment in each.

A firm using the **ABC system** divides its inventory into three groups, A, B, and C. The *A group* includes those items that require the largest dollar investment. In the typical distribution of inventory items, this group consists of the 20 percent of inventory items that account for 80 percent of the firm's dollar investment. The *B group* consists of the items accounting for the next largest investment. The *C group* typically consists of a large number of items accounting for a relatively small dollar investment. Dividing its inventory into A, B, and C items allows the firm to determine the level and types of inventory control procedures needed. Control of the A items should be most intensive due to the high dollar investment involved; the use of *perpetual inventory record keeping* that allows daily monitoring of these inventory levels is appropriate. B items are frequently controlled through *periodic checking*—possibly weekly—of their levels. C items can be controlled by using unsophisticated procedures such as a **red-line method,** in which a reorder is placed when enough inventory has been removed from a bin containing the inventory item to expose a red line that has been drawn around the inside of the bin. The economic order quantity (EOQ) model, discussed next, is appropriate for use in monitoring A and B items.

**red-line method**
Inventory management technique in which a reorder is placed when use of inventory items from a bin exposes a red line drawn inside the bin.

## The Basic Economic Order Quantity Model

**economic order quantity (EOQ) model**
Inventory management technique for determining the optimal order quantity for an item of inventory.

One of the most commonly cited sophisticated tools for determining the optimal order quantity for an item of inventory is the **economic order quantity (EOQ) model.** It takes into account various operating and financial costs and determines the order quantity that minimizes total inventory cost.

**Basic Costs**  Excluding the actual cost of the merchandise, the costs associated with inventory can be divided into three broad groups: order costs, carrying costs, and total cost. Each has certain key components and characteristics.

**order costs**
The fixed clerical costs of placing and receiving an inventory order.

**Order Costs.**  **Order costs** include the fixed clerical costs of placing and receiving an order: the cost of writing a purchase order, of processing the resulting paperwork, and of receiving an order and checking it against the invoice. Order costs are normally stated as dollars per order.

**Carrying Costs.** **Carrying costs** are the variable costs per unit of holding an item in inventory for a specified period. These costs are typically stated as dollars per unit per period. Carrying costs include storage costs, insurance costs, the cost of deterioration and obsolescence, and most important, the opportunity, or financial, cost of tying up funds in inventory. A commonly cited rule of thumb suggests that the cost of carrying an item in inventory for one year is between 20 and 30 percent of the cost (value) of the item.

**carrying costs**
The variable costs per unit of holding an item in inventory for a specified period.

**Total Cost.** The **total cost** of inventory is defined as the sum of the order and carrying costs. Total cost is important in the EOQ model, because the model's objective is to determine the order quantity that minimizes it.

**total cost**
The sum of the order costs and carrying costs of inventory.

**A Graphic Approach**   The stated objective of the EOQ model is to find the order quantity that minimizes the firm's total inventory cost. The economic order quantity can be found graphically by plotting order quantities on the *x*, or horizontal, axis and costs on the *y*, or vertical, axis. Figure 9.3 shows the general behavior of these costs. The total cost line represents the sum of the order costs and carrying costs for each order quantity. The minimum total cost occurs at the point labeled EOQ, where the order cost line and the carrying cost line intersect.

**A Mathematical Approach**   The formula given in Equation 9.2 can be used to determine the firm's EOQ for a given inventory item:

$$EOQ = \sqrt{\frac{2 \times S \times O}{C}}$$                    (9.2)

**Equation 9.2 Formula for the economic order quantity (EOQ)**

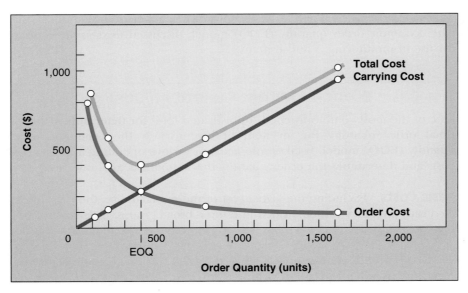

**FIGURE 9.3   A Graphic Presentation of an EOQ**

The total cost line represents the sum of the order costs and carrying costs for each order quantity. The EOQ, which is the order quantity that minimizes total inventory cost, occurs where the order cost line and carrying cost line intersect.

where

$$S = \text{usage in units per period}$$
$$Q = \text{order cost per order and}$$
$$C = \text{carrying cost per unit per period}$$

▶ E X A M P L E

Assume that RLB, Inc., a manufacturer of electronic test equipment, uses 1,600 units of an item annually. Its order cost is $50 per order and carrying cost is $1 per unit per year. Substituting $S = 1,600$, $O = \$50$, and $C = \$1$ into Equation 9.2 yields an EOQ of 400 units:

$$EOQ = \sqrt{\frac{2 \times 1,600 \times \$50}{\$1}} = \sqrt{160,000} = \underline{400 \text{ units}}$$

If the firm orders in quantities of 400 units, it minimizes its total inventory cost. The solution is depicted in Figure 9.3.

## The Reorder Point

**reorder point**
The point at which to reorder inventory.

**Equation 9.3 Expression for the reorder point**

Once the firm has calculated its economic order quantity, it must determine when to place orders. A reorder point is required that considers the lead time needed to place and receive orders. Assuming a constant usage rate for inventory, the **reorder point** can be determined by the following equation:

$$\text{Reorder point} = \text{lead time in days} \times \text{daily usage} \tag{9.3}$$

For example, if a firm knows that it requires 10 days to order and receive an inventory item, and if it uses 5 units of inventory daily, the reorder point is 50 units (10 days $\times$ 5 units per day). Thus as soon as the firm's inventory level reaches 50 units, an order is placed for an amount equal to the economic order quantity. If the estimates of lead time and daily usage are correct, the order is received exactly when the inventory level reaches zero. Because of the difficulty in precisely predicting lead times and daily usage rates, many firms typically maintain **safety stocks,** which are extra inventories that can be drawn down when actual outcomes are greater than expected.

**safety stocks**
Extra inventories that can be drawn down when actual lead times or usage rates are greater than expected.

## Materials Requirement Planning System

**materials requirement planning (MRP) system**
Inventory management system that compares production needs to available inventory balances and determines when orders should be placed for various items on the firm's *bill of materials.*

Many companies use a **materials requirement planning (MRP) system** to determine what to order, when to order, and what priorities to assign to ordering materials. MRP uses EOQ concepts to determine how much to order. It simulates, using a computer, each product's bill of materials structure, inventory status, and process of manufacturing. The *bill of materials* structure simply refers to every part or material that goes into making the finished product. For a given production plan, the computer simulates needed materials requirements by comparing production needs to available inventory balances. Based on the time it takes for a product that is in process to move through the various production stages, and the lead time required to get materials, the MRP system determines when orders should be placed for the various items on the bill of materials. The advantage of the MRP system is that it forces the firm to consider its inventory needs more thoughtfully and plan accordingly. The objective is to lower the firm's inventory investment without impairing production. If the firm's opportunity cost of capital for investments of equal risk is 25 percent, every dollar of investment released from inventory increases before-tax profits by $.25.

## Just-in-Time System

The **just-in-time (JIT) system** is used to minimize inventory investment. The philosophy is that materials should arrive at exactly the time they are needed for production. Ideally, the firm has only work-in-process inventory. Because its objective is to minimize inventory investment, a JIT system uses no, or very little, safety stocks. Extensive coordination must exist between the firm, its suppliers, and shipping companies to ensure that material inputs arrive on time. Failure of materials to arrive on time results in a shutdown of the production line until the materials arrive. Likewise, a JIT system requires high-quality parts from suppliers. When quality problems arise, production must be stopped until the problems are solved.

just-in-time (JIT) system
Inventory management system that minimizes inventory investment by having material inputs arrive at exactly the time they are needed for production.

The goal of the JIT system is manufacturing efficiency. It uses inventory as a tool for attaining efficiency by emphasizing quality, in terms of both the materials used and their timely delivery. When JIT is working properly, it forces process inefficiencies to surface and be resolved. A JIT system requires cooperation among all parties involved in the process: suppliers, shipping companies, and the firm's employees. Employees must encourage competitive excellence, continuous improvements, and 100-percent quality items. If they are not committed to these goals, the JIT system is likely to be unsuccessful.

## Progress Review Questions

**9-16.** Briefly describe each of the following techniques for managing inventory:
   **a.** ABC system
   **b.** Reorder point
   **c.** Materials requirement planning (MRP) system
   **d.** Just-in-time (JIT) system

**9-17.** What is the *EOQ model?* To which group of inventory items is it most applicable? What costs does it consider? What financial cost is involved?

# SUMMARY OF LEARNING GOALS

**Discuss the key aspects of credit selection, including the five C's of credit, obtaining credit information, analyzing credit information, credit scoring, and managing international credit.** Credit selection includes deciding whether to extend credit to a customer and how much credit to extend.

  LG  1

The five C's of credit—character, capacity, capital, collateral, and conditions—are used to guide credit investigations. Credit information can be obtained from a variety of external sources and can be analyzed in a number of ways. An analyst's subjective judgment is an important input to the final decision. At the consumer level, impersonal techniques, such as credit scoring, are often used. Credit management becomes much more complex for companies that operate internationally due to the presence of exchange rate risk and difficulty in shipping long distances across international borders and assessing and bearing the credit risks of foreign customers.

**LG 2**   **Understand how to isolate and measure the key variables and use them to evaluate quantitatively the effects of either relaxing or tightening a firm's credit standards.** At the mercantile level, credit standards—the minimum criteria for extension of credit to a customer—must be set by considering the trade-offs between the key variables, which are the profit contribution from sales, the cost of investment in accounts receivable, and the cost of bad debts. Generally, when credit standards are relaxed, the profit contribution from sales increases, as do the costs of investment in accounts receivable and bad debts. If the increased profit contribution exceeds the increased costs, the credit standards should be relaxed. A tightening of credit standards results in a decrease in each of the key variables; if the cost reductions exceed the reduced profit contribution, credit standards should be tightened.

**LG 3**   **Review the three components of a firm's credit terms, the effects of changes in each of them on key variables and profits, and the procedure for evaluating the quantitative effects of proposed cash discount changes.** Credit terms cover three things: (1) the cash discount, (2) the cash discount period, and (3) the credit period. Changes in each of these variables affect the firm's sales, investment in accounts receivable, bad debt expenses, and profit per unit. Quantitatively, a proposed increase (or initiation) of a cash discount is evaluated by comparing the profit increases attributable to the added sales, the reduction in accounts receivable investment, and the reduction in bad debts to the cost of the cash discount. If the profit increases exceed the cost, the discount increase should be undertaken. The proposed decrease (or elimination) of a cash discount is analyzed similarly, except that the profit and cost factors are reversed.

**LG 4**   **Explain the key features of collection policy, including aging accounts receivable, the basic trade-offs, and the types of collection techniques.** Collection policy determines the type and degree of effort exercised to collect overdue accounts. In addition to looking at the average collection period ratio, firms often age accounts receivable to evaluate the effectiveness of their credit and collection policies. Generally, increased collection expenditures have little effect on sales volume and reduce the investment in accounts receivable and bad debt expenses. A decrease in collection expenditures results in little effect on sales volume and an increase in the investment in accounts receivable and bad debt expenses. The basic collection techniques include letters, telephone calls, personal visits, the use of collection agencies, and, as a last resort, legal action.

**LG 5**   **Understand the types of inventory, differing viewpoints about inventory level, inventory as an investment, the relationship between inventory and accounts receivable, and international inventory management.** The respective viewpoints held by marketing, manufacturing, and purchasing managers regarding the appropriate levels of various types of inventory (raw materials, work in process, and finished goods) tend to conflict with that of the financial manager. The financial manager views inventory as an investment that consumes dollars and that should be maintained at a low level. Because it is more expensive to carry an item in inventory than to carry an account receivable, the financial manager must consider the relationship between inventory and accounts receivable when making decisions related to the production-sale process. Because international inventory management is more complex than the purely domestic situation, international inventory managers place greater emphasis on ensuring that sufficient quantities of materials are delivered where and when they are needed and in the right condition than on ordering economically optimal quantities.

**Describe the common techniques for managing inventory, including the ABC system, the basic economic order quantity (EOQ) model, the reorder point, the materials requirement planning (MRP) system, and the just-in-time (JIT) system.** The ABC system determines which inventories require the most attention according to dollar investment. One of the most common techniques for determining optimal order quantities is the economic order quantity (EOQ) model. Once the optimal order quantity has been determined, the firm can set the reorder point, the level of inventory at which an order is placed. Materials requirement planning (MRP) is a system that determines when orders should be placed for various items on a firm's bill of materials. Just-in-time (JIT) systems are used to minimize inventory investment by having materials arrive at exactly the time they are needed for production.

# SUMMARY OF KEY DEFINITIONS AND EQUATIONS

## Variable Definitions

$C$ = carrying cost per unit per period
EOQ = economic order quantity
$O$ = order cost per order
$S$ = usage in units per period

## Equations

$$\text{Average investment in accounts receivable} = \frac{\text{total variable cost of annual sales}}{\text{turnover of accounts receivable}} \qquad \text{[Eq. 9.1]}$$

where

$$\text{turnover of accounts receivable} = \frac{360}{\text{average collection period}}$$

Economic order quantity

[Eq. 9.2]
$$\text{EOQ} = \sqrt{\frac{2 \times S \times O}{C}}$$

[Eq. 9.3]
$$\text{Reorder point} = \text{lead time in days} \times \text{daily usage}$$

# 10 Sources of Short-Term Financing

Short-term financing, from both internal and external sources, gives a company's operating units the flexibility to carry out their business plans. Its treasury department determines the appropriate levels of short- and long-term debt and secures the financing on a timely basis at the lowest overall cost. The more seasonal a company's business, the greater its reliance on short-term financing.

> **Short-term financing . . . gives a company's operating units the flexibility to carry out their business plans.**

M/A-COM, a $340-million publicly traded electronics manufacturer, derives 45 to 50 percent of its revenue from sales to the government. The government places most of its orders with us in the third quarter, so we ship a disproportionate volume of products in the fall. Sales are at their lowest level in the winter months, so the need for short-term financing is greatest in February and March.

Historically, M/A-COM's defense business generated high cash flows, but sales from this market have declined steadily over the past few years. In 1992, the company decided to focus on commercial wireless communications and to reduce costs. It began to restructure in 1993, closing underutilized facilities and consolidating U.S. manufacturing into a single, state-of-the-art plant. This revitalization program required more funds than the cash flow generated from operations. As a result, M/A-COM looked to several forms of short-term financing, both internal and external.

Typically, a firm uses internal funds for short-term financing before going to external sources. M/A-COM implemented a companywide "manage for cash" program. Cash generation was measured monthly and included budget targets and incentive compensation goals. Managers improved cycle times, reduced inventory, centralized receivables collection, and set up electronic payment systems. Payables were reviewed more closely, and marketing personnel were encouraged to negotiate advance payments on large contracts. M/A-COM also reset intercompany payment terms worldwide. Now all intercompany payments are due in 30 days. This significantly improved U.S. cash flow.

The company also turned to external sources for its short-term cash requirements. Because M/A-COM is not large enough to issue commercial paper (short-term corporate IOUs), it arranged for bank financing. The company negotiated a revolving credit agreement, guaranteed credit availability for a specified amount and period, which allowed it to borrow as needed without restricting its ability to invest in commercial market opportunities. The "revolver" was unsecured, so the company did not have to put up assets as collateral.

A key factor in the successful negotiation of a flexible credit agreement is detailed regular communication with the banks. We met with the banks regularly to update them on the state of the business and progress on our operating plan. Executive management made periodic presentations to the bankers. In addition, the bankers received all information published on the company—press releases, financial statements, trade articles, and employee newsletters.

M/A-COM's bank relationships are very important to the company. Most of its bank business, including cash management, foreign exchange, and letters of credit, is placed with the revolving credit banks. As a result, the company has not only improved its prospects for maintaining adequate short-term financing but has created a true long-term partnership with its banks.

**Karen Edlund** is assistant treasurer of M/A-COM, which she joined in 1991. From 1985 until 1991, she worked for Dennison Manufacturing Company, now Avery Dennison, where she managed $200 million in retirement plan assets. She has a B.A. in French and economics from Middlebury College and a master's degree in finance from Boston College.

Short-term financing is debt that matures in one year or less and is used to fulfill seasonal and current asset needs. **Secured short-term financing** has specific assets pledged as collateral, whereas **unsecured short-term financing** does not. Both these forms of financing appear on the balance sheet as *current liabilities*—accounts payable, accruals, and notes payable. (*Notes payable* include all negotiated short-term financing.) For convenience, a summary table of the key features of the common sources of short-term financing is included as Table 10.3 in the chapter summary.

**secured short-term financing**
Financing that matures in one year or less and has specific assets pledged as collateral.

**unsecured short-term financing**
Financing that matures in one year or less and has no assets pledged as collateral.

## Spontaneous Sources

LG 1   LG 2

**spontaneous financing**
Financing that arises from the normal operations of the firm, the two major short-term sources of which are accounts payable and accruals.

**Spontaneous financing** arises from the normal operations of the firm. The two major spontaneous sources of short-term financing are *accounts payable* and *accruals.* Each of these sources is unsecured. As the firm's sales increase, accounts payable increases because of increased purchases required to produce at higher levels. The firm's accruals also increase as wages and taxes rise due to greater labor requirements and the increased taxes on the firm's increased earnings. There is normally no explicit cost attached to either of these current liabilities, although they do have certain implicit costs. The firm should take advantage of these often "interest-free" sources of unsecured short-term financing whenever possible.

### Accounts Payable

Accounts payable is the major source of unsecured short-term financing for business firms. Such accounts result from transactions in which merchandise is purchased but no formal note is signed to show the purchaser's liability to the seller. The purchaser, by accepting merchandise, in effect agrees to pay the supplier the amount required in accordance with the terms of sale. The credit terms extended in such transactions are normally stated on the supplier's invoice. The discussion of accounts payable here is presented from the viewpoint of the purchaser rather than the supplier of "trade credit."[1]

**Credit Terms**    The supplier's credit terms state the credit period, the size of the cash discount offered (if any), the cash discount period, and the date the credit period begins. Each of these aspects of a firm's credit terms is concisely stated in such expressions as "2/10 net 30 EOM." These expressions are a kind of shorthand containing the key information about the length of the credit period (30 days), the cash discount (2 percent), the cash discount period (10 days), and the time the credit period begins, which is the end of each month (EOM).

---

[1]An account payable of a purchaser is an account receivable on the supplier's books. Chapter 9 highlighted the key strategies and considerations involved in extending credit to customers.

**credit period**
The number of days until full payment of an account payable is required.

**Credit Period.** The **credit period** of an account payable is the number of days until payment in full is required. Regardless of whether a cash discount is offered, the credit period associated with any transaction must always be indicated. Credit periods usually range from zero to 120 days. Most credit terms refer to the credit period as the "net period." The word "net" indicates that the full amount of the purchase must be paid within the number of days indicated from the beginning of the credit period. For example, "net 30 days" indicates that the firm must make *full payment* within 30 days of the beginning of the credit period.

**cash discount**
A percentage deduction from the purchase price if the buyer pays within a specified time shorter than the credit period.

**Cash Discount.** A **cash discount,** if offered as part of the firm's credit terms, is a percentage deduction from the purchase price if the buyer pays within a specified time shorter than the credit period. Cash discounts normally range from between 1 and 5 percent. A 2 percent cash discount indicates that the purchaser of $100 of merchandise need pay only $98 if payment is made within the specified shorter interval. The purchaser, whose objective is to stretch accounts payable by paying as late as possible, must determine whether it is more advantageous to take the cash discount or to pay at the end of the full credit period. Techniques for analyzing the benefits of each alternative are discussed in a later section.

**cash discount period**
The number of days after the beginning of the credit period during which the cash discount is available.

**Cash Discount Period.** The **cash discount period** is the number of days after the beginning of the credit period during which the cash discount is available. Typically the cash discount period is between 5 and 20 days. Often large customers of smaller firms use their position as key customers to take cash discounts far beyond the end of the cash discount period. This strategy, although ethically questionable, is not uncommon.

**date of invoice**
Indicates that the beginning of the credit period is the date on the invoice for the purchase.

**end of month (EOM)**
Indicates that the credit period for all purchases made within a given month begins on the first day of the month immediately following.

**Beginning of the Credit Period.** The beginning of the credit period is stated as part of the supplier's credit terms. One of the most common designations for the beginning of the credit period is the **date of invoice.** Both the cash discount period and the net period are then measured from the invoice date. **End of month (EOM)** indicates that the credit period for all purchases made within a given month begins on the first day of the month immediately following. These terms simplify record keeping on the part of the firm extending credit. The following example may help to clarify the differences between credit period beginnings.

# EXAMPLE

The McKinley Company, a producer of computer graphics software, made two purchases from a certain supplier offering credit terms of 2/10 net 30. One purchase was made on September 10 and the other on September 20. The payment dates for each purchase, based on date of invoice and end of month (EOM) credit period beginnings, are given in Table 10.1. The payment dates if the firm takes the cash discount and if it pays the net amount are shown. From the point of view of the recipient of trade credit, a credit period beginning at the end of the month is preferable in both cases: Their purchases can be paid for without penalty at a later date than otherwise would be possible.

**TABLE 10.1  Payment Dates for the McKinley Company Given Various Assumptions**

| Beginning of Credit Period | September 10 Purchase | | September 20 Purchase | |
|---|---|---|---|---|
| | Discount Taken | Net Amount Paid | Discount Taken | Net Amount Paid |
| Date of invoice | Sept. 20 | Oct. 10 | Sept. 30 | Oct. 20 |
| End of month (EOM) | Oct. 10 | Oct. 30 | Oct. 10 | Oct. 30 |

To maintain their competitive position, firms within an industry generally offer the same terms. In many cases, stated credit terms are not the terms actually given to a customer. Special arrangements, or "deals," are made to provide certain customers with more favorable terms. The prospective purchaser is wise to look closely at the credit terms of suppliers when making a purchase decision. In many instances, concessions may be available.

**Analyzing Credit Terms**   The credit terms offered a firm by its suppliers allow it to delay payments for its purchases. Because the supplier's cost of having its money tied up in merchandise after it is sold is probably reflected in the purchase price, the purchaser is already indirectly paying for this benefit. The purchaser should therefore carefully analyze credit terms to determine the best trade credit strategy.

**Taking the Cash Discount.**  If a firm is extended credit terms that include a cash discount, it has two options. Its first option is to *take the cash discount.* If a firm intends to take a cash discount, it should pay on the last day of the discount period. There is no cost associated with taking a cash discount.

▶ E X A M P L E

Presti Corporation, operator of a small chain of video stores, purchased $1,000 worth of merchandise on February 27 from a supplier extending terms of 2/10 net 30 EOM. If the firm takes the cash discount, it has to pay $980 [$1,000 − (.02 × $1,000)] on March 10, thereby saving $20.

▶

**Giving Up the Cash Discount.**  The second option open to the firm is to *give up the cash discount* and pay on the final day of the credit period. Although there is no direct cost associated with giving up a cash discount, there is an implicit cost. The **cost of giving up a cash discount** is the implied rate of interest paid in order to delay payment of an account payable for an additional number of days. In other words, the amount of the discount that is given up is the interest being paid by the firm to keep its money by delaying payment for a number of days. This cost can be illustrated by a simple example. The example assumes that if the firm takes a cash discount, payment will be made on the final day of the cash discount period, and if the cash discount is given up, payment will be made on the final day of the credit period.

**cost of giving up a cash discount**
The implied rate of interest paid in order to delay payment of an account payable for an additional number of days.

# E X A M P L E

As in the preceding example, Presti Corporation has been extended credit terms of 2/10 net 30 EOM on $1,000 worth of merchandise. If it takes the cash discount on its February 27 purchase, payment will be required on March 10. If the cash discount is given up, payment can be made on March 30. To keep its money for an extra 20 days (from March 10 to March 30), the firm must give up an opportunity to pay $980 for its $1,000 purchase. In other words, it costs the firm $20 to delay payment for 20 days. Figure 10.1 shows the payment options open to the corporation.

To calculate the cost of giving up the cash discount, the *true purchase price* must be viewed as the discounted cost of the merchandise. For Presti Corporation, this discounted cost is $980. To delay paying the $980 for an extra 20 days, the firm must pay $20 ($1,000 − $980). The annual percentage cost of giving up the cash discount can be calculated using Equation 10.1.

**Equation 10.1** Formula for finding the cost of giving up a cash discount

$$\text{Cost of giving up cash discount} = \frac{CD}{100\% - CD} \times \frac{360}{N} \qquad (10.1)$$

where

$CD$ = the stated cash discount in percentage terms;

$N$ = the number of days payment can be delayed by giving up the cash discount

Substituting the values for $CD$ (2%) and $N$ (20 days) into Equation 10.1 results in an annualized cost of giving up the cash discount of 36.73 percent [(2% ÷ 98%) × (360 ÷ 20)]. A 360-day year is assumed.

A simple way to *approximate* the cost of a given up discount is to use the stated cash discount percentage, $CD$, in place of the first term of Equation 10.1.

**Equation 10.2** Formula for approximating the cost of giving up a cash discount

$$\text{Approximate cost of giving up cash discount} = CD \times \frac{360}{N} \qquad (10.2)$$

The smaller the cash discount, the closer the approximation to the actual cost of giving up the cash discount. Using this approximation, the cost of giving up the cash discount for Presti Corporation is 36 percent [2% × (360 ÷ 20)].

## FIGURE 10.1
**Payment Options for Presti Corporation**

As a result of its February 27 $1,000 purchase under credit terms of 2/10 net 30 EOM, Presti Corporation can either take the $20 discount and pay $980 on March 10 or forgo the discount and pay the full $1,000 20 days later on March 30.

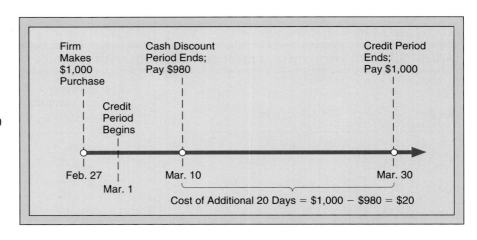

### Using the Cost of Giving Up a Cash Discount in Decision Making.

The financial manager must determine whether it is advisable to take a cash discount. It is important to recognize that taking cash discounts may represent a key source of additional profitability for firms that are currently giving them up.

▶ E X A M P L E

Omst Products, a large building supply company, has four possible suppliers, each offering different credit terms. Except for the differences in credit terms, their products and services are identical. Table 10.2 presents the credit terms offered by suppliers A, B, C, and D, respectively, and the cost of giving up the cash discounts in each transaction. The approximation method of calculating the cost of giving up a cash discount (Equation 10.2) has been used to simplify the analysis. The cost of giving up the cash discount from supplier A is 36 percent; from supplier B, 8 percent; from supplier C, 21.6 percent; and from supplier D, 28.8 percent.

If the firm needs short-term funds, which it could borrow from its bank at an interest rate of 13 percent, and if each of the suppliers (A, B, C, and D) is viewed *separately*, which (if any) of the suppliers' cash discounts should the firm give up? To answer this question, each supplier's terms must be evaluated as if it were the firm's sole supplier. In dealing with supplier A, the firm takes the cash discount because the cost of giving it up is 36 percent. The firm then borrows the funds it requires from its bank at 13 percent interest. In dealing with supplier B, the firm would do better to give up the cash discount because the cost of this action is less than the cost of borrowing money from the bank (8 percent versus 13 percent). In dealing with either supplier C or supplier D, the firm should take the cash discount because in both cases the cost of giving up the discount is greater than the 13 percent cost of borrowing from the bank.

▶ rowing from the bank.

The example shows that the cost of giving up a cash discount is relevant when evaluating a single supplier's credit terms in light of certain *bank borrowing costs*. When comparing various suppliers' credit terms, the cost of giving up the cash discount may not be the most important factor in the decision process. Other factors, such as the size of the cash discount, the length

**TABLE 10.2  Cash Discounts and Associated Costs for Omst Products**

| Supplier | Credit Terms | Approximate Cost of Giving Up Cash Discount |
|---|---|---|
| A | 2/10 net 30 EOM | 36.0% |
| B | 1/10 net 55 EOM | 8.0 |
| C | 3/20 net 70 EOM | 21.6 |
| D | 4/10 net 60 EOM | 28.8 |

of the cash discount period, and the length of the credit period, may also need to be considered. It is important to note that some firms, particularly small or poorly managed ones, routinely give up *all* discounts because either they lack alternative sources of unsecured short-term financing or they fail to recognize the high implicit costs of their actions.

**Effects of Stretching Accounts Payable**   If a firm anticipates *stretching accounts payable*, its cost of giving up a cash discount is reduced. Stretching accounts payable is sometimes suggested as a reasonable strategy for a firm as long as it does not damage its credit rating. As noted in Chapter 8, although this strategy is financially attractive, it raises an important ethical issue: It may cause the firm to violate the agreement it entered into with its supplier when it purchased merchandise. Clearly, a supplier does not look kindly on a customer who regularly and purposely postpones paying for purchases.

# E X A M P L E

Presti Corporation was extended credit terms of 2/10 net 30 EOM. The cost of giving up the cash discount, assuming payment on the last day of the credit period, was found to be approximately 36 percent [2% × (360 ÷20)]. If the firm is able to stretch its account payable to 70 days without damaging its credit rating, the cost of giving up the cash discount is only 12 percent [2% × (360 ÷ 60)]. Stretching accounts payable reduces the implicit cost of giving up a cash discount.

## Accruals

**accruals**
Liabilities for services received for which payment has yet to be made.

The second spontaneous source of short-term financing for a business is accruals. **Accruals** are liabilities for services received for which payment has yet to be made. The most common items accrued by a firm are wages and taxes. Because taxes are payments to the government, their accrual cannot be manipulated by the firm. However, the accrual of wages can be manipulated to some extent. This is accomplished by delaying payment of wages, thereby receiving an interest-free loan from employees who are paid sometime after they have performed the work. The pay period for employees who earn an hourly rate is often governed by union regulations or by state or federal law. However, in other cases the frequency of payment is at the discretion of the company's management.

# E X A M P L E

Chan Company, a large janitorial service company, currently pays its employees at the end of each work week. The weekly payroll totals $400,000. If the firm extended the pay period so as to pay its employees one week later throughout an entire year, the employees are in effect loaning the firm $400,000 for a year. If the firm could earn 10 percent annually on invested funds, such a strategy is worth $40,000 per year (.10 × $400,000). By delaying payment of accruals in this way, the firm can save this amount of money.

▼▼▼▼▼▼▼▼▼▼▼▼▼▼▼▼▼▼▼▼▼▼▼▼▼▼▼

## Progress Review Questions

**10-1.** What are the two key sources of spontaneous short-term financing for a firm? Why are these sources considered *spontaneous,* and how are they related to the firm's sales? Do they normally have a stated cost?

**10-2.** Is there a cost associated with taking a cash discount? Is there any cost associated with giving up a cash discount? How is the decision to take a cash discount affected by the firm's cost of borrowing short-term funds?

**10-3.** What are *accruals?* What items are most commonly accrued by the firm? How attractive are accruals as a source of financing to the firm?

▲▲▲▲▲▲▲▲▲▲▲▲▲▲▲▲▲▲▲▲▲▲▲▲▲▲▲

## Unsecured Bank Sources

Banks are a major source of unsecured short-term loans to businesses. Unlike the spontaneous sources of *unsecured short-term financing,* bank loans are negotiated and result from deliberate actions taken by the financial manager. The major type of loan made by banks to businesses is the **short-term self-liquidating loan.** Self-liquidating loans are intended merely to carry the firm through seasonal peaks in financing needs, caused primarily by buildups of accounts receivable and inventory. As receivables and inventories are converted into cash, the funds needed to retire these loans are automatically generated. In other words, the use to which the borrowed money is put provides the mechanism through which the loan is repaid (hence the term "self-liquidating"). Banks lend unsecured short-term funds in three basic ways: through single-payment notes, lines of credit, and revolving credit agreements. Before we look at these types of loans, it is necessary to lay some groundwork about loan interest rates.

> **short-term self-liquidating loan**
> An unsecured short-term loan in which the use to which the borrowed money is put provides the mechanism through which the loan is repaid.

### Loan Interest Rates

The interest rate on a bank loan is typically based on the prime rate of interest and can be a fixed or a floating rate. It should be evaluated using the *effective interest rate.* The differing ways of calculating this rate depend on whether interest is paid when the loan matures or in advance. Each of these aspects of loan interest rates is evaluated below.

**Prime Rate of Interest**   The **prime rate of interest (prime rate)** is the lowest rate of interest charged by the nation's leading banks on business loans to their most important and reliable business borrowers. The prime rate fluctuates with changing supply-and-demand relationships for short-term

> **prime rate of interest (prime rate)**
> The lowest rate of interest charged by the nation's leading banks on loans to their most reliable business borrowers.

funds.[2] Banks generally determine the rate charged on loans to various borrowers by adding some type of premium to the prime rate to adjust it for the borrower's "riskiness." The premium may amount to 4 percent or more. Most unsecured short-term notes carry premiums of less than 2 percent. In general, banks do not make short-term unsecured loans to businesses that are believed to be questionable risks.

**Fixed- and Floating-Rate Loans**   Loans can have either fixed or floating interest rates. On a **fixed-rate loan** the rate of interest is determined at a set increment above the prime rate on the date of the loan and remains at that fixed rate until maturity. On a **floating-rate loan** the increment above the prime rate is initially established, and the rate of interest is allowed to "float," or vary, above prime *as the prime rate varies* until maturity. Generally the increment above the prime rate on a floating-rate loan is *lower* than on a fixed-rate loan of equivalent risk because the lender bears less risk with a floating-rate loan. The highly volatile nature of the prime rate in recent years, coupled with the widespread use of computers by banks to monitor and calculate loan interest, has been responsible for the *current dominance of floating-rate loans.*

**Finding the Effective Interest Rate**   Once the *stated interest rate* is established, the method of computing interest is determined. Interest can be paid either when a loan matures or in advance. Regardless of which method is used, the relevant interest rate is the **effective interest rate,** which is the actual annual rate of interest. The general formula for finding the effective interest rate is:

**fixed-rate loan**
A loan with a rate of interest determined at a set increment above the prime rate at which it remains fixed until maturity.

**floating-rate loan**
A loan with a rate of interest set at an increment above the prime rate and allowed to "float" above prime *as the prime rate varies* until maturity.

**effective interest rate**
The actual annual rate of interest paid on a loan as opposed to its *stated rate of interest.*

**Equation 10.3** General formula for the effective interest rate.

$$\text{Effective interest rate} = \frac{\text{finance charges}}{\text{usable funds}} \times \frac{360}{N} \qquad (10.3)$$

where

finance charges = interest and any other loan charges incurred over the term of the loan;

usable funds = the amount of the loan principal actually received by the borrower; and

$N$ = the term of the loan in days (assumes a 360-day year consisting of twelve 30-day months).

When using Equation 10.3 to find the effective interest rate on a loan that *pays interest at maturity,* the finance charges equal the amount of interest paid over the term of the loan, and the usable funds equal the stated amount of loan principal. Most bank loans to businesses require the interest payment at maturity. When *interest is paid in advance,* it is deducted from the loan

---

[2]From 1975 through the third quarter of 1978 the prime rate was generally below 9 percent. From the end of 1978 until June of 1985 the prime rate remained above 9.5 percent. In late December 1980 the prime rate reached a record high 21.5 percent. The prime rate slowly dropped from 9.5 percent in June 1985 to 7.5 percent in late August 1986, and in March 1987 it began a slow rise to 9.0 percent by November of 1987. It remained around 9.0 percent until the middle of 1988 when it began to rise, peaking at 11.5 percent in 1989. The prime rate then declined to and remained at about 10.0 percent through the end of 1990. By the middle of 1991 it had declined to 8.5 percent from which it further declined, reaching 6.0 percent in mid-1992. The prime rate remained at 6.0 percent through early 1994 when actions of the Federal Reserve Board stimulated its rise to 7.75 percent by mid-August of that year. At that time the general expectation was a reasonably stable prime rate.

FINANCE IN

▲CTION

In the News

## Donald Trump, Short-Term Bridge Loans, and Artichokes

Some financing arrangements involve a complicated layering of different types of debt, so that the financial position of the borrower begins to resemble the leaves of an artichoke. Peeling off one layer of debt leads to a second layer, and this second layer leads to yet a third layer. In many cases, short-term bridge loans are the financial glue that holds these complex financing arrangements together.

New York real estate financier Donald Trump's financial structure provides a good example of this debt layering. In mid-1990, as East Coast real estate values began to plummet, Trump's ability to pay his debts took a similar turn for the worse. In order to raise $20 million and prevent default on his New Jersey casino debt, Trump's bankers arranged an eleventh-hour bridge loan for $20 million.

This temporary credit arrangement was contingent on the completion of a broader, long-term credit pact with Trump that called for the extension of $65 million in new financing to support Trump Tower in New York. In addition, this $65 million transaction allowed Trump to defer interest payments on some $2 billion in bank debt. The $20 million bridge loan

gave Trump's bankers the necessary time to work out the details for the larger financing transaction, with the proceeds from the $65 million loan used, in part, to repay the temporary bridge loan.

Unfortunately, things like marriage and financing plans don't always work out like The Donald thinks they will. Still reeling from a huge debt burden and declining sales revenue in 1992, Trump's Castle Casino in Atlantic City filed for bankruptcy. In the process, Trump's creditors gained a 50 percent ownership interest in his gaming business.

So what's next for Trump's financial empire? At last check, he was trying to regain total ownership of the casino properties from bondholders by asking them to swap their old bonds and ownership stake in the casino for new bonds carrying a higher interest rate. Given Trump's past record in meeting debt payments, however, it's a good bet that bondholders will think twice before accepting this latest offer.

Sources: *The American Banker*, June 27, 1990, p. 2.; *The Wall Street Journal*, August 30, 1993, p. A5-A.

amount so that the borrower actually receives less money than is requested. Loans for which interest is paid in advance are often called **discount loans.** While the finance charges in this case would equal the interest paid over the term of the loan, the usable funds would be found as follows:

> Usable funds on a discount loan = amount borrowed − interest    (10.4)

Because by paying interest in advance the borrower has less usable funds, the effective interest rate on these loans is higher than that rate on a similar loan that pays interest at maturity. Let us look at an example.

**discount loans**
Loans on which interest is paid in advance by deducting it from the amount borrowed.

**Equation 10.4** Formula for finding the amount of usable funds on a *discount loan.*

## ▶ E X A M P L E

Booster Company, a manufacturer of athletic apparel, wants to borrow $10,000 at a stated rate of 10 percent interest for one year. If the interest on the loan is paid at maturity, the firm pays $1,000 (.10 × $10,000) for the use of the $10,000 for the year (i.e., $N = 360$ days). Substituting into Equation 10.3, the effective interest rate is therefore

$$\frac{\$1,000}{\$10,000} \times \frac{360}{360} = .10 \times 1 = .10 = 10.0\%$$

If the money is borrowed at the same *stated* rate for one year but interest is paid in advance, the firm still pays $1,000 in interest, but it receives usable funds, found using Equation 10.4, of only $9,000 ($10,000 − $1,000). Thus substituting into Equation 10.3, the effective interest rate in this case is

$$\frac{\$1,000}{\$9,000} \times \frac{360}{360} = .111 \times 1 = .111 = 11.1\%$$

Paying interest in advance thus makes the effective interest rate (11.1 percent) greater than the stated interest rate (10.0 percent).

## Single-Payment Notes

**single-payment note**
A short-term, one-time loan payable as a single amount at its maturity.

A **single-payment note** can be obtained from a commercial bank by a credit-worthy business borrower. This type of loan is usually a "one-shot" deal made when a borrower needs additional funds for a short period. The resulting instrument is a *note*, signed by the borrower. The note states the terms of the loan, which include the length of the loan (the maturity date) and the interest rate charged. This type of short-term note generally has a maturity of 30 days to 9 months or more. The interest charged on the note is generally tied in some fashion to the prime rate of interest. A note may have either a fixed or floating rate. Let us look at an example.

## E X A M P L E

Golden Manufacturing, a producer of rotary mower blades, recently borrowed $100,000 from each of two banks: bank A and bank B. The loans were incurred on the same day, when the prime rate of interest was 9 percent. Each loan involved a 90-day note ($N = 90$ days) with interest to be paid at the end of 90 days. The interest rate was set at 1.5 percent above the prime rate on bank A's fixed-rate note. This means that over the 90-day period, the rate of interest remains at 10.5 percent (9% prime rate + 1.5% increment) regardless of fluctuations in the prime rate. The total interest on this loan is $2,625 [$100,000 × (10.5% × 90/360)]. The effective interest rate on this loan, calculated using Equation 10.3, is 10.50 percent [($2,625 ÷ $100,000) × (360 ÷ 90)].

On bank B's floating-rate note the interest rate was set at 1 percent above the prime rate. This means that the rate charged over the 90 days varies directly *with* the prime rate. Initially the rate is 10 percent (9% + 1%), but when the prime rate changes, so does the rate of interest on the note. For instance, if after 30 days the prime rate rises to 9.5 percent and after another 30 days drops to 9.25 percent, the firm pays 0.833 percent for the first 30 days (10% × 30/360), 0.875 percent for the next 30 days (10.5% × 30/360), and 0.854 percent for the last 30 days (10.25% × 30/360). Its total interest cost is $2,562 [$100,000 × (0.833% + 0.875% + 0.854%)], resulting in an effective interest rate on this loan, calculated using Equation 10.3, of 10.25 percent [($2,562 ÷ $100,000) × (360 ÷ 90)].

Clearly, in this case the floating-rate loan would have been less expensive (10.25%) than the fixed-rate loan (10.50%) due to its generally lower interest rates over the 90-day term of the note.

# Lines of Credit

A **line of credit** is an agreement between a commercial bank and a business specifying the amount of unsecured short-term borrowing the bank will make available to the firm over a given period. It is similar to the agreement under which issuers of bank credit cards, such as MasterCard, Visa, and Discover, extend pre-approved credit to cardholders. A line of credit agreement is typically made for a period of one year and often places certain constraints on the borrower. A line of credit is *not a guaranteed loan* but indicates that if the bank has sufficient funds available, it will allow the borrower to owe it up to a certain amount of money. The amount of a line of credit is *the maximum amount the firm can owe the bank* at any given time.

When applying for a line of credit the borrower may be required to submit such documents as its cash budget, its pro forma income statement, its pro forma balance sheet, and its recent financial statements. If the bank finds the customer acceptable, the line of credit is extended. The major attraction of a line of credit from the bank's point of view is that it eliminates the need to examine the creditworthiness of a customer each time it borrows money. A few characteristics of lines of credit require further explanation.

**Interest Rates**    The interest rate on a line of credit is normally stated as a floating rate—the *prime rate plus a percentage*. If the prime rate changes, the interest rate charged on new *as well as on outstanding* borrowing automatically changes. The amount a borrower is charged in excess of the prime rate depends on its creditworthiness. The more creditworthy the borrower, the lower the interest increment above prime, and vice versa.

**Operating Change Restrictions**    In a line of credit agreement, a bank may impose **operating change restrictions.** Such restrictions give the bank the contractual right to revoke the line if any major changes occur in the firm's financial condition or operations. The firm is usually required to submit for review periodically (quarterly or semiannually) up-to-date and, preferably, audited financial statements. In addition, the bank typically needs to be informed of shifts in key managerial personnel or in the firm's operations prior to changes taking place. Such changes may affect the future success and debt-paying ability of the firm and thus could alter its credit status. If the bank does not agree with the proposed changes and the firm makes them anyway, the bank has the right to revoke the line of credit agreement.

**Compensating Balances**    To ensure that the borrower will be a good customer, many short-term unsecured bank loans often require the borrower to maintain a **compensating balance** in a demand deposit account (checking account). The compensating balance is equal to a certain percentage of the amount borrowed. Compensating balances of 10 to 20 percent are frequently required. They may be required on single-payment notes as well as lines of credit. A compensating balance not only forces the borrower to be a good customer of the bank but may also raise the interest cost to the borrower, thereby increasing the bank's earnings. The following example illustrates this arrangement.

**line of credit**
An agreement specifying the amount of unsecured short-term borrowing a bank will make available to a firm over a given period.

**operating change restrictions**
Contractual restrictions that a bank may impose on a firm as part of a line of credit agreement.

**compensating balance**
A required checking account balance equal to a certain percentage of the borrower's short-term unsecured bank loan.

# EXAMPLE ◀

Exact Graphics, a graphics design firm, borrowed $1 million under a line of credit agreement. It must pay a stated interest rate of 10 percent and maintain a compensating balance equal to 20 percent of the amount borrowed, or $200,000, in its checking account. Thus it actually receives the use of only $800,000. To use the $800,000 for one year ($N = 360$ days) the firm pays interest of $100,000 (.10 × $1,000,000). The effective interest rate, calculated using Equation 10.3, on this loan is therefore 12.5 percent [($100,000 ÷ $800,000) × (360 ÷ 360)], 2.5 percent more than the stated rate of 10 percent.

If the firm normally maintains a balance of $200,000 or more in its checking account, it should be able to use the full $1 million, and the effective interest rate will equal the stated interest rate of 10 percent [($100,000 ÷ $1,000,000) × (360 ÷ 360)]. If the firm normally maintains a $100,000 balance in its checking account, only an additional $100,000 will be tied up, leaving it with $900,000 ($1,000,000 − $100,000) of usable funds. The effective interest rate in this case is 11.1 percent [($100,000 ÷ $900,000) × (360 ÷ 360)]. Thus a compensating balance raises the cost of borrowing *only* if it is larger than the firm's normal cash balance. ◀

**Annual Cleanups**  To ensure that money lent under a line of credit agreement is actually being used to finance seasonal needs, many banks require an **annual cleanup.** This means that the borrower must have a loan balance of zero—that is, owe the bank nothing—for a certain number of days during the year. Forcing the borrower to carry a zero loan balance for a certain period ensures that short-term loans do not turn into long-term loans.

**annual cleanup**
The requirement that for a certain number of days during the year borrowers under a line of credit carry a zero loan balance.

All of the characteristics of a line of credit agreement are negotiable to some extent. Today, banks bid competitively to attract large, well-known firms. A prospective borrower should attempt to negotiate a line of credit with the most favorable interest rate, for an optimal amount of funds, and with a minimum of restrictions. Borrowers today frequently pay fees to lenders instead of maintaining deposit balances as compensation for loans and other services provided by the lender. The lender attempts to get a good return with maximum safety. These negotiations should produce a line of credit suitable to both borrower and lender.

## Revolving Credit Agreements

**revolving credit agreement**
A line of credit *guaranteed* to a borrower by a bank for a stated period regardless of the scarcity of money.

A **revolving credit agreement** is nothing more than a *guaranteed line of credit.* It is guaranteed in the sense that the bank making the arrangement assures the borrower that a specified amount of funds will be made available regardless of the scarcity of money. The interest rate and other requirements for a revolving credit agreement are similar to those for a line of credit. It is not uncommon for a revolving credit agreement to be for a period greater than one year. Because the bank guarantees the availability of funds to the borrower, a **commitment fee** is normally charged on a revolving credit agreement. This fee often applies to the average unused balance of the borrower's credit line. It is normally about .5 percent of the *average unused portion* of the funds. An example will clarify the nature of a commitment fee.

**commitment fee**
The fee normally charged on a revolving credit agreement.

# ▶ E X A M P L E

The Blount Company, a major real estate developer, has a $2 million revolving credit agreement with its bank. Its average borrowing under the agreement for the past year ($N = 360$ days) was $1.5 million. The bank charges a commitment fee of .5 percent. Because the average unused portion of the committed funds was $500,000 ($2 million − $1.5 million), the commitment fee for the year was $2,500 (.005 × $500,000). Of course, Blount also had to pay interest on the actual $1.5 million borrowed under the agreement. Assuming $160,000 interest was paid on the $1.5 million borrowed, the *finance charges* totaled $162,500 ($2,500 commitment fee + $160,000 interest). The effective interest rate, calculated using Equation 10.3, on this agreement is 10.83 percent [($162,500 ÷ $1,500,000) × (360 ÷ 360)]. Although more expensive than a line of credit, a revolving credit agreement can be less risky from the borrower's viewpoint, because the availability of funds is guaranteed ▶ by the bank.

## Progress Review Questions

**10-4.** What is the primary source of *unsecured* short-term loans to business? When are loans considered *short-term self-liquidating loans?*

**10-5.** What is the *prime rate of interest?* How is it relevant to the cost of short-term bank borrowing? What is a *floating-rate loan?*

**10-6.** What is the *effective interest rate?* How is it calculated? How does the effective interest rate differ between a loan requiring interest payments *at maturity* and another similar loan requiring interest *in advance?*

**10-7.** What are the basic terms and characteristics of a *single-payment note?*

**10-8.** What is a *line of credit?* Describe each of the following features often included in these agreements:
  **a.** Operating change restrictions
  **b.** Compensating balance
  **c.** Annual cleanup

**10-9.** What is meant by a *revolving credit agreement?* How does this arrangement differ from the line of credit agreement? What is a *commitment fee?*

# Commercial Paper and International Loans

LG 4

Two other sources of unsecured short-term financing are commercial paper and international loans. These forms of financing are available primarily to large well-known firms and firms that are actively involved in international trade. Here we take a brief look at each of these sources of short-term financing.

## Commercial Paper

**commercial paper**
A form of financing consisting of short-term, unsecured promissory notes issued by firms with a high credit standing.

**Commercial paper** is a form of financing that consists of short-term, unsecured promissory notes issued by firms with a high credit standing. Generally, only quite large firms of unquestionable financial soundness and reputation are able to issue commercial paper. Most commercial paper has maturities ranging from 3 to 270 days. Although there is no set denomination, it is generally issued in multiples of $100,000 or more. A large portion of the commercial paper today is issued by finance companies; manufacturing firms account for a smaller portion of this type of financing. As noted in Chapter 8, businesses often purchase commercial paper, which they hold as marketable securities, to provide an interest-earning reserve of liquidity.

**Sale of Commercial Paper**    Commercial paper is *directly placed with investors* by the issuer or is *sold by commercial paper dealers.* For performing the marketing function, the commercial paper dealer is paid a fee. Regardless of the method of sale, most commercial paper is purchased from a firm by other businesses, banks, life insurance companies, pension funds, and money market mutual funds.

**Interest on Commercial Paper**    The interest paid by the issuer of commercial paper is determined by the size of the discount and the length of time to maturity. Commercial paper is sold at a discount from its *par,* or *face, value,* and the actual interest earned by the purchaser is determined by certain calculations. These can be illustrated by the following example.

## E X A M P L E

Deems Corporation, a large shipbuilder, has just issued $1 million worth of commercial paper that has a 90-day maturity and sells for $980,000. At the end of 90 days the purchaser of this paper will receive $1 million for its $980,000 investment. The interest paid on the financing is therefore $20,000 on a principal of $980,000. The effective interest rate for Deems Corporation commercial paper, calculated using Equation 10.3, is 8.2 percent [($20,000 ÷ $980,000) × (360 days ÷ 90 days)].

An interesting characteristic of commercial paper is that it *normally* has a yield of 1 to 3 percent below the prime bank lending rate. In other words, firms are able to raise funds through the sale of commercial paper more cheaply than by borrowing from a commercial bank. The reason is that many suppliers of short-term funds do not have the option of making low-risk business loans at the prime rate. They can invest only in marketable securities, such as Treasury bills and commercial paper. The yields on these marketable securities on July 27, 1994, when the prime rate of interest was 7.25 percent, were about 4.4 percent for 3-month Treasury bills and about 4.7 percent for 3-month commercial paper.

Although the stated interest cost of borrowing through the sale of commercial paper is normally lower than the prime bank loan rate, the *overall cost* of commercial paper may not be cheaper than a bank loan. Additional costs include the fees paid by most issuers to obtain the bank line of credit used to back the paper, fees paid to obtain third-party ratings used to make the paper more salable, and fees paid dealers for selling the paper. In addition, it is important for the firm to maintain a good working relationship with its bank. Therefore even if it is slightly more expensive to borrow from a bank, it may at times be advisable to do so to establish the necessary rapport. This strategy ensures that when money is tight, funds can be obtained promptly and at a reasonable interest rate.

## International Loans

In some ways, arranging short-term financing for international trade is no different from financing purely domestic operations. In both cases, producers must finance the production and storage of goods for sale and then continue to finance accounts receivable before collecting any cash payments from sales. In other ways, however, the short-term financing of international sales and purchases is fundamentally different from strictly domestic trade.

**International Transactions**    The important difference between international and domestic transactions is that payments are often made or received in a foreign currency. Not only does this require a U.S. company to pay the costs of doing business in the foreign exchange market, it also exposes the company to exchange rate risk if a delay occurs between the date that a foreign-currency invoice is created and the date it is paid. A U.S.-based company that exports goods and has accounts receivable denominated in a foreign currency faces the risk that the U.S. dollar will appreciate in value relative to the foreign currency. The risk to a U.S. importer with foreign-currency-denominated accounts payable is that the dollar will depreciate. Although exchange rate risk can often be protected against, doing so is costly and possible only for relatively few foreign currencies.

Other distinguishing features of international trade include the large size and longer maturity date of typical transactions. Therefore companies involved in international trade generally have to finance larger dollar amounts for longer periods than companies that operate domestically. Furthermore, because foreign companies are rarely well known in the United States, some financial institutions are reluctant to lend to U.S. exporters or importers, particularly smaller firms.

**Financing International Trade**    Many U.S. banks offer financing for international trade, and several specialized techniques have evolved. Perhaps the most important financing vehicle is the **letter of credit,** a letter written by a company's bank to the company's foreign supplier, stating that the bank guarantees payment of an invoiced amount if all the underlying agreements are met. The bank receives a fee for issuing a letter of credit. The letter of credit essentially substitutes a well-known bank's reputation and creditworthiness for that of its commercial customer, increasing the likelihood that foreign suppliers will sell to a U.S. importer. Likewise, a U.S. exporter is more willing to sell goods to a foreign buyer if the transaction is covered by a letter of credit issued by a well-known bank in the buyer's home country.

Firms that do business in foreign countries on an ongoing basis often finance their operations, at least in part, in the local market. A company that has an assembly plant in Mexico, for example, might choose to finance its

**letter of credit**
A letter written by a company's bank to the company's foreign supplier, stating that the bank guarantees payment of an invoiced amount if all the underlying agreements are met.

purchases of Mexican goods and services with peso funds borrowed from a Mexican bank. This not only minimizes exchange rate risk but also improves the company's business ties to the host community. Multinational companies, however, sometimes finance their international transactions through dollar-denominated loans from international banks. The depth and liquidity of *Eurocurrency loan markets* allows creditworthy borrowers to obtain financing on very attractive terms.

**Transactions Between Subsidiaries**  Much international trade involves transactions between corporate subsidiaries. A U.S. company might, for example, manufacture one part in an Asian plant and another part in the United States, assemble the product in Brazil, and sell it in Europe. The shipment of goods back and forth between subsidiaries creates accounts receivable and accounts payable, but the parent company has considerable discretion about how and when payments are made. In particular, the parent can minimize foreign exchange fees and other transaction costs by "netting" what affiliates owe each other and paying only the net amount due rather than having both subsidiaries pay each other the gross amounts due.

## Progress Review Questions

**10-10.** How is commercial paper used to raise short-term funds? Who can issue commercial paper? Who buys commercial paper? How is it sold?

**10-11.** What is the important difference between international and domestic transactions? How is a *letter of credit* used in financing international trade transactions? What is "netting," and how is it used in transactions between subsidiaries?

## Secured Sources

**secured loan**
A loan for which the lender requires collateral.

**collateral**
The security offered the lender by the borrower.

**security agreement**
The agreement between the borrower and the lender that specifies the collateral held against a secured loan.

Once a firm has exhausted its unsecured sources of short-term financing, it may be able to obtain additional short-term loans on a secured basis. A **secured loan** is a loan for which the lender requires collateral. The **collateral** commonly takes the form of an asset, such as accounts receivable or inventory. The lender obtains a security interest in the collateral through a contract (security agreement) with the borrower. The **security agreement** specifies the collateral held against the loan. In addition, the terms of the loan against which the security is held are attached to, or form part of, the security agreement. They specify the conditions required for the security interest to be removed, along with the interest rate on the loan, repayment dates, and other loan provisions. A copy of the security agreement is filed in a public office within the state—typically a county or state court. Filing provides subsequent lenders with information about which assets of a prospective borrower are unavailable for use as collateral. The filing requirement protects the lender by legally establishing the lender's security interest.

# Characteristics of Secured Short-Term Loans

Although many people believe that holding collateral as security reduces the risk of the loan, lenders do not usually view loans in this way. Lenders recognize that by having an interest in collateral they can reduce losses if the borrower defaults, but *as far as changing the risk of default, the presence of collateral has no effect.* A lender requires collateral to ensure recovery of some portion of the loan in the event of default. What the lender wants above all, however, is to be repaid as scheduled. In general, lenders prefer to make less risky loans at lower rates of interest than to be in a position in which they are forced to liquidate collateral.

**Collateral and Terms**  Lenders of secured short-term funds prefer collateral that has a life, or duration, closely matched to the term of the loan. This assures the lender that the collateral can be used to satisfy the loan in the event of a default. Current assets—accounts receivable and inventories—are the most desirable short-term loan collateral because they normally convert into cash much sooner than do fixed assets. Thus the short-term lender of secured funds generally accepts only liquid current assets as collateral.

Typically, the lender determines the desirable **percentage advance** to make against the collateral. This percentage advance constitutes the principal of the secured loan. It is normally between 30 and 100 percent of the book value of the collateral. It varies not only according to the type and liquidity of collateral but also according to the type of security interest being taken.

**percentage advance**
The percent of the book value of the collateral that constitutes the principal of a secured loan.

The interest rate charged on secured short-term loans is typically *higher* than the rate on unsecured short-term loans. Commercial banks and other institutions do not normally consider secured loans less risky than unsecured loans; they therefore require higher interest rates on them. In addition, negotiating and administering secured loans is more troublesome for the lender than negotiating and administering unsecured loans. The lender therefore normally requires added compensation in the form of a service charge, a higher interest rate, or both. *The higher cost of secured as opposed to unsecured borrowing is attributable to the greater risk of default and to the increased administration costs involved.* (Remember that firms typically borrow on a secured basis only after exhausting less costly unsecured sources of short-term funds.)

**Institutions Extending Secured Short-Term Loans**  The primary sources of secured short-term loans to businesses are commercial banks and commercial finance companies. Both institutions deal in short-term loans secured primarily by accounts receivable and inventory. The operations of banks have already been described. **Commercial finance companies** are lending institutions that make *only* secured loans—both short-term and long-term—to businesses. Unlike banks, finance companies are not permitted to hold deposits.

**commercial finance companies**
Lending institutions that make *only* secured loans to businesses.

Only when its unsecured and secured short-term borrowing power from the bank is exhausted does a borrower turn to a commercial finance company for additional secured borrowing. Because finance companies generally end up with higher risk borrowers, their interest charges on secured short-term loans are usually higher than those of commercial banks. The leading U.S. commercial finance companies include Associates Capital Company, The CIT Group, and GE Capital Services.

## The Use of Accounts Receivable as Collateral

Two commonly used means of obtaining short-term financing with accounts receivable are pledging accounts receivable and factoring accounts receivable. Actually, only a pledge of accounts receivable creates a secured short-term loan; factoring really entails the *sale* of accounts receivable at a discount. Although factoring is not actually a form of secured short-term borrowing, it does involve the use of accounts receivable to obtain needed short-term funds.

**pledge of accounts receivable**
The use of a firm's accounts receivable as collateral to obtain a short-term loan.

### Pledging Accounts Receivable

A **pledge of accounts receivable** is often used to secure a short-term loan. Because accounts receivable are normally quite liquid, they are an attractive form of short-term collateral. Both commercial banks and commercial finance companies extend loans against pledges of accounts receivable.

When a firm approaches a prospective lender to request a loan against accounts receivable, the lender first evaluates the firm's accounts receivable to determine their desirability as collateral. Next, the dollar value of the acceptable accounts is adjusted by the lender for expected returns on sales and other allowances. Then, the percentage to be advanced against the adjusted collateral is determined by the lender based on its overall evaluation of the quality of the acceptable receivables and the expected cost of their liquidation. This percentage represents the principal of the loan. It typically ranges between 50 and 90 percent of the face value of acceptable accounts receivable. Finally, to protect its interest in the collateral the lender files a **lien,** which is a publicly disclosed legal claim on the collateral.

**lien**
A publicly disclosed legal claim on collateral.

Pledges of accounts receivable are normally made on a **nonnotification basis.** This means that a customer whose account has been pledged as collateral is not notified of this action. Under the nonnotification arrangement, the borrower still collects the pledged account receivable and the lender trusts that the borrower will remit these payments as they are received. If a pledge of accounts receivable is made on a **notification basis,** the customer is notified to remit payment directly to the lender (or factor).

**nonnotification basis**
The basis on which a borrower, having pledged an account receivable, continues to collect the account payments without notifying the account customer.

The stated cost of a pledge of accounts receivable is normally 2 to 5 percent above the prime rate of interest offered by banks. In addition to the stated interest rate, a service charge of up to 3 percent may be levied by the lender to cover its administrative costs. Clearly, pledges of accounts receivable are typically a high-cost source of short-term financing.

**notification basis**
The basis on which an account customer whose account has been pledged (or factored) is notified to remit payments directly to the lender (or factor).

### Factoring Accounts Receivable

**Factoring accounts receivable** involves their outright sale at a discount to a financial institution. A **factor** is a financial institution that specializes in purchasing accounts receivable from businesses. Some commercial banks and commercial finance companies also factor accounts receivable. Although not actually the same as obtaining a short-term loan, factoring accounts receivable is similar to borrowing with accounts receivable as collateral. Factoring currently constitutes approximately one-third of the total financing secured by accounts receivable (including factoring) and inventory in the United States.

**factoring accounts receivable**
The outright sale of accounts receivable at a discount to obtain funds.

A factoring agreement normally states the exact conditions, charges, and procedures for the purchase of an account. The factor, like a lender against a pledge of accounts receivable, chooses accounts for purchase, selecting only those that appear to be acceptable credit risks. Where factoring is to be on a

**factor**
A financial institution that specializes in purchasing accounts receivable.

continuing basis, the factor actually makes the firm's credit decisions to guarantee the acceptability of accounts. Factoring is normally done on a *notification basis,* and the factor receives payment of the account directly from the customer. In addition, most sales of accounts receivable to a factor are made on a **nonrecourse basis.** This means that the factor agrees to accept all credit risks. Thus if a purchased account turns out to be uncollectible, the factor must absorb the loss.

Typically the factor is not required to pay the firm until the account is collected or until the last day of the credit period, whichever occurs first. The factor sets up an account similar to a bank deposit account for each customer. As payment is received or as due dates arrive, the factor deposits money into the seller's account, from which the seller is free to make withdrawals as needed. In many cases, if the firm leaves the money in the account, a *surplus* exists on which the factor pays interest. In other instances, the factor may make *advances* to the firm against uncollected accounts that are not yet due. These advances represent a negative balance in the firm's account, on which interest is charged.

Factoring costs include commissions, interest levied on advances, and interest earned on surpluses. The factor deposits in the firm's account the book value of the collected or due accounts purchased by the factor, less the commissions. The commissions are typically stated as a 1 to 3 percent discount

**nonrecourse basis**
The basis on which accounts receivable are sold to a factor with the understanding that the factor accepts all credit risks on the purchased accounts.

# FINANCE IN ACTION

## Small Business

### There's Gold in Them Thar Receivables

You say the bank has stopped returning your phone calls, and local investment bankers just look at your financial statements and laugh? Well cheer up, Bunkey, because help is on the way. Arctrade International Ltd. recently announced a new financing plan designed to help beleaguered small businesses raise cash. For firms with many slow-pay accounts receivable, Arctrade has a plan to convert those past sales into cash.

Through its trade finance subsidiary, AmWorld Commerce, Arctrade helps small businesses that are not viewed favorably by conventional providers of asset-based financing. Arctrade's service is called a trade assumption draft, or TAD for short. When a seller delivers goods to a buyer, the buyer signs a TAD, which represents a promise to pay Arctrade at a later date. The seller then takes the TAD to Arctrade

and collects 75 percent of the TAD's face value. The remaining 25 percent—less a few percentage points to cover processing and financing fees—is returned to the seller once Arctrade collects the money from the buyer.

Using the service, firms with many small accounts receivable, or firms selling internationally in many different markets, are able to avoid the hassle of collecting individual receivables. The program is designed for invoices ranging between $1,000 and $10,000, and the reduced receivables management costs often offset the financing charges imposed by Arctrade. All things considered, this simple idea offers a novel and creative way to turn those past-due receivable problems into a source of ready cash.

Source: J. Mello, Jr., "A Tad More Clout," *CFO Magazine,* January 1994, p. 10.

from the book value of factored accounts receivable. The *interest levied on advances* is generally 2 to 4 percent above the prime rate. It is levied on the actual amount advanced. The interest paid on surpluses or positive account balances left with a factor is generally around .5 percent per month. Although its cost may seem high, factoring has certain advantages that make it quite attractive to many firms. One is the ability it gives the firm to *turn accounts receivable immediately into cash* without having to worry about repayment. Another advantage of factoring is that it ensures a *known pattern of cash flows.* In addition, if factoring is undertaken on a continuing basis, the firm *can eliminate its credit and collection departments.*

## The Use of Inventory as Collateral

Inventory is generally second to accounts receivable in desirability as short-term loan collateral. Inventory is attractive as collateral because it normally has a market value greater than its book value, which is used to establish its value as collateral. A lender securing a loan with inventory will probably be able to sell it for at least book value if the borrower defaults on its obligations.

**Desirable Characteristics**   Raw materials, work in process, or finished goods may all be offered as collateral for a short-term loan; usually only raw materials or finished goods inventories are considered acceptable. The most important characteristic of inventory being evaluated as loan collateral is *marketability,* which must be considered in light of its physical properties. A warehouse of *perishable* items, such as fresh peaches, may be quite marketable, but if the cost of storing and selling the peaches is high, they may not be desirable collateral. *Specialized items,* such as moon-roving vehicles, are not desirable collateral either, because finding a buyer for them is likely to be difficult. When evaluating inventory as possible loan collateral, the lender looks for items with very stable market prices that have ready markets and that lack undesirable physical properties.

**Floating Inventory Liens**   A lender may be willing to secure a loan under a **floating inventory lien,** which is a claim on inventory in general. This arrangement is most attractive when the firm has a stable level of inventory that consists of a diversified group of relatively inexpensive merchandise. Inventories of items such as auto tires, screws and bolts, and shoes are candidates for floating-lien loans. Because it is difficult for a lender to verify the presence of the inventory, the lender generally advances less than 50 percent of the book value of the average inventory. The interest charge on a floating lien is 3 to 5 percent above the prime rate. Floating liens are often required by commercial banks as extra security on what is otherwise an unsecured loan. A floating-lien inventory loan may also be available from commercial finance companies.

**floating inventory lien**
A lender's claim on the borrower's general inventory as collateral for a secured loan.

**Trust Receipt Inventory Loans**   A **trust receipt inventory loan** can often be made against relatively expensive automotive, consumer-durable, and industrial equipment that can be identified by serial number. Under this agreement, the borrower keeps the inventory and the lender may advance 80 to 100 percent of its cost. The lender files a *lien* on all the items financed. The borrower is free to sell the merchandise and is *trusted* to remit the amount

**trust receipt inventory loan**
An agreement under which the lender advances a portion of the cost of the borrower's relatively expensive inventory items in exchange for the borrower's promise to repay the loan immediately, with accrued interest, on the sale of each item.

lent against each item, along with accrued interest, to the lender immediately after the sale. The lender then releases the lien on the appropriate item. The lender makes periodic checks of the borrower's inventory to make sure that the required amount of collateral remains in the hands of the borrower. The interest charge to the borrower is normally 2 percent or more above the prime rate.

Trust receipt loans are often made by manufacturers' wholly owned financing subsidiaries, known as *captive finance companies,* to their customers. *"Floor planning"* of automobile or equipment retailers is done under this arrangement. For example, General Motors Acceptance Corporation (GMAC), the financing subsidiary of General Motors, grants these types of loans to its dealers. Trust receipt loans are also available from commercial banks and commercial finance companies.

### Warehouse Receipt Loans
A **warehouse receipt loan** is an arrangement whereby a lender receives control of the pledged inventory collateral, which is warehoused (stored) by a designated agent on the lender's behalf. After selecting acceptable collateral, the lender hires a warehousing company to act as its agent and take possession of the inventory. The lender may be a commercial bank or a commercial finance company.

**warehouse receipt loan**
An arrangement in which the lender receives control of the pledged inventory collateral, which is warehoused by a designated agent.

Two types of warehousing arrangements are possible: terminal warehouses and field warehouses. A *terminal warehouse* is a central warehouse used to store the merchandise of various customers. Such a warehouse is normally used by the lender when the inventory can be delivered to the warehouse relatively inexpensively. Under a *field warehouse* arrangement, the lender hires a field warehousing firm to set up a warehouse on the borrower's premises or to lease part of the borrower's warehouse in which to store the pledged collateral. Whether or not a terminal or field warehouse is established, the warehousing company places a guard over the inventory. Only on written approval of the lender can any portion of the secured inventory be released.

The actual lending agreement specifically states the requirements for the release of inventory. As in the case of other secured loans, the lender accepts only collateral believed to be readily marketable and advances only a portion—generally 75 to 90 percent—of the collateral's value. The specific costs of warehouse receipt loans are generally higher than those of any other secured lending arrangements due to the need to hire and pay a third party (the warehousing firm) to guard and supervise the collateral. The basic interest charged on warehouse receipt loans is higher than that charged on unsecured loans, generally ranging from 3 to 5 percent above the prime rate. In addition to the interest charge, the borrower must absorb the costs of warehousing by paying the warehouse fee, which is generally between 1 and 3 percent of the amount of the loan. The borrower is normally also required to pay the insurance costs on the warehoused merchandise.

▼▼▼▼▼▼▼▼▼▼▼▼▼▼▼▼▼▼▼▼▼▼▼▼▼▼▼▼▼▼▼▼▼▼▼

## Progress Review Questions

**10-12.** What are the key differences between unsecured and secured forms of short-term borrowing? In what circumstances do firms borrow short-term money on a secured basis?

**10-13.** In general, what kind of interest rates and fees are levied on secured short-term loans? Why are these rates generally *higher* than the rates on unsecured short-term loans?

**10-14.** Compare, contrast, and describe the basic features of the following methods of using *accounts receivable* to obtain short-term financing. Be sure to mention the institutions offering each of them.
**a.** Pledging accounts receivable
**b.** Factoring accounts receivable

**10-15.** Describe the basic features and compare each of the following methods of using *inventory* as short-term loan collateral:
**a.** Floating lien
**b.** Trust receipt loan
**c.** Warehouse receipt loan

# SUMMARY OF LEARNING GOALS

**LG 1** **Describe the key features of the major sources of spontaneous short-term financing—accounts payable and accruals.** Spontaneous sources of short-term financing include accounts payable, which are the primary source of short-term funds, and accruals. Accounts payable result from credit purchases of merchandise, and accruals result primarily from wage and tax obligations. The key features of these forms of financing are summarized in part I of Table 10.3.

**LG 2** **Analyze credit terms offered by suppliers to determine, when the alternative is to borrow funds, whether to take or give up cash discounts and whether to stretch accounts payable.** Credit terms may differ with respect to the credit period, cash discount, cash discount period, and beginning of the credit period. The cost of giving up cash discounts is a factor in deciding whether to take or give up a cash discount. Cash discounts should be given up only when a firm in need of short-term funds must pay an interest rate on borrowing that is greater than the cost of giving up the cash discount. Stretching accounts payable can lower the cost of giving up a cash discount, thereby increasing the attractiveness of giving up the discount.

**LG 3** **Discuss the interest rates, basic types—single-payment notes, lines of credit, and revolving credit agreements, and the key features of these unsecured bank sources of short-term loans.** Banks are the major source of unsecured short-term loans to businesses. The interest rate on these loans is tied to the prime rate of interest by a risk premium and may be fixed or floating. It should be evaluated using the effective interest rate, which is calculated differently depending on whether interest is paid when the loan matures or in advance. Bank loans may take the form of a single-payment note, a line of credit, or a revolving credit agreement. The key features of the various forms of unsecured bank loans are summarized in part II of Table 10.3.

**TABLE 10.3  Summary of Key Features of Common Sources of Short-Term Financing**

| Type of Short-Term Financing | Source | Cost or Conditions | Characteristics |
| --- | --- | --- | --- |
| **I. Spontaneous sources** | | | |
| Accounts payable | Suppliers of merchandise | No stated cost except when a cash discount is offered for early payment. | Credit extended on open account for 0 to 120 days. The largest source of short-term financing. |
| Accruals | Employees and government | Free. | Result from the fact that wages (employees) and taxes (government) are paid at discrete points in time after the service has been rendered. Hard to manipulate this source of financing. |
| **II. Unsecured bank sources** | | | |
| Single-payment notes | Commercial banks | Prime plus 0–4% risk premium—fixed or floating rate. | A single-payment loan used to meet a funds shortage expected to last only a short period of time. |
| Lines of credit | Commercial banks | Prime plus 0–4% risk premium—fixed or floating rate. Often must maintain 10–20% compensating balance and clean up the line. | A prearranged borrowing limit under which funds, if available, will be lent to allow the borrower to meet seasonal needs. |
| Revolving credit agreements | Commercial banks | Prime plus 0–4% risk premium—fixed or floating rate. Often must maintain 10–20% compensating balance and pay a commitment fee of approximately .5% of the average unused balance. | A line of credit agreement under which the availability of funds is guaranteed. Often for a period greater than one year. |
| **III. Commercial paper** | Other businesses, banks, life insurance companies, pension funds, and money market mutual funds | Generally 1–3% below the prime rate of interest. | An unsecured short-term promissory note issued by the most financially sound firms. May be placed directly or sold through commercial paper dealers. |

| Type of Short-Term Financing | Source | Cost or Conditions | Characteristics |
| --- | --- | --- | --- |
| **IV. Secured sources** | | | |
| Accounts receivable collateral | | | |
| Pledging | Commercial banks and commercial finance companies | 2–5% above prime plus up to 3% in fees. Advance 50–90% of collateral value. | Selected accounts receivable are used as collateral. The borrower is trusted to remit to the lender upon collection of pledged accounts. Done on a nonnotification basis. |
| Factoring | Factors, commercial banks, and commercial finance companies | 1–3% discount from face value of factored accounts. Interest levied on advances of 2–4% above prime. Interest earned on surplus balances left with factor of about .5% per month. | Selected accounts are sold—generally without recourse—at a discount. All credit risks go with the accounts. Factor will loan (make advances) against uncollected accounts that are not yet due. Factor will also pay interest on surplus balances. Typically done on a notification basis. |
| Inventory collateral | | | |
| Floating liens | Commercial banks and commercial finance companies | 3–5% above prime. Advance less than 50% of collateral value. | A loan against inventory in general. Made when firm has stable inventory of a variety of inexpensive items. |
| Trust receipts | Manufacturers' captive financing subsidiaries, commercial banks, and commercial finance companies | 2% or more above prime. Advance 80–100% of cost of collateral. | Loan against relatively expensive automotive, consumer-durable, and industrial equipment that can be identified by serial number. Collateral remains in possession of borrower, who is trusted to remit proceeds to lender upon its sale. |
| Warehouse receipts | Commercial banks and commercial finance companies | 3–5% above prime plus a 1–3% warehouse fee. Advance 75–90% of collateral value. | Inventory used as collateral is placed under control of the lender by putting it in a terminal warehouse or through a field warehouse. A third party—a warehousing company—guards the inventory for the lender. Inventory is released only upon written approval of the lender. |

**Review the role of commercial paper in short-term financing and the use of international loans to finance international trade transactions.** Commercial paper, IOUs issued by firms with a high credit standing, is directly placed with investors by the issuer or is sold by commercial paper dealers. The key features of commercial paper are summarized in part III of Table 10.3. International sales and purchases expose firms to exchange rate risk; involve larger size and longer maturity dates on typical transactions; can be financed using a letter of credit, by borrowing in the local market, or through dollar-denominated loans obtained from international banks; and on transactions between subsidiaries "netting" can be used to minimize foreign exchange fees and other transaction costs.

**Describe the characteristics, acceptable collateral, and terms of secured short-term loans, and the key institutions extending these loans.** Secured short-term loans are those for which the lender requires collateral—typically, current assets, such as accounts receivable or inventory. Only a certain percentage of the book value of acceptable collateral is advanced by the lender. These loans are more expensive than unsecured loans; the presence of collateral does not lower the risk of default, and increased administrative costs result. Both commercial banks and commercial finance companies make secured short-term loans.

**Explain how accounts receivable (pledging and factoring) and inventory (floating lien, trust receipt, and warehouse receipt) can be used as collateral to secure short-term loans.** Accounts receivable is generally the most desirable form of short-term loan collateral. Both pledging, which is the use of accounts receivable as loan collateral, and factoring, which is the outright sale of accounts receivable at a discount, involve the use of accounts receivable to obtain needed short-term funds. Inventory can be used as short-term loan collateral under a floating lien, a trust receipt arrangement, or a warehouse receipt loan. The key features of these various forms of secured short-term loans are summarized in part IV of Table 10.3.

# SUMMARY OF KEY DEFINITIONS AND EQUATIONS

## Variable Definitions

$CD$ = the stated cash discount in percentage terms
finance charges = interest and any other loan charges incurred over the term of the loan

$N$ = the number of days payment can be delayed by giving up the cash discount or the term of the loan in days (assumes a 360-day year consisting of twelve 30-day months)

usable funds = the amount of the loan principal actually received by the borrower

## Equations

[Eq. 10.1]
$$\text{Cost of giving up cash discount} = \frac{CD}{100\% - CD} \times \frac{360}{N}$$

[Eq. 10.2]
$$\text{Approximate cost of giving up cash discount} = CD \times \frac{360}{N}$$

[Eq. 10.3]
$$\text{Effective interest rate} = \frac{\text{finance charges}}{\text{usable funds}} \times \frac{360}{N}$$

[Eq. 10.4]
$$\text{Usable funds on a discount loan} = \text{amount borrowed} - \text{interest}$$

# P A R T   IV

# Long-Term Financial Concepts

After studying this chapter, you should be able to

 **LG 1** Discuss the role of time value in finance, particularly the two common views—future value and present value—and the use of financial tables and business/financial calculators to find them.

 **LG 2** Understand the concept of future value, its calculation for a single amount, and the procedures and effects on future value of compounding interest more frequently than annually, specifically, semiannually or quarterly.

 **LG 3** Find the future value of an annuity using either financial tables or a hand-held business/financial calculator to simplify the calculations.

 **LG 4** Review the concept of present value, its calculation for a single amount, and the relationship of present to future value.

 **LG 5** Determine the present value of a mixed stream of cash flows, an annuity, and a perpetuity.

 **LG 6** Describe the procedures involved in (1) determining deposits to accumulate a future sum, (2) loan amortization, and (3) finding interest or growth rates.

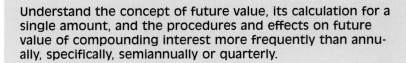
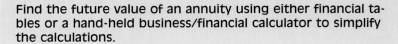
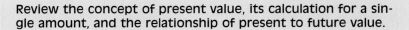

# 11 Time Value

# of Money

Most organizations make decisions involving the investment of resources for long periods of time. Typically, corporations have limited resources at their disposal, and they have to choose the best investments from among various alternatives. Many different methods can be used to deploy investment capital that take into consideration the time to re-

cover the project cost, rates of return, and risk.

The time value of money serves as a common denominator for making investment decisions. With knowledge of such time value concepts as present value, managers can analyze a project's future earnings and cash flow in terms of today's dollars. This allows them to make good investment decisions that increase shareholder value.

Businesses apply time value of money concepts in many

ways. Knowing how to apply time value techniques to investments, whether in tangible assets or securities, is a valuable skill. Reebok uses time value calculations in acquisition analysis as one way of determining how much to pay to acquire a firm. By looking at projected earnings and cash flow streams and applying present value techniques, we can determine what the company is worth to us today. The purchase price of an income-earning entity today has to reflect the present value of future earnings.

Calculating the return on investments, both short and long term, requires application of time value techniques. For example, companies that issue debt use time value techniques to determine the offering price based on the stated coupon versus the market interest rate.

Companies also purchase securities in the secondary market, where prices and yields change frequently. Financial managers have to make sure that the price they are quoted is correct. Although sophisticated computers and calculators perform the calculations, the quotes are sometimes wrong. You can't always rely on what someone else tells you or assume that the computer program is always right. I was involved in just this situation. The quoted price for some municipal securities seemed wrong, so I did the return calculations by hand. There were errors in the equipment providing the price quotes. Because I understood present-value concepts, I discovered the errors and avoided over-paying.

Understanding time value concepts helps managers in all departments ask the right questions and work effectively with financial managers to make informed decisions. Operations managers make decisions to build a new factory, buy new equipment, increase research and development spending, or hire more employees. This requires financial analysis that includes the application of time value techniques. Human resources managers use time value techniques to calculate the cost of offering long-term benefit plans and to advise employees on retirement plans. In addition, time value concepts apply to personal financial decisions—for example, calculations of loan and mortgage payments, analyzing whether to buy or lease a car, and estimating the values of security investment alternatives. Learning about time value pays off in many ways.

**Leo S. Vannoni** *joined Reebok International Ltd. as treasurer in 1993. From 1980 to 1993, he held financial management positions in the computer industry, serving as assistant treasurer of Stratus Computer; manager, international finance at Computervision Corp.; and senior treasury consultant for Digital Equipment Corporation. He received his B.A. in economics from Harvard College and his M.B.A. in finance from the Columbia University Graduate School of Business.*

> # Understanding time value concepts helps managers . . . ask the right questions and work effectively . . . to make informed decisions.

**I**magine that at age 25 you begin making annual cash deposits of $2,000 into a savings account that pays 5 percent annual interest. At the end of 40 years, at age 65, you would have made deposits totaling $80,000 (40 years × $2,000 per year). Assuming that you made no withdrawals, what would your account balance be at age 65? $100,000? $150,000? $200,000? No, your $80,000 would have grown to $242,000! Why? Because the time value of money allowed the deposits to earn interest that was compounded over the 40 years. Because opportunities to earn interest on funds are readily available, the time value of money affects everyone—individuals, businesses, and government.

# The Role of Time Value in Finance

LG  1

Since we view the firm as a going concern, its value and the decisions of the financial manager must be assessed in light of both its present and future cash flows—both inflows and outflows. Because firms as well as individuals are always confronted with opportunities to earn positive rates of return on their funds, that is, interest rates are always greater than zero, the timing of cash flows has important economic consequences. Taking a long-term view requires the financial manager to explicitly recognize the time value of money. Before developing the necessary computational procedures, we consider the two common views of time value—future value and present value—and the computational aids that are commonly used to streamline time-value calculations.

## Future Versus Present Value

Values and decisions can be assessed by using either future-value or present-value techniques. Although these techniques, when correctly applied—as demonstrated later in this chapter—result in the same decisions, they view the decision differently. Future-value techniques are used to find *future values,* which are typically measured at the *end* of a project's life, whereas present-value techniques are used to find *present values,* which are measured at the *start* of a project's life (time zero).

A **time line,** which is a horizontal line on which time zero is at the leftmost end and future periods are shown as you move from left to right, can be used to depict the cash flows associated with a given investment. An illustration of such a line covering five periods (in this case years) is given in Figure 11.1. The cash flow occurring at time zero and at the end of each year is shown above the line, the negative values representing *cash outflows* ($10,000 at time zero) and the positive values represent *cash inflows* ($3,000 inflow at the end of year 1, $5,000 inflow at the end of year 2, and so on). Time lines are frequently used in finance to allow the analyst to understand fully the cash flows associated with a given investment.

Because money has a time value (opportunities exist to earn positive rates of return), the cash flows associated with an investment, such as those depicted in Figure 11.1, must be measured at the same point in time. Typically, that point is either the end or the beginning of the investment's life. The fu-

**time line**
A horizontal line on which time zero is at the leftmost end and future periods are shown as you move from left to right; can be used to depict investment cash flows.

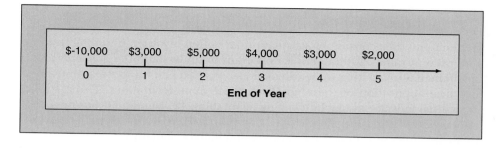

**FIGURE 11.1   Time Line Depicting an Investment's Cash Flows**
A $10,000 cash outflow occurs at time zero followed by cash inflows of $3,000, $5,000, $4,000, $3,000, and $2,000 at the ends of years 1 through 5, respectively.

ture-value technique uses *compounding* to find the future value of each cash flow at the end of the investment's life and then sums them to find the investment's future value. This approach is depicted above the time line in Figure 11.2; it can be seen that the future value of each cash flow is measured at the end of the investment's five-year life. The present-value technique, the other popular approach, uses *discounting* to find the present value of each cash flow at time zero and then sums them to find the investment's present value. Application of this approach is depicted below the time line in Figure 11.2. The meaning and mechanics of both compounding to find future value and discounting to find present value are covered later in this chapter. Although future value and present value, when correctly applied, result in the same decisions, *financial managers, because they make decisions at time zero, tend to rely primarily on present-value techniques.*

**FIGURE 11.2   Time Line Showing Future Value and Present Value**
The future-value technique uses compounding to find future value, and the present-value technique uses discounting to find present value.

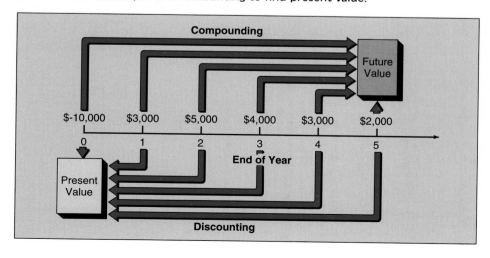

## Computational Aids

Tedious and time-consuming calculations are often involved in finding future and present values. Although it is important to understand the concepts and mathematics underlying these calculations, it is also helpful to streamline the practical application of these important time-value techniques. Three computational aids are available: (1) financial tables, (2) hand-held business/financial calculators, and (3) personal computers. Here we focus on the use of financial tables and hand-held business/financial calculators.

**Financial Tables**   Financial tables that include various future- and present-value interest factors can be easily developed from the appropriate formulas and used to simplify time-value calculations. The degree of decimal precision (rounding to the nearest .01, .001, and so on) varies, but the tables are typically indexed by the number of periods (varies by row) and the interest rate (varies by column). Figure 11.3 depicts this general layout of financial tables. If it were the appropriate table and we wished to find the interest factor for 10 years at a 20 percent interest rate, its value would be x.xxx, which is found at the intersection of the 10-year row and the 20 percent column, as shown. A full set of each of the four basic financial tables is included in Appendix A at the back of the book. The content and role of each of these tables are described later in the chapter, and they are used in the examples presented to demonstrate the application of time-value techniques.

**Business/Financial Calculators**   During the past 10 or so years, the power of the hand-held business/financial calculator has improved dramatically while its cost has become quite low. Today, a powerful hand-held business/financial calculator can be purchased for $15 to $25. Generally, the less expensive calculators are the generic *business calculators*, and the more expen-

### FIGURE 11.3   Layout and Use of a Financial Table

In financial tables, the number of periods varies by row, and the interest rate varies by column. For example, the factor for 10 years at a 20 percent interest rate, x.xxx, occurs at the intersection of the 10-year row and the 20% column.

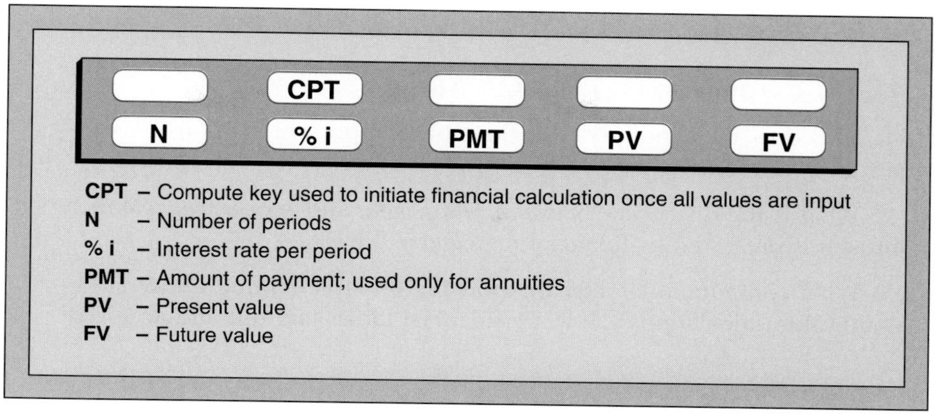

CPT   – Compute key used to initiate financial calculation once all values are input
N      – Number of periods
% i    – Interest rate per period
PMT  – Amount of payment; used only for annuities
PV    – Present value
FV    – Future value

**FIGURE 11.4   Important Financial Keys on the BA-35 Calculator**
The keys on the BA-35 calculator that are used for financial calculations include all of those appearing in its second row along with the CPT key in the first row.

sive ones are *financial calculators,* which include numerous preprogrammed, often menu-driven financial routines. In addition to describing the use of financial tables included in this text, this and subsequent chapters provide the calculator keystrokes for directly calculating interest factors and making other financial computations. For convenience, we use one of the least expensive ($15 to $20 at a discount store) and most popular business calculators, the Texas Instruments BA-35.

Using the BA-35, we focus primary attention on the keys appearing in its second row, along with the CPT key in the first row. Figure 11.4 depicts and defines these keys. We typically use only four of the five keys in the second row, with one of the four keys representing the unknown value being calculated. Occasionally, as we see in the discussion of finding bond values in Chapter 12, all five of the keys, with one representing the unknown value, are used. The keystrokes on other business/financial calculators are similar to those of the BA-35. Some of the more sophisticated and expensive calculators are menu-driven so that after you select the appropriate routine, the calculator prompts you to input each value. Nevertheless, any calculator with the basic future- and present-value functions can be used in lieu of financial tables. The capability and keystrokes of other business/financial calculators are explained in the reference guides that accompany them.

The use of both financial tables and business/financial calculators is demonstrated throughout this text, but I strongly urge you to use a calculator to streamline routine financial calculations *once you understand the basic underlying concepts.* Remember, an ability to solve problems with the aid of a calculator does not necessarily reflect a conceptual understanding of the material—which is the objective of this text. It is therefore important that you understand concepts before relying on the calculator to streamline required computations. Clearly, with a little practice, both the speed and accuracy of financial computations using a calculator (or personal computer) can be greatly enhanced. Note that because of the calculator's greater precision, slight rounding errors are likely to exist between values calculated by using financial tables and those found with a business/financial calculator.

▼▼▼▼▼▼▼▼▼▼▼▼▼▼▼▼▼▼▼▼▼▼▼▼▼▼▼▼▼▼

# Progress Review Questions

**11-1.** Why does the timing of cash flows have important economic consequences? What is a *time line,* and how is it used to depict cash flows?

**11-2.** What is the difference between *future value* and *present value?* Which approach is preferred by financial managers? Why?

**11-3.** What computational aids are available for streamlining future- and present-value calculations? How are financial tables laid out and accessed?

▲▲▲▲▲▲▲▲▲▲▲▲▲▲▲▲▲▲▲▲▲▲▲▲▲▲▲▲▲▲

# Future Value of a Single Amount

The **future value** of a single amount is found by applying compound interest over a specified period. Savings institutions advertise compound interest returns at a rate of *x* percent or *x* percent compounded annually, semiannually, quarterly, monthly, weekly, daily, or even continuously. The principles of future value are quite simple, whatever the period of time involved.

**future value**
The value of a present amount at a future date, found by applying compound interest over a specified period.

## The Concept of Future Value

We speak of **compounded interest** when we wish to indicate that the amount earned on a given deposit has become part of the principal at the end of a specified period. The term **principal** refers to the amount of money on which the interest is paid. Annual compounding is the most common type used in managerial finance calculations. The concept of future value with annual compounding can be illustrated by a simple example.

**compounded interest**
Interest earned on a given deposit that has become part of the principal at the end of a specified period.

**principal**
The amount of money on which interest is paid.

▶ **E X A M P L E**

If Rich Saver places $100 in a savings account paying 8 percent interest compounded annually, at the end of one year he will have $108 in the account. This $108 represents the initial principal of $100 plus 8 percent ($8) in interest. The future value at the end of the first year is calculated by using Equation 11.1.

$$\text{Future value at end of year 1} = \$100 \times (1 + .08) = \$108 \qquad (11.1)$$

**Equation 11.1**

If Rich leaves this money in the account for another year, he would be paid interest at the rate of 8 percent on the new principal of $108. At the end of this second year $116.64 would be in the account. This amount represents the principal at the beginning of year 2 ($108) plus 8 percent of the $108 ($8.64) in interest. The future value at the end of the second year is calculated using Equation 11.2.

$$\text{Future value at end of year 2} = \$108 \times (1 + .08) = \$116.64 \qquad (11.2)$$

**Equation 11.2**

Substituting the expression between the equal signs in Equation 11.1 for the $108 figure in Equation 11.2 gives us Equation 11.3.

**Equation 11.3**

$$\text{Future value at end of year 2} = \$100 \times (1 + .08) \times (1 + .08) \qquad (11.3)$$
$$= \$100 \times (1.08)^2$$
$$= \$116.64$$

## The Calculation of Future Value

The basic relationship in Equation 11.3 can be generalized to find the future value after any number of periods. Let

$FV_n$ = the future value at the end of period $n$

$PV$ = the initial principal, or present value

$k$ = the annual rate of interest paid
   (*Note:* On business/financial calculators, $i$ is typically used to represent this rate.)

$n$ = the number of periods—typically years—the money is left on deposit

By using this notation a general equation for the future value at the end of period $n$ can be formulated.

**Equation 11.4 General formula for future value**

$$FV_n = PV \times (1 + k)^n \qquad (11.4)$$

Equation 11.4 can be used to find the future value, $FV_n$, in an account paying $k$ percent interest compounded annually for $n$ periods if $PV$ dollars is deposited initially. A simple example will illustrate.

## E X A M P L E

Jane Frugal has placed $800 in a savings account paying 6 percent interest compounded annually. She wishes to determine how much money will be in the account at the end of five years. Substituting $PV = \$800$, $k = .06$, and $n = 5$ into Equation 11.4 gives the amount at the end of year 5.

$$FV_5 = \$800 \times (1 + .06)^5 = \$800 \times (1.338) = \$1,070.40$$

Jane will have $1,070.40 in the account at the end of the fifth year. This analysis can be depicted diagrammatically on a time line as shown in Figure 11.5.

**FIGURE 11.5 Time Line for Future Value of a Single Amount ($800 Initial Principal, Earning 6 Percent Annual Interest, at End of Five Years)**

An initial principal, *PV*, of $800 deposited into an account paying 6 percent annual interest, *k*, will have a future value at the end of 5 years, *FV₅*, of $1,070.40.

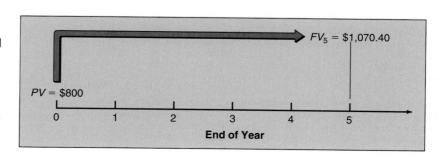

## Simplifying Future-Value Calculations

Solving the equation in the preceding example is quite time-consuming because one must raise 1.06 to the fifth power. A future-value interest table or a business/financial calculator can be used to simplify the calculations. A table for the amount generated by the payment of compound interest on an initial principal of $1 is given as Appendix Table A.1 (at the back of the book). The table provides values for $(1 + k)^n$ in Equation 11.4. This portion of Equation 11.4 is called the **future-value interest factor.** This factor is the multiplier used to calculate at a specified interest rate the future value of a present amount as of a given time. The future-value interest factor for an initial principal of $1 compounded at $k$ percent for $n$ periods is referred to as $FVIF_{k,n}$.

**future-value interest factor**
The multiplier used to calculate at a specified interest rate the future value of a present amount as of a given time.

$$\text{Future-value interest factor} = FVIF_{k,n} = (1 + k)^n \qquad (11.5)$$

**Equation 11.5 Formula for the future-value interest factor for a single amount**

By accessing the table with respect to the annual interest rate, $k$, and the appropriate periods, $n$, the factor relevant to a particular problem can be found.[1] By letting $FVIF_{k,n}$ represent the appropriate factor, we can rewrite Equation 11.4 as follows:

$$FV_n = PV \times (FVIF_{k,n}) \qquad (11.6)$$

**Equation 11.6 General formula for the future value of a single amount**

The expression indicates that to find the future value, $FV_n$, at the end of period $n$ of an initial deposit, we have merely to multiply the initial deposit, $PV$, by the appropriate future-value interest factor. An example illustrates this calculation using both a table and a hand-held business calculator.

▶ **E X A M P L E**

As noted in the preceding example, Jane Frugal placed $800 in her savings account at 6 percent interest compounded annually. She wishes to find out how much will be in the account at the end of five years.

**Table Use**   The future-value interest factor for an initial principal of $1 on deposit for five years at 6 percent interest compounded annually, $FVIF_{6\%,\ 5\ \text{yrs}}$, found in Table A.1, is 1.338. Multiplying the initial principal of $800 by this factor in accordance with Equation 11.6 results in a future value at the end of year 5 of $1,070.40.

**Calculator Use**[2]   The preprogrammed financial functions in the business calculator[3] can be used to calculate the future value directly. First punch in

---

[1]Although we commonly deal with years rather than periods, financial tables are frequently presented in terms of periods to provide maximum flexibility.

[2]Many calculators allow the user to set the number of payments per year. Most of these calculators are preset for monthly payments—12 payments per year. Because we work primarily with annual payments—one payment per year—it is important to *make sure that your calculator is set for one payment per year.* Consult the reference guide that accompanies your calculator for instructions for setting this value. Note that the BA-35 is always set for the desired payment frequency of one payment per year.

[3]The BA-35 calculator, like many other multifunction business calculators, has two preprogrammed functions: financial and statistical. It is therefore important always to make sure that the finance function keys have been activated before making financial calculations. On the BA-35 this is done by pressing **2nd** followed by **FIN. FIN** appears in the calculator display to confirm the activation of these functions. Also, to avoid including previous data in current calculations, *always clear* all registers before inputting values and making each computation.

$800, and depress **PV;** next punch in 5 and depress **N;** then punch in 6, and depress **%i** (which is equivalent to $k$ in our notation)[4]; finally, to calculate the future value, depress **CPT** and then **FV.** The future value of $1,070.58 should appear on the calculator display.

| Inputs: | 800 | 5 | 6 | | |
|---|---|---|---|---|---|
| Functions: | PV | N | % i | CPT | FV |
| Outputs: | | | | | 1070.58 |

The calculator is more accurate than the use of factors from Table A.1, which have been rounded to the nearest one-thousandth. Thus, a slight difference—in this case $0.18—frequently exists between the values found using these alternative methods. Clearly, the improved accuracy and ease of calculation tend to favor the use of the calculator when making financial calculations such as this.

## A Graphic View of Future Value

It is important to note that we measure future value at the *end* of the given period. The relationship between various interest rates, the number of periods interest is earned, and the future value of one dollar is illustrated in Figure 11.6. It clearly shows two relationships: (1) the higher the interest rate, the higher the future value, and (2) the longer the time period, the higher the future value. Note that for an interest rate of 0 percent, the future value always equals the present value ($1.00). But for any interest rate greater than zero, the future value is greater than the present value of $1.00 in Figure 11.6.

## Semiannual and Quarterly Compounding

Interest is often compounded more frequently than once a year. Savings institutions compound interest semiannually, quarterly, monthly, weekly, daily, or even continuously. This section discusses semiannual and quarterly compounding and explains how to use both a table and a hand-held business calculator to simplify calculations.

**semiannual compounding**
Compounding of interest over two periods within the year.

**Semiannual Compounding**   **Semiannual compounding** of interest involves two compounding periods within the year. Instead of the stated interest rate being paid once a year, one-half of the stated interest rate is paid twice a year.

## E X A M P L E

Rich Saver has decided to invest $100 in a savings account paying 8 percent interest *compounded semiannually.* If he leaves his money in the account for

---

[4]The known values *can be punched into the calculator in any order;* the order specified in this as well as other calculator use demonstrations included in this text results merely from convenience and personal preference.

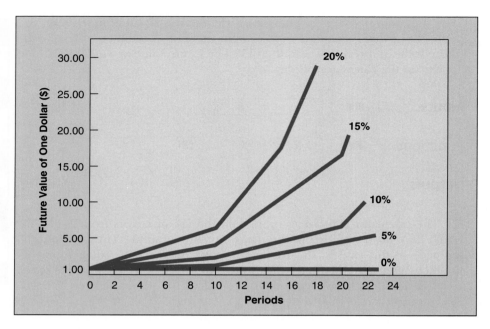

**FIGURE 11.6    Interest Rates, Time Periods, and Future Value of One Dollar**
The future value increases with increases in the interest rate and the period during which funds are left on deposit. At zero percent interest, the future value always equals the present value ($1.00), and for interest rates greater than zero, the future value is always greater than the present value of $1.00.

two years, he will be paid 4 percent interest compounded over four periods, each of which is six months long. Table 11.1 uses interest factors to show that at the end of one year, when the 8 percent interest is compounded semiannually, Rich will have $108.16. At the end of two years, he will have $116.99.

**Quarterly Compounding**    **Quarterly compounding** of interest involves four compounding periods within the year. One-fourth of the stated interest rate is paid four times a year.

**quarterly compounding**
Compounding of interest over four periods within the year.

## EXAMPLE

After further investigation of his savings opportunities, Rich Saver has found an institution that pays 8 percent interest *compounded quarterly*. If he leaves his money in this account for two years, he will be paid 2 percent interest compounded over eight periods, each of which is three months long. Table 11.2 uses interest factors to present the calculations required to determine the amount Rich will have at the end of two years. As the table shows, at the end of one year, when the 8 percent interest is compounded quarterly, Rich will have $108.24. At the end of two years, he will have $117.16.

Table 11.3 presents comparative values for Rich Saver's $100 at the end of years 1 and 2 given annual, semiannual, and quarterly compounding at the 8 percent rate. As the table shows, *the more frequently interest is compounded, the greater the amount of money accumulated.* This is true for any interest rate for any period of time.

## Annual Returns Can Be Deceiving

In most cases, it's a good idea to look at more than the most recent annual return posted by your favorite mutual fund. Take the case of Lexington Strategic Investments (LSI), a mutual fund that invests heavily in South African gold stocks. In 1993, the fund's total return was an eye-popping 265 percent, topping the charts on *Business Week*'s mutual funds scoreboard.

So far, the fund sounds like a winner, right? Let's look a little closer. Based on past performance, a $1,000 investment in the fund in 1984 is worth only $409 in 1994, making the fund's ef-

fective annual rate of return over the 10-year period *negative* 8.5 percent. In 6 of the last 10 years, the fund reported losses, rather than gains. Even in comparison with other mutual funds invested in gold, LSI's performance has been dreadful. Although the fund did indeed hit a home run in 1993, its 10-year batting average shows it hit plenty of foul balls before it finally connected at the plate.

Source: T. Peterson, "1993's Top Fund Has a Mixed Record," *Business Week*, January 17, 1994, p. 39.

**Simplifying the Calculations**   The future-value interest factors for one dollar, given in Table A.1, can be used to find the future value when interest is compounded *m* times each year. Instead of indexing the table for *k* percent and *n* years, as we do when interest is compounded annually, we index it for $(k \div m)$ percent and $(m \times n)$ periods. The usefulness of the table is usually somewhat limited, because it includes only selected rates for a limited number of periods. A business/financial calculator or personal computer is typically required. The following example demonstrates the use of both a table and a hand-held business calculator.

**TABLE 11.1   The Future Value from Investing $100 at 8 Percent Interest Compounded Semiannually over Two Years**

| Period | Beginning Principal (1) | Future-Value Interest Factor (2) | Future Value at End of Period [(1) × (2)] (3) |
|---|---|---|---|
| 6 months | $100.00 | 1.04 | $104.00 |
| 1 year | 104.00 | 1.04 | 108.16 |
| 18 months | 108.16 | 1.04 | 112.49 |
| 2 years | 112.49 | 1.04 | 116.99 |

**TABLE 11.2   The Future Value from Investing $100 at 8 Percent Interest Compounded Quarterly over Two Years**

| Period | Beginning Principal (1) | Future-Value Interest Factor (2) | Future Value at End of Period [(1) × (2)] (3) |
|---|---|---|---|
| 3 months | $100.00 | 1.02 | $102.00 |
| 6 months | 102.00 | 1.02 | 104.04 |
| 9 months | 104.04 | 1.02 | 106.12 |
| 1 year | 106.12 | 1.02 | 108.24 |
| 15 months | 108.24 | 1.02 | 110.40 |
| 18 months | 110.40 | 1.02 | 112.61 |
| 21 months | 112.61 | 1.02 | 114.86 |
| 2 years | 114.86 | 1.02 | 117.16 |

**TABLE 11.3   The Future Value from Investing $100 at 8 Percent for Years 1 and 2 Given Various Compounding Periods**

| End of Year | Compounding Period | | |
| | Annual | Semiannual | Quarterly |
|---|---|---|---|
| 1 | $108.00 | $108.16 | $108.24 |
| 2 | 116.64 | 116.99 | 117.16 |

▶ E X A M P L E

In the earlier examples, Rich Saver wished to find the future value of $100 invested at 8 percent compounded both semiannually and quarterly for two years. The number of compounding periods, $m$, was 2 and 4, respectively, in these cases. The interest rate and number of periods used in each case, along with the future-value interest factor, are shown in the table.

| Compounding Period | $m$ | Interest Rate $(k \div m)$ | Periods $(m \times n)$ | Future-Value Interest Factor from Table A.1 |
|---|---|---|---|---|
| Semiannual | 2 | 8% ÷ 2 = 4% | 2 × 2 = 4 | 1.170 |
| Quarterly | 4 | 8% ÷ 4 = 2% | 4 × 2 = 8 | 1.172 |

**Table Use**   The factor for 4 percent and four periods is used for semiannual compounding, and the factor for 2 percent and eight periods is used for quarterly compounding. Multiplying each of the factors by the initial $100 deposit results in a value of $117.00 (1.170 × $100) for semiannual compounding and a value of $117.20 (1.172 × $100) for quarterly compounding.

**Calculator Use**   If the calculator is used for the semiannual compounding calculation, as noted in the preceding table, the number of periods is 4, and the interest rate is 4 percent. First punch in $100, and depress **PV**; next punch in 4, and depress **N**; then punch in 4, and depress **%i**; finally, to calculate the future value, depress **CPT** followed by **FV**. The future value of $116.99 should appear on the calculator display.

| Inputs: | 100 | 4 | 4 | | |
|---|---|---|---|---|---|
| **Functions:** | PV | N | % i | CPT | FV |
| **Outputs:** | | | | | 116.99 |

For the quarterly compounding case, the number of periods is 8, and the interest rate is 2 percent. First punch in $100, and depress **PV**; next punch in 8, and depress **N**; then punch in 2, and depress **%i**; finally, to calculate the future value, depress **CPT** followed by **FV**. The future value of $117.17 should appear on the calculator display.

| Inputs: | 100 | 8 | 2 | | |
|---|---|---|---|---|---|
| **Functions:** | PV | N | % i | CPT | FV |
| **Outputs:** | | | | | 117.17 |

Comparing the values found by using the calculator with those based on the use of Table A.1, we can see that the calculator values generally agree with those values given in Table 11.3 but are more precise because the table factors have been rounded.

## Progress Review Questions

**11-4.** How is the *compounding process* related to the payment of interest on savings? What is the general equation for the future value, $FV_n$, in period $n$ if $PV$ dollars are deposited in an account paying $k$ percent annual interest?

**11-5.** What effect does (a) a *decrease* in the interest rate or (b) an *increase* in the holding period of a deposit have on its future value? Why?

**11-6.** What effect does compounding interest more frequently than annually have on the future value generated by a beginning principal? Why?

▲▲▲▲▲▲▲▲▲▲▲▲▲▲▲▲▲▲▲▲▲▲▲▲▲▲▲▲▲▲▲▲▲▲▲▲

# Future Value of an Annuity

LG ③

An **annuity** is a stream of equal annual cash flows. These cash flows can be *inflows* of returns earned on investments or *outflows* of funds invested to earn future returns. The calculations required to find the future value of an annuity on which interest is paid at a specified rate compounded annually can be illustrated by the following example.

**annuity**
A stream of equal annual cash flows

▶ E X A M P L E

Mollie Carr wishes to determine how much money she will have at the end of five years if she deposits $1,000 annually into a savings account paying 7 percent annual interest. The deposits are made *at the end* of each of the next five years. Table 11.4 presents the calculations required to find the future value of this annuity at the end of year 5. This situation is depicted diagrammatically on a time line in Figure 11.7. As the table and figure show, at the end of year 5, Mollie will have $5,751 in her account. Column 2 of the table indicates that since the deposits are made at the end of the year, the first deposit will earn interest for four years, the second for three years, and so on. The future-value interest factors in column 3 correspond to these interest-earning periods and the 7 percent rate of interest.

---

**TABLE 11.4  The Future Value of a $1,000 Five-Year Annuity Compounded at 7 Percent**

| End of Year | Amount Deposited (1) | Number of Years Compounded (2) | Future-Value Interest Factors from Table A.1 (3) | Future Value at End of Year [(1) × (3)] (4) |
|---|---|---|---|---|
| 1 | $1,000 | 4 | 1.311 | $1,311 |
| 2 | 1,000 | 3 | 1.225 | 1,225 |
| 3 | 1,000 | 2 | 1.145 | 1,145 |
| 4 | 1,000 | 1 | 1.070 | 1,070 |
| 5 | 1,000 | 0 | 1.000 | 1,000 |
| | | | Future value of annuity at end of year 5 | $5,751 |

**FIGURE 11.7   Time Line for Future Value of an Annuity ($1,000 End-of-Year Deposit, Earning 7 Percent, at End of Five Years)**

Annual end-of-year deposits, *PMT,* of $1,000 into an account paying 7 percent annual interest, *k,* will have a future value at the end of five years, *FVA₅,* of $5,751.

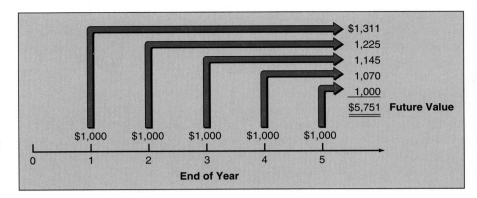

## Simplifying Future-Value-of-an-Annuity Calculations

**future-value interest factor for an annuity**
The multiplier used to calculate the future value of an annuity at a specified interest rate over a given period.

Annuity calculations can be simplified by using a future-value interest table for an annuity or a hand-held business/financial calculator. A table for the future value of a $1 annuity is given in Appendix Table A.2 (at the back of the book). The factors included in the table are based on the assumption that every deposit is made at the *end of the period*.[5] The formula for the **future-value interest factor for an annuity** when interest is compounded annually at $k$ percent for $n$ periods, $FVIFA_{k,n}$, is[6]

**Equation 11.7 Formula for the future-value interest factor for an annuity**

$$FVIFA_{k,n} = \sum_{t=1}^{n} (1 + k)^{t-1} \qquad (11.7)$$

This factor is the multiplier used to calculate the future value of an annuity at a specified interest rate over a given period.

Letting $FVA_n$ equal the future value of an *n*-year annuity, *PMT* equals the amount to be deposited annually at the end of each year, and $FVIFA_{k,n}$ represents the appropriate *future-value interest factor for a one-dollar annuity compounded at k percent for n years*, the relationship among these variables can be expressed as follows:

**Equation 11.8 General formula for the future value of an annuity**

$$FVA_n = PMT \times (FVIFA_{k,n}) \qquad (11.8)$$

An example illustrates this calculation using both a table and a hand-held business calculator.

## E X A M P L E

As noted in the preceding example, Mollie Carr wishes to find the future value ($FVA_n$) at the end of five years (*n*) of an annual *end-of-year deposit* of $1,000 (*PMT*) into an account paying 7 percent annual interest (*k*) during the next five years.

---

[5]The discussions of annuities throughout this text concentrate on the more common form of annuity—the *ordinary annuity*, which is an annuity that occurs at the *end* of each period. An annuity that occurs at the *beginning* of each period is called an *annuity due*. The financial tables for annuities included in this book are prepared for use with ordinary annuities.

[6]This formula merely states that the future-value interest factor for an *n*-year annuity is found by adding the sum of the first $n - 1$ future-value interest factors to 1.000, that is

$$FVIFA_{k,n} = 1.000 + \sum_{t=1}^{n-1} FVIF_{k,t}$$

**Table Use**   The appropriate future-value interest factor for a five-year annuity at 7 percent, $FVIFA_{7\%,5yrs}$, is found in Table A.2; it equals 5.751. Multiplying the $1,000 deposit by this factor in accordance with Equation 11.8 results in a future value for the annuity of $5,751.

**Calculator Use**   Using the calculator, first punch in the $1,000, and depress **PMT**; next punch in 5, and depress **N**; then punch in 7, and depress **%i**; finally, to calculate the future value of this annuity, depress **CPT** followed by **FV**. Ignoring the minus sign,[7] the future value of the annuity of $5,750.74 should appear on the calculator display. This is basically the same value as that obtained using the factor from Table A.2.

**Inputs:**   [ 1000 ]   [ 5 ]   [ 7 ]

**Functions:**   [ PMT ]   [ N ]   [ % i ]   [ CPT ]   [ FV ]

▶ **Outputs:**                                              [ 5,750.74 ]

▼▼▼▼▼▼▼▼▼▼▼▼▼▼▼▼▼▼▼▼▼▼▼▼▼▼▼▼▼▼▼▼

# Progress Review Question

**11-7.** Explain how one can conveniently determine the future value of an annuity that provides a stream of end-of-period cash inflows.

▲▲▲▲▲▲▲▲▲▲▲▲▲▲▲▲▲▲▲▲▲▲▲▲▲▲▲▲▲▲▲▲

# Present Value of a Single Amount

LG

It is often useful to determine the "present value" of a future amount of money. **Present value** is the current dollar value of a future amount—the amount of money that would have to be invested today at a given interest rate over a specified period to equal the future amount. Present value, like future value, is based on the belief that a dollar today is worth more than a dollar that will be received at some future date. The actual present value of a dollar depends largely on the investment opportunities of the recipient and the point in time at which the dollar is to be received. This section explores the present value of a single amount.

**present value**
The current dollar value of a future amount.

---

[7]Note that on many calculators, like the BA-35, the calculated future value of an annuity is preceded by a minus sign. Technically, this sign is intended to refer to the fact that this future value (*FVA*) is an outflow or withdrawal from the annuity account, because the amount of the annuity (*PMT*) is treated as an inflow or deposit into the annuity account. For our purposes the negative sign is not important and therefore should be ignored.

## The Concept of Present Value

**discounting cash flows**
The process of finding present values; the inverse of compounding interest.

The process of finding present values is often referred to as **discounting cash flows.** This process is actually the inverse of compounding interest. It is concerned with answering the question "If I can earn $k$ percent on my money, what is the most I am willing to pay for an opportunity to receive $FV_n$ dollars $n$ periods from today?" Instead of finding the future value of present dollars invested at a given rate, discounting determines the present value of a future amount, assuming that the decision maker has an opportunity to earn a certain return $k$ on the money. This annual rate of return is variously referred to as the *discount rate, required return, cost of capital,* or *opportunity cost.* These terms are used interchangeably in this text. The discounting process can be illustrated by a simple example.

### E X A M P L E

Mr. Cotter has been given an opportunity to receive $300 one year from now. If he can earn 6 percent on his investments in the normal course of events, what is the most he should pay now for this opportunity? To answer this question, we must determine how many dollars have to be invested at 6 percent today to have $300 one year from now. By letting $PV$ equal this unknown amount, and using the same notation as in the compounding discussion, the situation can be expressed as follows:

**Equation 11.9**

$$PV \times (1 + .06) = \$300 \tag{11.9}$$

Solving Equation 11.9 for $PV$ gives us Equation 11.10

**Equation 11.10**

$$PV = \frac{\$300}{1.06} \tag{11.10}$$

$$= \$283.02$$

which results in a value of $283.02 for $PV.$ In other words, the "present value" of $300 received one year from today, given an opportunity cost of 6 percent, is $283.02. Mr. Cotter should be indifferent to whether he receives $283.02 today or $300.00 one year from now. This is true because the present value of $283.02 is the cash equivalent today of $300 one year from now; investment of $283.02 today at the 6 percent opportunity cost would result in $300 at the end of one year. Clearly, if Mr. Cotter could receive either amount by paying less than $283.02 today, he should, of course, do so.

## The Calculation of Present Value

The present value of a future amount can be found mathematically by solving Equation 11.4 for $PV.$ In other words, one merely wants to obtain the present value, $PV,$ of some future amount, $FV_n,$ to be received $n$ periods from now, assuming an opportunity cost of $k.$ Solving Equation 11.4 for $PV$ gives us Equation 11.11, which is the general equation for the present value of a future amount.

**Equation 11.11  General formula for present value**

$$PV = \frac{FV_n}{(1 + k)^n} = FV_n \times \left[ \frac{1}{(1 + k)^n} \right] \tag{11.11}$$

Note the similarity between this general equation for present value and the equation in the preceding example (Equation 11.10). The use of this equation in finding the present value of a future amount can be illustrated by a simple example.

## ▶ E X A M P L E

Bob Lambert wishes to find the present value of $1,700 that will be received eight years from now. Bob's opportunity cost is 8 percent. Substituting $FV_8 = \$1,700$, $n = 8$, and $k = .08$ into Equation 11.11 yields Equation 11.12.

$$PV = \frac{\$1,700}{(1 + .08)^8}$$    (11.12)    **Equation 11.12**

To solve Equation 11.12, the term $(1 + .08)$ must be raised to the eighth power. The value resulting from this time-consuming calculation is 1.851. Dividing this value into $1,700 yields a present value for the $1,700 of $918.42 This analysis can be depicted diagrammatically on a time line as shown in ▶ Figure 11.8.

---

## Simplifying Present-Value Calculations

The present-value calculation can be simplified by using a **present-value interest factor.** This factor is the multiplier used to calculate at a specified discount rate the present value of an amount to be received in a future period. The present-value interest factor for the present value of $1 discounted at $k$ percent for $n$ periods is referred to as $PVIF_{k,n}$.

**present-value interest factor**
The multiplier used to calculate at a specified discount rate the present value of an amount to be received in a future period.

$$\text{Present-value interest factor} = PVIF_{k,n} = \frac{1}{(1 + k)^n}$$    (11.13)

**Equation 11.13 Formula for the present-value interest factor for a single amount**

Appendix Table A.3 (at the back of the book) presents present-value interest factors for $1. By letting $PVIF_{k,n}$ represent the appropriate interest factor, we can rewrite Equation 11.11 as follows:

$$PV = FV_n \times (PVIF_{k,n})$$    (11.14)

**Equation 11.14 General formula for the present value of a single amount**

This expression indicates that to find the present value, $PV$, of an amount to be received in a future period, $n$, we have merely to multiply the future amount, $FV_n$, by the appropriate present-value interest factor. An example illustrates this calculation using both a table and a hand-held business calculator.

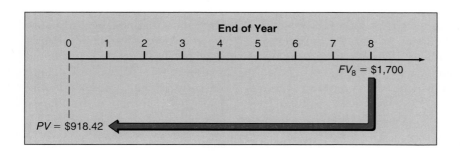

**FIGURE 11.8 Time Line for Present Value of a Single Amount ($1,700 Future Amount, Discounted at 8 Percent, from End of Eight Years)**

The present value, $PV$, of $1,700 to be received at the end of eight years, $FV_8$, using a discount rate, $k$, of 8 percent is $918.42.

# E X A M P L E

As noted in the preceding example, Bob Lambert wishes to find the present value of $1,700 to be received eight years from now, assuming an 8 percent opportunity cost.

**Table Use**  The present-value interest factor for 8 percent and eight years, $PVIF_{8\%, 8yrs}$, found in Table A.3, is .540. Multiplying the $1,700 future value by this factor in accordance with Equation 11.14 results in a present value of $918.

**Calculator Use**  Alternatively, the present value can be found by using the business calculator's financial functions. First punch in $1,700, and depress **FV**; next punch in 8, and depress **N**; then punch in 8, and depress **%i**; finally, to calculate the present value, depress **CPT** followed by **PV**. The present value, $918.46, should appear on the calculator display.

**Inputs:**    [ 1700 ]   [ 8 ]   [ 8 ]

**Functions:**   [ FV ]   [ N ]   [ % i ]   [ CPT ]   [ PV ]

**Outputs:**                                          [ 918.46 ]

Note that because of rounding in the calculation in Equation 11.12 and of the factors in Table A.3, the value obtained with the calculator—$918.46—is most accurate, although for purposes of this text these differences are deemed insignificant.

## A Graphic View of Present Value

It is important to note that present-value calculations assume that the future values are measured at the *end* of the given period. The relationship among various discount rates, time periods, and the present value of one dollar is illustrated in Figure 11.9. Everything else being equal, the figure clearly shows two relationships: (1) the higher the discount rate, the lower the present value, and (2) the longer the time period, the lower the present value. Also note that given a discount rate of 0 percent, the present value always equals the future value ($1.00). But for any discount rate greater than zero, the present value is less than the future value of $1.00 in Figure 11.9.

## Comparing Present Value and Future Value

A few important observations must be made with respect to present values. One is that the expression for the present-value interest factor for $k$ percent and $n$ periods, $1/(1 + k)^n$, is the inverse of the future-value interest factor for $k$ percent and $n$ periods, $(1 + k)^n$. This observation can be confirmed: Divide a present-value interest factor for $k$ percent and $n$ periods, $PVIF_{k,n}$, into 1.0 and compare the resulting value to the future-value interest factor given in

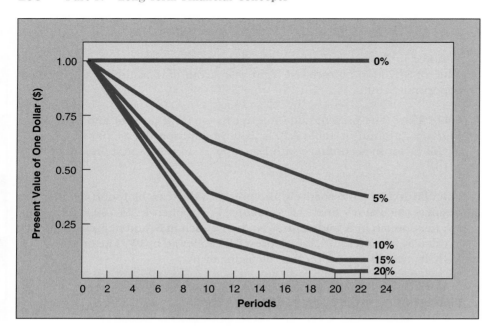

**FIGURE 11.9    Discount Rates, Time Periods, and Present Value of One Dollar**

The present value decreases with increases in the discount rate and the time until the future funds are received. At a 0% discount rate the present value always equals the future value ($1.00), and for discount rates greater than zero, the present value is always less than the future value of $1.00.

Table A.1 for $k$ percent and $n$ periods, $FVIF_{k,n}$. The two values should be equivalent. Because of the relationship between present-value interest factors and future-value interest factors, we can find the present-value interest factors given a table of future-value interest factors, and vice versa. For example, the future-value interest factor from Table A.1 for 10 percent and five periods is 1.611. Dividing this value into 1.0 yields .621, which is the present-value interest factor given in Table A.3 for 10 percent and five periods.

## Progress Review Questions

**11-8.** What is meant by the phrase "the present value of a future amount"? How are present-value and future-value calculations related?

**11-9.** What is the equation for the present value, $PV$, of a future amount $FV_n$, to be received in period $n$, assuming that the firm requires a minimum return of $k$ percent? How is this equation different from the equation for the future value of one dollar?

**11-10.** What effect does *increasing* (a) required return or (b) time periods have on the present value of a future amount? Why?

# Present Value of Cash Flow Streams

Quite often in finance there is a need to find the present value of a stream of cash flows to be received in various future periods. Two basic types of cash flow streams are possible: the mixed stream and the annuity. A **mixed stream** of cash flows reflects no particular pattern, whereas, as stated earlier, an *annuity* is a pattern of equal annual cash flows. Because certain shortcuts are possible when finding the present value of an annuity, mixed streams and annuities are discussed separately. In addition, the present value of a perpetuity is considered in this section.

**mixed stream**
A stream of cash flows that reflects no particular pattern.

## Present Value of a Mixed Stream

Finding the present value of a mixed stream of cash flows involves two steps. First, determine the present value of each future amount in the manner described in the preceding section. Then add all the individual present values to find the total present value of the stream. An example can be used to illustrate this procedure using Table A.3 or a hand-held business calculator.

## E X A M P L E

QTD Company, a shoe manufacturer, has been offered an opportunity to receive the mixed stream of cash flows shown in the table over the next five years. If the firm must earn 9 percent, at minimum, on its investments, what is the most it should pay for this opportunity?

| Year | Cash Flow |
|------|-----------|
| 1 | $400 |
| 2 | 800 |
| 3 | 500 |
| 4 | 400 |
| 5 | 300 |

**Table Use**   To solve this problem, we determine the present value of each cash flow discounted at 9 percent for the appropriate number of years. The sum of all these individual values is then calculated to get the present value of the total stream. The present-value interest factors required are obtained from Table A.3. Table 11.5 presents the calculations needed to find the present value of the cash flow stream, which turns out to be $1,904.60.

**Calculator Use**   A calculator can be used to find the present value of each individual cash flow, using the procedure demonstrated earlier; then the present values can be summed to get the present value of the stream of cash flows. Most more expensive financial calculators have a function that allows you to punch in all cash flows, specify the discount rate, and then directly calculate the present value of the entire cash flow stream. The inexpensive BA-35 business calculator used here does not contain that function. Because calculators provide more precise solutions than those based on the use of rounded table factors, using a calculator to find the present value of QTD Company's cash flow stream results in a value that is close to but not precisely equal to the $1,904.60 value calculated previously.

QTD should not pay more than $1,904.60 for the opportunity to receive these cash flows, because paying $1,904.60 provides exactly a 9 percent return. This situation is depicted diagrammatically on a time line in Figure 11.10.

## Present Value of an Annuity

The present value of an annuity can be found in a manner similar to that used for a mixed stream, but a shortcut is possible.

## ► E X A M P L E

Labco Company, a small producer of plastic toys, is attempting to determine the most it should pay to purchase a particular annuity. The firm requires a minimum return of 8 percent on all investments, and the annuity consists of cash flows of $700 per year for five years. Table 11.6 shows the long way of finding the present value of the annuity, which is the same as the method used for the mixed stream. This procedure yields a present value of $2,795.10, which can be interpreted in the same manner as for the mixed cash flow stream in the preceding example. Similarly, this situation is depicted graphically on a time line in Figure 11.11.

## Simplifying Present-Value-of-an-Annuity Calculations

Annuity calculations can be simplified by using a present-value interest table for an annuity or a business/financial calculator. The values for the present

### TABLE 11.5   The Present Value of a Mixed Stream of Cash Flows

| Year ($n$) | Cash Flow (1) | $PVIF_{9\%,n}^{a}$ (2) | Present Value [(1) × (2)] (3) |
|---|---|---|---|
| 1 | $400 | .917 | $ 366.80 |
| 2 | 800 | .842 | 673.60 |
| 3 | 500 | .772 | 386.00 |
| 4 | 400 | .708 | 283.20 |
| 5 | 300 | .650 | 195.00 |
| | | Present value of mixed stream | $1,904.60 |

[a]Present-value interest factors at 9 percent are from Table A-3.

**FIGURE 11.10  Time Line for Present Value of a Mixed Stream (End-of-Year Cash Flows, Discounted at 9 Percent, over Corresponding Number of Years)**

The $1,904.60 present value of the mixed stream of cash flows occurring at the end of each of the next five years is calculated by finding the sum of the present values of the individual cash flows using the 9 percent discount rate.

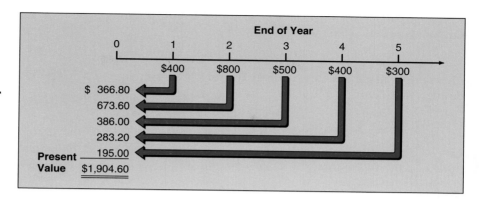

value of a $1 annuity are given in Appendix Table A.4 (at the back of the book). The interest factors in Table A.4 actually represent the sum of the first $n$ present-value interest factors in Table A.3 for a given discount rate. The formula for the **present-value interest factor for an annuity** with end-of-year cash flows that are discounted at $k$ percent for $n$ periods, $PVIFA_{k,n}$, is[8]

**Equation 11.15**
**Formula for the present-value interest factor for an annuity**

**present-value interest factor for an annuity**
The multiplier used to calculate the present value of an annuity at a specified discount rate over a given period.

$$PVIFA_{k,n} = \sum_{t=1}^{n} \frac{1}{(1+k)^t} \tag{11.15}$$

This factor is the multiplier used to calculate the present value of an annuity at a specified discount rate over a given period.

By letting $PVA_n$ equal the present value of an $n$-year annuity, $PMT$ equal the amount to be received annually at the end of each year, and $PVIFA_{k,n}$ represent the appropriate value for the *present-value interest factor for a one-dollar*

**TABLE 11.6   The Long Method for Finding the Present Value of an Annuity**

| Year ($n$) | Cash Flow (1) | $PVIF_{8\%,n}^{a}$ (2) | Present Value [(1) × (2)] (3) |
|---|---|---|---|
| 1 | $700 | .926 | $ 648.20 |
| 2 | 700 | .857 | 599.90 |
| 3 | 700 | .794 | 555.80 |
| 4 | 700 | .735 | 514.50 |
| 5 | 700 | .681 | 476.70 |
| | | Present value of annuity | $2,795.10 |

[a]Present-value interest factors at 8 percent are from Table A.3.

[8]This formula merely states that the present-value interest factor for an $n$-year annuity is found by summing the first $n$ present-value interest factors at the given rate, that is

$$PVIFA_{k,n} = \sum_{t=1}^{n} PVIF_{k,t}$$

*annuity discounted at k percent for n years,* the relationship among these variables can be expressed as follows:

$$PVA_n = PMT \times (PVIFA_{k,n}) \tag{11.16}$$

Equation 11.16 **General formula for the present value of an annuity**

An example illustrates this calculation using both a table and a hand-held business calculator.

▶ **E X A M P L E**

Labco Company, as noted in the preceding example, wishes to find the present value of a five-year annuity of $700 assuming an 8 percent opportunity cost.

**Table Use**   The present-value interest factor for an annuity at 8 percent for five years, $PVIFA_{8\%,5yrs}$, found in Table A.4 is 3.993. Multiplying the $700 annuity by this factor in accordance with Equation 11.16 results in a present value of $2,795.10.

**Calculator Use**   The present value of an annuity can alternatively be found by using the business calculator's financial functions. First punch in $700, and depress **PMT**; next punch in 5, and depress **N**; then punch in 8, and depress **%i**; finally, to calculate the present value of the annuity, depress **CPT** followed by **PV**. The present value of $2,794.90 should appear on the calculator display.

**Inputs:**   [ 700 ]   [ 5 ]   [ 8 ]

**Functions:**   [ PMT ]   [ N ]   [ % i ]   [ CPT ]   [ PV ]

**Outputs:**                                    [ 2794.90 ]

Note that because of rounding in the calculation in Table 11.6 and of the factors in Table A.4, the value obtained with the calculator—$2,794.90—is more accurate, although for purposes of this text these differences are deemed insignificant.

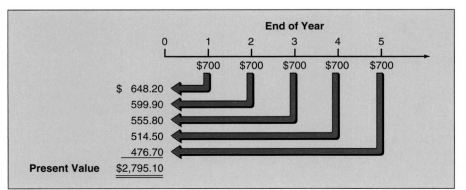

**FIGURE 11.11   Time Line for Present Value of an Annuity ($700 End-of-Year Cash Flows, Discounted at 8 Percent, over 5 Years)**

The $2,795.10 present value of the annuity cash flows of $700 occurring at the end of each of the next five years is calculated by finding the sum of the present values of the individual cash flows using the 8 percent discount rate.

# F I N A N C E I N

## C T I O N

In the News

### Need a New Printer? Here's One that Pays for Itself

In evaluating the total cost of new business assets, operating expenses often play a greater role than the initial purchase price. Take the case of laser printers, which typically sell for around $2,000. The average printer requires a toner cartridge that contains not only toner ink, but also a mechanical imaging drum that wears out every few thousand copies. Over the 300,000-copy life of the average printer, its owner will replace the toner cartridge every 3,000 to 5,000 copies. At $75 per cartridge, users pay about 2 cents for every printed page. Because the average printer runs about 30,000 copies a year over its 10-year service life, the annual operating cost of the printer runs around $600. At a 5 percent discount rate, the present value of total operating costs equals $4,633—well beyond the initial purchase price of most printers.

Kyocera Electronics recently introduced a new laser printer, which places black characters on white paper using a completely different technology. The firm's printers come with a permanent imaging drum made out of advanced ce-

ramics, and users replace only the toner ink every 7,000 copies. Because Kyocera's manufacturing technology is expensive and hazardous, the firm feels that other printer manufacturers will be unable or unwilling to copy its technology.

Why go to such trouble to make a simple laser printer? Because Kyocera's printing technology drops the cost-per-page from 2 cents to 0.7 cents. For a user running 30,000 copies each year, the annual operating cost of the Kyocera totals only $210. Over a 10-year service life, the present value of the printer's total operating costs equals $1,622 at a 5 percent discount rate. Compared with conventional laser printers, the total operating cost savings offered by the Kyocera is $3,011. Over time, the printer pays for itself, because the total operating cost savings completely offsets the initial purchase price of practically all basic laser printers.

Source: J. Xenakis, "How Green Is My Toner?," *CFO Magazine*, December 1993, p. 18.

## Present Value of a Perpetuity

**perpetuity**
An annuity with an infinite life, making continual annual payments

A **perpetuity** is an annuity with an infinite life—in other words, an annuity that never stops providing its holder with *PMT* dollars at the end of each year. It is sometimes necessary to find the present value of a perpetuity. The present-value interest factor for a perpetuity discounted at the rate $k$ is defined by Equation 11.17.

**Equation 11.17**
**Formula for the present-value interest factor for a perpetuity**

$$PVIFA_{k,\infty} = \frac{1}{k} \tag{11.17}$$

As noted, the appropriate factor, $PVIFA_{k,\infty}$, is found merely by dividing the discount rate $k$ (stated as a decimal) into 1. The validity of this method can be seen by looking at the factors in Table A.4 for 8 percent, 10 percent, 20 percent, and 40 percent. As the number of periods (typically years) approaches 50, the value of these factors approaches 12.500, 10.000, 5.000, and 2.500, respectively. Dividing .08, .10, .20, and .40 (for $k$) into 1 gives factors for finding the present value of perpetuities at these rates of 12.500, 10.000, 5.000, and 2.500. An example helps to clarify the application of the factor given in Equation 11.17.

► **E X A M P L E**

Fanny May wishes to determine the present value of a $1,000 perpetuity discounted at 10 percent. The appropriate present-value interest factor can be found by dividing 1 by .10, as noted in Equation 11.17. Substituting the resulting factor, 10, and the amount of the perpetuity, *PMT* = $1,000, into Equation 11.16 results in a present value of $10,000 for the perpetuity. In other words, the receipt of $1,000 every year for an indefinite period is worth only $10,000 today if Fanny May can earn 10 percent on her investments. The reason is that if she had $10,000 and earned 10 percent interest on it each year, $1,000 a year could be withdrawn indefinitely without affecting the initial $10,000, which would never be drawn upon.

## Progress Review Questions

**11-11.** How is the present value of a mixed stream of cash flows calculated? How can the calculations required to find the present value of an annuity be simplified?

**11-12.** What is a *perpetuity?* How might the present-value interest factor for such a stream of cash flows be determined?

## Special Applications of Time Value

Future-value and present-value techniques have a number of important applications. Three are presented in this section: (1) the calculation of the deposits needed to accumulate a future sum, (2) the calculation of amortization on loans, and (3) the determination of interest or growth rates.

### Deposits to Accumulate a Future Sum

Often an individual may wish to determine the annual deposit necessary to accumulate a certain amount of money a given number of years hence. Suppose a person wishes to buy a house five years from now and estimates that an initial down payment of $20,000 will be required at that time. She wishes to make equal annual end-of-year deposits in an account paying annual interest of 6 percent. She must determine what size annuity will result in a lump sum equal to $20,000 at the end of year 5. The solution to this problem is closely related to the process of finding the future value of an annuity.

In an earlier section of this chapter the future value of an *n*-year annuity, $FVA_n$, was found by multiplying the annual deposit, *PMT*, by the appropriate interest factor (from Table A.2 or using a hand-held business calculator), $FVIFA_{k,n}$. The relationship of the three variables was defined by Equation 11.8, which is rewritten here as Equation 11.18.

**Equation 11.18 General formula for the future value of an annuity**

$$FVA_n = PMT \times (FVIFA_{k,n}) \qquad (11.18)$$

We can find the annual deposit required to accumulate $FVA_n$ dollars, given a specified interest rate, $k$, and a certain number of years, $n$, by solving Equation 11.18 for $PMT$. Isolating $PMT$ on the left side of the equation gives us

**Equation 11.19 Formula for finding the annual deposit required to accumulate a specified future sum**

$$PMT = \frac{FVA_n}{FVIFA_{k,n}} \qquad (11.19)$$

Once this is done, we have only to substitute the known values of $FVA_n$ and $FVIFA_{k,n}$ into the right side of the equation to find the annual deposit required. An example demonstrates this calculation using Table A.2 as well as a hand-held business calculator.

## E X A M P L E

In the problem just stated, a person wished to determine the equal annual end-of-year deposits required to accumulate $20,000 at the end of five years given an interest rate of 6 percent.

**Table Use**   Table A.2 indicates that the future-value interest factor for an annuity at 6 percent for five years, $FVIFA_{6\%,5yrs}$, is 5.637. Substituting $FVA_5 =$ $20,000 and $FVIFA_{6\%,5yrs} = 5.637$ into Equation 11.19 yields an annual required deposit, $PMT$, of $3,547.99 ($20,000 ÷ 5.637). If $3,547.99 is deposited at the end of each year for five years at 6 percent, at the end of the five years $20,000 is in the account.

**Calculator Use**   Using the calculator, begin by punching in $20,000 and depressing **FV**; next punch in 5, and depress **N;** then punch in 6, and depress **%i;** finally, to calculate the annual deposit, depress **CPT** followed by **PMT.** The annual deposit amount appearing on the calculator display is $3,547.93 (ignore the minus sign). Note that this value, except for a slight rounding difference, agrees with the value found by using Table A.2 above.

| Inputs: | 20000 | 5 | 6 | | |
|---------|-------|---|---|---|---|
| Functions: | FV | N | % i | CPT | PMT |
| Outputs: | | | | | 3547.93 |

## Loan Amortization

**loan amortization**
The determination of the equal annual loan payments necessary to provide a lender with a specified interest return and to repay the loan principal over a specified period.

The term **loan amortization** refers to the determination of the equal annual loan payments necessary to provide a lender with a specified interest return and repay the loan principal over a specified period. The loan amortization process involves finding the future payments (over the term of the loan) the present value of which at the loan interest rate equals the amount of initial principal borrowed. Lenders use a **loan amortization schedule** to determine these payment amounts as well as the allocation of each payment to interest and principal. In the case of home mortgages, these tables are used to find the equal *monthly* payments necessary to amortize, or pay off, the mortgage at a specified interest rate over its repayment period, which is typically 15 to 30 years.

    Amortizing a loan actually involves creating an annuity out of a present amount. For example, an individual may borrow $6,000 at 10 percent and agree to make equal annual end-of-year payments over four years. To find the size of the payments, the lender determines the amount of a four-year annuity discounted at 10 percent that has a present value of $6,000. This process is actually the inverse of finding the present value of an annuity.

    Earlier in this chapter the present value, $PVA_n$, of an $n$-year annuity of $PMT$ dollars was found by multiplying the annual amount, $PMT$, by the present-value interest factor for an annuity (from Table A.4 or using a hand-held business calculator), $PVIFA_{k,n}$. This relationship, which was originally expressed as Equation 11.16, is rewritten here as Equation 11.20.

$$PVA_n = PMT \times (PVIFA_{k,n}) \tag{11.20}$$

**Equation 11.20 General formula for the present value of an annuity**

To find the equal annual payment, $PMT$, required to pay off, or amortize, the loan, $PVA_n$, over a certain number of years at a specified interest rate, we need to solve Equation 11.20 for $PMT$. Isolating $PMT$ on the left side of the equation gives us

$$PMT = \frac{PVA_n}{PVIFA_{k,n}} \tag{11.21}$$

**Equation 11.21 Formula for finding the annual payment required to pay off a loan**

Once this is done, we have only to substitute the known values of $PVA_n$ and $PVIFA_{k,n}$ into the right side of the equation to find the annual payment required.

▶ **E X A M P L E**

In the previous problem a person wished to determine the equal annual end-of-year payments necessary to amortize fully a $6,000, 10 percent loan over four years.

**Table Use**    Table A.4 indicates that the present-value interest factor for an annuity corresponding to 10 percent and four years, $PVIFA_{10\%,4yrs}$, is 3.170. Substituting $PVA_4 = \$6,000$ and $PVIFA_{10\%,4yrs} = 3.170$ into Equation 11.21 and solving for $PMT$ yields an annual loan payment of $1,892.74 ($6,000 ÷ 3.170). Thus, to repay the interest and principal on a $6,000, 10 percent, four-year loan, equal annual end-of-year payments of $1,892.74 are necessary.

**Calculator Use**    Using the calculator, begin by punching in $6,000 and depressing **PV**; next punch in 4, and depress **N**; then punch in 10, and depress **%i**; finally, to calculate the annual loan payment, depress **CPT** followed by **PMT**. The annual payment amount of $1,892.82 appearing on the display, except for a slight rounding difference, agrees with the value found using Table A.4.

**Inputs:**    [ 6000 ]   [ 4 ]   [ 10 ]

**Functions:**    [ PV ]   [ N ]   [ % i ]   [ CPT ]   [ PMT ]

**Outputs:**                                   [ *1892.82* ]

---

**loan amortization schedule**
A schedule showing the allocation to interest and principal of each of the equal payments to repay a loan.

The allocation of each loan payment to interest and principal can be seen in columns 3 and 4 of the *loan amortization schedule* given in Table 11.7. The portion of each payment representing interest (column 3) declines, and the portion going to principal repayment (column 4) increases over the repayment period. This is typical of amortized loans. With level payments, as the principal is reduced, the interest component declines, leaving a larger portion of each subsequent payment to repay principal.

## Interest or Growth Rates

It is often necessary to calculate the compound annual interest or growth rate of a stream of cash flows. In doing this, either future-value or present-value interest factors can be used. The approach using present-value interest tables is described in this section. The simplest situation is one in which a person wishes to find the rate of interest or growth in a cash flow stream.[9] This can be illustrated by the following example using both present-value tables and a hand-held business calculator.

## E X A M P L E

Al Taylor wishes to find the rate of interest or growth of the stream of cash flows shown in the table. With the first year (1991) as a base year, we see that interest has been earned (or growth experienced) for four years.

**TABLE 11.7  Loan Amortization Schedule ($6,000 Principal, 10 Percent Interest, Four-Year Repayment Period)**

| End of Year | Loan Payment (1) | Beginning-of-Year Principal (2) | Interest [.10 × (2)] (3) | Principal [(1) − (3)] (4) | End-of-Year Principal [(2) − (4)] (5) |
|---|---|---|---|---|---|
| | | | **Payments** | | |
| 1 | $1,892.74 | $6,000.00 | $600.00 | $1,292.74 | $4,707.26 |
| 2 | 1,892.74 | 4,707.26 | 470.73 | 1,422.01 | 3,285.25 |
| 3 | 1,892.74 | 3,285.25 | 328.53 | 1,564.21 | 1,721.04 |
| 4 | 1,892.74 | 1,721.04 | 172.10 | 1,720.64 | —[a] |

[a]Due to rounding, a slight difference ($.40) exists between the beginning-of-year-4 principal (in column 2) and the year-4 principal payment (in column 4).

[9]Because the calculations required for finding interest rates and growth rates, given certain cash flow streams, are the same, this section refers to the calculations as those required to find interest *or* growth rates.

| Year | Cash Flow |
|------|-----------|
| 1995 | $1,520 } 4 |
| 1994 | 1,440 } 3 |
| 1993 | 1,370 } 2 |
| 1992 | 1,300 } 1 |
| 1991 | 1,250 |

**Table Use**   The first step in finding the interest or growth rate is to divide the amount received in the earliest year by the amount received in the latest year. This gives the present-value interest factor for four years, $PVIF_{k,4yrs}$, which is .822 ($1,250 ÷ $1,520). The interest rate in Table A.3 associated with the factor closest to .822 for four years is the rate of interest or growth rate exhibited by the cash flows. Looking across year 4 of Table A.3 shows that the factor for 5 percent is .823—almost exactly the .822 value. Therefore the rate of interest or growth rate exhibited by the cash flows given is approximately (to the nearest whole percent) 5 percent.[10]

**Calculator Use**   Using the calculator, we treat the earliest value as a present value ($PV$) and the latest value as a future value ($FV_n$). First punch in the 1991 value of $1,250 and depress **PV**; next punch in the 1995 value of $1,520, and depress **FV**; then punch in the number of years of growth—4—and depress **N**; finally, to get the interest or growth rate, depress **CPT** followed by **%i**. The interest or growth rate appearing on the display is 5.01 percent, which is consistent with, but more precise than, the value found using Table A.3. (*Note:* Many calculators require either the $PV$ or $FV$ value to be input as a negative number to calculate an unknown interest or growth rate.)

**Inputs:**   [ 1250 ]  [ 1520 ]  [ 4 ]

**Functions:**   [ PV ]  [ FV ]  [ N ]  [ CPT ]  [ % i ]

▶ **Outputs:**                              [ 5.01 ]

Sometimes one wishes to find the interest rate associated with an equal-payment loan. The procedure for doing so can be demonstrated with an example using both financial tables and a hand-held business calculator.

▶ **E X A M P L E**

Jan Jong can borrow $2,000 to be repaid in equal annual end-of-year amounts of $514.14 for the next five years. She wants to calculate the interest rate on this loan.

[10]Rounding of interest or growth rate estimates to the nearest whole percent is assumed throughout this text. To obtain more precise estimates, *interpolation*—a mathematical technique for estimating unknown intermediate values—is required.

**Table Use**   Substituting $PVA_5 = \$2,000$ and $PMT = \$514.14$ into Equation 11.20 and rearranging the equation to solve for $PVIFA_{k,5yrs}$, we get

**Equation 11.22 Formula for finding the present-value interest factor given the initial loan principal and the annual loan payment**

$$PVIFA_{k,5yrs} = \frac{PVA_5}{PMT} = \frac{\$2,000}{\$514.14} = 3.890 \qquad (11.22)$$

The interest rate for five years associated with the factor closest to 3.890 in Table A-4 is 9 percent; therefore, the interest rate on the loan is approximately (to the nearest whole percent) 9 percent.

**Calculator Use**   Using the calculator, first punch in $514.14, and depress **PMT**; next punch in $2,000, and depress **PV**; then punch in 5, and depress **N**; finally, to get the interest rate, depress **CPT** followed by **%i**. The interest rate appearing on the display is 9 percent, which is consistent with, but more precise than, the approximate value found by using Table A.4. (*Note:* Many calculators require either the *PMT* or *PV* value to be input as a negative number to calculate an unknown interest rate on an equal-payment loan.)

**Inputs:**   | 514.14 |   | 2000 |   | 5 |

**Functions:**   | PMT |   | PV |   | N |   | CPT |   | % i |

**Outputs:**   | 9.00 | ◀

## Progress Review Questions

**11-13.** How can the size of the equal annual end-of-year deposits that are necessary to accumulate a certain future sum in a specified future period be determined? How might one use future-value interest factors to aid in this calculation?

**11-14.** Describe the procedure used to amortize a loan into a series of equal annual payments. What is a *loan amortization schedule?*

**11-15.** Which present-value interest factor is used to find (a) the growth rate associated with a stream of cash flows and (b) the interest rate associated with an equal-payment loan? How are each of these calculated?

# SUMMARY OF LEARNING GOALS

**LG 1**   **Discuss the role of time value in finance, particularly the two common views—future value and present value—and the use of financial tables and business/financial calculators to find them.** Financial managers use time value of money techniques to explicitly recognize their opportunities to earn positive returns when assessing the value of the expected cash flow streams associated with decision alternatives. While alternatives can be assessed by either compounding to find future value or discounting to find present value, financial managers, because they are at time zero when making decisions, rely primarily on present value techniques. Both financial tables, which provide various future- and present-value interest factors, and hand-held business/financial calculators like the BA-35 can be used to streamline the practical application of time-value techniques.

**Understand the concept of future value, its calculation for a single amount, and the procedures and effects on future value of compounding interest more frequently than annually, specifically, semiannually or quarterly.** Future value relies on compounded interest to measure the value of future amounts. When interest is compounded, the initial principal or deposit in one period, along with the interest earned on it, becomes the beginning principal of the following period, and so on. Interest can be compounded annually, semiannually, quarterly, monthly, weekly, daily, or even continuously. The more frequently interest is compounded, the larger the future amount that will be accumulated. This is true for any interest rate for any period. Semiannual compounding involves using one-half of the stated interest rate for twice the number of periods; quarterly compounding involves using one-fourth of the stated interest rate for four times the number of periods; and so on.

LG   2

**Find the future value of an annuity using either financial tables or a hand-held business/financial calculator to simplify the calculations.** The future value of an annuity, which is a pattern of equal annual cash flows, can be found using the future-value interest factor for an annuity. The product of the annual amount of the annuity and the future-value interest factor for the appropriate rate of interest and number of periods is the future value of the annuity. Alternatively, a business/financial calculator can be used to calculate quickly the future value of an annuity.

LG   3

**Review the concept of present value, its calculation for a single amount, and the relationship of present to future value.** When finding the present value of a future amount, we determine what amount of money today is equivalent to the given future amount, considering the fact that we can earn a certain return on the current money. The present value of a single amount can be found using either the present-value interest factor for one dollar or a business/financial calculator. Present value represents the inverse of future value.

LG   4

**Determine the present value of a mixed stream of cash flows, an annuity, and a perpetuity.** Occasionally it is necessary to find the present value of a stream of cash flows. For mixed streams, the individual present values must be found and summed. In the case of an annuity, the present value can be found by using the present-value interest factor for an annuity. For annuities, the product of the annual amount of the annuity and the present-value interest factor for the appropriate rate of interest and number of periods is the present value of the annuity. The present value of a perpetuity—an infinite-lived annuity—can be found by using 1 divided by the discount rate to represent the present-value interest factor.

LG   5

**Describe the procedures involved in (1) determining deposits to accumulate a future sum, (2) loan amortization, and (3) finding interest or growth rates.** The annual deposit needed to accumulate a given future sum can be found by solving the equation for the future value of an annuity for the annual payment. A loan can be amortized into equal annual payments by solving the equation for the present value of an annuity for the annual payment. Interest or growth rates can be estimated by finding the unknown interest rate in the equation for the present value of either a single amount or an annuity.

# SUMMARY OF KEY DEFINITIONS AND EQUATIONS

## Variable Definitions

$FV_n$ = future value or amount at the end of period $n$

$FVA_n$ = future value of an $n$-year annuity

$FVIF_{k,n}$ = future-value interest factor for an initial principal of $1 compounded at $k$ percent for $n$ periods

$FVIFA_{k,n}$ = future-value interest factor for an $n$-year annuity compounded at $k$ percent

$k$ = annual rate of interest

$n$ = number of periods—typically years—over which money earns a return

$PMT$ = amount deposited or received annually at the end of each year

$PV$ = initial principal, or present value

$PVA_n$ = present value of an $n$-year annuity

$PVIF_{k,n}$ = present-value interest factor for the present value of $1 discounted at $k$ percent for $n$ periods

$PVIFA_{k,n}$ = present-value interest factor for an $n$-year annuity discounted at $k$ percent

$t$ = period number index

## Equations

Future value (single amount)

[Eq. 11.4]

$$FV_n = PV \times (1 + k)^n$$

Future-value interest factor for a single amount

$$FVIF_{k,n} = (1 + k)^n$$ [Eq. 11.5]

Future value (single amount)

$$FV_n = PV \times (FVIF_{k,n})$$ [Eq. 11.6]

Future-value interest factor for an (ordinary) annuity

$$FVIFA_{k,n} = \sum_{t=1}^{n} (1 + k)^{t-1}$$ [Eq. 11.7]

Future value (annuity)

$$FVA_n = PMT \times (FVIFA_{k,n})$$ [Eq. 11.8]

Present value (single amount)

$$PV = \frac{FV_n}{(1 + k)^n} = FV_n \times \left[ \frac{1}{(1 + k)^n} \right]$$ [Eq. 11.11]

Present-value interest factor for a single amount

$$PVIF_{k,n} = \frac{1}{(1 + k)^n}$$ [Eq. 11.13]

Present value (single amount)

$$PV = FV_n \times (PVIF_{k,n})$$ [Eq. 11.14]

Present-value interest factor for an (ordinary) annuity

$$PVIFA_{k,n} = \sum_{t=1}^{n} \frac{1}{(1 + k)^t}$$ [Eq. 11.15]

Present value (annuity)

$$PVA_n = PMT \times (PVIFA_{k,n})$$ [Eq. 11.16]

Present-value interest factor for a perpetuity

$$PVIFA_{k,\infty} = \frac{1}{k}$$ [Eq. 11.17]

Annual deposit required to accumulate a specified future sum

$$PMT = \frac{FVA_n}{FVIFA_{k,n}}$$ [Eq. 11.19]

Annual payment required to pay off a loan

$$PMT = \frac{PVA_n}{PVIFA_{k,n}}$$ [Eq. 11.21]

After studying this chapter, you should be able to

 Review basic risk and return concepts, including risk aversion, risk of a single asset, and risk and time.

 Describe the risk and return characteristics of a portfolio in terms of correlation and diversification and the effect of international diversification on a portfolio.

Understand the two types of risk and the relationship between the relevant risk (measured by beta) and return as presented by the capital asset pricing model (CAPM).

 Discuss the key inputs and basic model used in the valuation process.

Apply the basic valuation model to bonds and preferred stocks, and evaluate the relationship between required returns and bond values.

 Perform basic common stock valuation using both the zero- and constant-growth models and other estimation approaches, and relate decision making to common stock value.

# 12 Risk, Return, and Valuation

Risk, return, and valuation are at the very core of financial management. Whether you make investment decisions, such as building a new plant or acquiring a company; manage a securities portfolio; or oversee international treasury operations, you must analyze the risk-return tradeoff. Put simply, this means that the higher the risk, the greater the return a company requires. The risk-return decisions a financial manager makes affect the value of the firm.

---

## Achieving the proper balance of risk and return is essential to maximizing a firm's value.

---

Measuring risk is a complex task. There is no single formula. A company's appetite for risk varies tremendously over time and is influenced by industry conditions. Market conditions also affect risk. Right now (early 1994) acquisition activity, especially in the telecommunications industry, is high. Interest rates on marketable securities are low, so it is incumbent on the financial manager to find acceptable acquisitions and capital projects that earn higher returns. Conversely, in the early 1980s when interest rates were very

high, firms would forgo capital investment projects, because they earned a substantial return on their marketable securities with minimal risk.

Risk-return analysis is an ongoing activity at Stratus Computer, Inc., a multinational firm with worldwide revenues exceeding $500 million. Stratus manufactures fault-tolerant computers that ensure continuous reliability in applications, such as telecommunications networks, international stock exchanges, banking networks, credit-card processing, air traffic control, and numerous other applications that cannot allow for computer downtime.

Part of Stratus' current business strategy is to integrate vertically by acquiring software companies and offering total computer solutions. This diversification reduces the overall risk of our business and increases the implicit value of the company going forward. Operating internationally—about 65 percent of Stratus' revenue comes from international sales—also reduces overall risk by diversifying in markets that have different business cycles.

Stratus approaches risk differently when it comes to acquisitions and other investment opportunities. We prepare three business cases—pessimistic, most likely, and optimistic—and use sensitivity analysis to see the range of possible returns. Qualitative factors are part of assessing risk. For example, revenue forecasts and market share estimates are based on subjective judgments. An additional risk when acquiring a software company is losing key employees. Profit potential and high

returns disappear very quickly without the software engineers. This risk is not easily quantified in any business case. Political risk management is also difficult to assess when international investments are considered.

Everything a manager does affects the firm's market value, as determined by its stock price. Achieving the proper balance of risk and return is essential to maximizing a firm's value. A manager has to know what risks are appropriate for the company—a skill that requires both good business judgment and a thorough understanding of business conditions.

**Charles Kane** *joined Stratus Computer, Inc., in 1989 as international controller and is currently director of finance. His prior experience includes five years in international treasury management at Prime Computer and five years as a CPA. He also teaches international finance in Boston College's masters of finance program. He received a B.A. in accounting from the University of Notre Dame and an M.B.A. in international finance from Babson College, Wellesley, MA.*

$\mathbf{I}$n Chapter 1 the goal of the financial manager, and therefore the firm, was specified as owner wealth maximization. For the publicly traded corporation, the financial manager's primary mission is to maximize the price of the firm's common stock. To do this the manager must learn to assess the two key determinants of share price: risk and return. **Valuation** is the process that links risk and return to determine the worth of an asset: bond, preferred stock, common stock, or fixed asset. Valuation relies on the use of the time-value techniques presented in Chapter 11. Like investors, financial managers must understand how to value assets in order to determine whether they are a "good buy." Each financial decision presents certain risk and return characteristics, and all major financial decisions must be viewed in terms of expected risk, expected return, and their combined effect on share price.

**valuation**
The process that links risk and return to determine the worth of an asset.

# Basic Risk and Return Concepts

LG  1   LG  2

Risk and return concepts can be viewed as they relate to a single asset held in isolation or to a **portfolio**—a collection, or group, of assets. Although portfolio risk is probably more important to the financial manager, the general concept of risk is more readily developed in terms of a single asset.

**portfolio**
A collection, or group, of assets.

## Fundamentals

Before developing risk and return concepts, we must define risk, return, and risk aversion.

**Risk Defined**   In the most basic sense, **risk** can be defined as the chance of financial loss. Assets having greater chances of loss are viewed as riskier than those with lesser chances of loss. More formally, the term *risk* is used interchangeably with *uncertainty* to refer to the *variability of returns associated with a given asset*. For instance, a government bond that guarantees its holder $100 interest after 30 days has no risk because no variability is associated with the return. An equivalent investment in a firm's common stock that may earn over the same period anywhere from $0 to $200 is very risky due to the high variability of the return. The more certain the return from an asset, the less variability and therefore the less risk.

**risk**
The chance of financial loss or, more formally, the variability of returns associated with a given asset.

**Return Defined**   As noted in Chapter 2 (see Equation 2.1), the **return** on an asset is the change in its value plus any cash distribution over a given period, expressed as a percentage of its initial value. The return on common stock is calculated by dividing the sum of any increase (or decrease) in share price and any cash dividends earned over a given period by its initial share price. For example, assume you purchased a share of stock one year ago for $20. If the stock is now selling for $22 per share and during the year you received a $1 cash dividend, your return over the year is 15 percent {[$2 increase in price ($22 − $20) + $1 cash dividend] ÷ $20 initial price}.

**return**
The change in value of an asset plus any cash distribution over a given period, expressed as a percentage of its initial value.

**Risk Aversion**   Financial managers generally seek to avoid risk. Most managers are **risk-averse,** because for a given increase in risk they require an increase in return. This behavior is believed consistent with the preference of the owners for whom the firm is being managed. Managers tend to accept only those risks with which they feel comfortable. And they generally tend to be conservative rather than aggressive when accepting risk. Accordingly, *a risk-averse financial manager requiring higher returns for greater risk is assumed throughout this text.*

**risk-averse**
The attitude toward risk in which an increased return is required for an increase in risk.

## Risk of a Single Asset

The risk of a single asset is measured in much the same way as the risk of an entire portfolio of assets. Yet it is important to differentiate between these two entities, because certain benefits accrue to holders of portfolios. It is also useful to assess risk from both a behavioral and a quantitative point of view. Sensitivity analysis can be used to get a feel for risk, and probabilities, probability distributions, the standard deviation, and the coefficient of variation can be used to assess risk more quantitatively.

**Sensitivity Analysis**   **Sensitivity analysis** is a behavioral approach that uses a number of possible return estimates to obtain a sense of the variability among outcomes. One common method involves the estimation of the pessimistic (worst), the most likely (expected), and the optimistic (best) returns associated with a given asset. In this case the asset's risk can be measured by the **range,** which is found by subtracting the pessimistic (worst) outcome from the optimistic (best) outcome. The greater the range for a given asset, the more variability, or risk, it is said to have.

**sensitivity analysis**
A behavioral approach for assessing risk that uses a number of possible return estimates to obtain a sense of the variability among outcomes.

**range**
A measure of an asset's risk, which is found by subtracting the pessimistic (worst) outcome from the optimistic (best) outcome.

## E X A M P L E

Alfred Company, a custom golfing-equipment manufacturer, is attempting to choose the better of two alternative investments: A and B. Each requires an initial outlay of $10,000 and each has a *most likely* annual rate of return of 15 percent. To evaluate the riskiness of these assets, management has made *pessimistic* and *optimistic* estimates of the returns associated with each. The three estimates for each asset, along with its range, are given in Table 12.1. Asset A appears to be less risky than asset B because its range of 4 percent (17% − 13%) is less than the range of 16 percent (23% − 7%) for asset B. The risk-averse financial decision maker prefers asset A over asset B: A offers the same most likely return as B (15%) but with lower risk (smaller range).

Although the use of sensitivity analysis and the range is rather crude, it does provide the decision maker with a feel for the behavior of returns. This behavioral insight can be used to assess roughly the risk involved. Of course, a variety of more quantitative risk measures exists.

**Probabilities**   Probabilities can be used to assess an asset's risk more precisely. The **probability** of a given outcome is the *chance* of it occurring. If an outcome has an 80 percent probability of occurrence, the given outcome is expected to occur 8 out of 10 times. If an outcome has a probability of 100 percent, it is certain to occur. Outcomes having a probability of zero never occur.

**probability**
The *chance* that a given outcome will occur.

**TABLE 12.1   Assets A and B**

|                            | Asset A   | Asset B   |
|----------------------------|-----------|-----------|
| Initial investment         | $10,000   | $10,000   |
| Annual rate of return      |           |           |
|   Pessimistic    | 13%       | 7%        |
|   Most likely    | 15        | 15        |
|   Optimistic     | 17        | 23        |
| Range                      | 4%        | 16%       |

## ▶ E X A M P L E

An evaluation of Alfred Company's past estimates indicates that the probabilities of the pessimistic, most likely, and optimistic outcomes' occurring are 25 percent, 50 percent, and 25 percent, respectively. The sum of these probabilities must equal 100 percent; that is, they must be based on all the alternatives considered. ▶

**Probability Distributions**   A **probability distribution** is a model that relates probabilities to the associated outcomes. The simplest type of probability distribution is the **bar chart,** which shows only a limited number of outcome-probability coordinates. The bar charts for Alfred Company's assets A and B are shown in Figure 12.1. Although both assets have the same most likely return, the range of return is much more dispersed for asset B than for asset A—16 percent versus 4 percent. If we knew all the possible outcomes and associated probabilities, a **continuous probability distribution** could be developed. This type of distribution can be thought of as a bar chart for a very large number of outcomes. Figure 12.2 presents continuous probability distributions for assets A and B. Note in Figure 12.2 that although assets A and B have the same most likely return (15 percent), the distribution of returns for asset B has much greater *dispersion* than the distribution for asset A. Clearly, asset B is riskier than asset A.

**Standard Deviation**   The most common statistical indicator of an asset's risk is the **standard deviation,** $\sigma_k$, which measures the dispersion around the *expected* value. The **expected value of a return,** $\bar{k}$, *is* the most likely return on an asset. This can be calculated using Equation 12.1.

$$\bar{k} = \sum_{i=1}^{n} k_i \times Pr_i \qquad (12.1)$$

where

    $k_i$ = return for the *ith* outcome
    $Pr_i$ = probability of occurrence of the *ith* outcome
    $n$ = number of outcomes considered

**probability distribution**
A model that relates probabilities to the associated outcomes.

**bar chart**
The simplest type of probability distribution showing only a limited number of outcomes and associated probabilities for a given event.

**continuous probability distribution**
A probability distribution showing all the possible outcomes and associated probabilities for a given event.

**standard deviation,** $\sigma_k$
Statistical indicator of an asset's risk; it measures the dispersion around the *expected* value.

**expected value of a return,** $\bar{k}$
The most likely return on a given asset.

**Equation (12.1)**
**Formula for calculating the expected return on an asset**

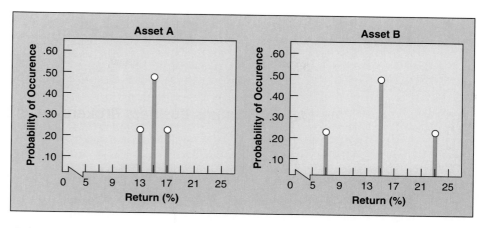

**FIGURE 12.1   Bar Charts for Asset A's and Asset B's Returns**
The bar charts show that although assets A and B have the same most likely return of 15 percent, the range of returns for asset B has much greater dispersion
than that of asset A. Asset B is therefore riskier.

## E X A M P L E

The calculations of the expected values for Alfred Company's assets A and B
are presented in Table 12.2. Column 1 gives the $Pr_i$'s, and column 2 gives the
$k_i$'s, $n$ equaling 3 in each case. The expected value for each asset's return is
15 percent.

The expression for the *standard deviation of returns*, $\sigma_k$, is given in Equation
12.2.

**FIGURE 12.2   Continuous Probability Distributions for Asset A's and
Asset B's Returns**
The continuous distribution of returns for asset B has much greater dispersion
than that of asset A, although both assets have the same most likely return of 15
percent. Asset B is therefore riskier.

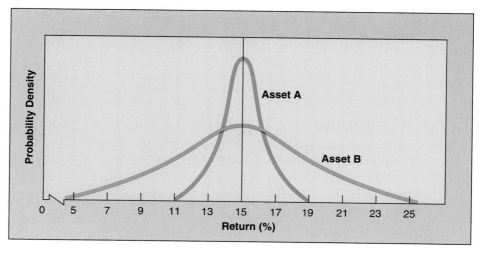

# FINANCE IN ACTION

**Small Business**

## Inc. Magazine Values Business Brokers' Nevada Casino

*Inc. Magazine*, the magazine targeted at small-business managers, gives readers a chance at the "American Dream" each month. Specifically, the last article in each edition reports on a business for sale. Recent examples include a Nevada casino, record-store chain, and travel agency. *Inc.* provides insight into the business, its financial outlook, a price rationale, and both pros and cons of purchase.

In one instance, investors willing to gamble could buy an Old West casino offered through the real estate firm of Business Brokers at year-end 1993. The casino, located 5 hours from Las Vegas, had a list price of $2.3 million. According to unnamed sources, *Inc.* reports that casinos tend to sell at three to four times earnings. Applying that multiple to the three-year average earnings of the casino for the prior three years

gives a value of $1.3 to $1.8 million. The higher price was justified, by the owners, based on a 65-room hotel and spacious parking lot.

*Inc.* sees the "pros" being that gambling is hot and that when casinos thrive they are very profitable. "Cons" consist of the casino not being near Las Vegas or Reno and the operation being open 24 hours a day, seven days a week. *Inc.* apparently applies a higher than normal discount rate in the analysis of the casino's cash flows, because the article concludes that "the patrons won't be the only ones gambling."

Source: Christopher Caggiano, "The American Dream: Business for Sale—Nevada Casino," *Inc.*, November 1993, p. 156.

$$\sigma_k = \sqrt{\sum_{i=1}^{n} (k_i - \bar{k})^2 \times Pr_i} \qquad (12.2)$$

**Equation 12.2** Formula for calculating the standard deviation when various return outcomes, the expected return, and associated probabilities are known

In general, the higher the standard deviation, the greater the risk.

## ▶ EXAMPLE

Table 12.3 on page 322 presents the calculation of standard deviations for Alfred Company's assets A and B, based on the data presented earlier. The standard deviation for asset A is 1.41 percent, and the standard deviation for asset B is 5.66 percent. The higher risk of asset B is clearly reflected in its higher standard deviation. ▶

**Coefficient of Variation**   The **coefficient of variation, *CV*,** is a measure of relative dispersion that is useful in comparing the risk of assets with differing expected returns. Equation 12.3 gives the expressions for the coefficient of variation.

**coefficient of variation, *CV***
A measure of relative dispersion used in comparing the risk of assets with differing expected returns.

$$CV = \frac{\sigma_k}{\bar{k}} \qquad (12.3)$$

**Equation 12.3** Formula for the coefficient of variation

The higher the coefficient of variation, the greater the risk.

**TABLE 12.2   Expected Values of Returns for Assets A and B**

| Possible Outcomes | Probability (1) | Returns (%) (2) | Weighted Value (%) [(1) × (2)] (3) |
|---|---|---|---|
| **Asset A** | | | |
| Pessimistic | .25 | 13 | 3.25 |
| Most likely | .50 | 15 | 7.50 |
| Optimistic | .25 | 17 | 4.25 |
| Total | 1.00 | Expected return | 15.00 |
| **Asset B** | | | |
| Pessimistic | .25 | 7 | 1.75 |
| Most likely | .50 | 15 | 7.50 |
| Optimistic | .25 | 23 | 5.75 |
| Total | 1.00 | Expected return | 15.00 |

# E X A M P L E

Substituting the standard deviation values (from Table 12.3) and the expected returns (from Table 12.2) for assets A and B into Equation 12.3, the coefficients of variation for A and B, respectively, are .094 (1.41% ÷ 15%) and .377 (5.66% ÷ 15%). Asset B has the higher coefficient of variation and is therefore riskier than asset A. Because both assets have the same expected return, the coefficient of variation has not provided any more information than the standard deviation.

The real utility of the coefficient of variation is for comparing assets that have *different* expected returns. A simple example illustrates this point.

# E X A M P L E

A firm is attempting to select the less risky of two alternative assets: X and Y. The expected return, standard deviation, and coefficient of variation for each of these assets' returns are given in the following table.

| Statistics | Asset X | Asset Y |
|---|---|---|
| (1) Expected return | 12% | 20% |
| (2) Standard deviation | 9%[a] | 10% |
| (3) Coefficient of variation [(2) ÷ (1)] | .75 | .50[a] |

[a]Preferred asset using the given risk measure.

**TABLE 12.3    The Calculation of the Standard Deviation of the Returns for Assets A and B**

### Asset A

| $i$ | $k_i$ | $\overline{k}$ | $k_i - \overline{k}$ | $(k_i - \overline{k})^2$ | $Pr_i$ | $(k_i - \overline{k})^2 \times Pr_i$ |
|---|---|---|---|---|---|---|
| 1 | 13% | 15% | −2% | 4% | .25 | 1% |
| 2 | 15 | 15 | 0 | 0 | .50 | 0 |
| 3 | 17 | 15 | 2 | 4 | .25 | 1 |

$$\sum_{i=1}^{3} (k_i - \overline{k})^2 \times Pr_i = 2\%$$

$$\sigma_{k_A} = \sqrt{\sum_{i=1}^{3} (k_i - \overline{k})^2 \times Pr_i} = \sqrt{2\%} = 1.41\%$$

### Asset B

| $i$ | $k_i$ | $\overline{k}$ | $k_i - \overline{k}$ | $(k_i - \overline{k})^2$ | $Pr_i$ | $(k_i - \overline{k})^2 \times Pr_i$ |
|---|---|---|---|---|---|---|
| 1 | 7% | 15% | −8% | 64% | .25 | 16% |
| 2 | 15 | 15 | 0 | 0 | .50 | 0 |
| 3 | 23 | 15 | 8 | 64 | .25 | 16 |

$$\sum_{i=1}^{3} (k_i - \overline{k})^2 \times Pr_i = 32\%$$

$$\sigma_{k_B} = \sqrt{\sum_{i=1}^{3} (k_i - \overline{k})^2 \times Pr_i} = \sqrt{32\%} = 5.66\%$$

If the firm compares the assets solely on the basis of their standard deviations, it will prefer asset X because asset X has a lower standard deviation than asset Y (9 percent versus 10 percent). However, comparing the coefficients of variation of the assets shows that management would be making a serious error in choosing asset X over asset Y. The relative dispersion, or risk, of the assets as reflected in the coefficient of variation is lower for Y than for X (.50 versus .75). Clearly, the use of the coefficient of variation to compare asset risk is effective because it also considers the relative size, or expected return, of the assets.

## Risk and Time

Risk can be viewed not only with respect to the current period but also as an *increasing function of time*. Figure 12.3 depicts probability distributions of returns for a 1-year, 10-year, 15-year, and 20-year forecast, assuming each year's expected returns are equal. A band representing ±1 standard deviation, $\sigma$,

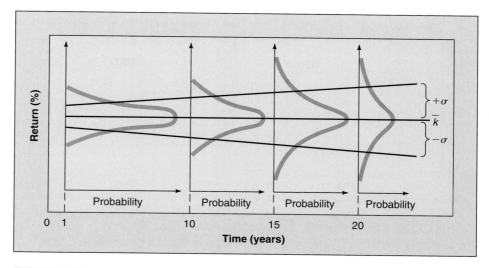

**FIGURE 12.3   Risk as a Function of Time**
The probability distributions of returns for a 1-year, 10-year, 15-year, and 20-year forecast, assuming each year's expected returns ($\bar{k}$) are equal, show that the variability of returns ($\sigma$)—and therefore the risk—increases with the passage of time.

from the expected return, $\bar{k}$, is indicated in the figure. It can be seen that the *variability of the returns, and therefore the risk, increases with the passage of time.* Generally, the longer lived an asset investment, the greater its risk. This relationship is due to increasing variability of returns resulting from increased forecasting errors for distant years.

## Risk of a Portfolio

The risk of any single proposed asset investment should not be viewed independent of other assets. New investments must be considered in light of their effect on the risk and return of the *portfolio* of assets. The financial manager's goal for the firm is to create an **efficient portfolio,** one that maximizes return for a given level of risk or minimizes risk for a given level of return. The statistical concept of *correlation* underlies the process of diversification that is used to develop an efficient portfolio of assets.

**Correlation**    **Correlation** is a statistical measure of the relationship, if any, between series of numbers representing data of any kind, from returns to test scores. If two series move in the same direction, they are **positively correlated;** if the series move in opposite directions, they are **negatively correlated.** The degree of correlation is measured by the **correlation coefficient,** which ranges from $+1$ for **perfectly positively correlated** series to $-1$ for **perfectly negatively correlated** series. These two extremes are depicted for series M and N in Figure 12.4. The perfectly positively correlated series move exactly together; the perfectly negatively correlated series move in exactly opposite directions.

**Diversification**    To reduce overall risk, it is best to combine or add to the portfolio assets that have a negative (or a low positive) correlation. By combining negatively correlated assets, the overall variability of returns, or risk,

**efficient portfolio**
A portfolio that maximizes return for a given level of risk or minimizes risk for a given level of return.

**correlation**
A statistical measure of the relationship, if any, between series of numbers representing data of any kind.

**positively correlated**
Two series of numbers that move in the same direction.

**negatively correlated**
Two series of numbers that move in opposite directions.

**correlation coefficient**
A measure of the degree of correlation between two series of numbers.

**perfectly positively correlated**
Two positively correlated series of numbers that have a *correlation coefficient* of +1.

**perfectly negatively correlated**
Two negatively correlated series of numbers that have a *correlation coefficient* of −1.

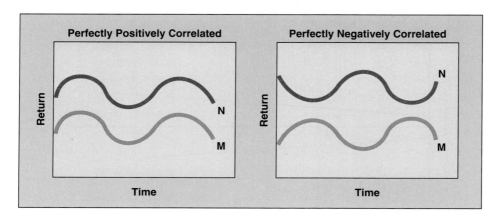

**FIGURE 12.4   The Correlation Between Series M and N**
The perfectly positively correlated series M and N in the left graph move exactly together. The perfectly negatively correlated series M and N in the right graph move in exactly opposite directions.

can be reduced. Figure 12.5 shows the effect of combining negatively correlated assets. Assets F and G individually have the same expected return $\bar{k}$. A portfolio containing these negatively correlated assets also has the return, $\bar{k}$, but has less risk (variability) than either of the individual assets. Even if assets are not negatively correlated, the lower the positive correlation between them, the lower the resulting risk.[1]

A portfolio that combines two assets having perfectly positively correlated returns *cannot* reduce the portfolio's overall risk below the risk of the least risky asset. Alternatively, a portfolio combining two assets with less than perfectly positive correlation *can* reduce total risk to a level below than of either of the components. In certain situations total risk may be zero. For example, assume you manufacture machine tools. This business is very *cyclical*, having high sales when the economy is expanding and low sales during a recession. If you acquire another machine tool company, which has sales positively correlated with those of your firm, the combined sales continue to be cyclical. Risk remains the same. As an alternative, however, you could acquire a sewing machine manufacturer, which is *countercyclical*. It has low sales during economic expansion and high sales during recession (because consumers are more likely to make their own clothes at such a time). Combination with the sewing machine manufacturer, which has negatively correlated sales, should reduce risk. The low machine tool sales during a recession are balanced out by high sewing machine sales, and vice versa. A numerical example provides a better understanding of the role of correlation in the diversification process.

---

[1]Some assets are *uncorrelated*. That is, they are completely unrelated in the sense that there is no interaction between their returns. Combining uncorrelated assets can reduce risk—not as effectively as combining negatively correlated assets, but more effectively than combining positively correlated assets. The correlation coefficient for uncorrelated assets is close to zero and acts as the midpoint between perfect positive and perfect negative correlation.

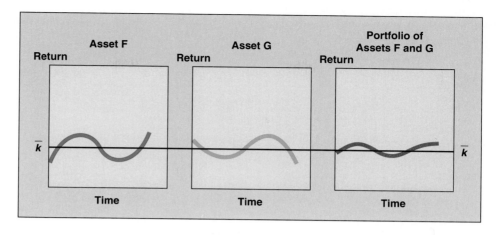

**FIGURE 12.5   Combining Negatively Correlated Assets to Diversity Risk**
The risk, or variability of returns, resulting from combining negatively correlated assets F and G, both having the same expected return, $\bar{k}$, results in a portfolio with the same level of expected return but less risk.

EXAMPLE   ◀

Table 12.4 presents the forecasted returns from three different assets—X, Y, and Z—over the next five years, along with their expected values and standard deviations. Each of the assets has an expected value of return of 12 percent and a standard deviation of 3.16 percent. The assets therefore have equal return and equal risk, although their return patterns are not necessarily identical. A comparison of the return patterns of assets X and Y shows that they are perfectly negatively correlated because they move in exactly opposite directions over time. A comparison of assets X and Z shows that they are perfectly positively correlated because they move in precisely the same direction. (*Note:* The returns for X and Z are identical.)

**Portfolio XY**   By combining equal portions of assets X and Y—the perfectly negatively correlated assets—portfolio XY (shown in Table 12.4) is created. The risk in the portfolio created by this combination, as reflected by its standard deviation, is reduced to 0 percent, and the expected return value remains at 12 percent. Because both assets have the same expected return values, are combined in equal parts, and are perfectly negatively correlated, the combination results in the complete elimination of risk. Whenever assets are perfectly negatively correlated, an optimum combination (similar to the 50:50 mix in the case of assets X and Y) exists for which the resulting standard deviation equals 0.

**Portfolio XZ**   By combining equal portions of assets X and Z—the perfectly positively correlated assets—portfolio XZ (shown in Table 12.4) is created. The risk in this portfolio, as reflected by its standard deviation, which remains at 3.16 percent, is unaffected by this combination, and the expected return value remains at 12 percent. Whenever perfectly positively correlated assets, such as X and Z, are combined, the standard deviation of the resulting portfolio cannot be reduced below that of the least risky asset; the maximum port-

## TABLE 12.4 Forecasted Returns, Expected Values, and Standard Deviations for Assets X, Y, and Z and Portfolios XY and XZ

| | Assets | | | Portfolios | |
|---|---|---|---|---|---|
| Year | X | Y | Z | XY[a] (50%X + 50%Y) | XZ[b] (50%X + 50%Z) |
| 1996 | 8% | 16% | 8% | 12% | 8% |
| 1997 | 10 | 14 | 10 | 12 | 10 |
| 1998 | 12 | 12 | 12 | 12 | 12 |
| 1999 | 14 | 10 | 14 | 12 | 14 |
| 2000 | 16 | 8 | 16 | 12 | 16 |
| **Statistics:** | | | | | |
| Expected value[c] | 12% | 12% | 12% | 12% | 12% |
| Standard deviation[d] | 3.16% | 3.16% | 3.16% | 0% | 3.16% |

[a]Portfolio XY, which consists of 50 percent of asset X and 50 percent of asset Y, illustrates *perfect negative correlation* because these two return streams behave in completely opposite fashion over the five-year period. Its return values are calculated as shown in the following table.

| | Forecasted Return | | | |
|---|---|---|---|---|
| Year | Asset X (1) | Asset Y (2) | Portfolio Return Calculation (3) | Expected Portfolio Return $k_p$ (4) |
| 1996 | 8% | 16% | $(.50 \times 8\%) + (.50 \times 16\%) =$ | 12% |
| 1997 | 10 | 14 | $(.50 \times 10) + (.50 \times 14) =$ | 12 |
| 1998 | 12 | 12 | $(.50 \times 12) + (.50 \times 12) =$ | 12 |
| 1999 | 14 | 10 | $(.50 \times 14) + (.50 \times 10) =$ | 12 |
| 2000 | 16 | 8 | $(.50 \times 16) + (.50 \times 8) =$ | 12 |

[b]Portfolio XZ, which consists of 50 percent of asset X and 50 percent of asset Z, illustrates *perfect positive correlation* because these two return streams behave identically over the five-year period. Its return values are calculated using the same method demonstrated in note a above for portfolio XY.

[c]Because the probabilities associated with the returns are not given, the formula given earlier in Equation 12.1 cannot be used to calculate expected value, $\bar{k}$. Instead, we use the general formula

$$\bar{k} = \frac{\sum_{i=1}^{n} k_i}{n}$$

where $k_i$ = return $i$, and $n$ = the number of outcomes considered. For portfolio XY

$$\bar{k}_{xy} = \frac{12\% + 12\% + 12\% + 12\% + 12\%}{5} = \frac{60\%}{5} = \underline{\underline{12\%}}$$

The same formula is applied to find the expected value of return for assets X, Y, and Z, and portfolio XZ.

[d]Because the probabilities associated with the returns are not given, the formula given earlier in Equation 12.2 cannot be used to calculate the standard deviations, $\sigma_k$. Instead, we use the general formula

$$\sigma_k = \sqrt{\frac{\sum_{i=1}^{n} (k_i - \bar{k})^2}{n - 1}}$$

where $k_i$ = return $i$, $\bar{k}$ = expected value of return, and $n$ = the number of outcomes considered. For portfolio XY:

$$\sigma_{k_{xy}} = \sqrt{\frac{(12\% - 12\%)^2 + (12\% - 12\%)^2 + (12\% - 12\%)^2 + (12\% - 12\%)^2 + (12\% - 12\%)^2}{5 - 1}}$$

$$= \sqrt{\frac{0\% + 0\% + 0\% + 0\% + 0\%}{4}} = \sqrt{\frac{0\%}{4}} = 0\%$$

The same formula is applied to find the standard deviation of returns for assets X, Y, and Z, and portfolio XZ.

folio standard deviation is that of the riskiest asset. Because assets X and Z have the same standard deviation (3.16 percent), the minimum and maximum standard deviations are both 3.16 percent. It is the only value that can be taken on by a combination of these assets. This result can be attributed to the unlikely situation that X and Z are identical assets.

Although detailed statistical explanations can be given for the behaviors illustrated in Table 12.4, the important point is that assets can be combined so that the resulting portfolio has less risk than that of either of the assets independently. And this can be achieved without any loss of return. Portfolio XY in the preceding example illustrates such behavior. The more negative (or less positive) the correlation between asset returns, the greater the risk-reducing benefits of diversification. In no case does creating portfolios of assets result in greater risk than that of the riskiest asset included in the portfolio. It is important to recognize that these relationships apply when considering the addition of an asset to an existing portfolio.

## International Diversification

The ultimate example of portfolio diversification involves including foreign assets in a portfolio. This strategy reduces risk in two ways. First, by including assets with payoffs denominated in foreign currencies, the correlations of the returns of the portfolio's assets are reduced when all investment returns are translated into dollars. Second, by including assets from countries that are less sensitive to the business cycle of the United States than are domestic financial assets, the portfolio's responsiveness to market movements is reduced.

**Returns from International Diversification**  Over long periods, returns from internationally diversified portfolios tend to be superior to those yielded by purely domestic ones. Over any single short or intermediate period, however, international diversification can yield subpar returns—particularly during periods when the dollar is appreciating in value relative to other currencies. When the U.S. currency gains in value, the dollar value of a foreign-currency-denominated portfolio of assets declines, and even if this portfolio yields a satisfactory return in local currency, the return to U.S. investors is reduced when translated into dollars. Furthermore, if the dollar is appreciating because the U.S. economy is performing relatively better than other economies, then foreign-currency-denominated portfolios tend to have lower local currency returns than U.S. domestic portfolios. Subpar local currency portfolio returns, coupled with an appreciating dollar, can yield truly dismal dollar returns to U.S. investors. Of course, if the U.S. economy is performing relatively poorly and the dollar is depreciating against most foreign currencies, then the dollar returns to U.S. investors on a portfolio of foreign assets can be very attractive indeed. The logic of international portfolio diversification assumes that these fluctuations in currency values and relative performance average out over long periods and that an internationally diversified portfolio tends to yield a comparable return at a lower level of risk than similar purely domestic portfolios.

**Risks of International Diversification**  U.S. investors should, however, also be aware of the potential dangers involved in international investing. In addition to the risk induced by potential currency fluctuations there are several other financial risks that are unique to international investing. The most important of these fall under the heading of political risk. **Political risk** arises from the danger that a host government might take actions harmful to foreign investors or from the possibility that political turmoil in a country might endanger investments made in that country by foreign nationals. Political risks are particularly acute in developing counties, where unstable or ideologically motivated governments often attempt to block return of profits by multinational companies and other foreign investors or even seize (nationalize) their assets in the host country.

Even where governments do not resort to deliberate exchange controls or seizure, international investors may suffer if a general shortage of hard currency prevents payment of dividends or interest to foreigners. When governments are forced to allocate scarce foreign exchange, they rarely give top priority to the interests of foreign investors. Instead, hard currency reserves are typically used to pay for necessary imports, such as food and industrial materials, and to pay interest on the government's own debts. Because most of the debt of developing countries is held by banks rather than individuals, portfolio investors are often harmed very badly when a country experiences political or economic problems.

**political risk**
Risk that arises from the danger that a host government might take actions that are harmful to foreign investors or from the possibility that political turmoil in a country might endanger investments made in that country by foreign nationals.

## Progress Review Questions

**12-1.** Define *risk* as it relates to financial decision making. How can the return on common stock be calculated? Why are financial managers commonly viewed as *risk-averse?*

**12-2.** How can *sensitivity analysis* be used to assess asset risk? What is one of the most common methods of sensitivity analysis? Define and describe the role of the *range* in sensitivity analysis.

**12-3.** How does a plot of the *probability distribution* of outcomes allow the decision maker to evaluate asset risk? What is the difference between a *bar chart* and a *continuous probability distribution?*

**12-4.** What does the *standard deviation* of a distribution of asset returns indicate? What is the *coefficient of variation?* When is the coefficient of variation preferred over the standard deviation for comparing asset risk?

**12-5.** What is an *efficient portfolio?* What is *correlation,* and how is it related to the process of diversification? How does diversification allow risky assets to be combined so that the risk of the portfolio is less than the risk of the individual assets in it?

**12-6.** How does international diversification enhance risk reduction? Why, particularly during periods when the dollar is appreciating, can international diversification result in subpar returns? What are *political risks,* and how do they affect international diversification?

# Risk and Return: The Capital Asset Pricing Model

**capital asset pricing model (CAPM)**
The basic theory that links risk and return for all assets.

The most important aspect of risk is the *overall risk* of the firm as viewed by investors in the marketplace. Overall risk significantly affects investment opportunities—and even more important, the owners' wealth. The basic theory that links together risk and return for all assets is commonly called the **capital asset pricing model (CAPM).** Here we use CAPM to understand the basic risk-return trade-offs involved in all types of financial decisions.

## Types of Risk

To understand the basic types of risk, consider what happens when we begin with a single security (asset) in a portfolio. Then we expand the portfolio by randomly selecting additional securities from, say, the population of all actively traded securities. Using the standard deviation of returns, $\sigma_k$, to measure the total portfolio risk, Figure 12.6 depicts the behavior of the total portfolio risk (*y*-axis) as more securities are added (*x*-axis). With the addition of securities, the total portfolio risk declines, due to the effects of diversification (as explained in the previous section), and tends to approach a limit. Research has shown that most of the benefits of diversification, in terms of risk reduction, can be gained by forming portfolios containing 15 to 20 randomly selected securities.

**total risk**
The combination of a security's nondiversifiable and diversifiable risk.

The **total risk** of a security can be viewed as consisting of two parts:

$$\text{Total security risk} = \text{nondiversifiable risk} + \text{diversifiable risk} \qquad (12.4)$$

**Equation 12.4** Formula showing the two parts of total security risk

**diversifiable risk**
The portion of an asset's risk attributable to firm-specific, random causes; can be eliminated through diversification.

**nondiversifiable risk**
The relevant portion of an asset's risk attributable to market factors that affect all firms; cannot be eliminated through diversification.

**Diversifiable risk** represents the portion of an asset's risk associated with random causes that can be eliminated through diversification. It is attributable to firm-specific events, such as strikes, lawsuits, regulatory actions, loss of a key account, and so forth. **Nondiversifiable risk** is attributable to market factors that affect all firms, and it cannot be eliminated through diversification. Factors, such as war, inflation, international incidents, and political events, account for nondiversifiable risk.

Because, as illustrated in Figure 12.6, any investor can create a portfolio of assets that eliminates all, or virtually all, diversifiable risk, the *only relevant risk is nondiversifiable risk*. Any investor (or firm) must therefore be concerned solely with nondiversifiable risk; it reflects the contribution of an asset to the risk, or standard deviation, of the portfolio. The measurement of nondiversifiable risk is thus of primary importance in selecting those assets possessing the most desired risk-return characteristics.

## The Model: CAPM

The capital asset pricing model (CAPM) links together nondiversifiable risk and return for all assets. We discuss the model in three parts. The first part defines and describes the beta coefficient, which is a measure of nondiversi-

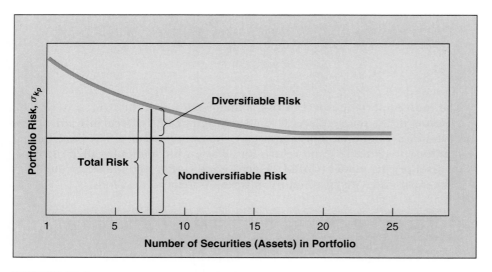

**FIGURE 12.6  Portfolio Risk and Diversification**
As randomly selected securities (assets) are combined to create a portfolio, the *total risk* of the portfolio declines until 15 to 20 securities are included. The portion of the risk eliminated is *diversifiable risk,* whereas that remaining is *nondiversifiable risk.*

fiable risk. The second part presents an equation of the model itself, and the final part graphically describes the relationship between risk and return.

**Beta Coefficient**  The **beta coefficient, *b*,** is used to measure nondiversifiable risk. It is an *index* of the degree of movement of an asset's return in response to a change in the *market return.* The beta coefficient for an asset can be found by examining the asset's historical returns relative to the returns for the market. The **market return** is the return on the market portfolio of all traded securities. The return on a portfolio of the stocks in *Standard & Poor's 500 Stock Composite Index* or some similar stock index is commonly used to measure the market return. Beta coefficients can be obtained for actively traded stocks from published sources, such as *Value Line Investment Survey,* or through brokerage firms. Betas for some selected stocks are given in Table 12.5. The beta coefficient for the market is considered to be equal to 1.0; all other betas are viewed in relation to this value. Asset betas may take on values that are either positive or negative, but positive betas are the norm. The majority of beta coefficients fall between 0.5 and 2.0. Table 12.6 provides some selected beta values and their associated interpretations.

**beta coefficient, *b***
An *index* of the degree of movement of an asset's return in response to a change in the *market return;* measures *nondiversifiable risk.*

**market return**
The return on the market portfolio of all traded securities.

**The Equation**  The *capital asset pricing model (CAPM),* given in Equation 12.5, uses the beta coefficient, *b,* to measure nondiversifiable risk.

$$k_j = R_F + [b_j \times (k_m - R_F)] \qquad (12.5)$$

where

$k_j$ = required return on asset $j$
$R_F$ = risk-free rate of return, commonly measured by the return on a
U.S. Treasury bill

**Equation 12.5**
**Expression for the capital asset pricing model (CAPM)**

---

**TABLE 12.5   Beta Coefficients for Selected Stocks (August 12, 1994)**

| Stock | Beta | Stock | Beta |
|---|---|---|---|
| Anheuser-Busch | 1.05 | IBM | .95 |
| Apple Computer | 1.25 | Merrill Lynch & Company | 1.80 |
| Boston Edison | .75 | Occidental Petroleum | .80 |
| CBS, Inc. | 1.00 | Procter & Gamble | 1.10 |
| Caesar's World | 1.40 | Seagram Company | 1.10 |
| Cascade Natural Gas | .55 | Sony Corporation | .85 |
| Delta Air Lines | 1.15 | Tandy Corporation | 1.35 |
| Exxon Corporation | .60 | Union Electric | .65 |
| General Motors | 1.10 | Universal Foods | .90 |
| Hilton Hotels | 1.45 | Xerox Corporation | 1.20 |

Source: *Value Line Investment Survey.* New York: Value Line Publishing, Inc., August 12, 1994.

$b_j$ = beta coefficient or index of nondiversifiable risk for asset $j$
$k_m$ = market return; the return on the market portfolio of assets

The required return on an asset, $k_j$, is an increasing function of beta, $b_j$, which measures nondiversifiable risk. In other words, *the higher the risk, the higher the required return, and vice versa*. The model can be broken into two parts: (1) the *risk-free rate*, $R_F$, and (2) the *risk premium*, $b_j \times (k_m - R_F)$. The $(k_m - R_F)$

---

**TABLE 12.6   Selected Beta Coefficients and Their Interpretations**

| Beta | Comment | Interpretation[a] |
|---|---|---|
| 2.0 | | Twice as responsive, or risky, as the market |
| 1.0 | Move in same direction as market | Same response or risk as the market (i.e., average risk) |
| .5 | | Only half as responsive, or risky, as the market |
| 0 | | Unaffected by market movement |
| −.5 | | Only half as responsive, or risky, as the market |
| −1.0 | Move in opposite direction to market | Same response or risk as the market (i.e., average risk) |
| −2.0 | | Twice as responsive, or risky, as the market |

[a]A stock that is twice as responsive as the market is expected to experience a 2 percent change in its return for each 1 percent change in the return of the market portfolio, whereas the return of a stock that is half as responsive as the market is expected to change by 1/2 of 1 percent for each 1 percent change in the return of the market portfolio.

portion of the risk premium is called the *market risk premium*. It represents the premium the investor must receive for taking the average amount of risk associated with holding the market portfolio of assets. Let us look at an example.

## ▶ E X A M P L E

Herbst Corporation, a growing computer software developer, wishes to determine the required return on an asset—asset Z—that has a beta, $b_z$, of 1.5. The risk-free rate of return is found to be 7 percent; the return on the market portfolio of assets is 11 percent. Substituting $b_z = 1.5$, $R_F = 7$ percent, and $k_m = 11$ percent into the capital asset pricing model given in Equation 12.5 yields a required return of

$$k_z = 7\% + [1.5 \times (11\% - 7\%)] = 7\% + 6\% = \underline{\underline{13\%}}$$

The market risk premium of 4 percent ($11\% - 7\%$), when adjusted for the asset's index of risk (beta) of 1.5, results in a risk premium of 6 percent ($1.5 \times 4\%$). This premium, when added to the 7 percent risk-free rate, results in a 13 percent required return. Other things being equal, the higher the beta, the greater the required return, and vice versa.

**The Graph: The Security Market Line**   When the capital asset pricing model is depicted graphically, it is called the **security market line (SML).** The SML is, in fact, a straight line. It reflects for each level of nondiversifiable risk (beta) the required return in the marketplace. In the graph, risk as measured by beta, $b$, is plotted on the *x*-axis, and required returns, $k$, are plotted on the *y*-axis. The risk-return trade-off is clearly represented by the SML. Let us look at an example.

**security market line (SML)**
The depiction of the *capital asset pricing model (CAPM)* as a graph that reflects the required return for each level of nondiversifiable risk (beta).

## ▶ E X A M P L E

In the preceding example for the Herbst Corporation, the risk-free rate, $R_F$, was 7 percent, and the market return, $k_m$, was 11 percent. Because the betas associated with $R_F$ and $k_m$, $b_{R_F}$ and $b_m$, are by definition 0 and 1, respectively[2], the SML can be plotted using these two sets of coordinates. (That is, $b_{R_F} = 0$, $R_F = 7\%$; and $b_m = 1$, $k_m = 11\%$.) Figure 12.7 presents the security market line that results from plotting the given coordinates. As traditionally shown, the security market line in Figure 12.7 presents the required return associated with all positive betas. The market risk premium of 4 percent ($k_m$ of $11\% - R_F$ of $7\%$) has been highlighted. With the beta for asset Z, $b_z$, of 1.5, its corresponding required return, $k_z$, is 13 percent. Also shown in the figure is asset Z's risk premium of 6 percent ($k_z$ of $13\% - R_F$ of $7\%$). For assets with betas greater than 1, the risk premium is greater than that for the market; for assets with betas less than 1, the risk premium is less than that for the market.

---

[2]Because $R_F$ is the rate of return on a risk-free asset, the beta, $b_{R_F}$, associated with the risk-free asset equals 0. The 0 beta on the risk-free asset reflects not only its absence of risk but also the fact that the asset's return is unaffected by movements in the market return.

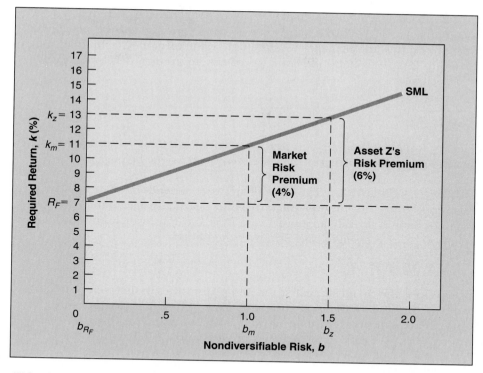

**FIGURE 12.7** **The Security Market Line with Herbst Corporation's Asset Z Data Shown**
At a beta of 0, the required return is the risk-free rate of 7 percent, and at a beta of 1.0, the required return is 11 percent (the 7% risk-free rate + a 4% market risk premium). The required return for asset Z, which has a beta of 1.5, is 13 percent (the 7% risk-free rate + a 6% risk premium).

## Progress Review Questions

**12-7.** What is the relationship of total risk, nondiversifiable risk, and diversifiable risk? Which risk is measured by *beta*? Why would someone argue that nondiversifiable risk is the only relevant risk?

**12-8.** What is the equation for the *capital asset pricing model (CAPM)*? Explain the meaning of each variable. Assuming a risk-free rate of 8 percent and a market return of 12 percent, draw the *security market line (SML)*.

LG 4

# Valuation Fundamentals

As stated at the beginning of this chapter, *valuation* is the process that links risk and return to determine the worth of an asset. It is a relatively simple process that can be applied to expected streams of benefits from bonds, stocks, income properties, oil wells, and so on to determine their worth at a given time. To do this, the manager uses the time value of money techniques presented in Chapter 11 and the concepts of risk and return developed earlier in this chapter.

## Key Inputs

The key inputs to the valuation process include cash flows (returns), timing, and the required return (risk). Each is described briefly below.

**Cash Flows (Returns)**   The value of any asset depends on the cash flow(s) it is expected to provide over the ownership period. To have value, an asset does not have to provide an annual cash flow; it can provide an intermittent cash flow or even a single cash flow over the period.

## ▶ E X A M P L E

Nancy Dorr, the financial analyst for Kemp Industries, a diversified holding company, wishes to estimate the value of three of its assets: common stock in Wortz United, an interest in an oil well, and an original painting by a well-known artist. Her cash flow estimates for each were as follows:

**Stock in Wortz United**   Expect to receive cash dividends of $300 per year indefinitely.

**Oil Well**   Expect to receive cash flow of $2,000 at the end of one year, $4,000 at the end of two years, and $10,000 at the end of four years, when the well is to be sold.

**Original Painting**   Expect to be able to sell the painting in five years for $85,000.

Having developed these cash flow estimates, Nancy has taken the first step toward placing a value on each of these assets. ▶

**Timing**   In addition to making cash flow estimates, we must know the timing of the cash flows.[3] It is customary to specify the timing along with the amounts of cash flow. For example, the cash flows of $2,000, $4,000, and $10,000 for the oil well in the example are expected to occur at the end of years 1, 2, and 4, respectively. In combination, the cash flow and its timing fully define the return expected from the asset.

**Required Return (Risk)**   Risk, as noted earlier, describes the chance that an expected outcome will not be realized. The level of risk associated with a given cash flow can significantly affect its value. In general, the greater the risk of (or the less certain) a cash flow, the lower its value. In terms of pres-

---

[3]Although cash flows can occur at any time during a year, for computational convenience as well as custom, we assume they occur at the *end* of the year unless otherwise noted.

ent value (see Chapter 11), greater risk can be incorporated into an analysis by using a higher required return, or discount rate. Recall that in the capital asset pricing model (CAPM) (see Equation 12.5), the greater the risk as measured by beta, $b$, the higher the required return, $k$. In the valuation process, too, the required return is used to incorporate risk into the analysis—the higher the risk, the greater the required return (discount rate), and vice versa.

# EXAMPLE

Let's return to Nancy Dorr's task of placing a value on the original painting owned by Kemp Industries. Remember that it is expected to provide a single cash flow of $85,000 from its sale at the end of five years. Let's consider two scenarios:

**Scenario 1—Certainty**  A major art gallery has contracted to buy the painting for $85,000 at the end of five years. Because this is considered a certain situation, Nancy views this asset as "money in the bank." She uses the prevailing risk-free rate, $R_F$, of 9 percent as the required return (discount rate) when calculating the value of the painting.

**Scenario 2—High Risk**  The value of original paintings by this artist has fluctuated widely over the past 10 years. Although Nancy expects to be able to get $85,000 for the painting, she realizes that its sale price in five years could range between $30,000 and $140,000. Due to the high uncertainty surrounding the painting's value, Nancy believes a 15 percent required return (discount rate) is appropriate.

The preceding example and the associated estimates of the appropriate required return illustrate the role this rate plays in capturing risk. The often subjective nature of such estimates is also clear.

## The Basic Valuation Model

Simply stated, the value of any asset is the *present value of all future cash flows it is expected to provide over the relevant period*. The period can be as short as one year or as long as infinity. The value of an asset is therefore determined by discounting the expected cash flows back to their present value. A required return commensurate with the asset's risk is used as the appropriate discount rate. Utilizing the present-value techniques presented in Chapter 11, we can express the value of any asset at time zero, $V_0$, as

**Equation 12.6 Formula for the value of any asset**

$$V_0 = \frac{CF_1}{(1 + k)^1} + \frac{CF_2}{(1 + k)^2} + \cdots + \frac{CF_n}{(1 + k)^n}$$

(12.6)

where

$V_0$ = value of the asset at time zero
$CF_t$ = cash flow expected at the end of year $t$
$k$ = appropriate required return (discount rate)
$n$ = relevant period

Using present-value interest factor notation, $PVIF_{k,n}$ from Chapter 11, we can rewrite Equation 12.6 as

$$V_0 = [CF_1 \times (PVIF_{k,1})] + [CF_2 \times (PVIF_{k,2})] + \cdots + [CF_n \times (PVIF_{k,n})] \quad (12.7)$$

Substituting the expected cash flows, $CF_t$, over the relevant period, $n$, and the appropriate required return, $k$, into Equation 12.7, we can determine the value of any asset.

**Equation 12.7 Formula for the value of any asset using present-value interest factor notation**

▶ E X A M P L E

Nancy Dorr, using appropriate required returns and Equation 12.7, calculated the value of each asset (using present-value interest factors from Table A.3) as shown in Table 12.7. The Wortz United stock has a value of $2,500; the oil well's value is $9,262; and the original painting has a value of $42,245. Had she instead used a calculator, the values of the oil well and original painting would have been $9,266.98 and $42,260.03, respectively. Note that whatever the pattern of the expected cash flow from an asset, the basic valuation equation can be used to determine its value.

▶

▼▼▼▼▼▼▼▼▼▼▼▼▼▼▼▼▼▼▼▼▼▼▼▼▼▼▼▼▼

## Progress Review Question

**12-9.** What are the three key inputs to the valuation process? Define and specify the general equation for the value of any asset, $V_0$, in terms of its expected cash flow, $CF_t$, in each year $t$, and the appropriate required return (discount rate), $k$.

▲▲▲▲▲▲▲▲▲▲▲▲▲▲▲▲▲▲▲▲▲▲▲▲▲▲▲▲▲

# Bond and Preferred Stock Values

 LG 5

The basic valuation equation can be customized for use in valuing specific securities: bonds, preferred stock, and common stock. Bonds and preferred stock are similar because they have stated contractual interest and dividend cash flows. The dividends on common stock, on the other hand, are not known in advance. Bond and preferred stock valuation is described in this section. Common stock valuation is discussed in the following section.

## Bond Valuation

*Bonds* are long-term debt instruments used by business and government to raise large sums of money. (Bonds are discussed fully in Chapter 18.) As noted in Chapter 2, most corporate bonds pay interest *semiannually* (every six months) at a stated *coupon interest rate*, have an initial *maturity* of from 10 to 30 years, and have a *par*, or *face*, *value* of $1,000 that must be repaid at maturity. An example illustrates the point.

**TABLE 12.7   Valuation of Kemp Industries' Assets by Nancy Dorr**

| Asset | Cash Flow, CF | | Appropriate Required Return (%) | Valuation |
|---|---|---|---|---|
| Wortz United stock[a] | $300/year indefinitely | | 12 | $V_0 = \$300 \times (PVIFA_{12\%,\infty})$ <br> $= \dfrac{\$300}{.12} = \underline{\underline{\$2{,}500}}$ |
| Oil well[b] | Year *(t)* | $CF_t$ | 20 | $V_0 = [\$2{,}000 \times (PVIF_{20\%,1})]$ |
| | 1 | $2,000 | | $+ [\$4{,}000 \times (PVIF_{20\%,2})]$ |
| | 2 | 4,000 | | $+ [\$0 \times (PVIF_{20\%,3})]$ |
| | 3 | 0 | | $+ [\$10{,}000 \times (PVIF_{20\%,4})]$ |
| | 4 | 10,000 | | $= [\$2{,}000 \times (.833)]$ |
| | | | | $+ [\$4{,}000 \times (.694)]$ |
| | | | | $+ [\$0 \times (.579)]$ |
| | | | | $+ [\$10{,}000 \times (.482)]$ |
| | | | | $= \$1{,}666 + \$2{,}776$ |
| | | | | $+ \$0 + \$4{,}820$ |
| | | | | $= \underline{\underline{\$9{,}262}}$ |
| Original painting[c] | $85,000 at end of year 5 | | 15 | $V_0 = \$85{,}000 \times (PVIF_{15\%,5})$ <br> $= \$85{,}000 \times (.497)$ <br> $= \underline{\underline{\$42{,}245}}$ |

[a]This is a perpetuity (infinite-lived annuity), and therefore the present-value interest factor given in Equation 11.17 is applied.
[b]This is a mixed stream of cash flows and therefore requires a number of *PVIF*s as noted.
[c]This is a lump-sum cash flow and therefore requires a single *PVIF*.

# E X A M P L E

Stills Company, a large defense contractor, on January 1, 1996, issued a 10 percent coupon interest rate, 10-year bond with a $1,000 par value that pays interest semiannually. Investors who buy this bond receive the contractual right to (1) $100 annual interest (10% coupon interest rate × $1,000 par value) distributed as $50 (1/2 × $100) at the end of each six months and (2) the $1,000 par value at the end of the tenth year.

**Basic Bond Valuation**   The value of a bond is the present value of the payments its issuer is obligated to make from the current time until it matures. The appropriate discount rate is the required return, $k_d$, which depends on prevailing interest rates and risk. The basic equation for the value of a bond is given by Equation 12.8.

$$B_0 = I \times \left[ \sum_{t=1}^{n} \frac{1}{(1 + k_d)^t} \right] + M \times \left[ \frac{1}{(1 + k_d)^n} \right] \quad (12.8)$$

$$= I \times (PVIFA_{k_d,n}) + M \times (PVIF_{k_d,n}) \quad (12.8a)$$

**Equation 12.8** Formula for the value of a bond

**Equation 12.8a** Simplified formula for the value of a bond using present-value interest factor notation

where

$B_0$ = the value of the bond at time zero
$I$ = *annual* interest paid in dollars[4]
$n$ = years to maturity
$M$ = par value in dollars
$k_d$ = required return on a bond

Equation 12.8a, along with the appropriate financial tables (A.3 and A.4) or a hand-held business/financial calculator, can be used to calculate bond value.

▶ **E X A M P L E**

Using the Stills Company data for the January 1, 1996, new issue and *assuming that interest is paid annually* and that the required return is equal to the bond's coupon interest rate, $I = \$100$, $k_d = 10$ percent, $M = \$1,000$, and $n = 10$ years.

**Table Use** Substituting the values noted above into Equation 12.8a yields

$$B_0 = \$100 \times (PVIFA_{10\%,10yrs}) + \$1,000 \times (PVIF_{10\%,10yrs})$$

$$= \$100 \times (6.145) + \$1,000 \times (.386)$$

$$= \$614.50 + \$386.00 = \underline{\$1,000.50}$$

The bond therefore has a value of approximately[5] $1,000.

**Calculator Use** Using the calculator, first punch in 10, and depress **N**; then punch in the required return, $k_d$, of 10, and depress **%i**; next punch in the annual interest, $I$, of $100, and depress **PMT**; then punch in the maturity value, $M$, of $1,000, and depress **FV**; finally to calculate the bond value, depress **CPT** followed by **PV**. The bond value of exactly $1,000 should appear on the calculator display.

**Inputs:**    [ 10 ]   [ 10 ]   [ 100 ]   [ 1000 ]

**Functions:**   [ N ]   [ % i ]   [ PMT ]   [ FV ]   [ CPT ]   [ PV ]

▶ **Outputs:**    [ *1,000* ]

---

[4]The payment of annual rather than semiannual bond interest is assumed throughout the following discussion. This assumption simplifies the calculations involved while maintaining the conceptual accuracy of the valuation procedures presented.

[5]Note that a slight rounding error ($.50) results here due to the use of the table factors, which are rounded to the nearest thousandth.

Note that the *bond value calculated in the example above is equal to its par value. This is always the case when the required return is equal to the coupon interest rate.* The computations involved in finding the bond value are depicted graphically on the time line in Figure 12.8.

**Required Returns and Bond Values**   Whenever the required return on a bond differs from the bond's coupon interest rate, the bond's value differs from its par, or face, value. The required return on the bond is likely to differ from the coupon interest rate for either of two reasons: (1) Economic conditions may have changed, causing a shift in the basic cost of long-term funds, or (2) The firm's risk has changed. Increases in the basic cost of long-term funds or in risk raise the required return, and vice versa.

Whatever the exact cause, the important point is that when the required return is greater than the coupon interest rate, the bond value, $B_0$, is less than its par value, $M$. In this case the bond is said to sell at a **discount,** which equals $M - B_0$. On the other hand, when the required rate of return falls below the coupon interest rate, the bond value is greater than par. In this situation the bond is said to sell at a **premium,** which equals $B_0 - M$. An example illustrates this point using Equation 12.8a, along with either financial tables or a hand-held business/financial calculator.

**discount**
The amount by which a bond sells at a value that is less than its par, or face, value.

**premium**
The amount by which a bond sells at a value that is greater than its par, or face, value.

# E X A M P L E

In the preceding example we saw that when the required return equaled the coupon interest rate, the bond's value equaled its $1,000 par value. If for

**FIGURE 12.8   Graphic Depiction of Bond Valuation (Stills Company's 10 Percent Coupon Interest Rate, 10-Year Maturity, $1,000 Par, January 1, 1996, Issue Paying Annual Interest; Required Return = 10 Percent)**

The $1,000.50 value of the Stills Company bond is found by adding the $614.50 present value (found using the 10 percent required return) of the 10 annual $100 interest payments to the $386.00 present value (also at 10 percent) of the $1,000 par value to be received in 10 years at maturity.

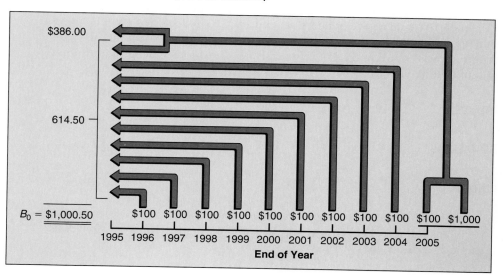

the same bond the required return rises to 12 percent, its value is found as follows:

**Table Use**

$$B_0 = \$100 \times (PVIFA_{12\%,10yrs}) + \$1,000 \times (PVIF_{12\%,10yrs})$$
$$= \$100 \times (5.650) + \$1,000 \times (.322) = \underline{\underline{\$887.00}}$$

**Calculator Use**   First punch in 10, and depress **N;** then punch in the required return of 12, and depress **%i;** next punch in the annual interest of $100, and depress **PMT;** then punch in the maturity value of $1,000, and depress **FV;** finally to calculate the bond value, depress **CPT** followed by **PV.** The bond value of $887.00 should appear on the calculator display.

**Inputs:**         [ 10 ]   [ 12 ]   [ 100 ]   [ 1000 ]

**Functions:**   [ N ]   [ % i ]   [ PMT ]   [ FV ]   [ CPT ]   [ PV ]

**Outputs:**                                                   [ 887.00 ]

The bond therefore sells at a *discount* of $113.00 ($1,000 par value − $887.00 value).

If, on the other hand, the required return fell to, say, 8 percent, the bond's value is found as follows:

**Table Use**

$$B_0 = \$100 \times (PVIFA_{8\%,10yrs}) + \$1,000 \times (PVIF_{8\%,10yrs})$$
$$= \$100 \times (6.710) + \$1,000 \times (.463) = \underline{\underline{\$1,134.00}}$$

**Calculator Use**   First punch in 10, and depress **N;** then punch in the required return of 8, and depress **%i;** next punch in the annual interest of $100, and depress **PMT;** then punch in the maturity value of $1,000, and depress **FV;** finally to calculate the bond value, depress **CPT** followed by **PV.** The bond value of $1,134.20 should appear on the calculator display. Note that this value is more precise than the $1,134 value calculated previously using the rounded financial table factors.

**Inputs:**         [ 10 ]   [ 8 ]   [ 100 ]   [ 1000 ]

**Functions:**   [ N ]   [ % i ]   [ PMT ]   [ FV ]   [ CPT ]   [ PV ]

**Outputs:**                                                   [ 1,134.20 ]

The bond therefore sells for a *premium* of about $134 ($1,134.00 value − $1,000 par value). The results of this and earlier calculations for Stills Company's bond values are summarized in Table 12.8.

**TABLE 12.8   Bond Values for Various Required Returns (Stills Company's 10 Percent Coupon Interest Rate, 10-Year Maturity, $1,000 Par Issue Paying Annual Interest)**

| Required return, $k_d$ (%) | Bond value, $B_0$ | Status |
|---|---|---|
| 12 | $ 887.00 | Discount |
| 10 | 1,000.00 | Par value |
| 8 | 1,134.00 | Premium |

## Preferred Stock Valuation

As noted in Chapter 2, preferred stock promises to pay a fixed periodic dividend. Because preferred stock never matures, its divided payments can be viewed as a perpetuity. Assuming that preferred stock dividends, $D_p$, are paid *annually*,[6] and the required return is $k_p$, the value of preferred stock, $PS_0$, can be given by Equation 12.9.

**Equation 12.9  Formula for the value of preferred stock**

$$PS_0 = D_p \times \left(\frac{1}{k_p}\right) = \frac{D_p}{k_p} \tag{12.9}$$

Recall from Chapter 11 that in the case of a perpetuity, the present-value interest factor, $PVIFA_{k_p,\infty} = 1/k_p$, must be used. The use of this factor to find the value of preferred stock can be noted in Equation 12.9. An example shows how this is done.

### E X A M P L E

Stills Company has an issue of preferred stock outstanding that has a stated annual dividend of $5. The required return on the preferred stock is estimated to be 13 percent. Substituting $D_p = \$5$ and $k_p = 13\%$ into Equation 12.9 yields a preferred stock value of $38.46 ($5 ÷ .13). Equation 12.9 can be used in this manner to find the value of any perpetuity.

## Progress Review Questions

**12-10.** In terms of the required return and the coupon interest rate, what relationship between them causes a bond to sell (a) at a discount? (b) at a premium? (c) at its par value? Explain.

**12-11.** Describe the procedure used to estimate the value of preferred stock. Why are preferred stock dividends treated as a perpetuity?

---

[6]The payment of annual rather than quarterly dividends is assumed for simplicity. Preferred stock is discussed in detail in Chapter 19.

# Common Stock Valuation

Common stockholders expect to be rewarded through the receipt of periodic cash dividends and an increasing—or at least nondeclining—share value. Like current owners, prospective owners and security analysts frequently estimate the firm's value. They choose to purchase the stock when they believe it to be *undervalued* (i.e., that its true value is greater than its market price). They sell when they feel it is *overvalued* (i.e., that its market price is greater than its true value).

## The Basic Stock Valuation Equation

Like bonds and preferred stock, the value of a share of common stock is equal to the present value of all future benefits it is expected to provide. That is, *the value of a share of common stock is equal to the present value of all future dividends it is expected to provide over an infinite time horizon.* By selling stock at a price above that originally paid, a stockholder can earn capital gains in addition to dividends. Yet what the stockholder is really selling is the right to all future dividends. Stocks that are not expected to pay dividends in the foreseeable future have a value attributable to a distant dividend expected to result from sale of the company or liquidation of its assets. Therefore, from a valuation viewpoint only dividends are relevant. By redefining terms, the basic valuation model in Equation 12.6 can be specified for common stock as given in Equation 12.10.

$$P_0 = \frac{D_1}{(1 + k_s)^1} + \frac{D_2}{(1 + k_s)^2} + \cdots + \frac{D_\infty}{(1 + k_s)^\infty} \quad (12.10)$$

**Equation 12.10 Basic formula for the value of common stock**

where

$P_0$ = value of common stock

$D_t$ = per-share dividend expected at the end of year $t$

$k_s$ = required return on common stock

The equation can be simplified somewhat by redefining each year's dividend, $D_t$, in terms of anticipated growth. We consider two cases here: zero growth and constant growth.

**Zero Growth**  The simplest approach to dividend valuation, the **zero-growth model,** assumes a constant, nongrowing dividend stream. In terms of the notation already introduced,

**zero-growth model**
An approach to dividend valuation that assumes a constant, nongrowing dividend stream.

$$D_1 = D_2 = \cdots = D_\infty$$

Letting $D_1$ represent the amount of the annual dividend, Equation 12.10 under zero growth reduces to

$$P_0 = D_1 \times \sum_{t=1}^{\infty} \frac{1}{(1 + k_s)^t} = D_1 \times (PVIFA_{k_s, \infty}) = \frac{D_1}{k_s} \quad (12.11)$$

**Equation 12.11 Formula for the value of a share of stock assuming zero dividend growth**

The equation shows that with zero growth, the value of a share of stock equals the present value of a perpetuity of $D_1$ dollars discounted at a rate $k_s$. Let us look at an example.

# EXAMPLE

The dividend of Addison Company, an established textile producer, is expected to remain constant at $3 per share indefinitely. If the required return on its stock is 15 percent, the stock's value is $20 ($3 ÷ .15).

**constant-growth model**
An approach to dividend valuation that assumes dividends grow at a constant rate that is less than the required return.

**Constant Growth**   The most widely cited dividend valuation approach, the **constant-growth model,** assumes that dividends grow at a constant rate, g, that is less than the required return, $k_s (g < k_s)$. Letting $D_0$ represent the most recent dividend, Equation 12.10 can be rewritten as follows:

**Equation 12.12**

$$P_0 = \frac{D_0 \times (1+g)^1}{(1+k_s)^1} + \frac{D_0 \times (1+g)^2}{(1+k_s)^2} + \cdots + \frac{D_0 \times (1+g)^\infty}{(1+k_s)^\infty} \quad (12.12)$$

If we simplify Equation 12.12, it can be rewritten as follows:

**Equation 12.13**
**Simplified formula for the value of a share of stock under the constant-growth, or Gordon, model**

$$P_0 = \frac{D_1}{k_s - g} \quad (12.13)$$

The constant-growth model in Equation 12.13 is commonly called the **Gordon model.** An example shows how it works.

**Gordon model**
Common name for the *constant-growth model.*

# EXAMPLE

Honee Company, a small cosmetics company, from 1990 through 1995 paid the per-share dividends shown in the table on the following page. The annual growth rate of dividends is assumed to equal the expected constant rate of dividend growth, g. Using Appendix Table A.3 for the present-value interest factor, *PVIF,* or a hand-held business/financial calculator and the technique for finding growth rates described in Chapter 11, we find that the annual growth rate of dividends equals 7 percent.[7] The company esti-

---

[7]The technique involves solving the following equation for g.

$$D_{1995} = D_{1990} \times (1+g)^5$$

$$\frac{D_{1990}}{D_{1995}} = \frac{1}{(1+g)^5} = PVIF_{g,5}$$

Two basic steps can be followed using the present-value table. First, dividing the earliest dividend ($D_{1990} = \$1.00$) by the most recent dividend ($D_{1995} = \$1.40$), a factor for the present value of one dollar, *PVIF,* of .714 ($1.00 ÷ $1.40) results. Although six dividends are shown, *they reflect only five years of growth.* Looking across the table at the present-value interest factors, *PVIF,* for five years, the factor closest to .714 occurs at 7 percent (.713). Therefore, the growth rate of the dividends, rounded to the nearest whole percentage, is 7 percent.
    Alternatively, using a business/financial calculator, begin by punching in the 1990 value of $1.00, and depress **PV;** next punch in the 1995 value of $1.40, and depress **FV;** then punch in the number of years of growth—5—and depress **N;** finally, to get the growth rate, depress **CPT** followed by **%i.** The growth rate of 6.96 percent, which we round to 7 percent, appears on the display. (*Note:* Many calculators require *either* the FV or PV value to be input as a negative number to calculate a growth rate.)

**Inputs:**   | 1.00 |   | 1.40 |   | 5 |

**Functions:**   | PV |   | FV |   | N |   | CPT |   | %i |

**Outputs:**   | 6.96 |

mates that its dividend in 1996, $D_1$, will equal \$1.50. The required return, $k_s$, is assumed to be 15 percent. Substituting these values into Equation 12.13, the value of the stock is

$$P_0 = \frac{\$1.50}{.15 - .07} = \frac{\$1.50}{.08} = \$18.75 \text{ per share}$$

| Year | Dividend ($) |
|------|--------------|
| 1995 | 1.40 |
| 1994 | 1.29 |
| 1993 | 1.20 |
| 1992 | 1.12 |
| 1991 | 1.05 |
| 1990 | 1.00 |

Assuming that the values of $D_1$, $k_s$, and $g$ are accurately estimated, Honee Company's stock value is \$18.75.

## Other Approaches to Common Stock Valuation

Many other approaches to common stock valuation exist, but only one is widely accepted. The more popular approaches include the use of book value, liquidation value, and some type of a price/earnings multiple.

**Book Value**   **Book value per share** is simply the amount per share of common stock to be received if all the firm's assets are sold for their exact book (accounting) value and if the proceeds remaining after paying all liabilities (including preferred stock) are divided among the common stockholders. This method lacks sophistication and can be criticized on the basis of its reliance on historical balance sheet data. It ignores the firm's expected earnings potential and generally lacks any true relationship to the firm's value in the marketplace. Let us look at an example.

**book value per share**
The amount per share of common stock to be received if all the firm's assets are sold for their book value and the remaining proceeds after paying all liabilities (including preferred stock) are divided among the common stockholders.

## ▶ E X A M P L E

Honee Company currently (December 31, 1995) has total assets of \$6 million; total liabilities including preferred stock of \$4.5 million; and 100,000 shares of common stock outstanding. Its book value per share therefore is

$$\frac{\$6,000,000 - \$4,500,000}{100,000 \text{ shares}} = \$15 \text{ per share}$$

Because this value assumes that assets are liquidated for their book value, it may not represent the minimum share value. As a matter of fact, although most stocks sell above book value, it is not unusual to find stocks selling below book value.

# FINANCE IN ACTION

In the News

## Kodak's Out-of-Focus Earnings Picture

Wall Street cheered Eastman Kodak's hiring of George Fisher, who had previously transformed Motorola into the world's dominant manufacturer of pagers and cellular phones. Since its 1988 earnings peak, Kodak had restructured itself five times without cutting costs or increasing sales. Kodak's stock price had been bid upward in anticipation of Fisher initiating fast and deep cost cuts.

The cheering stopped on December 15, 1993. After only two weeks on the job, Fisher abruptly announced that 1994's earnings were likely to be 20 percent below analysts' expectations. Furthermore, he announced that cost cutting would take place at a "measured pace." Fisher's statement didn't explain the reason for lower 1994 expectations, and Kodak's investor relations department stated that Fisher's an- nouncement was not a result of any new strategy.

Goldman Sachs, the largest investment banking firm, immediately removed Kodak from its "buy" list, and the Dean Witter brokerage firm reported that Kodak should have released the bad news earlier. Even though no dividend cut was announced, investors reacted by reducing Kodak's share price by 12 percent. The primary reason for the steep price decline lies in the reduced level of expected dividend growth. Zacks Investment Research, which surveys 2,800 brokers, found that the expected five-year growth rate was cut from 11.3 percent to 10.5 percent.

Source: Keith H. Hammonds, "Fisher's Way at Kodak," *Business Week*, December 27, 1993/January 3, 1994, p. 49.

**liquidation value per share**
The *actual* amount per share of common stock to be received if all the firm's assets are sold, liabilities (including preferred stock) are paid, and any remaining money is divided among the common stockholders.

**Liquidation Value**   **Liquidation value per share** is the *actual* amount per share of common stock to be received if all the firm's assets are sold, liabilities (including preferred stock) are paid, and any remaining money is divided among the common stockholders.[8] This measure is more realistic than book value, but it still fails to consider the earning power of the firm's assets. An example illustrates.

## EXAMPLE

Honee Company found that it would obtain only $5.25 million if it sold its assets today. The firm's liquidation value per share therefore is

$$\frac{\$5,250,000 - \$4,500,000}{100,000 \text{ shares}} = \underline{\$7.50 \text{ per share}}$$

Ignoring any expenses of liquidation, this amount is the firm's minimum value.

---

[8]In the event of liquidation, creditors' claims must be satisfied first, then those of the preferred stockholders. Anything left goes to common stockholders. A more detailed discussion of liquidation procedures is presented in Chapter 21.

**Price/Earnings Multiples**   The *price/earnings (P/E) ratio,* introduced in Chapter 4, reflects the amount investors are willing to pay for each dollar of earnings. The average P/E ratio in a particular industry can be used as the guide to a firm's value if it is assumed that investors value the earnings of a given firm the same as they do the "average" firm in that industry. The **price/earnings multiple approach** to value is a popular technique; the firm's expected earnings per share (EPS) are multiplied by the average price/earnings (P/E) ratio for the industry to estimate the firm's share value. The average P/E ratio for the industry can be obtained from a source such as *Standard & Poor's Industrial Ratios.*

The use of P/E multiples is especially helpful in valuing firms that are not publicly traded, whereas the use of the market price may be preferable for a publicly traded firm. In any case, the price/earnings multiple approach is considered superior to the use of book or liquidation values because it considers *expected* earnings. An example demonstrates the use of price/earnings multiples.

**price/earnings multiple approach**
A technique to estimate the firm's share value; calculated by multiplying the firm's expected earnings per share (EPS) by the average price/earnings (P/E) ratio for the industry.

▶ E X A M P L E

Honee Company is expected to earn $2.60 per share next year (1996). This expectation is based on an analysis of the firm's historical earnings trend and expected economic and industry conditions. The average price/earnings ratio for firms in the same industry is 7. Multiplying Honee's expected earnings per share of $2.60 by this ratio gives us a value for the firm's shares of $18.20, assuming that investors continue to measure the value of the average firm at 7 times its earnings.

▶

It is important to recognize that professional securities analysts typically use a variety of models and techniques to value stocks. For example, an analyst might use the constant-growth model, liquidation value, and price/earnings (P/E) multiples to estimate the true worth of a given stock. If the analyst feels comfortable with his or her estimates, the stock value is viewed as being not greater than the largest estimate. Of course, should the firm's estimated liquidation value per share exceed its "going concern" value per share estimated by using one of the valuation models (zero or constant growth) or the P/E multiple approach, it is viewed as being worth more dead than alive. In such an event the firm lacks sufficient earning power to justify its existence and should probably be liquidated. From an investor's perspective the stock in this situation is an attractive investment only if it can be purchased at a price below its liquidation value, which is highly unlikely.

## Decision Making and Common Stock Value

Valuation equations measure the stock value at a point in time based on expected return ($D_1$, $g$) and risk ($k_s$) data. The decisions of the financial manager, through their effect on these variables, can cause the value of the firm, $P_0$, to change.

**Changes in Expected Return**   Assuming that economic conditions remain stable, any management action that causes current and prospective stockholders to raise their dividend expectations should increase the firm's value. In Equation 12.13 we can see that $P_0$ increases for any increase in $D_1$ or $g$. Any action of the financial manager that increases the level of expected returns without changing risk (the required return) should be undertaken, because it positively affects owners' wealth. An example illustrates.

# E X A M P L E

In an earlier example using the constant-growth model, Honee Company was found to have a share value of $18.75. Imagine that on the following day the company announced a major technological breakthrough that would revolutionize its industry. Current and prospective stockholders are not expected to adjust their required return of 15 percent, but they do expect that future dividends will increase. Specifically, they feel that although the dividend next year, $D_1$, will remain at $1.50, the expected rate of growth will increase from 7 to 9 percent. Substituting $D_1 = \$1.50$, $k_s = .15$, and $g = .09$ into Equation 12.13 results in a share value of $25 [i.e., $1.50 ÷ (.15 − .09)]. The higher expected future dividends, reflected in the increase in the growth rate, $g$, caused the increase in value.

**Changes in Risk**   Although $k_s$ is defined as the required return, it is directly related to the nondiversifiable risk, which can be measured by the beta coefficient. The *capital asset pricing model (CAPM)* given in Equation 12.5 shows this relationship. With the risk-free rate, $R_F$, and the market return, $k_m$, held constant, the required return, $k_s$, depends directly on beta. In other words, any action taken by the financial manager that increases risk also increases the required return. In Equation 12.13 it can be seen that with all else constant, an increase in the required return, $k_s$, reduces share value, $P_0$, and vice versa. Thus any action of the financial manager that increases risk contributes toward a reduction in value, and vice versa. An example illustrates.

# E X A M P L E

Assume that Honee Company's 15 percent required return resulted from a risk-free rate, $R_F$, of 9 percent, a market return, $k_m$, of 13 percent, and a beta, $b$, of 1.50. Substituting into the capital asset pricing model (Equation 12.5), we get the 15 percent required return, $k_s$.

$$k_s = 9\% + [1.50 \times (13\% - 9\%)] = \underline{\underline{15\%}}$$

With this return, the value of the firm, $P_0$, was calculated to be $18.75 in the earlier example.

Now imagine that the financial manager makes a decision that, without changing expected dividends, increases the firm's beta to 1.75. Assuming that $R_F$ and $k_m$ remain at 9 and 13 percent, respectively, the required return increases to 16 percent (i.e., $9\% + [1.75 \times (13\% - 9\%)]$). The higher required return compensates stockholders for the increased risk. Substituting $D_1 = \$1.50$, $k_s = .16$, and $g = .07$ into the valuation equation, Equation 12.13, results in a share value of $16.67 [i.e., $1.50 ÷ (.16 − .07)]. As expected, the owners, by raising the required return (without any corresponding increase in expected return), cause the firm's stock value to decline. Clearly the financial manager's action was not in the owners' best interest.

**Combined Effect**   A financial decision rarely affects return and risk independently; most decisions affect both factors. In terms of the measures presented, with an increase in risk (beta, $b$) one expects an increase in return ($D_1$ or $g$, or both), assuming that $R_F$ and $k_m$ remain unchanged. Depending on the size of the changes in these variables, the net effect on value can be assessed.

▶ **E X A M P L E**

If we assume that the two changes illustrated for Honee Company in the preceding examples occur simultaneously as a result of an action of the financial decision maker, key variable values are $D_1 = \$1.50$, $k_s = .16$, and $g = .09$. Substituting into the valuation model, we obtain a share price of $21.43 [i.e., $\$1.50 \div (.16 - .09)$]. Return increased ($g$ from 7 to 9 percent) as did risk ($b$ from 1.50 to 1.75 and therefore $k_s$ from 15 to 16 percent). The net result of the decision is positive: the share price increased from $18.75 to $21.43. Assuming that the key variables are accurately measured, the decision appears to be in the best interest of the firm's owners, since it increases their wealth.

## Progress Review Questions

**12-12.** Describe, compare, and contrast the zero-growth and constant-growth approaches for estimating the value of common stock.

**12-13.** Explain each of the three other approaches to common stock valuation: (a) book value, (b) liquidation value, and (c) price/earnings (P/E) multiples. Which of these is considered the best?

**12-14.** Explain the linkages among financial decisions, return, risk, and stock value. How does the capital asset pricing model (CAPM) fit into this basic framework? Explain.

**12-15.** Assuming that all other variables remain unchanged, what effect does each of the following have on stock price? Explain your answer.
  **a.** The firm's beta increases.
  **b.** The firm's required return decreases.
  **c.** The dividend expected next year decreases.
  **d.** The rate of growth in dividends is expected to increase.

# SUMMARY OF LEARNING GOALS

**Review basic risk and return concepts, including risk aversion, risk of a single asset, and risk and time.** Risk is the chance of loss, or, more formally,

LG 1

refers to the variability of returns. Return is the change in value plus any cash distributions expressed as a percentage of the initial value. Most financial decision makers are risk-averse, because for a given increase in risk they require an increase in return. The risk of a single asset is measured in much the same way as the risk of a portfolio, or collection, of assets. Risk is an increasing function of time.

**LG 2**   **Describe the risk and return characteristics of a portfolio in terms of correlation and diversification and the effect of international diversification on a portfolio.** The financial manager's goal for the firm is to create an efficient portfolio, one that maximizes return for a given level of risk or minimizes risk for a given level of return. The risk of a portfolio, or collection, of assets may be reduced through diversification. New investments must be considered in light of their effect on the risk and return of the portfolio of assets. The correlation of asset returns affects the diversification process. International diversification, which involves including foreign assets in a portfolio of domestic assets, can be used to further reduce a portfolio's risk. Of course, with it comes the risk of currency fluctuation, political risks, and several other financial risks.

**LG 3**   **Understand the two types of risk and the relationship between the relevant risk (measured by beta) and return as presented by the capital asset pricing model (CAPM).** Total risk consists of nondiversifiable and diversifiable risk. Nondiversifiable risk is the only relevant risk because diversifiable risk can be easily eliminated through diversification. Nondiversifiable risk can be measured by the beta coefficient. The capital asset pricing model (CAPM) uses beta to relate an asset's risk relative to the market to the asset's required return. The graphic depiction of CAPM is the security market line (SML).

**LG 4**   **Discuss the key inputs and basic model used in the valuation process.** Key inputs to the valuation process include cash flows (returns), timing, and the required return (risk). The value, or worth, of any asset is equal to the present value of all future cash flows it is expected to provide over the relevant time period.

**LG 5**   **Apply the basic valuation model to bonds and preferred stocks, and evaluate the relationship between required returns and bond values.** The value of a bond is the present value of its interest payments plus the present value of its par, or face, value. The discount rate used to determine bond value is the required return, which may differ from the bond's coupon interest rate. A bond can sell at a discount, at par, or at a premium, depending on whether the required return is respectively greater than, equal to, or less than its coupon interest rate. The value of preferred stock is determined by applying the appropriate present-value interest factor for a perpetuity to its annual dividend.

**LG 6**   **Perform basic common stock valuation using both the zero- and constant-growth models and other estimation approaches, and relate decision making to common stock value.** The value of a share of common stock is the present value of all future dividends it is expected to provide over an infinite time horizon. Of the two cases of divided growth, zero and constant, the more widely cited is the constant-growth model. Other approaches for estimating common stock value include book value, liquidation value, and price/earnings (P/E) multiples. Because most financial decisions affect both return and risk, an assessment of their combined effect on value must be part of the financial decision-making process.

# SUMMARY OF KEY DEFINITIONS AND EQUATIONS

## Variable Definitions

$B_0$ = bond value

$b_j$ = beta coefficient or index of nondiversifiable risk for asset $j$

$CF_t$ = cash flow expected at the end of year $t$

$CV$ = coefficient of variation

$D_P$ = annual preferred stock dividend

$D_t$ = per-share dividend expected at the end of year $t$

$g$ = constant rate of growth in dividends

$I$ = annual interest on a bond

$k$ = appropriate required return (discount rate)

$k_d$ = required return on a bond

$k_i$ = return for the *ith* outcome

$k_j$ = required return on asset $j$

$k_m$ = market return; the return on the market portfolio of assets

$k_p$ = required return on preferred stock

$k_s$ = required return on common stock

$\bar{k}$ = expected value of return

$M$ = par value of a bond

$n$ = number of outcomes considered

$P_0$ = value of common stock

$Pr_i$ = probability of occurrence of the *ith* return

$PS_0$ = value of preferred stock

$PVIF_{k,n}$ = present-value interest factor for the present value of $1 discounted at $k$ percent for $n$ periods

$PVIFA_{k,n}$ = present-value interest factor for an $n$-year annuity discounted at $k$ percent

$R_F$ = risk-free rate of return

$V_0$ = value of any asset

$\sigma_k$ = standard deviation of returns

## Equations

Expected value of a return

[Eq. 12.1]
$$\bar{k} = \sum_{i=1}^{n} k_i \times Pr_i$$

Standard deviation of returns

[Eq. 12.2]
$$\sigma_k = \sqrt{\sum_{i=1}^{n} (k_i - \bar{k})^2 \times Pr_i}$$

Coefficient of variation

[Eq. 12.3]
$$CV = \frac{\sigma_k}{\bar{k}}$$

[Eq. 12.4]    Total security risk = non diversifiable risk + diversifiable risk

Capital asset pricing model (CAPM)

[Eq. 12.5]
$$k_j = R_F + [b_j \times (k_m - R_F)]$$

Value of any asset

[Eq. 12.6]
$$V_0 = \frac{CF_1}{(1+k)^1} + \frac{CF_2}{(1+k)^2} + \cdots + \frac{CF_n}{(1+k)^n}$$

Value of any asset using present-value interest factor

[Eq. 12.7]
$$V_0 = [CF_1 \times (PVIF_{k,1})] + [CF_2 \times (PVIF_{k,2})] + \cdots + [CF_n \times (PVIF_{k,n})]$$

Bond value

[Eq. 12.8]
$$B_0 = I \times \left[ \sum_{t=1}^{n} \frac{1}{(1+k_d)^t} \right] + M \times \left[ \frac{1}{(1+k_d)^n} \right]$$

[Eq. 12.8a]
$$B_0 = I \times (PVIFA_{k_d,n}) + M \times (PVIF_{k_d,n})$$

Preferred stock value

[Eq. 12.9]
$$PS_0 = \frac{D_p}{k_p}$$

Value of common stock

[Eq. 12.10]
$$P_0 = \frac{D_1}{(1+k_s)^1} + \frac{D_2}{(1+k_s)^2} + \cdots + \frac{D_\infty}{(1+k_s)^\infty}$$

Common stock value (zero-growth model )

[Eq. 12.11]
$$P_0 = \frac{D_1}{k_s}$$

Common stock value (constant-growth model )

[Eq. 12.13]
$$P_0 = \frac{D_1}{k_s - g}$$

L E A R N I N G    G O A L S

After studying this chapter, you should be able to

 LG 1   Understand the basic concept of cost of capital and the specific sources of capital underlying the cost of capital.

 LG 2   Determine the cost of long-term debt, using a popular approximation technique, and the cost of preferred stock.

LG 3   Calculate the cost of common stock equity and convert it into the cost of retained earnings and the cost of new issues of common stock.

 LG 4   Find the weighted average cost of capital (WACC) and discuss the alternative weighting schemes.

LG 5   Describe the rationale for and procedures used to determine the weighted marginal cost of capital (WMCC).

LG 6   Explain how the weighted marginal cost of capital (WMCC) can be used with the investment opportunities schedule (IOS) to make the firm's financing and investment decisions.

# 13 The Cost of Capital

The cost of capital allows a firm to evaluate the returns it earns on its investments. The earnings flow from any investment—building a new plant, buying equipment, or acquiring another company—is meaningless without a reference point against which that investment can be measured. The cost of capital serves as the "hurdle rate," the rate of

---

**The cost of capital serves as the "hurdle rate," the rate of return that projects must exceed to increase shareholder value.**

---

return that projects must exceed to increase shareholder value.

A firm's value is based on the whole company, not just one project. Therefore, a company must look at its overall, or weighted average, cost of capital, including all financing sources. Financial managers must understand the various components of cost of capital because each type of financing has a different cost. A company that bases an investment decision solely on the financing cost for a particular

project could accept a project with a return below its overall cost of capital. Without a cost of capital as the basis for investment decisions, a company can make poor investments.

EG&G is a $2.7 billion, technology-based corporation that provides scientific and technical services and products for government and industrial customers. Most of the firm's investment analysis is performed in the industrial product segments, which need capital for facilities, equipment, product development, and acquisitions.

EG&G's overall cost of capital stayed at about 13 percent for many years. Recently it was reduced to 11 percent, primarily due to lower long-term interest rates. The after-tax cost of debt is easy to calculate and is based on the current coupon interest rate that the company pays on new debt issues. The most difficult part of determining cost of capital is estimating the cost of equity, which has more variables to consider. We calculate its cost using the capital asset pricing model, which incorporates a risk-free rate, our stock's beta, and an equity risk premium.

The company's current strategy is to lower its cost of capital by reducing the amount of equity, the most expensive form of capital, and adding debt. Interest rates are currently (spring 1994) quite low, and EG&G's long-term goal is a debt-to-total-capital ratio of about 25 to 30 percent. Adding debt will lower our weighted average cost of capital and result in a new hurdle rate.

It is important to understand that cost of capital is just one

criterion used for investment decisions. Management must consider qualitative factors, including risk assessment and how the project helps to meet business objectives, and then use good business judgment to make the decision. Some companies must ration capital and cannot fund every project that has a return in excess of its cost of capital. Suppose two projects are expected to earn a 14 percent return. One requires a large investment now that won't be recovered for 10 years. The other's investment is smaller and will be recovered in four years. Clearly, the risk of the two projects is different, even though the return is acceptable. Conversely, companies do not reject all projects with low returns. For example, the acquisition of a new phone system may not have any return or may not have a return above the cost of capital, but it may be a necessary expense.

*Steven Wasserman received a B.B.A. from the University of Michigan and an M.B.A. from Babson College, Wellesley, Massachusetts. From 1978 to 1980 he was a financial analyst at National Medical Care and Continental Resources. He joined EG&G in 1981 as a staff accountant and held various financial positions before assuming his current position as director of investments and financial analysis in 1993.*

The cost of capital is an extremely important financial concept. It acts as a major link between the firm's long-term investment decisions (discussed in Part V) and the wealth of the owners as determined by investors in the marketplace. It is in effect the "magic number" used to decide whether a proposed corporate investment will increase or decrease the firm's stock price. Clearly, only those investments expected to increase stock price would be recommended. Due to its key role in financial decision making, the importance of the cost of capital cannot be overemphasized.

## An Overview of the Cost of Capital

LG 1

The **cost of capital** is the rate of return a firm must earn on its project investments to maintain the market value of its stock. It can also be thought of as the rate of return required by the market suppliers of capital to attract their funds to the firm. Holding risk constant, the implementation of projects with a rate of return above the cost of capital increases the value of the firm, and vice versa.

**cost of capital**
The rate of return a firm must earn on its project investments to maintain its market value and attract funds.

### The Basic Concept

The cost of capital is estimated at a given time. It reflects the expected average future cost of funds over the long run, based on the best information available. This view is consistent with the use of the cost of capital to make long-term financial investment decisions. Although firms typically raise money in lumps, the cost of capital should reflect the interrelatedness of financing activities. For example, if a firm raises funds with debt (borrowing) today, it is likely that some form of equity, such as common stock, will have to be used next time. Most firms maintain a deliberate, optimal mix of debt and equity financing. This mix is commonly called a **target capital structure**—a topic discussed in greater detail in Chapter 16. It is sufficient here to say that although firms raise money in lumps, they tend toward some desired *mix of financing* to maximize owner wealth.

**target capital structure**
The desired optimal mix of debt and equity financing that most firms attempt to achieve and maintain.

To capture the interrelatedness of financing under a target capital structure, we need a broad view. We need to look at the *overall cost of capital* rather than the cost of the specific source of funds used to finance a given expenditure. The importance of such a view can be illustrated by a simple example.

▶ E X A M P L E

A firm is *currently* faced with an opportunity. Assume the following:

**Best Project Available**

$$\text{Cost} = \$100,000$$

$$\text{Life} = 20 \text{ years}$$

$$\text{Return} = 7 \text{ percent}$$

**Cost of Least-Cost Financing Source Available**

Debt = 6 percent

Because it can earn 7 percent on the investment of funds costing only 6 percent, the firm undertakes the opportunity. Imagine that *one week later* a new opportunity is available:

**Best Project Available**

Cost = $100,000

Life = 20 years

Return = 12 percent

**Cost of Least-Cost Financing Source Available**

Equity = 14 percent

In this instance the firm rejects the opportunity because the 14 percent financing cost is greater than the 12 percent return expected.

The firm's actions were not in the best interests of its owners. It accepted a project yielding a 7 percent return and rejected one with a 12 percent return. Clearly, there is a better way. Due to the interrelatedness of financing decisions, the firm must use a combined cost. Over the long run the combined cost provides for better decisions. By weighting the cost of each source of financing by its target proportion in the firm's capital structure, a *weighted average cost* that reflects the interrelationship of financing decisions can be obtained. Assuming that a 50:50 mix of debt and equity is desired, the weighted average cost in this case is 10 percent [(.50 × 6% debt) + (.50 × 14% equity)]. Using this cost, the first opportunity would have been rejected (7% return < 10% weighted average cost), and the second one would have been accepted (12% return > 10% weighted average cost). Such an outcome is clearly more desirable.

## The Cost of Specific Sources of Capital

This chapter focuses on finding the costs of specific sources of capital and combining them to determine and apply the weighted average cost of capital. Our concern is only with the long-term sources of funds available to a business firm, because these sources supply the permanent financing. Long-term financing supports the firm's fixed-asset investments.[1]

Four basic sources of long-term funds are available for the business firm: long-term debt, preferred stock, common stock, and retained earnings. The right-hand side of a balance sheet can be used to illustrate these sources.

---

[1]The role of both long-term and short-term financing in supporting both fixed and current asset investments was addressed in Chapter 7. Suffice it to say that long-term funds are at minimum used to finance fixed assets.

| Balance Sheet | | |
|---|---|---|
| Assets | Current liabilities | |
| | Long-term debt | Sources of long-term funds |
| | Stockholders' equity<br>  Preferred stock<br>  Common stock equity<br>    Common stock<br>    Retained earnings | |

Although not all firms use each of these methods of financing, each firm is expected to have funds from some of these sources in its capital structure. The *specific cost* of each source of financing is the *after-tax* cost of obtaining the financing *today*. (The cost is not the historically based cost reflected by the existing financing on the firm's books.) Techniques for determining the specific cost of each source of long-term funds are presented on the following pages. Although these techniques tend to develop precisely calculated values, the resulting values are at best *rough approximations* due to the numerous assumptions and forecasts that underlie them. We round calculated costs to the nearest 0.1 percent throughout this chapter, but it is not unusual for practicing financial managers to use costs rounded to the nearest 1 percent due to the fact that these values are merely estimates.

## Progress Review Questions

**13-1.** What is the *cost of capital?* What role does it play in making long-term investment decisions? Why is use of a weighted average cost rather than the specific cost recommended?

**13-2.** You have just been told, "Because we are going to finance this project with debt, its required rate of return must exceed the cost of debt." Do you agree or disagree? Explain.

**13-3.** Why is the cost of capital most appropriately measured on an after-tax basis? What effect, if any, does this have on specific cost components?

# The Cost of Long-Term Debt

The **cost of long-term debt,** $k_i$, is the after-tax cost today of raising long-term funds through borrowing. For convenience we typically assume that the funds are raised through issuance and sale of bonds. In addition, consistent with Chapter 12, we assume that the bonds pay *annual*—rather than *semiannual*—interest.

**cost of long-term debt,** $k_i$
The after-tax cost today of raising long-term funds through borrowing.

## Net Proceeds

**net proceeds**
Funds actually received from the sale of a security.

**flotation costs**
The total costs of issuing and selling a security.

Most corporate long-term debts are incurred through the sale of bonds. The **net proceeds** from the sale of a bond, or any security, are the funds actually received from the sale. **Flotation costs**—the total costs of issuing and selling a security—reduce the net proceeds from the sale of a bond, whether sold at a premium, at a discount, or at its par (face) value.

## E X A M P L E

Debbo Company, a major hardware manufacturer, is contemplating selling $10 million worth of 20-year, 9 percent coupon (stated *annual* interest rate) bonds, each with a par value of $1,000. Because similar-risk bonds earn returns greater than 9 percent, the firm must sell the bonds for $980 to compensate for the lower coupon interest rate. The flotation costs paid to the investment banker are 2 percent of the par value of the bond (2% × $1,000), or $20. The net proceeds to the firm from the sale of each bond are therefore $960 ($980 − $20).

## Before-Tax Cost of Debt

The before-tax cost of debt, $k_d$, for a bond with a $1,000 par value can be approximated using the following equation:

**Equation 13.1 Formula for the approximate before-tax cost of debt**

$$k_d = \frac{I + \frac{\$1,000 - N_d}{n}}{\frac{N_d + \$1,000}{2}} \tag{13.1}$$

where

$I$ = annual interest in dollars
$N_d$ = net proceeds from the sale of debt (bond)
$n$ = number of years to the bond's maturity

## E X A M P L E

Substituting the appropriate values from the Debbo Company example into the approximation formula given in Equation 13.1, we get an approximate before-tax debt cost, $k_d$, of 9.4 percent. Note that the annual interest, $I$, is $90 (9% coupon interest rate × $1,000 par value).

$$k_d = \frac{\$90 + \frac{\$1,000 - \$960}{20}}{\frac{\$960 + \$1,000}{2}} = \frac{\$90 + \$2}{\$980}$$

$$= \frac{\$92}{\$980} = 9.4\%$$

## After-Tax Cost of Debt

As indicated earlier, the *specific cost* of financing must be stated on an after-tax basis. Because (as discussed in Chapter 2) interest on debt is tax-deductible, it reduces the firm's taxable income by the amount of de-

## Forest Oil Company Sells Junk to Save Money

From the sound of the title, you might think this is going to be another story about financial ethics. Actually, this story is about common sense and good financial management, because the kind of junk that Forest Oil sold in 1993 had nothing to do with the firm's products—it describes the firm's financing structure. The Denver-based natural gas producer issued $100 million in 11.25 percent coupon debt in 1993. Because the firm maintains a B+ credit rating from Standard & Poor's Corporation, the issue was classified as noninvestment grade, or "junk," debt.

So why did Forest Oil sell junk bonds? After all, aren't these securities very risky and somewhat unethical? Nothing could be farther from the truth. The firm sold the new securities as a money-saving measure, replacing $141 million in 12.5 percent coupon debt with the $100 million of 11.25 percent junk bonds. In the process,

Forest Oil cut its annual interest expense by $6.375 million. Many other small- and medium-sized firms with below-investment-grade credit ratings did likewise in 1993, as falling interest rates forced investors to seek higher returns by investing in companies unable to obtain a credit rating above BB. During the first nine months of 1993, the junk bond market absorbed $41 billion in new issues, compared with $38 billion in all of 1992 and just $10 billion in all of 1991. For investors, junk bonds meant higher returns in a market dominated by paltry 7 percent yields on investment-grade debt, and for corporate issuers junk bonds offered relief from the high cost of debt on bonds issued in previous years when market interest rates were substantially higher.

Source: A. Monroe, "Sitting Pretty," *CFO Magazine*, December 1993, p. 40.

ductible interest. The interest deduction therefore reduces taxes by an amount equal to the product of the deductible interest and the firm's tax rate, $T$. In light of this, the after-tax cost of debt, $k_i$, can be found by multiplying the before-tax cost, $k_d$, by 1 minus the tax rate as stated in the following equation:

$$k_i = k_d \times (1 - T) \qquad (13.2)$$

**Equation 13.2** Formula for the after-tax cost of debt

## ► E X A M P L E

We can use the 9.4 percent before-tax debt cost approximation for Debbo Company, which has a 40 percent tax rate, to demonstrate the after-tax debt cost calculation. Applying Equation 13.2 results in an after-tax cost of debt of 5.6 percent [i.e., $9.4\% \times (1 - .40)$]. Typically, the explicit cost of long-term debt is less than the explicit cost of any of the alternative forms of long-term financing. This is primarily due to the tax-deductibility of interest.

▼▼▼▼▼▼▼▼▼▼▼▼▼▼▼▼▼▼▼▼▼▼▼▼▼▼▼▼▼▼▼▼▼

## Progress Review Questions

**13-4.** What is meant by the *net proceeds* from the sale of a bond? In which circumstances is a bond expected to sell at a discount or at a premium?

**13-5.** What sort of general approximation can be used to find the before-tax cost of debt? How is the before-tax cost of debt converted into the after-tax cost?

▲▲▲▲▲▲▲▲▲▲▲▲▲▲▲▲▲▲▲▲▲▲▲▲▲▲▲▲▲▲▲▲▲▲▲▲▲

   LG ② 

# The Cost of Preferred Stock

Preferred stockholders must receive their *stated* dividends prior to the distribution of any earnings to common stockholders. Because preferred stock is a form of ownership, the proceeds from the sale of preferred stock are expected to be held for an infinite period. A complete discussion of the various characteristics of preferred stock is presented in Chapter 19. However, the one aspect of preferred stock that requires clarification at this point is dividends.

## Preferred Stock Dividends

The amount of preferred stock dividends that must be paid each year before earnings can be distributed to common stockholders may be stated in dollars or as a percentage of the stock's par, or face, value.

**Dollar Amounts**   Most preferred stock dividends are stated as "x dollars per year." When dividends are stated this way, the stock is often referred to as "x-dollar preferred stock." Thus a $4 preferred stock is expected to pay preferred stockholders $4 in dividends each year on each share of preferred stock owned.

**Percentage Amounts**   Sometimes preferred stock dividends are stated as an annual percentage rate. This rate represents the percentage of the stock's par, or face, value that equals the annual dividend. For instance, an 8 percent preferred stock with a $50 par value is expected to pay an annual dividend of $4 a share (.08 × $50 par = $4). Any dividends stated as percentages should be converted to annual dollar dividends before the cost of preferred stock is calculated.

## Calculating the Cost of Preferred Stock

**cost of preferred stock,** $k_p$
The annual preferred stock dividend divided by the net proceeds from the sale of the preferred stock.

The **cost of preferred stock,** $k_p$, is found by dividing the annual preferred stock dividend, $D_p$, by the net proceeds from the sale of the preferred stock, $N_p$. The net proceeds represent the amount of money to be received net of any flotation costs required to issue and sell the stock. For example, if a preferred stock is sold for $100 per share but $3 per share flotation costs are incurred, the net proceeds from the sale are $97. Equation 13.3 gives the cost of preferred stock, $k_p$, in terms of the annual dollar dividend, $D_p$, and the net proceeds from the sale of the stock, $N_p$.

**Equation 13.3** Formula for the cost of preferred stock

$$k_p = \frac{D_p}{N_p}$$

(13.3)

Because preferred stock dividends are paid out of the firm's *after-tax* cash flows, a tax adjustment is not required.

# ▶ E X A M P L E

Debbo Company is contemplating issuance of a 10 percent preferred stock expected to sell for its $87 per share par value. The cost of issuing and selling the stock is expected to be $5 per share. The firm wants to determine the cost of the stock. Because the dividend is stated as a percentage of the stock's $87 par value, the first step in finding this cost is to calculate the dollar amount of preferred dividends. The annual dollar dividend is $8.70 (.10 × $87). The net proceeds from the proposed sale of stock can be found by subtracting the flotation costs from the sale price. This gives a value of $82 per share. Substituting the annual dividend, $D_p$, of $8.70 and the net proceeds, $N_p$, of $82 into Equation 13.3 gives the cost of preferred stock, 10.6 percent ($8.70 ÷ $82).

Comparing the 10.6 percent cost of preferred stock to the 5.6 percent cost of long-term debt shows that the preferred stock is more expensive. This difference results primarily because the cost of long-term debt—interest—is tax-deductible.

▼▼▼▼▼▼▼▼▼▼▼▼▼▼▼▼▼▼▼▼▼▼▼▼▼▼▼▼▼▼▼▼▼

## Progress Review Question

**13-6.** How do you calculate the cost of preferred stock? Why do we concern ourselves with the net proceeds from the sale of the stock instead of its sale price?

▲▲▲▲▲▲▲▲▲▲▲▲▲▲▲▲▲▲▲▲▲▲▲▲▲▲▲▲▲▲▲▲▲

# The Cost of Common Stock

The *cost of common stock* is the return required on the stock by investors in the marketplace. There are two forms of common stock financing: (1) retained earnings and (2) new issues of common stock. As a first step in finding each of these costs we must estimate the cost of common stock equity.

## Finding the Cost of Common Stock Equity

The **cost of common stock equity, $k_s$,** is the rate at which investors discount the expected dividends of the firm to determine its share value. Two techniques for measuring the cost of common stock equity capital are available. One uses the constant-growth valuation model; the other relies on the capital asset pricing model (CAPM).

**Using the Constant-Growth Valuation Model** The **constant-growth valuation model**—the **Gordon model**—was presented in Chapter 12. It is based on the premise that the value of a share of stock is equal to the present value of all future dividends it is expected to provide over an infinite time horizon. The key expression derived in Chapter 12 and presented as Equation 12.13 is restated in Equation 13.4:

**cost of common stock equity, $k_s$**
The rate at which investors discount the expected dividends of the firm to determine its share value.

**constant-growth valuation (Gordon) model**
Assumes that the value of a share of stock equals the present value of all future dividends (assumed to grow at a constant rate) that it is expected to provide over an infinite time horizon.

**Equation 13.4**

$$P_0 = \frac{D_1}{k_s - g} \tag{13.4}$$

where

$P_0$ = value of common stock
$D_1$ = per-share dividend expected at the end of year 1
$k_s$ = required return on common stock
$g$ = constant rate of growth in dividends

Solving Equation 13.4 for $k_s$ results in the following expression for the *cost of common stock equity:*

**Equation 13.5 Formula for the cost of common stock equity**

$$k_s = \frac{D_1}{P_0} + g \tag{13.5}$$

Equation 13.5 indicates that the cost of common stock equity can be found by dividing the dividend expected at the end of year 1 by the current price of the stock and adding the expected growth rate. Because common stock dividends are paid from *after-tax* income, no tax adjustment is required.

### E X A M P L E

Debbo Company wishes to determine its cost of common stock equity capital, $k_s$. The market price, $P_0$, of its common stock is $50 per share. The firm expects to pay a dividend, $D_1$, of $4 at the end of the coming year, 1996. The dividends paid on the outstanding stock over the past six years (1990–1995) were as shown in the table.

| Year | Dividend |
|------|----------|
| 1995 | $3.80 |
| 1994 | 3.62 |
| 1993 | 3.47 |
| 1992 | 3.33 |
| 1991 | 3.12 |
| 1990 | 2.97 |

Using the table for the present-value interest factors, *PVIF* (Table A.3) or a business/financial calculator, in conjunction with the technique described for finding growth rates in Chapter 11, we can calculate the annual growth rate of dividends, $g$. It turns out to be approximately 5 percent (more precisely, 5.05 percent). Substituting $D_1 = \$4$, $P_0 = \$50$, and $g = 5$ percent into Equation 13.5 results in the cost of common stock equity.

$$k_s = \frac{\$4}{\$50} + 5.0\% = 8.0\% + 5.0\% = \underline{13.0\%}$$

The 13.0 percent cost of common stock equity capital represents the return required by existing shareholders on their investment in order to leave the market price of the firm's outstanding shares unchanged.

**Using the Capital Asset Pricing Model**   The **capital asset pricing model (CAPM),** developed and discussed in Chapter 12, describes the relationship between the required return, or cost of common stock equity capital, $k_s$, and the nondiversifiable risk of the firm as measured by the beta coefficient, $b$. The basic CAPM is given in Equation 13.6.

$$k_s = R_F + [b \times (k_m - R_F)] \tag{13.6}$$

where

$R_F$ = risk-free rate of return, commonly measured by the return on a
 U.S. Treasury bill
$k_m$ = market return; the return on the market portfolio of assets

Using CAPM, the cost of common stock equity is the return required by investors as compensation for the firm's nondiversifiable risk, which is measured by beta, $b$.

**Equation 13.6 Formula for the capital asset pricing model (CAPM)**

**capital asset pricing model (CAPM)**
Theory that describes the relationship between the required return and the nondiversifiable risk of the firm as measured by the beta coefficient.

## ▶ E X A M P L E

Debbo Company, which calculated its cost of common stock equity capital, $k_s$, using the constant-growth valuation model in the preceding example, also wishes to calculate this cost using the capital asset pricing model. From information provided by the firm's investment advisers and its own analyses, it is found that the risk-free rate, $R_F$, equals 7 percent; the firm's beta, $b$, equals 1.5; and the market return, $k_m$, equals 11 percent. Substituting these values into the CAPM (Equation 13.6), the company estimates the cost of common stock equity capital, $k_s$, as follows:

$$k_s = 7.0\% + [1.5 \times (11.0\% - 7.0\%)] = 7.0\% + 6.0\% = \underline{\underline{13.0\%}}$$

The 13.0 percent cost of common stock equity capital, which is the same as that found using the constant-growth valuation model, represents the required return of investors in Debbo Company common stock.

## The Cost of Retained Earnings

If earnings are not retained, dividends are charged to retained earnings and paid out of cash to the common stockholders. Thus the **cost of retained earnings, $k_r$,** to the firm is the same as the cost of an *equivalent fully subscribed issue of additional common stock*. This means that retained earnings increase the stockholders' equity in the same way as a new issue of common stock. Stockholders find the firm's retention of earnings acceptable only if they expect it will earn at least their required return on the reinvested funds.

Viewing retained earnings as a fully subscribed issue of additional common stock, we can set the firm's cost of retained earnings, $k_r$, equal to the cost of common stock equity as given by Equations 13.5 and 13.6.[2]

**cost of retained earnings, $k_r$**
The same as the cost of an equivalent fully subscribed issue of additional common stock, which is measured by the cost of common stock equity, $k_s$.

---

[2]Technically, if a stockholder receives dividends and wishes to invest them in additional shares of the firm's stock, he or she has to first pay personal taxes on the dividends and then pay brokerage fees prior to acquiring additional shares. Using $pt$ as the average stockholder's personal tax rate and $bf$ as the average brokerage fees stated as a percentage, the cost of retained earnings, $k_r$, can be specified as: $k_r = k_s \times (1 - pt) \times (1 - bf)$. Due to the difficulty in estimating $pt$ and $bf$, only the simpler definition of $k_r$ given in Equation 13.7 is used here.

**Equation 13.7 Formula for the cost of retained earnings**

$$k_r = k_s \qquad (13.7)$$

It is not necessary to adjust the cost of retained earnings for flotation costs because by retaining earnings the firm raises equity capital without incurring these costs.

## EXAMPLE

The cost of retained earnings for Debbo Company was actually calculated in the preceding examples because it is equal to the cost of common stock equity. Thus $k_r$ equals 13.0 percent. As we show in the next section, the cost of retained earnings is always lower than the cost of a new issue of common stock, due to the absence of flotation costs when financing projects with retained earnings.

## The Cost of New Issues of Common Stock

**cost of a new issue of common stock, $k_n$**
Cost determined by calculating the cost of common stock after considering both the amount of underpricing and the associated flotation costs.

**underpriced**
Stock sold at a price below its current market price.

Our purpose in finding the firm's overall cost of capital is to determine the after-tax cost of *new* funds required for financing projects. Attention must therefore be given to the **cost of a new issue of common stock, $k_n$.** As we explain later, this cost is important only when sufficient retained earnings are unavailable. The cost of a new issue of common stock is determined by calculating the cost of common stock after considering both the amount of underpricing and the associated flotation costs. Normally, a new issue must be **underpriced** to be sold, that is, it must be sold at a price below the current market price, $P_0$. In addition, flotation costs paid for issuing and selling the new issue reduce proceeds.

The cost of new issues can be calculated by determining the net proceeds after underpricing and flotation costs. We use the constant-growth valuation model expression for the cost of existing common stock, $k_s$, as a starting point. If we let $N_n$ represent the net proceeds from the sale of new common stock after allowing for underpricing and flotation costs, the cost of the new issue, $k_n$, can be expressed as follows:

**Equation 13.8 Formula for the cost of a new issue of common stock**

$$k_n = \frac{D_1}{N_n} + g \qquad (13.8)$$

The net proceeds from sale of new common stock, $N_n$, is less than the current market price, $P_0$. Therefore, the cost of new issues, $k_n$, is greater than the cost of existing issues, $k_s$, which as noted above is equal to the cost of retained earnings, $k_r$. The cost of new common stock is normally greater than any other long-term financing cost. Because common stock dividends are paid from after-tax cash flows, no tax adjustment is required.

## EXAMPLE

In the example using the constant-growth valuation model, we used an expected dividend, $D_1$, of \$4; a current market price, $P_0$, of \$50; and an expected growth rate of dividends, $g$, of 5 percent to calculate Debbo Company's cost of common stock equity capital, $k_s$. It was found to be 13.0 percent. To determine its cost of *new* common stock, $k_n$, Debbo Company has estimated that, on average, new shares can be sold for \$47. The \$3 per share underpricing is necessary due to the competitive nature of the market. A second cost associated with a new issue is an underwriting fee of $2.50 per share that is paid to cover the costs of issuing and selling the new issue. The total underpricing and flotation costs per share are therefore expected to be $5.50 ($3.00 per share underpricing plus $2.50 per share flotation).

Subtracting the $5.50 per share underpricing and flotation cost from the current $50 share price, $P_0$, results in expected net proceeds, $N_n$, of $44.50 per share ($50.00 − $5.50). Substituting $D_1 = \$4$, $N_n = \$44.50$, and $g = 5$ percent into Equation 13.8 results in a cost of new common stock, $k_n$, as follows:

$$k_n = \frac{\$4.00}{\$44.50} + 5.0\% = 9.0\% + 5.0\% = \underline{14.0\%}$$

Debbo Company's cost of new common stock, $k_n$, is therefore 14.0 percent. This is the value to be used in the subsequent calculation of the firm's overall cost of capital.

## Progress Review Questions

**13-7.** What premise about share value underlies the constant-growth valuation (Gordon) model that is used to measure the cost of common stock equity, $k_s$? What does each component of the equation represent?

**13-8.** If retained earnings are viewed as a fully subscribed issue of additional common stock, why is the cost of financing a project with retained earnings technically less than the cost of using a new issue of common stock?

# The Weighted Average Cost of Capital

LG **4**

Now that methods for calculating the cost of specific sources of financing have been reviewed, we can present techniques for determining the overall cost of capital. As noted earlier, the **weighted average cost of capital (WACC),** $k_a$, is found by weighting the cost of each specific type of capital by its proportion in the firm's capital structure. Let us look at the basic computational procedures and weighting schemes involved.

**weighted average cost of capital (WACC),** $k_a$
Cost determined by weighting the cost of each specific type of capital by its proportion in the firm's capital structure.

## Calculating the Weighted Average Cost of Capital

The weighted average cost of capital (WACC) can be calculated once the costs of the specific sources of financing have been determined. This calculation is performed by multiplying the specific cost of each form of financing by its proportion in the firm's capital structure and summing the weighted values. As an equation, the weighted average cost of capital, $k_a$, can be expressed as follows:

**Equation 13.9** Formula for the weighted average cost of capital (WACC)

$$k_a = (w_i \times k_i) + (w_p \times k_p) + (w_s \times k_{r \text{ or } n})$$   (13.9)

where

$w_i$ = proportion of long-term debt in capital structure
$w_p$ = proportion of preferred stock in capital structure
$w_s$ = proportion of common stock equity in capital structure
$w_i + w_p + w_s = 1.0$

Three important points should be noted about Equation 13.9:

1. For computational convenience it is best to convert the weights to decimal form and leave the specific costs in percentage terms.
2. *The sum of weights must equal 1.0.* Simply stated, all capital structure components must be accounted for.
3. The firm's common stock equity weight, $w_s$, is multiplied by either the cost of retained earnings, $k_r$, or the cost of new common stock, $k_n$. The specific cost used in the common stock equity term depends on whether the firm's common stock equity financing is obtained using retained earnings, $k_r$, or new common stock, $k_n$.

# E X A M P L E

Earlier in the chapter, we found the costs of the various types of capital for Debbo Company to be as follows:

Cost of debt, $k_i$ = 5.6 percent

Cost of preferred stock, $k_p$ = 10.6 percent

Cost of retained earnings, $k_r$ = 13.0 percent

Cost of new common stock, $k_n$ = 14.0 percent

The company uses the weights in the following table when calculating its weighted average cost of capital.

| Source of Capital | Weight |
|---|---|
| Long-term debt | 40% |
| Preferred stock | 10 |
| Common stock equity | 50 |
| Total | 100% |

Because the firm expects to have a sizable amount of retained earnings available ($300,000), it plans to use its cost of retained earnings, $k_r$, as the cost of common stock equity. Debbo Company's weighted average cost of capital is calculated in Table 13.1. (*Note:* For computational convenience the financing proportion weights are listed in decimal form in column 1 and the specific costs are shown in percentage terms in column 2.) The resulting weighted average cost of capital for Debbo is 9.8 percent. In view of this cost of capital and assuming an unchanged risk level, the firm should accept all projects that earn a return greater than or equal to 9.8 percent.

**TABLE 13.1    Calculation of the Weighted Average Cost of Capital for Debbo Company**

| Source of Capital | Weight (1) | Cost (2) | Weighted Cost [(1) × (2)] (3) |
|---|---|---|---|
| Long-term debt | .40 | 5.6% | 2.2% |
| Preferred stock | .10 | 10.6 | 1.1 |
| Common stock equity | .50 | 13.0 | 6.5 |
| Totals | 1.00 | | 9.8% |

Weighted average cost of capital = 9.8%

## Weighting Schemes

Weights can be calculated as *book value* or *market value* and as *historic* or *target*.

**Book Value Versus Market Value**    **Book value weights** use accounting values to measure the proportion of each type of capital in the firm's financial structure. **Market value weights** measure the proportion of each type of capital at its market value. Market value weights are appealing because the market values of securities closely approximate the actual dollars to be received from their sale. Moreover, because the costs of the various types of capital are calculated using prevailing market prices, it seems reasonable to use market value weights. In addition, the long-term investment cash flows to which the cost of capital is applied are estimated in terms of current as well as future market values. *Market value weights are clearly preferred over book value weights.*

**book value weights**
Weights that use accounting values to measure the proportion of each type of capital in the firm's financial structure.

**market value weights**
Weights that use market values to measure the proportion of each type of capital in the firm's financial structure.

**Historic Versus Target**    **Historic weights** can be either book or market value weights based on *actual* capital structure proportions. For example, past as well as current book value proportions constitute a form of historic weighting. Likewise, past or current market value proportions represent a historic weighting scheme. Such a weighting scheme is therefore based on real— rather than desired—proportions. **Target weights** reflect the firm's *desired* capital structure proportions. Like historic weights, they can also be based on either book or market values. Firms using target weights establish such proportions on the basis of the "optimal" capital structure they wish to achieve. When one considers the somewhat approximate nature of the calculations, the choice of weights may not be critical. However, from a strictly theoretical point of view the *preferred weighting scheme is target market value proportions,* and these are assumed throughout this chapter.

**historic weights**
Either book or market value weights based on *actual* capital structure proportions.

**target weights**
Either book or market value weights based on *desired* capital structure proportions.

## Progress Review Questions

**13-9.** What is the *weighted average cost of capital (WACC)*? How is it calculated?

**13-10.** Describe the logic underlying the use of *target capital structure weights,* and compare and contrast this approach with the use of *historic weights.*

# The Marginal Cost and Investment Decisions

The firm's weighted average cost of capital is a key input to the investment decision-making process. As demonstrated earlier in the chapter, the firm should make only those investments for which the expected return is greater than the weighted average cost of capital. Of course at any given time the firm's financing costs and investment returns are affected by the volume of financing or investment undertaken. The concepts of a *weighted marginal cost of capital* and an *investment opportunities schedule* provide the mechanisms whereby financing and investment decisions can be made simultaneously at any point in time.

## The Weighted Marginal Cost of Capital

**weighted marginal cost of capital (WMCC)**
The firm's weighted average cost of capital (WACC) associated with its next dollar of total new financing.

**weighted marginal cost of capital (WMCC) schedule**
Graph that relates the firm's weighted average cost of capital (WACC) to the level of total new financing.

The weighted average cost of capital may vary at any time depending on the volume of financing the firm plans to raise. *As the volume of financing increases, the costs of the various types of financing increase, raising the firm's weighted average cost of capital.* The **weighted marginal cost of capital (WMCC)** is simply the firm's weighted average cost of capital (WACC) associated with its next dollar of total new financing. The financial manager is interested in this marginal cost because it is relevant to current decisions.

A schedule or graph relating the firm's weighted average cost of capital to the level of total new financing is called the **weighted marginal cost of capital (WMCC) schedule.** The increasing financing costs are attributable to the fact that fund suppliers require greater returns in the form of interest, dividends, or growth as compensation for the increased risk introduced as larger volumes of *new* financing are incurred.

Another factor causing the weighted average cost of capital to increase relates to the use of common stock equity financing. The portion of new financing provided by common stock equity is taken from available retained earnings until exhausted and then obtained through new common stock financing. Remember that retained earnings are a less expensive form of common stock equity financing than the sale of new common stock. It should be clear, then, that once retained earnings are exhausted, the weighted average cost of capital rises with the addition of more expensive new common stock.

▶ E X A M P L E

In the preceding example the weighted average cost of capital (WACC) for Debbo Company was calculated in Table 13.1 using the 13.0 percent cost of retained earnings, $k_r$, as the cost of common stock equity. Once the $300,000 of available retained earnings is exhausted, the firm must use the more expensive new common stock financing ($k_n = 14.0\%$) to meet its common stock equity needs. Because the target capital structure dictates that common stock equity represent 50 percent of total capital, the $300,000 of retained earnings supports only $600,000 of *total new financing*. This value is found by dividing the available retained earnings of $300,000 by the common stock equity target proportion of 50 percent ($300,000 ÷ .50 = $600,000). Therefore, when the firm's total new financing increases beyond $600,000, the weighted average cost of capital rises: the cost of common stock equity increases from the 13.0 percent cost of retained earnings to the 14.0 percent cost of new common stock. Table 13.1 demonstrated the WACC calculation for the first $600,000 of total new financing. The WACC calculation for greater than $600,000 of total new financing is given in Table 13.2.

When the total new financing exceeds $600,000, the WACC rises from 9.8 percent (Table 13.1) to 10.3 percent (Table 13.2). Of course the firm may face other increases in the WACC due to increases in debt, preferred stock, and common stock equity costs as additional new funds are raised. Using calculations similar to those demonstrated previously, Debbo Company developed its *weighted marginal cost of capital (WMCC) schedule*, which is summarized in Table 13.3 and graphed in Figure 13.1. It is quite clear from both the tabular and graphic data that the WMCC is an *increasing* function of the amount of total new financing raised.

## The Investment Opportunities Schedule

At any given time a firm has certain investment opportunities available to it. These opportunities differ with respect to the size of investment anticipated, risk, and return. (For convenience, we assume that all opportunities have equal risk similar to the firm's risk.) The firm's **investment opportunities schedule (IOS)** is a ranking of investment possibilities from best (highest re-

**investment opportunities schedule (IOS)**
A ranking of investment possibilities from best (highest return) to worst (lowest return).

**TABLE 13.2  Calculation of the WACC for Debbo Company for Greater than $600,000 of Total New Financing**

| Source of Capital | Weight (1) | Cost (2) | Weighted Cost [(1) × (2)] (3) |
|---|---|---|---|
| Long-term debt | .40 | 5.6% | 2.2% |
| Preferred stock | .10 | 10.6 | 1.1 |
| Common stock equity | .50 | 14.0 | 7.0 |
| Totals | 1.00 | | 10.3% |

Weighted average cost of capital = 10.3%

**TABLE 13.3   Weighted Marginal Cost of Capital for Debbo Company**

| Range of Total New Financing | Weighted Average Cost of Capital |
|---|---|
| $0 to $600,000 | 9.8% |
| $600,000 to $1,000,000 | 10.3 |
| $1,000,000 and above | 11.5 |

turn) to worst (lowest return). As the cumulative amount of money invested in a firm's capital projects increases, its return on the projects decreases. Generally the first project selected has the highest return, the next project the second highest, and so on. In other words, the return on investments *decreases* as the firm accepts additional projects.

## EXAMPLE

Debbo Company's current investment opportunities schedule (IOS) lists the best (highest return) to the worst (lowest return) investment possibilities in column 1 of Table 13.4. In column 2 of the table, the initial investment required by each project is shown. In column 3 the cumulative total invested funds required to finance all projects better than and including the corresponding investment opportunity are given. Plotting the project returns

**FIGURE 13.1
Weighted Marginal Cost of Capital (WMCC) Schedule for Debbo Company**

Debbo Company's WMCC schedule shows that its weighted average cost of capital (WACC) increases from 9.8% between $0 and $600,000 of total new financing, to 10.3% between $600,000 and $1 million, to 11.5% for above $1 million.

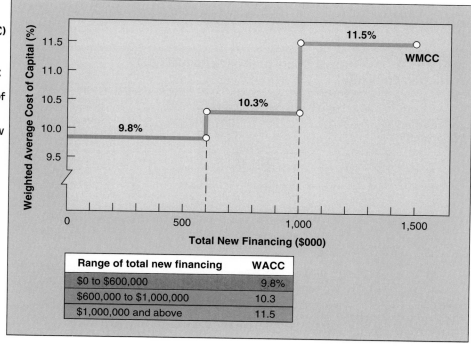

| Range of total new financing | WACC |
|---|---|
| $0 to $600,000 | 9.8% |
| $600,000 to $1,000,000 | 10.3 |
| $1,000,000 and above | 11.5 |

against the cumulative investment (column 1 against column 3 in Table 13.4) on a set of total new financing or investment-weighted average cost of capital or return axes results in the firm's investment opportunities schedule (IOS). A graph of the IOS for Debbo Company is given in Figure 13.2.

## Making Financing and Investment Decisions

As long as a project's rate of return is greater than the weighted marginal cost of new financing, the project should be accepted by the firm. Although the return decreases with the acceptance of more projects, the weighted marginal cost of capital increases because greater amounts of financing are required. The firm therefore *accepts projects up to the point where the marginal return on its investment equals its weighted marginal cost of capital.* Beyond that point its investment return is less than its capital cost. This approach is completely consistent with the firm's goal of owner wealth maximization. Returning to the Debbo Company example, we can demonstrate the application of this procedure.

▶ E X A M P L E

Figure 13.2 shows the Debbo Company's WMCC schedule and IOS on the same set of axes. Using these two functions in combination, the firm can determine its optimal capital budget ("X" in the figure). By raising $1.1 million of new financing and investing these funds in projects A, B, C, D, and E, the firm should maximize the wealth of its owners, because the 12.0 percent return on the last dollar invested (in project E) *exceeds* its 11.5 percent weighted average cost. Investment in project F is not feasible because its 11.0 percent return is *less than* the 11.5 percent cost of funds available for investment. The importance of the WMCC and the IOS for investment decision making should now be quite clear.

## TABLE 13.4   Investment Opportunities Schedule (IOS) for Debbo Company

| Investment Opportunity | Rate of Return (1) | Initial Investment (2) | Cumulative Investment[a] (3) |
|:---:|:---:|:---:|:---:|
| A | 15.0% | $100,000 | $ 100,000 |
| B | 14.5 | 200,000 | 300,000 |
| C | 14.0 | 400,000 | 700,000 |
| D | 13.0 | 100,000 | 800,000 |
| E | 12.0 | 300,000 | 1,100,000 |
| F | 11.0 | 200,000 | 1,300,000 |
| G | 10.0 | 100,000 | 1,400,000 |

[a]The cumulative investment represents the total amount invested in projects with higher returns plus the investment required for the given investment opportunity.

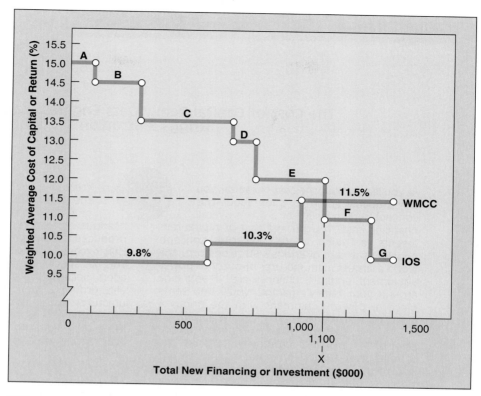

**FIGURE 13.2   Using the IOS and WMCC to Select Projects**
Debbo Company's investment opportunities schedule (IOS) depicts in descending order its investment possibilities. A total of $1.1 million should be raised and invested in projects A, B, C, D, and E because their marginal returns are in excess of the associated weighted marginal cost of capital (WMCC).

It is important to note that at the point at which the return equals the weighted average cost of capital, $k_a$—the optimal capital budget of $1,100,000 at point X in Figure 13.2—the firm's size as well as its shareholder value are optimized. In a sense the size of the firm is determined by the market—the availability of and returns on investment opportunities, and the availability and cost of financing. Of course, most firms operate under a management-imposed budget constraint that is below the optimum capital budget (where return = $k_a$). Suffice it to say that due to budget constraints, a gap frequently exists between the theoretically optimal capital budget and the firm's actual level of financing and investment.

## Progress Review Questions

**13-11.** What is the *weighted marginal cost of capital (WMCC)*? What does the *WMCC schedule* represent? Why does this schedule increase?

**13-12.** What is the *investment opportunities schedule (IOS)*? Is it typically depicted as an increasing or decreasing function of the level of investment at a given time? Why?

## The Cost of Capital Really Gets Engines Running at Briggs & Stratton

As you learn about the cost of capital, you will probably come to think about this concept as a measure of a firm's overall financing cost. In truth, the cost of capital represents a much more powerful concept. Consider the case of Briggs & Stratton Corp., the world's largest manufacturer of outdoor power equipment engines. Chances are, if you look around your family's garage, you'll find some piece of power equipment with the Briggs & Stratton name on it.

In 1993, Briggs & Stratton reported record sales of $1.1 billion. Even more impressive, the firm reported $70 million in net income, almost double the figure posted in 1992. The firm's return on equity surpassed 20 percent for the first time in corporate history, and two dividend in-

creases in a 12-month period helped push the firm's stock price to an all-time high of $80. So what's everyone at corporate headquarters talking about? Briggs & Stratton produced a cash operating profit (12.9 percent) that exceeded its cost of capital (12 percent). This has special significance for the firm's managers, because it placed the company in a truly elite group. Only about 25 percent of U.S. manufacturers are able to report that their operating profits exceed their cost of capital, providing a clear signal to investors that these firms are creating value for their shareholders.

Source: S. Barr, "Briggs & Stratton: Covering the Cost of Capital," *CFO Magazine*, January 1994, p. 23.

**13-13.** Use a graph to show how the weighted marginal cost of capital (WMCC) schedule and the investment opportunities schedule (IOS) can be used to find the level of financing and investment that maximizes owners' wealth. Why, on a practical basis, do many firms finance and invest at a level below this optimum?

# SUMMARY OF LEARNING GOALS

**Understand the basic concept of cost of capital and the specific sources of capital underlying the cost of capital.** The cost of capital is the rate of return that a firm must earn on its investments in order to maintain its market value and attract needed funds. To capture the interrelatedness of financing, an overall or weighted average cost of capital should be used rather than the cost of the specific source used to finance a

LG 1

given expenditure. This approach, by combining the costs of long-term financing sources, results in an expected average future cost of funds over the long run that can be used to make long-term investment decisions. The specific costs of the basic sources of capital (long-term debt, preferred stock, retained earnings, and common stock) can be calculated individually.

**Determine the cost of long-term debt, using a popular approximation technique, and the cost of preferred stock.** The cost of long-term debt is the after-tax cost today of raising long-term funds through borrowing. It can be approximated using a formula and a tax-adjustment calculation. The cost of preferred stock is the stated annual dividend expressed as a percentage of the net proceeds from the sale of preferred shares.

**Calculate the cost of common stock equity and convert it into the cost of retained earnings and the cost of new issues of common stock.** The cost of common stock equity can be calculated using the constant-growth valuation model or the capital asset pricing model (CAPM). The cost of retained earnings is equal to the cost of common stock equity. An adjustment in the cost of common stock equity to reflect underpricing and flotation cost is required to find the cost of new issues of common stock.

**Find the weighted average cost of capital (WACC) and discuss the alternative weighting schemes.** A firm's weighted average cost of capital (WACC) can be determined by combining the costs of specific types of capital after weighting each cost using historical book or market value weights or target book or market value weights. The theoretically preferred approach uses target weights based on market values.

**Describe the rationale for and procedures used to determine the weighted marginal cost of capital (WMCC).** A firm's weighted marginal cost of capital (WMCC) reflects the fact that as the volume of total new financing increases, the costs of the various types of financing increase, raising the firm's weighted average cost of capital (WACC). The WMCC is the firm's WACC associated with its next dollar of total new financing. The WMCC schedule relates the WACC to each level of total new financing.

**Explain how the weighted marginal cost of capital (WMCC) can be used with the investment opportunities schedule (IOS) to make the firm's financing and investment decisions.** The investment opportunities schedule (IOS) presents a ranking of currently available investments from those with the highest returns to those with the lowest returns. It is used in combination with the weighted marginal cost of capital (WMCC) to find the level of financing and investment that maximizes owners' wealth. With this approach the firm accepts projects up to the point where the marginal return on its investment equals its weighted marginal cost of capital.

# SUMMARY OF KEY DEFINITIONS AND EQUATIONS

## Variable Definitions

$b$ = beta coefficient or measure of nondiversifiable risk
$D_1$ = per-share dividend expected at the end of year 1
$D_p$ = annual preferred stock dividend
$g$ = constant rate of growth in dividends
$I$ = annual interest in dollars
$k_a$ = weighted average cost of capital
$k_d$ = before-tax cost of debt
$k_i$ = after-tax cost of debt
$k_m$ = market return; the return on the market portfolio of assets
$k_n$ = cost of a new issue of common stock
$k_p$ = cost of preferred stock
$k_r$ = cost of retained earnings
$k_s$ = cost of common stock equity or required return on common stock
$n$ = number of years to the bond's maturity
$N_d$ = net proceeds from the sale of debt (bond)
$N_n$ = net proceeds from sale of new common stock
$N_p$ = net proceeds from the sale of preferred stock
$P_0$ = value of common stock
$R_F$ = risk-free rate of return, commonly measured by the return on a U.S. Treasury bill
$T$ = firm's tax rate
$w_i$ = proportion of long-term debt in capital structure
$w_p$ = proportion of preferred stock in capital structure
$w_s$ = proportion of common stock equity in capital structure

## Equations

Approximate before-tax cost of debt

$$k_d = I + \frac{\dfrac{\$1,000 - N_d}{n}}{\dfrac{N_d + \$1,000}{2}}$$  [Eq. 13.1]

After-tax cost of debt

$$k_i = k_d \times (1 - T)$$  [Eq. 13.2]

Cost of preferred stock

[Eq. 13.3]
$$k_p = \frac{D_p}{N_p}$$

Cost of common stock equity
Using constant-growth valuation model

[Eq. 13.5]
$$k_s = \frac{D_1}{P_0} + g$$

Using capital asset pricing model (CAPM)

[Eq. 13.6]
$$k_s = R_F + [b \times (k_m - R_F)]$$

Cost of retained earnings

[Eq. 13.7]
$$k_r = k_s$$

Cost of new issues of common stock

[Eq. 13.8]
$$k_n = \frac{D_1}{N_n} + g$$

Weighted average cost of capital (WACC)

[Eq. 13.9]
$$k_a = (w_i \times k_i) + (w_p \times k_p) + (w_s \times k_{r \text{ or } n})$$

# Long-Term Investment Decisions

# CHAPTER

After studying this chapter, you should be able to

 **LG 1** Understand the key capital expenditure motives and the steps in the capital budgeting process, beginning with proposal generation and ending with follow-up.

 **LG 2** Define the basic terminology used to describe projects, funds availability, decision approaches, and cash flow patterns.

 **LG 3** Discuss the major components of relevant cash flows, differences in the development of expansion- versus replacement-decision cash flows, and international capital budgeting and long-term investments.

 **LG 4** Calculate the initial investment associated with a proposed capital expenditure, given relevant cost, depreciation, and tax data.

**LG 5** Determine the operating cash inflows relevant to a capital budgeting proposal using the income statement format.

**LG 6** Summarize the relevant cash flows associated with a capital budgeting proposal graphically on a time line.

# 14 Capital Budgeting and Cash Flow Principles

Capital budgeting is an integral part of strategic planning. If you are planning for long-term growth, you must set aside the capital to support that growth. At Hershey Foods, a major diversified food company producing chocolate, confectionery, and pasta products, our primary capital budgeting objective is selecting projects that fit the company's strategic objectives,

---

**The key to successful capital budgeting is developing reliable assumptions for the cash flow analysis . . .**

---

as determined by senior management.

Although industrial engineers in each division have primary responsibility for capital project analysis, they must rely on input from many departments. For example, they need marketing and sales information to develop revenue projections, and production cost estimates to forecast expenses. Capital budgeting is a cooperative effort.

Hershey's capital budgeting process starts each summer at the divisional level with approval of capital project lists for the coming year. These are submitted in October to the corporate planning committee, which looks at the company's total capital needs and approves a capital budget in January. During the year, the divisions prepare the project analyses. Then the corporate assistant controllers and the financial analysis staff review them for compliance with company policy and validity of assumptions before presentation to senior management for final approval.

Hershey groups projects based on risk and assigns each category a hurdle rate (a required rate of return that the project must meet) that increases with the project's risk. Cost-saving projects such as equipment to improve productivity carry the lowest risk, whereas taking an existing product into a new market is considered riskier. Introducing a new product in a new market is riskier still. For example, we require a greater return for a new candy bar than for a product extension of an established brand.

We perform a thorough analysis of capital projects over a 10-to-15-year time horizon. Proposals include a project summary, project alternatives, key assumptions, cash flows, the project scope and timeline, and funding information. The quality of the proposal is important, so managers need good communication skills.

The key to successful capital budgeting is developing reliable assumptions for the cash flow analysis used to determine project feasibility. Sound, supportable assumptions are especially important for higher risk ventures. Many factors must be analyzed. For example, we need to know if a product line extension will cannibalize (reduce) sales of the primary brand. The cash flows for Hershey's Kisses with Almonds included a cannibalization rate assumption to account for sales loss on the original chocolate Kiss.

Once a project is underway, the corporate finance staff monitors it closely. Each division's top three projects are audited one and three years after start-up, to compare actual with projected returns. It also helps the divisions to make better assumptions in the future.

**Scott McNelis** *received a B.A. in business administration from Franklin and Marshall College and an M.B.A. from Drexel University. He joined Hershey Foods in 1984 as a financial analyst in the corporate controller's department, and then moved to corporate planning and analysis. In 1991 he was promoted to manager, corporate financial analysis, where his responsibilities include analysis of capital projects, industry group analysis and benchmarking, and business acquisitions.*

**C**apital budgeting is the process of evaluating and selecting long-term investments consistent with the firm's goal of owner wealth maximization. Firms typically make a variety of long-term investments. The most common such investment for the manufacturing firm is in *fixed assets.* These assets are a necessity: without them production would be impossible. Fixed assets are quite often referred to as *earning assets* because they generally provide the basis for the firm's earning power and value. The three major classes of fixed assets are property (land), plant, and equipment. Chapters 16 through 20 address the key issues related to long-term financing of fixed assets. Here we concentrate on fixed-asset acquisition without regard to the specific method of financing used. Note that for ease of presentation and study, both this and the following chapter are devoted to coverage of capital budgeting.

**capital budgeting**
The process of evaluating and selecting long-term investments consistent with the firm's goal of owner wealth maximization.

# The Capital Budgeting Decision Process

Long-term investments represent sizable outlays of funds. Consequently, procedures are needed to analyze and select them properly. Attention must be given to the initial outlay and to subsequent cash flows associated with long-term or fixed-asset investments. As time passes, fixed assets may become obsolete or may require an overhaul; at these points, too, financial decisions may be required. This section of the chapter discusses capital expenditure motives and briefly describes the steps in the capital budgeting process.

## Capital Expenditure Motives

A **capital expenditure** is an outlay of funds by the firm that is expected to produce benefits over a period *greater than* one year. A **current expenditure** is an outlay resulting in benefits received *within* one year. Fixed-asset outlays are capital expenditures, but not all capital expenditures are classified as fixed assets. A $60,000 outlay for a new machine with a usable life of 15 years is a capital expenditure that appears as a fixed asset on the firm's balance sheet. A $60,000 outlay for advertising that produces benefits over a long period is also a capital expenditure. However, an outlay for advertising is rarely shown as a fixed asset.

**capital expenditure**
An outlay of funds that is expected to produce benefits over a period *greater than* one year.

**current expenditure**
An outlay of funds resulting in benefits received *within* one year.

Capital expenditures are made for many reasons. Although the motives may differ, the evaluation techniques are the same. The basic motives for capital expenditures are to expand, replace, or renew fixed assets or to obtain some other less tangible benefit over a long period.

**Expansion**    Perhaps the most common motive for a capital expenditure is to expand the level of operations—usually through acquisition of fixed assets. A growing firm often finds it necessary to acquire new fixed assets rapidly. Remember that fixed assets include property (land), plant, and equipment. In other words, the purchase of additional physical facilities, such as additional property or a new factory, is a capital expenditure.

### Replacement

As a firm's growth slows and it reaches maturity, most of its capital expenditures are for the replacement or renewal of obsolete or worn-out assets. This type of capital expenditure does not always result from the outright failure of a piece of equipment or the inability of an existing plant to function efficiently. The need to replace existing assets must be periodically examined by the firm's financial manager. A machine does not break down and say, "Please replace me!" But each time a machine requires a major repair, the firm should evaluate the outlay for the repair in terms of the outlay to replace the machine and the benefits of replacement.

### Renewal

The renewal of fixed assets is often an alternative to replacement. Renewal may involve rebuilding, overhauling, or retrofitting an existing machine or facility. For example, an existing drill press could be renewed by replacing its motor and adding a numeric control system. A physical facility could be renewed by rewiring, adding air conditioning, and so on. Firms wishing to improve efficiency may find that both replacing and renewing existing machinery are suitable solutions.

### Other Purposes

Some capital expenditures do not result in the acquisition or transformation of tangible fixed assets shown on the firm's balance sheet. Instead, they involve a long-term commitment of funds by the firm in expectation of a future return. These expenditures include outlays for advertising, research and development, management consulting, and new products. Advertising outlays are expected to provide benefits in the form of increased future sales. Research and development outlays are expected to provide future benefits in the form of new product ideas. Management-consulting outlays are expected to provide returns in the form of increased profits from increased efficiency of operation. New products are expected to contribute to a product mix that maximizes overall returns. Other capital expenditure proposals—such as the installation of pollution-control and safety devices mandated by the government—are difficult to evaluate because they provide intangible returns rather than clearly measurable cash flows.

## Steps in the Process

**capital budgeting process** Five distinct but interrelated steps used to evaluate and select long-term investments: proposal generation, review and analysis, decision making, implementation, and follow-up.

The **capital budgeting process** can be viewed as consisting of five distinct but interrelated steps that are used to evaluate and select long-term investments. It begins with proposal generation. This is followed by review and analysis, decision making, implementation, and follow-up. Each step in the process is important. Major time and effort, however, are devoted to review and analysis and decision making. These are the steps given the most attention in this and the following chapter.

### Proposal Generation

Proposals for capital expenditures are made by people at all levels within a business organization. To stimulate a flow of ideas that can result in potential cost savings, many firms offer cash rewards to employees whose proposals are ultimately adopted. Capital expenditure proposals typically travel from the originator to a reviewer at a higher level in the organization. For relatively minor expenditures, the review might be made at the next higher organizational level. Major expenditure proposals go before a higher level reviewer or review committee. Clearly, proposals requiring large outlays are much more carefully scrutinized than less costly ones.

**Review and Analysis**   Capital expenditure proposals—especially those requiring major outlays—are formally reviewed in the firm. The review seeks to assess a proposal's appropriateness in light of the firm's overall objectives and plans. More important, it evaluates the proposal's economic validity. The proposed costs and benefits are estimated and then converted into a series of relevant cash flows. Various capital budgeting techniques are applied to these cash flows to measure the investment merit of the potential outlay. In addition, various aspects of the *risk* associated with the proposal are considered. They are either incorporated into the economic analysis or rated and recorded along with the economic measures. Once the economic analysis is completed, a summary report, often with a recommendation, is submitted to the decision maker(s).

**Decision Making**   The size of proposed capital expenditures can vary significantly. Some expenditures, such as the purchase of a hammer that will provide benefits for three years, are by definition capital expenditures, even if the cost is only $15.[1] The purchase of a new machine costing $60,000 is also a capital expenditure because it is expected to provide long-term returns. The actual dollar outlay and the importance of a capital expenditure determine the organizational level at which the expenditure decision is made.

   **Dollar Outlay.**  Firms delegate capital expenditure authority on the basis of certain dollar limits. Generally, the board of directors reserves the right to make final decisions on capital expenditures requiring outlays beyond a certain amount; the authority for making smaller expenditures is given to other organizational levels. An example of a scheme for delegating capital expenditure decision authority is presented in Table 14.1. As the size of expenditures increases, the decision-making authority moves to higher levels within the organization. Of course, the detail and formality of the economic analysis on which the decision is based tend to increase in rigor with the dollar value of the proposal. The decision to buy a computer network is much more closely considered than the decision to buy new calculators for the clerical staff.

   **Importance.**  Firms operating under critical time constraints with respect to production often find it necessary to provide exceptions to a strict dollar-outlay scheme. In such cases the plant manager is often given the power

---

[1]Even though outlays to purchase items such as hammers are known to provide benefits over a period greater than a year, they are treated as current expenditures in the year of purchase. There is a certain dollar limit beyond which outlays are *capitalized* (i.e., treated as a fixed asset) and *depreciated* rather than *expensed*. This dollar limit depends largely on what the U.S. Internal Revenue Service permits. In accounting, the issue of whether to expense or capitalize an outlay is resolved using the *principle of materiality*. This rule suggests that any outlays deemed material (i.e., large) relative to the firm's scale of operations should be capitalized, whereas others should be expensed in the current period.

**TABLE 14.1   A Scheme for Delegating Capital Expenditure Decision Authority**

| Size of Expenditure | Decision-Making Authority |
| --- | --- |
| Over $500,000 | Board of directors or top management committee |
| $250,000–$500,000 | President and/or chair of board of directors |
| $100,000–$250,000 | Vice-president in charge of division |
| $10,000–$100,000 | Plant manager |
| Under $10,000 | Persons designated by plant manager |

to make decisions necessary to keep the production line moving, even though the outlays are larger than he or she is normally allowed to authorize. These exceptions must be allowed due to the high cost of interrupting production. It is wise to put some dollar limit on these critically important expenditures, but it can be set somewhat above the norm for that organizational level.

**Implementation**   Once a proposal has been approved and funding has been made available,[2] the implementation phase begins. For minor outlays, implementation is relatively routine; the expenditure is made and payment is rendered. For major expenditures, greater control is required to ensure that what has been proposed and approved is acquired at the budgeted costs. Often the expenditures for a single proposal may occur in phases, with each outlay requiring the signed approval of company officers.

**Follow-Up**   Follow-up involves monitoring the results during the operating phase of a project. The comparisons of actual costs and benefits with those expected and those of previous projects are vital. When actual outcomes deviate from projected outcomes, action may be required to cut costs, improve benefits, or possibly terminate the project. Follow-up is often ignored in practice, but it is an important activity that can contribute favorably to the firm's overall risk, return, and value.

▼▼▼▼▼▼▼▼▼▼▼▼▼▼▼▼▼▼▼▼▼▼▼▼▼▼▼▼▼▼

# Progress Review Questions

**14-1.** What is *capital budgeting?* How do capital expenditures relate to the capital budgeting process? Do all capital expenditures involve fixed assets? Explain.

**14-2.** What are the basic motives described in the chapter for making capital expenditures? Discuss, compare, and contrast them.

---

[2]Capital expenditures are often approved as part of the annual budgeting process, although funding is not made available until the budget is implemented—frequently as long as six months after approval.

**14-3.** Briefly describe each of the steps—proposal generation, review and analysis, decision making, implementation, and follow-up—involved in the capital budgeting process.

▲▲▲▲▲▲▲▲▲▲▲▲▲▲▲▲▲▲▲▲▲▲▲▲▲▲▲▲▲▲▲▲▲▲

# Capital Budgeting Terminology

LG  2

An understanding of some basic capital budgeting terminology is necessary before we can develop the concepts, tools, and techniques related to the review and analysis and decision-making steps in the capital budgeting process. In addition, we present a number of key assumptions used to simplify the discussion in the remainder of this chapter as well as in Chapter 15.

## Types of Projects

The firm may be confronted with a number of different types of projects. Depending on the types of projects being considered, different decision-making approaches may be required. The two most common project types are (1) independent and (2) mutually exclusive projects.

**Independent Projects**    **Independent projects** are projects with cash flows that are unrelated or independent of one another; the acceptance of one *does not eliminate* the others from further consideration. If a firm has unlimited funds to invest, all the independent projects that meet its minimum investment criteria can be implemented. For example, a firm with unlimited funds may be faced with three acceptable independent projects: (1) installing air conditioning in the plant, (2) acquiring a small supplier, and (3) purchasing a new computer system. Clearly, the acceptance of any one of these projects does not eliminate the others from further consideration; all three can be undertaken if funds are available to do so.

**independent projects**
Projects with cash flows that are unrelated or independent of one another; the acceptance of one *does not eliminate* the others from further consideration.

**Mutually Exclusive Projects**    **Mutually exclusive projects** are projects that have the same function and therefore compete with one another. The acceptance of one of a group of mutually exclusive projects *eliminates* from further consideration all other projects in the group. For example, a firm in need of increased production capacity could obtain it by (1) expanding its plant, (2) acquiring another company, or (3) contracting with another company for production. If each of these alternatives meets the firm's minimum acceptance criteria, some technique must be used to determine the "best" one. Clearly, the acceptance of one of these alternatives eliminates the need for either of the others.

**mutually exclusive projects**
Projects that compete with one another so that the acceptance of one *eliminates* the others from further consideration.

## The Availability of Funds

The availability of funds for capital expenditures affects the firm's decision environment.

## F I N A N C E  I N
## A C T I O N

International

### Good Intentions Don't Always Produce Tangible Capital Budgeting Projects

In most cases, corporations undertake capital budgeting projects in an isolated manner. Firms rarely collaborate with one another in developing new products or manufacturing processes, because the marketplace is a competitive environment. This tendency to "go it alone" against the competition is beginning to change, however, as American firms seek innovative ways to respond to the threat of foreign competition.

In the 1980s, most U.S. manufacturers of dynamic random access computer chips (DRAMs) were forced out of business by Japanese chip makers that dumped DRAM chips in the American market. The practice of dumping, or selling products below cost on foreign markets to gain overseas market share, provided dramatic growth for Japanese chipmakers. In addition, this practice reduced the supply of computer-related products introduced in the United States, as domestic producers were forced to depend on foreign chip suppliers to manufacture new products.

In response to this Japanese threat, 14 worried U.S. electronics companies, working with the financial support of the Department of Defense, formed Sematech, Inc. in 1990. This research consortium based in Austin, Texas, pools the financial resources of U.S. electronics firms to provide funding for capital budgeting projects across various computer equipment manufacturers and directs joint research efforts to accelerate U.S. chip-making technology past the level of technology in Japan. In 1990, Sematech provided $100 million in new funding for indi-

vidual electronics firms. One recipient of Sematech funds, CGA Corporation, introduced a new manufacturing process that prints circuit patterns as thin as 0.5 microns—far thinner than a human hair. In 1993, lacking significant demand for its products, CGA was forced to close.

At present, Sematech is embroiled in another controversy, because the consortium may be using taxpayer dollars to fund new technology that will be shared with Japan. Sematech funded SVG Lithography, Inc., a firm that recently agreed to share its technology with Canon Inc. of Japan. Sematech maintains that any U.S.-developed technology will be licensed to Canon, and the Japanese firm will have no equity position in its American partner. Opponents of the Sematech-supported venture claim that the association with Canon compromises Sematech's original purpose.

To date, Sematech's efforts to promote corporate cooperation and develop new American technology have yielded disappointing results. In spite of this spotty track record, the Clinton Administration has cited Sematech as a model of partnerships between industry and government and promised to continue the consortium's government funding. Now it's up to Sematech to produce some tangible capital budgeting projects.

Sources: *Business Week*, December 10, 1990, p. 186; P. Dunn, "Stepper Maker CGA Closes," *Electronic News*, May 24, 1993, p. 1; and R. Krause, "Sematech Scores Big in Tech Plan," *Electronic News*, March 1, 1993, p. 12.

**unlimited funds**
The financial situation in which a firm is able to accept all independent projects that provide an acceptable return.

**Unlimited Funds**   If a firm has **unlimited funds** for investment, making capital budgeting decisions is quite simple. All independent projects that provide returns greater than some predetermined level can be accepted. Most firms are not in such a situation. Typically only a certain number of dollars are budgeted for making capital expenditures.

**Capital Rationing**    Most firms operate under **capital rationing,** meaning that they have only a fixed number of dollars available for capital expenditures and that numerous projects compete for these limited dollars. The firm must therefore ration its funds by allocating them to projects that maximize share value. Procedures for dealing with capital rationing are presented in Chapter 15. The discussions that follow in this chapter assume unlimited funds.

**capital rationing**
The financial situation in which a firm has only a fixed number of dollars to allocate among competing capital expenditures.

## Approaches to Decision Making

Two basic approaches to capital budgeting decisions are available. These approaches are somewhat dependent on whether or not the firm is confronted with capital rationing. They are also affected by the type of project involved. The two are the *accept-reject approach* and the *ranking approach*.

**The Accept-Reject Approach**    The **accept-reject approach** involves evaluating capital expenditure proposals to determine whether they are acceptable. This is a simple approach that merely compares the projected return of the potential expenditure to the firm's minimum acceptable return. This approach can be used when the firm has unlimited funds, as a preliminary step when evaluating mutually exclusive projects, or in a situation in which capital must be rationed. In these cases only acceptable projects should be considered.

**accept-reject approach**
The evaluation of capital expenditure proposals to determine whether they are acceptable.

**The Ranking Approach**    The second method, the **ranking approach,** involves ranking proposals on the basis of some predetermined measure, such as the rate of return. The project with the highest return is ranked first, and the project with the lowest return is ranked last. Only acceptable projects should be ranked. Ranking is useful in selecting the "best" of a group of mutually exclusive projects and in evaluating projects with a view to capital rationing.

**ranking approach**
The ranking of capital expenditure proposals on the basis of some predetermined measure such as the rate of return.

When the firm is confronted with a number of projects, some of which are mutually exclusive and some of which are independent, it must first determine the best of each group of mutually exclusive alternatives. This reduces the mixed group of projects to a group of independent projects. The best of the acceptable independent projects can then be selected. All acceptable projects can be implemented if the firm has unlimited funds. If capital rationing is necessary, the mix of projects that maximizes the firm's overall value should be accepted. The following example illustrates the evaluation process.

▶ E X A M P L E

California Slimfast, a diet products concern with unlimited funds, wishes to evaluate eight projects: A through H. Projects A, B, and C are mutually exclusive; projects G and H are also mutually exclusive; and projects D, E, and F are independent of the other projects. The projects are listed along with their returns in the table at the top of the next page. To evaluate these projects, the firm must first determine the best of the mutually exclusive groups. On the basis of the return figures given in the table, project B would be selected from mutually exclusive projects A, B, and C because it has the highest return of this group. Project G would be preferred to project H because it has the higher return.

| Project | Status | Return (%) |
|---|---|---|
| A | | 16 |
| B | Mutually exclusive | 19 |
| C | | 11 |
| D | Independent | 15 |
| E | Independent | 13 |
| F | Independent | 21 |
| G | Mutually exclusive | 20 |
| H | | 17 |

After the selection of the best of the two groups of mutually exclusive projects, the five remaining independent projects can be ranked on the basis of their respective returns (as shown in the table below). Given that the firm has unlimited funds, and assuming that all projects are acceptable, ranking in this case is not necessary. California Slimfast could undertake all five projects (F, G, B, D, E). If the firm operates in an environment of capital rationing, however, ranking is useful in determining which projects to accept.

| Rank | Project | Return (%) |
|---|---|---|
| 1 | F | 21 |
| 2 | G | 20 |
| 3 | B | 19 |
| 4 | D | 15 |
| 5 | E | 13 |

## Types of Cash Flow Patterns

Cash flow patterns associated with capital investment projects can be classified as *conventional* or *nonconventional*. Another classification is as an *annuity* or a *mixed stream*.

**conventional cash flow pattern**
An initial outflow followed by a series of inflows.

### Conventional Cash Flows   A **conventional cash flow pattern** consists of an initial outflow followed by a series of inflows. This pattern is associated with many types of capital expenditures. For example, a firm may spend $10,000 today and as a result expect to receive cash inflows of $2,000 each year for the next eight years. This conventional pattern is diagrammed on the time line in Figure 14.1.[3]

**nonconventional cash flow patterns**
A pattern in which an initial outflow is *not* followed by a series of inflows.

### Nonconventional Cash Flows   A **nonconventional cash flow pattern** is any pattern in which an initial outflow is *not* followed by a series of inflows. For example, the purchase of a machine may require an initial cash outflow

[3]Arrows rather than plus or minus signs are frequently used on time lines to distinguish between cash inflows and cash outflows. Upward-pointing arrows represent cash inflows (positive cash flows) and downward-pointing arrows represent cash outflows (negative cash flows).

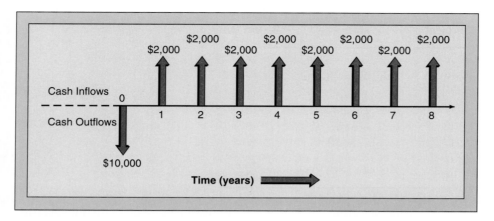

**FIGURE 14.1   Time Line for a Conventional Cash Flow Pattern**
This conventional cash flow pattern consists of an initial outflow ($10,000) followed by a series of inflows ($2,000 each year for eight years).

of $20,000 and may generate cash inflows of $5,000 each year for four years. In the fifth year after purchase, an outflow of $8,000 may be required to overhaul the machine, after which it generates inflows of $5,000 each year for five years. This nonconventional pattern is illustrated on the time line in Figure 14.2.

Difficulties often arise in evaluating projects with nonconventional patterns of cash flows. The discussions in the remainder of this chapter and in the following chapter are therefore limited to the evaluation of conventional patterns.

**Annuity or Mixed Stream**   As pointed out in Chapter 11, an **annuity** is a stream of equal annual cash flows. A series of cash flows exhibiting any pat-

**annuity**
A stream of equal annual
cash flows.

**FIGURE 14.2   Time Line for a Nonconventional Cash Flow Pattern**
This nonconventional cash flow pattern consists of an initial outflow ($20,000) followed by a series of inflows ($5,000 each year for four years) followed by another outflow ($8,000 in year 5) followed by a final series of inflows ($5,000 each year for five years).

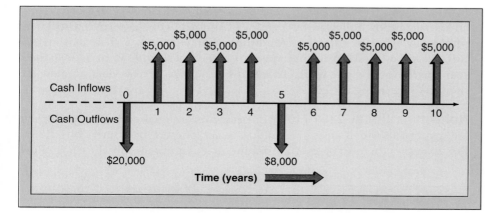

**mixed stream**
*A series of cash flows exhibiting any pattern other than that of an annuity.*

tern other than that of an annuity is a **mixed stream** of cash flows. The cash inflows of $2,000 per year (for eight years) in Figure 14.1 are inflows from an annuity. The unequal pattern of inflows in Figure 14.3 represents a mixed stream. As pointed out in Chapter 11, the techniques required to evaluate cash flows are much simpler to use when the pattern of flows is an annuity.

## Progress Review Question

**14-4.** Define and differentiate between each of the following sets of capital budgeting terms.
   **a.** Independent versus mutually exclusive projects
   **b.** Unlimited funds versus capital rationing
   **c.** Accept-reject versus ranking approaches
   **d.** Conventional versus nonconventional cash flow patterns
   **e.** Annuity versus mixed stream cash flows

LG **3**

# The Relevant Cash Flows

**relevant cash flows**
*The incremental after-tax cash outflow (investment) and resulting subsequent inflows associated with a proposed capital expenditure.*

**incremental cash flows**
*The additional cash flows—outflows or inflows—expected to result from a proposed capital expenditure.*

To evaluate capital expenditure alternatives, the **relevant cash flows** must be determined. These are the *incremental after-tax cash outflow (investment) and resulting subsequent inflows.* The **incremental cash flows** represent the *additional* cash flows—outflows or inflows—expected to result from a proposed capital expenditure. As noted in Chapter 3, cash flows, rather than accounting figures, are used; it is these flows that directly affect the firm's ability to pay bills and purchase assets. Furthermore, accounting figures and cash flows are not necessarily the same, due to the presence of certain noncash expenditures on the firm's income statement. The remainder of this chapter is devoted to the procedures for measuring the relevant cash flows associated with proposed capital expenditures.

## Major Cash Flow Components

**initial investment**
*The relevant cash outflow for a proposed project at time zero.*

**operating cash inflows**
*The incremental after-tax cash inflows resulting from use of a project during its life.*

The cash flows of any project having the *conventional pattern* include two basic components: (1) an initial investment and (2) operating cash inflows. All projects—whether for expansion, replacement, renewal, or some other purpose—have these components. Figure 14.3 shows on a time line the cash flows for a project. Each of the cash flow components is labeled. The **initial investment** is the relevant cash outflow at time zero. For the proposed project it is $50,000. The **operating cash inflows** are the incremental after-tax cash inflows resulting from use of the project during its life. In Figure 14.3, these gradually increase from $4,000 in the first year to $10,000 in the tenth and final year of the project.

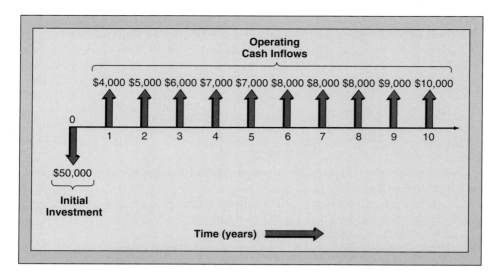

**FIGURE 14.3  Time Line for Major Cash Flow Components**
The major cash flow components for this project consist of the initial investment of $50,000 at time zero and the operating cash inflows, which increase from $4,000 in the first year to $10,000 in the tenth and final year.

## Expansion Versus Replacement Cash Flows

The development of relevant cash flows is most straightforward in the case of *expansion decisions*. In this case the initial investment and operating cash inflows are merely the after-tax cash outflow and inflows, respectively, associated with the proposed outlay. The development of relevant cash flows for *replacement decisions* is more complicated; the firm must find the *incremental* cash outflows and inflows that result from the proposed replacement. To find the initial investment in this case, the firm subtracts from the initial investment needed to acquire the new asset any after-tax cash inflows expected from liquidation today of the old asset being replaced. The operating cash inflows are found by taking the difference between the operating cash inflows from the new asset and from the replaced asset.

## ▶ E X A M P L E

Column 1 of Table 14.2 shows the initial investment and operating cash inflows for an *expansion decision* involving the acquisition of new asset A. As a result of a $13,000 purchase price, the firm expects operating cash inflows of $5,000 in each of the next five years.

If new asset A is being considered as a *replacement* for old asset A, the relevant cash flows are found by subtracting the expected cash flows attributed to old asset A from the expected cash flows for new asset A. The expected after-tax cash flows from new and old asset A are shown in columns 2 and 3, respectively, of Table 14.2. Because old asset A can be liquidated for $3,000, the initial investment in new asset A is $10,000 as shown in column 2. Replacement of old asset A eliminates its expected operating cash inflows in years 1 through 5 of $3,000, $2,500, $2,000, $1,500, and $1,000, respectively,

**TABLE 14.2   Expansion and Replacement Cash Flows**

| | Expansion | Replacement | | |
|---|---|---|---|---|
| | New Asset A (1) | New Asset A (2) | Old Asset A (3) | Relevant Cash Flows [(2) − (3)] (4) |
| Initial Investment | $13,000[a] | $10,000[b] | — | $10,000 |
| Year | | Operating Cash Inflows | | |
| 1 | $ 5,000 | $ 5,000 | $ 3,000 | $ 2,000 |
| 2 | 5,000 | 5,000 | 2,500 | 2,500 |
| 3 | 5,000 | 5,000 | 2,000 | 3,000 |
| 4 | 5,000 | 5,000 | 1,500 | 3,500 |
| 5 | 5,000 | 5,000 | 1,000 | 4,000 |

[a]Purchase price.
[b]$13,000 purchase price of new asset A less the $3,000 expected after-tax cash inflow from liquidating old asset A.

all shown in column 3 of Table 14.2. Therefore the relevant cash flows resulting from the *replacement decision* are the difference in expected cash flows between new asset A (column 2) and old asset A (column 3) as shown in column 4 of Table 14.2.

Actually, all capital budgeting decisions can be viewed as replacement decisions. Expansion decisions are merely replacement decisions in which all cash flows from the old asset are zero. In light of this fact, the following discussions emphasize replacement decisions.

# International Capital Budgeting and Long-Term Investments

Although the same basic capital budgeting principles are used for domestic and international projects, several additional factors must be addressed in evaluating foreign investment opportunities. International capital budgeting differs from the domestic version because (1) cash inflows and outflows occur in a foreign currency (the dollar value of these cash flows can change radically if exchange rates fluctuate), and (2) foreign investments potentially face significant political risk, including the risk that the company's assets may be seized. Both of these risks can be minimized through careful corporate planning.

Companies face both long- and short-term currency risks relating to both the invested capital and the cash flows resulting from it. Long-term currency risk can be minimized by at least partly financing the foreign investment in the local capital markets rather than with a dollar-denominated capital contribution from the parent company. This step ensures that the project's revenues, operating costs, and financing costs are in the local currency, rather than having the financing costs in dollars. Likewise, the dollar value of short-term, local currency cash flows can be protected by using special securities and strategies, such as futures, forwards, and options market instruments.

*Political risks* can be minimized by using both operating and financial strategies. For example, by structuring the investment as a joint venture and by selecting a competent and well-connected local partner, the U.S. company can minimize the risk that its operations will be seized or harassed. Furthermore, companies can protect themselves from having their investment returns blocked by local governments by structuring the financing of such investments as debt rather than as equity. Debt-service payments are legally enforceable claims, whereas equity returns (such as dividends) are not. Even if local courts do not support the claims of the U.S. company, the company can threaten to pursue its case in U.S. courts.

In spite of the above difficulties, **foreign direct investment,** which involves the transfer of capital, managerial, and technical assets to a foreign country, by U.S., European, and Japanese multinational companies has surged in recent years. For example, the market value of foreign assets owned by U.S.-based companies now exceeds $800 billion, although because many of these investments have been in place for over 20 years, the book value of these assets is less than $400 billion. Likewise, foreign direct investment in the United States now exceeds $500 billion in both market and book value, with British companies holding the largest stake, followed by Japanese, Canadian, Dutch, and German companies. Furthermore, foreign direct investment by U.S. companies now exceeds $50 billion per year and seems to be accelerating, particularly in East Asia and Latin America.

**foreign direct investment**
The transfer of capital, managerial, and technical assets to a foreign country.

## Progress Review Questions

**14-5.** Why is it important to evaluate capital budgeting projects on the basis of *incremental after-tax cash flows*? How can expansion decisions be treated as replacement decisions? Explain.

**14-6.** How does international capital budgeting differ from the domestic version? How can currency risk—both long- and short-term—and political risk be minimized when making *foreign direct investment?*

## Finding the Initial Investment

The term *initial investment* as used here refers to the relevant cash outflow to be considered when evaluating a prospective capital expenditure. Because our discussion of capital budgeting is concerned only with investments exhibiting conventional cash flows, the initial investment occurs at *time zero*—the time the expenditure is made. To calculate the initial investment, we subtract all cash inflows occurring at time zero from all cash outflows occurring at time zero.

Two basic cash flows must be considered when determining the initial investment associated with a capital expenditure: (1) the installed cost of the new asset and (2) the after-tax proceeds (if any) from the sale of an old asset. The basic format for determining the initial investment is given in Table 14.3. Note that if there are no installation costs and the firm is not replacing an existing asset, the purchase price of the asset is equal to the initial investment.

## Installed Cost of New Asset

**cost of new asset**
The net outflow required to acquire a new asset.

**installation costs**
Any added costs that are necessary to place an asset into operation.

**installed cost of new asset**
The cost of the asset plus its installation costs; equals the asset's depreciable value.

As shown in Table 14.3, the installed cost of the new asset is found by adding the cost of the new asset to its installation costs. The **cost of new asset** is the net outflow its acquisition requires. Usually, we are concerned with the acquisition of a fixed asset for which a definite purchase price is paid. **Installation costs** are any added costs that are necessary to place an asset into operation. They are considered part of the firm's capital expenditure. Each capital expenditure decision should be checked to make sure installation costs have not been overlooked. The Internal Revenue Service (IRS) requires the firm to add installation costs to the purchase price of an asset to determine its depreciable value, which is depreciated over a period of years. The **installed cost of new asset,** calculated by adding the cost of the asset to its installation costs, equals its depreciable value.

## After-Tax Proceeds from Sale of Old Asset

**after-tax proceeds from sale of old asset**
Found by subtracting applicable taxes from the proceeds from the sale of an old asset.

**proceeds from sale of old asset**
The cash inflows, net of any removal or cleanup costs, resulting from the sale of an existing asset.

Table 14.3 shows that the **after-tax proceeds from sale of old asset** decrease the firm's initial investment in the new asset. These proceeds are found by subtracting applicable taxes from (or adding any tax refunds to) the old asset's sale proceeds. The **proceeds from sale of old asset** are the net cash inflows it provides. This amount is net of any costs incurred in the process of removing the asset. Included in these *removal costs* are *cleanup costs,* particu-

---

**TABLE 14.3   The Basic Format for Determining Initial Investment**

Installed cost of new asset =
   Cost of new asset
+ Installation costs
− After-tax proceeds from sale of old asset =
   Proceeds from sale of old asset
∓ Tax on sale of old asset
Initial investment

larly those related to removal and proper disposal of chemical and nuclear wastes. These costs may not be trivial.

The proceeds from the sale of an old asset are normally subject to some type of tax.[4] This **tax on sale of old asset** depends on the relationship between its sale price, initial purchase price, and book value. The actual tax treatment is not controlled by the firm but rather is dictated by government tax laws, procedures, and forms, all of which are periodically revised. An understanding of (1) book value and (2) basic tax rules is necessary to determine the tax on sale of an asset.

**tax on sale of old asset**
Tax that depends on the relationship between the old asset's sale price, initial purchase price, and book value.

**Book Value**   The **book value** of an asset is its strict accounting value. It can be calculated using the following equation:

**book value**
The strict accounting value of an asset.

$$\text{Book value} = \text{installed cost of asset} - \text{accumulated depreciation} \qquad (14.1)$$

**Equation 14.1 Formula for book value**

▶ E X A M P L E

Two years ago Kontra Industries, a small electronics company, acquired a machine tool with an installed cost of $100,000. The asset was being depreciated under the modified accelerated cost recovery system (MACRS) using a five-year recovery period.[5] Table 3.6 (page 74), shows that under MACRS for a five-year recovery period, 20 percent and 32 percent of the installed cost are depreciated in years 1 and 2, respectively. In other words, 52 percent (20% + 32%) of the $100,000 cost, or $52,000 (.52 × $100,000), represents the accumulated depreciation at the end of year 2. Substituting into Equation 14.1, we get:

$$\text{Book value} = \$100,000 - \$52,000 = \$48,000$$

▶ The book value of Kontra's asset at the end of year 2 is therefore $48,000.

**Basic Tax Rules**   Four potential tax situations can occur when selling an asset. These situations differ, depending on the relationship between the asset's sale price, its initial purchase price, and its book value. The three key forms of taxable income and their associated tax treatments are defined and summarized in Table 14.4. The assumed tax rates used throughout this text are noted in the final column of the same table. The four possible tax situations resulting in one or more forms of taxable income are

1. The asset is sold for more than its initial purchase price.
2. The asset is sold for more than its book value but less than its initial purchase price.
3. The asset is sold for its book value.
4. The asset is sold for less than its book value.

An example illustrates.

---

[4]A brief discussion of the tax treatment of ordinary and capital gains income was presented in Chapter 2.

[5] For a review of MACRS, see Chapter 3. Under the *Tax Reform Act of 1986* most manufacturing machinery and equipment has a seven-year recovery period as noted in Table 3.5. Using this recovery period results in eight years of depreciation, which unnecessarily complicates examples and problems. To simplify, *machinery and equipment are treated as five-year assets in this and the following chapters.*

**TABLE 14.4   Tax Treatment on Sales of Assets**

| Form of Taxable Income | Definition | Tax Treatment | Assumed Tax Rate |
|---|---|---|---|
| Capital gain | Portion of the sale price that is in excess of the initial purchase price. | Regardless of how long the asset has been held, the total capital gain is taxed as ordinary income. | 40% |
| Recaptured depreciation | Portion of the sale price that is in excess of book value and represents a recovery of previously taken depreciation. | All recaptured depreciation is taxed as ordinary income. | 40% |
| Loss on sale of asset | Amount by which sale price is *less than* book value. | If asset is depreciable and used in business, loss is deducted from ordinary income. | 40% of loss is a tax savings |
| | | If asset is *not* depreciable or is *not* used in business, loss is deductible only against capital gains. | 40% of loss is a tax savings |

# EXAMPLE

The old asset purchased two years ago for $100,000 by Kontra Industries has a current book value of $48,000. What happens if the firm now decides to sell the asset and replace it? The tax consequences associated with sale of the asset depend on the sale price. Let us consider each of the four possible situations.

**The Sale of the Asset for More than its Initial Purchase Price**   If Kontra sells the old asset for $110,000, it realizes a capital gain of $10,000 (the amount by which the sale price exceeds the initial purchase price of $100,000) which is taxed as ordinary income.[6] The firm also experiences ordinary income in the form of **recaptured depreciation,** which is the portion of the sale price that is above book value and below the initial purchase price. In this case the recaptured depreciation amounts to $52,000 ($100,000 − $48,000). The taxes on the total gain of $62,000 are calculated as shown in the table at the top of the next page. These taxes should be used in calculating the initial investment in the new asset, using the format in Table 14.3. In effect, the taxes raise the amount of the firm's initial investment in the new asset by reducing the proceeds from the sale of the old asset.

**recaptured depreciation**
The portion of the sale price that is above book value and below the initial purchase price.

---

[6]The *Tax Reform Act of 1986* requires corporate capital gains to be treated as ordinary income. However, the structure for corporate capital gains is retained under the law for use in the likely event of future tax revisions. Therefore, this distinction is made throughout the text discussions.

| | Amount (1) | Rate (2) | Tax [(1) × (2)] (3) |
|---|---|---|---|
| Capital gain | $10,000 | .40 | $ 4,000 |
| Recaptured depreciation | 52,000 | .40 | 20,800 |
| Totals | $62,000 | | $24,800 |

**The Sale of the Asset for More than its Book Value but Less than its Initial Purchase Price**   If Kontra sells the old asset for $70,000, which is less than its original purchase price but more than its book value, there is no capital gain. However, the firm still experiences a gain in the form of recaptured depreciation of $22,000 ($70,000 − $48,000), which is taxed as ordinary income. Because the firm is assumed to be in the 40 percent tax bracket, the taxes on the $22,000 gain are $8,800. This amount in taxes should be used in calculating the initial investment in the new asset.

**The Sale of the Asset for its Book Value**   If the asset is sold for $48,000, its book value, the firm breaks even. Because *no tax results from selling an asset for its book value,* there is no effect on the initial investment in the new asset.

**The Sale of the Asset for Less than its Book Value**   If Kontra sells the asset for $30,000, an amount less than its book value, it experiences a loss of $18,000 ($48,000 − $30,000). If this is a depreciable asset used in the business, the loss may be used to offset ordinary operating income. If the asset is *not* depreciable or *not* used in the business, the loss can be used only to offset capital gains. In either case the loss saves the firm $7,200 ($18,000 × .40) in taxes. And, if current operating earnings or capital gains are not sufficient to offset the loss, the firm may be able to apply these losses to prior or future years' taxes.[7]

## Calculating the Initial Investment

It should be clear that a variety of tax and other considerations enter into the initial investment calculation. The following example illustrates how the basic variables described in the preceding discussions are used to calculate the initial investment according to the format in Table 14.3.

▶ E X A M P L E

Norman Company, a large diversified manufacturer of aircraft components, is trying to determine the initial investment required to replace an old machine with a new, much more sophisticated model. The proposed (new) machine's purchase price is $380,000, and an additional $20,000 is required to install it. It will be depreciated under MACRS using a five-year recovery pe-

---

[7]The tax law provides detailed procedures for *tax loss carrybacks* and *carryforwards.* Application of such procedures to capital budgeting is beyond the scope of this text, and they are therefore ignored in subsequent discussions.

riod. The present (old) machine was purchased three years ago at a cost of $240,000. It is being depreciated under MACRS using a five-year recovery period. The firm has found a buyer willing to pay $280,000 for the present machine and remove it at the buyer's expense. Both ordinary income and capital gains are taxed at a rate of 40 percent.

The only component of the initial investment calculation that is difficult to obtain is taxes. Because the firm is planning to sell the present machine for $40,000 more than its initial purchase price, it will realize a *capital gain of $40,000*. The book value of the present machine can be found by using the depreciation percentages from Table 3.6 (page 74) of 20 percent, 32 percent, and 19 percent for years 1 through 3, respectively. The resulting book value is $69,600 ($240,000 − [(.20 + .32 + .19) × $240,000]). An *ordinary gain of $170,400* ($240,000 − $69,600) in recaptured depreciation is also realized on the sale. The total taxes on the gain are $84,160 [($40,000 + $170,400) × .40]. Substituting these taxes along with the purchase price and installation costs of the proposed machine and the proceeds from the sale of the present machine into the format in Table 14.3 results in an initial investment of $204,160. This amount represents the net cash outflow required at time zero:

| | | |
|---|---:|---:|
| Installed cost of proposed machine | | |
|   Cost of proposed machine | $380,000 | |
| + Installation costs | 20,000 | |
|   Total installed cost: proposed (depreciable value) | | $400,000 |
| − After-tax proceeds from sale of present machine | | |
|   Proceeds from sale of present machine | $280,000 | |
|   − Tax on sale of present machine | 84,160 | |
|     Total after-tax proceeds: present | | 195,840 |
| Initial investment | | $204,160 |

## Progress Review Questions

**14-7.** Describe each of the following inputs to the initial investment, and use the basic format presented in this chapter to explain how the initial investment is calculated by using them.
  **a.** Cost of new asset
  **b.** Installation costs
  **c.** Proceeds from sale of old asset
  **d.** Tax on sale of old asset

**14-8.** What is the *book value* of an asset, and how is it calculated? Describe the three key forms of taxable income and their associated tax treatments.

**14-9.** What four tax situations may result from the sale of an asset that is being replaced? Describe the tax treatment in each situation.

**14-10.** Referring to the basic format for calculating initial investment presented in this chapter, explain how a firm determines the *depreciable value* of the new asset.

# Finding the Operating Cash Inflows

The benefits expected from a capital expenditure are measured by its *operating cash inflows,* which are *incremental after-tax cash inflows.* In this section we use the income statement format to develop clear definitions of the terms *after-tax, cash inflows,* and *incremental.*

## Interpreting the Term *After-Tax*

Benefits expected to result from proposed capital expenditures must be measured on an after-tax basis. The firm does not have the use of any benefits until it has satisfied the government's tax claims, and these claims depend on the firm's taxable income. Thus, the deduction of taxes *prior to* making comparisons between proposed investments is necessary for consistency. Consistency is required when evaluating capital expenditure alternatives because the intention is to compare like benefits.

## Interpreting the Term *Cash Inflows*

All benefits expected from a proposed project must be measured on a cash flow basis. Cash inflows represent dollars that can be spent, not merely "ac-

---

## FINANCE IN ACTION

**Ethics**

### It Pays to Keep Track of Your Cash Inflows

How should a company react when the cash inflows provided by a popular product suddenly skyrocket? At most firms, this would be cause for celebration, but managers at Havatampa, Inc. reacted in horror when they learned *why* the cash inflows from their best-selling Phillies Blunt cigar package recently increased. It seems inner-city youths are purchasing the cigars in record number, removing the tobacco, and refilling the hollow cigar with marijuana. When burned, the repackaged "cigar" produces a distinct, cigarlike odor that masks the smell of marijuana.

Digging a little deeper, Havatampa learned that its corporate trademark was becoming a status symbol within the inner-city drug culture; the firm's logo was appearing on pirated caps, T-shirts, and other apparel worn by inner-city kids. What could the firm do to protect its logo, and avoid profit-

ing from this unusual and unfortunate set of circumstances? Havatampa responded by approaching the small New York marketing company, Not From Concentrate, Inc., that was bootlegging the Havatampa logo and negotiated a deal. In return for avoiding any direct association with illegal drug use, the marketer received exclusive rights to reproduce the Havatampa logo on caps, T-shirts, and sweatshirts. Meanwhile, Havatampa is donating the royalties received from merchandise sold by the marketing firm to inner-city charities that fight drug abuse. Do you think that Havatampa's efforts go far enough in helping to eliminate the illicit and dangerous use of its product, or should the firm do more?

Source: J. Tilsner, "Reefer Madness at Havatampa," *Business Week,* January 24, 1994, p. 42.

counting profits," which are not necessarily available for paying the firm's bills. A simple technique for converting after-tax net profits into operating cash inflows was illustrated in Chapter 3. The basic calculation requires adding any *noncash charges* deducted as expenses on the firm's income statement back to net profits after taxes. Probably the most common noncash charge found on income statements is depreciation. It is the only noncash charge considered in this section. The following example shows how after-tax operating cash inflows can be calculated for a present and a proposed project.

# E X A M P L E

Norman Company's estimates of its revenue and expenses (excluding depreciation), with and without the proposed capital expenditure described in the preceding example, are given in Table 14.5. Note that both the expected usable life of the proposed machine and the remaining usable life of the present machine is five years. The amount to be depreciated with the proposed machine is calculated by summing the purchase price of $380,000 and the installation costs of $20,000. Because the proposed machine is to be depreciated under MACRS using a five-year recovery period,[8] 20, 32, 19,

**TABLE 14.5   Norman Company's Revenue and Expenses (Excluding Depreciation) for Proposed and Present Machines**

| Year | Revenue (1) | Expenses (Excl. Depr.) (2) |
|---|---|---|
| **With Proposed Machine** | | |
| 1 | $2,520,000 | $2,300,000 |
| 2 | 2,520,000 | 2,300,000 |
| 3 | 2,520,000 | 2,300,000 |
| 4 | 2,520,000 | 2,300,000 |
| 5 | 2,520,000 | 2,300,000 |
| **With Present Machine** | | |
| 1 | $2,200,000 | $1,990,000 |
| 2 | 2,300,000 | 2,110,000 |
| 3 | 2,400,000 | 2,230,000 |
| 4 | 2,400,000 | 2,250,000 |
| 5 | 2,250,000 | 2,120,000 |

[8]As noted in Chapter 3, it takes $n + 1$ years to depreciate an $n$-year class asset under the provisions of the *Tax Reform Act of 1986*. Therefore, MACRS percentages are given for each of six years for use in depreciating an asset with a five-year recovery period.

**TABLE 14.6   Depreciation Expense for Proposed and Present Machines for Norman Company**

| Year | Cost (1) | Applicable MACRS Depreciation Percentages (from Table 3.6) (2) | Depreciation [(1) × (2)] (3) |
|---|---|---|---|
| **With Proposed Machine** | | | |
| 1 | $400,000 | 20% | $ 80,000 |
| 2 | 400,000 | 32 | 128,000 |
| 3 | 400,000 | 19 | 76,000 |
| 4 | 400,000 | 12 | 48,000 |
| 5 | 400,000 | 12 | 48,000 |
| 6 | 400,000 | 5 | 20,000 |
| Totals | | 100% | $400,000 |
| **With Present Machine** | | | |
| 1 | $240,000 | 12% (year-4 depreciation) | $28,800 |
| 2 | 240,000 | 12  (year-5 depreciation) | 28,800 |
| 3 | 240,000 | 5  (year-6 depreciation) | 12,000 |
| 4 | | Because the present machine is at the end of the third year of its cost recovery at the time the analysis is performed, it has only the final three years of depreciation (years 4, 5, and 6) yet applicable. | 0 |
| 5 | | | 0 |
| 6 | | | 0 |
| Total | | | $ 69,600[a] |

[a]The total $69,600 represents the book value of the present machine at the end of the third year, as calculated in the preceding example.

12, 12, and 5 percent would be recovered in years 1 through 6, respectively. (See Chapter 3 and Table 3.6 on page 74 for more detail.) The resulting depreciation on this machine for each of the six years, as well as the remaining three years of depreciation on the present machine, are calculated in Table 14.6.[9]

The operating cash inflows in each year can be calculated using the income statement format shown in Table 14.7. Substituting the data from Tables 14.5 and 14.6 into this format and assuming a 40 percent tax rate, we get Table 14.8. It demonstrates the calculation of operating cash inflows for each year for both the proposed and the present machine. Because the

[9]It is important to recognize that although both machines provide five years of use, the proposed new machine is depreciated over the six-year period, whereas the present machine—as noted in the preceding example—was depreciated over three years and therefore has only its final three years (years 4, 5, and 6) of depreciation (i.e., 12, 12, and 5 percent, respectively, under MACRS) remaining.

proposed machine is depreciated over six years, the analysis must be performed over the six-year period to fully capture the tax effect of depreciation in year 6 for the new asset. The resulting operating cash inflows are shown in column 8 of the table. The year-6 cash inflow for the proposed machine of $8,000 results solely from the tax benefit of the year-6 depreciation deduction.

## Interpreting the Term *Incremental*

The final step in estimating the operating cash inflows to be used in evaluating a proposed project is to calculate the *incremental (relevant)* cash inflows. Incremental operating cash inflows are needed because our concern is *only* with how much more or less operating cash flows into the firm as a result of the proposed project.

## E X A M P L E

Table 14.9 demonstrates the calculation of Norman Company's incremental (relevant) operating cash inflows for each year. The estimates of operating cash inflows developed in Table 14.8 are given in columns 1 and 2. The column 2 values represent the amount of operating cash inflows that Norman Company will receive if it does not replace the present machine. If the proposed machine replaces the present machine, the firm's operating cash inflows for each year will be those shown in column 1. Subtracting the operating cash inflows with the present machine from the operating cash inflows with the proposed machine in each year results in the incremental operating cash inflows for each year, shown in column 3 of Table 14.9. These cash flows represent the

**TABLE 14.7   Calculation of Operating Cash Inflows Using an Income Statement Format**

Revenue
− Expenses (excluding depreciation)

Profits before depreciation and taxes
− Depreciation

Net profits before taxes
− Taxes

Net profits after taxes
+ Depreciation

Operating cash inflows

**TABLE 14.8    Calculation of Operating Cash Inflows for Norman Company's Proposed and Present Machines**

| Year | Revenue[a] (1) | Expenses (Excl. Depr.)[b] (2) | Profits Before Depreciation and Taxes [(1) − (2)] (3) | Depreciation[c] (4) | Net Profits Before Taxes [(3) − (4)] (5) | Taxes [.40 × (5)] (6) | Net Profits After Taxes [(5) − (6)] (7) | Operating Cash Inflows [(4) + (7)] (8) |
|---|---|---|---|---|---|---|---|---|
| **With Proposed Machine** | | | | | | | | |
| 1 | $2,520,000 | $2,300,000 | $220,000 | $ 80,000 | $140,000 | $56,000 | $ 84,000 | $164,000 |
| 2 | 2,520,000 | 2,300,000 | 220,000 | 128,000 | 92,000 | 36,800 | 55,200 | 183,200 |
| 3 | 2,520,000 | 2,300,000 | 220,000 | 76,000 | 144,000 | 57,600 | 86,400 | 162,400 |
| 4 | 2,520,000 | 2,300,000 | 220,000 | 48,000 | 172,000 | 68,800 | 103,200 | 151,200 |
| 5 | 2,520,000 | 2,300,000 | 220,000 | 48,000 | 172,000 | 68,800 | 103,200 | 151,200 |
| 6 | 0 | 0 | 0 | 20,000 | −20,000 | −8,000 | −12,000 | 8,000 |
| **With Present Machine** | | | | | | | | |
| 1 | $2,200,000 | $1,990,000 | $210,000 | $ 28,800 | $181,200 | $72,480 | $108,720 | $137,520 |
| 2 | 2,300,000 | 2,110,000 | 190,000 | 28,800 | 161,200 | 64,480 | 96,720 | 125,520 |
| 3 | 2,400,000 | 2,230,000 | 170,000 | 12,000 | 158,000 | 63,200 | 94,800 | 106,800 |
| 4 | 2,400,000 | 2,250,000 | 150,000 | 0 | 150,000 | 60,000 | 90,000 | 90,000 |
| 5 | 2,250,000 | 2,120,000 | 130,000 | 0 | 130,000 | 52,000 | 78,000 | 78,000 |
| 6 | 0 | 0 | 0 | 0 | 0 | 0 | 0 | 0 |

[a]From column 1 of Table 14.5.
[b]From column 2 of Table 14.5.
[c]From column 3 of Table 14.6.

**TABLE 14.9   Incremental (Relevant) Operating Cash Inflows for Norman Company**

| | Operating Cash Inflows | | |
| --- | --- | --- | --- |
| Year | Proposed Machine[a] (1) | Present Machine[a] (2) | Incremental (Relevant) [(1) − (2)] (3) |
| 1 | $164,000 | $137,520 | $26,480 |
| 2 | 183,200 | 125,520 | 57,680 |
| 3 | 162,400 | 106,800 | 55,600 |
| 4 | 151,200 | 90,000 | 61,200 |
| 5 | 151,200 | 78,000 | 73,200 |
| 6 | 8,000 | 0 | 8,000 |

[a]From column 8 of Table 14.8.

amounts by which each respective year's cash inflows increase as a result of replacing the present machine with the proposed machine. For example, in year 1, Norman Company's cash inflows increase by $26,480 if the proposed project is undertaken. Clearly, these are the relevant inflows to be considered when evaluating the benefits of making a capital expenditure for the proposed machine.

## Progress Review Questions

**14-11.** How is the *modified accelerated cost recovery system (MACRS)* used to depreciate an asset? How does depreciation enter into the operating cash inflow calculation?

**14-12.** Given the revenues, expenses (excluding depreciation), and depreciation associated with a present asset and a proposed replacement for it, how are the incremental (relevant) operating cash inflows associated with the decision calculated?

LG 6

# Summarizing the Relevant Cash Flows

The two cash flow components—the initial investment and the operating cash inflows—together represent a project's *relevant cash flows.* These cash flows can be viewed as the incremental after-tax cash flows attributable to the proposed project. They represent, in a cash flow sense, how much better or worse off the firm will be if it chooses to implement the proposal.

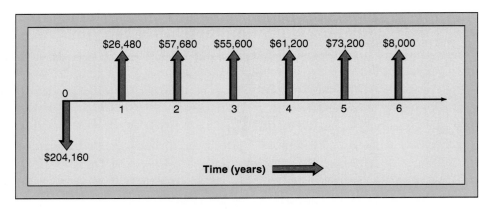

**FIGURE 14.4   Norman Company's Relevant Cash Flows with the Proposed Machine**

The relevant cash flows for Norman Company's proposed machine investment display a conventional pattern. An initial investment of $204,160 is followed by operating cash inflows of $26,480, $57,680, $55,600, $61,200, $73,200, and $8,000 in years 1 through 6, respectively.

▶ E X A M P L E

The relevant cash flows for Norman Company's proposed replacement expenditure can now be presented. They are shown graphically on a time line in Figure 14.4. As the figure shows, the relevant cash flows follow a conventional pattern (an initial outflow followed by a series of inflows). Techniques for analyzing this type of pattern to determine whether to undertake a proposed capital investment are discussed in Chapter 15.

## Progress Review Question

**14-13.** Diagram and describe the two elements representing the *relevant cash flows* for a conventional capital budgeting project.

▼          ▼          ▼

# SUMMARY OF LEARNING GOALS

**Understand the key capital expenditure motives and the steps in the capital budgeting process, beginning with proposal generation and ending with follow-up.** Capital budgeting is the process used to evaluate and select capital expenditures consistent with the goal of owner wealth maximization. Capital expenditures are long-term investments made to expand, replace, or renew fixed assets or to obtain some other less tangible benefit. The capital budgeting process contains five distinct but interrelated steps: proposal generation, review and analysis, decision making, implementation, and follow-up.

LG  1

**LG 2**   **Define the basic terminology used to describe projects, funds availability, decision approaches, and cash flow patterns.** Capital expenditure projects may be independent or mutually exclusive. Typically, firms have only limited funds for capital investments and must ration them among carefully selected projects. To make investment decisions when proposals are mutually exclusive or when capital must be rationed, projects must be ranked; otherwise, accept-reject decisions must be made. Conventional cash flow patterns consist of an initial outflow followed by a series of inflows; any other pattern is nonconventional. These patterns can be either annuities or mixed streams.

**LG 3**   **Discuss the major components of relevant cash flows, differences in the development of expansion- versus replacement-decision cash flows, and international capital budgeting and long-term investments.** The relevant cash flows necessary for making capital budgeting decisions are the initial investment and the operating cash inflows associated with a given proposal. For replacement decisions, these flows are found by determining the difference between the cash flows associated with the new asset and the old asset. Expansion decisions are viewed as replacement decisions in which all cash flows from the old asset are zero. International capital budgeting differs from the domestic version because (1) cash inflows and outflows occur in a foreign currency (the dollar value of these cash flows can change radically if exchange rates fluctuate), and (2) foreign investments potentially face significant political risk, including the risk that the company's assets may be seized.

**LG 4**   **Calculate the initial investment associated with a proposed capital expenditure, given relevant cost, depreciation, and tax data.** The initial investment is the initial outflow required, taking into account the installed cost of the new asset and the after-tax proceeds from the sale of the old asset. Finding the after-tax proceeds from sale of the old asset, which reduces the initial investment, involves cost, depreciation, and tax data. The book value of an asset is its strict accounting value, which is used to determine what, if any, taxes are owed as a result of selling an asset. Any of three forms of taxable income—capital gain, recaptured depreciation, or a loss—can result from sale of an asset. The form of taxable income that applies depends on whether it is sold for: (1) more than its initial purchase price, (2) more than book value but less than initially paid, (3) book value, or (4) less than book value.

**LG 5**   **Determine the operating cash inflows relevant to a capital budgeting proposal using the income statement format.** The operating cash inflows are the incremental after-tax operating cash inflows expected to result from implementing a proposal. The income statement format, which involves adding depreciation back to net profits after taxes, gives the operating cash inflows associated with the present and proposed projects. The relevant (incremental) cash inflows, which are used to evaluate the proposed project, are found by subtracting the operating cash inflows associated with the present project from those of the proposed project.

**LG 6**   **Summarize the relevant cash flows associated with a capital budgeting proposal graphically on a time line.** The two cash flow components—the initial investment and the operating cash inflows—together represent a project's relevant cash flows. These cash flows can be viewed as the incremental after-tax cash flows attributable to the proposed project. They represent, in a cash flow sense, how much better or worse off the firm will be if it chooses to implement the proposal.

After studying this chapter, you should be able to

 Calculate, interpret, and evaluate the two most commonly used unsophisticated capital budgeting techniques: average rate of return and payback period.

 Apply the sophisticated capital budgeting techniques—net present value (NPV), profitability index (PI), and internal rate of return (IRR)—to relevant cash flows to choose acceptable as well as preferred capital expenditures.

 Compare net present value and internal rate of return techniques in light of conflicting rankings from both theoretical and practical viewpoints.

 Discuss the two basic approaches—internal rate of return and net present value—for choosing projects under capital rationing.

 Recognize the basic behavioral approaches—sensitivity and scenario analysis, statistical approaches, decision trees, and simulation—for dealing with project risk and the unique risks and other issues facing multinational companies (MNCs).

 Understand the calculation and practical aspects of the two basic risk-adjustment techniques: certainty equivalents (CEs) and risk-adjusted discount rates (RADRs).

# Capital Budgeting Techniques:
# Certainty and Risk

Capital expenditures account for a major part of a company's cash outflows. Capital spending in 1993 for the Gillette Company—the world's leading producer of blades and razors, and a major producer of toiletries, writing instruments, toothbrushes, and personal appliances—was $352 million. Sound capital spending decisions help a company achieve its strategic objectives. Without knowledge of capital budgeting techniques, a manager may make capital investment decisions that are very costly to the company, both in terms of wasted dollars and reduced shareholder value.

## Capital budgeting techniques . . . are important decision-making tools. . . .

At Gillette, the primary tool to evaluate capital investment projects is the internal rate of return (IRR)—the discount rate at which the present value of the project's cash inflows equals its initial investment. This return is compared with a hurdle rate that is based on the cost of capital and adjusted for nonrevenue-producing assets, such as those required for environmental reasons. In addition to IRR, Gillette looks at payback, the amount of time it takes to recoup our investment. Payback is one way to measure risk.

Obviously, a project with a three-year payback is less risky than one with the same IRR and a six-year payback.

The specific decision criteria used should relate to the type of project. For example, Braun AG, which manufactures small electric personal household appliances, operates in a competitive situation that requires introduction of new models every few years. It places greater emphasis on payback to ensure the project is profitable before a model is discontinued.

Higher risk projects require a greater return over the hurdle rate than those which are certain. The company uses sensitivity analysis to adjust for risk. This shows how changing basic assumptions, such as projected sales volume or market share, affect return. For international projects, managers have to go beyond the basic IRR analysis to evaluate political risk, restrictions on dividends, exchange rate risks, and similar factors. Sometimes it is appropriate also to calculate a return on cash that compares the amount of cash put into a country to the amount expected to be taken out as dividends or profits.

Judgmental and qualitative assessments are critical to the capital investment decision process and may, in the end, have more influence than the quantitative analysis. Some decisions—product line extensions, lease-versus-purchase, cost reduction projects—are based mostly on quantitative criteria. However, many factors, especially for an international company, are not so easily quantified. A company may need to do a project to maintain its market share or accomplish a strategic goal, even though the return is lower than the norm. For example, our first project in China had an IRR that was lower than we normally accept. Management decided to proceed because China presented a major market opportunity, and establishing a strong presence there fit with the company's mission of being a worldwide blade and razor company.

Clearly, financial managers must have a thorough understanding of the business they're in. Capital budgeting techniques and the calculation of IRR, payback, and other measures are important decision-making tools, but they are not complete unless considered along with the strategic and tactical factors necessary to achieve the company's goals and objectives.

**Christopher Savage,** *a chartered accountant, joined Gillette in London in 1959. He moved to corporate headquarters in Boston in 1968 and held controller's positions in the international area until 1982. Since then he has served as controller, technical operations.*

T he relevant cash flows developed in Chapter 14 must be analyzed to assess whether a project is acceptable or to rank projects. A number of techniques are available for performing such analyses. The preferred approaches integrate time value procedures (Chapter 11), risk, return, and valuation concepts (Chapter 12), and the cost of capital (Chapter 13). They enable the financial manager to select capital expenditures that are consistent with the firm's goal of maximizing owners' wealth.

The focus of this chapter is the use of these techniques to evaluate capital expenditure proposals for decision-making purposes. Initially it is assumed that the firm has unlimited funds and that all projects' cash flows have the same level of risk. Because very few decisions are actually made under such conditions, these simplifying assumptions are relaxed in the discussions of capital rationing and risk presented later in the chapter. Here we begin with a look at both unsophisticated and sophisticated capital budgeting techniques.

## Unsophisticated Capital Budgeting Techniques

LG 1

**Unsophisticated capital budgeting techniques** do *not* explicitly consider the time value of money by discounting cash flows to find present value. There are two basic unsophisticated techniques for determining the acceptability of capital expenditure alternatives. One is to calculate the average rate of return; the other is to find the payback period.

We shall use the same basic problem to illustrate the application of all the techniques described in this chapter. The problem concerns Blano Company, a medium-sized metal fabricator. The firm is currently contemplating two projects: project A, requiring an initial investment of $42,000; and project B, requiring an initial investment of $45,000. The projected profits after taxes and incremental (relevant) operating cash inflows for the two projects are presented in Table 15.1.[1] The average profits after taxes and average operating cash inflows for each project are also included. The projects exhibit conventional cash flow patterns, which are assumed throughout the text.

**unsophisticated capital budgeting techniques**
Methods that do *not* explicitly consider the time value of money

### Average Rate of Return

The average rate of return is a popular technique used to evaluate proposed capital expenditures. Its appeal stems from the fact that the average rate of

---

[1] For simplification, five-year-lived projects with five years of cash inflows are used throughout this chapter. Projects with usable lives equal to the number of years of cash inflows are also included in the chapter problems found in the companion paperback *Applications* book. Recall from Chapter 14 that under the *Tax Reform Act of 1986* modified accelerated cost recovery system (MACRS) depreciation results in $n + 1$ years of depreciation for an $n$-year class asset. This means that projects commonly have at least one year of cash flow beyond their recovery period. In actual practice, usable lives of projects (and the associated cash inflows) may differ significantly from their depreciable lives. Generally, under MACRS, usable lives are longer than depreciable lives.

**TABLE 15.1   Capital Expenditure Data for Blano Company**

| Year | Project A | | Project B | |
|---|---|---|---|---|
| **Initial Investment** | **$42,000** | | **$45,000** | |
| Year | Profits After Taxes | Operating Cash Inflows | Profits After Taxes | Operating Cash Inflows |
| 1 | $7,700 | $14,000 | $21,250 | $28,000 |
| 2 | 4,760 | 14,000 | 2,100 | 12,000 |
| 3 | 5,180 | 14,000 | 550 | 10,000 |
| 4 | 5,180 | 14,000 | 550 | 10,000 |
| 5 | 5,180 | 14,000 | 550 | 10,000 |
| Average | $5,600 | $14,000 | $ 5,000 | $14,000 |

**average rate of return**
For a given project, the annual accounting rate of return expected on the average investment.

**Equation 15.1 Formula for the average rate of return**

**average profits after taxes**
The total after-tax profits expected over the project's life divided by the number of years of the project's life.

**average investment**
The initial investment divided by 2.

return is typically calculated from available accounting data (profits after taxes). The most common definition of the **average rate of return** for a given project is as follows:

$$\text{Average rate of return} = \frac{\text{average profits after taxes}}{\text{average investment}} \qquad (15.1)$$

**Average profits after taxes** are found by adding up the after-tax profits expected over the project's total life and dividing the total by the number of years of life. In the case of an annuity, the average after-tax profits are equal to any year's profits. The **average investment** is found by dividing the initial investment by 2. The average rate of return can be interpreted as the annual accounting rate of return expected on the average investment.

**The Decision Criterion**   When average rate of return is used to make accept-reject decisions, the decision criterion is as follows: *If the average rate of return is greater than the minimum acceptable average rate of return, accept the project; if the average rate of return is less than the minimum acceptable average rate of return, reject the project.*

# E X A M P L E

The average profits expected for projects A and B (given in Table 15.1) are $5,600 and $5,000, respectively. The average investment for project A is $21,000 ($42,000 ÷ 2) and for project B is $22,500 ($45,000 ÷ 2). Dividing the average profits after taxes by the average investment results in the average rate of return for each project:

$$\text{Project A: } \frac{\$\ 5,600}{\$21,000} = 26.67\%$$

$$\text{Project B: } \frac{\$\ 5,000}{\$22,500} = 22.22\%$$

If Blano's minimum acceptable average rate of return is 24 percent, then project A is accepted and project B rejected. If the minimum return is 28 percent, both projects are rejected. If the projects are being ranked for profitability, project A is preferred over project B because it has a higher average rate of return (26.67% versus 22.22%).

**Pros and Cons of the Average Rate of Return**   The most favorable aspect of using the average rate of return to evaluate projects is its ease of calculation. The only input required is projected profit, a figure that should be easily obtainable.

There are three major weaknesses of this approach. The key conceptual weakness is the inability to specify the appropriate average rate of return in light of the wealth maximization goal. The second weakness stems from the use of accounting profits rather than cash flow as a measure of return. (This weakness can be overcome by using average operating cash inflows in the numerator in Equation 15.1.) The third major weakness is that this method ignores the time factor in the value of money. The indifference to the time factor can be illustrated by the following example.

# ▶ E X A M P L E

Each of the three projects for which data are given in Table 15.2 has an average rate of return of 40 percent. Although the average rates of return are the same for all three projects, the financial manager is *not* indifferent to them. He or she prefers project Z to project Y and project Y to project X because project Z has the most favorable profit flow pattern, project Y has the next most favorable profit flow pattern, and project X has the least attractive profit flow pattern. Clearly the financial manager prefers to receive profits sooner than later.

**TABLE 15.2   Calculation of the Average Rate of Return for Three Alternative Capital Expenditure Projects**

|  | Project X | Project Y | Project Z |
|---|---|---|---|
| (1) Initial investment | $20,000 | $20,000 | $20,000 |
| (2) Average investment [(1) ÷ 2] | $10,000 | $10,000 | $10,000 |
| **Year** | **Profits After Taxes** | | |
| 1 | $2,000 | $4,000 | $6,000 |
| 2 | 3,000 | 4,000 | 5,000 |
| 3 | 4,000 | 4,000 | 4,000 |
| 4 | 5,000 | 4,000 | 3,000 |
| 5 | 6,000 | 4,000 | 2,000 |
| (3) Average profits after taxes | $4,000 | $4,000 | $4,000 |
| (4) Average rate of return [(3) ÷ (2)] | 40% | 40% | 40% |

# Payback Period

**payback period**
The exact amount of time required for a firm to recover its initial investment in a project as calculated from *cash inflows*.

Payback periods are another commonly used criterion for evaluating proposed investments. The **payback period** is the exact amount of time required for the firm to recover its initial investment in a project as calculated from *cash inflows*. In the case of an *annuity*, the payback period can be found by dividing the initial investment by the annual cash inflow. For a *mixed stream*, the yearly cash inflows must be accumulated until the initial investment is recovered.

### The Decision Criterion

When payback is used to make accept-reject decisions, the decision criterion is as follows: *If the payback period is less than the maximum acceptable payback period, accept the project; if the payback period is greater than the maximum acceptable payback period, reject the project.*

## E X A M P L E ◀

The data for Blano Company's projects A and B presented in Table 15.1 can be used to demonstrate the calculation of the payback period. For project A, which is an annuity, the payback period is 3.0 years ($42,000 initial investment ÷ $14,000 annual cash inflow). Because project B generates a mixed stream of cash inflows, the calculation of the payback period is not quite as clear-cut. In year 1, the firm will recover $28,000 of its $45,000 initial investment. At the end of year 2, $40,000 ($28,000 from year 1 + $12,000 from year 2) will be recovered. At the end of year 3, $50,000 ($40,000 from years 1 and 2 + $10,000 from year 3) will be recovered. Because the amount received by the end of year 3 is greater than the initial investment of $45,000, the payback period is somewhere between two and three years. Only $5,000 ($45,000 − $40,000) must be recovered during year 3. Actually, $10,000 is recovered, but only 50 percent of this cash inflow ($5,000 ÷ $10,000) is needed to complete the payback of the initial $45,000. The payback period for project B is therefore 2.5 years (2 years + 50 percent of year 3).

If Blano's maximum acceptable payback period is 2.75 years, project A is rejected and project B is accepted. If the maximum payback period is 2.25 years, both projects are rejected. If the projects are being ranked, project B is preferred over project A because it has a shorter payback period (2.5 years versus 3.0 years). ◀

### Pros and Cons of Payback Periods

The payback period's popularity, particularly among small firms, results from its ease of calculation and simple intuitive appeal. It is a more accurate measure than the average rate of return because it considers cash flows rather than accounting profits. The payback period is also a superior measure (compared with the average rate of return) in that it gives *some* implicit consideration to the timing of cash flows and therefore to the time value of money. Because it can be viewed as a measure of *risk exposure*, many firms use the payback period as a decision criterion or as a supplement to sophisticated decision techniques. The longer the firm must wait to recover its invested funds, the greater the possibility of a calamity, and vice versa. Therefore, the shorter the payback period, the lower the firm's exposure to such risk.

**TABLE 15.3   Calculation of the Payback Period for Two Alternative Investment Projects**

|  | Project X | Project Y |
|---|---|---|
| Initial Investment | $10,000 | $10,000 |
| Year | Cash Inflows | |
| 1 | $5,000 | $3,000 |
| 2 | 5,000 | 4,000 |
| 3 | 1,000 | 3,000 |
| 4 | 100 | 4,000 |
| 5 | 100 | 3,000 |
| **Payback period** | 2 years | 3 years |

The major weakness of the payback period is that, like the average rate of return, this method cannot specify the appropriate payback period in light of the wealth maximization goal. The reason it cannot is that it is not based on discounting cash flows to determine whether they add to the firm's value. Instead, the appropriate payback period is merely a subjectively determined maximum acceptable period of time over which a project's cash flows must break even (i.e., just equal the initial investment). A second weakness is that this approach fails to take *fully* into account the time factor in the value of money. By measuring how quickly the firm recovers its initial investment, it only implicitly considers the timing of cash flows. A third weakness is the failure to recognize cash flows that occur *after* the payback period. This weakness can be illustrated by an example.

▶ E X A M P L E

Data for two investment opportunities—X and Y—are given in Table 15.3. The payback period for project X is two years; for project Y it is three years. Strict adherence to the payback approach suggests that project X is preferable to project Y. However, if we look beyond the payback period, we see that project X returns only an additional $1,200 ($1,000 in year 3, $100 in year 4, and $100 in year 5), whereas project Y returns an additional $7,000 ($4,000 in year 4 and $3,000 in year 5). Based on this information, it appears that project Y is preferable to X. The payback approach ignores the cash inflows in years 3, 4, and 5 for project X and in years 4 and 5 for project Y.

▶

▼▼▼▼▼▼▼▼▼▼▼▼▼▼▼▼▼▼▼▼▼▼▼▼▼▼▼▼▼▼▼▼▼▼▼

## Progress Review Questions

**15-1.** What is the *average rate of return*? What weaknesses are associated with its use in evaluating a proposed capital expenditure? How can a tie in the rankings be resolved using this technique?

**15-2.** What is the *payback period?* How is it calculated? What weaknesses are commonly associated with the use of the payback period to evaluate a proposed investment?

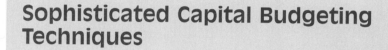

LG **2**   LG **3**

# Sophisticated Capital Budgeting Techniques

**sophisticated capital budgeting techniques**
Methods that give explicit consideration to the time value of money.

**Sophisticated capital budgeting techniques** give explicit consideration to the time value of money. These techniques include net present value, the profitability index, and the internal rate of return. They all discount the firm's cash flows using the cost of capital, which was discussed in detail in Chapter 13. The terms *discount rate* and *opportunity cost* are used interchangeably with *cost of capital* to refer to the minimum return that must be earned on a project to leave the firm's market value unchanged.

**net present value (NPV)**
The present value of a project's cash inflows minus its initial investment.

## Net Present Value

The **net present value (NPV),** as noted in Equation 15.2, is found by subtracting a project's initial investment, *II*, from the present value of its cash inflows, $CF_t$, discounted at a rate equal to the firm's cost of capital, *k:*

$$NPV = \text{present value of cash inflows} - \text{initial investment}$$

**Equation 15.2 Formula for net present value (NPV)**

$$NPV = \sum_{t=1}^{n} \frac{CF_t}{(1 + k)^t} - II \qquad (15.2)$$

**The Decision Criterion**   When NPV is used to make accept-reject decisions the decision criterion is as follows: *If NPV is greater than $0, accept the project; if NPV is less than $0, reject the project.* If NPV is greater than zero, the firm will earn a return greater than its cost of capital. Such action should enhance the market value of the firm and therefore the wealth of its owners.

## E X A M P L E

The net present value (NPV) approach can be illustrated using the Blano Company data presented in Table 15.1. If the firm has a 10 percent cost of capital, the net present values for projects A (an annuity) and B (a mixed stream) can be calculated as in Table 15.4. These calculations are based on the techniques presented in Chapter 11 using the appropriate present-value table factors.[2] The results show that the net present values of proj-

---

[2]Alternatively, a hand-held business/financial calculator such as the Texas Instruments BA-35 can be used to streamline these calculations as described in Chapter 11. Most of the more sophisticated (and more expensive) financial calculators are preprogrammed to find NPVs. With these calculators you merely punch in all cash flows along with the cost of capital or discount rate and depress **NPV** to find the net present value. Using such a calculator, the resulting values for projects A and B are $11,071 and $10,924, respectively.

**TABLE 15.4   The Calculation of NPVs for Blano Company's Capital Expenditure Alternatives**

### Project A

| | |
|---|---:|
| Annual cash inflow | $14,000 |
| × Present-value annuity interest factor, *PVIFA*ª | 3.791 |
| Present value of cash inflows | $53,074 |
| − Initial investment | 42,000 |
| Net present value (NPV) | $11,074 |

### Project B

| Year | Cash Inflows (1) | Present-Value Interest Factor, *PVIF*ᵇ (2) | Present Value [(1) × (2)] (3) |
|---|---:|:---:|---:|
| 1 | $28,000 | .909 | $25,452 |
| 2 | 12,000 | .826 | 9,912 |
| 3 | 10,000 | .751 | 7,510 |
| 4 | 10,000 | .683 | 6,830 |
| 5 | 10,000 | .621 | 6,210 |
| | | Present value of cash inflows | $55,914 |
| | | − Initial investment | 45,000 |
| | | Net present value (NPV) | $10,914 |

ªFrom Table A.4, for 5 years and 10 percent.
ᵇFrom Table A.3, for given year and 10 percent.

ects A and B are, respectively, $11,074 and $10,914. Both projects are acceptable, because the net present value of each is greater than zero. If the projects are being ranked, project A is considered superior to B because it has a higher net present value ($11,074 versus $10,914) than that of B.

## Profitability Index

The **profitability index (PI),** as noted in Equation 15.3, is calculated by dividing the present value of a project's cash inflows by its initial investment.

$$PI = \frac{\text{present value of cash inflows}}{\text{initial investment}}$$

$$PI = \frac{\sum_{t=1}^{n} \frac{CF_t}{(1+k)^t}}{II}$$

(15.3)

**profitability index (PI)**
The present value of a project's cash inflows divided by its initial investment.

**Equation 15.3 Formula for the profitability index (PI)**

**The Decision Criterion**   When the PI is used to make accept-reject decisions, the decision criterion is as follows: *If the PI is greater than 1, accept the project; if the PI is less than 1, reject the project.* When the PI is greater than 1, the net present value is greater than $0. Therefore the NPV and the PI approaches give the same accept-reject decisions. The acceptance of projects having PIs greater than 1 enhances the market value of the firm and therefore the wealth of its owners.

## E X A M P L E

Profitability indexes for Blano Company can be easily determined using the present values calculated in Table 15.4. The PIs for projects A and B are, respectively, 1.26 ($53,074 ÷ $42,000) and 1.24 ($55,914 ÷ $45,000). Because both PIs are greater than 1, both projects are acceptable. Ranked on a PI basis, project A is preferable to project B. Project A returns $1.26 present value for each dollar invested, whereas B returns only $1.24. This ranking is the same as that obtained using NPVs. However, *it is not unusual to get conflicting rankings using these two techniques.*

## Internal Rate of Return

**internal rate of return (IRR)**
The discount rate that equates the present value of cash inflows with the initial investment associated with a project, thereby making NPV = $0.

The **internal rate of return (IRR)** is the discount rate that equates the present value of cash inflows with the initial investment associated with a project. The IRR, in other words, is the discount rate that equates the NPV of an investment opportunity with zero (because the present value of cash inflows equals the initial investment). Mathematically, the IRR is found by solving Equation 15.2 for the value of $k$ that causes NPV to equal zero.

$$\$0 = \sum_{t=1}^{n} \frac{CF_t}{(1 + IRR)^t} - II$$

$$\sum_{t=1}^{n} \frac{CF_t}{(1 + IRR)^t} = II \qquad (15.4)$$

**Equation 15.4 Formula, based on setting NPV = $0, used to solve for the internal rate of return (IRR).**

As demonstrated shortly hereafter, the actual hand calculation of the IRR from Equation 15.4 is no easy chore.

**The Decision Criterion**   When the IRR is used to make accept-reject decisions, the decision criterion is as follows: *If the IRR is greater than the cost of capital, accept the project; if the IRR is less than the cost of capital, reject the project.* This criterion guarantees that the firm earns at least its required return. Such an outcome should enhance the market value of the firm and therefore the wealth of its owners.

**Calculating the IRR**   The IRR can be found either by using trial-and-error techniques or with the aid of a sophisticated financial calculator or a com-

# F I N A N C E   I N
# A C T I O N

In the News

## Payback, Net Present Value, and Internal Rate of Return Are Not Simply Fun and Games at Nintendo

In the 1987–1993 period, Nintendo and Sega Enterprises, both of Japan, licensed all of the technology running the 64 million game machines sold to households in the United States. The dominant player in the multibillion-dollar market is Nintendo, with over three-fourths of the sales. To keep competitors out, Nintendo and Sega have accepted negative internal rates of return on hardware, the boxes. Software, the games, provide sufficiently high internal rates of return for the firms to earn positive net present values overall and $1 billion in profits during 1993.

Perhaps more important in selecting individual games, however, is the payback period. Really successful titles, like Nintendo's Mortal Kombat, are enjoyed by buyers for one month. Afterwards, Nintendo has to upgrade the game so that Nintendo supplies kids with "interesting and new products all the time," according to Nintendo of America's president, Minoru Arakawa. In January, 1994, Nintendo released 13

new games, including Donkey Kong 1994, Ken Griffey Junior's Major League Baseball, and Wario Land.

Payback is the critical issue to Arakawa, because technology is quickly antiquated. For instance, in 1986, 1991, and 1993 Nintendo introduced the 8-bit, 16-bit, and 32-bit players, respectively. By 1995, Nintendo plans to have a 64-bit machine on the market.

To reduce the negative net present value of their hardware division, Nintendo is attempting to increase the uses of their boxes. In 1994, Nintendo began networking boxes so that owners could bank and trade stocks electronically. It also announced plans to develop a stationary bicycle that comes equipped with Nintendo hardware.

Sources: Rick Tetzeli, "Videogames: Serious Fun," *Fortune,* December 27, 1993; and "Showtime at the Nintendo Booth for the Consumer Electronics Show," *Dow Jones News Retrieval,* January 5, 1994.

puter.[3] Calculating the IRR for an annuity is considerably easier than calculating it for a mixed stream of operating cash inflows. The steps involved in calculating the IRR in each case are given in Table 15.5. These steps are illustrated by the following example.

▶ E X A M P L E

The two-step procedure given in Table 15.5 for finding the IRR of an *annuity* can be demonstrated using Blano Company's project A cash flows given in Table 15.1.

---

[3]The Texas Instruments BA-35 calculator—the business calculator used throughout this text—can be used to find the IRR of an annuity, but it lacks a function for finding the IRR of a mixed stream of cash flows. Most of the more sophisticated (and more expensive) financial calculators are preprogrammed to find IRRs. With these calculators you merely punch in all cash flows and depress **IRR** to find the internal rate of return. Computer software, such as the *Foundations of Managerial Finance (FMF) Disk* described in the *FMF Applications* book, and various spreadsheet programs, such as *Lotus 1-2-3,* are also available for calculating IRRs.

## TABLE 15.5   Steps for Calculating the Internal Rates of Return (IRRs) of Annuities and Mixed Streams

### For an Annuity

**Step 1:** Calculate the payback period for the project.[a]
**Step 2:** Use Table A-4 (the present-value interest factors for a $1 annuity, *PVIFA*) to find, for the life of the project, the factor closest to the payback value. The discount rate associated with that factor is the internal rate of return (IRR) to the nearest 1 percent.

### For a Mixed Stream[b]

**Step 1:** Calculate the average annual cash inflow.
**Step 2:** Divide the average annual cash inflow into the initial investment to get an "average payback period" (or present-value interest factor for a $1 annuity, *PVIFA*). The average payback is needed to estimate the IRR for the average annual cash inflow.
**Step 3:** Use Table A-4 (*PVIFA*) and the average payback period in the same manner as described in step 2 for finding the IRR of an annuity. The result is a *very rough* approximation of the IRR, based on the assumption that the mixed stream of cash inflows is an annuity.
**Step 4:[c]** Subjectively adjust the IRR obtained in step 3 by comparing the pattern of average annual cash inflows (calculated in step 1) to the actual mixed stream of cash inflows. If the actual cash flow stream seems to have higher inflows in the earlier years than the average stream, adjust the IRR up. If the actual cash inflows in the earlier years are below the average, adjust the IRR down. The amount of adjustment up or down typically ranges from 1 to 3 percentage points depending on how much the actual cash inflow stream's pattern deviates from the average annual cash inflows. For small deviations, an adjustment of around 1 percentage point may be best; for large deviations, adjustments of around 3 percentage points are generally appropriate. If the average cash inflows seem fairly close to the actual pattern, make no adjustment in the IRR.
**Step 5:** Using the IRR from step 4, calculate the net present value of the mixed-stream project. Be sure to use Table A-3 (the present-value interest factors for $1, *PVIF*), treating the estimated IRR as the discount rate.
**Step 6:** If the resulting NPV is greater than zero, subjectively raise the discount rate; if the resulting NPV is less than zero, subjectively lower the discount rate. The greater the deviation of the resulting NPV from zero, the larger the subjective adjustment. Typically, adjustments of 1 to 3 percentage points are used for relatively small deviations; larger adjustments are required for relatively large deviations.
**Step 7:** Calculate the NPV using the new discount rate. Repeat step 6. Stop as soon as two *consecutive* discount rates that cause the NPV to be positive and negative, respectively, have been found. Whichever of these rates causes the NPV to be closer to zero is the IRR to the nearest 1 percent.

[a]The payback period calculated actually represents the interest factor for the present value of an annuity *(PVIFA)* for the given life discounted at an unknown rate. Once determined, that rate represents the IRR for the project.
[b]Note that subjective estimates are suggested in steps 4 and 6. After working a number of these problems, a "feel" for the appropriate subjective adjustment, or "educated guess," may result.
[c]The purpose of this step is to provide a more accurate first estimate of the IRR. This step can be skipped.

**Step 1:** Dividing the initial investment of $42,000 by the annual cash inflow of $14,000 results in a payback period of 3.000 years ($42,000 ÷ $14,000 = 3.000).
**Step 2:** According to Table A.4, the *PVIFA* factors closest to 3.000 for five years are 3.058 (for 19 percent) and 2.991 (for 20 percent). The value closest to 3.000 is 2.991; therefore, the IRR for project A,

to the nearest 1 percent, is *20 percent*. The actual value, which is between 19 and 20 percent, can be found using interpolation, a calculator,[4] or a computer; it is 19.86 percent. (*Note:* For our purposes, values rounded to the nearest 1 percent suffice.) Project A with an IRR of 20 percent is quite acceptable, because this IRR is above the firm's 10 percent cost of capital (20 percent IRR > 10 percent cost of capital).

The seven-step procedure in Table 15.5 for finding the internal rate of return of a *mixed stream* of cash inflows can be illustrated using Blano Company's project B cash flows given in Table 15.1.

**Step 1:** Summing the cash inflows for years 1 through 5 results in total cash inflows of $70,000. That amount, when divided by the number of years in the project's life, results in an average annual cash inflow of $14,000 [($28,000 + $12,000 + $10,000 + $10,000 + $10,000) ÷ 5].

**Step 2:** Dividing the initial outlay of $45,000 by the average annual cash inflow of $14,000 (calculated in step 1) results in an "average payback period" (or present value of an annuity factor, *PVIFA*) of 3.214 years.

**Step 3:** In Table A.4, the factor closest to 3.214 for five years is 3.199, the factor for a discount rate of 17 percent. The starting estimate of the IRR is therefore 17 percent.

**Step 4:** Because the actual early-year cash inflows are greater than the average annual cash inflows of $14,000, a *subjective* increase of 2 percent is made in the discount rate. This makes the estimated IRR 19 percent.

**Step 5:** With the present-value interest factors *(PVIF)* for 19 percent and the correct year from Table A.3, the net present value of the mixed stream is calculated as shown in the following table.

| Year (*t*) | Cash Inflows (1) | $PVIF_{19\%,t}$ (2) | Present Value at 19% [(1) × (2)] (3) |
|---|---|---|---|
| 1 | $28,000 | .840 | $23,520 |
| 2 | 12,000 | .706 | 8,472 |
| 3 | 10,000 | .593 | 5,930 |
| 4 | 10,000 | .499 | 4,990 |
| 5 | 10,000 | .419 | 4,190 |
| | Present value of cash inflows | | $47,102 |
| | − Initial investment | | 45,000 |
| | Net present value (NPV) | | $ 2,102 |

---

[4]The procedure for using a hand-held business/financial calculator to find the unknown interest rate on an equal-payment loan described in Chapter 11 can also be used to find the IRR for an annuity. When applying this procedure, we treat the life of the annuity the same as the term of the loan, the initial investment the same as the loan principal, and the annual cash inflows the same as the annual loan payments. The resulting solution is the IRR for the annuity rather than the interest rate on the loan.

**Steps 6**

**and 7:** Because the net present value of $2,102, calculated in step 5, is greater than zero, we need to try a higher discount rate. Because the NPV deviates by only about 5 percent from the $45,000 initial investment, let's try a 2 percentage point increase to 21 percent. The calculations in the first table below indicate that the NPV of $494 for an IRR of 21 percent is reasonably close to, but still greater than, zero. Thus a higher discount rate should be tried. Because we are so close, let's try a 1 percentage point increase to 22 percent. As the calculations in the second table below show, the net present value using a discount rate of 22 percent is −$256.

| Year $(t)$ | Cash Inflows (1) | $PVIF_{21\%,t}$ (2) | Present Value at 21% [(1) × (2)] (3) |
|---|---|---|---|
| 1 | $28,000 | .826 | $23,128 |
| 2 | 12,000 | .683 | 8,196 |
| 3 | 10,000 | .564 | 5,640 |
| 4 | 10,000 | .467 | 4,670 |
| 5 | 10,000 | .386 | 3,860 |
| | Present value of cash inflows | | $45,494 |
| | − Initial investment | | 45,000 |
| | Net present value (NPV) | | $   494 |

| Year $(t)$ | Cash Inflows (1) | $PVIF_{22\%,t}$ (2) | Present Value at 22% [(1) × (2)] (3) |
|---|---|---|---|
| 1 | $28,000 | .820 | $22,960 |
| 2 | 12,000 | .672 | 8,064 |
| 3 | 10,000 | .551 | 5,510 |
| 4 | 10,000 | .451 | 4,510 |
| 5 | 10,000 | .370 | 3,700 |
| | Present value of cash inflows | | $44,744 |
| | − Initial investment | | 45,000 |
| | Net present value (NPV) | | −$   256 |

Because 21 and 22 percent are consecutive discount rates that give positive and negative net present values, we can stop the trial-and-error process. The IRR we are seeking is the discount rate for which the NPV is closest to zero. For this project, 22 percent causes the NPV to be closer to zero than 21 percent, so 22 percent is the IRR we use. If we use interpolation, a financial calculator, or a computer, the IRR is 21.65 percent; as indicated earlier, for our purposes the IRR rounded to the nearest 1 percent suffices. Therefore, the IRR of project B is approximately *22 percent*.

Project B is acceptable because its IRR of approximately 22 percent is greater than Blano Company's 10 percent cost of capital. This is the same conclusion reached using the NPV and PI as criteria. It is interesting to note that the IRR suggests that project B is preferable to A, which has an IRR of approximately 20 percent. This conflicts with the rankings of the projects obtained using NPV and PI. Such conflicts are not unusual; *there is no guarantee that these three techniques (NPV, PI, and IRR) rank projects in the same order. However, all methods should reach the same conclusion about the acceptability or nonacceptability of projects.*

## Comparison of NPV and IRR

Of the three sophisticated capital budgeting techniques, net present value (NPV) and internal rate of return (IRR) deserve the greatest attention. *For conventional projects, both techniques always generate the same accept-reject decision, but differences in their underlying assumptions can cause them to rank projects differently.* To understand the differences and preferences surrounding these techniques, we need to look at conflicting rankings and consider the question of which approach is better.

**Conflicting Rankings**   The possibility of *conflicting rankings* of projects by NPV and IRR should be clear from the Blano Company example. Ranking is an important consideration when projects are mutually exclusive or when capital rationing is necessary. When projects are mutually exclusive, ranking enables the firm to determine the best project from a financial viewpoint. When capital rationing is necessary, ranking projects may not determine the group of projects to accept, but it provides a logical starting point.

**Conflicting rankings** using NPV and IRR result from *differences in the magnitude and timing of cash flows.* Although these two factors explain conflicting rankings, the underlying cause is the implicit assumption concerning the reinvestment of **intermediate cash inflows**—cash inflows received prior to the termination of a project. NPV assumes that intermediate cash inflows are reinvested at the cost of capital, whereas IRR assumes that intermediate cash inflows are invested at a rate equal to the project's IRR.

**conflicting rankings**
Conflicts in the ranking given a project by NPV and IRR, resulting from *differences in the magnitude and timing of cash flows.*

**intermediate cash inflows**
Cash inflows received prior to the termination of a project.

**Which Approach Is Better?**   *On a purely theoretical basis, NPV is the better approach to capital budgeting.* Its theoretical superiority is based on a number of factors. Most important is the fact that the use of NPV assumes that any intermediate cash inflows are reinvested at the firm's cost of capital. The use of IRR assumes reinvestment at the often high rate specified by the IRR. The cost of capital tends to be a reasonable estimate of the rate at which the firm can actually reinvest intermediate cash inflows. Thus the use of NPV with its more conservative and more realistic reinvestment rate is, in theory, preferable. In addition, certain mathematical properties may cause a project with nonconventional cash flows to have zero or more than one IRR; this problem does not occur with the NPV approach.

Evidence suggests that in spite of the theoretical superiority of NPV, *financial managers prefer to use IRR*. In general, businesspeople prefer *rates of return* rather than actual *dollar returns*. Because interest rates, profitability, and so on are most often expressed as annual rates of return, the use of IRR makes sense to financial decision makers. They tend to find NPV more difficult to use because it does not really measure benefits *relative to the amount invested*. The widespread use of IRR should not be viewed as reflecting a lack of sophistication on the part of financial decision makers, however. A variety of methods and techniques are available for avoiding the pitfalls of IRR.

▼▼▼▼▼▼▼▼▼▼▼▼▼▼▼▼▼▼▼▼▼▼▼▼▼▼▼▼▼▼▼▼

## Progress Review Questions

**15-3.** What is the one characteristic that sophisticated capital budgeting techniques have in common that the unsophisticated techniques do not? What are the names commonly used to describe the rate at which cash flows are discounted to find present values?

**15-4.** What is the formula for finding the *net present value (NPV)* of a project with conventional cash flows? What is the acceptance criterion for NPV?

**15-5.** How is the *profitability index (PI)* calculated? What is its acceptance criterion? Is this measure consistent with the use of NPV? Explain.

**15-6.** What is the *internal rate of return (IRR)* on an investment? How is it determined? What is its acceptance criterion?

**15-7.** Do the net present value (NPV), profitability index (PI), and internal rate of return (IRR) always agree with respect to accept-reject decisions? With respect to ranking decisions? Explain.

**15-8.** What causes conflicts in the ranking of projects using net present value (NPV) and internal rate of return (IRR)? Explain how, on a purely theoretical basis, the assumption concerning the reinvestment of intermediate cash inflows tends to favor the use of net present value (NPV) over internal rate of return (IRR).

**15-9.** In practice, which of the two major capital budgeting techniques—net present value (NPV) or internal rate of return (IRR)—is preferred? Explain the rationale for this preference in light of the fact that it is inconsistent with theory.

▲▲▲▲▲▲▲▲▲▲▲▲▲▲▲▲▲▲▲▲▲▲▲▲▲▲▲▲▲▲▲▲

LG **4**

## Capital Rationing

Firms commonly operate under *capital rationing*—meaning that they have more acceptable independent projects than they can fund. *In theory*, capital rationing should not exist. As discussed in Chapter 13, firms should accept all projects that have returns > the cost of capital. Based on the techniques presented earlier this translates into accepting all projects for which NPV >

$0, PI > 1, or IRR > the cost of capital. However, *in practice* most firms operate under capital rationing. Generally, firms attempt to isolate and select the best acceptable projects subject to a capital expenditure budget set by management. Research has found that management internally imposes capital expenditure constraints to avoid what it deems to be "excessive" levels of new financing, particularly debt. In spite of the fact that failing to fund all acceptable independent projects is theoretically inconsistent with the goal of owner wealth maximization, here we discuss capital rationing procedures because they are widely used in practice.

The objective of *capital rationing* is to select the group of projects that provides the *highest overall net present value* and does not require more dollars than are budgeted. As a prerequisite to capital rationing, the best of any mutually exclusive projects must be chosen and placed in the group of independent projects. Two basic approaches to project selection under capital rationing are discussed here.

## Internal Rate of Return Approach

The **internal rate of return approach** involves graphing IRRs in descending order against the total dollar investment. This graph, which was discussed in some detail in Chapter 13, is called the *investment opportunities schedule (IOS)*. By drawing the cost of capital line and then imposing a budget constraint, the financial manager can determine the group of acceptable projects. The problem with this technique is that it does not guarantee the maximum dollar return to the firm. It merely provides a satisfactory solution to capital rationing problems.

**internal rate of return approach**
An approach to capital rationing that involves graphing project IRRs in descending order against the total dollar investment.

▶ E X A M P L E

Gould Company, a fast-growing plastics company, is confronted with six projects competing for its fixed budget of $250,000. The initial investment and IRR for each project are as shown in the table.

| Project | Initial Investment | IRR |
|---------|--------------------|-----|
| A | $ 80,000 | 12% |
| B | 70,000 | 20 |
| C | 100,000 | 16 |
| D | 40,000 | 8 |
| E | 60,000 | 15 |
| F | 110,000 | 11 |

The firm's cost of capital over the relevant range of total new financing is 10 percent. Figure 15.1 presents the investment opportunities schedule (IOS) resulting from ranking the six projects in descending order based on IRRs. According to the schedule, only projects B, C, and E should be accepted. Together, they absorb $230,000 of the $250,000 budget. Project D is not worthy of consideration because its IRR is less than the firm's 10 percent cost of

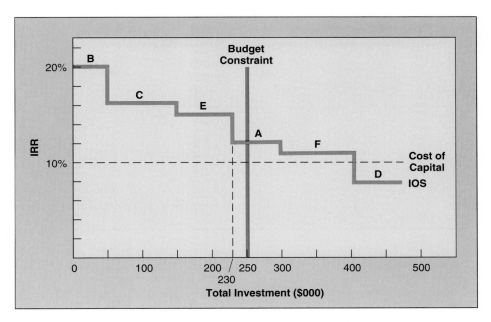

**FIGURE 15.1   Investment Opportunities Schedule (IOS) for Gould Company Projects**
Under the IRR approach to capital rationing, Gould Company's $250,000 budget constraint permits acceptance of only projects B, C, and E in spite of the fact that projects A and F have IRRs greater than the 10 percent cost of capital.

capital. The drawback of this approach, however, is that acceptance of projects B, C, and E is not guaranteed to maximize *total dollar returns* and therefore owners' wealth.

## Net Present Value Approach

**net present value approach**
An approach to capital rationing that is based on the use of present values to determine the group of projects that will maximize owners' wealth.

The **net present value approach** is based on the use of present values to determine the group of projects that will maximize owners' wealth. With it, the financial manager ranks projects on the basis of IRRs or PIs (profitability indexes) and then evaluates the present value of the benefits from each potential project. The goal is to *determine the combination of projects with the highest overall present value.* This is the same as maximizing net present value, because whether the entire budget is used or not, it is viewed as the total initial investment. The portion of the firm's budget that is not used does not increase the firm's value. At best, the unused money can be invested in marketable securities or returned to the owners in the form of cash dividends. In either case the wealth of the owners is not likely to be enhanced.

### E X A M P L E

The group of projects described in the preceding example is ranked in Table 15.6 on the basis of IRRs. The present value of the cash inflows associated with the projects is also included in the table. Projects B, C, and E, which together require $230,000, yield a present value of $336,000. However, if projects B, C, and A are implemented, the total budget of $250,000 is used, and

**TABLE 15.6    Rankings for Gould Company Projects**

| Project | Initial Investment | IRR | Present Value of Inflows at 10% | |
|---------|-------------------|-----|--------------------------------|---|
| B | $ 70,000 | 20% | $112,000 | |
| C | 100,000 | 16 | 145,000 | |
| E | 60,000 | 15 | 79,000 | |
| A | 80,000 | 12 | 100,000 | |
| F | 110,000 | 11 | 126,500 | Cutoff point |
| D | 40,000 | 8 | 36,000 | (IRR < 10%) |

the present value of the cash inflows is $357,000. This is greater than the return expected from selecting the projects on the basis of the highest IRRs. Implementing B, C, and A is preferable, because they maximize the present value for the given budget. *The firm's objective is to use its budget to generate the highest present value of inflows.* Assuming that any unused portion of the budget does not gain or lose money, the total NPV for projects B, C, and E is $106,000 ($336,000 − $230,000), whereas for projects B, C, and A, the total NPV is $107,000 ($357,000 − $250,000). Selection of projects B, C, and A therefore maximizes NPV.

## Progress Review Questions

**15-10.** What is *capital rationing?* In theory, should capital rationing exist? Why does it frequently occur in practice?

**15-11.** Compare and contrast the *internal rate of return approach* and *net present value approach* to capital rationing. Which is better? Why?

# Approaches for Dealing with Risk

LG    5

In the discussion of capital budgeting, **risk** refers to the chance that a project will prove unacceptable (i.e., NPV < $0, PI < 1, or IRR < cost of capital) or, more formally, to the degree of variability of cash flows. Projects with a small chance of being acceptable and a broad range of expected cash flows are riskier than projects having a high chance of being acceptable and a narrow range of expected cash flows. In the conventional capital budgeting projects assumed here, risk stems almost entirely from *cash inflows*, because the initial investment is generally known with relative certainty. Using the basic risk concepts presented in Chapter 12, we present here some behavioral approaches

**risk (in capital budgeting)** The chance that a project will prove unacceptable or, more formally, the degree of variability of cash flows.

for dealing with risk in capital budgeting: sensitivity and scenario analysis, statistical approaches, decision trees, and simulation. In addition, some international risk considerations are discussed.

## Sensitivity and Scenario Analysis

**sensitivity analysis**
A behavioral approach that uses a number of possible values for a given variable to assess its effect on a firm's return.

Two approaches for dealing with project risk to capture the variability of cash inflows and NPVs are sensitivity analysis and scenario analysis. **Sensitivity analysis,** as noted in Chapter 12, is a behavioral approach that uses a number of possible values for a given variable, such as cash inflows, to assess its effect on the firm's return, measured here by NPV. This technique is often useful in getting a feel for the variability of return in response to changes in a key variable. In capital budgeting, one of the most common sensitivity approaches is to estimate the NPVs associated with pessimistic (worst), most likely (expected), and optimistic (best) cash inflow estimates. The *range* can be determined by subtracting the pessimistic-outcome NPV from the optimistic-outcome NPV.

## E X A M P L E

Treadwell Tire Company, a tire retailer with a 10 percent cost of capital, is considering investing in either of two mutually exclusive projects: A and B. Each requires a $10,000 initial investment and is expected to provide equal annual cash inflows over their 15-year lives. The firm's financial manager made pessimistic, most likely, and optimistic estimates of the cash inflows for each project. The cash inflow estimates and resulting NPVs in each case are summarized in Table 15.7. The range of cash inflows is $1,000 for project A and $4,000 for project B. More important, the range of NPVs is $7,606 for project A and $30,424 for project B. It is clear that project A is less risky than project B. Given that both projects have the same most likely NPV of $5,212, the risk-averse decision maker takes project A because it has less risk and no possibility of loss.

**scenario analysis**
A behavioral approach that evaluates the effect on return of simultaneous changes in a number of variables.

**Scenario analysis** is a behavioral approach similar to sensitivity analysis but broader in scope. It is used to evaluate the impact of various circumstances on the firm's return. Rather than isolating the effect of a change in a single variable, scenario analysis is used to evaluate the effect on return of simultaneous changes in a number of variables. Decision makers can study the effects on return of changes in variables, such as cash inflows, cash outflows, and the cost of capital, resulting from differing assumptions about economic and competitive conditions. For example, the firm can evaluate the effect of both high inflation (scenario 1) and low inflation (scenario 2) on a project's NPV. Each scenario affects the firm's cash inflows, cash outflows, and cost of capital, thereby resulting in different levels of NPV. The decision maker can use these NPV estimates to roughly assess the risk involved with respect to the level of inflation. The widespread availability of computer-based spreadsheet programs (such as *Lotus 1-2-3*) has greatly enhanced the ease and popularity of use of scenario and sensitivity analysis.

## Statistical Approaches

The use of the standard deviation and coefficient of variation to measure the risk of a single asset held in isolation was presented in Chapter 12. These mea-

**TABLE 15.7  Sensitivity Analysis of Treadwell's Projects A and B**

|  | Project A | Project B |
|---|---|---|
| Initial Investment | $10,000 | $10,000 |
| **Annual Cash Inflows** | | |
| Outcome | | |
| Pessimistic | $1,500 | $    0 |
| Most likely | 2,000 | 2,000 |
| Optimistic | 2,500 | 4,000 |
| Range | $1,000 | $4,000 |
| **Net Present Values[a]** | | |
| Outcome | | |
| Pessimistic | $1,409 | −$10,000 |
| Most likely | 5,212 | 5,212 |
| Optimistic | 9,015 | 20,424 |
| Range | $7,606 | $30,424 |

[a]These values were calculated using the corresponding annual cash inflows. A 10 percent cost of capital and a 15-year life for the annual cash inflows were used.

sures can be applied to cash inflow or net present value (NPV) data to assess project risk behavior statistically. The following example illustrates the calculation of these statistics using NPV data.

▶ E X A M P L E

Treadwell Tire Company estimated the probabilities of the pessimistic, most likely, and optimistic NPV outcomes for projects A and B shown in Table 15.8. To find the standard deviation of each project, the first step is to calculate the *expected net present value of each project*. The *expected* NPV, $\overline{\text{NPV}}$, can be calculated using Equation 12.1 from Chapter 12, rewritten as

$$\overline{\text{NPV}} = \sum_{i=1}^{n} \text{NPV}_i \times Pr_i \qquad (15.5)$$

**Equation 15.5 Formula for the expected net present value**

where

$\text{NPV}_i$ = NPV for the *i*th outcome
$Pr_i$ = probability of occurrence of the *i*th NPV
$n$ = number of outcomes considered

Substituting the data from Table 15.8, we can calculate the expected NPV for each project:

**TABLE 15.8   NPVs and Associated Probability Estimates for Treadwell's Projects A and B**

| $i$ | Outcome$_i$ | NPV$^a{}_i$ | Probability, $Pr^b{}_i$ |
|---|---|---|---|
| | | **Project A** | |
| 1 | Pessimistic | $ 1,409 | .25 |
| 2 | Most likely | 5,212 | .50 |
| 3 | Optimistic | 9,015 | .25 |
| | | **Project B** | |
| 1 | Pessimistic | −$10,000 | .25 |
| 2 | Most likely | 5,212 | .50 |
| 3 | Optimistic | 20,424 | .25 |

$^a$From Table 15.7.
$^b$Values estimated subjectively, based on past experience.

$$\overline{\text{NPV}}_A = (\$1,409 \times .25) + (\$5,212 \times .50) + (\$9,015 \times .25)$$
$$= \$352.25 + \$2,606.00 + \$2,253.75 = \underline{\underline{\$5,212}}$$

$$\overline{\text{NPV}}_B = (-\$10,000 \times .25) + (\$5,212 \times .50) + (\$20,424 \times .25)$$
$$= -\$2,500 + \$2,606 + \$5,106 = \underline{\underline{\$5,212}}$$

Note that both projects have expected NPVs of $5,212, which also equals their most likely estimates.

Once the expected NPV, $\overline{\text{NPV}}$, has been calculated, the *standard deviation of NPV*, $\sigma_{\text{NPV}}$, can be found using Equation 12.2 from Chapter 12, rewritten as

**Equation 15.6 Formula for the standard deviation of NPV**

$$\sigma_{\text{NPV}} = \sqrt{\sum_{i=1}^{n} (\text{NPV}_i - \overline{\text{NPV}})^2 \times Pr_i} \tag{15.6}$$

The calculation of the standard deviation of NPV for projects A and B using Equation 15.6 is given in Table 15.9. It can be seen that project B's standard deviation of $10,756 is much higher than project A's standard deviation of $2,689. Project B is therefore clearly riskier than project A.

The *coefficient of variation, CV*, is an especially useful statistic for comparing the risk of projects of differing sizes. Because projects A and B have the same expected NPV, the coefficient of variation does not really improve the comparison. Applying Equation 12.3 from Chapter 12 to the NPV data, the coefficient of variation of NPV, $CV_{\text{NPV}}$, is defined as

**Equation 15.7 Formula for the coefficient of variation of NPV**

$$CV_{\text{NPV}} = \frac{\sigma_{\text{NPV}}}{\overline{\text{NPV}}} \tag{15.7}$$

Substituting $\sigma_{\text{NPV}}$ and $\overline{\text{NPV}}$ for projects A and B into Equation 15.7 yields

**TABLE 15.9　Calculation of the Standard Deviation of NPV for Treadwell's Projects A and B**

| $i$ | $NPV_i$ | $\overline{NPV}$ | $NPV_i - \overline{NPV}$ | $(NPV_i - \overline{NPV})^2$ | $Pr_i$ | $(NPV_i - \overline{NPV})^2 \times Pr_i$ |
|---|---|---|---|---|---|---|
| | | | **Project A** | | | |
| 1 | $1,409 | $5,212 | −$3,803 | $14,462,809 | .25 | $3,615,702 |
| 2 | 5,212 | 5,212 | 0 | 0 | .50 | 0 |
| 3 | 9,015 | 5,212 | 3,803 | 14,462,809 | .25 | 3,615,702 |

$$\sum_{i=1}^{3} (NPV_i - \overline{NPV})^2 \times Pr_i = \$7,231,404$$

$$\sigma_{NPV_A} = \sqrt{\sum_{i=1}^{3} (NPV_i - \overline{NPV})^2 \times Pr_i} = \sqrt{\$7,231,404} = \underline{\underline{\$2,689}}$$

| $i$ | $NPV_i$ | $\overline{NPV}$ | $NPV_i - \overline{NPV}$ | $(NPV_i - \overline{NPV})^2$ | $Pr_i$ | $(NPV_i - \overline{NPV})^2 \times Pr_i$ |
|---|---|---|---|---|---|---|
| | | | **Project B** | | | |
| 1 | −$10,000 | $5,212 | $15,212 | $231,400,000 | .25 | $ 57,850,000 |
| 2 | 5,212 | 5,212 | 0 | 0 | .50 | 0 |
| 3 | 20,424 | 5,212 | 15,212 | 231,400,000 | .25 | 57,850,000 |

$$\sum_{i=1}^{3} (NPV_i - \overline{NPV})^2 \times Pr_i = \$115,700,000$$

$$\sigma_{NPV_B} = \sqrt{\sum_{i=1}^{3} (NPV_i - \overline{NPV})^2 \times Pr_i} = \sqrt{\$115,700,000} = \underline{\underline{\$10,756}}$$

$$CV_{NPV_A} = \frac{\sigma_{NPV_A}}{NPV_A} = \frac{\$2,689}{\$5,212} = \underline{\underline{.516}}$$

$$CV_{NPV_B} = \frac{\sigma_{NPV_B}}{NPV_B} = \frac{\$10,756}{\$5,212} = \underline{\underline{2.064}}$$

Clearly project B, with a coefficient of variation of NPV of 2.064, is riskier than project A, which has a *CV* of .516.

## Decision Trees

**Decision trees** are a behavioral approach that uses diagrams to map the various investment decision alternatives and payoffs as well as their probabilities of occurrence. Their name derives from their resemblance to the branches of a tree (see Figure 15.2). Decision trees rely on estimates of the probabilities associated with the outcomes (payoffs) of competing courses of action. The payoffs associated with each course of action are weighted by the associated probability; the weighted payoffs for each course of action are summed; and the expected value of each course of action is then determined. The alternative providing the highest expected value is preferred.

**decision trees**
A behavioral approach that uses diagrams to map the various investment decision alternatives and payoffs as well as their probabilities of occurrence.

**FIGURE 15.2   Decision Tree for Convy, Inc.'s, Choice Between Projects I and J**

The $10,000 expected NPV of project I ($130,000 expected present value of cash inflows − $120,000 initial investment) is less than the $15,000 expected NPV of project J ($155,000 expected present value of cash inflows − $140,000 initial investment). Project J is therefore preferred.

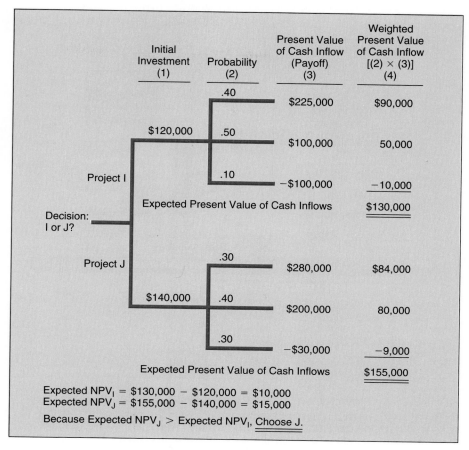

$$Expected\ NPV_I = \$130,000 - \$120,000 = \$10,000$$
$$Expected\ NPV_J = \$155,000 - \$140,000 = \$15,000$$

Because Expected $NPV_J$ > Expected $NPV_I$, Choose J.

# EXAMPLE

Convy, Inc., a manufacturer of picture frames, wishes to choose between two equally risky projects, I and J. To make this decision, Convy's management has gathered the necessary data, which are depicted in the decision tree in Figure 15.2. Project I requires an initial investment of $120,000; a resulting expected present value of cash inflows of $130,000 is shown in column 4. Project I's expected net present value, which is calculated below the decision tree, is therefore $10,000. Because the $15,000 expected net present value of project J, which is determined in a similar fashion, is greater than that for project I, project J is preferred.

## Simulation

**simulation**
A statistically based behavioral approach used in capital budgeting to get a feel for risk by applying predetermined probability distributions and random numbers to estimate risky outcomes.

**Simulation** is a statistically based behavioral approach used in capital budgeting to get a feel for risk by applying predetermined probability distributions and random numbers to estimate risky outcomes. By tying the various cash flow components together in a mathematical model and repeating the process numerous times, the financial manager can develop a probability distribution of project returns. Figure 15.3 presents a flowchart of the simulation of the net present value of a project. The process of generating random numbers and using the probability distributions for cash inflows and outflows

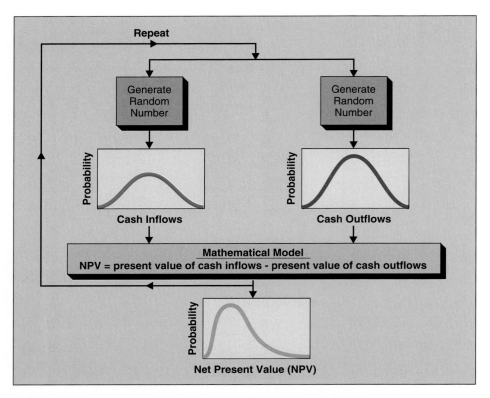

**FIGURE 15.3   Flowchart of a Net Present Value Simulation**
The basic NPV simulation uses random numbers with the probability distributions to determine cash inflows and cash outflows. These are substituted into
the mathematical model to determine NPV. This process is repeated a large number of times to create a probability distribution of NPV.

allows the decision maker to determine values for each of these variables.
Substituting these values into the mathematical model results in an NPV. By
repeating this process perhaps a thousand times, a probability distribution of
net present values is created.

Although only gross cash inflows and outflows are simulated in Figure
15.3, more sophisticated simulations using individual inflow and outflow components, such as sales volume, sale price, raw material cost, labor cost, maintenance expense, and so on, are quite common. From the distribution of returns, however they are measured (NPV, IRR, and so on), the decision maker
can determine not only the expected value of the return but also the probability of achieving or surpassing a given return. The use of computers has
made the simulation approach feasible. The output of simulation provides an
excellent basis for decision making; it allows the decision maker to view a continuum of risk-return trade-offs rather than a single-point estimate.

## International Risk Considerations

Although the basic techniques of capital budgeting are the same for purely
domestic firms as for multinational companies (MNCs), firms that operate in
several countries face risks unique to the international arena. Two types of

risk are particularly important and have been discussed briefly in earlier chapters: exchange rate risk and political risk—including, in the extreme, the risk that assets in foreign countries can be seized by the host government.

**exchange rate risk**
The danger that an unexpected change in the exchange rate between the dollar and the currency in which a project's cash flows are demoninated can reduce the market value of that project's cash flow.

**Exchange rate risk** refers to the danger that an unexpected change in the exchange rate between the dollar and the currency in which a project's cash flows are denominated can reduce the market value of that project's cash flow. Although a project's initial investment can, as usual, be predicted with some certainty in either local currency or dollar value, the dollar value of future cash inflows can be dramatically altered if the local currency depreciates against the dollar. In the short term, specific cash flows can be hedged by using financial instruments, such as currency futures and options. Long-term exchange rate risk can be minimized best by financing the project in whole or in part in local currency.

*Political risk* is much harder to protect against once a foreign project is accepted, because the foreign government can block the return of profits, seize the firm's assets, or otherwise interfere with a project's operation. This inability to manage risk after the fact makes it even more important that managers account for political risks before making an investment. They can do this either by adjusting a project's expected cash inflows to account for the probability of political interference or by using risk-adjusted discount rates (discussed later in this chapter) in the capital budgeting formulas. In general, it is much better to adjust individual project cash flows subjectively for political risk than to use a blanket adjustment for all projects.

In addition to unique risks that MNCs must face, several other special issues arise that are relevant only for international capital budgeting. These include tax law differences, the importance of *transfer pricing* in evaluating projects, and the need to analyze international projects from a strategic as well as a financial perspective. Because only after-tax cash flows are relevant for capital budgeting, financial managers must carefully account for taxes paid to foreign governments on profits (or even on revenues) earned within their borders. They must also address the effect of these tax payments on the parent company's U.S. tax liability, because full or partial credit is generally allowed for foreign tax payments.

**transfer prices**
Prices that subsidiaries charge each other for the goods and services traded between them.

Much of the international trade involving MNCs is, in reality, simply the shipment of goods and services from one of a parent company's wholly owned subsidiaries to another subsidiary located abroad. The parent company therefore has great discretion in setting the **transfer prices,** which are the prices that subsidiaries charge each other for the goods and services traded between them, because they are not traded in open markets with objectively determined prices. The importance and widespread use of transfer pricing in international trade makes capital budgeting in MNCs very difficult unless the transfer prices used accurately reflect actual costs and incremental cash flows.

Finally, MNCs often must approach international capital projects from a strategic point of view, rather than from a strictly financial perspective. For example, an MNC may feel compelled to invest in a country to ensure continued access, even if the project itself may not have a positive net present value. This motivation was important for Japanese automakers who set up assembly plants in the United States even when the strong dollar of the early 1980s made export from Japan more economically rational. For much the same reason, U.S. investment in Europe surged during the years before the market integration of the European Community in 1992. MNCs often invest in production facilities in the home country of major rivals to deny these competitors a profitable, uncontested home market. Finally, MNCs may feel compelled to invest in certain industries or countries to achieve a broad corporate objective, such as completing a product line or diversifying raw material sources, even when the project's cash flows may not be sufficiently profitable.

## Progress Review Questions

**15-12.** Define *risk* in terms of the cash inflows from a project. Briefly describe each of the following behavioral approaches, and explain how each can be used to deal with project risk:
  **a.** Sensitivity and scenario analysis
  **b.** Statistics
  **c.** Decision trees
  **d.** Simulation

**15-13.** Briefly define and explain how each of the following items that are unique to multinational companies (MNCs) affect their capital budgeting decisions.
  **a.** Exchange rate risk
  **b.** Political risk
  **c.** Tax law differences
  **d.** Transfer pricing
  **e.** Strategic rather than financial viewpoint

## Risk-Adjustment Techniques

LG 6

The approaches for dealing with risk presented so far allow the financial manager to get a "feel" for project risk. Unfortunately, they do not provide a straightforward basis for evaluating risky projects. We now illustrate the two major risk-adjustment techniques using the net present value (NPV) decision method.[5] The NPV decision rule of accepting only those projects with NPVs greater than $0 continues to hold. The basic equation for NPV was presented earlier in Equation 15.2. Because the initial investment, which occurs at time zero, is known with certainty, a project's risk is embodied in the present value of cash inflows.

Two methods can be used to adjust the present value of cash inflows for risk: (1) the cash inflows themselves can be adjusted, or (2) the discount rate can be adjusted. Here we describe and compare the two techniques: the cash inflow adjustment process using *certainty equivalents,* and the discount rate adjustment process using *risk-adjusted discount rates.* In addition, we discuss the practical aspects of certainty equivalents and risk-adjusted discount rates.

---

[5]The IRR can just as well be used, but because NPV is theoretically preferable, it is used instead.

## Certainty Equivalents

The theoretically preferred approach for risk adjustment is the use of **certainty equivalents (CEs).** They represent the percentage of estimated cash inflow that investors are satisfied to receive for *certain* rather than the cash inflows that are *possible* for each year. A project under consideration is therefore adjusted for risk in two steps: by first converting its expected cash inflows to certain amounts using the certainty equivalents and by then discounting the cash inflows at the risk-free rate, $R_F$. The **risk-free rate, $R_F$,** is the rate of return one earns on a virtually riskless investment such as a U.S. Treasury bill. It is used to discount the certain cash inflows and should not be confused with a risk-adjusted discount rate. (If a risk-adjusted rate were used, the risk would in effect be counted twice.) Although the process described here of converting risky cash inflows to certain cash inflows is somewhat subjective, the technique is theoretically sound.

## E X A M P L E

Blano Company wishes to consider risk in the analysis of two projects: A and B. The basic data for these projects were initially presented in Table 15.1, and the analysis of the projects using net present value and assuming the projects had equivalent risks was presented in Table 15.4. Ignoring risk differences and using net present value, we saw earlier that at the firm's 10 percent cost of capital, project A was preferred over project B; its NPV of $11,074 was greater than B's NPV of $10,914. Assume, however, that on further analysis the firm found that project A was actually riskier than project B. To consider the differing risks, the firm estimated the certainty equivalent factors for each project's cash inflows for each year. Columns 2 and 7 of Table 15.10 show the estimated values for projects A and B, respectively. Multiplying the risky cash inflows (given in columns 1 and 6) by the corresponding certainty equivalent factors (CEs) (columns 2 and 7, respectively) gives the certain cash inflows for projects A and B shown in columns 3 and 8, respectively.

On investigation, Blano's management estimated the prevailing risk-free rate of return, $R_F$, to be 6 percent. Using that rate to discount the certain cash inflows for each of the projects results in the net present values of $4,541 for project A and $10,141 for project B, as shown at the bottom of columns 5 and 10, respectively, in Table 15.10. (The calculated values using a hand-held business/financial calculator are $4,544 and $10,151 for projects A and B, respectively.) Note that as a result of the risk adjustment, project B is now preferred. The usefulness of the certainty equivalent approach for risk adjustment should be quite clear; the only difficulty lies in the need to estimate subjectively the certainty equivalents.

## Risk-Adjusted Discount Rates

A more practical approach for risk adjustment involves the use of *risk-adjusted discount rates (RADRs)*. Instead of adjusting the cash inflows for risk, as was done in the certainty equivalent approach, this approach adjusts the discount rate. The **risk-adjusted discount rate (RADR)** is the rate of return that must be earned on a given project to compensate the firm's owners adequately, that is, to maintain or improve the firm's share price. The higher the risk of a project, the higher the RADR and therefore the lower the net present value for a given stream of cash inflows.

**TABLE 15.10　Analysis of Blano Company's Projects A and B Using Certainty Equivalents**

### Project A

| Year *(t)* | Cash Inflows (1) | Certainty Equivalent Factors[a] (2) | Certain Cash Inflows [(1) × (2)] (3) | $PVIF_{6\%,t}$ (4) | Present Value [(3) × (4)] (5) |
|---|---|---|---|---|---|
| 1 | $14,000 | .90 | $12,600 | .943 | $11,882 |
| 2 | 14,000 | .90 | 12,600 | .890 | 11,214 |
| 3 | 14,000 | .80 | 11,200 | .840 | 9,408 |
| 4 | 14,000 | .70 | 9,800 | .792 | 7,762 |
| 5 | 14,000 | .60 | 8,400 | .747 | 6,275 |
| | | | Present value of cash inflows | | $46,541 |
| | | | − Initial investment | | 42,000 |
| | | | Net present value (NPV) | | $ 4,541 |

### Project B

| Year *(t)* | Cash Inflows (6) | Certainty Equivalent Factors[a] (7) | Certain Cash Inflows [(6) × (7)] (8) | $PVIF_{6\%,t}$ (9) | Present Value [(8) × (9)] (10) |
|---|---|---|---|---|---|
| 1 | $28,000 | 1.00 | $28,000 | .943 | $26,404 |
| 2 | 12,000 | .90 | 10,800 | .890 | 9,612 |
| 3 | 10,000 | .90 | 9,000 | .840 | 7,560 |
| 4 | 10,000 | .80 | 8,000 | .792 | 6,336 |
| 5 | 10,000 | .70 | 7,000 | .747 | 5,229 |
| | | | Present value of cash inflows | | $55,141 |
| | | | − Initial investment | | 45,000 |
| | | | Net present value (NPV) | | $10,141 |

[a]These values were estimated by management; they reflect the risk managers perceive in the cash inflows.

*Note:* The basic cash flows for these projects were presented in Table 15.1, and the analysis of the projects using NPV and assuming equal risk was presented in Table 15.4.

Using the coefficient of variation, *CV*, as a measure of project risk, the firm can develop a **market risk-return function**—a graph of the discount rates associated with each level of project risk. An example of such a function is given in Figure 15.4. It relates the risk-adjusted discount rate, RADR, to the project risk as measured by the coefficient of variation, *CV*. This function is similar to the capital asset pricing model (CAPM) presented in Chapter 12.

**market risk-return function**
A graph of the discount rates associated with each level of project risk.

The risk-return function in Figure 15.4 indicates that project cash inflows associated with a riskless event ($CV = 0$) should be discounted at a 6 percent rate. This rate of return therefore represents the risk-free rate, $R_F$ (point $a$ in the figure). For all levels of risk greater than certainty ($CV > 0$), the associated required rate of return is indicated. Points $b$, $c$, and $d$ indicate that rates of return of approximately 9, 11, and 14 percent are required on projects with coefficients of variation of .6, 1.0, and 1.5, respectively.

Figure 15.4 is a *market risk-return function.* This means that investors discount cash inflows with the given levels of risk at the corresponding rates. Therefore, in order not to damage its market value, the firm must use the correct discount rate for evaluating a project. If a firm discounts a risky project's cash inflows at too low a rate and accepts the project, the firm's market price may drop as investors recognize that investing in the firm itself has become riskier. The amount by which the required discount rate for a project exceeds the risk-free rate is called the **risk premium.** It of course increases with increasing project risk. A simple example clarifies the use of the risk-adjusted discount rate, RADR, in evaluating capital budgeting projects.

**risk premium**
The amount by which the required discount rate for a project exceeds the risk-free rate.

# E X A M P L E ◀

Blano Company wishes to use risk-adjusted discount rates to determine, according to NPV, whether to implement project A or project B. In addition to the data presented earlier, Blano's management has estimated the coefficient of variation for project A as 1.5 and for project B as 1.0. According to Figure 15.4, the RADR for project A is approximately 14 percent; for project B, it is approximately 11 percent. Due to the riskier nature of project A, its risk premium is 8 percent ($14\% - 6\%$); for project B the risk premium is 5 percent ($11\% - 6\%$). The net present value of each project, using its RADR, is cal-

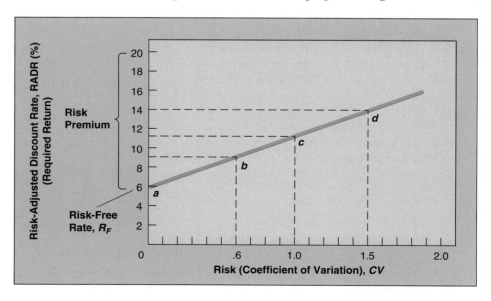

**FIGURE 15.4    A Market Risk-Return Function**
The market risk-return function shows the risk-adjusted discount rate, RADR, or required return associated with each level of risk measured by the coefficient of variation, *CV.* At *CV*s of 0 (no risk), .6, 1.0, and 1.5, the RADRs are approximately 6 percent (risk-free rate, $R_F$), 9 percent, 11 percent, and 14 percent, respectively.

## Tootsie Roll's Risk-Adjustment Technique Limits Expansion

Tootsie Roll started out making candy a century ago, and that's all it does today at its four factories in the United States and one in Mexico City. Although Tootsie Roll has collected 17 candy brands through the years, it remains a slow and selective buyer. When examining new purchases, Ellen and Melvin Gordon use a high risk-adjusted discount rate for candy brands and a very high discount rate for any other investment.

Several factors have contributed to Tootsie Roll's usage of high risk-adjusted discount rates. Ellen and Melvin Gordon, who have been president and CEO of Tootsie Roll for 30 years, have seen many competitors fail in their attempts to market novelty candy brands such as the Reggie Bar. As holders of 47 percent of Tootsie Roll's shares they can control the expansion process at Tootsie Roll. Although both are over 62 years

old, they have not announced a succession plan. Most importantly, perhaps, Tootsie Roll has paid a cash dividend every year for the past 50 years, a dividend that has increased every year since the Gordons took over in 1963. Expansion could possibly reduce the funds they would have available for increasing dividends.

The lack of expansion has limited Tootsie Roll sales to North America until recently. When asked about Tootsie Roll's relatively high price/earnings ratio, a stockbroker at Kidder Peabody noted that the Gordons cannot hold on forever. Perhaps the next managers of Tootsie Roll will take more risk through employment of a lower risk-adjusted discount rate.

Source: John LaBate, "Companies to Watch: Tootsie Roll Industries," *Fortune,* January 10, 1994, p. 109.

culated in Table 15.11. (The calculated values using a hand-held business/financial calculator are $6,063 and $9,798 for projects A and B, respectively.) The results clearly show that project B is preferable; its risk-adjusted net present value (NPV) of $9,802 is greater than the $6,062 risk-adjusted NPV for project A. This is the same conclusion that resulted using certainty equivalents in the preceding example. As noted earlier (see Table 15.4), when the discount rates are not adjusted for risk, project A is preferred to project B. The usefulness of risk-adjusted discount rates should now be clear; the real difficulty of this approach lies in estimating the market risk-return function.

## CE Versus RADR in Practice

*Certainty equivalents (CEs) are theoretically superior to risk-adjusted discount rates (RADRs) for project risk adjustment. However, because of the complexity of developing CEs, RADRs are most often used in practice.* Their popularity stems from two major facts: (1) They are consistent with the general disposition of financial decision makers toward rates of return. (2) They are easily estimated and applied. The first reason is clearly a matter of personal preference. The second is based on the computational convenience and well-developed procedures involved in the use of RADRs. In practice, risk is often subjectively categorized rather than related to a continuum of RADRs associated with each

**TABLE 15.11  Analysis of Blano Company's Projects A and B Using Risk-Adjusted Discount Rates**

### Project A

| | |
|---|---|
| Annual cash inflow | $14,000 |
| $\times\ PVIFA_{14\%,5\ yrs}$ | 3.433 |
| Present value of cash inflows | $48,062 |
| $-$ Initial investment | 42,000 |
| Net present value (NPV) | $ 6,062 |

### Project B

| Year (t) | Cash Inflows (1) | $PVIF_{11\%,t}$ (2) | Present Value [(1) × (2)] (3) |
|---|---|---|---|
| 1 | $28,000 | .901 | $25,228 |
| 2 | 12,000 | .812 | 9,744 |
| 3 | 10,000 | .731 | 7,310 |
| 4 | 10,000 | .659 | 6,590 |
| 5 | 10,000 | .593 | 5,930 |
| | | Present value of cash inflows | $54,802 |
| | | $-$ Initial investment | 45,000 |
| | | Net present value (NPV) | $ 9,802 |

*Note:* By using Figure 15.4 and the coefficients of variation of 1.5 and 1.0 for projects A and B, respectively, a discount rate of 14 percent is used for project A and a discount rate of 11 percent is used for project B.

level of risk, as illustrated by the market risk-return function in Figure 15.4. Firms often establish a number of *risk classes,* with an RADR assigned to each. Each project is then subjectively placed in the appropriate risk class, and the corresponding RADR is used to evaluate it. This is sometimes done on a division-by-division basis. Each division is given its own set of risk classes and associated RADRs, similar to those in Table 15.12. The use of *divisional costs of capital* and associated risk classes allows the large multidivisional firm to incorporate differing levels of divisional risk into the capital budgeting process. At the same time it recognizes differences in the levels of individual project risk. An example helps to illustrate the general use of risk classes and RADRs.

# EXAMPLE

Assume that the management of Blano Company decides to use a more subjective but practical RADR approach to analyze projects. Each project is placed in one of four risk classes according to its perceived risk. The classes range from I for the lowest risk projects to IV for the highest risk projects. Associated with each class is an RADR appropriate to the level of risk of projects in the

## TABLE 15.12   Blano Company's Risk Classes and RADRs

| Risk Class | Description | Risk-Adjusted Discount Rate, RADR |
|:---:|---|:---:|
| I | *Below-average risk:* Projects with low risk. Typically involve routine replacement without renewal of existing activities. | 8% |
| II | *Average risk:* Projects similar to those currently implemented. Typically involve replacement or renewal of existing activities. | 10% |
| III | *Above-average risk:* Projects with higher than normal, but not excessive, risk. Typically involve expansion of existing or similar activities. | 14% |
| IV | *Highest risk:* Projects with very high risk. Typically involve expansion into new or unfamiliar activities. | 20% |

class. A brief description of each class, along with the associated RADR, is given in Table 15.12. It shows that lower risk projects tend to involve routine replacement or renewal activities; higher risk projects involve expansion, often into new or unfamiliar activities.

The financial manager of Blano assigns project A to class III and project B to class II. The cash flows for project A are therefore evaluated using a 14 percent RADR; project B's are evaluated using a 10 percent RADR.[6] The net present value of project A at 14 percent was calculated in Table 15.11 to be $6,062. The NPV for project B at a 10 percent RADR was found in Table 15.4 to be $10,914. Clearly, with RADRs based on the use of risk classes, project B is preferred over project A. As noted earlier, this result is contrary to the findings in Table 15.4, where no attention was given to the differing risk of projects A and B.

# Progress Review Questions

**15-14.** Describe the underlying logic and basic procedures involved in using (1) *certainty equivalents (CEs)* and (2) *risk-adjusted discount rates (RADRs)* in the risk-adjustment process.

**15-15.** Compare and contrast certainty equivalents (CEs) and risk-adjusted discount rates (RADRs) from both a theoretical and a practical point of view. In practice, how are *risk classes* often used to apply RADRs? Explain.

---

[6]Note that the 10 percent RADR for project B using the risk classes in Table 15.12 differs from the 11 percent RADR found earlier for project B using the market risk-return function. This difference is attributable to the less precise nature of the use of risk classes.

# SUMMARY OF LEARNING GOALS

**LG 1**   **Calculate, interpret, and evaluate the two most commonly used unsophisticated capital budgeting techniques: average rate of return and payback period.** The average rate of return measures the annual accounting rate of return expected on the average investment. Its ease of calculation is appealing, although it lacks any link to the wealth maximization goal, fails to consider cash flows, and ignores the time value of money. The payback period measures the amount of time required by the firm to recover its initial investment. Shorter payback periods are preferred. Its appeal lies in its consideration of cash flows, the implicit consideration given to timing, and its ability to measure risk exposure. The weaknesses of the payback period include its lack of linkage to the wealth maximization goal, failure to consider time value explicitly, and the fact that it ignores cash flows that occur after the payback period.

**LG 2**   **Apply the sophisticated capital budgeting techniques—net present value (NPV), profitability index (PI), and internal rate of return (IRR)—to relevant cash flows to choose acceptable as well as preferred capital expenditures.** Sophisticated capital budgeting techniques use the cost of capital to consider the time factor in the value of money. They include net present value (NPV), the profitability index (PI), and the internal rate of return (IRR). All of these techniques provide the same accept-reject decisions for a given project but often conflict when ranking projects.

**LG 3**   **Compare net present value and internal rate of return techniques in light of conflicting rankings from both theoretical and practical viewpoints.** On a purely theoretical basis, NPV is preferred over IRR, because NPV assumes reinvestment of intermediate cash inflows at the cost of capital and does not exhibit the mathematical problems often occurring when calculating IRRs for nonconventional cash flows. In practice, the IRR is more commonly used by major firms because it is consistent with the general preference of businesspeople toward rates of return.

**LG 4**   **Discuss the two basic approaches—internal rate of return and net present value—for choosing projects under capital rationing.** The two basic approaches for choosing projects under capital rationing are the internal rate of return approach and the net present value approach. Of the two, the net present value approach better achieves the objective of using the budget to generate the highest present value of inflows.

**LG 5**   **Recognize the basic behavioral approaches—sensitivity and scenario analysis, statistical approaches, decision trees, and simulation—for dealing with project risk and the unique risks and other issues facing multinational companies (MNCs).** Risk in capital budgeting is concerned with either the chance that a project will prove unacceptable or, more formally, the degree of variability of cash flows. Sensitivity analysis and scenario analysis are two behavioral approaches for dealing with project risk to capture the variability of cash inflows and NPVs. Statistical approaches for measuring project risk include the standard deviation and the coefficient of variation. A decision tree relies on estimates of probabilities associated with the outcomes of competing courses of action to determine the expected values used to select a preferred action. Simulation, which results in a probability distribution of project returns, usually requires a computer and allows the decision maker to understand the risk-return trade-offs involved in a proposed investment. Firms that operate in several countries face risks that are unique to the international arena. Two types of risk are particularly important: exchange rate risk and political risk. Multinational firms also face other special issues, such as tax law differences, the importance of transfer pricing in evaluating projects, and the need to analyze international projects from a strategic as well as a financial perspective.

**Understand the calculation and practical aspects of the two basic risk-adjustment techniques: certainty equivalents (CEs) and risk-adjusted discount rates (RADRs).** Certainty equivalents (CEs) are used to adjust risky cash inflows to certain amounts, which are discounted at a risk-free rate in order to find the NPV. The risk-adjusted discount rate (RADR) technique involves a market-based adjustment of the discount rate used to calculate NPV. CEs are the theoretically superior risk-adjustment technique. RADRs are more commonly used in practice because decision makers prefer rates of return and find them easier to estimate and apply.

# S U M M A R Y   O F   K E Y
# D E F I N I T I O N S   A N D
# E Q U A T I O N S

## Variable Definitions

$CF_t$ = cash inflow in period $t$

$CV_{NPV}$ = coefficient of variation of NPV

$II$ = initial investment

IRR = internal rate of return

$k$ = cost of capital

$n$ = number of outcomes considered

NPV = net present value

$NPV_i$ = NPV for the $i$th outcome

PI = profitability index

$Pr_i$ = probability of occurrence of the $i$th NPV

$\sigma_{NPV}$ = standard deviation of NPV

## Equations

Average rate of return

[Eq. 15.1]
$$\text{Average rate of return} = \frac{\text{average profits after taxes}}{\text{average investment}}$$

Net present value (NPV)

[Eq. 15.2]
$$\text{NPV} = \sum_{t=1}^{n} \frac{CF_t}{(1+k)^t} - II$$

Profitability index (PI)

[Eq. 15.3]
$$\text{PI} = \frac{\displaystyle\sum_{t=1}^{n} \frac{CF_t}{(1+k)^t}}{II}$$

Internal rate of return (IRR)

[Eq. 15.4]
$$\sum_{t=1}^{n} \frac{CF_t}{(1+\text{IRR})^t} = II$$

Expected net present value

[Eq. 15.5]
$$\overline{\text{NPV}} = \sum_{i=1}^{n} \text{NPV}_i \times Pr_i$$

Standard deviation of NPV

[Eq. 15.6]
$$\sigma_{\text{NPV}} = \sqrt{\sum_{i=1}^{n} (\text{NPV}_i - \overline{\text{NPV}})^2 \times Pr_i}$$

Coefficient of variation of net present value (NPV)

[Eq. 15.7]
$$CV_{\text{NPV}} = \frac{\sigma_{\text{NPV}}}{\overline{\text{NPV}}}$$

# P A R T VI

# Long-Term Financing Decisions

After studying this chapter, you should be able to

LG 1  Understand capital structure, including the basic types of capital, external assessment of capital structure, and the capital structure of non-U.S. firms.

LG 2  Explain graphically, using a modified form of the zero-growth valuation model and the firm's debt, equity, and weighted average cost of capital functions, the "optimal" capital structure.

LG 3  Discuss the graphic presentation, risk considerations, and basic shortcoming of using the EBIT-EPS approach to compare capital structures.

LG 4  Describe cash dividend payment procedures, dividend reinvestment plans, the relevance of dividend policy and related arguments, and the key factors that affect dividend policy.

LG 5  Describe and evaluate the three basic types of dividend policies: constant-payout-ratio, regular, and low-regular-and-extra.

LG 6  Contrast the basic features, objectives, and procedures for paying other forms of dividends, including stock dividends, stock splits, and stock repurchases.

## 16

# Capital Structure and Dividend Policy

From a practical standpoint, capital structure gives you tremendous insight into how a company views itself, its position in its industry, and its competitive posture. For example, does an aggressive (heavily leveraged) capital structure mean the company is growing or that it is short of cash and must borrow to maintain growth? Looking at the capital structure and understanding its composition—debt versus equity—tells a lot about a company.

## Capital structure and dividend policies affect the marketplace's perception and valuation of a firm.

A company's dividend policy provides information on how the company views its future. A positive dividend policy—increasing yearly dividends on an ongoing basis—tells you that a company is confident of its ability to sustain growth in the long term. On the other hand, a policy of paying out as dividends a very low percentage of earnings raises other questions, for example, is the company using its dollars to fund growth at above-average levels? If the percentage of earnings paid out as dividends is high, you might ask whether this is the best use of funds or if there is enough funding for long-term growth. Clearly, financial managers need to be aware of what their capital structure and dividend policy strategies tell the investing public.

Companies should consistently review their capital structure in terms of their need for funds, the interest rate environment, and alternative returns. The desired levels of debt and equity should take dividends into account, to see if the percentage of earnings paid out should be maintained or increased, which depends on the other uses a company has for the money it generates.

A firm's optimal capital structure depends on its strategic goals. High-growth companies usually have more debt than equity. The risk-return trade-off must also be considered. If additional risk is incurred by borrowing $100 million, what kind of return can be earned by investing it in company growth to maximize market value?

In my opinion, it is more important for a company to understand its own situation than to match industry debt-to-equity ratios, which typically cover a broad range. Being similar to other firms isn't relevant—*if* the reasons for choosing a particular capital structure policy make sense. Too much emphasis is often placed on comparisons with other companies, rather than a company's willingness to spend money to grow. In any industry, if you don't spend dollars to develop and promote new products and services, you won't grow at all.

A company's dividend policy depends on its ability to generate cash, returns on cash investments, and earnings growth. It's less important for a young, growing company to pay dividends than for an established company to do so. A cash dividend policy can open up a company to a broader range of investors. Some institutions cannot buy stock unless it pays dividends. Thus, some companies pay a modest dividend to improve the marketability of their stock.

Capital structure and dividend policies affect the marketplace's perception and valuation of a firm. Corporate financial managers should not focus too much on short-term objectives and lose sight of the long-term consequences of these strategic decisions on the company and its shareholders.

George Novello *is a managing director and head of equity mutual funds for Greenwich Street Advisors, a division of Smith Barney Shearson. He began his investment management and brokerage experience at Alliance Capital, moving to E.F. Hutton in 1978. From 1986 to 1988 he was Hutton's associate director of research.*

445

**C**apital structure and dividend policy are important areas of long-term financial decision making. Both are deeply rooted in financial theory and play an important role in maximizing shareholder wealth. The firm's **capital structure**—the mix of long-term debt and equity maintained by the firm—can significantly affect its value by affecting risk and return. Poor capital structure decisions can result in a high cost of capital, thereby lowering project net present values (NPVs) and making more of them unacceptable. Effective decisions can lower the cost of capital, resulting in higher NPVs and more acceptable projects, thereby increasing the value of the firm.

As noted in Chapter 12, expected cash dividends are the key return variable from which owners and investors determine share price. In each period, any earnings that remain after satisfying obligations to creditors, the government, and preferred stockholders can be retained by the firm, paid out as cash dividends, or divided between retained earnings and cash dividends. Retained earnings can be invested in assets that help the firm expand or maintain its present rate of growth. On the other hand, the owners of the firm generally desire some current return on their equity investment—the payment of a cash dividend, which reduces the amount of earnings retained. Here we first discuss the important aspects of capital structure and then consider dividend policy.

**capital structure**
The mix of long-term debt and equity maintained by the firm.

---

# The Firm's Capital Structure

LG  1

Capital structure is one of the most complex areas of financial decision making due to its interrelationship with other financial decision variables.[1] To achieve the firm's goal of owner wealth maximization, the financial manager must be able to assess the firm's capital structure and understand its relationship to risk, return, and value. This and the following two sections link together the concepts presented in Chapters 4, 5, 12, and 13.

## Types of Capital

The term **capital** denotes the long-term funds of the firm. All of the items on the right-hand side of the firm's balance sheet, excluding current liabilities, are sources of capital. The following simplified balance sheet illustrates the basic breakdown of total capital into its two components: debt capital and equity capital.

**capital**
The long-term funds of the firm; all items on the right-hand side of the firm's balance sheet, excluding current liabilities.

---

[1]Of course, although capital structure is financially important, it, like many business decisions, is generally not as important as the firm's products or services. In a practical sense a firm can probably more readily increase its value by improving quality and reducing costs than by fine-tuning its capital structure.

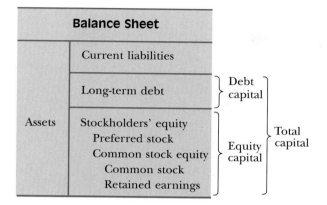

**Debt capital** includes all of the firm's long-term borrowing. The various types and characteristics of long-term debt are discussed in detail in Chapter 18. Remember from Chapter 13 that the cost of debt is less than the cost of other forms of financing. The relative inexpensiveness of debt capital is due to the fact that the lenders take the least risk of any long-term contributors of capital. Their risk is less than that of others because (1) they have a higher priority of claim against any earnings or assets available for payment, (2) they have a far stronger legal pressure against the company to make payment than do preferred or common stockholders, and (3) the tax-deductibility of interest payments substantially lowers the debt cost to the firm.

**Equity capital** consists of the long-term funds provided by the firm's owners, the stockholders. Unlike borrowed funds that must be repaid at a specified future date, equity capital is expected to remain in the firm for an indefinite time. The two basic sources of equity capital are (1) preferred stock and (2) common stock equity, which includes common stock and retained earnings. As demonstrated in Chapter 13, common stock is typically the most expensive form of equity, followed by retained earnings and preferred stock, respectively. The characteristics of retained earnings are briefly discussed as part of the dividend presentation later in this chapter; preferred and common stock are discussed further in Chapter 19.

Our concern here is the relationship between debt and equity capital. Key differences between these two types of capital are summarized in Table 16.1. It should be clear that due to its secondary position relative to debt, suppliers of equity capital take greater risk and therefore must be compensated with higher expected returns than suppliers of debt capital.

## External Assessment of Capital Structure

In Chapter 5 we saw that *financial leverage* results from the use of fixed-payment financing, such as debt and preferred stock, to magnify return and risk. Debt ratios, which measure the firm's degree of financial leverage, were presented in Chapter 4. A direct measure of the degree of indebtedness is the *debt ratio:* The higher this ratio, the greater the firm's financial leverage. The measures of the firm's ability to meet fixed payments associated with debt include the *times interest earned ratio* and the *fixed-payment coverage ratio.* These ratios provide indirect information on leverage. The smaller these ratios, the

**TABLE 16.1   Key Differences Between Debt and Equity Capital**

| Characteristic | Type of Capital | |
| --- | --- | --- |
| | Debt | Equity |
| Voice in management[a] | No | Yes |
| Claims on income and assets | Senior to equity | Subordinate to debt |
| Maturity | Stated | None |
| Tax treatment | Interest deduction | No deduction |

[a]In default, debtholders and preferred stockholders *may* receive a voice in management; otherwise, only common stockholders have voting rights.

less able the firm is to meet payments as they come due. In general, low debt-payment ratios are associated with high degrees of financial leverage. The more risk a firm is willing to take, the greater is its financial leverage. In theory, the firm should maintain financial leverage consistent with a capital structure that maximizes owners' wealth.

*An acceptable degree of financial leverage for one industry or line of business can be highly risky in another due to differing operating characteristics between industries or lines of business.* Table 16.2 presents the debt and times interest earned ratios for selected industries and lines of business. Significant industry differences can be seen in these data. For example, the debt ratio for electronic computer manufacturers is 58.3 percent, whereas for auto retailers it is 79.0 percent. Of course, differences in debt positions are also likely to exist *within* an industry or line of business.

## Capital Structure of Non-U.S. Firms

Modern capital structure theory (highlighted in the next section) has developed largely within the framework of the U.S. financial system, and most studies of these theories have employed data from U.S. companies. In recent years, however, both corporate executives and academic researchers have focused much greater attention on financing patterns shown by European, Japanese, Canadian, and other non-U.S. companies. They have found striking similarities and important differences between U.S. and international companies.

In general, non-U.S. companies have much higher debt ratios than do their U.S. counterparts. There are several reasons for this, most of which are related to the fact that financial markets are much more developed in the United States than elsewhere and have played a much greater role in corporate financing than has been the case in other countries. In most European countries and especially in Japan and other Pacific rim nations, large commercial banks are much more actively involved in the financing of corporate activity than has been true in the United States. Furthermore, in many of these countries, banks are allowed to make large equity investments in non-financial corporations—a practice prohibited for U.S. banks. Finally, share ownership tends to be much more tightly controlled among founding family,

**TABLE 16.2  Debt Ratios for Selected Industries and Lines of Business**

| Industry or Line of Business | Debt Ratio | Times Interest Earned Ratio |
|---|---|---|
| **Manufacturing industries** | | |
| Books: publishing and printing | 63.1% | 2.6 |
| Dairy products | 62.3 | 2.4 |
| Electronic computers | 58.3 | 2.0 |
| Fertilizers | 56.8 | 2.5 |
| Iron and steel foundries | 61.3 | 2.2 |
| Jewelry and precious metals | 56.5 | 2.3 |
| Machine tools and metalworking equipment | 57.3 | 1.9 |
| Wines, distilled liquors, liqueurs | 56.5 | 2.4 |
| Women's dresses | 62.0 | 3.3 |
| **Wholesaling industries** | | |
| Furniture | 65.9 | 2.1 |
| General groceries | 67.3 | 2.3 |
| Hardware and paints | 59.2 | 2.2 |
| Men's and boys' clothing | 63.7 | 2.6 |
| Petroleum products | 65.7 | 2.0 |
| **Retailing industries** | | |
| Autos, new and used | 79.0 | 1.4 |
| Department stores | 56.3 | 1.6 |
| Radios, TV, consumer electronics | 65.8 | 2.2 |
| Restaurants | 71.0 | 2.4 |
| Shoes | 65.7 | 2.2 |
| **Service industries** | | |
| Accounting, auditing, bookkeeping | 52.7 | 5.4 |
| Advertising agencies | 75.0 | 3.0 |
| Auto repair—general | 63.5 | 2.3 |
| Insurance agents and brokers | 78.9 | 2.4 |
| Physicians | 67.2 | 2.4 |
| Travel agencies | 71.7 | 2.5 |

Source: *RMA Annual Statement Studies, 1992* (fiscal years ended 4/1/91 through 3/31/92). Philadelphia: Robert Morris Associates, 1992. Copyright © 1992 by Robert Morris Associates.

*Note:* Robert Morris Associates recommends that these ratios be regarded only as general guidelines and not as absolute industry norms. No claim is made as to the reprsentativeness of their figures.

institutional, and even public investors in Europe and Asia than is the case for most large U.S. corporations, many of which have up to one million individual shareholders. This tight ownership structure of non-U.S. firms allows them to tolerate a higher level of indebtedness.

On the other hand, important similarities exist between U.S. corporations and corporations in other countries. First, the same industry patterns of capital structure tend to be revealed around the world. For example, in almost all countries, pharmaceutical and other high-growth industrial firms tend to have lower debt ratios than do steel companies, airlines, and electric utility companies. Second, the capital structures of the largest U.S.-based multinational companies, which have access to many different financial markets and financing techniques around the world, typically resemble the capital structures of multinational companies from other countries more than they resemble those of smaller national companies. Finally, the worldwide trend is away from reliance on banks for corporate financing and toward greater reliance on security issuance, so over time the differences in the capital structures of U.S. and non-U.S. firms will probably lessen.

▼▼▼▼▼▼▼▼▼▼▼▼▼▼▼▼▼▼▼▼▼▼▼▼▼▼▼▼▼▼▼

## Progress Review Questions

**16-1.** What is a firm's *capital structure?* How do *debt* and *equity* capital differ?

**16-2.** What ratios can be used to assess the degree of financial leverage in the firm's capital structure?

**16-3.** Discuss the differences, and the reasons for them, in the capital structures of U.S. and non-U.S. corporations. In what ways are the capital structures of U.S. and non-U.S. corporations similar?

▲▲▲▲▲▲▲▲▲▲▲▲▲▲▲▲▲▲▲▲▲▲▲▲▲▲▲▲▲▲▲

# The Optimal Capital Structure

A firm's capital structure is closely related to its cost of capital. Many debates over whether an "optimal" capital structure exists are found in the financial literature. This controversy began in the late 1950s and is not yet resolved. Those who believe that an optimal capital structure exists follow the **traditional approach.** Those who believe such a structure does *not* exist are supporters of the **M and M approach,** named for its initial proponents, Franco Modigliani and Merton H. Miller.

To provide some insight into what is meant by an optimal capital structure, we examine the basic financial relationships associated with the traditional approach.[2] It is generally believed that *the value of the firm is maximized*

**traditional approach**
The theory that an optimal capital structure exists, and that the value of the firm is maximized when the cost of capital is minimized.

**M and M approach**
Named for its initial proponents, Modigliani and Miller, the theory that an optimal capital structure does *not* exist.

---

[2]You may wonder why attention is given only to the traditional approach and not to the Modigliani and Miller approach. The chief reason is that the M and M model is algebraically somewhat rigorous, and it is more important at this level to become familiar with the key concepts that affect managerial decisions than to delve deeply into the theory of finance. Business people tend to believe the traditional as opposed to the M and M approach.

*when the cost of capital is minimized.* Using a modification of the simple zero-growth valuation model (see Equation 12.11 in Chapter 12), we can define the value of the firm, *V*, by Equation 16.1, where EBIT equals earnings before interest and taxes, *T* is the tax rate, EBIT × (1 − *T*) represents the after-tax operating earnings available to debt and equity holders, and $k_a$ is the weighted average cost of capital:

**Equation 16.1**

$$V = \frac{\text{EBIT} \times (1 - T)}{k_a} \tag{16.1}$$

Clearly, if we assume that EBIT is constant, the value of the firm, *V*, is maximized by minimizing the weighted average cost of capital, $k_a$.

## Cost Functions

Figure 16.1A plots three cost functions—the after-tax cost of debt, $k_i$; the cost of equity, $k_s$; and the weighted average cost of capital, $k_a$—as a function of financial leverage measured by the debt ratio (debt-to-total assets). The *cost of debt*, $k_i$, remains low due to the tax subsidy (interest is tax-deductible) but slowly increases with increasing leverage in order to compensate lenders for increasing risk. The *cost of equity*, $k_s$, is above the cost of debt. It increases with increasing financial leverage, but generally more rapidly than the cost of debt. The increase in the cost of equity occurs because, in order to compensate for the higher degree of financial risk, the stockholders require a higher return as leverage increases.

The *weighted average cost of capital, $k_a$*, results from a weighted average of the firm's debt and equity capital costs. At a debt ratio of zero, the firm is 100 percent equity-financed. As debt is substituted for equity and as the debt ratio increases, the weighted average cost of capital declines because the debt cost is less than the equity cost ($k_i < k_s$). As the debt ratio continues to in-

**FIGURE 16.1  Capital Costs and the Optimal Capital Structure**

**A.** As financial leverage increases, the cost of debt, $k_i$, remains constant and then rises, whereas the cost of equity, $k_s$, always rises. The resulting weighted average cost of capital, $k_a$, is U-shaped or saucer-shaped, causing the optimal capital structure to occur at its minimum, *M*. **B.** At the optimal capital structure, *M*, the value of the firm is maximized at *V\**.

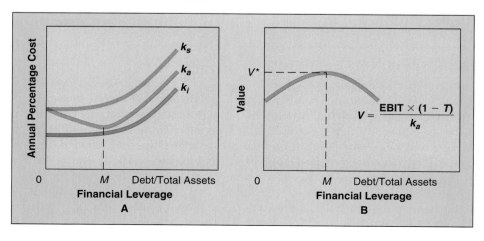

# FINANCE IN ACTION

## Special K's and United Airlines' Capital Structures Are Distinctive Brands

Kellogg, the Battle Creek maker of Rice Krispies, Special K, Corn Flakes, and other cereals, is under attack. Producers of store-brand cereals, led by Ralston Purina, have been able to copy Kellogg's uncomplicated products. As a result, Kellogg's market share declined from over 41% to 37% in five years.

In fact, Kellogg's annual domestic volume hasn't grown much above the billion-pound level sold in 1988. Yet, Kellogg has prided itself on providing investors with a high return on equity. To keep the increase in net income per dollar of stockholders' equity soaring above the 30 percent rate, Kellogg has aggressively bought back many of its shares over the past 10 years. In 1993 alone it retired $600 million worth of its own shares, or 5 percent of the shares outstanding.

United Airlines, the nation's second largest domestic carrier, will have a unique group of shareholders as it pursues its twin goals of maximizing shareholder wealth and minimizing agency problems. Under an arrangement agreed to in early 1994, United's pilots and machinists

unions will receive a minimum of 53 percent of United's stock. The unions will have three board seats and effective veto power over major decisions.

As shareholders, the employees are expected to work to maximize United's profitability and reduce its risk. To aid profitability, union members will grant $5.5 billion in wage concessions over the 1993–1997 period. To reduce the firm's risk, the agreement allows United to match the lower pay scales and relaxed work rules of upstart competitors, such as Southwest Airlines. Under this deal, United's labor costs will be slashed by about 15 percent. Furthermore, as majority shareholders, employees will have an incentive to remain competitive. Shareholders were expected to receive $173—$46 above the value a year earlier—for called shares.

Sources: Andrew E. Serwer, "What Price Brand Loyalty?," *Fortune*, January 10, 1993, pp. 103–104; and Aaron Berstein and Kevin Kelly, "This Give-and-Take May Actually Fly," *Business Week*, December 27, 1993/January 3, 1994, p. 37.

crease, the increased debt and equity costs eventually cause the weighted average cost of capital to rise (after point $M$ in Figure 16.1**A**). This behavior results in a U-shaped, or saucer-shaped, weighted average cost of capital function, $k_a$.

## A Graphic View of the Optimal Structure

Because the maximization of value, $V$, is achieved when the overall cost of capital, $k_a$, is at a minimum (see Equation 16.1), the **optimal capital structure** is therefore that at which the weighted average cost of capital, $k_a$, is minimized. In Figure 16.1**A** the point $M$ represents the minimum weighted average cost of capital—the point of optimal financial leverage and hence of optimal capital structure for the firm. As shown in Figure 16.1**B**, at that point, $M$, the value of the firm is maximized at $V^*$. Generally, the lower the firm's weighted average cost of capital, the higher are project net present values (NPVs) and the greater the number of acceptable projects. Simply stated,

**optimal capital structure**
The capital structure at which the weighted average cost of capital is minimized, thereby maximizing the firm's value.

minimizing the weighted average cost of capital allows management to undertake a larger number of more profitable projects, thereby further increasing the value of the firm.

As a practical matter, there is no way to calculate the optimal capital structure implied by Figure 16.1. Because it is impossible to either know or remain at the precise optimal capital structure, firms generally try to operate in a range that places them near what they believe to be the optimal capital structure. The fact that retained earnings and other new financings cause the firm's actual capital structure to change further justifies the focus on a capital structure range rather than a single optimum.

▼▼▼▼▼▼▼▼▼▼▼▼▼▼▼▼▼▼▼▼▼▼▼▼▼▼▼▼▼▼▼▼▼▼▼

## Progress Review Questions

**16-4.** Under the traditional approach to capital structure, what happens to the cost of debt, the cost of equity, and the weighted average cost of capital as the firm's financial leverage increases from zero? Where is an *optimal capital structure* under this approach, and what is its relationship to the firm's value at that point?

**16-5.** Why does achievement of the optimal capital structure allow management to undertake a larger number of more profitable (higher NPV) projects? As a practical matter, do firms generally attempt to achieve a precise optimal capital structure? Explain.

▲▲▲▲▲▲▲▲▲▲▲▲▲▲▲▲▲▲▲▲▲▲▲▲▲▲▲▲▲▲▲▲▲▲▲

 LG 3

# The EBIT-EPS Approach to Capital Structure

**EBIT-EPS approach**
An approach for selecting the capital structure that maximizes earnings per share (EPS) over the expected range of earnings before interest and taxes (EBIT).

The graphic comparison of financing plans on a set of EBIT-EPS axes was briefly described in Chapter 5. Here, a similar EBIT-EPS approach is used to evaluate alternative capital structures. The **EBIT-EPS approach** to capital structure involves selecting the capital structure that maximizes earnings per share (EPS) over the expected range of earnings before interest and taxes (EBIT). Here the main emphasis is on the effects of various capital structures on *owners' returns*. Because one of the key variables affecting the market value of the firm's shares is its earnings, EPS can be conveniently used to analyze alternative capital structures.

## Presenting a Financing Plan Graphically

To analyze the effects of a firm's capital structure on the owners' returns, we consider the relationship between earnings before interest and taxes (EBIT) and earnings per share (EPS). A constant level of EBIT is assumed in order to isolate the effect on returns of the financing costs associated with alternative capital structures (financing plans). EPS is used to measure the owners' returns, which are expected to be closely related to share price.

**The Data Required**   To graph a financing plan, we need to know at least two EBIT-EPS coordinates. The approach for obtaining coordinates can be illustrated by the following example.

# ▶ E X A M P L E

The current capital structure of JSG Company, a soft-drink manufacturer, is as shown in the table below. Note that JSG's capital structure currently contains only common stock equity; the firm has no debt or preferred stock. If for convenience we assume the firm has no current liabilities, its debt ratio (total liabilities ÷ total assets) is currently 0 percent ($0 ÷ $500,000); it therefore has *zero* financial leverage. Assume the firm is in the 40 percent tax bracket.

| Current Capital Structure | |
| --- | --- |
| Long-term debt | $          0 |
| Common stock equity (25,000 shares @ $20) | 500,000 |
| Total capital (assets) | $500,000 |

EBIT-EPS coordinates for JSG's current capital structure can be found using the technique presented in Chapter 5. Because the EBIT-EPS graph is a straight line, any two EBIT values can be used to find coordinates. Here we arbitrarily use values of $100,000 and $200,000.

| | | |
| --- | --- | --- |
| EBIT (assumed) | $100,000 | $200,000 |
| − Interest (rate × $0 debt) | 0 | 0 |
| Earnings before taxes | $100,000 | $200,000 |
| − Taxes (.40) | 40,000 | 80,000 |
| Earnings after taxes | $ 60,000 | $120,000 |
| EPS | $\dfrac{\$60,000}{25,000 \text{ sh.}} = \$2.40$ | $\dfrac{\$120,000}{25,000 \text{ sh.}} = \$4.80$ |

The two EBIT-EPS coordinates resulting from these calculations are ▶ (1) $100,000 EBIT and $2.40 EPS and (2) $200,000 EBIT and $4.80 EPS.

**Plotting the Data**   The two sets of EBIT-EPS coordinates developed for JSG Company's current zero-leverage (debt ratio = 0 percent) situation can be plotted on a set of EBIT-EPS axes, as shown in Figure 16.2. Because our concern is only with positive levels of EPS, the graph has not been extended below the *x*-axis. The figure shows the level of EPS expected for each level of EBIT.

## Comparing Alternative Capital Structures

The graphic display of financing plans (similar to Figure 16.2) can be used to compare alternative capital structures. The following example illustrates this procedure.

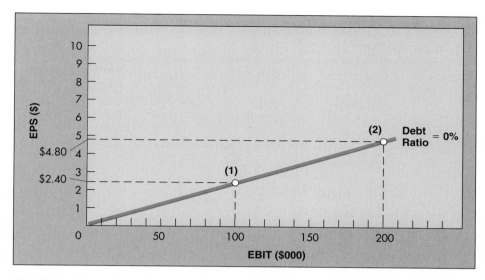

**FIGURE 16.2  Graphic Presentation of JSG Company's Zero-Leverage Financing Plan**

Plotting the two coordinates (1) $100,000 EBIT and $2.40 EPS and (2) $200,000 EBIT and $4.80 EPS on the EBIT-EPS axes results in a straight line representing JSG Company's zero-leverage (debt ratio = 0 percent) financing plan. The figure shows the level of EPS for each level of EBIT.

## E X A M P L E

JSG Company, whose current zero-leverage capital structure was described in the preceding example, is contemplating shifting its capital structure to either of two leveraged positions. To maintain its $500,000 of total capital, JSG's capital structure is shifted to greater leverage by issuing debt and using the proceeds to retire an equivalent amount of common stock. The two alternative capital structures result in debt ratios of 30 percent and 60 percent, respectively. The basic information on the current and two alternative capital structures is summarized in Table 16.3.

Using the data in Table 16.3, we can calculate the coordinates needed to plot the 30 percent and 60 percent debt capital structures. For convenience, using the same $100,000 and $200,000 EBIT values used earlier to plot the current capital structure, we get the information in the following table.

| | Capital Structure | | | |
|---|---|---|---|---|
| | 30% Debt | | 60% Debt | |
| EBIT (assumed) | $100,000 | $200,000 | $100,000 | $200,000 |
| − Interest (Table 16.3) | 15,000 | 15,000 | 49,500 | 49,500 |
| Earnings before taxes | $ 85,000 | $185,000 | $ 50,500 | $150,500 |
| − Taxes (.40) | 34,000 | 74,000 | 20,200 | 60,200 |
| Earnings after taxes | $ 51,000 | $111,000 | $ 30,300 | $ 90,300 |
| EPS | $\dfrac{\$51,000}{17,500 \text{ sh.}} = \$2.91$ | $\dfrac{\$111,000}{17,500 \text{ sh.}} = \$6.34$ | $\dfrac{\$30,300}{10,000 \text{ sh.}} = \$3.03$ | $\dfrac{\$90,300}{10,000 \text{ sh.}} = \$9.03$ |

**TABLE 16.3   Basic Information on JSG Company's Current and Alternative Capital Structures**

| Capital Structure Debt Ratio (1) | Total Assets[a] (2) | Debt [(1) × (2)] (3) | Equity [(2) − (3)] (4) | Interest Rate on Debt[b] (5) | Annual Interest [(3) × (5)] (6) | Shares of Common Stock Outstanding [(4) ÷ $20][c] (7) |
|---|---|---|---|---|---|---|
| 0% (current) | $500,000 | $    0 | $500,000 | 0  % | $    0 | 25,000 |
| 30 | 500,000 | 150,000 | 350,000 | 10 | 15,000 | 17,500 |
| 60 | 500,000 | 300,000 | 200,000 | 16.5 | 49,500 | 10,000 |

[a]Because for convenience the firm is assumed to have no current liabilities, total assets equals total capital of $500,000.

[b]The interest rate on all debt increases with increases in the debt ratio due to the greater leverage and risk associated with higher debt ratios.

[c]The $20 value represents the book value of common stock equity.

The two sets of EBIT-EPS coordinates developed in the table at the bottom of the preceding page, along with those developed earlier for the current zero-leverage capital structure, are summarized in Table 16.4. They are used to plot the 30 percent and 60 percent capital structures (along with the 0 percent structure) on the EBIT-EPS axes in Figure 16.3. An analysis of the figure shows that over certain ranges of EBIT, each capital structure reflects superiority over the others in terms of maximizing EPS. The zero-leverage capital structure (debt ratio = 0 percent) is superior to either of the other capital structures for levels of EBIT between $0 and $50,000. Between $50,000 and $95,500 of EBIT, the capital structure associated with a debt ratio of 30 percent is preferred. At a level of EBIT in excess of $95,500, the capital structure associated with a debt ratio of 60 percent provides the highest earnings per share.[3]

## Considering Risk in EBIT-EPS Analysis

When interpreting EBIT-EPS analysis, the financial analyst must consider the risk of each capital structure alternative. Graphically, the risk of each capital structure can be viewed in light of the *financial breakeven point* (EBIT-axis intercept) and the *degree of financial leverage* reflected in the slope of the capital structure line. The higher the financial breakeven point and the steeper the slope of the capital structure line, the greater the financial risk. Further assessment of risk can be performed using ratios. With increased financial leverage, as measured using the debt ratio, we expect a corresponding decline in the firm's ability to make scheduled interest payments, as measured using the times interest earned ratio.

---

[3]An algebraic technique can be used to find the *indifference points* between the capital structure alternatives. Due to its relative complexity, this technique is not presented. Instead, emphasis is given here to the visual estimation of these points from the graph.

**TABLE 16.4   EBIT-EPS Coordinates for JSG Company's Selected Capital Structures**

| | EBIT | |
|---|---|---|
| | $100,000 | $200,000 |
| **Capital Structure Debt Ratio** | **Earnings per Share (EPS)** | |
| 0% | $2.40 | $4.80 |
| 30 | 2.91 | 6.34 |
| 60 | 3.03 | 9.03 |

# EXAMPLE

Reviewing the three capital structures plotted for JSG Company in Figure 16.3, we can see that as the debt ratio increases, so does the financial risk of each alternative. Both the financial breakeven point and the slope of the capital structure lines increase with increasing debt ratios. If we use the $100,000 EBIT value, the times interest earned ratio (EBIT ÷ interest) for the zero-leverage capital structure is infinity ($100,000 ÷ $0). For the 30 percent debt case it is 6.67 ($100,000 ÷ $15,000). For the 60 percent debt case it is 2.02 ($100,000 ÷ $49,500). Because lower times interest earned ratios reflect higher risk, these ratios support the earlier conclusion that the risk of the

**FIGURE 16.3   A Graphic Comparison of Selected Capital Structures for JSG Company**

The zero-leverage capital structure (debt ratio = 0 percent) maximizes EPS when EBIT is between $0 and $50,000. Between $50,000 and $95,500 of EBIT, the capital structure with the 30 percent debt ratio is preferred. For EBIT in excess of $95,500, the capital structure with the 60 percent debt ratio maximizes EPS.

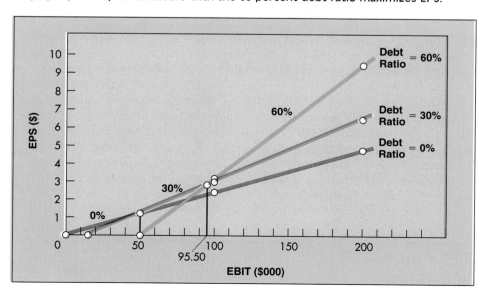

capital structures increases with increasing financial leverage. The capital structure for a debt ratio of 60 percent is riskier than that for a debt ratio of 30 percent, which in turn is riskier than the capital structure for a debt ratio of 0 percent.

## Basic Shortcoming of EBIT-EPS Analysis

The most important point to recognize when using EBIT-EPS analysis is that this technique tends to concentrate on *maximizing earnings rather than maximizing owners' wealth*. Although there may be a positive relationship between these two objectives, the use of an EPS-maximizing approach ignores risk. Because risk increases with increases in financial leverage, the maximization of EPS *does not* ensure owners' wealth maximization. To select the best capital structure, the financial manager must integrate both return (EPS) and risk (via the required return, $k_s$) into a valuation framework consistent with the capital structure theory presented earlier. Although more sophisticated approaches that consider both return and risk are available, their complexity puts them beyond the scope of this text.

▼▼▼▼▼▼▼▼▼▼▼▼▼▼▼▼▼▼▼▼▼▼▼▼▼▼▼▼▼▼

## Progress Review Question

**16-6.** Explain the *EBIT-EPS approach* to capital structure. Include in your explanation a graph indicating the financial breakeven point; label the axes. Is this approach consistent with maximization of value? Explain.

▲▲▲▲▲▲▲▲▲▲▲▲▲▲▲▲▲▲▲▲▲▲▲▲▲▲▲▲▲▲

# Dividend Fundamentals

Dividend policy, like capital structure, can significantly affect the firm's share price. Dividends represent a source of cash flow to stockholders and provide them with information about the firm's current and future performance. Because **retained earnings**—earnings not distributed as dividends—are a form of *internal* financing, the dividend decision can significantly affect the firm's *external* financing requirements. In other words, if the firm needs financing, the larger the cash dividend paid, the greater the amount of financing that must be raised externally. Such financing is obtained through borrowing or through the sale of preferred or common stock. (Remember that although dividends are charged to retained earnings, they are actually paid out of cash.) To provide an understanding of the fundamentals of dividend policy, we discuss the procedures for paying cash dividends, dividend reinvestment plans, the relevance of dividend policy, and the key factors affecting dividend policy.

**retained earnings**
Earnings not distributed as dividends; a form of *internal* financing.

## Cash Dividend Payment Procedures

The payment of cash dividends to corporate stockholders is decided by the firm's board of directors. The directors normally hold a quarterly or semiannual dividend meeting at which they evaluate the past period's financial performance and future outlook. They then determine whether and in what amount dividends should be paid. Insight into recent dividends paid, if any, can typically be found in their annual stockholders' reports. The payment date of the cash dividend, if one is declared, must also be established.

**Amount of Dividends**   Whether dividends should be paid and, if they are, how large they should be are important decisions that depend largely on the firm's dividend policy. Most firms pay some cash dividends each period. The amount is generally fixed, although significant increases or decreases in earnings may justify changing it. Most firms have a set policy with respect to the amount of the periodic dividend, but the firm's directors can change this amount at the dividend meeting.

**Relevant Dates**   If the directors of the firm declare a dividend, they also indicate the record and payment dates associated with the dividend. Typically, the directors issue a statement indicating their dividend decision, the record date, and the payment date. This statement is generally quoted in *The Wall Street Journal, Barron's,* and other financial news media.

> **date of record (dividends)**
> The date, set by the firm's directors, on which all persons whose names are recorded as stockholders will receive a declared dividend at a specified future time.

> **holders of record**
> Owners of the firm's shares on the *date of record*.

> **ex dividend**
> Period beginning four *business days* prior to the date of record during which a stock is sold without the right to receive the current dividend.

> **payment date**
> The actual date on which the firm mails the dividend payment to the holders of record.

**Record Date.**  All persons whose names are recorded as stockholders on the **date of record,** which is set by the directors, receive a declared dividend at a specified future time. These stockholders are often referred to as **holders of record.** Due to the time needed to make bookkeeping entries when a stock is traded, the stock begins selling **ex dividend** four *business days* prior to the date of record. A simple way to determine the first day on which the stock sells ex dividend is to subtract four from the date of record; if a weekend intervenes, subtract six days. Purchasers of a stock selling ex dividend do not receive the current dividend. Ignoring general market fluctuations, the stock's price is expected to drop by the amount of the declared dividend on the ex dividend date.

**Payment Date.**  The payment date is also set by the directors. It is generally set a few weeks after the record date. The **payment date** is the actual date on which the firm mails the dividend payment to the holders of record. An example should clarify the various dates and accounting entries.

# EXAMPLE

At the quarterly dividend meeting of Junot Company, a distributor of office products, held June 10, the directors declared an $.80 per share cash dividend for holders of record on Monday, July 1. The firm had 100,000 shares of common stock outstanding. The payment date for the dividend was August 1. Before the dividend was declared, the key accounts of the firm were as follows:

| | | | |
|---|---|---|---|
| Cash | $200,000 | Dividends payable | $        0 |
| | | Retained earnings | 1,000,000 |

When the dividend was announced by the directors, $80,000 of the retained earnings ($.80 per share × 100,000 shares) was transferred to the dividends payable account. The key accounts thus became:

| Cash | $200,000 | Dividends payable | $ 80,000 |
| | | Retained earnings | 920,000 |

Junot Company's stock began selling ex dividend four *business days* prior to the date of record, which was June 25. This date was found by subtracting six days (since a weekend intervened) from the July 1 date of record. Purchasers of Junot's stock on June 24 or earlier received the rights to the dividends; those purchasing the stock on or after June 25 did not. Assuming a stable market, Junot's stock price was expected to drop by approximately $.80 per share when it began selling ex dividend on June 25. When the August 1 payment date arrived, the firm mailed dividend checks to the holders of record as of July 1. This produced the following balances in the key accounts of the firm:

| Cash | $120,000 | Dividends payable | $    0 |
| | | Retained earnings | 920,000 |

The net effect of declaration and payment of the dividend was to reduce the firm's total assets (and stockholders' equity) by $80,000.

## Dividend Reinvestment Plans

Today many firms offer **dividend reinvestment plans (DRPs),** which enable stockholders to use dividends received on the firm's stock to acquire additional shares—even fractional shares—at little or no transaction (brokerage) cost. (A small number of these companies, such as Exxon, Texaco, and W.R. Grace, allow investors to make their *initial purchases* of the firm's stock directly from the company without going through a broker.) Under current tax law, cash dividends from all plans (or the value of the stocks received through a DRP) are taxed as ordinary income. In addition, when the acquired shares are sold, if the proceeds are in excess of the original purchase price, the capital gain is also taxed as ordinary income.

Dividend reinvestment plans can be handled by a company in either of two ways. Both allow the stockholder to elect to have dividends reinvested in the firm's shares. In one approach, a third-party trustee is paid a fee to buy the firm's outstanding shares in the open market on behalf of the shareholders who wish to reinvest their dividends. This type of plan benefits participating shareholders by allowing them to use their dividends to purchase shares generally at a lower transaction cost than they would otherwise pay. The second approach involves buying newly issued shares directly from the firm without paying any transaction costs. This approach allows the firm to raise new capital while permitting owners to reinvest their dividends, frequently at about 5 percent below the current market price. Clearly, the existence of a DRP may enhance the appeal of a firm's shares.

**dividend reinvestment plans (DRPs)**
Plans that enable stockholders to use dividends received on the firm's stock to acquire additional full or fractional shares at little or no transaction (brokerage) cost.

## The Relevance of Dividend Policy

During the past 35 or so years the results of a great deal of research concerning dividend policy have been reported in the financial literature. Although this research has provided some interesting arguments and insights about dividend policy, capital budgeting and capital structure decisions are generally considered far more important than dividend decisions. In other words, good investment and financing decisions should not be sacrificed for a dividend policy of questionable importance. A number of key questions have yet to be resolved: Does dividend policy matter? What effect does dividend policy have on share price? Is there a model that can be used to evaluate alternative dividend policies in view of share value? Here we begin by describing the residual theory of dividends. It is used as a backdrop for discussion of the key arguments in support of dividend irrelevance and then those in support of dividend relevance.

**residual theory of dividends**
A theory that the dividend paid by a firm should be the amount left over after all acceptable investment opportunities have been undertaken.

### The Residual Theory of Dividends

One school of thought—the **residual theory of dividends**—suggests that the dividend paid by a firm should be viewed as a *residual*—the amount left over after all acceptable investment opportunities have been undertaken. According to this approach, as long as the firm's equity need is in excess of the amount of retained earnings, no cash dividend is paid. If an excess of retained earnings exists, the residual amount is then distributed as a cash dividend. This view of dividends tends to suggest that the required return of investors, $k_s$, is *not* influenced by the firm's dividend policy—a premise that in turn suggests that dividend policy is irrelevant.

### Dividend Irrelevance Arguments

The residual theory of dividends suggests that dividends are irrelevant—that they represent an earnings residual rather than an active decision variable that affects the firm's value. The major advocates of this view are Franco Modigliani and Merton H. Miller (commonly referred to as M and M). They argue that the firm's value is determined solely by the earning power and risk of its assets (investments) and that the manner in which it splits its earnings stream between dividends and internally retained (and reinvested) funds does not affect this value.

However, some studies have shown that large dividend changes affect share price in the same direction—increases in dividends result in increased share price, and vice versa. In response, M and M argue that these effects are attributable not to the dividend itself but rather to the **informational content** of dividends with respect to future earnings. As a result, an increase in dividends causes investors to bid up the share price, and a decrease in dividends causes a decrease in share price.

**informational content**
The information provided by the dividends of a firm with respect to future earnings, which causes owners to bid up or down the price of the firm's stock.

**clientele effect**
The argument that a firm attracts shareholders whose preferences with respect to the payment and stability of dividends correspond to the payment pattern and stability of the firm itself.

M and M further argue that a **clientele effect** exists: A firm attracts shareholders whose preferences with respect to the payment and stability of dividends correspond to the payment pattern and stability of the firm itself. In other words, investors desiring stable and predictable dividends as a source of income hold the stock of firms that pay about the same dividend amount each period; investors preferring to earn capital gains are more attracted to growing firms that reinvest a large portion of their earnings, which results in a fairly unstable pattern of dividends. Because the shareholders get what they expect, M and M argue that the value of their firm's stock is unaffected by dividend policy.

In summary, M and M and other dividend irrelevance proponents argue that—all else being equal—an investor's required return, $k_s$, and therefore the value of the firm, are unaffected by dividend policy for the following reasons:

1. The firm's value is determined solely by the earning power and risk of its assets.

2. If dividends do affect value, they do solely because of their informational content, which indicates management's earnings expectations.
3. A clientele effect exists that causes a firm's shareholders to receive the dividends that they expect.

These views of M and M with respect to dividend irrelevance are consistent with the residual theory, which focuses on making the best investment decisions in order to maximize share value. The proponents of dividend irrelevance conclude that because dividends are irrelevant to a firm's value, the firm does not need to have a dividend policy.

**Dividend Relevance Arguments**   The key argument in support of dividend relevance is attributed to Myron J. Gordon and John Lintner, who suggest that stockholders prefer current dividends and that there is, in fact, a direct relationship between the dividend policy of the firm and its market value. Fundamental to this proposition is their **bird-in-the-hand argument.** It suggests that investors are generally risk-averse and attach less risk to current as opposed to future dividends or capital gains. Simply stated, "a bird in the hand is worth two in the bush." Current dividend payments are therefore believed to reduce investor uncertainty, causing investors to discount the firm's earnings at a lower rate, $k_s$, thereby—all else being equal—placing a higher value on the firm's stock. Conversely, if dividends are reduced or not paid, investor uncertainty increases, raising the required return, $k_s$, and lowering the stock's value.

> **bird-in-the-hand argument**
> The belief, in support of dividend relevance arguments, that current dividend payments ("a bird in the hand") reduce investor uncertainty and result in a higher value for the firm's stock.

Although many other arguments and counter-arguments relating to the question of dividend relevance have been put forward, researchers have yet to develop a model that can be used to evaluate alternative policies in view of share value. In practice, however, the actions of financial managers and stockholders alike tend to support the belief that dividend policy affects stock value.[4] Because our concern centers on the day-to-day behavior of business firms, the remainder of this chapter is consistent with the belief that dividends *are relevant*—that each firm must develop a dividend policy that fulfills the goals of owners and maximizes their wealth as reflected in the firm's share price.

## Factors Affecting Dividend Policy

Before discussing the basic types of dividend policies, we should consider the factors involved in formulating dividend policy. These include legal constraints, contractual constraints, internal constraints, the firm's growth prospects, owner considerations, and market considerations.

**Legal Constraints**   Most states prohibit corporations from paying out as cash dividends any portion of the firm's "legal capital," which is measured by the par value of common stock. Other states define legal capital to include

---

[4]A common exception is small firms, because they frequently treat dividends as a residual remaining after all acceptable investments have been initiated. This course of action occurs because small firms usually do not have ready access to financial markets. The use of retained earnings therefore acts as a key source of financing for growth, which is generally an important goal of a small firm.

not only the par value of the common stock but also any paid-in capital in excess of par. These "capital impairment restrictions" are generally established to provide a sufficient equity base to protect creditors' claims. An example clarifies the differing definitions of capital.

# EXAMPLE

The stockholders' equity account of Moeller Flour Company, a large grain processor, is presented in the following table.

### Moeller Flour Company's Stockholders' Equity

| | |
|---|---|
| Common stock at par | $100,000 |
| Paid-in capital in excess of par | 200,000 |
| Retained earnings | 140,000 |
| Total stockholders' equity | $440,000 |

In states where the firm's legal capital is defined as the par value of its common stock, the firm can pay out $340,000 ($200,000 + $140,000) in cash dividends without impairing its capital. In states where the firm's legal capital includes all paid-in capital, the firm can pay out only $140,000 in cash dividends.

An earnings requirement limiting the amount of dividends to the sum of the firm's present and past earnings is sometimes imposed. In other words, the firm cannot pay more in cash dividends than the sum of its most recent and past retained earnings. However, *the firm is not prohibited from paying more in dividends than its current earnings.*[5]

# EXAMPLE

Assume Moeller Flour Company, from the preceding example, in the year just ended has $30,000 in earnings available for common stock dividends. An analysis of the stockholders' equity account shown in the table above indicates that the firm has past retained earnings of $140,000. Thus it can legally pay dividends of up to $170,000.

If a firm has overdue liabilities or is legally insolvent or bankrupt (if the fair market value of its assets is less than its liabilities), most states prohibit its payment of cash dividends. In addition, the Internal Revenue Service prohibits firms from accumulating earnings in order to reduce the owners' taxes. A firm's owners must pay income taxes on dividends when received, but the owners are not taxed on capital gains in market value until the stock is sold. A firm may retain a large portion of earnings in order to delay the payment

---

[5] A firm having an operating loss in the current period can still pay cash dividends as long as sufficient retained earnings against which to charge the dividend are available and, of course, as long as it has the cash with which to make the payments.

of taxes by its owners. If the IRS can determine that a firm has accumulated an excess of earnings in order to allow owners to delay paying ordinary income taxes, it may levy an **excess earnings accumulation tax** on any retained earnings above $250,000—the amount currently exempt from this tax for all firms except personal service corporations.

**Contractual Constraints**    Often the firm's ability to pay cash dividends is constrained by certain restrictive provisions in a loan agreement. Generally, these constraints prohibit the payment of cash dividends until a certain level of earnings has been achieved, or they may limit the amount of dividends paid to a certain dollar amount or percentage of earnings. Constraints on dividend payments help to protect creditors from losses due to insolvency on the part of the firm. The violation of a contractual constraint is generally grounds for a demand of immediate payment by the funds supplier affected.

**Internal Constraints**    The firm's ability to pay cash dividends is generally constrained by the amount of excess cash available rather than the level of retained earnings against which to charge them. Although it is possible for a firm to borrow funds to pay dividends, lenders are generally reluctant to make such loans because they produce no tangible or operating benefits that will help the firm repay the loan. Although a firm may have high earnings, its ability to pay dividends may be constrained by a low level of liquid assets (cash and marketable securities).

**excess earnings accumulation tax**
The tax levied by the IRS on retained earnings above $250,000, when it has determined that a firm has accumulated an excess of earnings in order to allow owners to delay paying ordinary income taxes.

▶ **E X A M P L E**

The Moeller Flour Company's stockholders' equity account presented earlier indicates that if the firm's legal capital is defined as all paid-in capital, the firm can pay $140,000 in dividends. If the firm has total liquid assets of $50,000 ($20,000 in cash + marketable securities worth $30,000) and $35,000 of this is needed for operations, the maximum cash dividend the firm can pay is $15,000 ($50,000 − $35,000).

**Growth Prospects**    The firm's financial requirements are directly related to the degree of asset expansion anticipated. If the firm is in a growth stage, it may need all the funds it can get to finance capital expenditures. A growing firm also requires funds to maintain and improve its assets. High-growth firms typically find themselves constantly in need of funds. Their financial requirements may be characterized as large and immediate. Firms exhibiting little or no growth may, nevertheless, periodically need funds to replace or renew assets.

A firm must evaluate its financial position from the standpoint of profitability and risk in order to develop insight into its ability to raise capital externally. It must determine not only its ability to raise funds but also the cost and speed with which financing can be obtained. Generally, a large, mature firm has adequate access to new capital, whereas the funds available to a rapidly growing firm may not be sufficient to support its numerous acceptable projects. A growth firm is likely to have to depend heavily on internal financing through retained earnings to take advantage of profitable projects; it is likely to pay out only a very small percentage of its earnings as dividends. A more stable firm that needs long-term funds only for planned outlays is in a better position to pay out a large proportion of its earnings, especially if it has ready sources of financing.

**Owner Considerations**   In establishing a dividend policy, the firm's primary concern should be to maximize owners' wealth. Although it is impossible to establish a policy that maximizes each owner's wealth, the firm must establish a policy that has a favorable effect on the wealth of the *majority* of owners.

One consideration is the *tax status of a firm's owners*. If a firm has a large percentage of wealthy stockholders who are in a high tax bracket, it may decide to pay out a *lower* percentage of its earnings to allow the owners to delay the payment of taxes until they sell the stock. Of course, when the stock is sold, if the proceeds are in excess of the original purchase price, the capital gain is taxed as ordinary income. Lower income shareholders, however, who need dividend income, prefer a *higher* payout of earnings.

A second consideration is the *owners' investment opportunities*. A firm should not retain funds for investment in projects yielding lower returns than the owners can obtain from external investments of equal risk. The firm should evaluate the returns expected on its own investment opportunities and, using present-value techniques, determine whether greater returns are obtainable from external investments, such as government securities or other corporate stocks. If it appears that the owners have better opportunities externally, the firm should pay out a higher percentage of its earnings. If the firm's investment opportunities are at least as good as similar-risk external investments, a lower payout is justifiable.

A final consideration is the *potential dilution of ownership*. If a firm pays out a higher percentage of earnings, new equity capital has to be raised with common stock. The result may be the dilution of both control and earnings for the existing owners. By paying out a low percentage of its earnings, the firm can minimize such possibility of dilution.

**Market Considerations**   Because the wealth of the firm's owners is reflected in the market price of the firm's shares, an awareness of the market's probable response to certain types of policies is helpful in formulating a suitable dividend policy. Stockholders are believed to value a *fixed or increasing level of dividends* as opposed to a fluctuating pattern of dividends. In addition, stockholders are believed to value a policy of *continuous dividend payment*. Because regularly paying a fixed or increasing dividend eliminates uncertainty about the frequency and magnitude of dividends, the earnings of the firm are likely to be discounted at a lower rate. This should result in an increase in the market value of the stock and therefore increased owners' wealth.

A final market consideration is the *informational content* of dividends. Shareholders often view the firm's dividend payment as an indicator of future success. A stable and continuous dividend conveys to the owners that the firm is in good health and that there is no reason for concern. If the firm skips a dividend payment in a given period due to a loss or to very low earnings, shareholders are likely to react unfavorably. The nonpayment of the dividend creates uncertainty about the future, and this uncertainty is likely to result in lower stock value. Owners and investors generally construe a dividend payment during a period of losses as an indication that the loss is merely temporary.

▼▼▼▼▼▼▼▼▼▼▼▼▼▼▼▼▼▼▼▼▼▼▼▼▼▼▼▼▼▼▼▼

## Progress Review Questions

**16-7.** How do the date of record and the holders of record relate to the payment of cash dividends? What does the term *ex dividend* mean? Who sets the dividend payment date?

**16-8.** What is a *dividend reinvestment plan?* What benefit is available to plan participants? Describe the two ways in which companies can handle such plans.

**16-9.** Describe the *residual theory of dividends.* Does following this approach lead to a stable dividend? Is this approach consistent with dividend relevance? Explain.

**16-10.** Describe, compare, and contrast the basic arguments relative to the irrelevance or relevance of dividend policy given by
  **a.** Franco Modigliani and Merton H. Miller (M and M)
  **b.** Myron J. Gordon and John Lintner

**16-11.** Briefly describe each of the following factors affecting dividend policy:
  **a.** Legal constraints
  **b.** Contractual constraints
  **c.** Internal constraints
  **d.** Growth prospects
  **e.** Owner considerations
  **f.** Market considerations

▲▲▲▲▲▲▲▲▲▲▲▲▲▲▲▲▲▲▲▲▲▲▲▲▲▲▲▲▲▲▲▲

# Types of Dividend Policies

The firm's **dividend policy** represents a plan of action to be followed whenever the dividend decision must be made. The dividend policy must be formulated with two basic objectives in mind: maximizing the wealth of the firm's owners and providing for sufficient financing. These two objectives are interrelated. They must be fulfilled in light of a number of factors—legal, contractual, internal, growth, owner-related, and market-related—that limit the policy alternatives. Three of the more commonly used dividend policies are described in the following sections. A particular firm's cash dividend policy may incorporate elements of each.

## Constant-Payout-Ratio Dividend Policy

One type of dividend policy occasionally adopted by firms is the use of a constant payout ratio. The **dividend-payout ratio,** calculated by dividing the firm's cash dividend per share by its earnings per share, indicates the percentage of each dollar earned that is distributed to the owners in the form of cash. With a **constant-payout-ratio dividend policy,** the firm establishes that a certain percentage of earnings is paid to owners in each dividend period. The problem

**dividend policy**
The firm's plan of action to be followed whenever a decision concerning dividends must be made.

**dividend-payout ratio**
Indicates the percentage of each dollar earned that is distributed to the owners in the form of cash.

**constant-payout-ratio dividend policy**
A dividend policy based on the payment of a certain percentage of earnings to owners in each dividend period.

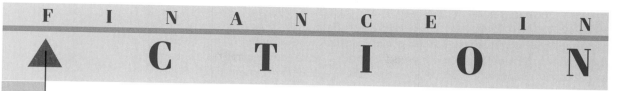

# FINANCE IN ACTION

## Ethics

### First Boston Identifies High-Dividend-Yield Shares and Federated Funds Recommends Avoiding Shares with "Too High" Dividend Yields

Considering the range of dividend policies available to the financial manager, one may wonder what constitutes an average dividend yield and high dividend yield. At year-end 1993, the dividend yield on the *Standard & Poors 500* stood at 2.7 percent. The year-end yields on the industrial, transportation, and utility indexes were 2.7 percent, 1.1 percent, and 5.8 percent, respectively.

First Boston, a closed-end mutual fund traded on the New York Stock Exchange, cites all shares offering over 3.8 percent as being high dividend yield shares. In addition to utilities, First Boston's high-dividend-yield listing perennially includes banks and oil companies. In 1994, the pharmaceutical industry replaced telephone companies as another industry offering high dividend yields.

Chris Wiles, financial analyst at Federated Funds, warns investors to avoid abnormally high dividends. As a rule of thumb, Wiles only buys firms with dividend yields under 6 percent. Even then, Wiles requires at least a 3 percent capital gain for selection. Otherwise, the high dividend yield may be a consequence of poor performance (i.e., a low share price) that may lead to a subsequent dividend cut.

Sources: "Databank," *The Wall Street Journal*, January 3, 1994, p. 21; and Susan E. Kuhn, "How to Get Good Returns without Stretching for Yield," *Fortune*, January 1993, p. 22.

with this policy is that if the firm's earnings drop or if a loss occurs in a given period, the dividends may be low or even nonexistent. Because dividends are often considered an indicator of the firm's future condition and status, the firm's stock price may thus be adversely affected by this type of action. An example clarifies the problems stemming from a constant-payout-ratio policy.

## EXAMPLE

Nader Industries, a miner of potassium, has a policy of paying out 40 percent of earnings in cash dividends. In periods when a loss occurs, the firm's policy is to pay no cash dividends. Nader's earnings per share, dividends per share, and average price per share for the past six years were as shown in the following table.

| Year | Earnings/Share | Dividends/Share | Average Price/Share |
| --- | --- | --- | --- |
| 1995 | $−0.50 | $0.00 | $42.00 |
| 1994 | 3.00 | 1.20 | 52.00 |
| 1993 | 1.75 | 0.70 | 48.00 |
| 1992 | −1.50 | 0.00 | 38.00 |
| 1991 | 2.00 | 0.80 | 46.00 |
| 1990 | 4.50 | 1.80 | 50.00 |

Dividends increased in 1992–1993 and in 1993–1994 and decreased in 1990–1991, 1991–1992, and 1994–1995. The data show that in years of decreasing dividends the firm's stock price dropped; when dividends increased, the price of the stock increased. Nader's sporadic dividend payments appear to make its owners uncertain about the returns they can expect from their investment in the firm and therefore tend to generally depress the stock's price. Although a constant-payout-ratio dividend policy is used by some firms, it is *not* recommended.

## Regular Dividend Policy

Another type of dividend policy, the **regular dividend policy,** is based on the payment of a fixed-dollar dividend in each period. The regular dividend policy provides the owners with generally positive information, indicating that the firm is okay and thereby minimizing their uncertainty. Often, firms using this policy increase the regular dividend once a *proven* increase in earnings has occurred. Under this policy, dividends are almost never decreased.

**regular dividend policy**
A dividend policy based on the payment of a fixed-dollar dividend in each period.

► E X A M P L E

The dividend policy of Norman Oil Company, an oil exploration company, is to pay annual dividends of $1.00 per share until per-share earnings have exceeded $4.00 for three consecutive years. The annual dividend is then raised to $1.50 per share, and a new earnings plateau is established. The firm does not anticipate decreasing its dividend unless its liquidity is in jeopardy. Norman's earnings per share, dividends per share, and average price per share for the past 12 years were as shown in the following table.

| Year | Earnings/Share | Dividends/Share | Average Price/Share |
|------|----------------|-----------------|---------------------|
| 1995 | $4.50 | $1.50 | $47.50 |
| 1994 | 3.90 | 1.50 | 46.50 |
| 1993 | 4.60 | 1.50 | 45.00 |
| 1992 | 4.20 | 1.00 | 43.00 |
| 1991 | 5.00 | 1.00 | 42.00 |
| 1990 | 2.00 | 1.00 | 38.50 |
| 1989 | 6.00 | 1.00 | 38.00 |
| 1988 | 3.00 | 1.00 | 36.00 |
| 1987 | 0.75 | 1.00 | 33.00 |
| 1986 | 0.50 | 1.00 | 33.00 |
| 1985 | 2.70 | 1.00 | 33.50 |
| 1984 | 2.85 | 1.00 | 35.00 |

Whatever the level of earnings, Norman Oil paid dividends of $1.00 per share through 1992. In 1993 the dividend was raised to $1.50 per share because earnings in excess of $4.00 per share had been achieved for three years. In 1993 the firm also had to establish a new earnings plateau for further dividend increases. Norman Oil Company's average price per share exhibited a stable, increasing behavior in spite of a somewhat volatile pattern of earnings.

**target dividend-payout ratio**
A policy under which the firm attempts to pay out a certain percentage of earnings as a stated dollar dividend, which it adjusts toward a target payout as proven earnings increases occur.

Often, a regular dividend policy is built around a **target dividend-payout ratio.** Under this policy the firm attempts to pay out a certain percentage of earnings, but rather than let dividends fluctuate, it pays a stated dollar dividend and adjusts it toward the target payout as proven earnings increases occur. For instance, Norman Oil Company appears to have a target payout ratio of around 35 percent. The payout was about 35 percent ($1.00 ÷ $2.85) when the dividend policy was set in 1984, and when the dividend was raised to $1.50 in 1993, the payout ratio was about 33 percent ($1.50 ÷ $4.60).

### Low-Regular-and-Extra Dividend Policy

**low-regular-and-extra dividend policy**
A dividend policy based on paying a low regular dividend, supplemented by an additional dividend when earnings warrant it.

**extra dividend**
An additional dividend optionally paid by the firm if earnings are higher than normal in a given period.

Some firms establish a **low-regular-and-extra dividend policy,** paying a low regular dividend, supplemented by an additional dividend when earnings warrant it. If earnings are higher than normal in a given period, the firm may pay this additional dividend, which is designated an **extra dividend.** By designating the amount by which the dividend exceeds the regular payment as an extra dividend, the firm avoids giving shareholders false hopes. The use of the "extra" designation is especially common among companies that experience cyclical shifts in earnings.

By establishing a low regular dividend that is paid each period, the firm gives investors the stable income necessary to build confidence in the firm, and the extra dividend permits them to share in the "earnings" if the firm experiences an especially good period. Firms using this policy must raise the level of the regular dividend once proven increases in earnings have been achieved. The extra dividend should not be a regular event, or it becomes meaningless. The use of a target dividend-payout ratio in establishing the regular dividend level is advisable.

▼▼▼▼▼▼▼▼▼▼▼▼▼▼▼▼▼▼▼▼▼▼▼▼▼▼▼▼

## Progress Review Question

**16-12.** What are (a) a *constant-payout-ratio dividend policy,* (b) a *regular dividend policy,* and (c) a *low-regular-and-extra dividend policy?* What are the effects of these policies?

▲▲▲▲▲▲▲▲▲▲▲▲▲▲▲▲▲▲▲▲▲▲▲▲▲▲▲▲

LG **6**

# Other Forms of Dividends

A number of other forms of dividends are available to the firm. In this section we discuss two other methods of paying dividends—stock dividends and stock repurchases—as well as a closely related topic, stock splits.

**stock dividend**
The payment to existing owners of a dividend in the form of stock.

### Stock Dividends

A **stock dividend** is the payment to existing owners of a dividend in the form of stock. Often, firms pay stock dividends as a replacement for or a supplement to cash dividends. Although stock dividends do not have a real value, stockholders may perceive them to represent something they did not have before and therefore to have value.

**Accounting Aspects**  In an accounting sense, the payment of a stock dividend is a shifting of funds between capital accounts rather than a use of funds. When a firm declares a stock dividend, the procedures with respect to announcement and distribution are the same as those described earlier for a cash dividend. The accounting entries associated with the payment of stock dividends vary depending on whether or not it is a **small (ordinary) stock dividend**—a stock dividend representing less than 20 to 25 percent of the common stock outstanding at the time the dividend is declared. Because small stock dividends are most common, the accounting entries associated with them are illustrated in the following example.

**small (ordinary) stock dividend**
A stock dividend that represents less than 20 to 25 percent of the common stock outstanding at the time the dividend is declared.

▶ **E X A M P L E**

The current stockholders' equity on the balance sheet of Wieta Company, a distributor of prefabricated cabinets, is as shown in the following accounts.

| | |
|---|---:|
| Preferred stock | $ 300,000 |
| Common stock (100,000 shares at $4 par) | 400,000 |
| Paid-in capital in excess of par | 600,000 |
| Retained earnings | 700,000 |
| Total stockholders' equity | $2,000,000 |

If Wieta declares a 10 percent stock dividend and the market price of its stock is $15 per share, $150,000 of retained earnings (10% × 100,000 shares × $15 per share) is capitalized. The $150,000 is distributed between common stock and paid-in capital in excess of par accounts based on the par value of the common stock. The resulting stockholders' equity on the balance sheet is as shown in the following accounts.

| | |
|---|---:|
| Preferred stock | $ 300,000 |
| Common stock (110,000 shares at $4 par) | 440,000 |
| Paid-in capital in excess of par | 710,000 |
| Retained earnings | 550,000 |
| Total stockholders' equity | $2,000,000 |

Because 10,000 new shares (10% × 100,000) have been issued and the prevailing market price is $15 per share, $150,000 ($15 per share × 10,000 shares) is shifted from retained earnings to the common stock and paid-in capital accounts. A total of $40,000 ($4 par × 10,000 shares) is added to common stock, and the remaining $110,000 [($15 − $4) × 10,000 shares] is added to the paid-in capital in excess of par. The firm's total stockholders' equity has not changed; funds have only been *redistributed* among stockholders' equity accounts.

▶

**The Shareholder's Viewpoint**  The shareholder receiving a stock dividend receives nothing of value. After the dividend is paid, the per-share value of the shareholder's stock decreases in proportion to the dividend in such a way that the market value of his or her total holdings in the firm remains unchanged. The shareholder's proportion of ownership in the firm also remains the same, and *as long as the firm's earnings remain unchanged,* so does his or her share of total earnings. (Clearly, if the firm's earnings and cash dividends increase at the time the stock dividend is issued, an increase in share value is likely to result.) A continuation of the preceding example clarifies this point.

# EXAMPLE

Mr. X owned 10,000 shares of the Wieta Company's stock. The company's most recent earnings were $220,000, and earnings are not expected to change in the near future. Before the stock dividend, Mr. X owned 10 percent (10,000 shares ÷ 100,000 shares) of the firm's stock, which was selling for $15 per share. Earnings per share were $2.20 ($220,000 ÷ 100,000 shares). Because Mr. X owned 10,000 shares, his earnings were $22,000 ($2.20 per share × 10,000 shares). After receiving the 10 percent stock dividend, Mr. X has 11,000 shares, which again is 10 percent (11,000 shares ÷ 110,000 shares) of the ownership. The market price of the stock can be expected to drop to $13.64 per share [$15 × (1.00 ÷ 1.10)]. Thus the market value of Mr. X's holdings is $150,000 (11,000 shares × $13.64 per share). This is the same as the initial value of his holdings (10,000 shares × $15 per share). The future earnings per share drops to $2 ($220,000 ÷ 110,000 shares) because the same $220,000 in earnings must now be divided among 110,000 shares. Because Mr. X still owns 10 percent of the stock, his share of total earnings is still $22,000 ($2 per share × 11,000 shares). In summary, if the firm's earnings remain constant and total cash dividends do not increase, a stock dividend results in a lower per-share market value for the firm's stock.

**The Company's Viewpoint**   Stock dividends are more costly to issue than cash dividends, but the advantages generally outweigh these costs. Firms find the stock dividend a means of giving owners something without having to use cash. Generally, when a firm is growing rapidly and needs to preserve cash to finance this growth, a stock dividend is used. As long as the stockholders recognize that the firm is reinvesting the cash flow generated from earnings in a manner that should tend to maximize future earnings, the market value of the firm should at least remain unchanged. If the stock dividend is paid so that cash can be retained to satisfy past-due bills, a decline in market value may result.

## Stock Splits

**stock split**
A method commonly used to lower the market price of a firm's stock by increasing the number of shares belonging to each shareholder.

Although not a type of dividend, *stock splits* have an effect on a firm's share price similar to that of stock dividends. A **stock split** is a method commonly used to lower the market price of a firm's stock by increasing the number of shares belonging to each shareholder. Quite often, a firm believes that its stock is priced too high and that lowering the market price will enhance trading activity. Stock splits are often made prior to new issues of a stock to enhance the marketability of the stock and stimulate market activity.

A stock split has no effect on the firm's capital structure. It commonly increases the number of shares outstanding and reduces the stock's per-share par value. In other words, when a stock is split, a specified number of new shares are exchanged for a given number of outstanding shares. In a 2-for-1 split, two new shares are exchanged for each old share; in a 3-for-2 split, three new shares are exchanged for each two old shares, and so on.

▶ E X A M P L E

Brandt Company, a forest products concern, had 200,000 shares of $2 par-value common stock and no preferred stock outstanding. Because the stock is selling at a high market price, the firm has declared a 2-for-1 stock split. The total before- and after-split stockholders' equity is shown in the following table.

| Before Split | |
| --- | --- |
| Common stock (200,000 shares at $2 par) | $ 400,000 |
| Paid-in capital in excess of par | 4,000,000 |
| Retained earnings | 2,000,000 |
| Total stockholders' equity | $6,400,000 |

| After 2-for-1 Split | |
| --- | --- |
| Common stock (400,000 shares at $1 par) | $ 400,000 |
| Paid-in capital in excess of par | 4,000,000 |
| Retained earnings | 2,000,000 |
| Total stockholders' equity | $6,400,000 |

▶ The insignificant effect of the stock split on the firm's books is obvious.

Stock can be split in any way desired. Sometimes a **reverse stock split** is made: a certain number of outstanding shares are exchanged for one new share. For example, in a 1-for-2 split, one new share is exchanged for two old shares; in a 2-for-3 split, two new shares are exchanged for three old shares, and so on. Reverse stock splits are initiated when a stock is selling at too low a price to appear respectable.

It is not unusual for a stock split to cause a slight increase in the market value of the stock. This is attributable to the informational content of stock splits and the fact that *total* dividends paid commonly increase slightly after a split.

**reverse stock split**
A method used to raise the market price of a firm's stock by exchanging a certain number of outstanding shares for one new share of stock.

## Stock Repurchases

During the past 5 to 10 years, firms have increased their repurchasing of outstanding common stock in the marketplace. The practical motives for **stock repurchase** include obtaining shares to be used in acquisitions, having shares available for employee stock option plans, or merely retiring shares. Here we focus on the repurchase of shares for retirement, because this motive for repurchase is similar to the payment of cash dividends.

**stock repurchase**
The repurchasing by the firm of outstanding shares of its common stock in the marketplace.

**Accounting Entries** The accounting entries that result when common stock is repurchased are a reduction in cash and the establishment of a contra capital account called "treasury stock," which is shown as a deduction from stockholders' equity. The label **treasury stock** is used to indicate the presence of repurchased shares on the balance sheet. The repurchase of stock can be viewed as a cash dividend because it involves the distribution of cash to the firm's owners, who are the sellers of the shares.

**treasury stock**
The label used on the firm's balance sheet to designate repurchased shares of stock; shown as a deduction from stockholders' equity.

**Viewed as a Cash Dividend** When common stock is repurchased for retirement, the underlying motive is to distribute excess cash to the owners. As a result of any repurchase, the owners receive cash for their shares. Generally as long as earnings remain constant, the repurchase of shares reduces the number of outstanding shares, raising the earnings per share and therefore the market price per share. In addition, certain owner tax benefits may result from stock repurchases. The repurchase of common stock results in a type of reverse dilution because the earnings per share and the market price of stock are increased by reducing the number of shares outstanding. The net effect of the repurchase is similar to the payment of a cash dividend. A simple example clarifies this point.

## E X A M P L E

Farrell Company, a national sportswear chain, has released the following financial data:

| | |
|---|---|
| Earnings available for common stockholders | $1,000,000 |
| Number of shares of common outstanding | 400,000 |
| Earnings per share ($1,000,000 ÷ 400,000) | $2.50 |
| Market price per share | $50 |
| Price/earnings (P/E) ratio ($50 ÷ $2.50) | 20 |

The firm is contemplating using $800,000 of its earnings either to pay cash dividends or to repurchase shares. If the firm pays cash dividends, the amount of the dividend is $2 per share ($800,000 ÷ 400,000 shares). If the firm pays $52 per share to repurchase stock, it can repurchase approximately 15,385 shares ($800,000 ÷ $52 per share). As a result of this repurchase, 384,615 shares (400,000 shares − 15,385 shares) of common stock remain outstanding. Earnings per share (EPS) rise to $2.60 ($1,000,000 ÷ 384,615). If the stock still sells at 20 times earnings (P/E = 20), applying the *price/earnings (P/E) multiple approach* presented in Chapter 12, its market price rises to $52 per share ($2.60 × 20). In both cases the stockholders receive $2 per share—a $2 cash dividend in the dividend case or a $2 increase in share price ($50 per share to $52 per share) in the repurchase case.

The advantages of stock repurchases are an increase in per-share earnings and certain owner tax benefits. The tax advantage stems from the fact that if the cash dividend is paid, the owners have to pay ordinary income taxes on it, whereas the $2 increase in the market value of the stock due to the repurchase is not taxed until the owner sells the stock. Of course, when the stock is sold, if the proceeds are in excess of the original purchase price, the capital gain is taxed as ordinary income. The IRS allegedly watches firms that regularly repurchase stock and levies a penalty if it believes the repurchases have been made to delay the payment of taxes by the stockholders. Enforcement in this area appears to be relatively lax.

## Progress Review Questions

**16-13.** What is a *stock dividend?* Why do firms issue stock dividends? Comment on the following statement: "I have a stock that promises to pay a 20 percent stock dividend every year, and therefore it guarantees that I will break even in five years."

**16-14.** What is a *stock split?* What is a *reverse stock split?* Compare a stock split with a stock dividend.

**16-15.** What is the logic behind *repurchasing shares* of common stock to distribute excess cash to the firm's owners? How might this raise the per-share earnings and market price of outstanding shares?

# SUMMARY OF LEARNING GOALS

**Understand capital structure, including the basic types of capital, external assessment of capital structure, and the capital structure of non-U.S. firms.** A firm's capital structure is determined by the mix of long-term debt and equity it uses in financing its operations. Debt and equity capital differ with respect to voice in management, claims on income and assets, maturity, and tax treatment. Capital structure can be externally assessed using the debt ratio, times interest earned ratio, and the fixed-payment coverage ratio. Non-U.S. companies tend to have much higher leverage ratios than do their U.S. counterparts, primarily because U.S. capital markets are much better developed. Similarities between U.S. corporations and those of other countries include industry patterns of capital structure, large multinational company capital structures, and the trend toward greater reliance on securities issuance and less reliance on banks for financing.

**Explain graphically, using a modified form of the zero-growth valuation model and the firm's debt, equity, and weighted average cost of capital functions, the "optimal" capital structure.** The zero-growth valuation model can be used to define the firm's value as its after-tax earnings before interest and taxes (EBIT) divided by its weighted average cost of capital. Assuming that EBIT is constant, the value of the firm is maximized by minimizing its weighted average cost of capital (WACC). The optimal capital structure is therefore the one that minimizes the WACC. Graphically, although both debt and equity costs rise with increasing financial leverage, the lower cost of debt causes the WACC to decline and then rise with increasing financial leverage. As a result, the firm's WACC exhibits a U-shape having a minimum value, which defines the optimum capital structure—the one that maximizes the owners' wealth.

**LG 3**    **Discuss the graphic presentation, risk considerations, and basic shortcoming of using the EBIT-EPS approach to compare capital structures.** The EBIT-EPS approach can be used to evaluate various capital structures in light of the returns they provide the firm's owners and their degree of financial risk. Under the EBIT-EPS approach, the preferred capital structure is the one expected to provide maximum earnings per share (EPS) over the firm's expected range of EBIT. Graphically, this approach reflects risk in terms of the financial breakeven point and the slope of the capital structure line. The major shortcoming of EBIT-EPS analysis is that by ignoring risk it concentrates on maximization of earnings rather than maximization of owners' wealth.

**LG 4**    **Describe cash dividend payment procedures, dividend reinvestment plans, the relevance of dividend policy and related arguments, and the key factors that affect dividend policy.** The cash dividend decision is normally a quarterly decision made by the corporate board of directors that establishes the record date and payment date. Generally, the larger the dividend charged to retained earnings and paid in cash, the greater the amount of financing that must be raised externally. Some firms offer dividend reinvestment plans that allow stockholders to acquire shares in lieu of cash dividends, often at an attractive price. A company offering such a plan can either have a trustee buy outstanding shares on behalf of participating shareholders, or it can issue new shares to any participants. The residual theory suggests that dividends should be viewed as the residual earnings left after all acceptable investment opportunities have been undertaken. Dividend irrelevance, which supports the residual theory, is argued by Modigliani and Miller using a perfect world wherein information content and clientele effects exist. Gordon and Lintner argue dividend relevance based on the uncertainty-reducing effect of dividends, supported by their bird-in-the-hand argument. The actions of financial managers and stockholders alike tend to support the belief that dividend policy is relevant—it affects stock value. Certain legal, contractual, and internal constraints as well as growth prospects, owner considerations, and certain market considerations affect a firm's dividend policy, which should maximize the wealth of its owners while providing for sufficient financing.

**LG 5**    **Describe and evaluate the three basic types of dividend policies: constant-payout-ratio, regular, and low-regular-and-extra.** With a constant-payout-ratio dividend policy, the firm pays a fixed percentage of earnings out to the owners each period. The problem with this policy is that dividends move up and down with earnings, and no dividend is paid when the firm experiences a loss. Under a regular dividend policy, the firm pays a fixed-dollar dividend each period; it increases the amount of the dividend only after a proven increase in earnings has occurred. The regular dividend policy is appealing because it provides the owners with generally positive information, indicating the firm is okay and thereby minimizing their uncertainty. The low-regular-and-extra dividend policy is similar to the regular dividend policy, except that it pays an "extra dividend" in periods when the firm's earnings are higher than normal. By establishing a low regular dividend that is paid each period, the firm using this policy gives investors stable predictable income and pays a bonus when the firm experiences an especially good period. The regular and the low-regular-and-extra dividend policies are generally preferred over the constant-payout-ratio dividend policy because of the uncertainty-reducing effect of their stable patterns of dividends.

**Contrast the basic features, objectives, and procedures for paying other forms of dividends, including stock dividends, stock splits, and stock repurchases.** Occasionally firms may pay stock dividends as a replacement for or supplement to cash dividends. The payment of stock dividends involves a shifting of funds between capital accounts rather than a use of funds. Stock splits are sometimes used to enhance trading activity of a firm's shares by lowering or raising the market price of its stock by increasing or decreasing, respectively, the number of shares belonging to each shareholder. A stock split has no effect on the firm's capital structure. Stock repurchases can be made in lieu of cash dividend payments to retire outstanding shares and delay the payment of taxes. Whereas stock dividends and stock repurchases can be viewed as dividend alternatives, stock splits are used to deliberately adjust the market price of shares. Only stock repurchases involve the actual outflow of cash; both stock dividends and stock splits involve accounting adjustments in the capital accounts.

LG   6

# C H A P T E R

**17**

## L E A R N I N G    G O A L S

After studying this chapter, you should be able to

 **LG 1** Understand the role of long-term financing, including internal and external sources, the need for external funds, and the methods used by both established and emerging small corporations to raise external funds.

 **LG 2** Explain the role of investment banking in long-term business financing: the bankers' roles as underwriter, agent, adviser, and market maker, the use of shelf registration, and the formation of syndicates by underwriters.

 **LG 3** Discuss investment banker compensation: the underwriting spread, the cost of public offerings, and the cost of private placements.

 **LG 4** Describe the key activities of the firm in an initial public offering—selecting an investment banker and going public—and public offering versus private placement.

 **LG 5** Review the restrictions and dilemmas frequently faced by the financial manager when making subsequent public offerings of new common stock.

 **LG 6** Summarize recent trends in the investment banking industry—the demise of largely debt-financed acquisitions and the rise of financial engineering—and how it is likely to change in the future.

# Investment Banking: Its Role in Raising Long-Term Funds

All companies want to take advantage of growth opportunities. Long-term financing allows a company to expand so that it can remain competitive without depleting its cash reserves. Raising funds in the capital markets at the lowest cost is critical to maintaining an organization's viability. Investment bankers help companies structure, price, and sell long-term financing, and provide ongoing advice.

## Investment bankers help companies structure, price, and sell long-term financing, and provide ongoing advice.

Like other businesses, health care providers raise long-term financing to add new facilities and renovate existing ones. They must keep overall costs—financing as well as operating—as low as possible to provide community access to health care. In addition to obtaining new funding, financial managers should monitor the firm's outstanding long-term debt. Fluctuations in market interest rates may create opportunities for the firm to reduce interest expense by refinancing its debt.

Wilson N. Jones Memorial Hospital, a 224-bed nonprofit community hospital with annual gross revenues of about $100 million, is one of three hospitals in our market area. Maintaining a strong position in the community is an important strategic goal for the hospital.

Recently the hospital raised $50,575,000 in long-term debt. As a nonprofit institution, we can sell municipal bonds—debt issued through a local authority whose interest is tax-exempt. The issue included both refinancing and new debt. Refinancing reduced the hospital's annual interest cost by 5 percent. Proceeds from the new debt were used to finance construction of a 25-bed rehabilitation center and renovate operating rooms.

The hospital used an investment banking firm to underwrite the issue (buy the bonds for a predetermined price and then sell them to investors). The investment banker also assisted in the bond-rating process and pricing the issue. Bond ratings are grades indicating investment quality, issued by independent rating agencies that conduct a thorough financial analysis of the organization.

The investment banker a firm chooses should have expertise in the firm's particular industry. Most major and regional investment banks have specialized health care financing groups. In our case, the ability to sell bonds to individual investors locally was also important.

The underwriter helped us decide whether to pay an additional premium for municipal bond insurance, which raises the company's bond rating to that of the insurer. There is a tradeoff between the amount of the premium and the lower coupon interest rate resulting from the higher rating. The insurance raised the hospital's rating three full grades to the highest, AAA, lowering the coupon by about .6 of a basis point (.6%), which also opened up new markets for the bonds.

Working with underwriters is valuable because they closely monitor market conditions and can advise clients on pricing the issue. The bond market is extremely variable, fluctuating daily. In fact, there was such a high demand for our bonds that we were able to recall them and reduce the rate. Our underwriter continued to work with us after the bonds were sold, helping us to earn high rates when we invested issue proceeds.

**Christopher Knight** *became controller of Wilson N. Jones Memorial Hospital, Sherman, Texas, in 1992. He was controller of St. Joseph's Hospital, Fort Worth, Texas, from 1989 to 1992 and from 1982 to 1989 held financial management positions at West Virginia University Hospital and Aliquippa Hospital, Aliquippa, Pennsylvania. He holds a bachelor's degree in accounting and an M.B.A. from Waynesburg State University, Waynesburg, PA.*

**L**ong-term financing—financing with an initial maturity of more than one year—enables firms to finance corporate growth and the replacement of worn-out equipment and to pay off debts and other obligations as they come due. Frequently these funds are obtained internally by retaining corporate profits rather than paying them out to shareholders as dividends. At other times, managers raise long-term funds externally through the sale of new debt, preferred stock, or common stock. Issuing and selling new securities can be a difficult task. The financial manager must know how to structure the terms of the new issue, how to satisfy the legal and regulatory requirements of security issuance, and how to market and sell new securities effectively to investors. Financial managers often hire investment banking firms to assist in the design and marketing of new security issues to investors. In this chapter we discuss the various ways in which financial managers raise long-term funds, the role of investment banking, compensating investment bankers, initial and subsequent sales of new common stock, and recent trends in the investment banking industry.

**long-term financing**
Financing with an initial maturity of more than one year.

## Raising Long-Term Funds

Financial managers face a wide variety of choices when they raise long-term funds. They can raise either debt or equity. Debt (discussed in Chapter 18) is an **external source of funds**—it is raised outside of the firm—obtained either through negotiated loans (discussed in Chapter 18 but ignored here) or the sale of bonds. Equity (discussed in Chapter 19) can be obtained either as an **internal source of funds**—funds generated within the firm—from retained earnings or raised externally through the sale of preferred or common stock. Figure 17.1 shows the various sources of internal and external long-term financing that are discussed throughout this chapter.

**external sources of funds**
Funds raised outside the firm from negotiated loans and the sale of bonds and stock.

**internal sources of funds**
Funds generated inside the firm from retained earnings.

### When Do Firms Need External Funds?

Most growing firms are unable through internally generated retained earnings to obtain all of the long-term funds needed. These firms must use externally generated funds to fulfill their long-term financing needs. Firms also frequently seek external funding during periods when internally generated funds are in short supply. This typically occurs when the economy enters a recession, business activity slows down, and corporate profits fall. When economic recovery begins at the end of a recessionary period, corporate profits begin to recover, internal sources of funds increase, and corporate use of external funding declines. Because the availability of internal funds varies directly with the business cycle, the use of external funds rises when economic activity declines and falls when economic activity increases.

### How Do Firms Raise External Funds?

Corporations wishing to raise external funds can do so either through a public offering or a private placement of the securities. Here we take a brief look at these alternatives for selling new debt or equity.

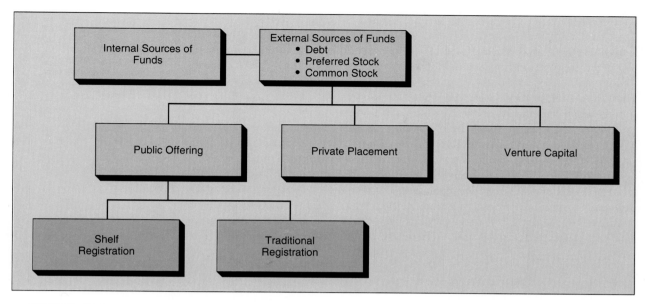

**FIGURE 17.1   Sources of Long-Term Corporate Financing**
Firms can raise long-term funds internally through retained earnings or externally through the sale of debt, preferred stock, or common stock. External financing may be raised through public offering or private placement. Emerging small corporations frequently must rely on venture capital for their long-term financing.

**public offering**
The sale of a firm's securities to the general public.

**investment banker**
A firm that serves as an intermediary between the corporation (or government) issuing securities and the investing public who purchases them in the primary capital market.

**private placement**
The sale of new securities directly to selected groups of investors, without SEC registration.

In a **public offering,** the firm offers its securities for sale to the general public. To do so it must register the securities with the Securities and Exchange Commission (SEC). Most public offerings are made with the assistance of an **investment banker**—a firm that serves as an intermediary between the corporation (or government) issuing securities and the investing public who purchases them in the primary capital market. (Recall from Chapter 2 that a *primary market* is the market in which securities are initially issued; in contrast, preowned securities are traded in *secondary markets* such as the New York Stock Exchange.) In addition, the investment banker may serve in a variety of additional roles for its clients.

An alternative to public offering is the private placement of new securities with selected investors. Under a **private placement,** new securities are sold by the issuer directly to selected groups of investors such as insurance companies and pension funds. Privately placed securities do *not* require SEC registration. Because these institutional investors are sophisticated enough to request and examine relevant investment information with respect to the issuer and the securities, assistance from the federal government is not necessary. Although private placement allows the issuer to avoid the time and expense of SEC registration, it limits the issuer to a far smaller group of potential investors.

## External Funds for Emerging Small Corporations: Venture Capital

Financially starved emerging small corporations typically lack the asset base, revenue and credit history, and proven growth needed to sell securities publicly. Although these firms may have good potential for success, typically they can neither attract nor afford to hire an investment banker to assist in raising funds through a private placement. Thus, emerging small corporations frequently seek financing in the form of venture capital. **Venture capital** is financing provided to an emerging business firm by specialized financial intermediaries known as *venture capitalists*. Although venture capital firms sometimes provide debt financing, in most cases they obtain common stock ownership in the businesses they finance. They typically finance innovative businesses that operate in rapidly growing segments of the economy and have a good chance of success.

> **venture capital**
> Financing provided to an emerging business by specialized financial intermediaries known as *venture capitalists*.

Usually, the common stock issued by start-up corporations is not publicly traded, and venture capitalists that hold it therefore face a substantial liquidity risk. Because many emerging businesses fail before public sale of their common equity can occur, venture capitalists also face a significant risk of losing their entire investment in a firm. Only a small number of ventures earn positive cash returns, but these returns are generally so large that they more than compensate for the losses incurred in connection with failed ventures.

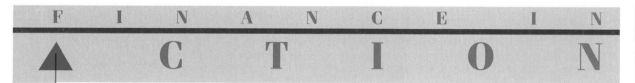

## FINANCE IN ACTION

### Small Business

## Think You've Got a Great Idea for a New Business?

OK—you've just discovered the best business idea since Edwin Land invented the Polaroid camera, and all you need now is a little start-up capital to begin raking in the bucks. What do you do?

Before you call your friendly neighborhood venture capitalist to pitch your idea, it pays to do your homework. According to New York City investment banking firm, D. H. Blair & Company, which reviews over 3,000 new business plans each year, you don't get much time to win the attention, and financing, of most venture capital firms. You need to be well organized, and have a business plan that really stands out from the other 2,999 plans sitting next to yours in the "in" basket.

So how do you knock their socks off? D. H. Blair suggests the following pointers:

- Make it simple and brief. Prepare a well-written executive summary to introduce your report. The summary should explain why you think your business will succeed, highlight your financial goals, and demonstrate your skills as a manager.
- Provide an analysis of your competition. This shows that you have thoroughly studied your market and that you know what you're up against.
- Detail your management experience, showing that you have the skills, ability, and track record to transform your idea into a successful business.
- Prepare realistic pro forma financial statements that show how your start-up costs will be paid and how your investors will realize a return on their investment.

What turns off most venture capitalists? According to D. H. Blair, sending a product sample that does not work along with your business plan, delivering a handwritten business plan, having friends write letters of recommendation to vouch for your business skills, and being persistent to the point that you become a pest in the venture capitalist's office are the fastest ways to lose the attention—and financial backing—of firms that fund private placements.

Source: Ellyn E. Spragins, "How to Write a Business Plan that Will Get You in the Door," *Inc.*, November 1990, p. 159.

## Progress Review Questions

**17-1.** Define and differentiate between *internal* and *external* sources of funds. When do firms typically raise external funds?

**17-2.** How does a *public offering* differ from a *private placement*? What is an *investment banker*?

**17-3.** What is *venture capital*? What are the two key risks borne by venture capitalists?

---

LG **2**

# The Role of Investment Banking

Some corporations, and even the U.S. government, bring new securities to market without the service of an investment banker to act as an intermediary between them and the investing public. Most corporations, however, hire an investment banker, such as Merrill Lynch, Kidder Peabody, and Lehman Brothers, to put together, market, and distribute their securities offerings. The investment banking industry is greatly concentrated—the 10 largest firms account for more than 75 percent of both the number of offerings and their dollar volume during the typical year. In the investment banking industry, size confers prestige. The largest firms have an extensive network of contacts in the capital market. These contacts are important to nonfinancial corporations seeking to issue new securities, because the issuer's new securities can achieve the widest possible distribution within the financial community. In this section we define each of the roles frequently played by investment bankers, the use of shelf registration by issuers, and the formation of syndicates by underwriters.

## Defining the Roles

As noted earlier, investment bankers can serve in a variety of roles when acting as intermediary between corporate (or government) security issuers and the investing public. Their most common roles in security offerings are as underwriter, agent, adviser, and market maker. Here we briefly describe each of these.

**underwriter**
The role served by an investment banker who purchases a security issue from an issuer at a prearranged price and plans to resell the securities to other investors at a higher price, thereby profiting from the transaction.

**price risk**
The risk that the price of a new security will fall while it is being held by an investment banking firm.

**Underwriter**   When an investment banker serves as an **underwriter** it purchases the security issue from the issuing firm at a prearranged price and then resells the securities to other investors. The investment banker buys the securities at a lower price than it plans to resell them for, thereby expecting to make a profit on the *spread* between the purchase and sale price. The investment banker bears **price risk** in an underwriting. If the price of the securities falls while they are held by the investment banking firm, it—not the issuing corporation—experiences the loss. Consequently, investment bankers must maintain close contact with the capital markets in order to estimate accurately how a particular issue will be received by investors. It is the investment bankers' knowledge of financial markets, along with their expertise in structuring new offerings and skill in marketing and distributing new securities, that explains why most nonfinancial corporations hire them to assist in raising funds externally. Generally, large investment bankers always make offerings of securities for large firms and governments on a strict underwriting basis.

### Agent

Rather than sell securities for client firms on a strict underwriting basis, an investment banker can serve as the issuing firm's **agent**—a party authorized by the issuer to sell securities on its behalf to third parties. As an agent, the investment banker may agree to take new securities from the issuer and sell them on a **best efforts basis.** In this case the investment banker agrees to sell, typically on a commission basis, as many securities as possible at a preestablished price. Any securities remaining unsold at conclusion of the offering are simply returned to the issuer; the investment banker bears no underwriting or *price risk.* Best efforts offerings are typically used when the issuer is a smaller, lesser known corporation and are handled typically by smaller investment banking firms. Investment bankers also act as agents in *private placements.* In this situation the issuer pays the investment banker a fee for directly placing a security issue with groups of investors, such as insurance companies and pension funds. Offerings that are privately placed by investment bankers typically involve smaller issues than are sold through public offering.

**agent**
A party authorized by an issuing firm to sell securities on its behalf to third parties.

**best efforts basis**
Arrangement in which an investment banker agrees to act as an *agent* to sell as much of a securities issue as possible at a preset price but does not purchase the securities from the issuer for resale.

### Adviser

Investment bankers use their knowledge and expertise in financial markets to advise corporate issuers about the type of security to offer, the appropriate terms and timing of the issue, and the best financial market in which to sell the issue. They also assist the firm in preparing and filing the accounting and legal documents necessary for security issuance. Investment bankers help issuers price securities by determining their value. If the offering price is set too high, the new securities do not sell and the investment banker loses money on the underwriting transaction. If the offering price is set too low, a portion of the firm's value is transferred from existing stockholders to purchasers of the new shares. In this case, both the management and stockholders of the issuing firm will be dissatisfied with the investment banker's performance. Because an investment banker has a feel for the pulse of the capital markets, it can also, for a fee, provide corporations with useful advice on mergers, acquisitions, refinancings, and other important financial decisions.

### Market Maker

Investment bankers use their industry contacts with other investment banking firms to create the widest possible distribution for new issues and *make a market* in them. Making a market means that the investment banker maintains an inventory of underwritten securities, quotes purchase and sale prices on them, and stands ready to buy and sell those securities at the quoted prices for a limited time following the original public issue. When a firm announces a new security issue, the announcement often causes a change in the firm's existing stock price because it provides new information to investors outside the firm. The investment banker attempts to communicate the purpose, intent, and value of the new security offering throughout the investment community to enhance its marketability by giving investors the same information that is available to the firm's management. The investment banker also places its reputation behind the new issues it underwrites, thereby strengthening each issue's perceived quality, legitimacy, and marketability.

## Shelf Registration

Corporations issuing new securities often try to "time the market." Their goal is to bring new common stock to market when stock prices are relatively high and new bonds to market when interest rates are relatively low. Under traditional SEC registration requirements, it takes a minimum of several weeks to register new securities. Typically, months pass between the time a firm first decides to issue new securities and the date they are finally sold.

**shelf registration**
Securities registration procedure that allows certain firms to sell securities during a two-year period under a "master registration statement" filed with the SEC.

To overcome lengthy registration delays, since 1982 the SEC has allowed an alternative registration procedure called **shelf registration.** Firms with more than $150 million in outstanding common stock may file a "master registration statement." The statement describes the firm's planned funding needs and forecasts security issues over a two-year period. At any time during the two years following the effective date of the shelf registration, the firm, after filing a "short statement," can sell securities already approved under the master statement.

Shelf registration of new securities has become extremely popular. But does shelf registration allow financial managers to time the market effectively? The evidence is mixed. In some cases, shelf registration reduces the transactions costs of bringing new securities to market, because it minimizes the paperwork necessary to initiate security sales. The shelf registration process does not, however, appear to have a significant effect on reducing the cost of debt and equity capital for new issues. Why? Because even with streamlined registration procedures, it isn't easy to time the market when issuing new securities.

## Underwriting

Investment bankers use a variety of different methods to reduce the *price risk* they face when underwriting new security issues. Whereas small public issues may be completely controlled by a single investment banker, larger offerings are distributed in the capital market using an **underwriting syndicate**—a group of investment banking firms that collectively participate in buying and selling a portion of the new issue. The **managing (or lead) underwriter** of the syndicate negotiates with the issuing corporation the terms of the issue, its price, and the fees payable to the investment banking syndicate. Then the managing underwriter invites other investment banking firms to join the syndicate and underwrite a portion of the issue.

**underwriting syndicate**
Group of investment banking firms that collectively participate in buying and selling a portion of a new security issue.

**managing (or lead) underwriter**
Underwriter of a syndicate that negotiates the terms, price, and fees of the issue with the issuing corporation.

**tombstone advertisements**
Advertisements for security issues.

Investors can easily determine the membership and organizational structure of an underwriting syndicate from its **tombstone advertisements** published in the financial press. Figure 17.2 shows a tombstone that appeared in *The Wall Street Journal* to announce a 1993 common stock issue by Louis Dreyfus Natural Gas Corp. The "tombstone" which gets its name from the stark, businesslike appearance of the announcement, alerts the investment community of a firm's intention to issue new securities. Notice that the tombstone pro-

This announcement is neither an offer to sell nor a solicitation of an offer to buy any of these Securities. The offer is made only by the Prospectus.

# 7,000,000 Shares

## Louis Dreyfus Natural Gas Corp.
### Common Stock

### Price $18 a Share

Copies of the Prospectus may be obtained in any State from only such of the undersigned as may legally offer these Securities in compliance with the securities laws of such State.

## 5,600,000 Shares

This portion of the offering is being offered in the United States and Canada by the undersigned.

MORGAN STANLEY & CO.
*Incorporated*

DONALDSON, LUFKIN & JENRETTE
*Securities Corporation*

PAINEWEBBER INCORPORATED

| | | |
|---|---|---|
| BEAR, STEARNS & CO. INC. | CS FIRST BOSTON | DILLON, READ & CO. INC. |
| A.G. EDWARDS & SONS, INC. | HOWARD, WEIL, LABOUISSE, FRIEDRICHS *Incorporated* | |
| KIDDER, PEABODY & CO. *Incorporated* | LEHMAN BROTHERS | J.P. MORGAN SECURITIES INC. |
| OPPENHEIMER & CO., INC. | PRUDENTIAL SECURITIES INCORPORATED | |
| SALOMON BROTHERS INC. | SMITH BARNEY SHEARSON INC. | |
| UBS SECURITIES INC. | DEAN WITTER REYNOLDS INC. | |
| KEMPER SECURITIES, INC. | C.J. LAWRENCE/DEUTSCHE BANK SECURITIES *Corporation* | |
| McDONALD & COMPANY *Securities, Inc.* | WHEAT FIRST BUTCHER & SINGER *Capital Markets* | |
| FAHNESTOCK & CO. INC. | HANIFEN, IMHOFF INC. | |
| HARRIS NESBITT THOMSON SECURITIES INC. | MABON SECURITIES CORP. | |
| PETRIE PARKMAN & CO. | THE PRINCIPAL/EPPLER, GUERIN & TURNER, INC. | |
| RAUSCHER PIERCE REFSNES, INC. | SUTRO & CO. INCORPORATED | TUCKER ANTHONY *Incorporated* |

## 1,400,000 Shares

This portion of the offering is being offered outside the United States and Canada by the undersigned.

MORGAN STANLEY INTERNATIONAL

DONALDSON, LUFKIN & JENRETTE
*Securities Corporation*

PAINEWEBBER INTERNATIONAL

| | | |
|---|---|---|
| ABN AMRO BANK N.V. | BNP CAPITAL MARKETS LIMITED | INDOSUEZ CAPITAL |
| BARCLAYS DE ZOETE WEDD LIMITED | | DEUTSCHE BANK *Aktiengesellschaft* |
| PARIBAS CAPITAL MARKETS | SOCIETE GENERALE | UBS LIMITED |

November 17, 1993

— Managing Underwriters

— Underwriting Syndicate Members

**FIGURE 17.2**
**Tombstone Advertisement for Louis Dreyfus Natural Gas Corp.**

The "tombstone" for Louis Dreyfus Natural Gas Corp.'s common stock offering of November 17, 1993, shows that a total of 7,000,000 shares are offered at $18.00 per share by a large syndicate of underwriters managed by three firms: Morgan Stanley & Co.; Donaldson, Lufkin & Jenrette; and PaineWebber Incorporated.

vides information concerning the number of shares offered and their issue price. It also lists each investment banker participating in the underwriting syndicate.

The order in which investment banking firms appear in the tombstone is meaningful. At the top, the advertisement identifies the managing underwriters as Morgan Stanley & Co.; Donaldson, Lufkin & Jenrette; and PaineWebber Incorporated. Next, national investment banking firms taking a major position in the underwriting are listed in alphabetical order. This listing begins with Bear, Stearns & Co., Inc. and ends with UBS Securities Inc. The next alphabetical list identifies underwriters that purchase a small number of shares in the offering, followed by an alphabetical listing of regional investment banking firms that purchase an even smaller portion of the offering.

Distribution relationships can be quite complex, as the underwriters try to make the new shares widely available through a number of retail brokerage firms. Members of the underwriting syndicate solicit sales from institutional and individual investors, and often form a **selling group** composed of brokerage houses located throughout the United States. Members of the selling group promote the securities through their branch offices and retail stockbrokers in their particular market area.

**selling group**
Group of brokerage houses who promote a securities issue through their branch offices and retail stockbrokers in their area.

## Progress Review Questions

**17-4.** Describe the investment banker's role as an *underwriter* of securities issues. How do investment bankers bear *price risk* when serving in this role?

**17-5.** How does an offering done on a *best efforts basis* differ from an underwriting of a new security issue? Describe the investment bankers' role as an *agent* in offerings made on both a best efforts basis and in private placements.

**17-6.** Briefly describe the investment bankers' role as an *adviser* to corporate security issuers. How does an investment banker serve as a *market maker*?

**17-7.** What is *shelf registration*? How does this procedure work? What benefit does this procedure provide to the corporation?

**17-8.** Describe the role of an *underwriting syndicate* in the distribution of a new security issue. What is the significance of the order in which investment banking firms are listed in a *tombstone advertisement*? What is a *selling group*?

LG 3

# Compensating Investment Bankers

Determining the compensation received by investment bankers for structuring, underwriting, and marketing corporate security offerings is quite simple. Of course, the compensation scheme for a public offering differs from that for a private placement. Here we review each of them.

## The Cost of Public Offerings

Public security offerings underwritten by a single investment banker or syndicate of investment bankers are purchased from the issuing corporation at a lower price than that at which they are to be resold to the public. This difference represents the investment banker's **gross commission** (or **gross underwriting spread**).

The gross commission is easy to determine by examining the front cover of the **prospectus,** which is a portion of the registration statement filed by the issuer with the SEC that details the firm's operating and financial position. Figure 17.3 shows the front cover of a prospectus describing the terms and conditions associated with the issue of 7,000,000 shares of common stock by Louis Dreyfus Natural Gas Corp. in November 1993. The managing underwriters in this transaction—Morgan Stanley & Co.; Donaldson, Lufkin & Jenrette; and PaineWebber Incorporated—paid $16.895 per share for the stock and planned to resell it to the public for $18.00. The *gross commission* represents $1.105 per share and totals $7,735,000 ($1.105 × 7,000,000 shares).

The distribution of the gross commission depends on the syndicate agreement. In most cases, the gross commission from the underwriting transaction is divided four ways as listed below:

1. First, the managing underwriter pays all **out-of-pocket costs** incurred in connection with the issue. These costs include lawyers' fees, accountants' fees, SEC filing fees, printing and engraving costs, postage, and miscellaneous costs.
2. Next, the managing underwriter subtracts a **management fee,** which is its payment for coordinating and sponsoring the syndicate. This fee usually equals about 15 percent of the gross commission.
3. Then the managing underwriter divides the total **underwriting fee** on a pro rata basis among the syndicate participants who purchased securities from the issuing corporation. The underwriting fee also equals about 15 percent of the gross commission.
4. Finally, the balance of the gross commission is divided among all members of the syndicate based on the number of shares that each member sold. This represents the **selling concession** paid to members of the selling group that distributed shares in the capital market.

An example can demonstrate the calculation and distribution of the gross commission realized by the managing underwriter.

▶ E X A M P L E

Plath Industries, a diversified producer of building products, recently issued 1,000,000 shares of new common stock through an underwritten offering arranged by Flatbush Securities, Inc. As the managing underwriter for the sale, Flatbush formed a syndicate composed of three other investment banking firms—Alpha Company, Beta Company, and Delta Company—to purchase and resell Plath's common stock to the public. According to the prospectus describing the issue, Flatbush paid Plath $28.00 per share for the new stock, and set the initial offering price at $30.00. Flatbush's out-of-pocket costs for the transaction totaled $450,000. It sold 200,000 shares at $28.70 a share to

---

**gross commission (gross underwriting spread)**
The difference between the price at which an investment banker sells a securities issue to the public and the price at which it bought the issue from the issuing firm.

**prospectus**
The portion of the registration statement filed by a securities issuer with the SEC that details the firm's operating and financial position.

**out-of-pocket costs**
Costs of a managing underwriter incurred in connection with a securities issue.

**management fee**
Fee paid a managing underwriter for coordinating and sponsoring an underwriting syndicate.

**underwriting fee**
Fee divided on a pro rata basis among members of an underwriting syndicate.

**selling concession**
Fee paid to members of an underwriting syndicate based on the number of shares each member sold.

**FIGURE 17.3   Front Cover of Prospectus for Louis Dreyfus Natural Gas Corp.'s Common Stock Offering**

The front cover of the prospectus for Louis Dreyfus Natural Gas Corp.'s November 1993 common stock issue indicates that the managing underwriters—Morgan Stanley & Co.; Donaldson, Lufkin & Jenrette; and PaineWebber Incorporated—paid $16.895 per share and planned to sell 7,000,000 shares to the public for $18.00 each. They will net a gross commission of $1.105 per share for a total of $7,735,000.

PROSPECTUS

# 7,000,000 Shares

# Louis Dreyfus Natural Gas Corp.
## Common Stock

All of the shares of Common Stock offered hereby are being sold by the Company. Of the 7,000,000 shares offered, 5,600,000 shares are being offered initially in the United States and Canada by the U.S. Underwriters and 1,400,000 shares are being offered initially outside the United States and Canada by the International Underwriters. See "Underwriters." Prior to the Offering, there has been no public market for the Common Stock of the Company. See "Underwriters" for a discussion of the factors considered in determining the initial public offering price.

The Common Stock has been approved for listing on the New York Stock Exchange.

SEE "INVESTMENT CONSIDERATIONS" FOR A DISCUSSION OF CERTAIN FACTORS TO BE CONSIDERED IN CONNECTION WITH AN INVESTMENT IN THE COMMON STOCK.

THESE SECURITIES HAVE NOT BEEN APPROVED OR DISAPPROVED BY THE SECURITIES AND EXCHANGE COMMISSION NOR HAS THE COMMISSION PASSED UPON THE ACCURACY OR ADEQUACY OF THIS PROSPECTUS. ANY REPRESENTATION TO THE CONTRARY IS A CRIMINAL OFFENSE.

## PRICE $18 A SHARE

|  | Price to Public | Underwriting Discounts and Commissions(1) | Proceeds to Company(2) |
|---|---|---|---|
| Per Share .................... | $18.00 | $1.105 | $16.895 |
| Total(3) .................... | $126,000,000 | $7,735,000 | $118,265,000 |

(1) The Company has agreed to indemnify the Underwriters against certain liabilities, including liabilities under the Securities Act of 1933, as amended. See "Underwriters."

(2) Before deducting expenses payable by the Company estimated at $1,251,000.

(3) The Company has granted the U.S. Underwriters an option, exercisable within 30 days of the date hereof, to purchase up to an aggregate of 1,050,000 additional shares at the price to public less underwriting discounts and commissions for the purpose of covering over-allotments, if any. If the U.S. Underwriters exercise such option in full, the total price to public, underwriting discounts and commissions and proceeds to Company will be $144,900,000, $8,895,250 and $136,004,750, respectively. See "Underwriters."

The shares are offered, subject to prior sale, when, as and if accepted by the Underwriters named herein and subject to approval of certain legal matters by Davis Polk & Wardwell, counsel for the Underwriters. It is expected that delivery of the shares will be made on or about November 18, 1993 at the office of Morgan Stanley & Co. Incorporated against payment therefor in New York Funds.

## MORGAN STANLEY & CO.
Incorporated

## DONALDSON, LUFKIN & JENRETTE
Securities Corporation

## PAINEWEBBER INCORPORATED

November 11, 1993

each of its three partners in the underwriting group and planned to distribute the remaining 400,000 shares directly to the public. The investment bankers earned an underwriting fee of $0.30 from each share and were paid a selling concession of $1.00 per share on each share they sold. The stock was well received in the market, and the syndicate sold out the entire issue in one day.

The *gross commission* in this transaction was $2.00 per share ($30.00 offering price − $28.00 purchase price), or $2,000,000 for the entire issue ($2.00 per share × 1,000,000 shares).

The gross commission is broken down and divided among syndicate members as noted in Table 17.1. This breakdown of the gross commission is depicted in terms of price paid per share in Figure 17.4. It is summarized and evaluated on a percentage basis relative to both the initial offering price and the gross commission in Table 17.2 on page 492. Table 17.2 shows that the selling concession accounts for 50 percent of the gross commission. The out-of-pocket costs, management fee, and underwriting fee account for 22.5 percent, 12.5 percent, and 15 percent, respectively, of the gross commission.

Table 17.3 on page 493 provides historical data concerning recent costs of public offerings of common stock, preferred stock, and corporate bonds. The table separates the underwriting spread from the out-of-pocket costs. The gross commissions in the table represent the amount paid to investment banking firms. Notice that the *gross commissions for debt are significantly below the gross commissions for equity.* This difference is reflected in both the underwriting spread and the out-of-pocket costs. Clearly, firms issue more debt than equity because it is cheaper to sell new debt securities. In addition, note that the gross commissions decline for all types of securities as the issue size increases. This is particularly true of the out-of-pocket costs, which are much like fixed costs. From a cost standpoint, it is much cheaper for firms to issue a large quantity of securities at infrequent intervals than to issue small quantities of securities on a regular basis.

## The Cost of Private Placements

Nonunderwritten issues, private placements, and transactions handled by investment bankers on a best efforts basis involve a slightly different compen-

**FIGURE 17.4 Breakdown of Gross Commission in Terms of Price Paid per Share for Plath Industries' Common Stock Offering**

The gross commission of $2.00 ($30.00 sale price to public – $28.00 paid by Flatbush Securities, Inc. to Plath Industries) on Plath Industries' common stock offering by Flatbush Securities, Inc. was broken into $.45 in out-of-pocket costs, a $.25 management fee, a $.30 underwriting fee, and a $1.00 selling concession.

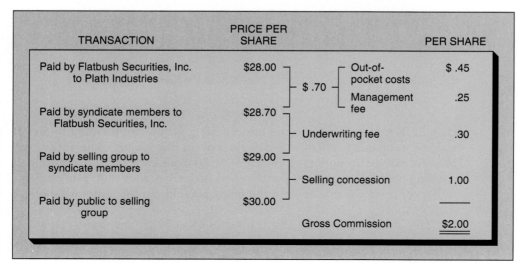

**TABLE 17.1   Distribution of the Gross Commission for Plath Industries' Common Stock Offering**

|  | Total | Per Share[a] |
|---|---|---|
| **1. Out-of-Pocket Costs** <br> Paid by Flatbush Securities, Inc. | $ 450,000 | $0.45 |
| **2. Management Fee** | 250,000 | 0.25 |

[($0.25 per share) × ($1,000,000 shares)]. This fee was paid to Flatbush as the lead underwriter. Notice that the total cost paid by Flatbush for each share was $28.45, representing the $28.00 paid to Plath and $0.45 in out-of-pocket costs associated with the issue. Flatbush resold shares to the investment banking syndicate for $28.70 each, earning a management fee of $0.25 on each share ($28.70 − $28.45).

**3. Underwriting Fee**

| | | |
|---|---|---|
| Flatbush Securities | $120,000 | |
| Alpha Company | 60,000 | |
| Beta Company | 60,000 | |
| Delta Company | 60,000 | |
| Total | 300,000 | 0.30 |

Shares resold to selling group for $29.00 ($30.00 price to public − $1 selling concession). Syndicate pays $28.70 for shares. The underwriting fee on each share was therefore $0.30 ($29.00 price to selling group − $28.70 price to syndicate). Flatbush sold 200,000 shares to each of its underwriting partners ($0.30 × 200,000 = $60,000), and retained 400,000 shares for distribution to the public ($0.30 × 400,000 = $120,000).

**4. Selling Concession**

| | | |
|---|---|---|
| Flatbush Securities | $400,000 | |
| Alpha Company | 200,000 | |
| Beta Company | 200,000 | |
| Delta Company | 200,000 | |
| Total | 1,000,000 | 1.00 |

The selling concession was $1.00 per share ($30,000 price to public − $29.00 price to selling group). Flatbush sold 400,000 shares to the public; each of the other three underwriters sold 200,000 shares each.

| **Gross Commission** | $2,000,000 | $2.00 |
|---|---|---|

[a]Per-share values were calculated by dividing the total cost by 1,000,000: the number of shares issued.

sation mechanism. Because in these situations investment bankers do not purchase and resell securities, they cannot be compensated on the basis of a price mark-up at the time of public sale. Instead, investments bankers establish a charge based on the advising, marketing, and distribution services they provide. In most cases, advising services carry a fixed charge. Marketing and distribution services are billed according to the number of securities the issuer

**TABLE 17.2   Analysis of the Gross Commission for Plath Industries' Common Stock Offering**

| Component | Total | Value<sup>a</sup> Per Share | Percent of Initial Offering Price | Percent of Gross Commission |
|---|---|---|---|---|
| Out-of-pocket costs | $  450,000 | $0.45 | $0.45/$30 = 1.5% | $0.45/$2 =  22.5% |
| Management fee | 250,000 | 0.25 | 0.25/ 30 = 0.9 | 0.25/ 2 =  12.5 |
| Underwriting fee | 300,000 | 0.30 | 0.30/ 30 = 1.0 | 0.30/ 2 =  15.0 |
| Selling concession | 1,000,000 | 1.00 | 1.00/ 30 = 3.3 | 1.00/ 2 =  50.0 |
| Total | $2,000,000 | $2.00 | $2.00/$30 = 6.7% | $2.00/$2 = 100.0% |

<sup>a</sup>From Table 17.1

sells during the time the investment banker is acting as its agent. Thus, these transactions earn investment bankers advisory fees and selling commissions rather than the gross commission earned in public offerings.

## Progress Review Questions

**17-9.** What are the components of the investment banker's *gross commission*? How are these components allocated among members of an *underwriting syndicate*?

**17-10.** How is the investment banker compensated for its work in private placements and other nonunderwritten transactions? Compare this compensation scheme to that for a public offering.

## The Initial Public Offering

LG 4

In the preceding sections we described how firms raise long-term funds and the role played by investment bankers in that process. Here, we examine the decisions faced by financial managers when they first raise external funds through a public stock issue. Typically, start-up businesses rely on private equity investments from their founders, venture capitalists, and other individuals personally known by the firm's founders. As they grow, these businesses may expand their equity base through the accumulation of retained earnings or the private placement of additional shares of common stock with interested parties close to the firm, or both. In time, however, many privately held

**TABLE 17.3**  **The Cost of Public Security Offerings as a Percentage of Offering Price**

| Issue Size (in Millions) | Common Stock | | | Preferred Stock | | | Corporate Bonds | | |
|---|---|---|---|---|---|---|---|---|---|
| | Underwriting Spread[a] (%) | Out-of-Pocket Costs[b] (%) | Gross Commission[c] (%) | Underwriting Spread[a] (%) | Out-of-Pocket Costs[b] (%) | Gross Commission[c] (%) | Underwriting Spread[a] (%) | Out-of-Pocket Costs[b] (%) | Gross Commission[c] (%) |
| Under $10.0 | 8.68 | 6.16 | 14.84 | 8.83 | 2.65 | 11.48 | 4.72 | 1.46 | 6.18 |
| 10.0–24.9 | 6.41 | 2.19 | 8.60 | 5.62 | 1.15 | 6.77 | 1.89 | 0.56 | 2.45 |
| 25.0–49.9 | 5.62 | 1.26 | 6.88 | 2.69 | 0.76 | 3.45 | 2.17 | 0.59 | 2.76 |
| 50.0–99.9 | 5.12 | 0.89 | 6.01 | 1.95 | 0.31 | 2.26 | 1.43 | 0.31 | 1.74 |
| 100.0–199.9 | 4.74 | 0.57 | 5.31 | 2.65 | 0.31 | 2.96 | 1.07 | 0.19 | 1.26 |
| 200.0–500.0 | 4.66 | 0.38 | 5.04 | 3.27 | 0.18 | 3.45 | 1.07 | 0.12 | 1.19 |
| Over 500 | 5.87 | 0.23 | 6.10 | 3.50 | 0.30 | 3.80 | 1.78 | 0.16 | 1.94 |
| Average | 5.87 | 1.67 | 7.54 | 4.07 | 0.81 | 4.88 | 2.02 | 0.48 | 2.50 |

[a]Represents the sum of the management fee, underwriting fee, and selling concession.

[b]Represents the out-of-pocket costs, including lawyers' fees, accountants' fees, SEC filing fees, printing and engraving costs, postage, mailing, and miscellaneous costs.

[c]Represents the sum of the underwriting spread and the out-of-pocket costs given in the two preceding columns.

Source: Securities Data Company, Inc.

firms reach the point at which further expansion requires the public sale of common stock. When a privately held firm publicly issues common stock for the first time, it is said to be **"going public,"** and its stock issue is called an **initial public offering (IPO).** This section reviews important decisions and procedures that managers of privately held firms encounter when they decide to go public. Note that most of these decisions and procedures are applicable to subsequent sales of securities by established public companies as well.

**going public**
Offering to the general public common stock previously held by private investors.

**initial public offering (IPO)**
The stock issue of a firm that offers shares to the public for the first time.

## Selecting an Investment Banker

A firm that wishes to go public must first select an investment banker to assist with the IPO. It then must determine whether the issue should be underwritten or distributed on a best efforts basis. If the firm finds investment bankers willing to underwrite the issue, it probably hires them to make the offering. An underwritten offering ensures the firm that it will raise a specified amount of money in exchange for a given number of shares.

Next, the firm must decide whether to hire its investment banker on the basis of *competitive bidding* or a *negotiated offering.* Under **competitive bidding,** the issuer specifies the type of security it intends to sell and invites a number of investment bankers to bid for the issue. The bidder offering the highest price for the issue is awarded it. Competitive bidding is common among registered public utilities. The Public Utility Holding Company Act of 1935 requires these firms to select an investment banker using the competitive bid-

**competitive bidding**
The process in which a number of investment bankers bid for the right to sell a securities issue and the one making the highest bid is the winner.

ding process. *Among industrial firms, however, competitive bidding is infrequently used.* Most likely an issuer uses a negotiated offering to select an investment banker. Under a **negotiated offering** the issuer interviews a variety of investment bankers and selects the one that is expected to best meet its needs at the lowest cost. In this case, the issuer negotiates the total underwriting cost of the issue directly with the investment banker.

**negotiated offering**
The process in which a securities issuer interviews a number of investment bankers and selects the one that it thinks will best meet its needs at the lowest cost.

## Going Public

Once the firm has selected an investment banker, the firm's board of directors must make sure the corporate charter authorizes the proposed public sale of new common stock. If it doesn't, the corporate charter must be amended (with the approval of shareholders) to authorize the issuance of new common stock. Next, the firm must comply with state and federal regulations governing new stock issues.

**Securities Regulation**    Prior to 1933, regulation of security sales was left to individual state governments. Because securities regulations were not consistent across all states, however, the federal government stepped into the picture with a series of legislative measures after the stock market crash of 1929. The **Securities Act of 1933** currently regulates the public sale of new security issues; the **Securities Exchange Act of 1934** provides federal rules governing the sale of securities in secondary markets—both organized and over the counter. The fundamental objective of the Securities Act of 1933 is to provide full disclosure of all relevant information to potential investors. *The act does not, however, require the federal government to assess the investment merits of new security issues.* It merely charges the government with ensuring the full disclosure of all relevant information with respect to new security issues, and allows the government to halt the offering of securities that contain false or misleading claims.

**Securities Act of 1933**
Federal law that regulates the public sale of new security issues.

**Securities Exchange Act of 1934**
Federal law that regulates the sale of securities in secondary markets.

The Securities Act of 1933 requires SEC approval for all interstate public offerings in excess of $500,000 that involve securities with a maturity of more than 270 days. Public offerings by railroads, banks, and public utilities are excluded from SEC registration requirements because these firms are regulated by other federal agencies. The **registration statement** filed with the SEC contains financial, legal, and technical information regarding the new issue and the business of the issuer. The registration statement must be filed with the SEC for a minimum of 20 days before approval is granted. The sale of new securities cannot begin until the registration statement is approved.

**registration statement**
Statement with information about a new security issue that must be filed with and approved by the SEC before public sale of the issue can take place.

To complete the registration statement, the issuer must identify the type and terms of the security being offered for sale. At first glance, this might appear to be quite simple. In reality, it can be very difficult. The issuer must specify the key features of the debt or equity offering, including items such as the coupon interest rate, maturity date, and any collateral in the case of a debt issue. Items, such as voting rights, planned dividend payments, and expected dilution of earnings per share, are specified for an equity issue.

**Market Listing**    Once the firm specifies the type of security it plans to sell, it must identify where the securities will trade. The common stock of most small firms trades in the over-the-counter market, because not enough interest is usually generated in it to justify listing it on a regional or national stock exchange. As a firm grows and achieves a wider ownership base, it may decide to apply for listing on a regional stock exchange. For example, a firm based in Los Angeles might decide to list its stock on the Pacific Stock Exchange, and a Chicago firm may list its stock on the Midwest Stock Exchange. Growing still larger, a firm might decide to apply for listing on one of the national exchanges—like the New York Stock Exchange or the American Stock Exchange—or even on a foreign stock exchange located in Hong Kong, London, Sydney, or Tokyo. Of course, listing is not automatic. The firm must apply for listing, meet the specified listing requirements of the given exchange, and pay fees to have its stock listed on an organized exchange.

### Pricing the Issue

One of the critical functions of the managing underwriter is to price the new security. When a firm's stock is offered to the public for the first time, this job can be particularly difficult. Without existing shares trading in the market, the investment banker has few reference points to suggest how the market will value the new shares. As a consequence, the managing underwriter uses a variety of stock valuation models, such as the *constant-growth model* introduced in Chapter 12, to price the new shares at their market value.

### Preparing Documents

Next the firm begins the document preparation process. Public offerings require submission of a registration statement to the SEC. The federal government reviews the registration statement, but the issuer can circulate among potential investors a *prospectus.* The cover of Louis Dreyfus Natural Gas Corp.'s 67-page common stock prospectus is shown in Figure 17.3. As noted earlier, a prospectus is the portion of the registration statement that has important operating and financial data. To circulate the prospectus during this period, a **"red herring"**—a statement indicating the tentative nature of the offer—must be printed in red ink on its cover. After the registration statement receives SEC approval, the red herring will be removed and the prospectus will become final. Note that when the new security is offered for sale the prospectus must be made available to all interested parties.

**red herring**
A statement printed in red ink on the cover of a prospectus indicating the tentative nature of a securities offering before its approval by the SEC.

### Selling the Issue

After the registration statement is approved, the underwriter or underwriting syndicate purchases the new securities from the issuing firm and begins to sell them to the general public. The underwriters closely monitor the price that retail buyers are paying for the new stock. It is essential that the demand for, and therefore the price of, the stock remain strong. Any weakness in demand for the stock causes a price decline and reduces the underwriters' gross commission. If the retail price begins to move below the initial offering price printed on the prospectus, the underwriters may reverse direction and begin purchasing shares in the open market. This activity, called **market stabilization,** usually lasts for two or three days following the initial offering. For new issues that are particularly difficult to sell, however, the stabilization period can last as long as 30 days. This activity is legal as long as its intent is disclosed in the registration statement filed with the SEC. Market stabilization is in the best interest of both the issuer and the underwriters; it reduces the underwriters' risk, thereby justifying payment of a higher price to the issuer by the underwriters.

**market stabilization**
The purchase by underwriters of a security they are attempting to sell if the retail price of the shares moves below the initial offering price.

Once the underwriters' inventory of shares is completely exhausted, their job is still not finished. The managing underwriter, in particular, continues to monitor the aftermarket behavior of the security's price for periods extending up to one year. The investment banker's reputation and future underwriting business are significantly affected by its track record in correctly pricing and marketing new securities issues. Hence, the managing underwriter watches the price movement of the new stock and through its trading activities tries to make sure that the issue is neither significantly overvalued nor undervalued.

## Public Offering Versus Private Placement

When considering the sale of equity to raise needed funds, the financial manager must decide whether to go public or privately place their stock with a single investor or small group of investors. Attention must be given not only to the firm's unique circumstances and prevailing market conditions, but also to an evaluation of the fundamental advantages and disadvantages of public offerings. Here we take a brief look at these advantages and disadvantages and the recent trend toward public offerings.

**Advantages of Public Offerings**    Because investors can easily resell publicly traded securities in secondary markets, such securities offer *greater liquidity* to current and prospective stockholders. When a firm's securities are

## FINANCE IN ACTION

### Careers

### Sure It's a Tough Job, but Someone's Gotta Do It

Now that you've set your sights on a career in investment banking, just how much do you think you should be paid? If you were fortunate enough to be part of the investment banking industry in 1993, the answer is plenty. After a banner underwriting year, New York's investment banks realized pretax income of $8.8 billion in 1993, shattering 1992's record-breaking $6.2 billion in before-tax income. And the securities industry shared the wealth with its key employees.

Year-end bonuses in 1993 were up nearly 30 percent over 1992 levels. Hundreds of bonuses totaling $3 million or more were paid to top managing directors and partners at leading investment banks. Wall Street's most profitable player, Goldman Sachs & Co., offered bonuses of at least $5 million to each of its 160 partners. Although star traders and fund managers took home the largest paychecks, junior traders did pretty well too. Investment bankers just five years out of business school realized bonuses in the neighborhood of $250,000, and clerical personnel took home year-end paychecks that averaged about 30 percent of their annual base compensation. As you might expect, all this money makes for very happy employees. At year-end 1993, many investment bankers wouldn't even return phone calls from headhunters offering new employment opportunities.

Source: A. Stone, "Sorry, This Year Your Bonus Is Only $5 Million," *Business Week*, January 17, 1994, p. 27.

publicly held, it *can more readily issue additional securities* to raise more funds. This gives the firm wider access to a larger pool of financing, largely attributable to the greater market awareness resulting from public trading. In addition it is *easy to determine the market value of the firm's shares* when they are publicly traded. In contrast, privately held firms have more difficulty determining the market value of their shares, because they are not regularly exchanged by investors in a competitive marketplace. Another advantage is the *listing prestige* often resulting from having shares listed on a major stock exchange. For example, a firm whose shares are listed on the New York Stock Exchange (NYSE) can publicize that its shares trade in the same market as the largest, best known U.S. corporations. Finally, a public stock issue *allows the founders to sell their shares to the public and use the proceeds to diversify their investment portfolios.* It in effect creates a convenient mechanism that allows the founders to "cash out" if they so choose.

### Disadvantages of Public Offerings

Although going public has many advantages, it may not be the best course of action for all small firms. The out-of-pocket and underwriting *costs associated with public security sales are significant.* Firms can avoid, or at least reduce, these costs by using private placements to raise external funds. Another disadvantage is that SEC registration for public sale *requires firms publicly to disclose a great deal of operating and financial information.* Publicly held firms must make quarterly and annual financial statements available to the SEC, all shareholders, and the general public. These disclosures not only provide competitors with potentially useful information but also are costly. Another concern is that if investors focus on the short-term operating results of publicly held firms, *managers may operate these businesses to enhance short-run profits at the expense of long-run value.* For example, managers might postpone or forego major expenditures on research and development as well as equipment renovation, even where these projects would increase the long-run value of the firm, in order to increase short-run profits. (*Note:* This controversial criticism is probably valid only for stocks that are publicly traded but not widely followed by professional investors.) Public trading also *exposes the firm to the risk of a hostile takeover* by a corporate outsider that accumulates a controlling interest in the firm. Clearly, this possibility may result in a change in management and a loss of control by the firm's founders. Even if a firm does not become vulnerable to a hostile takeover, public sale results in the *dilution of ownership.* This occurs because when the owner-managers of a privately held firm take it public, they transfer some ownership rights to outside investors, thus reducing their proportionate ownership rights and control of the firm.

### The Trend Toward Public Offerings

Given the advantages and disadvantages of going public, it is not surprising that some firms choose public offerings, and others select private placements. Interestingly, the trend in recent years is toward increasing use of public offerings. Although in 1992 slightly more than 85 percent of both debt and common stock issues were sold through public offerings, the biggest change has occurred in debt issues. For example, between 1988 and 1992 the percentage of new debt issues that were publicly offered grew from about 61 percent to 85 percent. During the same period the percentage of new publicly offered common stock issues increased from about 70 percent to 85 percent. This trend can be attributed to the bull (i.e., rising) market for bonds and stocks, the advantages of going public cited above, and an increased willingness on the part of institutional investors to purchase new corporate debt and equity securities through public offerings.

▼▼▼▼▼▼▼▼▼▼▼▼▼▼▼▼▼▼▼▼▼▼▼▼▼▼▼▼▼▼

## Progress Review Questions

**17-11.** What is an *initial public offering (IPO)?* Why might a privately held firm decide to go public?

**17-12.** Describe, compare, and contrast the use of *competitive bidding* and the use of a *negotiated offering* to hire an investment banker.

**17-13.** What role does the *Securities Act of 1933* play in protecting investors? Does SEC approval of a security issue indicate that it is a good investment? Describe the roles of the *registration statement, prospectus,* and *red herring* as they relate to SEC registration.

**17-14.** List and briefly describe the key advantages and disadvantages commonly cited for going public. What is the recent trend with regard to public offerings? Explain.

▲▲▲▲▲▲▲▲▲▲▲▲▲▲▲▲▲▲▲▲▲▲▲▲▲▲▲▲▲▲

LG 5

## Beyond The IPO: Selling Additional Common Stock

If the managing underwriter does a good job of managing an IPO, for a time the new stock trades in the market at very close to its initial offering price. When this happens, the issuer is typically satisfied with the services provided by the underwriter and is likely to use the same investment banker to manage future offerings of additional equity. Here we examine some of the activities involved in subsequent public offerings of new common stock.

### Corporate Charter Restrictions

When a firm wishes to sell additional common stock, it must first make sure that it has enough **authorized shares** to support the issue. A firm's corporate charter defines the number of authorized shares it can issue. The firm cannot sell more shares than the charter authorizes without obtaining approval from its owners through a shareholder vote. Because it is often difficult to amend the charter to authorize the issuance of additional shares, firms generally attempt to authorize more shares than they initially plan to issue. Authorized shares become **outstanding shares** when they are sold to the public. If the firm repurchases any of its outstanding shares, these shares are recorded as *treasury stock* and shown as a deduction from stockholders' equity on the firm's balance sheet. **Issued shares** is the number of shares of common stock that has been put into circulation; it represents the sum of outstanding shares and treasury stock.

**authorized shares**
The number of shares of common stock that a firm's corporate charter allows without further shareholder approval.

**outstanding shares**
The number of shares of common stock held by the public.

**issued shares**
The number of shares of common stock that has been put into circulation; outstanding shares plus treasury stock.

# EXAMPLE

On December 31 of the year just ended Golden Enterprises, a producer of medical pumps, has the stockholders' equity account shown below.

| | |
|---|---:|
| Stockholders' equity | |
| Common stock—$.80 par value: | |
| Authorized 35,000,000 shares; issued 15,000,000 shares | $ 12,000,000 |
| Paid-in capital in excess of par | 63,000,000 |
| Retained earnings | 31,000,000 |
| | $106,000,000 |
| Less: Cost of treasury stock (1,000,000 shares) | 4,000,000 |
| Total stockholders' equity | $102,000,000 |

If Golden decides to sell additional common stock, how many shares can it sell without gaining approval from its shareholders? Note that the firm has 35 million authorized shares, 15 million issued shares, and 1 million shares of treasury stock. Thus, 14 million shares are outstanding (15 million issued shares − 1 million shares of treasury stock), and Golden can issue 21 million additional shares (35 million authorized shares − 14 million outstanding shares) without seeking shareholder approval to amend its corporate charter. This total includes the treasury shares currently held by Golden, which the firm can always reissue to the public without obtaining shareholder approval for their sale.

# Dilemmas Facing the Financial Manager

If a corporation has enough authorized shares to support the sale of additional stock, it follows a sequence of activities similar to an IPO to bring new stock to market. This means using the same process as the one described previously for an initial public offering. In addition, subsequent public offerings of new common stock create a few dilemmas for financial managers.

**Timing the Sale**   When selling new common stock, financial managers try to time the sale to get the highest possible price for the shares. If stock markets are *efficient* (i.e., stock prices are close to their true values), however, such actions are futile. Although financial managers may occasionally time equity sales to occur at peak pricing periods in the market, they will not be able to do so consistently.

Although the stock market is reasonably efficient, evidence suggests that some periods are better than others for issuing new stock. For example, it is not a good idea to offer new shares near the expiration date of *options* contracts written on a firm's common stock (discussed in Chapter 20). Stock prices can behave unpredictably during these periods. Second, it may be better to offer stocks that have historically paid high dividends before, rather than after, their ex dividend dates. As noted in Chapter 16, share prices are expected to drop by the amount of the declared dividend on the *ex dividend* date. Finally, it is usually a good idea to sell new issues when the demand for new stock is relatively high and the supply of new issues is relatively low. This means that financial managers are better off bringing new shares to market when investor optimism is high, and they are better off postponing new issues when numerous firms are actively trying to publicly sell new issues of common stock.

**Underpricing the Issue**    When publicly held firms issue new shares of common stock, they often set the initial offering price slightly below the market price of the firm's outstanding common stock. This provides some insurance that all of the new stock offered will be absorbed by the market. If the offering price is set too low, however, the value of the new shares quickly rises in the first few days after issuance. This presents a problem for the issuer: it suggests that the new stock was underpriced at the time it was issued. If so, the issuer has sold valuable securities to its new shareholders at a price below their true worth. As a result, the firm's cost of common stock equity (see Chapter 13) increases, and the wealth of its current owners declines as a result of a drop in share price. A transfer of wealth effectively results; the new shareholders gain by receiving more value than they paid for, and the existing shareholders' shares drop correspondingly in value.

**Market Impact of Public Offering**    When a publicly held corporation announces its plans to issue additional stock, the price of the firm's outstanding shares typically drops. Investors believe that the firm's managers feel the stock is overvalued and have therefore chosen to finance with common stock rather than debt. It may also occur because investors do not have the same information as the firm's managers regarding its investment opportunities. Shareholders may feel that the new stock issue will lower earnings per share, because the announced increase in the number of outstanding shares exceeds the growth in earnings they expect. Unless managers can convince them otherwise, these shareholders will not view the new equity issue as good news. Some may even sell their shares, which would hurt the market for them shortly after the firm announces its intent to sell new shares. Clearly, the financial manager must carefully and effectively communicate to its shareholders and the investment community positive information about the firm's motivations, plans, and expectations for the sale of additional common stock.

## Progress Review Questions

**17-15.** Define and differentiate between *authorized, outstanding,* and *issued* shares. How can the relationship among these values affect the firm's ability to issue additional shares of stock?

**17-16.** Briefly discuss each of the following dilemmas that frequently face a corporation that has adequate authorized shares and wishes to sell additional common stock.
   **a.** Timing the sale of new shares
   **b.** Underpricing the new shares
   **c.** Anticipating the market effect of the offering

# Recent Trends in the Investment Banking Industry

**leveraged buyouts (LBOs)**
Largely debt-financed acquisitions of firms by acquirers.

**junk bonds**
Low-rated, high-risk debt securities used by acquirers to finance acquisitions of firms.

Investment banking is an extremely dynamic industry. Investment bankers vigorously compete with one another to attract new clients and win new underwriting business. They take advantage of changes in economic conditions, regulation, and social attitudes to bring innovative new securities to market. During the 1980s, many investment bankers used deregulation within the financial services industry, changes in tax laws, and the growing public acceptance of largely debt-financed acquisitions, called **leveraged buyouts (LBOs),** to gain new business underwriting low-rated, high-risk debt securities known as **junk bonds.** In these LBOs acquirers raised substantial amounts of money by issuing junk bonds through a few investment banking firms. They then used the proceeds to acquire controlling equity interests in firms that they believed were undervalued. (See Chapter 21 for a discussion of leveraged buyouts.) Once the acquirer gained control of the firm, it planned to use the firm's operating cash flows to repay the debt that financed its acquisition. If operating cash flows were inadequate to meet the interest and principal payments on the debt, acquirers believed they could always sell some of the acquired firm's assets to other investors and use the sale proceeds to reduce their heavy debt burdens.

## The Demise of Largely Debt-Financed Acquisitions

Initially, many debt-financed acquisitions proceeded according to the plan noted above. Many investors profited: junk bond underwriters captured huge underwriting profits; shareholders of acquired firms realized substantial capital gains; acquirers made fortunes through speculative and short-term investments; and junk bondholders realized sizeable returns on their investments while apparently taking little risk. Each new deal involved bigger numbers and more leverage—it seemed like the party would never end. However, toward the end of the 1980s, it did. Economic growth slowed to a crawl, and in mid-1990 the domestic economy officially entered a recession. With little economic growth to stimulate corporate sales, the operating cash flows of highly leveraged firms plummeted. Without the cash flow needed to meet the excessive debt burdens, managers of newly acquired firms sold assets to raise cash. In a recessionary economy, however, few new buyers came forward to buy the assets. Many bond issues entered default when corporations could no longer make required interest and principal payments on these debts.

At the same time, the demise of the savings and loan industry and the growing crisis among commercial banks and insurance companies took many institutional purchasers of junk bonds out of the market. With savings and loans posting record losses in the late 1980s, the government passed the *Financial Institutions Reform, Recovery, and Enforcement Act of 1989* to salvage federal deposit insurance programs as well as the remains of the savings and loan industry. This legislation prohibited federally insured financial institutions from owning junk bonds. It also ordered savings and loans to sell their existing junk bond investments over a relatively short period. In addition, commercial bank regulators tightened federal regulations governing loans to highly leveraged borrowers.

These changes resulted in fewer individual and institutional investors seeking to buy junk bonds, and therefore significantly reduced the volume of funds flowing into the junk bond market. With little new money entering the market and a growing list of junk bond defaults, the value of existing junk bonds sank dramatically. Financial institutions and investment bankers who were holding large portfolios of junk bonds watched in horror. Their asset values collapsed and the value of their equity turned negative. Drexel, Burnham, Lambert, the largest underwriter of junk bond issues in the 1980s, filed for bankruptcy in early 1990. At the same time, many savings and loans and insurance companies holding large junk bond portfolios faced financial ruin.

What did we learn from the excessive use of leverage in the 1980s? First, risk and return are closely linked. To achieve higher returns, investors must take larger risks. In addition, leverage can be addictive. Naive investors and financial managers frequently overlooked the risks contained in highly leveraged transactions and focused instead on the attractive returns they would earn through the use of debt financing. In the end, however, it was the risk—not the high expected returns—that they remembered. Although the *prudent use* of debt financing is good for stockholders, bondholders, financial managers, and investment bankers, the lesson of the 1980s is that the *excessive use* of debt can really hurt all of them.

## The Rise of Financial Engineering

How are investment bankers surviving and prospering today, given the collapse of their junk bond underwriting business? Although it is true that many corporations continue to reduce their use of debt financing, the market for new debt issues certainly has not disappeared. Of course investment bankers actively continue to underwrite new and subsequent equity offerings and serve as agents, advise, and make markets for client firms. In addition, investment bankers continue to develop new and innovative financing arrangements that meet the needs of firms seeking to raise external funds and provide risk-return characteristics that attract investors.

The process of bringing innovative financial products and procedures to market is known as **financial engineering.** Financial engineering includes the introduction of new consumer investments such as IRA and Keogh accounts, the creation of new securities such as money market preferred stock, the development of new procedures such as shelf registration, and the identification of innovative solutions to corporate finance problems such as the creation and sale of junk bond portfolios.

**financial engineering**
The process of bringing new innovative financial products and procedures to market.

A variety of factors explain the motives for financial engineering within the investment banking industry. First, investment bankers must constantly monitor and respond to changes in tax laws and securities regulation. These changes create opportunities to design new securities that save corporate borrowers money and provide attractive returns for investors. Second, environmental changes often signal the need for innovative financing arrangements. Increased interest rate movements in the 1980s offered investment bankers an opportunity to design securities that exploit as well as minimize the risk of interest rate changes. A number of these securities were soon introduced to help borrowers and lenders cope with rapidly changing interest rates. Finally, the competition between investment banking firms encourages financial engineering. The firms that develop innovative securities and new solutions to corporate financing problems can use these products and services to solicit business from new clients, thereby gaining market share and a reputation for financial innovation.

## Investment Banking in the Future

With the eventual entry of commercial banks into the investment banking industry sometime before the end of this decade, competition among investment bankers will surely accelerate. Increased competition means more financial engineering, and hence a steady flow of new financial products and procedures. What will future innovations look like, and how will we know they are significant innovations when we see them? In general, any innovation that enhances shareholder value is likely to succeed. This can be accomplished in a variety of ways.

First, if investment bankers can develop new securities that are less costly to the issuer than existing securities with similar terms, they will create shareholder value. The lower cost will lower the firm's cost of capital (see Chapter 13) and (assuming constant earnings) will increase the firm's value (see Chapter 12). Second, if investment bankers can develop products and procedures that reduce the riskiness of payment streams made by issuing corporations to investors, they will create shareholder value. Lower risk means that investors will accept lower returns, the issuers' cost of capital will be reduced, and (again assuming constant earnings) shareholder value will increase. Third, if investment bankers can develop ways for corporations to build fixed asset portfolios less expensively than individual investors can build portfolios of fixed assets, then shareholder value will increase. Corporations will issue securities backed by their fixed assets, and because it will be cheaper for investors to buy these securities than to assemble their own portfolios of fixed assets, new investment dollars will flow to the firm at a reasonable cost. Once again, the lower cost financing resulting from this innovation will create shareholder value.

Investment bankers will use a number of other techniques in the future to create shareholder value. Underwritten instruments with lower transaction costs help build value, so investment bankers will search for new financing arrangements that require lower underwriting spreads. Securities that reduce the issuer's tax liability create shareholder value, so investment bankers will carefully examine the tax code to identify new ways to engineer securities that minimize corporate taxes. Finally, new issues that convey more information to investors concerning the strength of the issuer create value, because these securities reduce the information gap between a firm's managers and outside investors. Equal access to information will reduce a costly barrier to the investor's understanding of the firm's condition and outlook, and will increase the value of the firm.

# Progress Review Question

**17-17.**

**a.** Describe the following two recent trends in the investment banking industry:

   i. Demise of *largely debt-financed acquisitions*
   ii. Rise in *financial engineering*

**b.** Discuss the future of investment banking.

# SUMMARY OF LEARNING GOALS

**Understand the role of long-term financing, including internal and external sources, the need for external funds, and the methods used by both established and emerging small corporations to raise external funds.** Businesses routinely need long-term funds to finance corporate growth and the replacement of worn-out equipment and to pay off debts and other obligations as they come due. The internal source of funds is funds generated within the firm from retained earnings. External sources of funds are raised outside of the firm through negotiated loans or the sale of bonds, preferred stock, or common stock. Firms use external funds to finance growth when their internally generated funds are inadequate to meet their long-term financing need. Firms typically raise external funds through either a public offering or a private placement of new debt or equity securities. Emerging small corporations frequently seek financing in the form of venture capital. Venture capital is financing invested in an emerging business firm by specialized financial intermediaries known as venture capitalists. Although they sometimes provide debt financing, in most cases they obtain common stock ownership in the businesses they finance.

LG 1

**Explain the role of investment banking in long-term business financing: the bankers' role as underwriter, agent, adviser, and market maker, the use of shelf registration, and the formation of syndicates by underwriters.** Investment bankers act as financial intermediaries between the issuers and buyers of new securities. Their most common roles in security offerings are as underwriter, agent, adviser, and market maker. The investment banker's primary function is underwriting, which involves buying a security issue from the issuing firm at a lower price than the investment banker plans to sell it for, thereby guaranteeing the issuer a specified amount from the issue and assuming the risk of price changes between the points of purchase and sale. Investment bankers also assist in private placement and can be hired to serve as the issuer's agent and sell its securities on a best efforts basis. A secondary, but important, function performed by investment bankers involves providing advice to issuers on appropriate financing, mergers, acquisitions, and refinancing decisions. Investment bankers also use their industry contacts with other investment banking firms to create the widest possible distribution for new issues and make a market in them. Shelf registration of new securities has become extremely popular because, in most cases, it minimizes the paperwork necessary to initiate security sales, thus reducing the transactions cost of bringing new securities to market. Investment bankers may form an underwriting syndicate—a group of investment banking firms that collectively participate in buying and selling a portion of the new issues—to reduce the price risk.

LG 2

**Discuss investment banker compensation: the underwriting spread, the cost of public offerings, and the cost of private placements.** Investment bankers are compensated with a gross commission (or gross underwriting spread)—the difference between the price at which an investment banker sells a se-

 LG 3

curities issue to the public and the price at which it bought the issue from the issuing firm—on underwritten issues and a fee paid on a per share basis for nonunderwritten issues, direct placements, and best efforts sales. In the case of private (direct) placement, investment bankers do not purchase and resell securities and, thus, they cannot be compensated on the basis of a price mark-up at the time of public sale. They establish a charge based on the advising, marketing, and distribution services they provide.

**LG 4**

**Describe the key activities of the firm in an initial public offering—selecting an investment banker and going public—and public offering versus private placement.** In an initial public offering, the firm must select an investment banker either on the basis of competitive bidding or a negotiated offering. With the help of the investment banker, the firm then obtains authorization to issue new common stock to the public, identifies the market in which the securities will trade, prices the new security, submits documents to and obtains approval from the SEC, and sells the securities to the general public. An alternative to public offering is private (direct) placement of securities—primarily bonds and preferred stocks. In private placements an investment banker is usually employed to assist in finding a buyer and to provide pricing advice.

**LG 5**

**Review the restrictions and dilemmas frequently faced by the financial manager when making subsequent public offerings of new common stock.** When a publicly held firm wishes to sell additional equity it must first make sure that a sufficient number of authorized and unissued shares are available. If not, it needs to obtain shareholder approval for issuance of additional shares. The dilemmas faced by the financial manager when making subsequent public offerings of common stock include timing the sale to get the highest possible price, avoiding excessive underpricing that reduces the wealth of current owners, and effectively communicating to its shareholders positive information about the motives for the offering.

**LG 6**

**Summarize recent trends in the investment banking industry—the demise of largely debt-financed acquisitions and the rise of financial engineering—and how it is likely to change in the future.** During the 1980s, many investment bankers used deregulation within the financial services industry, changes in tax laws, and the growing public acceptance of largely debt-financed acquisitions, called leveraged buyouts (LBOs), to gain new business underwriting low-rated, high-risk debt securities known as "junk bonds." A slowdown in the rate of economic growth, the demise of the savings and loan industry, and the growing crisis among commercial banks and insurance companies brought on the collapse of the junk bond market. Also, many highly debt-financed firms, as a result of diminished cash flows, found themselves unable to make payments on their debts. In the future, investment bankers will face increased competition. To survive, they will focus on financial engineering, the introduction of innovative financial products and procedures intended to reduce the cost of capital and increase the issuer's shareholder value. The new financial products and procedures will be aimed at lowering financing costs—directly, through risk reduction, or by lowering transactions costs—to enhance shareholder value.

# 18 Long-Term Debt and Leasing

Ryder System Inc., a $4.2 billion international transportation services company, is the largest truck-leasing and rental company in the world, the second largest student transportation services company, and the nation's largest over-the-road carrier of new autos. The company's fastest growing area is dedicated logistics, in which Ryder, in addition to vehicles, provides

> **To keep interest rates low, you must actively manage your debt portfolio as market conditions and your asset base change.**

drivers, routing, and scheduling to optimize its customers' distribution networks.

The company is asset-intensive, with average annual capital expenditures of over $1 billion. When business is growing, the need for capital increases. The level of debt and equity in a company's capital structure determines its cost of capital, which affects its competitive position, pricing strategy, and capital investment decisions. Typically, debt is more cost-effective than equity because interest is tax-deductible. Companies try

to lower their cost of capital through the optimal use of debt and equity.

Companies use many different strategies to fund their debt requirement. Public companies can use private bank term debt or raise public debt in the capital markets. Ryder's access to both the private and public debt markets results in the availability of several financing instruments, including commercial paper, medium-term notes, bonds, leasing, and the use of derivative instruments, among others in the market.

A company's debt cost depends on its credit quality. Other factors, such as tax position, can also influence cost. In a normal interest rate environment, long-term debt, which is typically fixed, is more expensive than short-term debt, which is typically floating, but provides liquidity and predictability of interest costs. The amount of fixed- and floating-rate debt a company has is tied to market conditions and a company's risk tolerance. For example, in 1992 and 1993, some companies had more floating-rate debt than usual because rates were low and trending downward.

"Match funding" the average debt maturity to the average life of the underlying pool of assets is a strategy Ryder uses. The actual maturities depend on the market, the yield curve, and maturities in the existing debt portfolio. Ryder has intermediate maturity debt, which is appropriate for our asset base (primarily trucks). A utility company, on the other hand, finances power plants, which have longer average lives, with debt that has longer average maturities.

Leasing is another long-term financing technique, and Ryder acts as both lessor and lessee of equipment. Ryder's large equipment capital expenditures generate more tax depreciation than it can use. Ryder uses leveraged leasing to lower its financing cost by leasing equipment from companies that need tax benefits to shelter income. We analyze the net present-value cost of the lease-versus-purchase transaction and choose the most economic alternative.

Being a financial manager today is definitely more interesting and challenging than ever. With interest rates so volatile and new financial tools coming to market each day, you can't just issue a 30-year bond and consider it done. To keep interest costs low, you must actively manage your debt portfolio as market conditions and your asset base change.

*Glynis Bryan, assistant treasurer of Ryder System Inc., received a B.A. in psychology from York University, Toronto, Canada, and an M.B.A. in finance from Florida International University, Miami. She joined Ryder in 1984 and served in finance positions in several business units before assuming her current position in 1993.*

Long-term debt and leasing are important forms of *long-term financing*. Long-term debt can be obtained with a *term loan,* which is negotiated from a financial institution, or through the sale of *bonds,* which are marketable debt sold to a number of institutional and individual lenders. Long-term debt provides financial leverage (see Chapter 5) and is a desirable component of capital structure (see Chapter 16) because it tends to lower the weighted average cost of capital (see Chapter 13).[1]

*Leasing,* like long-term debt, allows the firm to obtain use of, but not ownership of, fixed assets in exchange for a series of contractual, periodic lease payments. The use of leasing has grown in popularity over the past 30 or so years. We begin this chapter with discussions of long-term debt financing followed by a review of leasing.

# Characteristics of Long-Term Debt Financing

LG 1

The long-term debts of a business typically have maturities of between 5 and 20 years. When a long-term debt is within one year of its maturity, accountants show the balance of the long-term debt as a current liability; at that point it becomes a short-term obligation. Similar treatment is given to portions of long-term debts payable in the coming year. These entries are normally labeled "current portion of long-term debt." Here we discuss long-term debt provisions and costs. In subsequent sections we turn our attention to term loans and corporate bonds.

## Standard Debt Provisions

A number of **standard debt provisions** are included in long-term debt agreements. These provisions specify certain criteria of satisfactory record keeping and reporting, tax payment, and general business maintenance on the part of the borrowing firm. Standard debt provisions do not normally place a burden on the financially sound business. Commonly included standard provisions appear in the following list:

**standard debt provision**
Provisions in long-term debt agreements specifying certain operating criteria, which normally do not place a burden on the financially sound business borrower.

1. The borrower is required to *maintain satisfactory accounting records* in accordance with generally accepted accounting principles (GAAP).
2. The borrower is required to periodically *supply audited financial statements,* which are used by the lender to monitor the firm and enforce the debt agreement.
3. The borrower is required to *pay taxes and other liabilities when due.*
4. The borrower is required to *maintain all facilities in good working order,* thereby behaving as a "going concern."

---

[1]Of course, as noted in Chapter 16, the introduction of large quantities of debt into the firm's capital structure can result in high levels of financial risk, which cause the weighted average cost of capital to rise.

## Restrictive Debt Provisions

**restrictive covenants**
Contractual clauses in long-term debt agreements that place certain operating and financial constraints on the borrower.

Long-term debt agreements, whether resulting from a term loan or a bond issue, normally include certain **restrictive covenants,** contractual clauses that place certain operating and financial constraints on the borrower. Because the lender is committing funds for a long period, it of course seeks to protect itself. Restrictive covenants, coupled with standard debt provisions, allow the lender to monitor and control the borrower's activities in order to protect itself against increases in borrower risk. These covenants remain in force for the life of the debt agreement. The most common restrictive covenants are as follows:

1. The borrower is required to *maintain a minimum level of net working capital.* Net working capital below the minimum is considered indicative of inadequate liquidity, a common precursor to loan default and ultimate failure.

2. Borrowers are *prohibited from selling accounts receivable* to generate cash. Doing so can cause a long-run cash shortage if proceeds are used to meet current obligations.

3. Long-term lenders commonly impose *fixed-asset restrictions* on the firm. These constrain the firm with respect to the liquidation, acquisition, and encumbrance of fixed assets; any of these actions can damage the firm's ability to repay its debt.

4. Many debt agreements *constrain subsequent borrowing* by prohibiting additional long-term debt or by requiring that additional borrowing be "*subordinated*" to the original loan. **Subordination** means that all subsequent or less important creditors agree to wait until all claims of the *senior debt* are satisfied before having their claims satisfied.

**subordination**
The stipulation in a long-term debt agreement that all subsequent or less important creditors agree to wait until all claims of the *senior debt* are satisfied before having their claims satisfied.

5. Borrowers may be *prohibited from entering into certain types of leases.* This provision limits additional fixed-payment obligations.

6. Occasionally the lender *prohibits combinations* by requiring the borrower to agree not to consolidate, merge, or combine in any way with another firm, because such an action can significantly change the borrower's business and financial risk.

7. To prevent liquidation of assets through large salary payments, the lender may *prohibit or limit salary increases for specified employees.*

8. The lender may include *management restrictions* requiring the borrower to maintain certain "key employees" without whom the future of the firm is uncertain.

9. Occasionally the lender includes a covenant *limiting the borrower's security investment* alternatives. This restriction protects the lender by controlling the risk and marketability of the borrower's security investments.

10. Occasionally a covenant specifically requires the borrower to *spend the borrowed funds on a proven financial need.*

11. A relatively common provision *limits the firm's annual cash dividend payments* to a maximum of 50 to 70 percent of its net earnings or a specified dollar amount.

In the process of negotiating the terms of long-term debt, borrower and lender must ultimately agree to acceptable restrictive covenants. A good financial manager knows in advance the relative effect of proposed restrictions. He or she "holds the line" on those that may have a severely negative or damaging effect. The violation of any standard or restrictive provision by the borrower gives the lender the right to demand immediate repayment of the debt. Generally the lender evaluates any violation to determine whether it is serious enough to jeopardize the loan. On the basis of such an evaluation the lender may demand immediate repayment of the loan, waive the violation and continue the loan, or waive the violation but alter the terms of the initial debt agreement.

## Cost of Long-Term Debt

The cost of long-term debt is generally greater than that of short-term borrowing. In addition to standard and restrictive provisions, the long-term debt agreement specifies the interest rate, the timing of payments, and the dollar amount of payments. The major factors affecting the cost, or interest rate, of long-term debt are loan maturity, loan size, and more importantly, borrower risk and the basic cost of money.

**Loan Maturity**   Generally, long-term loans have higher interest rates than short-term loans. The longer the term of a loan, the less accuracy there is in predicting future interest rates and therefore the greater the lender's risk of missing an opportunity to loan money at a higher rate. In addition, the longer the term, the greater the repayment risk associated with the loan. To compensate for both the uncertainty of future interest rates and the higher probability that the borrower will default, the lender typically charges a higher interest rate on long-term loans.

**Loan Size**   The size of the loan affects the interest cost of borrowing in an inverse manner. As loan size increases, loan administration costs per dollar borrowed tend to decrease. On the other hand, the risk to the lender increases, because larger loans result in less diversification. The size of the loan sought by each borrower must therefore be evaluated to determine the net administrative cost-risk trade-off.

**Borrower Risk**   As noted in Chapter 5, the higher the firm's operating leverage, the greater its business risk. Also, the higher the borrower's debt ratio, the greater its financial risk. (Likewise, the lower the firm's times interest earned ratio or its fixed-payment coverage ratio, the greater its financial risk.) The lender's main concern is with the borrower's ability to repay fully the loan as prescribed in the debt agreement. The overall assessment of the borrower's business and financial risk, along with information on past payment patterns, is used by the lender in setting the interest rate on any loan.

**Basic Cost of Money**   The cost of money is the basis for determining the actual interest rate charged. Generally the rate on U.S. Treasury securities with *equivalent maturities* is used as the basic (lowest risk) cost of money. To determine the actual interest rate to be charged, the lender adds premiums for loan size and borrower risk to this basic cost of money for the given maturity. Alternatively, some lenders use the rate charged on similar-maturity loans to firms believed to have equivalent risk. Instead of having to determine a risk premium, the lender can use the risk premium prevailing in the marketplace for similar loans.

## Progress Review Questions

**18-1.** What are the two key methods of raising long-term debt financing? What motives does the lender have for including certain *restrictive covenants* in a debt agreement? How do these covenants differ from so-called *standard debt provisions?*

**18-2.** What sort of negotiation process is required in settling on a set of restrictive loan covenants? What are the consequences of violation of a standard or restrictive provision by the borrower?

**18-3.** What is the general relationship between the cost of short-term and long-term debt? Why? In addition to loan maturity, what other major factors affect the cost, or interest rate, of long-term debt?

# Term Loans

**term (long-term) loan**
A loan with an initial maturity of more than one year, made by a financial institution to a business.

A **term (long-term) loan** is a loan with an initial maturity of more than one year, made by a financial institution to a business. These loans generally have maturities of 5 to 12 years; shorter maturities are available, but minimum 5-year maturities are common. Term loans are often made to finance *permanent* working capital needs, to pay for machinery and equipment, or to liquidate other loans.

## Characteristics of Term Loan Agreements

**term loan agreement**
A formal contract specifying the conditions under which a financial institution has made a long-term loan.

The actual **term loan agreement** is a formal contract ranging from a few to a few hundred pages. The following items are commonly specified in the document: the amount and maturity of the loan, payment dates, interest rate, standard provisions, restrictive provisions, collateral (if any), purpose of the loan, action to be taken if the agreement is violated, and stock-purchase warrants. Of these, only payment dates, collateral requirements, and stock-purchase warrants require further discussion.

**Payment Dates**   Term loan agreements generally specify monthly, quarterly, semiannual, or annual loan payments. Generally these equal payments fully repay the interest and principal over the life of the loan. Occasionally a term loan agreement requires periodic payments over the life of the loan followed by a large lump-sum payment at maturity. This so-called **balloon payment** represents the entire loan principal if the periodic payments represent only interest.

**balloon payment**
At the maturity of a loan, a large lump-sum payment.

**Collateral Requirements**   Term lending arrangements may be *unsecured* or *secured,* similar to those for short-term loans (see Chapter 10). Whether *collateral* is required depends on the lender's evaluation of the borrower's financial condition. Common forms of collateral include machinery and equipment, plant, inventory, pledges of accounts receivable, and pledges of securities. Any collateral required and its disposition under various circumstances are specifically described in the term loan agreement. In addition, the lender files necessary legal documents to (1) establish clearly its right to seize and liquidate loan collateral if the borrower defaults and (2) serve notice to subsequent lenders of a prior claim on the asset(s).

**Stock-Purchase Warrants**   A trend in term lending is for the corporate borrower to give the lender certain financial perquisites in addition to the payment of interest and repayment of principal. **Stock-purchase warrants** are instruments that give their holders the right to purchase a certain number of shares of the firm's common stock at a specified price over a certain period. These are used to entice institutional lenders to make long-term loans, possibly under better-than-normal terms. Stock-purchase warrants are discussed in greater detail in Chapter 20.

**stock-purchase warrants**
Instruments that give their holders the right to purchase a certain number of shares of the firm's common stock at a specified price over a certain period.

## Term Lenders

The primary lenders making term loans to business are commercial banks, insurance companies, pension funds, regional development companies, the federal government's Small Business Administration, small business investment companies, commercial finance companies, and equipment manufacturers' financing subsidiaries. Although the characteristics and provisions of term lending agreements made by these lenders are similar, a number of basic differences exist. Table 18.1 summarizes the key characteristics and types of loans made.

▼▼▼▼▼▼▼▼▼▼▼▼▼▼▼▼▼▼▼▼▼▼▼▼▼▼▼▼▼▼▼

## Progress Review Questions

**18-4.** What types of payment dates are generally required in a term (long-term) loan agreement? What is a *balloon payment?*

**18-5.** What role do commercial banks, insurance companies, pension funds, regional development companies, the Small Business Administration, small business investment companies, commercial finance companies, and equipment manufacturers play in lending long-term funds to businesses?

▲▲▲▲▲▲▲▲▲▲▲▲▲▲▲▲▲▲▲▲▲▲▲▲▲▲▲▲▲▲▲

# Corporate Bonds

A **corporate bond** is a certificate indicating that a corporation has borrowed a certain amount of money from an institution or an individual and promises to repay it in the future under clearly defined terms. Most bonds are issued with maturities of 10 to 30 years and with a par, or face, value of $1,000. The coupon interest rate on a bond represents the percentage of the bond's par value that is to be paid annually, typically in two equal semiannual payments.

**corporate bond**
A certificate indicating that a corporation has borrowed a certain amount of money and promises to repay it in the future under clearly defined terms.

**TABLE 18.1 Characteristics and Types of Term Loans Made by Major Term Lenders**

| Lender | Characteristics | Types of Loans |
|---|---|---|
| Commercial bank | Makes some term loans to businesses. | Generally less than 12-year maturity except for real estate. Often participates in large loans made by a group of banks because banks are legally limited[a] in the amount they can loan a single borrower. Loans typically secured by collateral. |
| Insurance company | Life insurers are most active lenders. | Maturities of 10 to 20 years. Generally to larger firms and in larger amounts than commercial bank loans. Both unsecured and secured loans. |
| Pension fund | Invests a small portion of its funds in term loans to businesses. | Generally mortgage loans to large firms. Similar to insurance company loans. |
| Regional development company | An association generally attached to local or regional governments. Attempts to promote business development in a given area by offering attractive financing deals. Obtains funds from various governmental bodies and through sale of tax-exempt bonds. | Term loans are made at competitive rates. |
| Small Business Administration (SBA) | An agency of the federal government that makes loans to eligible small and minority-owned businesses.[b] | Joins with private lender and lends or guarantees repayment of all or part of the loan. Most loans are made for less than $750,000 at or below commercial bank interest rates. The average loan amount is around $300,000. |
| Small business investment company (SBIC) | Licensed by the government. Makes both debt and equity investments in small firms. | Makes loans to small firms with high growth potential. Term loans with 5- to 20-year maturities and interest rates above those on bank loans. Generally receives, in addition, an equity interest in the borrowing firm. |
| Commercial finance company (CFC) | Involved in financing equipment purchases. Often a subsidiary of the manufacturer of equipment. | Makes secured loans for purchase of equipment. Typically installment loans with less-than-10-year maturities at higher-than-bank interest rates. |
| Equipment manufacturers' financing subsidiary | A type of "captive finance company" owned by the equipment manufacturer. | Makes long-term installment loans on equipment sales. Similar to commercial finance companies. |

[a]Commercial banks are legally prohibited from loaning amounts in excess of 15 percent (plus an additional 10 percent for loans secured by readily marketable collateral) of the bank's unimpaired capital and surplus to any one borrower. This restriction is intended to protect depositors by forcing the commercial bank to spread its risk across a number of borrowers.

[b]To be eligible for an SBA loan, small business owners must first attempt to obtain private financing from a bank or other lending institution. If they are turned down, they can then apply to the SBA. The law does not allow the SBA to make a loan to a business that can get funds from a bank or other private source.

The bondholders, who are the lenders, are promised the semiannual interest payments and, at maturity, repayment of the principal amount (par value).

## Legal Aspects of Corporate Bonds

Because a corporate bond issue may be for hundreds of millions of dollars obtained by selling portions of the debt to numerous unrelated persons, certain legal arrangements are required to protect purchasers. Bondholders are legally protected primarily through the indenture and the trustee.

**Bond Indenture**   A **bond indenture** is a complex and lengthy legal document stating the conditions under which a bond has been issued. It specifies both the rights of the bondholders and the duties of the issuing corporation. In addition to specifying the interest and principal payments and dates, and containing various standard and restrictive provisions, it frequently contains sinking-fund requirements and, if the bond is secured, provisions with respect to a security interest.

**bond indenture**
A legal document stating the conditions under which a bond has been issued.

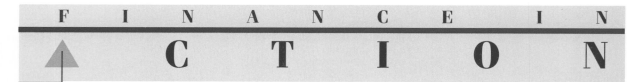

# FINANCE IN
# ACTION

### Creative Debt Financing Flourishes When Interest Rates Are Low

**In the News**

In the low interest rate environment that prevailed in the early 1990s, many financial managers saw an opportunity to use debt in innovative and creative ways. For example, Phoenix Reinsurance Corp. used long-term debt as variable capital to achieve greater leverage on its expanding equity base. Phoenix issued $26 million in convertible preferred stock and $50 million in common stock in 1992, and then added $75 million in 10-year, 9.75 percent debt in 1993 to create greater financial leverage against its new equity issues. The firm plans to treat the new debt as "variable" capital, retiring it after five years when the leverage benefits are no longer needed to boost the company's return on equity.

At Community Health Systems, Inc., an owner-operator of nonurban hospitals in the greater Houston area, $120 million in senior debt was replaced with permanent subordinated debt in 1993. The transaction elevated the firm's total debt ratio slightly; however, the ratio of senior debt to capital decreased from 63 percent to less than 33 percent, making the company's bankers very happy. In this case, Community Health Systems revised its capital structure using multilayered debt, rather than equity, because the stock market was not, well, hospitable to new equity issues from health care firms. Uncertainty about the long-term effects of the Clinton Administration's health care reform plan led the company to avoid an equity offering and to spruce up its capital structure using $100 million in 10-year, subordinated debentures carrying a 10.25 percent coupon.

Source: A. Monroe, "Sitting Pretty," *CFO Magazine*, December 1993, p. 40.

**Sinking-Fund Requirements.**  The standard and restrictive provisions for long-term debt and for bond issues were described in an earlier section of this chapter. However, an additional restrictive provision often included in a bond indenture is a **sinking-fund requirement.** Its objective is to provide for the systematic retirement of bonds prior to their maturity. To carry out this requirement, the corporation makes semiannual or annual payments to a *trustee,* who uses these funds to retire bonds by purchasing them in the marketplace. This process is simplified by inclusion of a *call feature,* which permits the issuer to repurchase bonds at a stated price prior to maturity. The trustee "calls" bonds only when sufficient bonds cannot be purchased in the marketplace or when the market price of the bond is above the stated (call) price.

**Security Interest.**  The bond indenture is similar to a loan agreement in that any collateral pledged against the bond is specifically identified in the document. Usually, the title to the collateral is attached to the indenture, and the disposition of the collateral in various circumstances is specifically described. The protection of bond collateral is crucial to increasing the safety and thereby enhancing the marketability of a bond issue.

**Trustee**  A **trustee** is a third party to a bond indenture. The trustee can be an individual, a corporation, or, most often, a commercial bank trust department. The trustee, whose services are paid for, acts as a "watchdog" on behalf of the bondholders, making sure that the issuer does not default on its contractual responsibilities. The trustee is empowered to take specified actions on behalf of the bondholders if the terms of the indenture are violated.

## General Features of a Bond Issue

Three common features of a bond issue are (1) a conversion feature, (2) a call feature, and (3) stock-purchase warrants. These features provide both the issuer and the purchaser with certain opportunities for replacing, retiring, and (or) supplementing the bond with some type of equity issue.

**Conversion Feature**  The **conversion feature** of certain so-called *convertible bonds* allows bondholders to change each bond into a stated number of shares of stock. Bondholders convert their bonds only when the market price of the stock is greater than the conversion price, hence providing a profit for the bondholder. Chapter 20 discusses convertible bonds in detail.

**Call Feature**  The **call feature** is included in almost all corporate bond issues. It gives the issuer the opportunity to repurchase bonds prior to maturity. The **call price** is the stated price at which bonds may be repurchased prior to maturity. Sometimes the call privilege may be exercised only during a certain period. As a rule, the call price exceeds the par value of a bond by an amount equal to one year's interest. For example, a $1,000 bond with a 10 percent coupon interest rate is callable for around $1,100 [$1,000 + (10% × $1,000)]. The amount by which the call price exceeds the bond's par value is commonly referred to as the **call premium.** This premium compensates bondholders for having the bond called away from them, and it is the cost to the issuer of calling the bonds. A higher call premium is required by investors

---

**sinking-fund requirement**
A restrictive provision often included in a bond indenture providing for the systematic retirement of bonds prior to their maturity.

**trustee**
A paid third party to a bond indenture, whose job it is to ensure that the issuer does not default on its contractual responsibilities to the bondholders.

**conversion feature**
A feature of so-called *convertible bonds* that allows bondholders to change each bond into a stated number of shares of stock.

**call feature**
A feature of most corporate bonds that allows the issuer to repurchase bonds at a stated price prior to maturity.

**call price**
The stated price at which a bond may be repurchased, by use of a call feature, prior to maturity.

**call premium**
The amount by which a bond's call price exceeds its par value.

when interest rates are high because there is an increased likelihood rates will decline, the issuer will exercise the call, and the bondholders will experience large opportunity losses.

The call feature is generally advantageous to the issuer, because it enables the issuer to retire outstanding debt prior to maturity. Thus when interest rates fall, an issuer can call an outstanding bond and reissue a new bond at a lower interest rate. When interest rates rise, the call privilege is not exercised, except possibly to meet sinking-fund requirements. Of course, to sell a callable bond the issuer must pay a higher interest rate than on noncallable bonds of equal risk. Bondholders must be compensated for the risk of having the bonds called away from them.

**Stock-Purchase Warrants**   Like term loans, bonds occasionally have warrants attached as "sweeteners" to make them more attractive to prospective buyers. As noted earlier, a *stock-purchase warrant* gives its holder the right to purchase a certain number of shares of common stock at a specified price over a certain period. An in-depth discussion of stock-purchase warrants is included in Chapter 20.

## Bond Ratings

The riskiness of publicly traded bond issues is assessed by independent agencies such as Moody's and Standard & Poor's. Moody's has 9 major ratings; Standard & Poor's has 10. These agencies derive their ratings by using financial ratio and cash flow analyses. Table 18.2 summarizes the ratings. There is normally an inverse relationship between the quality or rating of a bond and the rate of return it must provide bondholders. High-quality (high-rated) bonds provide lower returns than lower quality (low-rated) bonds. This reflects the risk-return trade-off of the lender. When considering bond financing, the financial manager must therefore be concerned with the expected ratings of the firm's bond issue because these ratings can significantly affect salability and cost.

## Popular Types of Bonds

Bonds can be classified in a variety of ways. Here we break them into traditional and contemporary bonds. Traditional bonds are the basic types that have been around for years. Contemporary bonds are newer, more innovative types of bonds that have been developed or become popular in recent years. The traditional types of bonds are summarized in terms of their key characteristics and priority of lenders' claim in Table 18.3 on page 518. Note that the first three types—**debentures, subordinated debentures,** and **income bonds**—are unsecured; the last three—**mortgage bonds, collateral trust bonds,** and **equipment trust certificates**—are secured.

Table 18.4 on page 519 summarizes the key characteristics of five contemporary types of bonds: **zero (or low)-coupon bonds, junk bonds, floating-rate bonds, extendable notes,** and **putable bonds.** These bonds can be either unsecured or secured. Contemporary bonds have been introduced in recent years in response to changing capital market conditions and investor preferences: Zero (or low)-coupon bonds are designed to provide tax benefits to both issuer and purchaser; junk bonds were recently widely used to finance mergers and take-overs; both floating-rate bonds and extendable notes give purchasers in-

**debentures**
See Table 18.3.

**subordinated debentures**
See Table 18.3.

**income bonds**
See Table 18.3.

**mortgage bonds**
See Table 18.3.

**collateral trust bonds**
See Table 18.3.

**equipment trust certificates**
See Table 18.3.

**zero (or low)-coupon bonds**
See Table 18.4.

**junk bonds**
See Table 18.4.

**floating-rate bonds**
See Table 18.4.

**extendable notes**
See Table 18.4.

**putable bonds**
See Table 18.4.

**TABLE 18.2 Moody's and Standard & Poor's Bond Ratings[a]**

| Moody's | Interpretation | Standard & Poor's | Interpretation |
|---|---|---|---|
| Aaa | Prime quality | AAA | Bank investment quality |
| Aa | High grade | AA | |
| | | | |
| A | Upper medium grade | A | |
| Baa | Medium grade | BBB | |
| | | | |
| Ba | Lower medium grade or speculative | BB B | Speculative |
| B | Speculative | | |
| | | | |
| Caa | From very speculative to | CCC | |
| Ca | near or in default | CC | |
| C | Lowest grade | C | Income bond |
| | | D | In default |

[a]Some ratings may be modified to show relative standing within a major rating category; for example, Moody's uses numerical modifiers (1, 2, 3), whereas Standard & Poor's uses plus (+) and minus (−) signs.

Source: Moody's Investors Services, Inc., and Standard & Poor's Corporation.

flation protection; and putable bonds give the bondholder an option to sell the bond at par. These contemporary bonds allow the firm to raise funds more easily at a reasonable cost by better meeting the needs of investors. Changing capital market conditions, investor preferences, and corporate financing needs are likely to result in development of further innovations in bond financing.

## International Long-Term Debt Financing

Companies and governments borrow internationally by tapping one of three principal financial markets: the Eurobond, foreign bond, and Eurocurrency loan markets. Each of these provides established, creditworthy borrowers with the opportunity to obtain large amounts of long-term debt financing quickly and efficiently, in their choice of currency, and with very flexible repayment terms. Each of these markets is briefly described below.

**Eurobonds**   A **Eurobond** is a bond issued by an international borrower and sold to investors in countries with currencies other than the currency in which the bond is denominated. A dollar-denominated bond issued by a U.S. corporation and sold to Belgian investors is an example of a Eurobond. The Eurobond market first developed in the early 1960s, when several European and U.S. borrowers discovered that many European investors wanted to hold dollar-denominated, bearer bonds that both sheltered investment income from taxation (because coupon interest payments were made to the "bearer" of the bond and names were not reported to tax authorities) and provided protection against exchange rate risk.

**Eurobond**
A bond issued by an international borrower and sold to investors in countries with currencies other than the currency in which the bond is denominated.

**TABLE 18.3** Summary of Characteristics and Priority of Claim of Traditional Types of Bonds

| Bond Type | Characteristics | Priority of Lenders' Claim |
|---|---|---|
| Debentures | Unsecured bonds that only creditworthy firms can issue. Convertible bonds are normally debentures. | Claims are same as those of any general creditor. May have other unsecured bonds subordinated to them. |
| Subordinated debentures | Claims are not satisfied until those of the creditors holding certain (senior) debts have been fully satisfied. | Claim is that of a general creditor but not as good as a senior debt claim. |
| Income bonds | Payment of interest is required only when earnings are available from which to make such payment. Commonly issued in reorganization of a failed or failing firm. | Claim is that of a general creditor. Not in default when interest payments are missed because they are contingent only on earnings being available. |
| Mortgage bonds | Secured by real estate or buildings. Can be *open-end* (other bonds issued against collateral), *limited open-end* (a specified amount of additional bonds can be issued against collateral), or *closed-end;* may contain an *after-acquired clause* (property subsequently acquired becomes part of mortgage collateral). | Claim is on proceeds from sale of mortgaged assets; if not fully satisfied, lender becomes a general creditor. The *first-mortgage* claim must be fully satisfied prior to distribution of proceeds to *second-mortgage* holders, and so on. A number of mortgages can be issued against the same collateral. |
| Collateral trust bonds | Secured by stock and (or) bonds that are owned by the issuer. Collateral value is generally 25 to 35 percent greater than bond value. | Claim is on proceeds from stock and (or) bond collateral; if not fully satisfied, the lender becomes a general creditor. |
| Equipment trust certificates | Used to finance "rolling stock"—airplanes, trucks, boats, railroad cars. A trustee buys such an asset with funds raised through the sale of trust certificates and then leases it to the firm. After making the final scheduled lease payment, the firm receives title to the asset. A type of leasing. | Claim is on proceeds from sale of asset; if proceeds do not satisfy outstanding debt, trust certificate lenders become general creditors. |

From its founding until the mid-1980s, "blue chip" U.S. corporations were the largest single class of Eurobond issuers, and many of these companies were able to borrow in this market at interest rates below those the U.S. government paid on Treasury bonds. As the market matured, issuers were able to choose the currency in which they borrowed, and European and Japanese borrowers rose to prominence. In more recent years the Eurobond market has become much more balanced in terms of the mix of borrowers, total issue volume, and currency of denomination. Today, most Eurobond issues are in fact executed as one part of a complicated financial engineering transaction known as a "currency swap," wherein companies headquartered in different countries issue bonds in their home country currencies and then exchange principal and interest payments with each other.

**Foreign Bonds** Whereas a Eurobond is issued by an international borrower in a single currency (initially dollars) in a variety of countries, a **foreign bond** is a bond issued in a host country's financial market, in the host

**foreign bond**
A bond issued in a host country's financial market, in the host country's currency, by a foreign borrower.

**TABLE 18.4   Summary of Characteristics of Contemporary Types of Bonds**

| Bond Type | Characteristics[a] |
|---|---|
| Zero (or low)-coupon bonds | Issued with no (zero) or a very low coupon (stated) interest rate and sold at a large discount from par. A significant portion (or all) of the investor's return comes from gain in value (i.e., par value minus purchase price). Generally callable at par value. Because the issuer can annually deduct the current year's interest accrual without having to actually pay the interest until the bond matures (or is called), its cash flow each year is increased by the amount of the tax shield provided by the interest deduction. |
| Junk bonds | Debt rated Ba or lower by Moody's or BB or lower by Standard & Poor's. During the 1980s commonly used by rapidly growing firms to obtain growth capital, most often as a way to finance mergers and takeovers of other firms. High-risk bonds with high yields—typically yielding 3 percent more than the best quality corporate debt. As a result of a number of major defaults during the early 1990s, the popularity of these bonds has been somewhat reduced. |
| Floating-rate bonds | Stated interest rate is adjusted periodically within stated limits in response to changes in specified money or capital market rates. Popular when future inflation and interest rates are uncertain. Tend to sell at close to par as a result of the automatic adjustment to changing market conditions. Some issues provide for annual redemption at par at the option of the bondholder. |
| Extendable notes | Short maturities, typically 1 to 5 years, which can be redeemed or renewed for a similar period at the option of their holders. Similar to a floating-rate bond. An issue might be a series of 3-year notes renewable over a period of 15 years; every 3 years the notes can be extended for another 3 years, at a new rate competitive with market interest rates prevailing at the time of renewal. |
| Putable bonds | Bonds that can be redeemed at par (typically $1,000) at the option of their holder either at specific dates such as 3 to 5 years after the date of issue and every 1 to 5 years thereafter, or when and if the firm takes specified actions such as being acquired, acquiring another company, or issuing a large amount of additional debt. In return for the right to "put the bond" at specified times or actions by the firm, the bond's yield is lower than that of a nonputable bond. |

[a]The claims of lenders (i.e., bondholders) against issuers of each of these types of bonds vary depending on their other features. Each of these bonds can be unsecured or secured.

country's currency, by a foreign borrower. A Deutsche-mark-denominated bond issued in Germany by a U.S. company is an example of a foreign bond. The three largest foreign bond markets are Japan, Switzerland, and the United States.

**Eurocurrency loan market**
A large number of international banks that make long-term, floating-rate, hard-currency (typically U.S. dollar-denominated) loans in the form of lines of credit to international corporate and government borrowers.

**Eurocurrency Loan Market**   The **Eurocurrency loan market** consists of a large number of international banks that stand ready to make long-term, floating-rate, hard-currency (typically U.S. dollar-denominated) loans to international corporate and government borrowers. These bank loans are usually structured as lines of credit on which borrowers can draw. Most large (over $500 million) loans are syndicated, meaning that pieces of each loan are sold to dozens of banks, thereby providing a measure of diversification to the lenders. Individual syndicated loans have ranged as large as $14 billion, and loans of $1 billion are quite common. Furthermore, in total size the Eurocurrency market dwarfs all other international financial markets. Finally, the Eurocurrency market became an overwhelmingly important corporate financing market during the 1980s.

## Bond-Refunding Options

A firm that wishes to retire or refund a bond prior to maturity has two options. Both require some foresight on the part of the issuer.

**Serial Issues**    The borrower can issue **serial bonds,** a certain proportion of which matures each year. When serial bonds are issued, a schedule showing the interest rate associated with each maturity is given. An example is a $30 million, 20-year bond issue for which $1.5 million of the bonds ($30 million ÷ 20 years) mature each year. The interest rates associated with shorter maturities, of course, differ from the rates associated with longer maturities. Although serial bonds cannot necessarily be retired at the option of the issuer, they do permit the issuer to systematically retire the debt.

**serial bonds**
An issue of bonds for which a certain proportion matures each year.

**Refunding Bonds by Exercising a Call**    If interest rates drop following the issuance of a bond, the issuer may wish to refund (refinance) the debt with new bonds at the lower interest rate. If a call feature has been included in the issue, the issuer can easily retire it. In an accounting sense, bond refunding increases earnings per share and reduces risk by lowering interest expense. Of course, the desirability of refunding a bond through exercise of a call is not necessarily obvious; its long-term consequences require the use of present-value techniques. This **bond-refunding decision** is another application of the capital budgeting techniques described in Chapters 14 and 15. Here the firm must find the net present value (NPV) of the bond-refunding cash flows. The *initial investment* is the incremental after-tax cash outflows associated with calling the old bonds and issuing new bonds. The *annual cash flow savings* are the after-tax cash savings expected to result from the reduced debt payments on the new lower interest bond. These cash flows are the same each year. The resulting cash flow pattern surrounding this decision is *conventional*—an outflow followed by a series of inflows. The bond-refunding decision can be made using the following three-step procedure:

**bond-refunding decision**
The decision facing firms when bond interest rates drop: whether to refund (refinance) existing bonds with new bonds at the lower interest rate.

Step 1: *Find the initial investment.* To do so, the firm estimates the incremental after-tax cash outflow required at time zero to call the old bond and issue a new bond in its place.
Step 2: *Find the annual cash flow savings.* This savings is the difference between the annual after-tax debt payments with the old and new bond. This cash flow stream is an annuity with a life equal to the maturity of the new bond.
Step 3: *Find the net present value (NPV).* To get this figure, the firm subtracts the initial investment from the present value of annual cash flow savings. The *after-tax cost of debt* is used as the discount rate because the decision involves very low risk.[2] *If the resulting NPV is greater than zero, the proposed refunding is recommended.* Otherwise, it is rejected.

---

[2]Because the refunding decision involves the choice between retaining an existing debt or substituting a new, lower cost debt, it is viewed as a low-risk decision that does not significantly affect the firm's financial risk. The low-risk nature of the decision warrants the use of a very low rate, such as the firm's after-tax cost of debt.

Application of these bond-refunding decision procedures can be illustrated with a simple example. However, a few tax-related points must be clarified first.

**Call Premiums.** The amount by which the call price exceeds the par value of the bond is the *call premium*. It is paid by the issuer to the bondholder to buy back outstanding bonds prior to maturity. The call premium is treated as a tax-deductible expense in the year of the call.

**Bond Discounts and Premiums.** When bonds are sold at a discount or at a premium, the firm is required to amortize (write off) the discount or premium in equal portions over the life of the bond. The amortized discount is treated as a tax-deductible expenditure, whereas the amortized premium is treated as taxable income. If a bond is retired prior to maturity, any unamortized portion of a discount or premium is deducted from or added to pretax income at that time.

**Flotation or Issuance Costs.** Any costs incurred in the process of issuing a bond must be amortized over the life of the bond. The annual write-off is therefore a tax-deductible expenditure. If a bond is retired prior to maturity, any unamortized portion of this cost is deducted from pretax income at that time.

# EXAMPLE ◀

Lavery Company, a manufacturer of copper pipe, is contemplating calling $30 million of 30-year, $1,000 bonds (30,000 bonds) issued 5 years ago with a coupon interest rate of 14 percent. The bonds have a call price of $1,140 and initially netted proceeds of $29.1 million due to a discount of $30 per bond. The initial flotation cost was $360,000. The company intends to sell $30 million of 12 percent coupon interest rate, 25-year bonds in order to raise funds for retiring the old bonds. The firm intends to sell the new bonds at their par value of $1,000. The flotation costs on the new issue are estimated to be $440,000. The firm is currently in the 40 percent tax bracket and estimates its after-tax cost of debt to be 8 percent.

**Step 1:** *Find the initial investment.* A number of calculations are required to find the initial investment.

**a.** *Call premium* The call premium per bond is $140 ($1,140 call price − $1,000 par value). Because the total call premium is deductible in the year of the call, its after-tax cost is

| | |
|---|---:|
| Before tax ($140 × 30,000 bonds) | $4,200,000 |
| Less: Taxes (.40 × $4,200,000) | 1,680,000 |
| After-tax cost of call premium | $2,520,000 |

**b.** *Flotation cost of new bond* This cost was given as $440,000.

**c.** *Unamortized discount on old bond* The $900,000 discount ($30,000,000 par value − $29,100,000 net proceeds from sale) on the old bond was being amortized over 30 years. Because only five of the 30 years' amortization of the discount has been applied, the remaining 25 years of unamortized discount can be deducted as a lump sum, thereby reducing taxes by $300,000 (25/30 × $900,000 × .40).

**TABLE 18.5    Finding the Initial Investment for Lavery Company's Bond-Refunding Decision**

| | | |
|---|---:|---:|
| **a.** Call premium | | |
| Before tax [($1,140 − $1,000) × 30,000 bonds] | $4,200,000 | |
| Less: Taxes (.40 × $4,200,000) | 1,680,000 | |
| After-tax cost of call premium | | $2,520,000 |
| **b.** Flotation cost of new bond | | 440,000 |
| **c.** Tax savings from unamortized discount on old bond [25/30 × ($30,000,000 − $29,100,000) × .40] | | (300,000) |
| **d.** Tax savings from unamortized flotation cost of old bond (25/30 × $360,000 × .40) | | (120,000) |
| Initial investment | | $2,540,000 |

> **d.** *Unamortized flotation cost of old bond* The $360,000 initial flotation cost on the old bond was being amortized over 30 years. Because only 5 of the 30 years' amortization of this cost has been applied, the remaining 25 years of unmortized flotation cost can be deducted as a lump sum, thereby reducing taxes by $120,000 (25/30 × $360,000 × .40).

Summarizing these calculations in Table 18.5, we find the initial investment to be $2,540,000. This means that Lavery Company must pay out $2,540,000 now to implement the proposed bond refunding.

> **Step 2:** *Find the annual cash flow savings.* To find the annual cash flow savings, we need to make a number of calculations.
>
> **a.** *Interest cost of old bond* The after-tax annual interest cost of the old bond is

| | |
|---|---:|
| Before tax (.14 × $30,000,000) | $4,200,000 |
| Less: Taxes (.40 × $4,200,000) | 1,680,000 |
| After-tax interest cost | $2,520,000 |

> **b.** *Amortization of discount on old bond* The $900,000 discount ($30,000,000 par value − $29,100,000 net proceeds from sale) on the old bond was being amortized over 30 years, resulting in an annual write-off of $30,000 ($900,000 ÷ 30). Because it is a tax-deductible noncash charge, the amortization of this discount results in an annual tax savings of $12,000 (.40 × $30,000).
>
> **c.** *Amortization of flotation cost on old bond* The $360,000 flotation cost on the old bond was being amortized over 30 years, resulting in an annual write-off of $12,000 ($360,000 ÷ 30). Because it is a tax-deductible noncash charge, the amortization of the flotation cost results in an annual tax savings of $4,800 (.40 × $12,000).
>
> **d.** *Interest cost of new bond* The after-tax annual interest cost of the new bond is

**TABLE 18.6    Finding the Annual Cash Flow Savings for Lavery Company's Bond-Refunding Decision**

| | Old Bond | |
|---|---|---|
| **a.** Interest cost | | |
| Before tax (.14 × $30,000,000) | $4,200,000 | |
| Less: Taxes (.40 × $4,200,000) | 1,680,000 | |
| After-tax interest cost | | $2,520,000 |
| **b.** Tax savings from amortization of discount [($900,000ᵃ ÷ 30) × .40] | | (12,000) |
| **c.** Tax savings from amortization of flotation cost [($360,000 ÷ 30) × .40] | | (4,800) |
| (1)  Annual after-tax debt payment | | $2,503,200 |

| | New bond | |
|---|---|---|
| **d.** Interest cost | | |
| Before tax (.12 × $30,000,000) | $3,600,000 | |
| Less: Taxes (.40 × $3,600,000) | 1,440,000 | |
| After-tax interest cost | | $2,160,000 |
| **e.** Tax savings from amortization of flotation cost [($440,000 ÷ 25) × .40] | | (7,040) |
| (2)  Annual after-tax debt payment | | $2,152,960 |
| Annual cash flow savings [(1) − (2)] | | $  350,240 |

ᵃ$30,000,000 par value − $29,100,000 net proceeds from sale

| | |
|---|---|
| Before tax (.12 × $30,000,000) | $3,600,000 |
| Less: Taxes (.40 × $3,600,000) | 1,440,000 |
| After-tax interest cost | $2,160,000 |

**e.** *Amortization of flotation cost on new bond*  The $440,000 flotation cost on the new bond is amortized over 25 years, resulting in an annual write-off of $17,600 ($440,000 ÷ 25). Because it is a tax-deductible noncash charge, the amortization of the flotation cost results in an annual tax savings of $7,040 (.40 × $17,600).

These calculations are summarized in Table 18.6. Totaling the first three values (**a,b,** and **c**), we find the annual after-tax debt payment for the old bond to be $2,503,200. Totaling the values for the new bond (**d** and **e**), we find the annual after-tax debt payment for the new bond to be $2,152,960. Subtracting the new bond's annual debt payment from that of the old bond, we find the annual cash flow savings to be $350,240 ($2,503,200 −

**TABLE 18.7    Finding the Net Present Value of Lavery Company's Bond-Refunding Decision**

| | |
|---|---:|
| Present value of annual cash flow savings (from Table 18.6) | |
| $350,240 \times PVIFA_{8\%,25yrs}$ | |
| $350,240 \times 10.675 =$ | $3,738,812 |
| Less: Initial investment (from Table 18.5) | 2,540,000 |
| Net present value (NPV) of refunding[a] | $1,198,812 |

Decision: The proposed refunding is *recommended* because the NPV of refunding of $1,198,812 is greater than $0.

[a]Using a hand-held business/financial calculator, the present value of the annual cash flow savings is $3,738,734, which results in a NPV of refunding of $1,198,734.

$2,152,960). This means that implementation of the proposed bond refunding results in an annual cash flow savings of $350,240.

> **Step 3:** *Find the net present value (NPV).* The net present value (NPV) of the proposed bond refunding is calculated in Table 18.7. The present value of the annual cash flow savings of $350,240 at the 8 percent after-tax cost of debt over the 25 years is $3,738,812. Subtracting the initial investment of $2,540,000 from the present value of annual cash flow savings results in a net present value (NPV) of $1,198,812. Because a positive NPV results, *the proposed bond refunding is recommended.*

## Progress Review Questions

**18-6.** What types of maturities, denominations, and interest payments are associated with a typical corporate bond? Describe the role of the *bond indenture* and the *trustee.*

**18-7.** What does it mean if a bond has a *conversion feature?* A *call feature? Stock-purchase warrants?* How are bonds rated, and why?

**18-8.** Describe the basic characteristics of each of the following popular types of bonds:
  **a.** Debentures
  **b.** Subordinated debentures
  **c.** Income bonds
  **d.** Zero (or low)-coupon bonds
  **e.** Junk bonds
  **f.** Floating-rate bonds
  **g.** Extendable notes
  **h.** Putable bonds

**18-9.** Describe, compare, and contrast the basic features of the following secured bonds:

**a.** Mortgage bond
**b.** Collateral trust bond
**c.** Equipment trust certificate

**18.10.** Describe and compare the basic characteristics of the following sources of international long-term debt financing:
**a.** Eurobonds
**b.** Foreign bonds
**c.** Eurocurrency loans

**18-11.** What two options may be available to a firm that wants to retire or refund an outstanding bond issue prior to maturity? Must these options be provided for in advance of issuance? Why might the issuer wish to retire or refund a bond prior to its maturity?

**18-12.** Why does the *bond-refunding decision* lend itself to the application of capital budgeting techniques? Describe the three-step procedure that is used to make these decisions.

▲▲▲▲▲▲▲▲▲▲▲▲▲▲▲▲▲▲▲▲▲▲▲▲▲▲▲▲▲▲▲▲

# Characteristics of Leases

**leasing**
The process by which a firm can obtain the use of certain fixed assets for which it must make a series of contractual, periodic, tax-deductible payments.

**lessee**
The receiver of the services of the assets under a lease contract.

**lessor**
The owner of assets that are being leased.

**operating lease**
A *cancelable* contractual arrangement whereby the lessee agrees to make periodic payments to the lessor, often for five or fewer years, for an asset's services; generally the total payments over the term of the lease are *less* than the lessor's initial cost of the leased asset.

Through **leasing,** a firm can obtain the use of certain fixed assets for which it must make a series of contractual, periodic, tax-deductible payments. The **lessee** is the receiver of the services of the assets under the lease contract; the **lessor** is the owner of the assets. Leasing can take a number of forms. Here we discuss the basic types of leases and leasing arrangements, with special emphasis on the effects of leasing on the lessee corporation. The lease contract is also briefly described.

## Basic Types of Leases

The two basic types of leases available to a businesses are *operating* and *financial* leases. (Financial leases are often called *capital leases* by accountants.) Each is briefly described in the following sections.

**Operating Leases**  An **operating lease** is normally a contractual arrangement whereby the lessee agrees to make periodic payments to the lessor, often for five or fewer years, to obtain an asset's services. Such leases are generally *cancelable* at the option of the lessee, who may be required to pay a predetermined penalty for cancellation. Assets leased under operating leases have a usable life *longer* than the term of the lease. Usually, however, they become less efficient and technologically obsolete if leased for a longer period of years. Computer systems are prime examples of assets the relative efficiency of which is expected to diminish with new technological developments. The operating lease is therefore a common arrangement for obtaining such systems, as well as for other relatively short-lived assets such as automobiles.

If an operating lease is held to maturity, the lessee at that time returns the leased asset to the lessor, who may lease it again or sell the asset. Normally the asset still has a positive market value at the termination of the lease. In some instances, the lease contract gives the lessee the opportunity to purchase the leased asset. Generally the total payments made by the lessee to the lessor are *less* than the lessor's initial cost of the leased asset.

### Financial (or Capital) Leases

A **financial (or capital) lease** is a *longer term* lease than an operating lease. Financial leases are *noncancelable* and therefore obligate the lessee to make payments for the use of an asset over a predefined period. Even if the lessee does not require the service of the leased asset, it is contractually obligated to make payments over the life of the lease contract. Financial leases are commonly used for leasing land, buildings, and large pieces of equipment. The noncancelable feature of the financial lease makes it quite similar to certain types of long-term debt. The lease payment becomes a fixed, tax-deductible expenditure that must be paid at predefined dates over a definite period. Like debt, failure to make the contractual lease payments can result in bankruptcy for the lessee.

Another distinguishing characteristic of the financial lease is that the total payments over the lease period are *greater* than the lessor's initial cost of the leased asset. In other words, the lessor must receive more than the asset's purchase price to earn its required return on the investment. Technically, under *Financial Accounting Standards Board* (*FASB*) Standard No. 13, "Accounting for Leases," a financial (or capital) lease is defined as one having *any* of the following elements:

1. The lease transfers ownership of the property to the lessee by the end of the lease term.
2. The lease contains an option to purchase the property at a "bargain price." Such an option must be exercisable at a "fair market value."
3. The lease term is equal to 75 percent or more of the estimated economic life of the property (exceptions exist for property leased toward the end of its usable economic life).
4. At the beginning of the lease, the present value of the lease payments is equal to 90 percent or more of the fair market value of the leased property.

The emphasis in this chapter is on financial leases because they result in inescapable long-term financial commitments by the firm.

## Leasing Arrangements

Lessors use three primary techniques for obtaining assets to be leased. The method depends largely on the desires of the prospective lessee. A **direct lease** results when a lessor owns or acquires the assets that are leased to a given lessee. In other words, the lessee did not previously own the assets it is leasing. A second technique commonly used by lessors to acquire leased assets is to purchase assets already owned by the lessee and lease them back. A **sale-leaseback arrangement** is normally initiated by a firm that needs funds for operations. By selling an existing asset to a lessor and then *leasing it back,* the lessee receives cash for the asset immediately while obligating itself to make fixed periodic payments for use of the leased asset. Leasing arrangements that include one or more third-party lenders are leveraged leases. Unlike direct and sale-leaseback arrangements, under a **leveraged lease** the lessor acts as

**financial (or capital) lease**
A *noncancelable* lease that obligates the lessee to make payments for the use of an asset over a predefined period; the term of the lease is longer than for an operating lease, and total payments over the term of the lease are *greater* than the lessor's initial cost of the leased asset.

**direct lease**
A lease under which a lessor owns or acquires the assets that are leased to a given lessee.

**sale-leaseback arrangement**
A lease under which the lessee sells an asset for cash to a prospective lessor and then leases back the same asset, making fixed periodic payments for its use.

**leveraged lease**
A lease under which the lessor acts as an equity participant, supplying only about 20 percent of the cost of the asset, while a lender supplies the balance.

# FINANCE IN ACTION

F I N A N C E   I N

C T I O N

**International**

## Lease Financing Drives U.S. Auto Sales for Japanese Car Makers

Times are currently tough for Japanese manufacturers in the U.S. market for cars and light trucks. In 1993, for the second year in a row, their share of the American market fell, reaching 23.2 percent by the end of the year. In 1994, it looks as if Japanese automobile manufacturers will again lose market share, as the rising value of the yen and deep recessions in the Japanese and European auto markets trim corporate sales revenue. To avoid financial losses, most Japanese manufacturers will probably boost retail auto prices in 1994, widening the retail price advantage enjoyed by American auto manufacturers to $1,700 per car.

So how can the Japanese manufacturers compete in American markets? In a word: leasing. Because Japanese cars usually hold their values over time better than Detroit's products, vehicle leasing almost completely eliminates the pricing advantage enjoyed by the big three U.S. auto makers. Japanese manufacturers can pass along the higher resale value of their cars in the form of lower lease payments, so American consumers can acquire higher priced Japanese cars for the same monthly payment they would pay to acquire a cheaper American car. Lease payments on a midline Honda Accord valued at $18,300 in 1994 are just $239 per month—lower than the lease payments on a comparably equipped, $15,769 Pontiac Grand Am SE. The lease payment advantage enjoyed by Japanese auto manufacturers won't last forever, but it gives these firms time to address the real problem behind their higher retail auto prices: excessive operating costs.

Source: L. Armstrong, "Trying to Rev Up," *Business Week*, January 24, 1994, p. 32.

---

**maintenance clauses**
Provisions common in operating leases that require the lessor to maintain the assets and to make insurance and tax payments.

**renewal options**
Provisions especially common in operating leases that grant the lessee the option to re-lease assets at the expiration of the lease.

**purchase options**
Provisions frequently included in both operating and financial leases that allow the lessee to purchase the leased asset at maturity, typically for a prespecified price.

an equity participant, supplying only about 20 percent of the cost of the asset, and a lender supplies the balance. In recent years leveraged leases have become especially popular in structuring leases of very expensive assets.

A lease agreement normally specifies whether the lessee is responsible for maintenance of the leased assets. Operating leases normally include **maintenance clauses** requiring the lessor to maintain the assets and to make insurance and tax payments. Financial leases almost always require the lessee to pay maintenance and other costs. The lessee is usually given the option to renew a lease at its expiration. **Renewal options,** which grant lessees the right to re-lease assets at expiration, are especially common in operating leases because their term is generally shorter than the usable life of the leased assets. **Purchase options** allow the lessee to purchase the leased asset at maturity, typically for a prespecified price. Such options are frequently included in both operating and financial leases.

The lessor can be one of a number of parties. In operating lease arrangements, the lessor is quite likely to be the manufacturer's leasing subsidiary or an independent leasing company. Financial leases are frequently handled by independent leasing companies or by the leasing subsidiaries of large financial institutions, such as commercial banks and life insurance companies. Life insurance companies are especially active in real estate leasing. Pension funds, like commercial banks, have also been increasing their leasing activities.

## The Lease Contract

The key items of the lease contract normally include a description of the leased assets; the term, or duration, of the lease; provisions for its cancellation; lease payment amounts and dates; maintenance and associated cost provisions; renewal options; purchase options; and other provisions specified in the lease negotiation process. Although some provisions are optional, the leased assets, the terms of the agreement, the lease payment, and the payment interval must all be clearly specified in every lease agreement. Furthermore, the consequences of the violation of any lease provisions by either the lessee or lessor must be clearly stated in the contract.

## Progress Review Questions

**18-13.** What is *leasing?* Define, compare, and contrast *operating leases* and *financial (or capital) leases.* How does the Financial Accounting Standards Board (FASB) Standard No. 13 define a financial (or capital) lease?

**18-14.** Describe three methods used by lessors to acquire assets to be leased. Do financial leases typically include: *maintenance clauses? renewal options? purchase options?* Explain each.

## Leasing as a Source of Financing

LG 6

Leasing is considered a source of financing provided by the lessor to the lessee. The lessee receives the service of a certain fixed asset for a specified period, in exchange for which the lessee commits itself to a fixed periodic payment. The only other way the lessee can obtain the services of the given asset is to purchase it outright, and the outright purchase of the asset requires financing. The following discussions of the lease-versus-purchase decision, the effects of leasing on future financing, and the advantages and disadvantages of leasing explain the role of leasing as a source of financing.

## The Lease-Versus-Purchase Decision

The **lease-versus-purchase (or lease-versus-buy) decision** is one that commonly confronts firms contemplating the acquisition of new fixed assets. The alternatives available are (1) lease the assets, (2) borrow funds to purchase the assets, or (3) purchase the assets using available liquid resources. Alternatives 2 and 3, although they differ, are analyzed in a similar fashion. Even if the firm has the liquid resources with which to purchase the assets, the use of these funds is viewed as equivalent to borrowing. Therefore, here we need to compare only the leasing and purchasing alternatives.

The lease-versus-purchase decision is made using basic present-value techniques. The following steps are involved in the analysis:

**lease-versus-purchase (or lease-versus-buy) decision**
The decision facing firms needing to acquire new fixed assets: whether to lease the assets or to purchase them, using borrowed funds or available liquid resources.

**Step 1:** *Find the after-tax cash outflows for each year under the lease alternative.* This step generally involves a fairly simple tax adjustment of the annual lease payments. In addition, the cost of exercising a purchase option in the final year of the lease term must frequently be included.

**Step 2:** *Find the after-tax cash outflows for each year under the purchase alternative.* This step involves adjusting the sum of the scheduled loan payment and maintenance cost outlay for the tax shields resulting from the tax deductions due to maintenance, depreciation, and interest.

**Step 3:** *Calculate the present value of the cash outflows* associated with the lease (from step 1) and purchase (from step 2) alternatives using the *after-tax cost of debt* as the discount rate. The after-tax cost of debt is used because this decision involves very low risk.

**Step 4:** *Choose the alternative with the lower present value of cash outflows* from step 3. This is the *least-cost* financing alternative.

Due to the relative complexity of the tax adjustments required to determine the after-tax lease and purchase outflows in steps 1 and 2, only steps 3 and 4 are demonstrated in the following example:

# E X A M P L E

Moore Company, a small machine shop, is contemplating acquiring a new machine tool costing $24,000. Arrangements can be made to lease or purchase the machine. The firm is in the 40 percent tax bracket, and its after-tax cost of debt is 6 percent.

**Lease:**   The firm could obtain a five-year lease requiring annual end-of-year lease payments of $6,000.[3] All maintenance costs would be paid by the lessor, whereas insurance and other costs would be borne by the lessee. The lessee would exercise its option to purchase the equipment for $4,000 when the lease terminates.

**Purchase:**   The firm could finance the purchase of the machine with a 9 percent, five-year loan requiring end-of-year installment payments of $6,170. The machine would be depreciated under MACRS using a five-year recovery period. The firm would pay $1,500 per year for a service contract that covers all maintenance costs; insurance and other costs would be borne by the firm. The firm plans to keep the equipment and use it beyond its five-year recovery period.

Assume that after applying various depreciation, interest, and tax adjustments, the after-tax cash outflows associated with the lease and purchase alternatives are determined as shown, respectively, in columns 1 and 4 of Table 18.8. Applying the appropriate 6 percent present-value interest factors given in columns 2 and 5 to the after-tax cash outflows in columns 1 and 4 results in the present values of lease and purchase cash outflows given in columns 3

---

[3]Lease payments are generally made at the beginning of the year. To simplify the following discussions, end-of-year payments are assumed.

**TABLE 18.8   A Comparison of the Cash Outflows Associated with Leasing Versus Purchasing for Moore Company**

| | Leasing | | | Purchasing | | |
|---|---|---|---|---|---|---|
| End of Year | After-Tax Cash Outflows[a] (1) | Present-Value Factors[b] (2) | Present Value of Outflows [(1) × (2)] (3) | After-Tax Cash Outflows[a] (4) | Present-Value Factors[b] (5) | Present Value of Outflows [(4) × (5)] (6) |
| 1 | $ 3,600 | .943 | $ 3.395 | $ 4,286 | .943 | $ 4,042 |
| 2 | 3,600 | .890 | 3,204 | 3,278 | .890 | 2,917 |
| 3 | 3,600 | .840 | 3,024 | 4,684 | .840 | 3,935 |
| 4 | 3,600 | .792 | 2,851 | 5,527 | .792 | 4,377 |
| 5 | 7,600 | .747 | 5,677 | 5,714 | .747 | 4,268 |
| | Present value of cash outflows | | $18,151 | Present value of cash outflows | | $19,539 |

[a]Values developed using techniques beyond the scope of this text.
[b]From Table A-3, *PVIF* for 6 percent and the corresponding year.

and 6, respectively. The sum of the present values of the cash outflows for the leasing alternative is given in column 3 of Table 18.8, and the sum for the purchasing alternative is given in column 6 of Table 18.8. Because the present value of cash outflows for leasing ($18,151) is lower than that for purchasing ($19,539), *the leasing alternative is preferred.* Leasing results in an incremental savings of $1,388 ($19,539 − $18,151) and is therefore the less costly alternative.[4]

## Effects of Leasing on Future Financing

Because leasing is considered a type of financing, it affects the firm's future financing. Lease payments are shown as a tax-deductible expense on the firm's income statement. Anyone analyzing the firm's income statement probably recognizes that an asset is being leased, although the actual details of the amount and term of the lease are unclear. The following sections discuss the lease disclosure requirements established by the Financial Accounting Standards Board (FASB) and the effect of leases on financial ratios.

**Lease Disclosure Requirements**   The Financial Accounting Standards Board (FASB) in Standard No. 13, "Accounting for Leases," requires explicit disclosure of *financial (capital) lease* obligations on the firm's balance sheet. Such a lease must be shown as a **capitalized lease,** meaning the present value

**capitalized lease**
A *financial* (or *capital*) *lease* that has the present value of all its payments included as an asset and corresponding liability on the firm's balance sheet, as required by FASB Standard No. 13.

[4]Using a hand-held business/financial calculator, the present value of the cash outflows for the lease are $18,154 and for the purchase are $19,541, resulting in an incremental savings of $1,387.

of all its payments is included as an asset and corresponding liability on the firm's balance sheet. An operating lease, on the other hand, need not be capitalized, but its basic features must be disclosed in a footnote to the financial statements. Standard No. 13, of course, establishes detailed guidelines to be used in capitalizing leases to reflect them as an asset and corresponding liability on the balance sheet. Subsequent standards have further refined lease capitalization and disclosure procedures. Let us look at an example.

# EXAMPLE

Graber Company, a manufacturer of water purifiers, is leasing an asset under a 10-year lease requiring annual end-of-year payments of $15,000. The lease can be capitalized merely by calculating the present value of the lease payments over the life of the lease. However, the rate at which the payments should be discounted is difficult to determine.[5] If 10 percent is used, the present, or capitalized, value of the lease is $92,175 ($15,000 × 6.145). (The calculated value using a hand-held business/financial calculator is $92,169.) The capitalized value is shown as an asset and corresponding liability on the firm's balance sheet.

**Leases and Financial Ratios**  Because the consequences of missing a financial lease payment are the same as those of missing an interest or principal payment on debt, a financial analyst must view the lease as a long-term financial commitment of the lessee. As a result of FASB No. 13, the inclusion of financial (capital) leases as an asset and corresponding liability (i.e., long-term debt) provides for a balance sheet that more accurately reflects the firm's financial status. It thereby permits various types of financial ratio analyses to be performed directly on the statement by any interested party.

## Advantages and Disadvantages of Leasing

Leasing has a number of commonly cited advantages and disadvantages that should be considered when making a lease-versus-purchase decision. Although not all these advantages and disadvantages hold in every case, it is not unusual for a number of them to apply in a given situation.

**Advantages**  The commonly cited advantages of leasing are as follows:

1. Leasing allows the lessee, in effect, to *depreciate land,* which is prohibited if the land is purchased. Because the lessee who leases land is permitted to deduct the *total lease payment* as an expense for tax purposes, the effect is the same as if the firm had purchased the land and then depreciated it.
2. Because it results in the receipt of service from an asset possibly without increasing the assets or liabilities on the firm's balance sheet, leas-

---

[5]The Financial Accounting Standards Board in Standard No. 13 established certain guidelines for the appropriate discount rate to use when capitalizing leases. Most commonly, the rate that the lessee would have incurred to borrow the funds to buy the asset with a secured loan under terms similar to the lease repayment schedule is used. This simply represents the *before-tax cost of a secured debt.*

ing may result in *misleading financial ratios*. With the passage of FASB No. 13, this advantage no longer applies to financial leases, although in the case of operating leases it remains a potential advantage.

3. The use of sale-leaseback arrangements may permit the firm to *increase its liquidity* by converting an *existing* asset into cash, which can then be used as working capital. A firm short of working capital or in a liquidity bind can sell an owned asset to a lessor and lease the asset back for a specified number of years.

4. Leasing provides *100 percent financing*. Most loan agreements for the purchase of fixed assets require the borrower to pay a portion of the purchase price as a down payment. As a result the borrower is able to borrow only 90 to 95 percent of the purchase price of the asset.

5. Leasing offers certain *financial advantages when a firm becomes bankrupt* or is reorganized. In such an event, the maximum claim of lessors against the corporation is three years of lease payments, and the lessor of course gets the asset back. If debt is used to purchase an asset, the creditors have a claim equal to the total outstanding loan balance.

6. In a lease arrangement, the firm may *avoid the cost of obsolescence* if the lessor fails to anticipate accurately the obsolescence of assets and sets the lease payment too low. This is especially true in the case of operating leases, which generally have relatively short lives.

7. A lessee *avoids many of the restrictive covenants* that are normally included as part of a long-term loan. Requirements with respect to minimum net working capital, subsequent borrowing, changes in management, and so on are *not* normally found in a lease agreement.

8. In the case of low-cost assets that are infrequently acquired, leasing—especially operating leases—may provide the firm with needed *financing flexibility*. That is, the firm does not have to arrange other financing for these assets and can somewhat conveniently obtain them through a lease.

**Disadvantages**   The commonly cited disadvantages of leasing are the following:

1. A lease does not have a stated interest cost. Thus in many leases the *return to the lessor is quite high;* the firm might be better off borrowing to purchase the asset.

2. At the end of the term of the lease agreement, the *salvage value* of an asset, if any, is realized by the lessor. If the lessee had purchased the asset, it could have claimed its salvage value. Of course, an expected salvage value when recognized by the lessor results in lower lease payments.

3. Under a lease, the lessee is generally *prohibited from making improvements* on the leased property or asset without the approval of the lessor. If the property were owned outright, this difficulty would not arise. Of course, lessors generally encourage leasehold improvements when they are expected to enhance the asset's salvage value.

4. If a lessee leases (under a financial lease) an *asset that subsequently becomes obsolete,* it still must make lease payments over the remaining term of the lease. This is true even if the asset is unusable.

# Progress Review Questions

**18-15.** Describe the four basic steps involved in the *lease-versus-purchase decision* process. Why must present-value techniques be used in this process?

**18-16.** What type of lease must be treated as a *capitalized lease* on the balance sheet? How does the financial manager capitalize a lease?

**18-17.** List and discuss the commonly cited advantages and disadvantages that should be considered when making a lease-versus-purchase decision.

# SUMMARY OF LEARNING GOALS

**LG 1** **Describe the basic characteristics of long-term debt financing, including standard debt provisions, restrictive debt provisions, and cost.** Standard and restrictive provisions are included in long-term debt agreements to protect the lender. Standard debt provisions do not ordinarily place a burden on a financially sound business. Restrictive covenants tend to place certain operating and financial constraints on the borrower. The cost (interest rate) of long-term debt is normally higher than the cost of short-term borrowing. Major factors affecting the cost of long-term debt are loan maturity, loan size, and more important, borrower risk and the basic cost of money.

**LG 2** **Understand the characteristics of term (long-term) loan agreements and the various term lenders to business.** The conditions of a term (long-term) loan are specified in the term loan agreement. Term loans generally require periodic installment payments; some require balloon payments at maturity. Term loans may be either unsecured or secured. Some term lenders receive stock-purchase warrants. Term loans can be obtained from a number of major lenders ranging from commercial banks and insurance companies to the federal government's Small Business Administration to the financing subsidiaries of equipment manufacturers. Table 18.1 provides a complete listing of term lenders along with the characteristics and types of loans they make.

**LG 3** **Discuss the legal aspects of corporate bonds, general features of a bond issue, bond ratings, popular types of bonds, and international long-term debt financing.** Corporate bonds are certificates indicating that a corporation has borrowed a certain amount that it promises to repay in the future under clearly defined terms. Most bonds are issued with maturities of 10 to 30 years and a par value of $1,000. All conditions of the bond issue are detailed in the indenture, which is enforced by the trustee. A bond issue may include a conversion feature, a call feature, or stock-purchase warrants. Bond ratings by independent agencies indicate the risk of a bond issue. A variety of traditional and contemporary types of bonds, some unsecured and others secured, are available; Tables 18.3 and 18.4 list them and summarize their characteristics. The Eurobond, foreign bond, and Euro-currency loan markets allow established creditworthy companies and governments to borrow quickly and efficiently large amounts of debt internationally, in their choice of currency, and with very flexible repayment terms.

**Explain the logic and computational procedures involved in bond-refunding options, particularly exercising a call to refund a bond with new bonds issued at a lower interest rate.** Firms sometimes retire or refund (refinance) bonds prior to their maturity. When serial bonds are issued, retirement is on a planned basis. Bonds are refunded (refinanced) when a drop in interest rates is sufficient to result in a positive net present value (NPV) from calling the old bonds and replacing them with new, lower interest rate bonds. The NPV is found by first finding the initial investment, which is the estimated incremental after-tax cash outflow required at time zero to call the old bond and issue the new bond in its place. Next, the annual cash flow savings is found by determining the difference between the annual after-tax debt payments with the old and new bond. Finally, the after-tax cost of debt is used to find NPV by subtracting the initial investment from the present value of annual cash flow savings.

LG 4

**Review the basic types of leases, leasing arrangements, and the lease contract.** A lease, like long-term debt, allows the firm to make contractual, tax-deductible payments to obtain the use of fixed assets. Operating leases are generally five or fewer years in term, cancelable, and renewable, and they provide for maintenance by the lessor. Financial leases are longer term, noncancelable, and not renewable, and they require the lessee to maintain the asset. FASB Standard No. 13 provides specific guidelines for defining a financial (or capital) lease. A lessor can obtain assets to be leased through a direct lease, a sale-leaseback arrangement, or a leveraged lease. It can be a manufacturer's leasing subsidiary, an independent leasing company, or the leasing subsidiary of a large financial institution. The lease contract normally includes a description of the leased assets, the term (duration) of the lease, provisions for its cancellation, lease payment amounts and dates, maintenance and associated cost provisions, renewal options, purchase options, and other provisions specified in the lease negotiation process.

LG 5

**Analyze the lease-versus-purchase decision, the effects of leasing on future financing, and the advantages and disadvantages of leasing.** A lease-versus-purchase decision can be evaluated by calculating the after-tax cash outflows associated with the leasing and purchasing alternatives. The more desirable alternative is the one that has the lower present value of after-tax cash outflows. FASB Standard No. 13 requires firms to show financial (or capital) leases as assets and corresponding liabilities on their balance sheets; operating leases must be shown in footnotes to the financial statements. A number of commonly cited advantages and disadvantages should be considered when making lease-versus-purchase decisions.

LG 6

## L E A R N I N G   G O A L S

After studying this chapter, you should be able to

 LG 1   Differentiate between debt and equity capital in terms of ownership rights, claims on income and assets, maturity, and tax treatment.

 LG 2   Understand preferred stock, including the basic rights of preferred stockholders, features normally included as part of a preferred stock issue, and special types of preferred stock.

 LG 3   Explain the key advantages and disadvantages of preferred stock financing.

 LG 4   Discuss common stock, including important aspects of voting rights and international common stock.

 LG 5   Describe stock rights, including the mechanics of rights offerings, management decisions, theoretical values, and market behavior.

 LG 6   Review the key advantages and disadvantages of common stock financing.

# 19 Preferred and Common Stock

Equity capital is the foundation of the firm's capital structure. It represents the ownership of the firm and thus shares in the risks and rewards (profits) of the firm. A company's equity is like the down payment for a mortgage when buying a house. Equity is the risk capital, or the down payment, that allows all other financing to take place. Without common stock equity, a firm cannot expect a lender to provide debt financing.

Preferred equity has some of the attributes of common stock and some similarities with debt. Like equity, preferred stock generally has per-

## Equity capital is the foundation of the firm's capital structure.

petual life (although you can retire it by paying a premium). Like debt, it has a fixed cost in the form of its dividend and may carry restrictive covenants. The company can skip a dividend, however, but usually must make up missed dividends before paying common dividends.

Not all companies use preferred stock. Utilities are big consumers of capital and use many financing sources, including preferred stock. Companies that need to raise equity may issue preferred stock, especially when their

common stock prices are depressed. The sale of common stock would dilute the current owner's equity. This was true for utilities in the mid-1970s and early 1980s and for banks in the late 1980s and early 1990s. Service companies, on the other hand, generally have relatively small capital requirements and do not often use preferred stock.

Common stock, the least restrictive form of financing, gives a company financial flexibility. It is the "cushion" that gives comfort to a lender, who may require fewer restrictions on debt if the equity base is solid. But it is also the most costly capital, and financial managers must balance the mix of debt and equity to best meet a company's individual needs. Obviously, a company wants to sell its equity at the highest possible price. Market conditions, economic cycles, and industry cycles influence the relative cost of common equity. For example, when interest rates are low, prices of utility common stock tend to be higher, and vice versa. Recently, low interest rates have pushed prices of electric utilities' common stock to all-time highs, making this an advantageous time to build equity.

A firm's financing strategy evolves over time based on its profitability and capital requirements. Thus, it's important to build flexibility into financing arrangements. For example, Duquesne Light currently has about 4 percent preferred stock in its capital structure. In the early 1980s, however, it had about 10 percent preferred stock. At that time heavy financing requirements due to a large capital program made preferred stock

a good choice because the common stock was undervalued. Duquesne Light has subsequently retired all of that preferred stock and has the option of replacing it with common stock at twice its depressed value.

Financial managers must respond to changes in the environment and understand the different financing alternatives available to get the lowest overall cost of capital. With new financing alternatives being introduced each year and with finance being an integral part of any company's operation, it's an exciting time to be an active participant in the financial marketplace. Understanding financial concepts will put you in a better position to help the firm and your career, no matter what area of business you choose.

**Gary Schwass** *is vice-president, treasurer, and chief financial officer of DQE, an energy services holding company, president of its credit company, and vice-president— Financial Group and chief financial officer of Duquesne Light Company, an electric utility serving Pittsburgh, Pennsylvania. Before joining Duquesne Light as treasurer in 1985, he was executive director of financial planning at Consumers Power Company. He received a B.S. in mathematics and psychology from Western Michigan University and an M.B.A. in finance from Eastern Michigan University.*

A firm needs to maintain an equity base large enough to allow it to take advantage of low-cost debt and build an optimal capital structure (see Chapter 16). Equity capital can be raised *internally* through retained earnings, or *externally* by selling preferred or common stock. Although preferred stock, as noted in the discussion of cost of capital in Chapter 13, is a less costly form of financing than common stock and retained earnings, it is not frequently used. Here we begin with brief discussions of equity capital and preferred stock, and then concentrate our attention on the characteristics, features, and role of common stock.

# The Nature of Equity Capital

LG  1

The key differences between debt and equity capital were summarized in Chapter 16 (see specifically Table 16.1). These differences relate to ownership rights, claims on the firm's income and assets, maturity, and tax treatment.

## Ownership Rights

Unlike creditors (lenders), holders of equity capital (preferred and common stockholders) are owners of the firm. Holders of equity capital often have voting rights that permit them to select the firm's directors and to vote on special issues. In contrast, debtholders may receive voting privileges only when the firm has violated the conditions of a *term loan agreement* or *bond indenture*.

## Claims on Income and Assets

Holders of equity capital have claims on both income and assets that are secondary to the claims of creditors. Their *claims on income* cannot be paid until the claims of all creditors have been satisfied. These claims include both interest and scheduled principal payments. Once these claims have been satisfied, the firm's board of directors can decide whether to distribute dividends to the owners. Of course, as explained in Chapter 16, a firm's ability to pay dividends may be limited by legal, contractual, or internal constraints.

The equity holders' *claims on assets* of the firm are secondary to the claims of creditors. If the firm becomes bankrupt,[1] assets are sold and the proceeds distributed in this order: to employees and customers, to the government, to secured creditors, to unsecured creditors, and finally to equity holders. Because equity holders are the last to receive any distribution of assets during bankruptcy proceedings, they expect greater returns from dividends and stock price appreciation.

As was noted in Chapter 13, the costs of the various forms of equity financing are generally higher than debt costs. This is partially explained by the fact that the suppliers of equity capital take more risk as a result of their

---

[1]The procedures followed when a firm becomes bankrupt are described in Chapter 21.

claims on income and assets being subordinate to those of debtholders. Despite its being more costly, equity capital is necessary for the firm to grow and mature. All firms must initially be financed with some common stock equity.

## Maturity

Unlike debt, equity capital is a permanent form of financing. It does not "mature," and therefore repayment of the initial amount paid in is not required. Because equity does not mature and is liquidated only during bankruptcy proceedings, the owners must recognize that although a ready market may exist for the firm's shares, the price that can be realized may fluctuate. This potential fluctuation of the market price of equity makes the overall returns to a firm's owners even riskier.

## Tax Treatment

As noted in Chapter 2, interest payments to debtholders are treated as tax-deductible expenses on the firm's income statement, whereas dividend payments to preferred and common stockholders are not tax-deductible. The tax-deductibility of interest primarily accounts for the fact that the cost of debt is generally less than the cost of equity (as pointed out in Chapter 13).

## Progress Review Question

**19-1.** How do debt and equity capital differ? What are the key differences between them with respect to ownership rights, claims on income and assets, maturity, and tax treatment?

LG 2  LG 3

## Preferred Stock

*Preferred stock* gives its holders certain privileges that make them senior to common stockholders. Because of this, firms generally do not issue large quantities of preferred stock. Preferred stockholders are promised a fixed periodic return, which is stated either as a percentage or as a dollar amount. In other words, a 5 percent preferred stock or a $5 preferred stock can be issued. The way the dividend is specified depends on whether the preferred stock has a par value. **Par-value preferred stock** has a stated face value. The annual dividend is stated as a percentage on par-value preferred stock and in dollars on **no-par preferred stock,** which does not have a stated face value. Thus a 5 percent preferred stock with a $100 par value is expected to pay $5 (5% × $100) in dividends per year, and a $5 preferred stock with no par value is also expected to pay its $5 stated dividend each year.

Preferred stock is most often issued by public utilities, by acquiring firms in merger transactions, or by firms that are experiencing losses and need ad-

**par-value preferred stock** Preferred stock with a stated face value that is used with the specified dividend percentage to determine the annual dollar dividend.

**no-par preferred stock** Preferred stock with no stated face value but with a stated annual dollar dividend.

ditional financing. Public utilities issue preferred stock to increase their financial leverage while increasing equity and avoiding the higher risk associated with debt financing. Preferred stock is used in connection with mergers to give the acquired firm's shareholders a fixed-income security that, when exchanged for their stock, results in certain tax advantages. In addition, preferred stock is frequently used by firms that are experiencing losses to raise needed funds. These firms can sell preferred stock more easily than common stock because preferred stock gives its holder a claim that is senior to that of common stockholders and therefore is less risky than common stock. Frequently, special features, such as conversion or warrants (described in Chapter 20) are included to enhance the attractiveness of the preferred stock and lower its cost to the issuer.

## Basic Rights of Preferred Stockholders

The basic rights of preferred stockholders with respect to voting, the distribution of earnings, and the distribution of assets are somewhat more favorable than the rights of common stockholders. Because preferred stock is a form of ownership and has no maturity date, its claims on income and assets are secondary to those of the firm's creditors.

**Voting Rights**   Preferred stock is often considered a *quasi-debt* because, much like interest on debt, it specifies a fixed periodic (dividend) payment. Of course, as ownership, preferred stock is unlike debt in that it has no maturity date. Because their claim on the firm's income is fixed and takes precedence over the claim of common stockholders, preferred stockholders are therefore not exposed to the same degree of risk as common stockholders. They are consequently *not* normally given the right to vote.

**Distribution of Earnings**   Preferred stockholders are given preference over common stockholders with respect to the distribution of earnings. If the stated preferred stock dividend is *passed* (not paid) by the board of directors, the payment of dividends to common stockholders is prohibited. It is this preference in dividend distribution that makes common stockholders the true risk-takers with respect to receipt of periodic returns.

**Distribution of Assets**   Preferred stockholders are usually given preference over common stockholders in the liquidation of assets resulting from a firm's bankruptcy. However, they must wait until all creditors have been satisfied. The amount of the claim of preferred stockholders in liquidation is normally equal to the par, or stated, value of the preferred stock. The preferred stockholder's preference over the common stockholder places the common stockholder in the riskier position with respect to recovery of investment.

## Features of Preferred Stock

A number of features are generally included as part of a preferred stock issue. These features, along with a statement of the stock's par value, the amount of dividend payments, the dividend payment dates, and any restrictive covenants, are specified in an agreement similar to a *term loan agreement* or *bond indenture* (see Chapter 18).

**Restrictive Covenants**  The restrictive covenants commonly found in a preferred stock issue are aimed at assuring the continued existence of the firm and, most important, regular payment of the stated dividend. These covenants include provisions related to passing dividends, the sale of senior securities, mergers, sales of assets, net working capital requirements, and the payment of common stock dividends or common stock repurchases. The violation of preferred stock covenants usually permits preferred stockholders either to obtain representation on the firm's board of directors or to force the retirement of their stock at or above its par, or stated, value.

**cumulative preferred stock**
Preferred stock for which all passed (unpaid) dividends in arrears must be paid along with the current dividend prior to the payment of dividends to common stockholders.

**noncumulative preferred stock**
Preferred stock for which passed (unpaid) dividends do not accumulate.

**Cumulation**  Most preferred stock is **cumulative** with respect to any dividends passed. That is, all dividends in arrears must be paid along with the current dividend prior to the payment of dividends to common stockholders. If preferred stock is **noncumulative,** passed (unpaid) dividends do not accumulate. In this case only the current dividend must be paid prior to paying dividends to common stockholders. Because the common stockholders, who are the firm's true owners, can receive dividends only after the dividend claims of preferred stockholders have been satisfied, it is in the firm's best interest to pay preferred dividends when they are due.[2] The following example helps to clarify the distinction between cumulative and noncumulative preferred stock.

# E X A M P L E

Utley Company, a manufacturer of specialty automobiles, currently has outstanding an issue of $6 preferred stock on which quarterly dividends of $1.50 are to be paid. Due to a cash shortage, the last two quarterly dividends were passed. The directors of the company have been receiving a large number of complaints from common stockholders, who have of course not received any dividends in the past two quarters either. If the preferred stock is cumulative, the company has to pay its preferred stockholders $4.50 per share ($3.00 of dividends in arrears plus the current $1.50 dividend) prior to paying dividends to its common stockholders. If the preferred stock is noncumulative, the firm must pay only the current $1.50 dividend to its preferred stockholders prior to paying dividends to its common stockholders.

**nonparticipating preferred stock**
Preferred stock for which holders receive only the specified dividend payments.

**participating preferred stock**
Preferred stock that provides for dividend payments based on certain formulas allowing preferred stockholders to participate with common stockholders in the receipt of dividends beyond a specified amount.

**Participation**  Most issues of preferred stock are **nonparticipating,** which means that preferred stockholders receive only the specified dividend payments. Occasionally, **participating preferred stock** is issued. This type provides for dividend payments based on certain formulas allowing preferred stockholders to participate with common stockholders in the receipt of dividends beyond a specified amount. This feature is included only when the firm considers it absolutely necessary in order to obtain badly needed funds.

**Call Feature**  Preferred stock is generally *callable*, which means that the issuer can retire outstanding stock within a certain period at a specified price. The call feature generally cannot be exercised until a period of years has

---

[2]Most preferred stock is cumulative because it is difficult to sell noncumulative stock. Common stockholders obviously prefer issuance of noncumulative preferred because it does not place them in quite as risky a position. But it is often in the best interest of the firm to sell *cumulative* preferred stock due to its lower cost.

elapsed since the issuance of the stock. The call price is normally set above the initial issuance price but may decrease according to a predetermined schedule as time passes. Making preferred stock callable provides the issuer with a method of bringing the fixed-payment commitment of the preferred issue to an end.

**Conversion Feature**   Preferred stock quite often contains a **conversion feature** that allows preferred stockholders to change each share into a stated number of shares of common stock. Sometimes the conversion ratio, or number of shares of common stock, changes according to a prespecified formula. A detailed discussion of conversion is presented in Chapter 20.

**conversion feature**
A feature that allows preferred stockholders to change each share into a stated number of shares of common stock.

## Special Types of Preferred Stock

Most preferred stock has a fixed dividend, but some firms issue **adjustable-rate (or floating-rate) preferred stock (ARPS).** Such stocks have a dividend rate tied to interest rates on specific government securities. Rate adjustments are commonly made quarterly, and typically the rate must be maintained within certain preset limits. The investment appeal of ARPS is that its dividend rate will rise as interest rates increase. From the firm's perspective, adjustable-rate preferreds have appeal because they can be sold at an initially lower dividend rate, and the scheduled dividend rate falls if interest rates decline.

**adjustable-rate (or floating-rate) preferred stock (ARPS)**
Preferred stock with a dividend rate tied to interest rates on specific government securities.

A relatively recent innovation in preferred stock financing, **payment-in-kind (PIK) preferred stock,** usually doesn't pay cash dividends, but rather pays in additional shares of preferred stock. These, in turn, pay dividends in even more preferred stock. Typical dividend rates on PIK preferred stock range from 15 to 18 percent. After a stated period, generally five or six years, PIK preferreds are supposed to begin paying cash dividends or provide holders with a chance to swap for another, more traditional security. These preferreds are essentially the equivalent of *junk bonds* (see Chapters 17 and 18) and, like them, are issued to finance corporate takeovers. A good deal of uncertainty surrounds PIK preferreds. If the issuer runs into trouble, holders may end up with nothing—little chance of receiving cash dividends and little possibility of legal recourse against the issuer. Because they are primarily used to finance takeovers, PIK preferreds are not viewed as a major corporate financing tool.

**payment-in-kind (PIK) preferred stock**
Preferred stock that pays dividends in additional shares of preferred stock rather than cash.

## Advantages and Disadvantages of Preferred Stock

It is difficult to generalize about the advantages and disadvantages of preferred stock due to the variety of features that may be incorporated in a preferred stock issue. The attractiveness of preferred stock is also affected by current interest rates and the firm's existing capital structure. Nevertheless, some key advantages and disadvantages are often cited.

**Advantages**   One commonly cited advantage of preferred stock is its *ability to increase financial leverage*. Because preferred stock obligates the firm to pay only fixed dividends to its holders, its presence helps to increase the firm's financial leverage. (The effects of preferred stock on a firm's financial leverage were discussed in Chapter 5.) Increased financial leverage magnifies the effects of increased earnings on the common stockholders' returns.

A second advantage is the *flexibility* provided by preferred stock. Although preferred stock provides added financial leverage in much the same way as bonds, it differs from bonds in that the issuer can pass a dividend payment without suffering the consequences that result when an interest or principal payment is missed on a bond. Preferred stock allows the issuer to keep its levered position without running as great a risk of being forced out of business in a lean year as it might if it missed interest or principal payments on actual debt.

A third advantage of preferred stock has been its *use in corporate restructuring—mergers, leveraged buyouts (LBOs), and divestitures* (see Chapter 21). Often preferred stock is exchanged for the common stock of an acquired firm, with the preferred dividend set at a level equivalent to the historic dividend of the acquired firm. This exchange allows the acquiring firm to state at the time of the acquisition that only a fixed dividend will be paid. All other earnings can be reinvested to perpetuate the growth of the new enterprise. In addition, the owners of the acquired firm are assured of a continuing stream of dividends equivalent to that which may have been provided prior to the restructuring.

**Disadvantages**   Three major disadvantages are often cited for preferred stock. One is the *seniority of the preferred stockholder's claim*. Because holders of preferred stock are given preference over common stockholders with respect to the distribution of earnings and assets, the presence of preferred stock in a sense jeopardizes common stockholders' returns. If a firm has preferred stockholders to pay, and if the firm's after-tax earnings vary significantly, its ability to pay at least token dividends to common stockholders may be seriously impaired.

A second disadvantage of preferred stock is cost. The *cost of preferred stock financing is generally higher than that of debt financing*. The reason is that, unlike the payment of interest to bondholders, the payment of dividends to preferred stockholders is not guaranteed. Because preferred stockholders are willing to accept the added risk of purchasing preferred stock rather than long-term debt, they must be compensated with a higher return. Another factor causing the cost of preferred stock to be greater than that of long-term debt is the fact that interest on debt is tax-deductible, whereas preferred stock dividends must be paid from after-tax earnings.

A third disadvantage of preferred stock is that it is *generally difficult to sell*. Most investors find preferred stock unattractive relative to bonds (due to the issuer's ability to pass dividends) and to common stock (due to its limited return). As a consequence, most preferred stock includes special features, such as conversion or warrants, to enhance its marketability.

## Progress Review Questions

**19-2.**   What is *preferred stock*? What claims do preferred stockholders have with respect to the distribution of earnings (dividends) and assets? What types of firms and circumstances are typically involved in the issuance of preferred stock?

**19-3.**   What are *cumulative* and *noncumulative* preferred stock? Which form is more common? Why?

**19-4.** What is a *call feature* in a preferred stock issue? What is an *adjustable-rate (or floating-rate) preferred stock (ARPS)*? What is *payment-in-kind (PIK) preferred stock*?

**19-5.** What are the key advantages and disadvantages of using preferred stock financing as a source of new long-term funds?

▲▲▲▲▲▲▲▲▲▲▲▲▲▲▲▲▲▲▲▲▲▲▲▲▲▲▲▲▲▲▲▲▲▲

# Common Stock

The true owners of business firms are the common stockholders, who invest their money with the expectation of receiving future returns. A common stockholder is sometimes referred to as a *residual owner,* because in essence he or she receives what is left—the residual—after all other claims on the firm's income and assets have been satisfied. As a result of this generally uncertain position, the common stockholder expects to be compensated with adequate dividends and, ultimately, capital gains. Here we discuss the fundamental aspects of common stock: ownership; par value; authorized, outstanding, and issued shares; voting rights; dividends; stock repurchases; the distribution of earnings and assets; and international common stock.

## Ownership

The common stock of a firm can be **privately owned** by a single individual, **closely owned** by a small group of investors such as a family, or **publicly owned** by a broad group of unrelated individual and(or) institutional investors. Typically, small corporations are privately or closely owned; if their shares are traded, this occurs privately or on the over-the-counter exchange. Large corporations, which are emphasized in the following discussions, are publicly owned, and their shares are generally actively traded on the organized or over-the-counter exchanges, which were briefly described in Chapter 2.

**privately owned (stock)**
All common stock of a firm owned by a single individual.

**closely owned (stock)**
All common stock of a firm owned by a small group of investors such as a family.

**publicly owned (stock)**
Common stock of a firm owned by a broad group of unrelated individual and(or) institutional investors.

## Par Value

Common stock may be sold with or without a par value. A **par value** is a relatively useless value arbitrarily placed on the stock in the firm's corporate charter. It is generally quite low, somewhere in the range of $1. Firms often issue stock with **no-par value,** in which case they may assign it a value or place it on the books at the price at which it is sold. A low par value may be advantageous in states where certain corporate taxes are based on the par value of stock; if a stock has no par value, the tax may be based on an arbitrarily determined per-share figure. The accounting entries resulting from the sale of common stock can be illustrated by a simple example.

**par value**
A relatively useless value arbitrarily placed on stock in the firm's corporate charter.

**no-par value**
Describes stock issued without a *par value.*

▶ **E X A M P L E**

Moxie Company, a soft drink manufacturer, has issued 1,000,000 shares of $2 par-value common stock, receiving proceeds of $50 per share. This results in the following entries appearing on the firm's books:

# F I N A N C E   I N

# A C T I O N

International

## Which Teléfonos de Mexico Shares Will Ring up Higher Profits?

Firms obviously seek the highest price for shares at initial public offerings. To attract as many investors as possible, firms may issue shares with multiple classes that differ in terms of the voting rights or dividend payment. Large firms also often issue shares on foreign exchanges. In the United States, the shares of foreign corporations are normally held by U.S. banks that issue receipts to investors, known as American depositary receipts (ADRs).

Complications and confusion can arise when multiple ADRs exist as a consequence of multiple classes of shares for the same foreign firm. A prime example is the shares issued by Teléfonos de Mexico (TelMex), the Mexican telephone conglomerate with a backlog of 450,000 potential customers. The firm has three primary classes of shares with varying rights as outlined in the following table.

| Class | ADR | Rights/Ownership |
| --- | --- | --- |
| AA | None | Control of TelMex/owned by Grupo Carso, France Telecom, and Southwestern Bell |
| L | New York Stock Exchange (NYSE) | 20 class L shares per ADR/most limited voting rights |
| A | Over-the-counter (OTC) exchange | 1 class A share per ADR/moderate voting rights |

Ironically, investors have greatest control, though indirect control, through purchase of Southwestern Bell shares. Greatest liquidity is available through purchase of TelMex shares listed on the NYSE. The lowest price of owner-ship comes with purchasing OTC-listed shares, which are claims on only one TelMex share.

Source: Richard S. Teitelbaum, "TelMex Is Hot, but Which Way to Buy It?," *Fortune*, January 10, 1994, p. 24.

| | |
| --- | --- |
| Common stock (1,000,000 shares at $2 par) | $ 2,000,000 |
| Paid-in capital in excess of par | 48,000,000 |
| Common stock equity | $50,000,000 |

Sometimes the entry labeled "paid-in capital in excess of par" may be labeled "capital surplus." This value is important because, as noted in Chapter 16, firms are usually prohibited by state law from distributing any paid-in capital as dividends.

## Authorized, Outstanding, and Issued Shares

As noted in Chapter 17, the corporate charter states the number of *authorized shares* of common stock. Not all authorized shares are necessarily *outstanding shares* that are under ownership of the firm's shareholders. Because it is often difficult to amend the charter to authorize the issuance of additional shares, firms generally attempt to authorize more shares than they plan to issue. It is possible for the corporation to have more *issued shares* of common stock than are currently outstanding if it has repurchased stock. Repurchased stock, as noted in Chapter 16, is called *treasury stock*. The amount of treasury stock is therefore found by subtracting the number of outstanding shares from the number of issued shares.

## Voting Rights

Generally, each share of common stock entitles the holder to one vote in the election of directors and in other special elections. Votes are generally assignable and must be cast at the annual stockholders' meeting.

In recent years many firms have issued two or more classes of common stock, unequal voting rights being their key difference. The issuance of different classes of stock has been frequently used as a defense against a **hostile merger** in which an outside group, without management support, tries to gain voting control of the firm by buying its shares in the marketplace. At other times a class of **nonvoting common stock** is issued when the firm wishes to raise capital through the sale of common stock but does not want to give up its voting control. This and other approaches to issuing classes of stock with unequal voting rights result in some **supervoting shares.** By giving their holders more votes per share, supervoting shares allow them to better control the firm's future. An interesting variation on this theme was put in place by J. M. Smucker Co. (food, confectionery). The firm initially had only one class of stock, which, once it was held for four years, provided 10 votes per share. Because the Smucker family owned 30 percent of the stock, this procedure, when it was initiated a number of years ago, effectively ruled out a hostile merger of the company.

When different classes of common stock are issued on the basis of unequal voting rights, class A common is typically—but not universally—designated as nonvoting, and class B common has voting rights. Generally, higher classes of shares are given preference with respect to the distribution of earnings (dividends) and assets (in liquidation) over the lower class shares. The lower class shares in exchange receive more voting rights. In other words, because class A shares are not given voting rights, they are generally given preference over class B shares in terms of the distribution of dividends and assets. Treasury stock, which resides within the corporation, generally *does not* have voting rights, *does not* earn dividends, and *does not* have a claim on assets in liquidation. Three aspects of voting require special attention: proxies, majority voting, and cumulative voting.

**Proxies**   Because most small stockholders cannot attend the annual meeting to vote, they may sign a **proxy statement** giving their votes to another party. The solicitation of proxies from shareholders is closely controlled by the Securities and Exchange Commission, to protect against the possibility that proxies will be solicited on the basis of false or misleading information. Existing management generally receives the stockholders' proxies, because it is able to solicit them at company expense. Occasionally, when the ownership of the firm is widely disseminated, outsiders may attempt to gain control by waging a **proxy battle.** They attempt to solicit a sufficient number of votes to unseat the existing management. To win a corporate election, votes from a majority of the shares voted are required. Proxy battles generally occur when

**hostile merger**
A maneuver in which an outside group, without management support, tries to gain voting control of a firm by buying its shares in the marketplace.

**nonvoting common stock**
Common stock that carries no voting rights; issued when the firm wishes to raise capital through the sale of common stock but does not want to give up its voting control.

**supervoting shares**
Stock that carries with it more votes per share than a share of regular common stock.

**proxy statement**
A statement giving the votes of a stockholder or stockholders to another party.

**proxy battle**
The attempt by a nonmanagement group to gain control of the management of a firm by soliciting a sufficient number of proxy votes.

the existing management is performing poorly; however, the odds of a non-management group winning a proxy battle are generally slim.

**Majority Voting**    In the **majority voting system,** each stockholder is entitled to one vote for each share of stock owned. The stockholders vote for each position on the board of directors separately, and each stockholder is permitted to vote all of his or her shares for *each* director he or she favors. The directors receiving the majority of the votes are elected. It is impossible for minority interests to select a director, because each shareholder can vote his or her shares for as many of the candidates as he or she wishes. As long as management controls a majority of the votes, it can elect all the directors. An example clarifies this point.

**majority voting system**
The system whereby, in the election of a board of directors, each stockholder is entitled to one vote for each share of stock owned and can vote all shares for each director.

# E X A M P L E    ◀

Dill Company, a producer of high-quality paper, is in the process of electing three directors. One thousand shares of stock are outstanding, 60 percent of which management controls. The management-backed candidates are A, B, and C; the minority candidates are D, E, and F. By voting its 600 shares (60% × 1,000) for *each* of its candidates, management can elect A, B, and C. The minority shareholders, with only 400 votes for each of their candidates, cannot elect any directors. Management's candidates receive 600 votes each, and other candidates receive 400 votes each.    ◀

**Cumulative Voting**    Nearly half of all the states, including California, Illinois, and Michigan, require corporations chartered by them to use a **cumulative voting system** in the election of directors; other states permit cumulative voting as long as it is provided for in the corporation's charter. This system gives a number of votes equal to the total number of directors to be elected to each share of common stock. The votes can be given to *any* director(s) the stockholder desires. The advantage of this system is that it provides the minority shareholders with an opportunity to elect at least some directors.

**cumulative voting system**
The system under which each share of common stock is allotted a number of votes equal to the total number of corporate directors to be elected and votes can be given to *any* director(s).

# E X A M P L E    ◀

Esco Company, a competitor of Dill Company, is also in the process of electing three directors. In this case, however, each share of common stock entitles the holder to three votes, which may be voted in any manner desired. Again, 1,000 shares are outstanding, and management controls 600. It therefore has a total of 1,800 votes (3 × 600), whereas the minority shareholders have 1,200 votes (3 × 400). In this situation, the majority shareholders can elect only two directors, and the minority shareholders can elect at least one director. The majority shareholders can split their votes evenly among the three candidates (give them 600 votes each); but if the minority shareholders give all their votes to one of their candidates, he or she will win.    ◀

**Equation 19.1 Formula for the number of shares necessary to elect a certain number of directors under cumulative voting**

A commonly cited formula for determining the number of shares necessary to elect a certain number of directors, *NE*, under cumulative voting is given by Equation 19.1:

$$NE = \frac{O \times D}{TN + 1} + 1 \qquad (19.1)$$

where

$NE$ = number of shares needed to elect a certain number of directors
$O$ = total number of shares of common stock outstanding
$D$ = number of directors desired
$TN$ = total number of directors to be elected

▶ E X A M P L E

Substituting the values in the preceding example for $O$ (1,000) and $TN$ (3) into Equation 19.1 and letting $D = 1$, 2, and 3 yields values of $NE$ equal to 251, 501, and 751. Because the minority stockholders control only 400 shares, they can elect only one director.

The advantage of cumulative voting from the viewpoint of minority shareholders should be clear from the example. However, even with cumulative voting, certain election procedures such as staggered terms for directors can be used to prevent minority representation on a board. Also, the majority shareholders may control a large enough number of shares, or the total number of directors to be elected may be small enough to prevent minority representation.

## Dividends

The payment of corporate dividends is at the discretion of the board of directors. Most corporations pay dividends quarterly. Dividends may be paid in cash, stock, or merchandise. Cash dividends are the most common; merchandise dividends are the least common. *Stock splits,* which have some similarity to *stock dividends,* are sometimes used to enhance the trading activity of a stock (see Chapter 16).

The common stockholder is not promised a dividend, but he or she comes to expect certain payments based on the historical dividend pattern of the firm. Before dividends are paid to common stockholders, the claims of the government, all creditors, and preferred stockholders must be satisfied. Because of the importance of the dividend decision to the growth and valuation of the firm, a portion of Chapter 16 was devoted to a discussion of dividend policy.

## Stock Repurchases

Another characteristic of common stock, alluded to earlier in the discussion of authorized, outstanding, and issued shares, is the repurchase of stock. Firms occasionally repurchase stock in order to change their capital structure or to increase the returns to the owners. The effect of repurchasing common stock is similar to that of the payment of cash dividends to stockholders. The repurchase of stock is popular among firms that are in a very liquid position with no attractive investment opportunities. Because stock repurchases are similar to cash dividend payments, they too were discussed in Chapter 16.

## Distribution of Earnings and Assets

As mentioned in previous sections, holders of common stock have no guarantee of receiving any periodic distribution of earnings in the form of dividends, nor are they guaranteed anything in the event of liquidation. However, one thing they are assured of is that they cannot lose any more than they have invested in the firm. Moreover, the common stockholder can receive unlimited returns through dividends and through the appreciation in the value of his or her holdings. In other words, although nothing is guaranteed, the *possible* rewards for providing risk capital can be considerable and even great.

## International Common Stock

Although the international market for common stock is not—and probably never will be—as large as the international market for debt securities, cross-border trading and issuance of common stock have increased dramatically during the past 15 years. Much of this increase can be accounted for by a growing desire on the part of securities investors to diversify their investment portfolios internationally.

**International Stock Issues**   Besides investors, corporations have also discovered the benefits of issuing stock outside of their home markets. For example, several top U.S. multinational companies have chosen to list their stock in half a dozen or more stock markets—the London, Frankfurt, and Tokyo markets being the most popular. Issuing stock internationally both broadens the ownership base and helps a company integrate itself into the local business scene. A local stock listing both increases local business press coverage and serves as effective corporate advertising. Having locally traded stock can also facilitate corporate acquisitions because shares can then be used as an acceptable method of payment.

**American depositary receipts (ADRs)**
Claims issued by U.S. banks representing ownership of shares of a foreign company's stock held on deposit by the U.S. bank in the foreign market and issued in dollars to U.S. investors.

**American Depositary Receipts**   Foreign corporations have also discovered the benefits of trading their stock in the United States. The disclosure and reporting requirements mandated by the U.S. Securities and Exchange Commission have historically discouraged all but the largest foreign firms from directly listing their shares on the New York or American Stock Exchanges. For example, in mid-1993, Daimler Benz announced that it would become the first large German company to seek such a listing. Instead, most foreign companies tap the U.S. market through **American depositary receipts (ADRs).** These are claims issued by U.S. banks representing ownership of shares of a foreign company's stock held on deposit by the U.S. bank in the foreign market. Because ADRs are issued in dollars, by a U.S. bank, to U.S. investors, they are subject to U.S. securities laws yet still give investors the opportunity to diversify their portfolios internationally.

**Recent Trends**   Two very important recent trends have arisen in international equity issues. The first is the increasing frequency with which European companies are making multinational equity issues within the European Community in preparation for the open market and unified currency expected to develop during the 1990s. These multinational equity issues have coincided with a surge in cross-border mergers and acquisitions undertaken for the same purpose. The second, and more fundamental, trend affecting global equity trading is the increasing frequency and size of share issues involving *privatization* of formerly state-owned enterprises. As privatization continues to spread through Western and Eastern Europe, the Commonwealth of Independent States, and, ultimately, the People's Republic of China, these equity issues will play a major role in international equity trading.

▼▼▼▼▼▼▼▼▼▼▼▼▼▼▼▼▼▼▼▼▼▼▼▼▼▼▼▼▼▼▼▼▼▼

# Progress Review Questions

**19-6.** Why is the common stockholder considered the true owner of a firm? What risks do common stockholders take that other suppliers of long-term capital do not?

**19-7.** What are *proxies*? How are they used? What are *proxy battles,* and why are they initiated? Why is it difficult for minority shareholders to win such battles?

**19-8.** How do majority and cumulative voting systems differ? Which of these voting systems is preferred by the minority shareholders? Why?

**19-9.** Discuss the following with regard to international equity issues:
  **a.** The reasons for the increase in cross-border common stock trading and issuance
  **b.** The advantages, to both U.S.-based and foreign corporations, of issuing stock outside of their home markets
  **c.** The use of American depositary receipts (ADRs)
  **d.** Recent trends in international equity issues

▲▲▲▲▲▲▲▲▲▲▲▲▲▲▲▲▲▲▲▲▲▲▲▲▲▲▲▲▲▲▲▲

# Stock Rights and Other Considerations

LG ⑤   LG ⑥

In addition to common stock fundamentals, stock rights, and the advantages and disadvantages of common stock are important considerations.

## Stock Rights

**Stock rights** allow stockholders to purchase additional shares of stock in direct proportion to their number of owned shares. Today, rights are primarily used by smaller corporations whose shares are either *closely owned* or *publicly owned* and not actively traded. In these situations rights are an important common stock financing tool without which shareholders would run the risk of losing their proportionate control of the corporation. Rights are rarely used by large publicly owned corporations whose shares are widely held and actively traded. Maintenance of proportionate control in such firms is not a major concern of their shareholders.

### Preemptive Rights
**Preemptive rights** allow common stockholders to maintain their *proportionate* ownership in the corporation when new issues are made. Although most states permit shareholders to be extended this privilege in the corporate charter, only two states require corporations chartered by them to provide these rights to common stockholders. Preemptive rights allow existing shareholders to maintain their voting control and protect against the dilution of their ownership and earnings. **Dilution of ownership** usually results in the dilution of earnings, because each present shareholder

**stock rights**
Allow stockholders to purchase additional shares of stock in direct proportion to their number of owned shares.

**preemptive rights**
Allow common stockholders to maintain their *proportionate* ownership in the corporation when new issues are made.

**dilution of ownership**
Occurs when a new stock issue results in each present stockholder having a claim on a *smaller* part of the firm's earnings than previously.

has a claim on a *smaller* part of the firm's earnings than previously. Of course, if total earnings simultaneously increase, the long-run effect may be an overall increase in earnings per share.

From the firm's viewpoint, the use of rights offerings to raise new equity capital may be easier and less costly and generate more interest than a public offering of stock. An example may help clarify the use of rights.

# EXAMPLE

Dominic Company, a large national advertising firm, currently has 100,000 shares of common stock outstanding and is contemplating issuing an additional 10,000 shares through a rights offering. Each existing shareholder receives one right per share, and each right entitles the shareholder to purchase one-tenth of a share of new common stock (10,000 ÷ 100,000). Therefore, 10 rights are required to purchase one share of stock. The holder of 1,000 shares (1 percent) of the outstanding common stock receives 1,000 rights. Because each permits the purchase of one-tenth of a share of new common stock, the holder is able to purchase 100 shares ($\frac{1}{10}$ × 1,000 shares) of new common stock. If the shareholder exercises the rights, he or she ends up with a total of 1,100 shares of common stock, or 1 percent of the total number of shares outstanding (110,000). Thus the shareholder maintains the same proportion of ownership he or she had prior to the rights offering.

**Mechanics of Rights Offerings**   When a company makes a rights offering, the board of directors must set a **date of record,** which is the last date on which the recipient of a right must be the legal owner indicated in the company's stock ledger. Due to the time needed to make bookkeeping entries when a stock is traded, stocks usually begin selling **ex rights**—without the rights being attached to the stock—four *business days* prior to the date of record.

**date of record (rights)**
The last date on which the recipient of a right must be the legal owner indicated in the company's stock ledger.

**ex rights**
Period, beginning four *business days* prior to the date of record, during which a stock is sold without announced rights being attached.

**subscription price**
The price, set below the prevailing market price, at which stock rights are exercisable for a specified period.

The issuing firm sends rights to *holders of record,* who may exercise their rights, sell them, or let them expire. Rights are negotiable instruments, and many are traded actively enough to be listed on the various securities exchanges. They are exercisable for a specified period, generally not more than a few months. The price at which they may be exercised, called the **subscription price,** is set somewhat below the prevailing market price. Because fractions of shares are not always issued, it is sometimes necessary to purchase additional rights or sell extra rights. The value of a right depends largely on the number of rights needed to purchase a share of stock and the amount by which the right's subscription price is below the current market price. If the rights have a very low value and a rights holder owns only a small number of shares, the rights may be allowed to expire.

**Management Decisions**   A firm's management must make two basic decisions when preparing for a rights offering. The first is the price at which the rights holders can purchase a new share of common stock. The subscription price must be set *below* the current market price, but how far below depends on several things: management's evaluation of the sensitivity of the market demand to a price change, the degree of dilution of ownership and earnings expected, and the size of the offering. Management considers the rights offering successful if approximately 90 percent of the rights are exercised.

## FINANCE IN ACTION

Small Business

### Houston Biotechnological Eyes a Solution in Stock Rights

Houston Biotechnological needed cash but didn't want to diminish shareholder control. The Woodlands, Texas, manufacturer of eye-care solutions needed $3.3 million to upgrade its business. Given the risky nature of the pharmaceutical industry and already outstanding debt, further debt carried an unacceptably high interest rate. The search for capital began in 1991, when weak investor demand made prospects for a conventional stock offering dim. Equity deals and research-and-development partnerships examined in 1992 consistently offered Houston Biotech less than the CEO felt the company was worth.

Consequently, Houston Biotech turned to its existing investors for assistance. Shares were offered to them based on their stake in Houston Biotech. Those with $10,000, for instance, could buy 500 new shares at a price of $5 each. To entice shareholders, those purchasing additional shares were given the right to buy 250 extra shares at a price of $5 each in 1994 or 1995. After 1995, those buying into the rights offering could obtain additional shares at a price of $10 each.

Overall, about 15 percent of the eligible shareholders bought additional shares. In a short time, Houston Biotech had raised the needed funds. Furthermore, equity will also become available if existing investors exercise their stock-purchase warrants.

Source: Bruce E. Posner, "New 'Rights' for Old Investors," *Inc.*, December 1993, p. 167.

Once management has determined the subscription price, it must determine the number of rights required to purchase a share of stock. Because the amount of funds to be raised is known in advance, the subscription price can be divided into this value to get the total number of shares that must be sold. Dividing the total number of shares outstanding by the total number of shares to be sold gives management the number of rights required to purchase a share of stock.

## ▶ EXAMPLE

Lorne Company, a closely owned hand-tool manufacturer, intends to raise $1 million through a rights offering. The firm currently has 160,000 shares outstanding, which have been most recently trading for $53 to $58 per share. The company has consulted an investment banking firm, which has recommended setting the subscription price for the rights at $50 per share. It believes that at this price the offering will be fully subscribed. The firm must therefore sell an additional 20,000 shares ($1,000,000 ÷ $50 per share). This means that eight rights (160,000 ÷ 20,000) are needed to purchase a new share at $50. Each right entitles its holder to purchase one-eighth of a share of common stock.

**Value of a Right**   Theoretically, the value of a right should be the same if the stock is selling *with rights* or *ex rights*. In either case, the market value of a right may differ from its theoretical value.

**With Rights.**   Once a rights offering has been declared, shares trade with rights for only a few days. Equation 19.2 is used to find the theoretical value of a right when the stock is trading with rights, $R_w$:

**Equation 19.2** Formula for the theoretical value of a right when the stock is trading *with rights*

$$R_w = \frac{M_w - S}{N + 1} \tag{19.2}$$

where

$R_w$ = theoretical value of a right when the stock is selling with rights
$M_w$ = market value of the stock with rights
$S$ = subscription price of the stock
$N$ = number of rights needed to purchase one share of stock

# E X A M P L E

Lorne Company's stock is currently selling with rights at a price of $54.50 per share, the subscription price is $50 per share, and eight rights are required to purchase a new share of stock. According to Equation 19.2, the value of a right is $.50 [($54.50 − $50.00) ÷ (8 + 1)]. A right should therefore be worth $.50 in the marketplace.

**Ex Rights.**   When a share of stock is traded ex rights, meaning that the value of the right is no longer included in the stock's market price, the share price of the stock is expected to drop by the value of a right. Equation 19.3 is used to find the market value of the stock trading ex rights, $M_e$. The same notation is used as in Equation 19.2:

**Equation 19.3** Formula for the market value of stock trading *ex rights*

$$M_e = M_w - R_w \tag{19.3}$$

The theoretical value of a right when the stock is trading ex rights, $R_e$, is given by Equation 19.4:

**Equation 19.4** Formula for the theoretical value of a right when the stock is trading *ex rights*

$$R_e = \frac{M_e - S}{N} \tag{19.4}$$

The use of these equations can be illustrated by returning to the Lorne Company example.

# E X A M P L E

According to Equation 19.3, the market price of the Lorne Company stock selling ex rights is $54 ($54.50 − $.50). Substituting this value into Equation 19.4 gives the value of a right when the stock is selling ex rights, which is $.50 [($54.00 − $50.00) ÷ 8]. The theoretical value of the right when the stock is selling with rights or ex rights is therefore the same.

**Market Behavior of Rights**   As indicated earlier, stock rights are negotiable instruments, often traded on securities exchanges. The market price of a right generally differs from its theoretical value. The extent to which it differs depends on how the firm's stock price is expected to behave during the period when the right is exercisable. By buying rights instead of the stock itself, investors can achieve much higher returns on their money when stock prices rise.

## Advantages and Disadvantages of Common Stock

A number of key advantages and disadvantages of common stock are often cited.

**Advantages** The basic advantages of common stock stem from the fact that it is a source of financing that places a *minimum of constraints* on the firm. Because dividends do *not* have to be paid on common stock, and their nonpayment does not jeopardize the receipt of payment by other securities holders, common stock financing is quite attractive. The fact that common stock has *no maturity,* thereby eliminating a future repayment obligation, also enhances its desirability as a form of financing. Another advantage of common stock over other forms of long-term financing is its *ability to increase the firm's borrowing power.* The more common stock a firm sells, the larger its equity base and therefore the more easily and cheaply long-term debt financing can be obtained.

**Disadvantages** The disadvantages of common stock financing include the *potential dilution of earnings.* Clearly, when additional shares are issued, more shares have a claim on the firm's earnings. This often results in a short-run decline in earnings per share (EPS), which in turn can, and often does, negatively affect the stock's market price. A related disadvantage is the *potential dilution of control.* Particularly for smaller corporations, the issuance of additional shares can shift ownership proportions, and therefore voting control, from one party to another. Another disadvantage of common stock financing is its *high cost.* As we saw in Chapter 13, common stock equity is normally the most expensive form of long-term financing. It is expensive because common stock is a riskier security than either debt or preferred stock and because dividends are not tax-deductible.

▼▼▼▼▼▼▼▼▼▼▼▼▼▼▼▼▼▼▼▼▼▼▼▼▼▼▼▼▼▼▼▼

## Progress Review Questions

**19-10.** What are *stock rights?* What is a right *subscription price?* How is it determined? Given the subscription price, what must the firm know to determine the number of rights to offer?

**19-11.** Compare the theoretical value of rights when a stock is selling *with rights* with its *ex rights* value. Do these values typically equal their market price? Why?

**19-12.** What are the key advantages and disadvantages of using common stock financing as a source of new long-term funds?

▲▲▲▲▲▲▲▲▲▲▲▲▲▲▲▲▲▲▲▲▲▲▲▲▲▲▲▲▲▲▲▲

# SUMMARY OF LEARNING GOALS

**Differentiate between debt and equity capital in terms of ownership rights, claims on income and assets, maturity, and tax treatment.** Holders of equity capital (common and preferred stock) are owners of the firm. Holders of

LG 1

common stock have voting rights that permit them to select the firm's directors and vote on special issues; holders of preferred stock and debt capital typically have no voting rights. Preferred and common stockholders have claims on income and assets that are secondary to the claims of creditors, have no maturity date, and do not receive tax benefits similar to those given to debtholders.

**LG 2**   **Understand preferred stock, including the basic rights of preferred stockholders, features normally included as part of a preferred stock issue, and special types of preferred stock.** Preferred stockholders are given preference over common stockholders with respect to the distribution of earnings and assets and, as a result, do not normally receive voting privileges. Preferred stock issues may have certain restrictive covenants, cumulative dividends, participation in earnings, a call feature, and a conversion feature. Special types of preferred stock include adjustable-rate (or floating-rate) preferred stock (ARPS) and payment-in-kind (PIK) preferred stock. Whereas most preferred stock is similar to debt in that it has stated fixed annual cash dividends, these special types do not.

**LG 3**   **Explain the key advantages and disadvantages of preferred stock financing.** The basic advantages for preferred stock financing include its ability to increase the firm's leverage, the flexibility of the obligation, and its use in corporate restructuring. Disadvantages include the seniority of its claim over that of the common stockholders, its relatively high cost compared with debt financing, and the general difficulty of selling it.

**LG 4**   **Discuss common stock, including important aspects of voting rights and international common stock.** The common stock of a firm can be privately owned, closely owned, or publicly owned. It can be sold with or without a par value. Not all shares authorized in the corporate charter are outstanding. If a firm has treasury stock, it has issued more shares than are outstanding. Some firms issue two or more classes of common stock, with unequal voting rights being their key difference. Proxies can be used to transfer voting rights from one party to another. Either majority voting or cumulative voting may be used by the firm to elect its directors. Common stockholders are guaranteed neither the periodic distribution of earnings in the form of dividends nor the receipt of funds in the event of liquidation. International trading of common stock dramatically increased during the past 15 years as corporations discovered the benefits of using stock outside of their home markets and foreign corporations discovered the benefits of trading their stock in the U.S. either through listing on U.S. exchanges or through the issuance of American depositary receipts (ADRs). This trend is expected to continue.

**LG 5**   **Describe stock rights, including the mechanics of rights offerings, management decisions, theoretical values, and market behavior.** Holders of common stock—especially in smaller corporations—may receive stock rights that give them an opportunity to purchase new common stock at a reduced price on a pro rata basis. A certain number of rights is required to purchase the new shares at the reduced price, which causes each right to have a monetary value. Rights may be exercised, sold, purchased, or allowed to expire. A firm's management must determine the price at which the rights holders can purchase a new share of common stock and the number of rights required to purchase a share of stock. Theoretically, the value of a right should be the same if the stock is selling with rights or ex rights. In either case, the market value of a right may differ from its theoretical value. The extent to which it differs depends on how the firm's stock price is expected to behave during the period when the right is exercisable.

**Review the key advantages and disadvantages of common stock financing.** Basic advantages of common stock include the minimum of constraints it places on the firm, its lack of a maturity date, and its ability to increase the firm's borrowing power. Disadvantages include the potential dilution of earnings and control, and its high cost.

# SUMMARY OF KEY DEFINITIONS AND EQUATIONS

## Variable Definitions

$D$ = number of directors desired
$M_e$ = market value of the stock trading ex rights
$M_w$ = market value of the stock with rights
$N$ = number of rights needed to purchase one share of stock
$NE$ = number of shares needed to elect a certain number of directors
$O$ = total number of shares of common stock outstanding
$R_e$ = theoretical value of a right when the stock is trading ex rights
$R_w$ = theoretical value of a right when the stock is selling with rights
$S$ = subscription price of the stock
$TN$ = total number of directors to be elected

## Equations

Number of shares necessary to elect a certain number of directors under cumulative voting

$$NE = \frac{O \times D}{TN + 1} + 1$$    [Eq. 19.1]

Theoretical value of a right when the stock is trading with rights

$$R_w = \frac{M_w - S}{N + 1}$$    [Eq. 19.2]

Market value of stock trading ex rights

[Eq. 19.3]

$$M_e = M_w - R_w$$

Theoretical value of a right when the stock is trading ex rights

[Eq. 19.4]

$$R_e = \frac{M_e - S}{N}$$

## L E A R N I N G   G O A L S

After studying this chapter, you should be able to

**LG 1** Describe the basic types of convertible securities and their general features, including the conversion ratio, conversion period, conversion (or stock) value, and effect on earnings.

**LG 2** Discuss the key motives for convertible financing, the considerations involved in forcing conversion, and the difficulties associated with overhanging issues.

**LG 3** Demonstrate the procedures for determining the straight bond value, conversion (or stock) value, and market value of a convertible bond.

**LG 4** Explain the basic characteristics of stock-purchase warrants and compare them with rights and convertibles.

**LG 5** Calculate the theoretical value of a warrant and use its market value to determine the warrant premium.

**LG 6** Define options and discuss the basics of calls and puts, options markets, options trading, the role of call and put options in fund raising, and using options to protect against foreign currency exposures.

# 20 Convertibles, Warrants, and Options

Convertible securities, warrants, and options are long-term financing alternatives that give companies greater financial flexibility. It is therefore important for financial managers to be familiar with these financing techniques. All types of companies can benefit from using convertibles, warrants, and options. In particular, they allow young companies to obtain growth capital when other forms of financing are not available or cost-effective.

# Convertible securities, warrants, and options . . . give companies greater financial flexibility.

Convertible debt and convertible preferred stock give the holder the right to convert the original security into a given number of shares of common stock at a specified price. Convertible securities are popular with firms in their developing stages. Although such firms have a strong "story to tell," they are not yet ready to issue stock in the public markets. Their equity would either not be marketable or wouldn't command a good price. Convertibles therefore provide an attractive intermediate financing source.

They allow companies to raise funds from investors who want the opportunity to participate in the potential financial success of these new firms. These investors are willing to make a loan to the company today in hopes of converting to equity that has increased in value at a later date. Another advantage of convertibles is their tremendous flexibility. Issuers can customize the financing terms to meet their needs.

Convertibles are also used by established companies. Telecommunications utilities use convertible securities to meet capital ratio requirements and maintain their credit ratings. A convertible bond may be treated as equity by the rating agency so that the company's debt ratio stays within accepted limits.

Options, which include warrants, calls, and puts, also give companies access to lower cost capital. Warrants allow the holder to buy a stated number of common stock shares at a set price for a specified period. For a promising young company, adding warrants makes its bonds more salable. Investors who feel that the company has a bright future are attracted by the possibility of purchasing stock at a discount in the future. Warrants can also be granted or traded independently of a bond. For example, investment bankers sometimes accept warrants in lieu of fees, on a very selective basis, from emerging companies that could not otherwise afford financial advisory services.

Calls and puts are two popular types of options. A call provides the right to buy, and a put provides the right to sell, a certain number of shares of common stock at a set price by a specified date. In addition to their role as secondary market investments that are traded, they are used by corporate financial managers to customize financing transactions to the needs of a particular issuer or buyer. For example, a lender may offer a lower cost loan if the debt-financing transaction includes a call or put. Options may be used in deals involving private financing, minority investments (where a company acquires an interest of less than 50 percent of another firm), and strategic partnership investments. For example, telecommunications companies often include them when they form strategic alliances with other high-tech firms to gain access to particular markets or products.

**Samme Thompson** *is a senior vice-president at Kidder, Peabody & Co., specializing in telecommunications and information technology company financing. Before joining Kidder in 1987, he was head of strategic planning for AT&T Information Systems and a telecommunications consultant at McKinsey & Co. Mr. Thompson received a Bachelor's degree in electrical engineering from Prairie View A&M in Texas and his M.B.A. from the University of Pittsburgh.*

Chapters 18 and 19 presented the various methods of raising long-term financing externally: term loans, bonds, leasing, preferred stock, and common stock. In addition, three vehicles—the conversion feature, stock-purchase warrants, and options—are available for use by the firm in its long-term financing activities.

The *conversion feature*, which can be part of either a bond or preferred stock, permits the firm's capital structure to be changed without increasing the total financing. *Stock-purchase warrants* can be attached to either a long-term loan or a bond. They permit the firm to raise additional funds at some point in the future by selling common stock, thereby shifting the company's capital structure to a less highly levered position. *Options* are a special type of security that provides the holder with the right to purchase or sell specified assets at a stated price on or before a set expiration date. Here we focus on the characteristics and role in long-term financing of convertibles, warrants, and options.

# Convertible Securities

A **conversion feature** is an option included as part of a bond or a preferred stock issue that allows its holder to change the security into a stated number of shares of common stock. The conversion feature typically enhances the marketability of an issue.

**conversion feature**
An option included as part of a bond or a preferred stock issue that allows its holder to change the security into a stated number of shares of common stock.

## Types of Convertible Securities

Corporate bonds and preferred stocks may be convertible into common stock. The most common type of convertible security is the bond. Convertibles normally have an accompanying *call feature*. This feature permits the issuer to retire or encourage conversion of outstanding convertibles when appropriate.

**Convertible Bonds**    A **convertible bond** is a bond that at some future time can be changed into a specified number of shares of common stock. It is almost always a *debenture*—an unsecured bond—with a call feature. Because the conversion feature provides the purchaser of a convertible bond with the possibility of becoming a stockholder on favorable terms, convertible bonds are generally a less expensive form of financing than similar-risk nonconvertible, or **straight bonds.** The conversion feature adds a degree of speculation to a bond issue, although the issue still maintains its value as a bond. Convertible bonds are sometimes convertible only for a specified period of years.

**convertible bond**
A bond that at some future time can be changed into a specified number of shares of common stock.

**straight bond**
A bond that has no conversion feature.

**Convertible Preferred Stock**    **Convertible preferred stock** is preferred stock that at some future time can be changed into a specified number of shares of common stock. It can normally be sold with a lower stated dividend than a similar-risk nonconvertible, or **straight preferred stock.** The reason is that the convertible preferred holder is assured of the fixed dividend payment associated with a preferred stock and also may receive the appreciation

**convertible preferred stock**
Preferred stock that at some future time can be changed into a specified number of shares of common stock.

**straight preferred stock**
Preferred stock that has no conversion feature.

resulting from increases in the market price of the underlying common stock. Convertible preferred stocks are usually convertible over an unlimited time horizon. Although convertible preferred stock behaves in a fashion similar to convertible bonds, the following discussions concentrate on the more popular convertible bonds.

## General Features of Convertible Securities

The general features of convertible securities include the conversion ratio, the conversion period, the conversion (or stock) value, and the effect on earnings.

**conversion ratio**
The ratio at which a convertible security can be exchanged for common stock.

**conversion price**
The per-share price effectively paid for common stock as the result of conversion of a convertible security.

**Conversion Ratio**   The **conversion ratio** is the ratio at which a convertible security can be exchanged for common stock. The conversion ratio can be stated in two ways.

1. Sometimes the conversion ratio is stated by indicating that the security is convertible into a given number of shares of common stock. In this situation the conversion ratio is *given*. To find the **conversion price**, which is the per-share price effectively paid for common stock as the result of conversion, the par value (not the market value) of the convertible security must be divided by the conversion ratio.

### E X A M P L E

Western Company, a manufacturer of denim products, has outstanding a bond that has a $1,000 par value and is convertible into 25 shares of common stock. The bond's conversion ratio is 25. The conversion price for the bond is $40 per share ($1,000 ÷ 25).

2. Sometimes, instead of the conversion ratio, the conversion price is given. The conversion ratio can be obtained by dividing the par value of the convertible by the conversion price.

### E X A M P L E

Ginsberg Company, a franchiser of seafood restaurants, has outstanding a convertible 20-year bond with a par value of $1,000. The bond is convertible at $50 per share into common stock. The conversion ratio is 20 ($1,000 ÷ $50).

The issuer of a convertible security normally establishes a conversion ratio or conversion price that sets the conversion price per share at the time of issuance above the current market price of the firm's stock. If the prospective purchasers do not expect conversion ever to be feasible, they purchase a straight security or some other convertible issue. A predictable chance of conversion must be provided for in order to enhance the marketability of a convertible security.

**Conversion Period**   Convertible securities are almost always convertible anytime during the life of the security. Occasionally, conversion is permitted only for a limited number of years, say, for 5 or 10 years after issuance of the convertible.

**Conversion Value**    The **conversion (or stock) value** is the value of the convertible security measured in terms of the market price of the common stock into which it can be converted. The conversion value can be found simply by multiplying the conversion ratio by the current market price of the firm's common stock.

**conversion (or stock) value**
The value of a convertible security measured in terms of the market price of the common stock into which it can be converted.

▶ **E X A M P L E**

Sperling Company, a petroleum processor, has outstanding a $1,000 bond that is convertible into common stock at $62.50 a share. The conversion ratio is therefore 16 ($1,000 ÷ $62.50). Because the current market price of the common stock is $65 per share, the conversion value is $1,040 (16 × $65). Because the conversion value is above the bond value of $1,000, conversion is a viable option for the owner of the convertible security.

**Effect on Earnings**    The presence of **contingent securities,** which include convertibles as well as warrants and options (described later in this chapter), affects the reporting of the firm's earnings per share (EPS). Firms with contingent securities that if converted or exercised increase by more than 3 percent the number of shares outstanding are required to report earnings in two other ways: on a *primary* basis and on a *fully diluted* basis. **Primary EPS** treats as common stock all contingent securities *that derive the major portion of their value from their conversion privileges or common stock characteristics.* These securities are technically called **common stock equivalents (CSEs).** Primary EPS is calculated by dividing earnings available for common stockholders (adjusted for interest and preferred stock dividends that would *not* be paid given assumed conversion) by the sum of the number of shares outstanding and the CSE. **Fully diluted EPS** treats as common stock *all* contingent securities. It is calculated by dividing earnings available for common stockholders (adjusted for interest and preferred stock dividends that would *not* be paid given assumed conversion of *all* outstanding convertibles) by the number of shares of common stock that are outstanding if *all* contingent securities are converted and exercised. Rather than demonstrate these accounting calculations, suffice it to say that firms with outstanding convertibles, warrants, and/or options must report primary and fully diluted EPS on their income statements.

**contingent securities**
Convertibles, warrants, and options. Their presence affects the reporting of a firm's earnings per share (EPS).

**primary EPS**
Earnings per share (EPS) calculated under the assumption that all contingent securities *that derive the major portion of their value from their conversion privileges or common stock characteristics* are converted and exercised, and are therefore common stock.

**common stock equivalents (CSEs)**
All contingent securities that derive a major portion of their value from their conversion privileges or common stock characteristics.

**fully diluted EPS**
Earnings per share (EPS) calculated under the assumption that *all* contingent securities are converted and exercised and are therefore common stock.

## Motives for Convertible Financing

Using convertible securities to raise long-term funds can help the firm achieve its cost of capital and capital structure goals (see Chapters 13 and 16, respectively). Specifically, convertibles can be used as a form of deferred common stock financing, as a "sweetener" for financing, and for raising temporarily cheap funds.

**Deferred Common Stock Financing**    The use of convertible securities provides for future common stock financing. When a convertible security is issued, both issuer and purchaser expect the security to be converted into common stock at some point in the future. If the purchaser did not have this expectation, he or she would not accept the lower interest rate normally associated with convertible issues. Because the security is first sold with a conversion price above the current market price of the firm's stock, conversion is initially not attractive.

The issuer of a convertible alternatively can sell common stock, but only at or below its current market price. By selling the convertible, the issuer in effect makes a *deferred sale* of common stock. As the market price of the firm's common stock rises to a higher level, conversion may occur. By deferring the issuance of new common stock until the market price of the stock has increased, the firm needs to issue fewer shares, thereby minimizing the *dilution of both earnings and ownership*. This benefit of using convertible securities as a form of deferred common stock financing is illustrated by the following example.

# E X A M P L E

Mitton Manufacturing Company, a producer of lighting fixtures, needs $1 million of new long-term financing. The firm is considering the sale of either common stock or a convertible bond. The current market price of the common stock is $20 per share. To sell the new issue, the stock would have to be underpriced by $1 and sold for $19 per share. This means that approximately 52,632 shares ($1,000,000 ÷ $19 per share) would have to be sold. The alternative is to issue 30-year, 12 percent (coupon interest rate), $1,000 par-value convertible bonds. The conversion price would be set at $25 per share, and the bond could be sold at par (for $1,000). Thus, 1,000 bonds ($1,000,000 ÷ $1,000 per bond) must be sold. The firm currently has outstanding 200,000 shares of common stock. Most recently the earnings available for common stock were $500,000, or $2.50 per share ($500,000 ÷ 200,000 shares).

If we assume that the earnings available for common stock remains at the $500,000 level, the dilution benefit of using a convertible security to defer common stock financing can easily be illustrated. The earnings per share with both common stock financing and a convertible bond are given in the table.

| Financing Alternative | Number of Shares Outstanding | Earnings per Share |
|---|---|---|
| Common stock | 252,632 | $1.98 |
| Convertible bond | | |
| Before conversion | 200,000 | $2.50[a] |
| After conversion[b] | 240,000 | $2.08 |

[a]To simplify this example, the additional interest expense on the convertible bond has been ignored.

[b]Assuming that all bonds are converted.

After conversion of the convertible bond, 40,000 additional shares of common stock are outstanding. The use of the convertible bond has not only resulted in a smaller dilution of earnings per share ($2.08 per share versus $1.98 per share) but also in a smaller number of shares outstanding (240,000 versus 252,632), thereby preserving the voting control of the owners.

**A "Sweetener" for Financing**   The conversion feature often makes a bond issue more attractive to the purchaser. Because the purchaser is given an opportunity to become a common stockholder and share in the firm's future success, *convertibles can normally be sold with lower interest rates than nonconvertibles*. Therefore, from the firm's viewpoint, including a conversion feature reduces the effective interest cost of debt. The purchaser of the issue sacrifices a portion of his or her interest return for the potential opportunity to become a common stockholder in the future.

**Raising Temporarily Cheap Funds**   By using convertible bonds, the firm can temporarily raise debt, which is typically less expensive than common stock (see Chapter 13), to finance projects. Once such projects are on line, the firm may wish to shift its capital structure to a less highly leveraged position. A conversion feature gives the issuer the opportunity, through actions of convertible holders, to shift its capital structure at a future time.

## Forcing Conversion

When the price of the firm's common stock rises above the conversion price, the market price of the convertible security normally rises to a level close to its conversion value. When this happens, many convertible holders do not convert because they already have the market price benefit obtainable from conversion and can still receive fixed periodic interest payments. Because of this behavior, virtually all convertible securities have a *call feature* that enables the issuer to encourage, or *"force," conversion*. The call price of the security generally exceeds the security's par value by an amount equal to one year's stated interest on the security. Although the issuer must pay a premium for calling a security, the call privilege is generally not exercised until the con-

---

**F I N A N C E  I N**

**A C T I O N**

**Small Business**

### Silverado Foods Bridges Its Financial Hunger Gap with Convertible Notes

Lawrence Field, founder and CEO of Silverado Foods, wasn't impressed with the price offered him by a venture-capital firm in 1994. Instead, Field bet that his Tulsa, Oklahoma firm, maker of a string of food products, including gourmet popcorn, would be worth a lot more by 1996. The flexibility to buy other businesses as well as a distribution system for Silverado's products in the interim was obtained through $3.3 million of convertible notes.

The financing, provided by New York City's Commonwealth Associates Growth Fund, consisted of two-year notes with an interest rate of 9 percent. Commonwealth Associates can convert the notes into 25 percent of the company's stock when Silverado makes an initial public offering.

Field plans to have the company go public in 1996 and use some of the proceeds to pay off the notes. In fact, with sales of only $3 million in 1993, it appears highly unlikely that Field would be able to generate the cash internally that is needed to pay off the notes. However, the convertible notes, which when used in this fashion are often referred to as "bridge financing," give Field two additional years to increase Silverado's value.

Source: Bruce G. Posner, "Betting on the Bridge," *Inc.*, December 1993, p. 167.

version value of the security is 10 to 15 percent *above the call price*. This type of premium above the call price helps to assure the issuer that when the call is made, the holders of the convertible will convert it instead of accepting the call price.

## E X A M P L E

Armstead Company, a textile distributor, currently has outstanding a 12 percent (coupon interest rate), $1,000 convertible bond. The bond is convertible into 50 shares of common stock at a conversion price of $20 per share ($1,000 ÷ 50 shares) and callable at $1,120. Because the bond is convertible into 50 shares of common stock, calling it is equivalent to paying each bondholder $22.40 per share ($1120 ÷ 50 shares). If the firm issues the call when the stock is selling for $24 per share, a convertible bondholder is likely to take the $1,120 instead of converting the bond even though he or she realizes only $22.40 per share instead of $24. The holder recognizes that the stock price is likely to drop as soon as the conversion occurs. Also, if the holder wishes to sell the stock after conversion, he or she must pay brokerage fees and taxes on the transaction.

If the Armstead Company waited until the market price exceeded the call price by 10 to 15 percent—if, say, the call was made when the market price of the stock reached $25—most of the convertible holders would probably convert the bond. The market price of $25 per share is approximately 11.6 percent above the call price per share of $22.40—high enough to cover any movements in the stock price or brokerage fees and taxes associated with conversion. At least 30 days' advance notice is normally given prior to a call.

## Overhanging Issues

**overhanging issue**
A convertible security that cannot be forced into conversion using the call feature.

The market price of a security sometimes does not reach a level sufficient to stimulate the conversion of associated convertibles. A convertible security that cannot be forced into conversion using the call feature is called an **overhanging issue.** An overhanging issue can be quite detrimental to a firm. If the firm calls the issue, the bondholders are likely to accept the call price rather than convert the bonds and effectively pay an excessive price for the stock. In this case not only does the firm have to pay the call premium, but it also requires additional financing to pay for the call itself. If the firm raised these funds through the sale of equity, a large number of shares must be issued due to their low market price. This, in turn, can result in the dilution of existing ownership. Another source of financing the call is the use of debt or preferred stock, but this use leaves the firm's capital structure no less leveraged than prior to the call. An example can be used to demonstrate the problems associated with an overhanging issue.

## E X A M P L E

Armstead Company's 12 percent (coupon interest rate), $1,000 convertible bond described in the preceding example is convertible into 50 shares of common stock at a conversion price of $20 per share, and callable at $1,120. At the $1,120 call price, calling the bonds is equivalent to paying each bondholder $22.40 per share ($1,120 ÷ 50 shares). If the common stock is selling for less than this amount, say at $21 per share, and the firm wishes to force conversion, such an action becomes impossible. Calling the bond does *not* force conversion because the bondholders accept the $1,120 call price rather than the 50 shares of common stock, which are worth only $1,050 ($21 per share × 50 shares). Furthermore, the firm must finance the call by selling common stock, additional bonds, or preferred stock. Clearly, this convertible bond is an overhanging issue because the firm cannot force its bondholders to convert to common stock.

## Determining the Value of a Convertible Bond

The key characteristic of convertible securities that greatly enhances their marketability is their ability to minimize the possibility of a loss while providing a possibility of capital gains. Here we discuss the three values of a convertible bond: (1) the straight bond value, (2) the conversion (or stock) value, and (3) the market value.

### Straight Bond Value

The **straight bond value** of a convertible bond is the price at which it would sell in the market without the conversion feature. This value is found by determining the value of a nonconvertible bond with similar payments issued by a firm having the same risk. The straight bond value is typically the *floor,* or minimum, price at which the convertible bond is traded. The straight bond value equals the present value of the bond's interest and principal payments discounted at the interest rate the firm must pay on a nonconvertible bond.

**straight bond value**
The price at which a convertible bond would sell in the market without the conversion feature.

## ▶ E X A M P L E

Rich Company, a southeastern discount store chain, has just sold a $1,000, 20-year convertible bond with a 12 percent coupon interest rate. The bond interest is paid at the end of each year, and the principal is repaid at maturity.[1] A straight bond could have been sold with a 14 percent coupon interest rate, but the conversion feature compensates for the lower rate on the convertible. The straight bond value of the convertible is calculated as shown in the table.

| Year(s) | Payments (1) | Present-Value Interest Factor at 14 Percent (2) | Present Value [(1) × (2)] (3) |
|---------|--------------|------------------------------------------------|-------------------------------|
| 1–20 | $ 120[a] | 6.623[b] | $794.76 |
| 20 | 1,000 | .073[c] | 73.00 |
| | | Straight bond value | $867.76 |

[a]$1,000 at 12% = $120 interest per year.
[b]Present-value interest factor for an annuity, *PVIFA*, discounted at 14% for 20 years, from Table A-4.
[c]Present-value interest factor for $1, *PVIF*, discounted at 14% for year 20, from Table A-3.

---

[1]Consistent with Chapter 12, we continue to assume the payment of annual rather than semiannual bond interest. This assumption simplifies the calculations involved while maintaining the conceptual accuracy of the procedures presented.

This value, $867.76, is the minimum price at which the convertible bond is expected to sell. (The calculated value using a hand-held business/financial calculator is $867.54.) Generally, only in certain instances where the stock's market price is below the conversion price is the bond expected to sell at this level.

**Conversion Value**   The *conversion (or stock) value* of a convertible security was defined earlier as the value of the convertible measured in terms of the market price of the common stock into which the security can be converted. When the market price of the common stock exceeds the conversion price, the conversion (or stock) value exceeds the par value. An example clarifies the point.

# E X A M P L E

Rich Company's convertible bond described previously is convertible at $50 per share. This means each bond can be converted into 20 shares because each bond has a $1,000 par value. The conversion values of the bond when the stock is selling at $30, $40, $50, $60, $70, and $80 per share are shown in the table.

| Market Price of Stock | Conversion Value |
|---|---|
| $30 | $  600 |
| 40 | 800 |
| 50 (conversion price) | 1,000 (par value) |
| 60 | 1,200 |
| 70 | 1,400 |
| 80 | 1,600 |

When the market price of the common stock exceeds the $50 conversion price, the conversion value exceeds the $1,000 par value. Because the straight bond value (calculated in the preceding example) is $867.76, the bond, in a stable environment, never sells for less than this amount, however low its conversion value is. If the market price per share is $30, the bond still sells for $867.76—not $600—because its value as a bond dominates.

**Market Value**   The market value of a convertible is likely to be greater than its straight value or its conversion value. The amount by which the market value exceeds its straight or conversion value is called the **market premium.** The general relationship of the straight bond value, conversion value, market value, and market premium for Rich Company's convertible bond is shown in Figure 20.1. The straight bond value acts as a floor for the security's value up to the point X. At that point the stock price is high enough to cause the conversion value to exceed the straight bond value. The market value of the convertible often exceeds both its straight and conversion values, thus resulting in a market premium. The premium is attributed to the fact that the convertible gives investors a chance to experience attractive capital gains from increases in the stock price while taking less risk. The reduced risk is attrib-

**market premium**
The amount by which the market value of a convertible security exceeds its straight or conversion value.

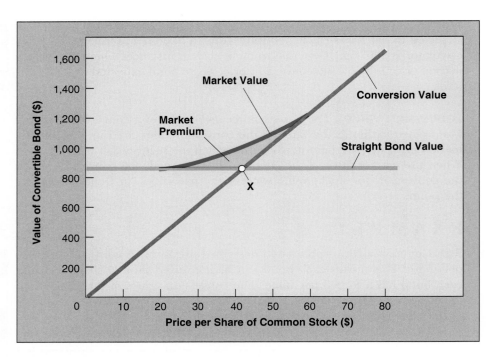

**FIGURE 20.1   The Values and Market Premium for Rich Company's Convertible Bond**

The $867.76 straight value of Rich Company's convertible bond acts as a floor for its value up to point X. At that point the stock price is high enough to cause the conversion value to exceed the straight bond value. The market value of the convertible bond exceeds these values, creating a market premium.

utable to the fact that the floor (straight bond value) provides protection against losses resulting from a decline in the stock price caused by falling profits or other factors. The market premium tends to be greatest when the straight bond value and conversion (or stock) value are nearly equal. This probably results from the fact that investors perceive the benefits of these two sources of value to be greatest at this point.

## Progress Review Questions

**20-1.** What is the *conversion feature?* What is a *conversion ratio?* How do convertibles and other *contingent securities* affect EPS?

**20-2.** Briefly describe each of the following motives for using convertible financing:
  **a.** Deferred common stock financing
  **b.** A "sweetener" for financing
  **c.** Raising temporarily cheap funds

**20-3.** When the market price of the stock rises above the conversion price, why may a convertible security *not* be converted? How can the *call feature* be used to force conversion in this situation? What is an *overhanging issue?*

**20-4.** What is meant by the *straight bond value* of a convertible security? How is this value calculated, and why is it often viewed as a floor for the convertible's value?

**20-5.** What is the *conversion (or stock) value* of a convertible security? How can the conversion value be calculated if you know the conversion ratio and the current market price of the firm's stock?

**20-6.** Describe the general relationship among the straight bond value, conversion value, market value, and market premium associated with a convertible bond.

▲▲▲▲▲▲▲▲▲▲▲▲▲▲▲▲▲▲▲▲▲▲▲▲▲▲▲▲▲▲▲

# Stock-Purchase Warrants

**stock-purchase warrant**
An instrument that gives its holder the right to purchase a certain number of shares of common stock at a specified price over a certain period.

Stock-purchase warrants are quite similar to stock rights, which were described in detail in Chapter 19. A **stock-purchase warrant** gives the holder the right to purchase a certain number of shares of common stock at a specified price over a certain period. (Of course, holders of warrants earn no income from them until the warrant is exercised or sold.) Warrants also bear some similarity to convertibles in that they provide for the injection of additional equity capital into the firm at some future date.

## Characteristics of Stock-Purchase Warrants

Some of the basic characteristics of stock-purchase warrants are discussed here.

**Warrants as "Sweeteners"**   Warrants are often attached to debt issues as "sweeteners," or added benefits. When a firm makes a large bond issue, the attachment of stock-purchase warrants may add to the marketability of the issue while lowering the required interest rate. As sweeteners, warrants are similar to conversion features. Often, when a new firm is raising its initial capital, suppliers of debt require warrants to permit them to share in whatever success the firm achieves. In addition, established companies sometimes offer warrants with debt to compensate for risk and thereby lower the interest rate or provide for less restrictive provisions.

**exercise (or option) price**
The price at which holders of warrants can purchase a specified number of shares of common stock.

**Exercise Prices**   The price at which holders of warrants can purchase a specified number of shares of common stock is normally referred to as the **exercise, or option, price.** This price is normally set 10 to 20 percent above the market price of the firm's stock at the time of issuance. Until the market price of the stock exceeds the exercise price, holders of warrants are not advised to exercise them, because the stock can be purchased more cheaply in the marketplace.

**Life of a Warrant**   Warrants normally have a life of no more than 10 years, although some have infinite lives. Although, unlike convertible securities, warrants cannot be called, their limited life stimulates holders to exercise them when the exercise price is below the market price of the firm's stock.

**Warrant Trading**    A warrant is usually *detachable,* which means that the bondholder may sell the warrant without selling the security to which it is attached. Many detachable warrants are listed and actively traded on organized securities exchanges and on the over-the-counter exchange. The majority of actively traded warrants are listed on the American Stock Exchange. Warrants, as demonstrated in a later section, often provide investors with better opportunities for gain (with increased risk) than the underlying common stock.

## Comparison of Warrants and Rights

The similarity between a warrant and a right should be clear. Both result in new equity capital, although the warrant provides for *deferred* equity financing. The life of a right is typically not more than a few months; a warrant is generally exercisable for a period of years. Rights are issued at a subscription price below the prevailing market price of the stock; warrants are generally issued at an exercise price 10 to 20 percent above the prevailing market price.

## Comparison of Warrants and Convertibles

The exercise of a warrant shifts the firm's capital structure to a less highly leveraged position because new common stock is issued without any change in debt. If a convertible bond is converted, the reduction in leverage is even more pronounced, because common stock is issued in exchange for a reduction in debt. In addition, the exercise of a warrant provides an influx of new capital; with convertibles the new capital is raised when the securities are originally issued rather than when converted. The influx of new equity capital resulting from the exercise of a warrant does not occur until the firm has achieved a certain degree of success, which is reflected in an increased price for its stock. In this instance, the firm conveniently obtains needed funds.

## The Value of Warrants

Like a convertible security, a warrant has both a market and a theoretical value. The difference between these values, or the **warrant premium,** depends largely on investor expectations and the ability of investors to get more leverage from the warrants than from the underlying stock.

**warrant premium**
The difference between the actual market value and the theoretical value of a warrant.

**Theoretical Value of a Warrant**    The *theoretical value* of a stock-purchase warrant is the amount the warrant is expected to sell for in the marketplace. Equation 20.1 gives the theoretical value of a warrant.

$$TVW = (P_0 - E) \times N \qquad (20.1)$$

where

**Equation 20.1** Formula for the theoretical value of a stock-purchase warrant

$TVW$ = theoretical value of a warrant
$P_0$ = current market price of a share of common stock
$E$ = exercise price of the warrant
$N$ = number of shares of common stock obtainable with one warrant

The use of Equation 20.1 is illustrated by the following example:

# E X A M P L E

LK Electronics, a major producer of transistors, has outstanding warrants that are exercisable at $40 per share and that entitle holders to purchase three shares of common stock. The warrants were initially attached to a bond issue to sweeten the bond. The common stock of the firm is currently selling for $45 per share. Substituting $P_0 = \$45$, $E = \$40$, and $N = 3$ into Equation 20.1 yields a theoretical warrant value of $15 [($45 − $40) × 3]. Therefore, LK's warrants should sell for $15 in the marketplace.

**Market Value of a Warrant**   The market value of a stock-purchase warrant is generally above the theoretical value of the warrant. Only when the theoretical value of the warrant is very high or the warrant is near its expiration date are the market and theoretical values close. The general relationship between the theoretical and market values of LK Electronics' warrants is presented graphically in Figure 20.2. The market value of warrants generally exceeds the theoretical value by the greatest amount when the stock's market price is close to the warrant exercise price per share. In addition, the amount of time until expiration also affects the market value of the warrant. Generally speaking, the closer the warrant is to its expiration date, the more likely is its market value to equal its theoretical value.

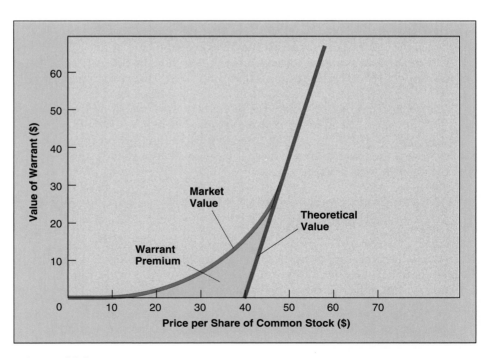

**FIGURE 20.2   The Values and Warrant Premium for LK Electronics' Stock-Purchase Warrants**

The theoretical value of LK Electronics' warrants is zero when the market price of the common stock is below the $40 exercise price, and greater than zero beyond that point. The market value of the warrant exceeds the theoretical value, creating a warrant premium.

## Warrant Premium

The *warrant premium,* or amount by which the market value of LK Electronics' warrants exceeds the theoretical value of these warrants, is also shown in Figure 20.2. This premium results from a combination of positive investor expectations and the ability of the investor with a fixed sum to invest to obtain much larger potential returns (and risk) by trading in warrants rather than the underlying stock. An example clarifies the effect of expected stock price movements and investor leverage opportunities on warrant market values.

▶ E X A M P L E

John Investor has $2,430 which he is interested in investing in LK Electronics. The firm's stock is currently selling for $45 per share, and its warrants are selling for $18 per warrant. Each warrant entitles the holder to purchase three shares of LK's common stock at $40 per share. Because the stock is selling for $45 per share, the theoretical warrant value, calculated in the preceding example using Equation 20.1, is $15 [($45 − $40) × 3].

The warrant premium is believed to result from positive investor expectations and leverage opportunities. John Investor can spend his $2,430 in either of two ways. He can purchase 54 shares of common stock at $45 per share or 135 warrants at $18 per warrant (ignoring brokerage fees). If Mr. Investor purchases the stock, its price rises to $48, and if he then sells the stock, he gains $162 ($3 per share × 54 shares). If instead of purchasing the stock he purchases the 135 warrants and the stock price increases by $3 per share, Mr. Investor makes approximately $1,215. Because the price of a share of stock rises by $3, the price of each warrant can be expected to rise by $9 (each warrant can be used to purchase three shares of common stock). A gain of $9 ▶ per warrant on 135 warrants means a total gain of $1,215 on the warrants.

The greater leverage associated with trading warrants should be clear from the preceding example. Of course, because leverage works both ways it results in greater risk. If the market price falls by $3, the loss on the stock is $162, whereas the loss on the warrants is close to $1,215. Clearly, the use of warrants by investors is riskier.

▼▼▼▼▼▼▼▼▼▼▼▼▼▼▼▼▼▼▼▼▼▼▼▼▼▼▼▼▼▼▼▼▼

## Progress Review Questions

**20-7.** What are *stock-purchase warrants?* What are the similarities and key differences between the effects of warrants and rights on the firm's capital structure and its ability to raise new capital?

**20-8.** What are the similarities and key differences between the effects of warrants and convertible securities on the firm's capital structure and its ability to raise new capital?

**20-9.** What is the general relationship between the theoretical and market values of a warrant? In what circumstances are these values quite close? What is a *warrant premium?*

▲▲▲▲▲▲▲▲▲▲▲▲▲▲▲▲▲▲▲▲▲▲▲▲▲▲▲▲▲▲▲▲▲

# Options

# Options

**option**
An instrument that gives its holder an opportunity to purchase or sell a specified asset at a stated price on or before a set *expiration date*.

In the most general sense, an **option** can be viewed as an instrument that gives its holder an opportunity to purchase or sell a specified asset at a stated price on or before a set *expiration date*. Today the interest in options centers on common stock options. The development of organized options exchanges has created markets in which to trade these options, which themselves are securities. Three basic forms of options are rights, warrants, and calls and puts. Rights were discussed in Chapter 19, and warrants were described in the preceding section.

## Calls and Puts

**call option**
An option to *purchase* a specified number of shares of a stock (typically 100) on or before some future date at a stated price.

**striking price**
The price at which the holder of a call option can buy (or the holder of a put option can sell) a specified amount of stock at any time prior to the option's expiration date.

**put option**
An option to *sell* a given number of shares of a stock (typically 100) on or before a specified date at a stated price.

The two most common types of options are calls and puts. A **call option** is an option to *purchase* a specified number of shares of a stock (typically 100) on or before some future date at a stated price. Call options usually have initial lives of one to nine months, occasionally one year. The **striking price** is the price at which the holder of the option can buy the stock at any time prior to the option's expiration date. This price is generally set at or near the prevailing market price of the stock at the time the option is issued. For example, if the firm's stock is currently selling for $50 per share, a call option on the stock initiated today is likely to have a striking price set at $50 per share. To purchase a call option, the investor must pay a specified price of normally a few hundred dollars.

A **put option** is an option to *sell* a given number of shares of a stock (typically 100) on or before a specified future date at a stated striking price. Like the call option, the striking price of the put is close to the market price of the underlying stock at the time of issuance. The lives and costs of puts are similar to those of calls.

## Options Markets

Options transactions can be made in two ways. The first involves making a transaction through one of about 20 call and put options dealers with the help of a stockbroker. The other, more popular, mechanism is the organized options exchanges. The dominant exchange is the *Chicago Board Options Exchange (CBOE),* which was established in 1973. Other exchanges on which options are traded include the American Stock Exchange, the New York Stock Exchange, and several regional stock exchanges. Each exchange provides an organized marketplace in which purchases and sales of both call and put options can be made in an orderly fashion. The options traded on the options exchanges are standardized and thus are considered registered securities. Each option is for 100 shares of the underlying stock. The price at which options transactions can be made is determined by the forces of supply and demand.

## Options Trading

The most common motive for purchasing call options is the expectation that the market price of the underlying stock will rise by more than enough to cover the cost of the option and thereby allow the purchaser of the call to profit.

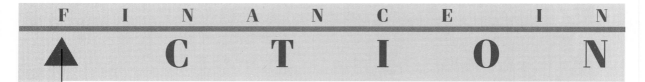

## YES's Options Are Managed by Excommunists to Protect Capitalists

Firms with $5.0 million to invest can obtain the services of Yield Enhancement Strategies (YES). The money-management operation, located in New York and Jerusalem, is staffed by Russian-born rocket scientists. Why? According to YES's manager, analysis of missile trajectory curves is similar to options-related analysis.

Having no knowledge of capital markets and little exposure to capitalism, new hires are put in a six-month training course at the Salomon Brothers investment banking firm. Much of the training is dedicated to options because a considerable portion of YES's trading is designed to exploit perceived mispricing of currency options in Europe and the United States. Businesses using YES's service are, consequently, protecting foreign profits from fluctuating exchange rates.

According to Managed Account Reports, an industry newsletter and data base, Russian training in mathematics, physics, and probability analysis has led YES to an impressive return. Through early 1994, YES earned an annual return of approximately 10 percent. According to one staff member (YES does not disclose names to avoid losing staff), aerospace deflection determination is useful knowledge when trying to manage risk and obtain an inflation-beating rate of return as a bonus. Obviously, options are not a means of financing undertaken by a typical financial manager.

Source: Neal Sandler, "Real Rocket Science Comes to High Finance," *Business Week*, January 17, 1994, pp. 69, 72.

## ► E X A M P L E

Assume that Sam Peters pays $250 for a three-month *call option* on Altex Corporation, a maker of aircraft components, at a striking price of $50. This means that by paying $250 Sam is guaranteed that he can purchase 100 shares of Altex at $50 per share at any time during the next three months. The stock price must climb $2.50 per share ($250 ÷ 100 shares) to $52.50 per share to cover the cost of the option (ignoring any brokerage fees or dividends). If the stock price rises to $60 per share during the period, Sam's net profit is $750 [(100 shares × $60/share) − (100 shares × $50/share) − $250]. Because this return is earned on a $250 investment, it illustrates the high potential return on investment that options offer. Of course, if the stock price does not rise above $50 per share, Sam loses the $250 because he has no reason to exercise the option. If the stock price rises to between $50 and $52.50 per share, Sam probably exercises the option in order to reduce his loss to an amount less than $250.

Put options are purchased in the expectation that the share price of a given security will decline over the life of the option. Purchasers of puts commonly own the shares and wish to protect a gain they have realized since their initial purchase. By buying a put, they lock in the gain because it enables them to sell their shares at a known price during the life of the option. Investors gain from put options when the price of the underlying stock declines by more than the per-share cost of the option. The logic underlying the purchase of a put is exactly the opposite of that underlying the use of call options.

# EXAMPLE

Assume that Dawn Kelly pays $325 for a six-month *put option* on Allante United, a baked-goods manufacturer, at a striking price of $40. Dawn purchased the put option in expectation that the stock price would drop due to the introduction of a new product line by Allante's chief competitor. By paying $325 Dawn is assured that she can sell 100 shares of Allante at $40 per share at any time during the next six months. The stock price must drop by $3.25 per share ($325 ÷ 100 shares) to $36.75 per share to cover the cost of the option (ignoring any brokerage fees or dividends). If the stock price drops to $30 per share during the period, Dawn's net profit is $675 [(100 shares × $40/share) − (100 shares × $30/share) − $325]. Because the return is earned on a $325 investment, it again illustrates the high potential return on investment that options offer. Of course, if the stock price rises above $40 per share, Dawn loses the $325 because she has no reason to exercise the option. If the stock price falls to between $36.75 and $40.00 per share, Dawn probably exercises the option in order to reduce her loss to an amount less than $325.

## The Role of Call and Put Options in Fund Raising

Although call and put options are extremely popular investment vehicles, they play *no* direct role in the fund-raising activities of the financial manager. These options are issued by investors, not businesses. *They are not a source of financing to the firm.* Corporate pension managers, whose job it is to invest and manage corporate pension funds, may use call and put options as part of their investment activities to earn a return or to protect or lock in returns already earned on securities. The presence of options trading in the firm's stock can—by increasing trading activity—stabilize the firm's share price in the marketplace, but the financial manager has no direct control over this. Buyers of options have neither any say in the firm's management nor any voting rights; only stockholders are given these privileges. Despite the popularity of call and put options as an investment vehicle, the financial manager has very little need to deal with them, especially as part of fund-raising activities.

## Using Options to Protect Against Foreign Currency Exposures

Since 1983 the Philadelphia Stock Exchange (PHLX) has offered exchange-traded options contracts on the Canadian dollar, the Japanese yen, and several important European currencies. Currency options proved to be an immediate hit and today are used by a wide range of traders—from the largest multinational companies to small exporters and importers, as well as by individual speculators and investors. Unlike futures and forward contracts, options offer the key benefit of effectively protecting against the risk of adverse price movements while preserving the possibility of profiting if prices move in your favor. The key drawback to using options to protect against foreign currency exposures is its high cost relative to using more traditional futures or forward contracts. The use of currency options is best demonstrated by an example.

## ▶ E X A M P L E

Assume that an exporter just booked a sale denominated in Swiss francs with payment due on delivery in three months. The company can protect against the risk of the dollar depreciating by purchasing a Swiss franc put option. This gives the company the right to sell Swiss francs at a fixed price (say, $.65/Sf). This option becomes very valuable if the Swiss Franc depreciates from today's $.66/Sf to, say, $.60/Sf before expiration of the contract. On the other hand, if the Swiss franc appreciates from $.66/Sf to, say, $.72/Sf, the U.S. exporter allows the put option to expire unexercised and instead converts the Swiss francs received in payment on the sales contract into dollars on the open market at the new, higher dollar price. The exporter is protected from adverse price risk but is still able to profit from favorable price movements.

▶ ▼▼▼▼▼▼▼▼▼▼▼▼▼▼▼▼▼▼▼▼▼▼▼▼▼▼▼▼▼▼▼▼▼▼▼▼▼▼

## Progress Review Questions

**20-10.**  What is an *option*? Define the *striking price* of an option. Are rights and warrants options?

**20-11.**  Define *calls* and *puts*. What is the logic of buying a call and buying a put?

**20-12.**  What role, if any, do call and put options play in the fund-raising activities of the financial manager?

**20-13.**  How can the firm use currency options to protect its international business transactions against the risk of adverse movements in foreign exchange rates? Describe the key benefit and drawback of using currency options rather than the more traditional futures and forward contracts.

▲▲▲▲▲▲▲▲▲▲▲▲▲▲▲▲▲▲▲▲▲▲▲▲▲▲▲▲▲▲▲▲▲▲▲▲▲

# S U M M A R Y   O F   L E A R N I N G   G O A L S

**Describe the basic types of convertible securities and their general features, including the conversion ratio, conversion period, conversion (or stock) value, and effect on earnings.** Corporate bonds and preferred stock may both be convertible into common stock. The conversion ratio indicates the

LG  1

number of shares for which a convertible can be exchanged and determines the conversion price. A conversion privilege is almost always available anytime during the life of the security. The conversion (or stock) value is the value of the convertible measured in terms of the market price of the common stock into which it can be converted. The presence of convertibles and other contingent securities (warrants and options) often requires the firm to report earnings (EPS) on both a primary basis and a fully diluted basis.

**LG 2**   **Discuss the key motives for convertible financing, the considerations involved in forcing conversion, and the difficulties associated with overhanging issues.** The key motives for the use of convertibles are to obtain deferred common stock financing, to "sweeten" bond issues, and to raise temporarily cheap funds. When conversion becomes attractive, the firm may use the call feature to encourage, or "force," conversion. When conversion cannot be forced, the firm has an overhanging issue. Such an issue can be detrimental to the firm because either forcing conversion or paying the call price to retire the bonds is not economically justifiable.

**LG 3**   **Demonstrate the procedures for determining the straight bond value, conversion (or stock) value, and market value of a convertible bond.** The straight bond value of a convertible is the price at which it would sell in the market without the conversion feature. It typically represents the minimum value at which a convertible bond trades. The conversion (or stock) value of the convertible is found by multiplying the conversion ratio by the current market price of the underlying common stock. The market value of a convertible generally exceeds both its straight and conversion values, thus resulting in a market premium. The premium, which is largest when the straight and conversion values are nearly equal, is attributed to the attractive gains potential from the stock and the risk protection provided by the straight value of the convertible.

**LG 4**   **Explain the basic characteristics of stock-purchase warrants and compare them with rights and convertibles.** Stock-purchase warrants are often attached to debt issues to "sweeten" them and lower their interest cost. Warrants, like rights, provide their holders with the privilege of purchasing a certain number of shares of common stock at the specified exercise price. Warrants generally have limited lives, are detachable, and may be listed and traded on securities exchanges. Warrants are similar to stock rights, except that the life of a warrant is generally longer than that of a right, and the exercise price of a warrant is initially set above the underlying stock's current market price. Warrants are also similar to convertibles, but exercising them has a less pronounced effect on the firm's leverage and brings in new funds.

**LG 5**   **Calculate the theoretical value of a warrant and use its market value to determine the warrant premium.** The theoretical value of a warrant is the amount one expects it to sell for in the marketplace. It is found by multiplying the difference between the current market price of the stock and the exercise price of the warrant by the number of shares of common stock obtainable with one warrant. The market value of a warrant usually exceeds its theoretical value, creating a warrant premium. The premium results from positive investor expectations and the ability of investors to get more leverage from trading warrants than from trading the underlying stock.

**Define options and discuss the basics of calls and puts, options markets, options trading, the role of call and put options in fund raising, and using options to protect against foreign currency exposures.** An option provides its holder with an opportunity to purchase or sell a specified asset at a stated price on or before a set expiration date. Rights, warrants, and calls and puts are all options. Calls are options to purchase common stock, and puts are options to sell common stock. Options exchanges, such as the Chicago Board Options Exchange (CBOE), provide organized market-places in which purchases and sales of both call and put options can be made in an orderly fashion. The options traded on the exchanges are stan-dardized, and the price at which they trade is determined by the forces of supply and demand. Call and put options do not play a direct role in the fund-raising activities of the financial manager. On the other hand, cur-rency options can be used, in lieu of futures and forward contracts, to pro-tect the firm's international transactions against the risk of adverse move-ments in foreign exchange rates.

# SUMMARY OF KEY DEFINITIONS AND EQUATION

## Variable Definitions

$E$ = exercise price of the warrant
$N$ = number of shares of common stock obtainable with one warrant
$P_0$ = current market price of a share of common stock
$TVW$ = theoretical value of a warrant

## Equation

Theoretical value of a warrant

$$TVW = (P_0 - E) \times N$$

[Eq. 20.1]

# P A R T VII

# Special Managerial Finance Topics

After studying this chapter, you should be able to

 **LG 1** Understand merger fundamentals, including basic terminology, motives for merging, and types of mergers.

 **LG 2** Describe the objectives and procedures used in leveraged buyouts (LBOs) and divestitures.

 **LG 3** Demonstrate the procedures used to analyze mergers, including valuing the target company and the effect of stock swap transactions on earnings per share.

 **LG 4** Discuss the merger negotiation process, the role of holding companies, and international mergers.

 **LG 5** Understand the types and major causes of business failure and the use of voluntary settlements to sustain or liquidate the failed firm.

 **LG 6** Explain bankruptcy legislation and the procedures involved in reorganizing or liquidating a bankrupt firm.

# 21 Mergers, LBOs, Divestitures, and Failure

Mergers and divestitures are among the more exciting areas in managerial finance. Understanding the *strategic* significance of these business decisions and not just the numbers adds interesting challenges and nuances to the job of financial manager.

Knowledge of mergers and acquisitions is also important for the small-businessperson. Selling the business for a profit can be part of the entrepreneur's strategy or become necessary as retirement approaches. Also, the small-business owner may need to sell part of the company to

---

## Mergers and divestitures are among the more exciting areas in managerial finance.

---

venture capitalists to fund growth. Without a basic understanding of valuation techniques and deal structures, he or she might not receive a fair price for the business.

Acquisitions play a large role in Blockbuster Entertainment Corporation's business plan. Our video rental business, which generates more cash than the firm needs to operate and grow, faces a technological threat; video-on-demand services could be available within 10 years. So our current strategy is to diversify by acquiring companies in entertainment-

related businesses. We use our unique strengths—buying power in Hollywood, widespread entertainment retail presence, and highly efficient retail computer systems—to make the acquired firms more profitable and efficient.

Some acquisitions moved us into related but different businesses. For example, Blockbuster acquired Sound Warehouse/Music Plus, a U.S. chain, and did a joint venture with Virgin Retail, with stores in Europe and Asia, to apply its entertainment retailing expertise to the music industry, which is less threatened by technological change.

When analyzing an acquisition, Blockbuster starts with strategic criteria. We want companies that fit our long-range business goals and can benefit from our strengths. Once a prospect passes this test, we assess its financial attractiveness. First, we analyze publicly available documents such as SEC filings (annual and quarterly financial reports) and stock analyst reports. After a confidentiality agreement is executed, we receive more detailed management reports and financial statements. We forecast the company's cash flows and accounting earnings considering the changes we plan to make in the business. Finally, we decide whether the return is worth the risk.

Blockbuster uses several techniques to value the target. First develop a detailed computer model and run discounted cash flow calculations on various scenarios. We use the capital asset pricing model to develop a discount rate. Second, we look at comparable companies to determine reasonable multiples of earn-

ings and cash flow. This gives us a check against our discounted cash flow model.

To remain financially flexible, Blockbuster typically pays for acquisitions with stock, rather than issuing debt. Buyers and sellers frequently differ over the desired means of financing, a point that often becomes a major part of the deal. Some sellers want more cash, whereas others want stock because of tax and other considerations. Negotiating is probably one of the most exciting aspects of mergers and acquisitions. You must identify the key points, develop alternative ways to get what you want, and know your "break points" on each item. Considerable gamesmanship is involved, so if the other party throws his papers down and storms out of the room, don't worry—you're just getting started!

*After receiving his B.S. in economics from Florida State University and M.B.A. from the University of North Carolina, **William Flaherty** joined Ryder System Inc. During his four years there he was senior financial analyst in London and financial consultant to the regional vice-presidents. He joined Blockbuster Entertainment Corporation in 1992 and as director, corporate development—media, is responsible for media acquisitions and new ventures.*

Mergers, LBOs, divestitures, and failure are important areas of long-term financial decision making. Although decisions in these areas are typically made much less frequently than capital budgeting, capital structure, and dividend decisions, their outcomes can significantly affect a firm's value. Mergers are sometimes used by firms to expand externally by acquiring control of another firm. Although the overriding objective for a merger should be to improve, and hopefully, maximize the firm's share value, a number of more immediate motivations frequently exist. These include diversification, tax considerations, and increasing owner liquidity. Sometimes mergers are pursued to acquire needed assets rather than the going concern. Although the "merger mania" of the 1980s has cooled somewhat, brisk merger activity continues to take place today.

Unfortunately not all firms are able to sustain themselves indefinitely; many fail each year. In some instances they can be reorganized voluntarily or under bankruptcy law with the cooperation of outsiders. If reorganization is not feasible, voluntary or legal procedures can be used to liquidate the firm in an orderly fashion. It is important that the financial manager understand the fundamental aspects of both mergers and business failure. Here we first discuss mergers, LBOs, and divestitures, followed by a brief review of business failure.

## Merger Fundamentals

LG **1**

In this section we discuss merger fundamentals, including terminology, motives, and types. In the following sections we briefly describe the related topics of leveraged buyouts and divestitures and review the procedures used to analyze and negotiate mergers.

### Basic Terminology

The high level of merger activity occurring during the last 10 to 15 years has resulted in the coining of numerous new terms to describe various actions, strategies, participants, and techniques. In the broadest sense, activities involving expansion or contraction of a firm's operations or changes in its asset or financial (ownership) structure are called **corporate restructuring.** The topics addressed in this chapter—mergers, LBOs, and divestitures—are some of the most common forms of corporate restructuring. Below we define some basic merger terminology; other terms are introduced and defined as needed in subsequent discussions.

**corporate restructuring**
The activities involving expansion or contraction of a firm's operations or changes in its asset or financial (ownership) structure.

**merger**
The combination of two or more firms, in which the resulting firm maintains the identity of one of the firms, usually the larger one.

**consolidation**
The combination of two or more firms to form a completely new corporation.

#### Mergers, Consolidations, and Holding Companies

A **merger** occurs when two or more firms are combined and the resulting firm maintains the identity of one of the firms. Usually the assets and liabilities of the smaller firm are merged into those of the larger firm. **Consolidation,** on the other hand, involves the combination of two or more firms to form a completely new corporation. The new corporation normally absorbs the assets and liabilities of the companies from which it is formed. Due to the similarity of mergers and consolidations, the term *merger* is used throughout this chapter to refer to both. A **holding company** is a corporation that has voting control of one or more other corporations. Having control in large, widely held companies generally requires ownership of between 10 and 20 percent of the outstanding stock. The companies controlled by a holding company are normally referred to as its **subsidiaries.** Control of a subsidiary is typically obtained by purchasing (generally for cash) a sufficient number of shares of its stock.

**Acquiring Versus Target Companies**   The firm in a merger transaction that attempts to acquire another firm is commonly called the **acquiring company.** The firm that the acquiring company is pursuing is referred to as the **target company.** Generally the acquiring company identifies, evaluates, and negotiates with the management and/or shareholders of the target company. Occasionally the management of a target company initiates its acquisition by seeking to be acquired.

**Friendly Versus Hostile Takeovers**   Mergers can occur on either a friendly or a hostile basis. Typically, after isolating the target company, the acquirer initiates discussions with its management. If the target management is receptive to the acquirer's proposal it may endorse the merger and recommend shareholder approval. If the stockholders approve the merger, the transaction is typically consummated through either a cash purchase of shares by the acquirer or through an exchange of the acquirer's stock, bonds, or some combination for the target firm's shares. This type of negotiated transaction is known as a **friendly merger.** If, on the other hand, the takeover target's management does not support the proposed takeover for any of a number of possible reasons, it can fight the acquirer's actions. In this case the acquirer can attempt to gain control of the firm by buying sufficient shares of the target company in the marketplace. This is typically accomplished using a **tender offer,** which is a formal offer to purchase a given number of shares of a firm's stock at a specified price. This type of unfriendly transaction is commonly referred to as a *hostile merger.* Clearly hostile mergers are more difficult to consummate because the target firm's management acts to deter the acquisition. Nevertheless, hostile takeovers are sometimes successful.

**Strategic Versus Financial Mergers**   Mergers are undertaken for either strategic or financial reasons. **Strategic mergers** involve merging firms to achieve various economies of scale by eliminating redundant functions, increasing market share, improving raw material sourcing and finished product distribution, and so on. In these mergers the operations of the acquiring and target firms are combined to achieve economies and thereby cause the performance of the merged firm to exceed that of the premerged firms. The mergers of Bristol-Myers and Squibb (both pharmaceutical firms), the *New York Times* and the *Boston Globe* (both publishers), Southwest Airlines and Morris Air (both airlines), and AT&T (telecommunications) and NCR (computers) are examples of strategic mergers. An interesting variation of the strategic merger involves the purchase of specific product lines (rather than the whole company) for strategic reasons. Examples include Colgate-Palmolive (consumer products) buying the Softsoap Liquid line from Minnetonka Labs, and Shaw Industries' (textiles) purchase of the carpet division of Armstrong World Industries.

---

**holding company**
A corporation that has voting control of one or more other corporations.

**subsidiaries**
The companies controlled by a holding company.

**acquiring company**
The firm in a merger transaction that attempts to acquire another firm.

**target company**
The firm in a merger transaction that the acquiring company is pursuing.

**friendly merger**
A merger transaction endorsed by the target company's management, approved by its stockholders, and easily consummated.

**tender offer**
A formal offer to purchase a given number of shares of a firm's stock at a specified price.

**strategic merger**
A merger transaction undertaken to achieve economies of scale.

**Financial mergers,** on the other hand, are based on the acquisition of companies that can be restructured to improve their cash flow. These mergers involve the acquisition of the target firm by an acquirer, which may be another company or a group of investors—often the firm's existing management. The objective of the acquirer is to cut costs drastically and sell off certain unproductive or noncompatible assets to increase the firm's cash flows. The increased cash flows are used to service the sizable debt typically incurred to finance these transactions. Financial mergers are not based on the firm's ability to achieve economies of scale, but rather on the acquirer's belief that through restructuring, the firm's hidden value can be unlocked. The ready availability of expensive, high-risk *junk bond* financing throughout the 1980s fueled the financial merger mania during that period. Examples of financial mergers include the takeover of RJR Nabisco by Kohlberg Kravis Roberts (KKR), Campeau Corporation's (real estate) acquisition of Allied Stores and Federated Department Stores, and Merv Griffin's acquisition of Resorts International (hotels/casinos) from Donald Trump. With the collapse of the junk bond market in the early 1990s, financial mergers have fallen on relatively hard times. The heavy debt burdens involved in many of the glamorous financial mergers of the 1980s caused many of them to subsequently file for bankruptcy. As a result, the strategic merger, which does not rely as heavily on debt, tends to dominate today.

**financial merger**
A merger transaction undertaken to restructure the acquired company to improve its cash flow and unlock its hidden value.

## Motives for Merging

The overriding goal for merging is the maximization of the owners' wealth as reflected in the acquirer's share price. Specific motives include growth or diversification, synergy, fund raising, increased managerial skill or technology, tax considerations, increased ownership liquidity, and defense against takeover. These motives should be pursued when they are believed consistent with owner wealth maximization.

### Growth or Diversification
Companies that desire rapid growth in *size* or *market share* or diversification in the *range of their products* may find that a merger can be used to fulfill their objective. Instead of going through the time-consuming process of internal growth or diversification, the firm may achieve the same objective in a short time by merging with an existing firm. In addition, such a strategy is often less costly than the alternative of developing the necessary production capability and capacity. If a firm that wants to expand operations in existing or new product areas can find a suitable going concern, it may avoid many of the risks associated with the design, manufacture, and sale of additional or new products. Moreover, when a firm expands or extends its product line by acquiring another firm, it also removes a potential competitor.[1]

### Synergy
The *synergy* of mergers is the economies of scale resulting from the merged firms' lower overhead. Synergy is said to be present when a whole is greater than the sum of its parts (often stated as "1 plus 1 equals 3"). The

---

[1] Certain legal constraints on growth exist—especially when the elimination of competition is expected. The various antitrust laws, which are closely enforced by the Federal Trade Commission (FTC) and the Justice Department, prohibit business combinations that eliminate competition, especially when the resulting enterprise would be a monopoly.

economies of scale that generally result from a merger lower the combined overhead, thereby increasing earnings to a level greater than the sum of the earnings of each of the independent firms. Synergy is most obvious when firms merge with other firms in the same line of business because many redundant functions and employees can thereby be eliminated.

### Fund Raising

Often firms combine to enhance their fund-raising ability. A firm may be unable to obtain funds for its own internal expansion but able to obtain funds for external business combinations. Quite often one firm may combine with another that has high liquid assets and low levels of liabilities. The acquisition of this type of "cash-rich" company immediately increases the firm's borrowing power by decreasing its financial leverage. This result should allow funds to be raised externally at lower cost.

### Increased Managerial Skill or Technology

Occasionally a firm has good potential that it finds itself unable to develop fully due to deficiencies in certain areas of management or an absence of needed product or production technology. If the firm cannot hire the management or develop the technology it needs, it might combine with a compatible firm that has the needed managerial personnel or technical expertise. Of course any merger, whatever the specific motive for it, should contribute to the maximization of owners' wealth.

**tax loss carryforward**
In a merger, the tax loss of one of the firms that can be applied against a limited amount of future income of the merged firm over the shorter of either 15 years or until the total tax loss has been fully recovered.

### Tax Considerations

Quite often tax considerations are a key motive for merging. In such a case the tax benefit generally stems from the fact that one of the firms has a **tax loss carryforward.** This means that the company's tax loss can be applied against a limited amount of future income of the merged firm over the shorter of either 15 years or until the total tax loss has been fully recovered.[2] Two situations can actually exist. A company with a tax loss can acquire a profitable company to utilize the tax loss. In this case the acquiring firm boosts the combination's after-tax earnings by reducing the taxable income of the acquired firm. A tax loss may also be useful when a profitable firm acquires a firm that has such a loss. In either situation, however, the merger must be justified not only on the basis of the tax benefits but also on grounds consistent with the goal of owner wealth maximization. Moreover, the tax benefits described can be used only in mergers. They cannot be used in the formation of holding companies because only in the case of mergers are operating results reported on a consolidated basis. An example clarifies the use of the tax loss carryforward.

# EXAMPLE   ◀

Maxwell Company, a wheel bearing manufacturer, has a total of $450,000 in tax loss carryforwards resulting from operating tax losses of $150,000 a year in each of the past three years. To use these losses and to diversify its operations, C.B. Company, a molder of plastics, has acquired Maxwell through a

---

[2]The *Tax Reform Act of 1986,* to deter firms from combining solely to take advantage of tax loss carryforwards, initiated an annual limit on the amount of taxable income against which such losses can be applied. The annual limit is determined by formula and is tied to the premerger value of the corporation with the loss. Although not fully eliminating this motive for combination, the act makes it more difficult for firms to justify combinations solely on the basis of tax loss carryforwards.

merger. C.B. expects to have *earnings before taxes* of $300,000 per year. We assume that these earnings are realized, that they fall within the annual limit legally allowed for application of the tax loss carryforward resulting from the merger (see footnote 2 on the preceding page), that the Maxwell portion of the merged firm just breaks even, and that C.B. is in the 40 percent tax bracket. The total taxes paid by the two firms and their after-tax earnings without and with the merger are calculated as shown in Table 21.1.

With the merger the total tax payments are less: $180,000 (total of line 7) versus $360,000 (total of line 2). With the merger the total after-tax earnings are more: $720,000 (total of line 8) versus $540,000 (total of line 3). The merged firm is able to deduct the tax loss either for 15 years subsequently or until the total tax loss has been fully recovered, whichever period is shorter. In this example the shorter is at the end of year 2.

**Increased Ownership Liquidity**   The merger of two small firms or a small and a larger firm may provide the owners of the small firm(s) with greater liquidity. This is due to the higher marketability associated with the shares of larger firms. Instead of holding shares in a small firm that has a very "thin" market, the owners receive shares that are traded in a broader market and can thus be liquidated more readily. The ability to convert shares into cash quickly is welcome. And owning shares for which market price quotations are readily available provides owners with a better sense of the value of their holdings. Especially in the case of small, closely held firms, the improved liquidity of ownership obtainable through merger with an acceptable firm may have considerable appeal.

**TABLE 21.1   Total Taxes and After-Tax Earnings for C.B. Company Without and With Merger**

**Total Taxes and After-Tax Earnings Without Merger**

| | 1 | 2 | 3 | Total for 3 Years |
|---|---|---|---|---|
| (1) Earnings before taxes | $300,000 | $300,000 | $300,000 | $900,000 |
| (2) Taxes [.40 × (1)] | 120,000 | 120,000 | 120,000 | 360,000 |
| (3) Earnings after taxes [(1) − (2)] | $180,000 | $180,000 | $180,000 | $540,000 |

**Total Taxes and After-Tax Earnings With Merger**

| | 1 | 2 | 3 | Total for 3 Years |
|---|---|---|---|---|
| (4) Earnings before losses | $300,000 | $300,000 | $300,000 | $900,000 |
| (5) Tax loss carryforward | 300,000 | 150,000 | 0 | 450,000 |
| (6) Earnings before taxes [(4) − (5)] | $ 0 | $150,000 | $300,000 | $450,000 |
| (7) Taxes [.40 × (6)] | 0 | 60,000 | 120,000 | 180,000 |
| (8) Earnings after taxes [(4) − (7)] | $300,000 | $240,000 | $180,000 | $720,000 |

**Defense against Takeover**   Occasionally when a firm becomes the target of an unfriendly takeover, it acquires another company as a defense. Such a strategy typically works like this: The original target firm takes on additional debt to finance its defensive acquisition; because of the debt load, the target firm becomes too large and too highly leveraged financially to be of any further interest to its suitor. To be effective, a defensive takeover must create greater value for shareholders than they would have realized had the firm been merged with its suitor. An example of such a defense was the 1988 incurrence of about $2.5 billion in debt a year after Harcourt Brace Jovanovich's (HBJ's) (publishing, insurance, theme parks) acquisition of Holt, Rinehart and Winston (publishing) from CBS, Inc. (broadcasting) to ward off its suitor, Robert Maxwell (British takeover specialist, now deceased). To service the huge debt incurred in this transaction, HBJ subsequently sold its Sea World theme parks to Anheuser-Busch Co. (alcoholic beverages) but subsequently defaulted on many of its debts. After much negotiation, HBJ (now called Harcourt General) was acquired by General Cinema in 1991. In retrospect it appears that HBJ's defense may have been its downfall. Clearly the use of a merger with a large amount of debt financing as a takeover defense, although effectively deterring the takeover, can result in subsequent financial difficulty and possibly failure.

## Types of Mergers

The four types of mergers are the (1) horizontal merger, (2) vertical merger, (3) congeneric merger, and (4) conglomerate merger. A **horizontal merger** results when two firms in the *same line of business* are merged. An example is the merger of two machine-tool manufacturers. This form of merger results in the expansion of a firm's operations in a given product line while eliminating a competitor. A **vertical merger** occurs when a firm acquires a *supplier or a customer.* For example, the merger of a machine-tool manufacturer with its supplier of castings is a vertical merger. The economic benefit of this type of merger stems from the firm's increased control over the acquisition of raw materials or the distribution of finished goods.

A **congeneric merger** is achieved by acquiring a firm in the *same general industry* but neither in the same line of business nor a supplier or customer. An example is the merger of a machine-tool manufacturer with a manufacturer of industrial conveyor systems. The benefit of this type of merger is the resulting ability to use the same sales and distribution channels to reach customers of both businesses. A **conglomerate merger** involves the combination of firms in *unrelated businesses.* The merger of a machine-tool manufacturer with a chain of fast-food restaurants is an example of this kind of merger. The key benefit of the conglomerate merger is its ability to *reduce risk* by merging firms with different seasonal or cyclical patterns of sales and earnings.

**horizontal merger**
A merger of two firms in the *same line of business.*

**vertical merger**
A merger in which a firm acquires a *supplier or a customer.*

**congeneric merger**
A merger in which one firm acquires another firm in the *same general industry* but neither in the same line of business nor a supplier or customer.

**conglomerate merger**
A merger combining firms in *unrelated businesses.*

▼▼▼▼▼▼▼▼▼▼▼▼▼▼▼▼▼▼▼▼▼▼▼▼▼▼▼▼▼

## Progress Review Questions

**21-1.** Define and differentiate each of the following sets of terms:
  **a.** Mergers, consolidations, and holding companies
  **b.** Acquiring versus target company

    **c.** Friendly versus hostile mergers
    **d.** Strategic versus financial mergers

**21-2.** Briefly describe each of the following motives for merging:
    **a.** Growth or diversification
    **b.** Synergy
    **c.** Fund raising
    **d.** Increased managerial skill or technology
    **e.** Tax considerations
    **f.** Increased ownership liquidity
    **g.** Defense against takeover

**21-3.** Briefly describe each of the following types of mergers:
    **a.** Horizontal merger
    **b.** Vertical merger
    **c.** Congeneric merger
    **d.** Conglomerate merger

▲▲▲▲▲▲▲▲▲▲▲▲▲▲▲▲▲▲▲▲▲▲▲▲▲▲▲▲▲▲▲▲▲▲▲▲

# Leveraged Buyouts and Divestitures

LG 2

Before addressing the mechanics of merger analysis and negotiation, we cover two topics that are closely related to mergers: leveraged buyouts and divestitures. A leveraged buyout is a method of structuring a financial merger, whereas divestiture involves the sale of a firm's assets.

## Leveraged Buyouts

A popular technique widely used during the 1980s to make acquisitions is the *leveraged buyout (LBO)*. It involves the use of a large amount of debt to purchase a firm. LBOs are a clear-cut example of a *financial merger* undertaken to create a high-debt private corporation with improved cash flow and value. Typically 90 percent or more of the purchase price of an LBO is financed with debt. A large part of the borrowing is secured by the acquired firm's assets. The lenders, due to the high risk, take a portion of the firm's equity. Expensive, high-risk *junk bonds* have been routinely used to raise the large amounts of debt needed to finance LBO transactions. Of course, the purchasers in an LBO expect to use the improved cash flow to service the large amount of junk bond and other debt incurred in the buyout. The acquirers in LBOs are other firms or groups of investors that frequently include key members of the acquired firm's existing management.

    An attractive candidate for acquisition through leveraged buyout should possess three basic attributes:

1. It must have a good position in its industry with a solid profit history and reasonable expectations of growth.
2. The firm should have a relatively low level of debt and a high level of "bankable" assets that can be used as loan collateral.

3. It must have stable and predictable cash flows that are adequate to meet interest and principal payments on the debt and provide adequate working capital.

Of course, a willingness on the part of existing ownership and management to sell the company on a leveraged basis is also needed.

The leveraged buyout of Gibson Greeting Cards by a group of investors and managers headed by William Simon, former Secretary of the Treasury, is the classic example of a highly successful LBO. In the early 1980s Simon's group, Wesray, purchased Gibson from RCA for $81 million. The group put up $1 million and borrowed the remaining $80 million, using the firm's assets as collateral. Within three years after Gibson had been acquired, Wesray had publicly sold 50 percent of the company for $87 million. Wesray still owned 50 percent of Gibson and had earned $87 million on a $1 million investment. Indeed success of this magnitude is not typical, but it does point out the potential rewards from the use of LBOs to finance acquisitions.

Many LBOs did not live up to original expectations. The largest ever was the $24.5 billion buyout of RJR Nabisco by KKR, mentioned earlier. RJR was later taken public, and the company is still struggling with the very heavy debt burden from the LBO. Campeau Corporation's buyouts of Allied Stores and Federated Department Stores resulted in its later filing for bankruptcy protection, from which reorganized companies later emerged. In recent years, other highly publicized LBOs have defaulted on the debt (primarily high-risk junk bonds) incurred to finance the buyout. Although the LBO remains a viable financing technique under the right circumstances, its use in the future will be greatly diminished from the frenzied pace of the 1980s. Whereas the LBOs of the 1980s were used, often indiscriminately, for hostile takeovers, today LBOs are most often used to finance management buyouts.

## Divestitures

**operating unit**
A part of a business, such as a plant, division, product line, or subsidiary, that contributes to the actual operations of the firm.

**divestiture**
The selling of some of a firm's assets for various strategic motives.

It is important to recognize that companies often achieve external expansion by acquiring an **operating unit**—plant, division, product line, subsidiary, etc.—of another company. In such a case the seller generally believes that the value of the firm will be enhanced by converting the unit into cash or some other more productive asset. The selling of some of a firm's assets is called **divestiture.** Unlike selling assets in the case of business failure, the motive for divestiture is often positive: to generate cash for expansion of other product lines, to get rid of a poorly performing operation, to streamline the corporation, or to restructure the corporation's business consistent with its strategic goals.

Firms can use a variety of methods to divest themselves of operating units. One involves the *sale of a product line to another firm.* Examples include Dow Jones & Co.'s (newspaper publishing) sale of Richard D. Irwin (publishing) to Times Mirror (newspapers) to concentrate on its business publishing and Clorox Company's (soap and cleaning products) sale of its Lucite/Olympic Paint business to focus entirely on its supermarket-distributed products. These outright sales can be accomplished on a cash or stock swap basis using the procedures described later in this chapter. A second method that has become quite popular in recent years involves the *sale of the unit to existing management.* This sale is often achieved through the use of a *leveraged buyout (LBO).*

Sometimes divestiture is achieved through a **spin-off** which results in an operating unit becoming an independent company. A spin-off is accomplished by issuing shares in the operating unit being divested on a pro rata basis to the parent company's shareholders. Such an action allows the unit to be separated from the corporation and to trade as a separate entity. An example was the decision by The Quaker Oats Company to spin off Fisher-Price Toys to focus entirely on its supermarket-distributed brand-name products. Like outright sale, this approach achieves the divestiture objective, although it does not bring additional cash or stock to the parent company. The final and least popular approach to divestiture involves *liquidation of the operating unit's individual assets.*

> **spin-off**
> A form of divestiture in which an operating unit becomes an independent company by issuing shares in it on a pro rata basis to the parent company's shareholders.

Whatever the method used to divest a firm of an unwanted operating unit, the goal typically is to create a leaner and more focused operation. This, in turn, enhances the efficiency as well as the profitability of the enterprise and creates maximum value for shareholders. Recent divestitures seem to suggest that many operating units are worth much more to others than to the firm itself. Comparisons of postdivestiture and predivestiture market values have shown that the "breakup value" of many firms is significantly greater than their combined value. As a result of market valuations, divestiture often creates value in excess of the cash or stock received in the transaction. Unlike LBOs, the use of divestitures in corporate restructuring is expected to remain popular.

## Progress Review Questions

**21-4.** What is a *leveraged buyout (LBO)*? What are the three key attributes of an attractive candidate for acquisition using an LBO?

**21-5.** What is a *divestiture*? What is an *operating unit*? What are four common methods used by firms to divest themselves of operating units?

## Analyzing and Negotiating Mergers

This portion of the chapter describes the procedures used to analyze and negotiate mergers. Initially, we consider valuing the target company and using stock swap transactions to acquire companies. Next, we look at the merger negotiation process. Then, we review the major advantages and disadvantages of holding companies. Finally, we briefly discuss international mergers.

### Valuing the Target Company

Once the acquiring company isolates a target company it wishes to acquire, it must estimate the target's value. The value is then used, along with a proposed financing scheme, to negotiate the transaction—on a friendly or hostile basis. The value of the target is estimated using the valuation techniques presented in Chapter 12 and applied to long-term investment decisions in Chapters 14 and 15. Similar capital budgeting techniques are applied whether the target firm is being acquired for its assets or as a going concern.

**Acquisitions of Assets**   Occasionally a firm is acquired not for its income-earning potential but as a collection of assets (generally fixed assets) that are needed by the acquiring company. The price paid for this type of acquisition depends largely on which assets are being acquired. Consideration must also be given to the value of any tax losses. To determine whether the purchase of assets is financially justified, the acquirer must estimate both the costs and benefits of the target assets. This is a capital budgeting problem (see Chapters 14 and 15) because an initial cash outlay is made to acquire assets, and, as a result, future cash inflows are expected.

# EXAMPLE

PR Company, a major manufacturer of electric transformers, is interested in acquiring certain fixed assets of Zoom Company, an industrial electronics company. Zoom, which has tax loss carryforwards from losses over the past five years, is interested in selling out, but it wishes to sell out entirely, not just get rid of certain fixed assets. A condensed balance sheet for Zoom Company is shown below.

| Balance Sheet Zoom Company | | | |
|---|---|---|---|
| **Assets** | | **Liabilities and Stockholders' Equity** | |
| Cash | $ 2,000 | Total liabilities | $ 80,000 |
| Marketable securities | 0 | Stockholders' equity | 120,000 |
| Accounts receivable | 8,000 | Total liabilities and | |
| Inventories | 10,000 | stockholders' equity | $200,000 |
| Machine A | 10,000 | | |
| Machine B | 30,000 | | |
| Machine C | 25,000 | | |
| Land and buildings | 115,000 | | |
| Total assets | $200,000 | | |

PR Company needs only machines B and C and the land and buildings. However, it has made some inquiries and has arranged to sell the accounts receivable, inventories, and machine A for $23,000. Because there is also $2,000 in cash, PR gets $25,000 for the excess assets. Zoom wants $20,000 for the entire company, which means that PR must pay the firm's creditors $80,000 and its owners $20,000. The actual outlay required of PR after liquidating the unneeded assets is $75,000 [($80,000 + $20,000) − $25,000]. In other words, to obtain the use of the desired assets (machines B and C and the land and buildings) and the benefits of Zoom's tax losses, PR must pay

**TABLE 21.2    Net Present Value of Zoom Company's Assets**

| Year(s) | Cash Inflow (1) | Present-Value Factor at 11% (2) | Present Value [(1) × (2)] (3) |
|---|---|---|---|
| 1–5 | $14,000 | 3.696[a] | $51,744 |
| 6 | 12,000 | 0.535[b] | 6,420 |
| 7 | 12,000 | 0.482[b] | 5,784 |
| 8 | 12,000 | 0.434[b] | 5,208 |
| 9 | 12,000 | 0.391[b] | 4,692 |
| 10 | 12,000 | 0.352[b] | 4,224 |
| | | Present value of inflows | $78,072 |
| | | Less: Cash outlay required | 75,000 |
| | | Net present value[c] | $ 3,072 |

[a]The present-value interest factor for an annuity, *PVIFA*, with a five-year life discounted at 11 percent obtained from Table A-4.

[b]The present-value interest factor, *PVIF*, for $1 discounted at 11 percent for the corresponding year obtained from Table A-3.

[c]Using a hand-held business/financial calculator the net present value is $3,063.

$75,000. The *after-tax cash inflows* expected to result from the new assets and applicable tax losses are $14,000 per year for the next five years and $12,000 per year for the following five years. The desirability of this asset acquisition can be determined by calculating the net present value of this outlay using PR Company's 11 percent cost of capital, as shown in Table 21.2. *Because the net present value of $3,072 is greater than zero, PR's value should be increased by acquiring Zoom Company's assets.*

**Acquisitions of Going Concerns**    Acquisitions of target companies that are going concerns are best analyzed using capital budgeting techniques similar to those described for asset acquisitions. The basic difficulty in applying the capital budgeting approach to the acquisition of a going concern is the *estimation of cash flows* and certain *risk considerations*. The methods of estimating expected cash flows from an acquisition are similar to those used in estimating capital budgeting cash flows. Typically, *pro forma income statements* reflecting the postmerger revenues and costs attributable to the target company are prepared (see Chapter 6). They are then adjusted to reflect the expected cash flows over the relevant period. Whenever a firm considers acquiring a target company that has different risk behaviors, it should adjust the cost of capital appropriately prior to applying the appropriate capital budgeting techniques (see Chapter 15). An example clarifies this procedure.

▶ **E X A M P L E**

Edge Company, a major media company, is contemplating the acquisition of Wall Company, a small independent film producer that can be purchased for $60,000. Edge currently has a high degree of financial leverage, which is reflected in its 13 percent cost of capital. Because of the low financial leverage of the Wall Company, Edge estimates that its overall cost of capital will drop to 10 percent after the acquisition. Because the effect of the less risky capital structure resulting from the acquisition of Wall Company cannot be reflected in the expected cash flows, the postmerger cost of capital (10 percent) must be used to evaluate the cash flows expected from the acquisition. The post-merger cash flows attributable to the target company are forecast over a 30-year time horizon. These estimated cash flows (all inflows) are $5,000 for years 1 through 10, $13,000 for years 11 through 18, and $4,000 for years 19 through 30. The net present value (i.e., value) of the target company, Wall Company, is calculated in Table 21.3.

*Because the net present value of the target company of $2,357 is greater than zero, the merger is acceptable.* It is interesting to note that, if the effect of the changed capital structure on the cost of capital is not considered, the acquisition is found unacceptable because the net present value *at a 13 percent cost of capital* is −$11,864, which is less than zero. (The calculated value using a hand-held business/financial calculator is −$11,868.)

## Stock Swap Transactions

Once the value of the target company is determined, the acquirer must develop a proposed financing package. The simplest, but probably least common, case is a pure cash purchase. Beyond this extreme case a virtually infinite number of financing packages exist. They use various combinations of cash, debt, preferred stock, and common stock. Here we look at the other

**TABLE 21.3   Net Present Value of the Wall Company Acquisition**

| Year(s) | Cash Inflow (1) | Present-Value Factor at 10%[a] (2) | Present Value [(1) × (2)] (3) |
|---|---|---|---|
| 1–10 | $ 5,000 | 6.145 | $30,725 |
| 11–18 | 13,000 | $(8.201 - 6.145)$[b] | 26,728 |
| 19–30 | 4,000 | $(9.427 - 8.201)$[b] | 4,904 |
| | | Present value of inflows | $62,357 |
| | | Less: Cash purchase price | 60,000 |
| | | Net present value[c] | $ 2,357 |

[a]Present-value interest factors for annuities, *PVIFA*, obtained from Table A-4.

[b]These factors are found using a shortcut technique that can be applied to annuities for periods of years beginning at some point in the future. By finding the appropriate interest factor for the present value of an annuity given for the last year of the annuity and subtracting the present-value interest factor of an annuity for the year immediately preceding the beginning of the annuity, the analyst can obtain the appropriate interest factor for the present value of an annuity beginning sometime in the future. You can check this shortcut by using the long approach and comparing the results.

[c]The net present value calculated using a hand-held business/financial calculator is $2,364.

extreme—**stock swap transactions** in which the acquisition is paid for using an exchange of common stock. The acquiring firm exchanges its shares for shares of the target company according to a predetermined ratio. The *ratio of exchange* of shares is determined in the merger negotiations. This ratio affects the various financial yardsticks that are used by existing and prospective shareholders to value the merged firm's shares. With the demise of LBOs, the use of stock swaps to finance mergers has grown in popularity during the past few years.

**stock swap transaction**
An acquisition method in which the acquiring firm exchanges its shares for shares of the target company according to a predetermined ratio.

**Ratio of Exchange**   When one firm swaps its stock for the shares of another, the firms must determine the number of shares of the acquiring firm to be exchanged for each share of the target firm. The first requirement, of course, is that the acquiring company have sufficient shares available to complete the transaction. Often a firm's repurchase of shares (which was discussed in Chapter 16) is necessary to obtain sufficient shares for such a transaction. The acquiring firm generally offers more for each share of the target company than the current market price of its publicly traded shares. The actual **ratio of exchange** is merely the ratio of the amount *paid* per share of the target company to the per-share market price of the acquiring firm. It is calculated in this manner because the acquiring firm pays the target firm in stock, which has a value equal to its market price. An example clarifies the calculation.

**ratio of exchange**
The ratio of the amount *paid* per share of the target company to the per-share market price of the acquiring firm.

## FINANCE IN ACTION

### Merck Merges with Medco Containment to Improve Its Health

In the News

The biggest merger completed in 1993 was Merck's acquisition of Medco Containment Services. Medco became a subsidiary of Merck, keeping its name and operating under its existing management team. Medco is the leading pharmaceutical benefits manager, or drug discounter, and Merck is a leading drug maker.

Under the agreement, 60 percent of Medco's shares were exchanged for Merck shares at a rate of 1.214 Merck shares per Medco share. The remaining 40 percent of Medco's shares were to be exchanged for $39 a share, or a total of $2.4 billion. The total value of the merger was $6.05 billion.

Shareholders in Medco had the option of accepting either shares in Merck or cash. Given that Merck traded at $34.625 on the merger closing day, or $42.04 per converted Medco share, it's not surprising that only 19 percent of Medco's shareholders chose the cash option. Consequently, Medco shareholders that requested conversion to Merck shares only received about three-fourths of the shares (60 percent of shares available ÷ 81 percent of shares requested) they would otherwise have been entitled to receive. Their remaining Medco shares were converted into cash much to the chagrin of its shareholders.

Source: Randall Smith, "Merger Activity Shifts into High Gear as the Information Superhighway Opens," *The Wall Street Journal,* January 3, 1994, p. R8.

# EXAMPLE

Bigge Company, a leather products concern, whose stock is currently selling for $80 per share, is interested in acquiring Tiny Company, a producer of belts. To prepare for the acquisition, Bigge has been repurchasing its own shares over the past three years. Tiny's stock is currently selling for $75 per share, but in the merger negotiations, Bigge has found it necessary to offer Tiny $110 per share. Because Bigge does not have sufficient financial resources to purchase the firm for cash and it does not wish to raise these funds, Tiny has agreed to accept Bigge's stock in exchange for its shares. As stated, Bigge's stock currently sells for $80 per share, and it must pay $110 per share for Tiny's stock. Therefore the ratio of exchange is 1.375 ($110 ÷ $80). This means that Bigge Company must exchange 1.375 shares of its stock for each share of Tiny's stock.

**Effect on Earnings per Share**   Ordinarily the resulting earnings per share differ from the premerger earnings per share for both the acquiring firm and the target firm. They depend largely on the ratio of exchange and the premerger earnings per share of each firm. It is best to view the initial and long-run effects of the ratio of exchange on earnings per share (EPS) separately.

**Initial Effect.** When the ratio of exchange is equal to 1 and both the acquiring firm and the target firm have the *same* premerger earnings per share, the merged firm's earnings per share initially remain constant. In this rare instance, both the acquiring and target firms also have equal price/earnings (P/E) ratios. In actuality the earnings per share (EPS) of the merged firm are generally above the premerger EPS of one firm and below the premerger EPS of the other, after making the necessary adjustment for the ratio of exchange. These differences can be illustrated by a simple example.

# EXAMPLE

Bigge Company is contemplating acquiring Tiny Company by swapping 1.375 shares of its stock for each share of Tiny's stock. The current financial data related to the earnings and market price for each of these companies are given in Table 21.4. Although Tiny's stock currently has a market price of $75 per share, Bigge has offered it $110 per share. As seen in the preceding example, this results in a ratio of exchange of 1.375.

**TABLE 21.4   Bigge Company and Tiny Company Financial Data**

| Item | Bigge Company | Tiny Company |
|---|---|---|
| (1) Earnings available for common stock | $500,000 | $100,000 |
| (2) Number of shares of common stock outstanding | 125,000 | 20,000 |
| (3) Earnings per share (EPS) [(1) ÷ (2)] | $4 | $5 |
| (4) Market price per share | $80 | $75 |
| (5) Price/earnings (P/E) ratio [(4) ÷ (3)] | 20 | 15 |

To complete the merger and retire the 20,000 shares of Tiny Company stock outstanding, Bigge must issue and (or) use treasury stock totaling 27,500 shares (1.375 × 20,000 shares). Once the merger is completed, Bigge has 152,500 shares of common stock (125,000 + 27,500) outstanding. If the earnings of each of the firms remain constant, the merged company is expected to have earnings available for the common stockholders of $600,000 ($500,000 + $100,000). The earnings per share of the merged company should therefore equal approximately $3.93 ($600,000 ÷ 152,500 shares).

It appears at first glance that Tiny Company's shareholders have sustained a decrease in per-share earnings from $5 to $3.93, but because each share of Tiny Company's original stock is equivalent to 1.375 shares of the merged company, the equivalent earnings per share are actually $5.40 ($3.93 × 1.375). In other words, as a result of the merger Bigge Company's original shareholders experience a decrease in EPS from $4 to $3.93 to the benefit of Tiny Company's shareholders, whose EPS increase from $5 to $5.40. These results are summarized in Table 21.5.

The postmerger earnings per share (EPS) for owners of the acquiring and target companies can be explained by comparing the price/earnings (P/E) ratio paid by the acquiring company with its initial P/E ratio. This relationship is summarized in Table 21.6. By paying more than its current value per dollar of earnings to acquire each dollar of earnings (P/E paid > P/E of acquiring company), the acquiring firm transfers the claim on a portion of its premerger earnings to the owners of the target firm. Therefore on a postmerger basis the target firm's EPS increases and the acquiring firm's EPS decreases. Note that this outcome is *almost always* the case. The acquirer typically pays a 50 percent, on average, premium above the target firm's market price, thereby resulting in the P/E paid being much above its own P/E. Examples include Bristol-Myers paying 26 times Squibb's EPS when its own P/E was 16, and Procter & Gamble paying 27 times Noxell's EPS when its own P/E was only 17. If the acquiring company pays less than its current value per dollar of earnings to acquire each dollar of earnings (P/E paid < P/E of acquiring com-

---

**TABLE 21.5   Summary of the Effects on Earnings per Share of a Merger Between Bigge Company and Tiny Company at $110 per Share**

| | Earnings per Share (EPS) | |
| --- | --- | --- |
| **Stockholders** | **Before Merger** | **After Merger** |
| Bigge Company | $4.00 | $3.93[a] |
| Tiny Company | 5.00 | 5.40[b] |

[a] $\dfrac{\$500,000 + \$100,000}{125,000 + (1.375 \times 20,000)} = \$3.93$

[b] $\$3.93 \times 1.375 = \$5.40$

**TABLE 21.6   Effect of Price/Earnings (P/E) Ratios on Earnings per Share (EPS)**

| Relationship Between P/E Paid and P/E of Acquiring Company | Effect on EPS | |
| --- | --- | --- |
| | Acquiring Company | Target Company |
| P/E paid > P/E of acquiring company | Decrease | Increase |
| P/E paid = P/E of acquiring company | Constant | Constant |
| P/E paid < P/E of acquiring company | Increase | Decrease |

pany), the opposite effects result. The P/E ratios associated with the Bigge-Tiny merger can be used to explain the effect of the merger on earnings per share.

## EXAMPLE

Bigge Company's P/E ratio is 20, whereas the P/E ratio paid for Tiny Company's earnings was 22 ($110 ÷ $5). Because the P/E paid for Tiny Company is greater than the P/E for Bigge Company (22 versus 20), the effect of the merger is to decrease the EPS for original holders of shares in Bigge Company (from $4.00 to $3.93) and to increase the effective EPS of original holders of shares in Tiny Company (from $5.00 to $5.40).

**Long-Run Effect.** The long-run effect of a merger on the earnings per share (EPS) of the merged company depends largely on whether the earnings of the merged firm grow. Often, although a decrease in the per-share earnings of the stock held by the original owners of the acquiring firm is expected initially, the long-run effects of the merger on EPS are quite favorable. What, then, enables the acquiring company to experience higher future EPS than it would have without the merger? The key factor is that the earnings attributable to the target company's assets grow at a faster rate than those resulting from the acquiring company's premerger assets. An example clarifies this point.

## EXAMPLE

In 1995 Bigge Company acquired Tiny Company by swapping 1.375 shares of its common stock for each share of Tiny Company. Other key financial data and the effects of this exchange ratio were discussed in the preceding examples. The total earnings of Bigge Company were expected to grow at an annual rate of 3 percent without the merger; Tiny Company's earnings were expected to grow at a 7 percent annual rate without the merger. The same growth rates are expected to apply to the component earnings streams with the merger.[3] Table 21.7 shows the future effects on EPS for Bigge Company without and with the proposed Tiny Company merger, based on these growth rates.

---

[3]Frequently, due to synergy, the combined earnings stream is greater than the sum of the individual earnings streams. This possibility is ignored here.

**TABLE 21.7   Effects of Earnings Growth on EPS for Bigge Company Without and With the Tiny Company Merger**

| Year | Without Merger | | With Merger | |
|------|----------------|----------------|----------------|----------------|
| | Total Earnings[a] | Earnings per Share[b] | Total Earnings[c] | Earnings per Share[d] |
| 1995 | $500,000 | $4.00 | $600,000 | $3.93 |
| 1996 | 515,000 | 4.12 | 622,000 | 4.08 |
| 1997 | 530,450 | 4.24 | 644,940 | 4.23 |
| 1998 | 546,364 | 4.37 | 668,868 | 4.39 |
| 1999 | 562,755 | 4.50 | 693,835 | 4.55 |
| 2000 | 579,638 | 4.64 | 719,893 | 4.72 |

[a]Based on a 3 percent annual growth rate.
[b]Based on 125,000 shares outstanding.
[c]Based on 3 percent annual growth in Bigge Company's earnings and 7 percent annual growth in Tiny Company's earnings.
[d]Based on 152,500 shares outstanding [125,000 shares + (1.375 × 20,000 shares)].

Table 21.7 indicates that the earnings per share without the merger are greater than the EPS with the merger for the years 1995 through 1997. After 1997, however, the EPS with the merger will be higher than they would have been without the merger as a result of the faster earnings growth rate of Tiny Company (7% versus 3%). Although a few years are required for this difference in the growth rate of earnings to pay off, it can be seen that in the future Bigge Company will receive an earnings benefit as a result of merging with Tiny Company at a 1.375 ratio of exchange. The relationships in Table 21.7 are graphed in Figure 21.1. The long-run earnings advantage of the merger is clearly depicted by this graph.

**Effect on Market Price per Share**   The market price per share does not necessarily remain constant after the acquisition of one firm by another. Adjustments occur in the marketplace in response to changes in expected earnings, the dilution of ownership, changes in risk, and certain other operating and financial changes. Using the ratio of exchange, we can calculate a **ratio of exchange in market price,** which indicates the market price per share of the acquiring firm *paid* for each dollar of market price per share of the target firm. This ratio, the *MPR*, is defined by Equation 21.1:

$$MPR = \frac{MP_{\text{acquiring}} \times RE}{MP_{\text{target}}}$$

(21.1)

where

$$
\begin{aligned}
MPR &= \text{market price ratio of exchange} \\
MP_{\text{acquiring}} &= \text{market price per share of the acquiring firm} \\
MP_{\text{target}} &= \text{market price per share of the target firm} \\
RE &= \text{ratio of exchange}
\end{aligned}
$$

**ratio of exchange in market price**
The ratio of the market price per share of the acquiring firm *paid* for each dollar of market price per share of the target firm.

**Equation 21.1**
Formula for the ratio of exchange in market price

The following example can be used to illustrate the calculation of this ratio:

# E X A M P L E

In the Bigge-Tiny example, the market price of Bigge Company's stock was $80 and that of Tiny Company's was $75. The ratio of exchange was 1.375. Substituting these values into Equation 21.1 yields a ratio of exchange in market price of 1.47 [($80 × 1.375) ÷ $75]. This means that $1.47 of the market price of Bigge Company is given in exchange for every $1.00 of the market price of Tiny Company.

The ratio of exchange in market price is normally always greater than 1. This fact indicates that to acquire a firm, a premium above its market price must be paid by the acquirer. Even so, the original owners of the acquiring firm may still gain because the merged firm's stock may sell at a price/earnings ratio above the individual premerger ratios. This results from the improved risk and return relationship perceived by shareholders and other investors.

# E X A M P L E

The financial data developed earlier for the Bigge-Tiny merger can be used to explain the market price effects of a merger. If the earnings of the merged company remain at the premerger levels, and if the stock of the merged company sells at an assumed multiple of 21 times earnings, the values in Table 21.8 can be expected. In spite of the fact that Bigge Company's earnings per share decline from $4.00 to $3.93 (see Table 21.5), the market price of its shares increases from $80.00 (see Table 21.4) to $82.53 as a result of the merger.

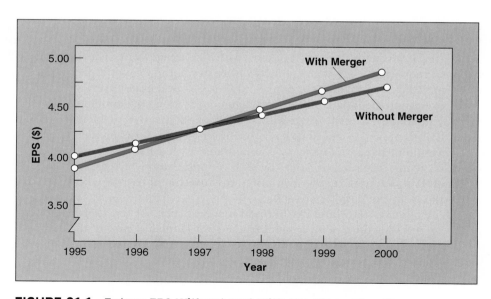

**FIGURE 21.1   Future EPS Without and With the Bigge-Tiny Merger**
The earnings per share (EPS) for Bigge Company in the period from 1995 through 1997 will be lower with the proposed Tiny Company merger than without it. After 1997 the postmerger EPS will be greater with than without the proposed merger.

**TABLE 21.8 Postmerger Market Price of Bigge Company Using a P/E Ratio of 21**

| Item | Merged Company |
|---|---|
| (1) Earnings available for common stock | $600,000 |
| (2) Number of shares of common stock outstanding | 152,500 |
| (3) Earnings per share (EPS) [(1) ÷ (2)] | $3.93 |
| (4) Price/earnings (P/E) ratio | 21 |
| (5) Expected market price per share [(3) × (4)] | $82.53 |

Although the kind of behavior exhibited in this example is not unusual, the financial manager must recognize that only with proper management of the merged enterprise can its market value be improved. If the merged firm cannot achieve sufficiently high earnings in view of its risk, there is no guarantee that its market price will reach the forecast value. Nevertheless, a policy of acquiring firms with low P/Es can produce favorable results for the owners of the acquiring firm. Acquisitions are especially attractive when the acquiring firm's stock price is high, because fewer shares must be exchanged to acquire a given firm.

## The Merger Negotiation Process

A merger is often handled by an **investment banker**—a financial intermediary hired by the acquirer to find suitable target companies and assist in negotiations. A firm seeking a potential acquisition can hire an investment banker to find firms meeting its requirements. Once a target company is selected, the investment banker negotiates with its management or investment banker. Frequently, when management wishes to sell the firm or a division of the firm, it hires an investment banker to seek out potential buyers.

If attempts to negotiate with the management of the target company break down, the acquiring firm, often with the aid of its investment banker, can make a direct appeal to shareholders by using *tender offers* (as explained later). The investment banker is typically compensated with a fixed fee, a commission tied to the transaction price, or with a combination of fees and commissions. Frequently, particularly in LBOs, the investment banker takes an equity position in the target company.

Many observers attribute the frenzied merger activity of the 1980s largely to the aggressive actions of investment bankers who initiated most of the many transactions that took place. The huge fees extracted by investment bankers, as well as attorneys, from their clients in these transactions in effect fueled the market. Today, with the collapse of the junk bond market and the related demise of LBOs and other forms of purely financial mergers, the investment banking community—especially the segment of investment bankers involved in mergers and acquisitions—is smaller and less active than during the 1980s. Although the merger business is not expected to disappear, investment banking revenues from this activity are not expected to experience significant growth in the future. (Detailed discussions of investment banking are included in Chapter 17.)

**investment bankers** Financial intermediary hired by the prospective participants in a merger to find suitable partners and assist in negotiations.

**Management Negotiations**   To initiate the negotiation process, the acquiring firm must make an offer either in cash or based on a stock swap with a specified ratio of exchange. The target company must then review the offer and, in light of alternative offers, accept or reject the terms presented. A desirable merger candidate usually receives more than a single offer. Normally, certain nonfinancial issues must be resolved. These may include the disposition and compensation of the existing management, product-line policies, financing policies, and the independence of the target firm. The key factor, of course, is the per-share price offered in cash or reflected in the ratio of exchange. Although the negotiations are generally based on the expectation of a merger, sometimes they do break down.

**Tender Offers**   When management negotiations for an acquisition break down, tender offers may be used to negotiate a then "hostile merger" directly with the firm's stockholders. As noted earlier, a *tender offer* is a formal offer to purchase a given number of shares of a firm's stock at a specified price. The offer is made to all the stockholders at a premium above the market price. Occasionally the acquirer makes a **two-tier offer** in which the terms offered are more attractive to those who tender (present) shares early. For example, the acquirer offers to pay $25 per share for the first 60 percent of the outstanding shares tendered, and only $23 per share for the remaining shares. The stockholders are advised of a tender offer through announcements in financial newspapers or through direct communications from the offering firm. Sometimes a tender offer is made to add pressure to existing merger negotiations. In other cases the tender offer may be made without warning as an attempt at an abrupt corporate takeover.

**two-tier offer**
A *tender offer* in which the terms offered are more attractive to those who tender shares early.

**Fighting Hostile Takeovers**   If the management of a target firm does not favor a merger or considers the price offered in a proposed merger too low, it is likely to take defensive actions to ward off the hostile tender offer. Such actions are generally developed with the assistance of investment bankers and lawyers who, for generally sizable fees, help the firm develop and employ effective **takeover defenses.** Numerous strategies for fighting hostile takeovers were developed during the 1980s. Some obvious strategies are informing stockholders of the alleged damaging effects of a takeover, acquiring another company, and attempting to sue the acquiring firm on antitrust or other grounds. In addition, many other defenses (some with colorful names) exist—"white knight," "poison pills," "greenmail," leveraged recapitalization, "golden parachutes," and "shark repellents." We now take a brief look at each of these strategies.

**takeover defenses**
Strategies for fighting hostile merger.

**"white knight"**
A takeover defense in which the target firm finds an acquirer more to its liking than the initial hostile acquirer and prompts the two to compete to take over the firm.

With the **"white knight"** strategy, the target firm finds a more suitable acquirer (the "white knight") and prompts it to compete with the initial hostile acquirer to take over the firm. The basic premise of this strategy is that if being taken over is nearly certain, the target firm ought to attempt to be taken over by the firm deemed most acceptable to its management. Use of a **"poison pill"** typically involves the creation of securities that give their holders certain rights that become effective when a takeover is attempted. The "pill" allows the shareholders to receive special voting rights or securities that, once issued, cause the firm to be much less desirable to the hostile acquirer. **"Greenmail"** is a strategy under which the firm repurchases through private negotiation a large block of stock at a premium from one or more shareholders to end a hostile takeover attempt by those shareholders. Clearly, greenmail is a form of corporate blackmail by the holders of a large block of shares.

**"poison pill"**
A takeover defense in which a firm issues securities that give their holders certain rights that become effective when a takeover is attempted and that make the target firm less desirable to a hostile acquirer.

**"greenmail"**
A takeover defense under which a target firm repurchases through private negotiation a large block of stock at a premium from one or more shareholders to end a hostile takeover attempt by those shareholders.

Another hostile takeover defense involves the use of a **leveraged recapitalization,** which is the payment of a large debt-financed cash dividend. This strategy significantly increases the firm's financial leverage, thereby deterring the takeover attempt. As a further deterrent the recapitalization is often structured to increase the equity and control of the existing management. "**Golden parachutes**" are provisions in the employment contracts of key executives that provide them with sizable compensation if the firm is taken over. Golden parachutes deter hostile takeovers to the extent that cash outflows required by these contracts are large enough to make the takeover unattractive to the acquirer. Another defense is use of "**shark repellents.**" These antitakeover amendments to the corporate charter constrain the firm's ability to transfer managerial control of the firm as a result of a merger. Although this defense can entrench existing management, many firms have had such amendments ratified by shareholders.

Because takeover defenses tend to insulate management from shareholders, the potential for litigation is great when these strategies are employed. Lawsuits are sometimes filed against management by dissident shareholders. In addition, federal and state governments frequently intervene when a proposed takeover is deemed in violation of federal or state law. A number of states have legislation on their books limiting or restricting hostile takeovers within their boundaries. Although new takeover defenses will surely be developed in the future, so too will new legislation be passed to regulate merger activity. Lawmakers want to protect the interests not only of stockholders but also of employees, customers, suppliers, creditors, and other "stakeholders" in target firms.

**leveraged recapitalization**
A takeover defense in which the target firm pays a large debt-financed cash dividend, increasing the firm's financial leverage.

**"golden parachutes"**
Provisions in the employment contracts of key executives that provide sizable compensation if the firm is taken over.

**"shark repellents"**
Antitakeover amendments to a corporate charter that constrain the firm's ability to transfer managerial control as a result of a merger.

## Holding Companies

As defined earlier, a *holding company* is a corporation that has voting control of one or more other corporations. The holding company may need to own only a small percentage of the outstanding shares to have this voting control. In the case of companies with a relatively small number of shareholders, as much as 30 to 40 percent of the stock may be required. In the case of firms with a widely dispersed ownership, 10 to 20 percent of the shares may be sufficient to gain voting control. A holding company wishing to obtain voting control of a firm may use direct market purchases or tender offers to acquire needed shares. Although there are relatively few holding companies and they are far less important than mergers, it is helpful to understand their key advantages and disadvantages.

**Advantages of Holding Companies**    The primary advantage of holding companies is the *leverage effect*. It permits the firm to control a large amount of assets with a relatively small dollar investment. In other words, the owners of a holding company can *control* significantly larger amounts of assets than they could *acquire* through mergers. The following example illustrates the leverage effect.

▶ E X A M P L E

Hauck Company, a holding company, currently holds voting control of two subsidiaries: company X and company Y. The balance sheets for Hauck Company and its two subsidiaries are presented in Table 21.9. It owns approximately 17

## TABLE 21.9   Balance Sheets for Hauck Company and Its Subsidiaries

| Assets | | Liabilities and Stockholders' Equity | |
|---|---|---|---|
| **Hauck Company** | | | |
| Common stock holdings | | Long-term debt | $ 6 |
| Company X | $10 | Preferred stock | 6 |
| Company Y | 14 | Common stock equity | 12 |
| Total | $24 | Total | $24 |
| **Company X** | | | |
| Current assets | $ 30 | Current liabilities | $ 15 |
| Fixed assets | 70 | Long-term debt | 25 |
| Total | $100 | Common stock equity | 60 |
| | | Total | $100 |
| **Company Y** | | | |
| Current assets | $ 20 | Current liabilities | $ 10 |
| Fixed assets | 140 | Long-term debt | 60 |
| Total | $160 | Preferred stock | 20 |
| | | Common stock equity | 70 |
| | | Total | $160 |

percent ($10 ÷ $60) of company X and 20 percent ($14 ÷ $70) of company Y. It is assumed that these holdings are sufficient for voting control.

The owners of Hauck Company's $12 worth of equity have control over $260 worth of assets (company X's $100 worth and company Y's $160 worth). Thus the owners' equity represents only about 4.6 percent ($12 ÷ $260) of the total assets controlled. From the discussions of ratio analysis, leverage, and capital structure in Chapters 4, 5, and 16, you should recognize that this is quite a high degree of leverage. If an individual stockholder or even another holding company owns $3 of Hauck Company's stock, which is assumed sufficient for its control, it in actuality controls the whole $260 of assets. The investment itself in this case represents only 1.15 percent ($3 ÷ $260) of the assets controlled.

The high leverage obtained through a holding company arrangement greatly magnifies earnings and losses for the holding company. Quite often a **"pyramiding"** of holding companies occurs: one holding company controls other holding companies, thereby causing an even greater magnification of earnings and losses. The greater the leverage, the greater the risk involved. The risk-return trade-off is a key consideration in the holding company decision.

**"pyramiding"**
An arrangement among holding companies wherein one holding company controls others, thereby causing an even greater magnification of earnings and losses.

Another commonly cited advantage of holding companies is *risk protection*. The failure of one of the companies (such as Y in the preceding example) does not result in the failure of the entire holding company. Because each subsidiary is a separate corporation, the failure of one company should cost the holding company, at maximum, no more than its investment in that subsidiary. Other advantages include the following: (1) Certain state *tax benefits* may be realized by each subsidiary in its state of incorporation. (2) *Lawsuits* or *legal actions* against a subsidiary do not threaten the remaining companies. (3) It is *generally easy to gain control* of a firm because stockholder or management approval is not typically necessary.

**Disadvantages of Holding Companies**   A major disadvantage of the holding company arrangement is the *increased risk* resulting from the leverage effect. When general economic conditions are unfavorable, a loss by one subsidiary may be magnified. For example, if subsidiary company X in Table 21.9 experiences a loss, its inability to pay dividends to Hauck Company can result in Hauck Company's inability to meet its scheduled payments.

Another disadvantage is *double taxation*. Prior to paying dividends a subsidiary must pay federal and state taxes on its earnings. Although a 70 percent tax exclusion is allowed on dividends received by one corporation from another, the remaining 30 percent received is taxable. (If the holding company owns between 20 and 80 percent of the stock in a subsidiary, the exclusion is 80 percent; if it owns more than 80 percent of the stock in the subsidiary, 100 percent of the dividends are excluded.) If a subsidiary were part of a merged company, double taxation would *not* exist.

The fact that holding companies are *difficult to analyze* is another disadvantage. Security analysts and investors typically have difficulty understanding holding companies due to their complexity. As a result these firms tend to sell at low multiples of earnings (P/Es). This means that the shareholder value of holding companies may suffer.

A final disadvantage of holding companies is the generally *high cost of administration* resulting from maintaining each subsidiary company as a separate entity. A merger, on the other hand, is likely to result in certain administrative economies of scale. The need for coordination and communication between the holding company and its subsidiaries may further elevate these costs.

## International Mergers

Perhaps in no other area does U.S. financial practice differ more fundamentally from practices in other countries than in the field of mergers. Outside of the United States (and, to a lesser degree, Great Britain), hostile takeovers are virtually nonexistent, and in some countries (such as Japan), takeovers of any kind are uncommon. The emphasis in the United States and Great Britain on shareholder value and reliance on public capital markets for financing is generally inapplicable in continental Europe. This occurs because companies there are generally smaller and other stakeholders, such as employees, bankers, and governments, are accorded greater consideration. The U.S. approach is also a poor fit for Japan and other Asian nations.

**Changes in Western Europe**   Today, there are signs that Western Europe is moving more toward a U.S.-style approach to shareholder value and public capital market financing. Since the final plan for European economic integration was unveiled in 1988, the number, size, and importance of cross-border European mergers have exploded. Nationally focused companies want to achieve economies of scale in manufacturing, encourage international product development strategies, and develop distribution networks across the continent. They are also driven by the need to compete with U.S. companies, which have been operating on a continentwide basis in Europe for decades.

These larger European-based companies will probably prove to be even more formidable competitors once national barriers are fully removed in the mid-1990s. Although the vast majority of these cross-border mergers (and joint ventures, which have also increased recently) are friendly in nature, a few have been actively resisted by target firm managements. It seems clear that as European companies come to rely more on public capital markets for financing, and as the market for common stock becomes more truly European in character—rather than French or British or German, active markets for European corporate equity will inevitably evolve.

**Foreign Takeover of U.S. Companies**   Both European and Japanese companies have been active as acquirers of U.S. companies in recent years. In fact, during the 1980s, foreign takeovers of U.S. companies for the first time exceeded in number and dollar volume the acquisitions by U.S. firms of companies in Europe, Canada, and the Pacific rim excluding Japan. Foreign companies purchased U.S. firms for two major reasons: to gain access to the world's single largest, richest, and least regulated market and to acquire world-class technology at a bargain price. Because the dollar has depreciated against most major currencies since 1987, the effective price of purchasing U.S. assets has declined. British companies have historically been the most active acquirers of U.S. firms. For example, Grand Metropolitan acquired Pillsbury Corp. in 1989. In the late 1980s, Japanese corporations surged to prominence with a series of very large acquisitions, including two in the entertainment industry: Sony's purchase of Columbia Pictures and Matsushita's acquisition of MCA. More recently, German firms have become especially active acquirers of U.S. companies as the cost of producing export goods in Germany has become prohibitively expensive. (German workers now have the world's highest wages and shortest work week.) It seems inevitable that in the years ahead, foreign companies will continue to acquire U.S. firms even as U.S. companies continue to seek attractive acquisitions or joint-venture partners abroad.

## Progress Review Questions

**21-6.** Describe the procedures typically used by an acquirer to value a target company, whether it is being acquired for its assets or as a going concern.

**21-7.** What is the *ratio of exchange?* Is it based on the current market prices of the shares of the acquiring and target firms? Why may a long-run view of the merged firm's earnings per share change a merger decision?

**21-8.** What role do *investment bankers* often play in the merger negotiation process? What is a *tender offer?* When and how is it used?

**21-9.** Briefly describe each of the following *takeover defenses* against a hostile merger:
  **a.** "White knight"
  **b.** "Poison pill"
  **c.** "Greenmail"
  **d.** Leveraged recapitalization
  **e.** "Golden parachutes"
  **f.** "Shark repellents"

**21-10.** What are the key advantages and disadvantages cited for the holding company arrangement? What is "*pyramiding*," and what are its consequences?

**21-11.** Discuss the differences in merger practices between U.S. companies and companies in other countries. What changes are occurring in international merger activity, particularly in Western Europe and Japan?

▲▲▲▲▲▲▲▲▲▲▲▲▲▲▲▲▲▲▲▲▲▲▲▲▲▲▲▲▲▲▲▲▲▲

# Business Failure Fundamentals

A business failure is an unfortunate circumstance. Although the majority of firms that fail do so within the first year or two of life, other firms grow, mature, and fail much later. The failure of a business can be viewed in a number of ways and can result from one or more causes.

## Types of Business Failure

A firm may fail because its *returns are negative or low*. A firm that consistently reports operating losses probably experiences a decline in market value. If the firm fails to earn a return greater than its cost of capital, it can be viewed as having failed. Negative or low returns, unless remedied, are likely to result eventually in one of the following more serious types of failure.

A second type of failure, **technical insolvency,** occurs when a firm is unable to pay its liabilities as they come due. When a firm is technically insolvent, its assets are still greater than its liabilities, but it is confronted with a *liquidity crisis.* If some of its assets can be converted into cash within a reasonable period, the company may be able to escape complete failure. If not, the result is the third and most serious type of failure, **bankruptcy.** Bankruptcy occurs when a firm's liabilities exceed the fair market value of its assets. A bankrupt firm has a *negative* stockholders' equity.[4] This means that the claims of creditors cannot be satisfied unless the firm's assets can be liquidated for more than their book value. Although bankruptcy is an obvious form of failure, the *courts treat technical insolvency and bankruptcy in the same way.* They are both considered to indicate the financial failure of the firm.

**technical insolvency**
Business failure that occurs when a firm is unable to pay its liabilities as they come due.

**bankruptcy**
Business failure that occurs when a firm's liabilities exceed the fair market value of its assets.

---

[4]On a balance sheet the firm's assets equal the sum of its liabilities and stockholders' equity, therefore, the only way a firm that has more liabilities than assets can balance its balance sheet is to have a *negative* stockholders' equity.

## Major Causes of Business Failure

The primary cause of business failure is *mismanagement,* which accounts for more than 50 percent of all cases. Numerous specific managerial faults can cause the firm to fail. Overexpansion, poor financial actions, an ineffective sales force, and high production costs can all singly, or in combination, cause the ultimate failure of the firm. Because all major corporate decisions are eventually measured in terms of dollars, the financial manager may play a key role in avoiding or causing a business failure. It is his or her duty to monitor the firm's financial pulse.

*Economic activity*—especially economic downturns—can contribute to the failure of a firm. If the economy goes into a recession, sales may decrease abruptly, leaving the firm with high fixed costs and insufficient revenues to cover them. In addition, rapid rises in interest rates just prior to a recession can contribute further to cash flow problems and make it more difficult for the firm to obtain and maintain needed financing. If the recession is prolonged, the likelihood of survival decreases even more. Recently, a number of major business failures, such as those of Olympia and York (real estate), Megafoods Stores (supermarkets), and Executive Life (life insurance and annuities), have resulted from overexpansion and a recessionary economy.

A final cause of business failure is *corporate maturity.* Firms, like individuals, do not have infinite lives. Like a product, a firm goes through the stages of birth, growth, maturity, and eventual decline. The firm's management should attempt to prolong the growth stage through research, the development of new products, and mergers. Once the firm has matured and has begun to decline, it should seek to be acquired by another firm or liquidate before it fails. Effective management planning should help the firm to postpone decline and ultimate failure.

## Voluntary Settlements

**voluntary settlement**
An arrangement between a technically insolvent or bankrupt firm and its creditors, enabling it to bypass many of the costs involved in legal bankruptcy proceedings.

When a firm becomes technically insolvent or bankrupt, it may arrange with its creditors a **voluntary settlement,** which enables it to bypass many of the costs involved in legal bankruptcy proceedings. The settlement is normally initiated by the debtor firm. Such an arrangement may enable the firm to continue to exist or to be liquidated in a manner that gives the owners the greatest chance of recovering part of their investment. The debtor, possibly with the aid of a key creditor, arranges a meeting between the firm and all its creditors. At the meeting a committee of creditors is selected to investigate and analyze the debtor's situation and recommend a plan of action. The recommendations of the committee are discussed with both the debtor and the creditors, and a plan for sustaining or liquidating the firm is drawn up.

**extension**
An arrangement whereby the firm's creditors receive payment in full, although not immediately.

**composition**
A cash settlement of creditor claims by the debtor firm under which a uniform percentage of each dollar owed is paid.

**Voluntary Settlement to Sustain the Firm**   Normally the rationale for sustaining a firm is a reasonable belief that the firm's recovery is feasible. By sustaining the firm the creditor can continue to receive business from it. A number of strategies are commonly used. An **extension** is an arrangement whereby the firm's creditors receive payment in full, although not immediately. Normally when creditors grant an extension, they agree to require cash payments for purchases until all past debts have been paid. A second arrangement, called **composition,** is a pro rata cash settlement of creditor claims.

# FINANCE IN ACTION

## Ethics

### Downsizing Without Firing at Hewlett-Packard

"If we cannot offer employees job security, how can we expect them to be committed to the future of our firm?" was the question facing Hewlett-Packard's managers in 1990. The answer came in the form of early retirement, voluntary severance programs, and redeployment. In the 1990–1994 period, H-P redeployed 5,000 employees from low-margin printed circuit board divisions to higher margin laser printer divisions.

H-P could simply have fired employees in one state and hired new employees in another state. However, according to H-P's manager of human resource planning, H-P experienced a 10-fold return in terms of employee loyalty, creativity, and productivity when H-P moved em-

ployees and their belongings and kept them on the team. Operating expenses as a percentage of sales have declined from 38 percent to 31 percent.

One, somewhat unexpected, result was that some departments eliminated themselves. For instance, a 15-member sales support team worked itself out of a job by redesigning coverage in Pennsylvania. As a reward, none of the members were restructured out of a position at H-P. In fact, Hewlett-Packard promoted some to district managers.

Source: Ronald Henkoff, "Getting Beyond Downsizing," *Fortune*, January 10, 1994, pp. 58–64.

---

Instead of receiving full payment of their claims, as in the case of an extension, creditors receive only a partial payment. A uniform percentage of each dollar owed is paid in satisfaction of each creditor's claim. A third arrangement is **creditor control.** In this case the creditor committee may decide that the only circumstance in which maintaining the firm is feasible is if the operating management is replaced. The committee may then take control of the firm and operate it until all claims have been settled. Sometimes, a plan involving some combination of extension, composition, and creditor control results. An example is a settlement in which the debtor agrees to pay a total of 75 cents on the dollar in three annual installments of 25 cents on the dollar, and the creditors agree to sell additional merchandise to the firm on 30-day terms if the existing management is replaced by a new management acceptable to them.

**creditor control**
An arrangement in which the creditor committee replaces the firm's operating management and operates the firm until all claims have been settled.

**Voluntary Settlement Resulting in Liquidation**    After the situation of the firm is investigated by the creditor committee, recommendations made, and talks among the creditors and the debtor held, the only acceptable course of action may be liquidation of the firm. Liquidation can be carried out in two ways: privately or through the legal procedures provided by bankruptcy law. If the debtor firm is willing to accept liquidation, legal procedures may not be required. Generally, the avoidance of litigation enables the creditors to obtain *quicker* and *higher* settlements. However, all the creditors must agree to a private liquidation for it to be feasible.

The objective of the voluntary liquidation process is to recover as much per dollar owed as possible. Under voluntary liquidation, common stockholders, who are the firm's true owners, cannot receive any funds until the claims of all other parties have been satisfied. A common procedure is to have a meeting of the creditors at which they make an **assignment.** This procedure passes the power to liquidate the firm's assets to an adjustment bureau, trade association, or a third party, which is designated the *assignee.* The assignee's job is to liquidate the assets, obtaining the best price possible. The assignee is sometimes referred to as the *trustee* because it is entrusted with the title to the company's assets and the responsibility to liquidate them efficiently. Once the trustee has liquidated the assets, it distributes the recovered funds to the creditors and owners (if any funds remain for the owners). The final action in a private liquidation is for the creditors to sign a release attesting to the satisfactory settlement of their claims.

**assignment**
A voluntary liquidation procedure by which a firm's creditors pass the power to liquidate the firm's assets to a third party, designated the *assignee* or *trustee.*

## Progress Review Questions

**21-12.** What are the three types of business failure? What is the difference between *technical insolvency* and *bankruptcy?* What are the major causes of business failure?

**21-13.** Define an *extension* and a *composition,* and explain how they might be combined to form a voluntary settlement plan to sustain the firm. How is a voluntary settlement resulting in liquidation handled?

LG 6

# Reorganization and Liquidation in Bankruptcy

If a voluntary settlement for a failed firm cannot be agreed on, the firm can be forced into bankruptcy by its creditors. As a result of bankruptcy proceedings, the firm may be either reorganized or liquidated.

## Bankruptcy Legislation

As already stated, *bankruptcy* in the legal sense occurs when the firm cannot pay its bills or when its liabilities exceed the fair market value of its assets. In either of these situations a firm may be declared legally bankrupt. However, creditors generally attempt to avoid forcing a firm into bankruptcy if it appears to have opportunities for future success.

The governing bankruptcy legislation in the United States today is the **Bankruptcy Reform Act of 1978,** which significantly modified earlier bankruptcy legislation. This law contains eight odd-numbered (1 through 15) chapters and one even-numbered (12) chapter. A number of these chapters apply in the instance of failure; the two key ones are Chapters 7 and 11. **Chapter 7** details the procedures to be followed when liquidating a failed firm. This

**Bankruptcy Reform Act of 1978**
The current governing bankruptcy legislation in the United States.

**Chapter 7**
The portion of the *Bankruptcy Reform Act of 1978* that details the procedures for liquidating a failed firm.

chapter typically comes into play once it has been determined that a fair, equitable, and feasible basis for the reorganization of a failed firm does not exist. (Although a firm may of its own accord choose not to reorganize and may instead go directly into liquidation.) **Chapter 11** outlines the procedures for reorganizing a failed (or failing) firm, whether its petition is filed voluntarily or involuntarily. If a workable plan for reorganization cannot be developed, the firm is liquidated under Chapter 7.

**Chapter 11**
The portion of the *Bankruptcy Reform Act of 1978* that outlines the procedures for reorganizing a failed (or failing) firm, whether its petition is filed voluntarily or involuntarily.

## Reorganization in Bankruptcy

Reorganization petitions are of two basic types: voluntary and involuntary. Any firm that is not a municipal or financial institution can file a petition for **voluntary reorganization** on its own behalf. **Involuntary reorganization** is initiated by an outside party, usually a creditor. An involuntary petition against a firm can be filed if one of three conditions is met:

1. The firm has past-due debts of $5,000 or more.
2. Three or more creditors can prove they have aggregate unpaid claims of $5,000 against the firm. If the firm has fewer than 12 creditors, any creditor owed more than $5,000 can file the petition.
3. The firm is *insolvent,* which means (a) that it is not paying its debts as they come due, (b) that within the immediately preceding 120 days a custodian (a third party) was appointed or took possession of the debtor's property, or (c) that the fair market value of the firm's assets is less than the stated value of its liabilities.

**voluntary reorganization**
A petition filed by a failed firm on its own behalf for reorganizing its structure and paying its creditors.

**involuntary reorganization**
A petition initiated by an outside party, usually a creditor, for the reorganization of a failed firm and payment of its creditors.

**Procedures** The procedures for initiation and execution of corporate reorganizations involve five separate steps: filing, appointment, development and approval of a reorganization plan, acceptance of the plan, and payment of expenses.

**Filing.** A reorganization petition under Chapter 11 must be filed in a federal bankruptcy court. If an involuntary petition is challenged by the debtor, a hearing must be held to determine whether the firm is insolvent. If so, the court enters an "Order for Relief" that formally initiates the process.

**Appointment.** On filing a reorganization petition, the filing firm becomes the **debtor in possession (DIP)** of the assets. If creditors object to the filing firm being the debtor in possession, they can ask the judge to appoint a trustee.

**debtor in possession (DIP)**
The term for a firm that files a reorganization petition under Chapter 11 and then develops, if feasible, a reorganization plan.

**Reorganization Plan.** After reviewing its situation, the debtor in possession submits to the court a plan of reorganization and a disclosure statement summarizing the plan. A hearing is held to determine whether the plan is *fair, equitable,* and *feasible* and whether the disclosure statement contains adequate information. The court's approval or disapproval is based on its evaluation of the plan in light of these standards. A plan is considered *fair and equitable* if it *maintains the priorities* of the contractual claims of the creditors, preferred stockholders, and common stockholders. The court must also find the reorganization plan *feasible,* meaning it must be *workable.* The reorganized corporation must have sufficient working capital, sufficient funds to cover fixed charges, sufficient credit prospects, and sufficient ability to retire or refund debts as proposed by the plan.

**Acceptance of the Reorganization Plan.** Once approved, the plan, along with the disclosure statement, is given to the firm's creditors and shareholders for their acceptance. Under the *Bankruptcy Reform Act,* creditors and owners are separated into groups with similar types of claims. In the case of creditor groups, approval by holders of at least two-thirds of the dollar amount of claims as well as a numerical majority of creditors in the group is required. In the case of ownership groups (preferred and common stockholders), two-thirds of the shares in each group must approve the reorganization plan for it to be accepted. Once accepted and confirmed by the court, the plan is put into effect as soon as possible.

**Payment of Expenses.** After the reorganization plan has been approved or disapproved, all parties to the proceedings whose services were beneficial or contributed to the approval or disapproval of the plan file a statement of expenses. If the court finds these claims acceptable, the debtor must pay these expenses within a reasonable time.

**Role of the Debtor in Possession**  Because reorganization activities are largely in the hands of the debtor in possession (DIP), it is useful to understand the DIP's responsibilities. The DIP's first responsibility is the valuation of the firm to determine whether reorganization is appropriate. To do this, the DIP must estimate both the *liquidation value* of the enterprise and its value as a *going concern*. If the DIP finds that its value as a going concern is less than its liquidation value, it recommends liquidation. If the opposite is found to be true, the DIP recommends reorganization. If the reorganization of the firm is recommended by the DIP, a plan of reorganization must be drawn up.

The key portion of the reorganization plan generally concerns the firm's capital structure. Because most firms' financial difficulties result from high fixed charges, the company's capital structure is generally *recapitalized,* or altered, to reduce these charges. Under **recapitalization,** debts are generally exchanged for equity, or the maturities of existing debts are extended. When recapitalizing the firm, the DIP places a great deal of emphasis on building a mix of debt and equity that allows the firm to meet its debts and provide a reasonable level of earnings for its owners.

Once the optimal capital structure has been determined, the DIP must establish a plan for exchanging outstanding obligations for new securities. The guiding principle is to *observe priorities*. Senior claims (those with higher legal priority) must be satisfied prior to junior claims (those with lower legal priority). To comply with this principle, senior suppliers of capital must receive a claim on new capital equal to their previous claims. The common stockholders are the last to receive any new securities. (It is not unusual for them to receive nothing.) Security holders do not necessarily have to receive the same type of security they held before; often they receive a combination of securities. Once the debtor in possession has determined the new capital structure and distribution of capital, it submits the reorganization plan and disclosure statement to the court as described.

**recapitalization**
The reorganization procedure under which a failed firm's debts are generally exchanged for equity or the maturities of existing debts are extended.

## Liquidation in Bankruptcy

The liquidation of a bankrupt firm usually occurs once the courts have determined that reorganization is not feasible. A petition for reorganization must normally be filed by the managers or creditors of the bankrupt firm. If no petition is filed, if a petition is filed and denied, or if the reorganization plan is denied, the firm must be liquidated. Three important aspects of liquidation in bankruptcy are the procedures, the priority of claims, and the final accounting.

**Procedures**   When a firm is decreed bankrupt, the judge may appoint a *trustee* to perform the many routine duties required in administering the bankruptcy. The trustee takes charge of the property of the bankrupt firm and protects the interest of its creditors. A meeting of creditors must be held within 20 to 40 days. At this meeting the creditors are made aware of the prospects for the liquidation. The meeting is presided over by the bankruptcy court clerk. The trustee is then given the responsibility to liquidate the firm, keep records, examine creditors' claims, disburse money, furnish information as required, and make final reports on the liquidation. In essence the trustee is responsible for the liquidation of the firm. Occasionally the court calls subsequent creditor meetings, but only a final meeting for closing the bankruptcy is required.

**Priority of Claims**   It is the trustee's responsibility to liquidate all the firm's assets and to distribute the proceeds to the holders of *provable claims*. The courts have established certain procedures for determining the provability of claims. The priority of claims, which is specified in Chapter 7 of the *Bankruptcy Reform Act,* must be maintained by the trustee when distributing the funds from liquidation. Any **secured creditors** have specific assets pledged as collateral and in liquidation receive proceeds from the sale of those assets. If these proceeds are inadequate to meet their claim, the secured creditors become **unsecured, or general, creditors** for the unrecovered amount since specific collateral no longer exists. These and all other unsecured creditors divide, on a pro rata basis, any funds remaining after all prior claims are satisfied. If the proceeds from the sale of secured assets are in excess of the claims against them, the excess funds become available to meet claims of unsecured creditors. The complete order of priority of claims is listed in Table 21.10.

In spite of the priorities listed in items 1 through 7, secured creditors have first claim on proceeds from the sale of their collateral. The claims of unsecured creditors, including the unpaid claims of secured creditors, are satisfied next and, finally, the claims of preferred and common stockholders. The application of these priorities by the trustee in bankruptcy liquidation proceedings can be illustrated by a simple example.

▶ E X A M P L E

Dempsey Company, a manufacturer of portable computers, has the balance sheet presented in Table 21.11 on page 614. The trustee, as was her obligation, has liquidated the firm's assets, obtaining the highest amounts she could get. She managed to obtain $2.3 million for the firm's current assets and $2 million for the firm's fixed assets. The total proceeds from the liquidation were therefore $4.3 million. Obviously, the firm is legally bankrupt, because its liabilities of $5.6 million dollars exceed the $4.3 million fair market value of its assets.

The next step is to distribute the proceeds to the various creditors. The only liability not shown on the balance sheet is $800,000 in expenses for administering the bankruptcy proceedings and satisfying unpaid bills incurred

**secured creditors**
Creditors who have specific assets pledged as collateral and in liquidation of the firm receive proceeds from the sale of those assets.

**unsecured, or general, creditors**
Creditors who have a general claim against all the firm's assets other than those specifically pledged as collateral.

**TABLE 21.10   Order of Priority of Claims in Liquidation of a Failed Firm**

1. The expenses of administering the bankruptcy proceedings.

2. Any unpaid interim expenses incurred in the ordinary course of business between filing the bankruptcy petition and the entry of an Order for Relief in an involuntary proceeding. (This step is *not* applicable in a voluntary bankruptcy.)

3. Wages of not more than $2,000 per worker that have been earned by workers in the 90-day period immediately preceding the start of bankruptcy proceedings.

4. Unpaid employee benefit plan contributions that were to be paid in the 180-day period preceding the filing of bankruptcy or the termination of business, whichever occurred first. For any employee, the sum of this claim plus eligible unpaid wages (item 3) cannot exceed $2,000.

5. Claims of farmers or fishermen in a grain-storage or fish-storage facility, not to exceed $2,000 for each producer.

6. Unsecured customer deposits, not to exceed $900 each, resulting from purchasing or leasing a good or service from the failed firm.

7. Taxes legally due and owed by the bankrupt firm to the federal government, state government, or any other governmental subdivision.

8. Claims of secured creditors, who receive the proceeds from the sale of collateral held, regardless of the priorities above. If the proceeds from the liquidation of the collateral are insufficient to satisfy the secured creditors' claims, the secured creditors become unsecured creditors for the unpaid amount.

9. Claims of unsecured creditors. The claims of unsecured, or general, creditors and unsatisfied portions of secured creditors' claims (item 8) are all treated equally.

10. Preferred stockholders, who receive an amount up to the par, or stated, value of their preferred stock.

11. Common stockholders, who receive any remaining funds, which are distributed on an equal per-share basis. If different classes of common stock are outstanding (see Chapter 19), priorities may exist.

between the time of filing the bankruptcy petition and the entry of an Order for Relief. The distribution of the $4.3 million among the firm's creditors is shown in Table 21.12. The table shows that once all prior claims on the proceeds from liquidation are satisfied, the unsecured creditors get the remaining funds. The pro rata distribution of the $700,000 among the unsecured creditors is given in Table 21.13 on page 615. The disposition of funds in the Dempsey Company liquidation should be clear from Tables 21.12 and 21.13. Because the claims of the unsecured creditors have not been fully satisfied, the preferred and common stockholders receive nothing.

**Final Accounting**   After the trustee has liquidated all the bankrupt firm's assets and distributed the proceeds to satisfy all provable claims in the appropriate order of priority, he or she makes a final accounting to the bankruptcy court and creditors. Once the court approves the final accounting, the liquidation is complete.

## TABLE 21.11    Balance Sheet for Dempsey Company

| Assets | | Liabilities and Stockholders' Equity | |
|---|---|---|---|
| Cash | $ 10,000 | Accounts payable | $ 200,000 |
| Marketable securities | 5,000 | Notes payable—bank | 1,000,000 |
| Accounts receivable | 1,090,000 | Accrued wages[a] | 320,000 |
| Inventories | 3,100,000 | Unpaid employee benefits[b] | 80,000 |
| Prepaid expenses | 5,000 | Unsecured customer deposits[c] | 100,000 |
| Total current assets | $4,210,000 | Taxes payable | 300,000 |
| Land | $2,000,000 | Total current liabilities | $2,000,000 |
| Net plant | 1,810,000 | First mortgage[d] | $1,800,000 |
| Net equipment | 80,000 | Second mortgage[d] | 1,000,000 |
| Total fixed assets | $3,890,000 | Unsecured bonds | 800,000 |
| Total | $8,100,000 | Total long-term debt | $3,600,000 |
| | | Preferred stock (5,000 shares) | $ 400,000 |
| | | Common stock (10,000 shares) | 500,000 |
| | | Paid-in capital in excess of par | 1,500,000 |
| | | Retained earnings | 100,000 |
| | | Total stockholders' equity | $2,500,000 |
| | | Total | $8,100,000 |

[a]Represents wages of $800 per employee earned within 90 days of filing bankruptcy for 400 of the firm's employees.
[b]These unpaid employee benefits were due in the 180-day period preceding the firm's bankruptcy filing, which occurred simultaneously with the termination of its business.
[c]Unsecured customer deposits not exceeding $900 each.
[d]The first and second mortgages are on the firm's total fixed assets.

## TABLE 21.12    Distribution of the Liquidation Proceeds of Dempsey Company

| | |
|---|---|
| Proceeds from Liquidation | $4,300,000 |
| − Expenses of administering bankruptcy and paying interim bills | $ 800,000 |
| − Wages owed workers | 320,000 |
| − Unpaid employee benefits | 80,000 |
| − Unsecured customer deposits | 100,000 |
| − Taxes owed governments | 300,000 |
| Funds Available for Creditors | $2,700,000 |
| − First mortgage, paid from the $2 million proceeds from the sale of fixed assets | $1,800,000 |
| − Second mortgage, partially paid from the remaining $200,000 of fixed assets proceeds | 200,000 |
| Funds Available for Unsecured Creditors | $ 700,000 |

**TABLE 21.13   Pro Rata Distribution of Funds Among Unsecured Creditors of Dempsey Company**

| Unsecured Creditors' Claims | Amount | Settlement at 25%[a] |
|---|---|---|
| Unpaid balance of second mortgage | $  800,000[b] | $200,000 |
| Accounts payable | 200,000 | 50,000 |
| Notes payable—bank | 1,000,000 | 250,000 |
| Unsecured bonds | 800,000 | 200,000 |
| Totals | $2,800,000 | $700,000 |

[a]The 25 percent rate is calculated by dividing the $700,000 available for unsecured creditors by the $2.8 million owed unsecured creditors. Each is entitled to a pro rata share.

[b]This figure represents the difference between the $1 million second mortgage and the $200,000 payment on the second mortgage from the proceeds from the sale of the collateral remaining after satisfying the first mortgage.

# Progress Review Questions

**21-14.** What is the concern of Chapter 11 of the *Bankruptcy Reform Act of 1978?* How is the *debtor in possession (DIP)* involved in (a) the valuation of the firm, (b) the recapitalization of the firm, and (c) the exchange of obligations using the priority rule?

**21-15.** What is the concern of Chapter 7 of the *Bankruptcy Reform Act of 1978?* Under which conditions is a firm liquidated in bankruptcy? Describe the procedures (including the role of the *trustee*) involved in liquidating the bankrupt firm.

**21-16.** In which order are the following claims settled when distributing the proceeds from liquidating a bankrupt firm?
 **a.** Claims of preferred stockholders
 **b.** Claims of secured creditors
 **c.** Expenses of administering the bankruptcy
 **d.** Claims of common stockholders
 **e.** Claims of unsecured, or general, creditors
 **f.** Taxes legally due
 **g.** Unsecured deposits of customers
 **h.** Certain eligible wages
 **i.** Unpaid employee benefit plan contributions
 **j.** Unpaid interim expenses incurred between the time of filing and the entry of an Order for Relief
 **k.** Claims of farmers or fishermen in a grain-storage or fish-storage facility

# SUMMARY OF LEARNING GOALS

**Understand merger fundamentals, including basic terminology, motives for merging, and types of mergers.** Mergers, including consolidations, result from the combining of firms. Typically the acquiring company pursues and attempts to merge with the target company, on either a friendly or a hostile basis. Mergers are undertaken either for strategic reasons to achieve economies of scale or for financial reasons to restructure the firm to improve its cash flow. Although the overriding goal of merging is maximization of owners' wealth (share price), other specific merger motives include growth or diversification, synergy, fund raising, increased managerial skill or technology, tax considerations, increased ownership liquidity, and defense against takeover. The four basic types of mergers are horizontal—the merger of two firms in the same line of business; vertical—acquisition of a supplier or customer; congeneric—acquisition of a firm in the same general industry but neither in the same business nor a supplier or customer; and conglomerate—merger between unrelated businesses.

**Describe the objectives and procedures used in leveraged buyouts (LBOs) and divestitures.** A popular technique for structuring financial mergers during the 1980s was the leveraged buyout (LBO), which involves use of a large amount of debt to purchase a firm. Attractive LBO candidates must have good profits and growth prospects, low debt and a high level of assets that can be used as collateral, and stable and predictable cash flows that can be used to repay the debt and provide adequate working capital. While still used today, LBOs are fewer in number and generally used for management buyouts. Divestiture involves the sale of a firm's assets, typically an operating unit, to another firm or existing management, the spin-off of assets into an independent company, or the liquidation of assets. Motives for divestiture include cash generation and corporate restructuring consistent with strategic goals. The result is typically a more focused and efficient company.

**Demonstrate the procedures used to analyze mergers, including valuing the target company and the effect of stock swap transactions on earnings per share.** The value of a target company can be estimated by using valuation techniques. Capital budgeting techniques are applied to the relevant cash flows whether the target firm is being acquired for its assets or as a going concern. All proposed mergers with positive net present values are considered acceptable. In a stock swap transaction in which the acquisition is paid for by an exchange of common stock, a ratio of exchange must be established. This ratio measures the amount paid per share of the target company relative to the per-share market price of the acquiring firm. The resulting relationship between the price/earnings (P/E) ratio paid by the acquiring firm and its initial P/E affects the merged firm's earnings per share (EPS) and market price. If the P/E paid is greater than the P/E of the acquiring company, the EPS of the acquiring company decreases and the EPS of the target company increases; if the P/E paid is less than the P/E of the acquiring firm, the converse is the case.

**Discuss the merger negotiation process, the role of holding companies, and international mergers.** Investment bankers are commonly hired by the acquirer to find a suitable target company and assist in negotiations. A merger can be negotiated with the target firm's management or, in the case of a hostile merger, directly with the firm's shareholders by using tender offers. When the management of the target firm does not favor the merger, it can employ any of a number of takeover defenses, which include a "white knight," "poison pills," "greenmail," leveraged recapitalization, "golden parachutes," and "shark repellents." A holding company can be created by one firm gaining control of other companies, often by owning as little as 10 to 20 percent of their stock. The chief advantages of holding companies are the leverage effect, risk protection, tax benefits, protection against lawsuits, and the fact that it is generally easy to gain control of a subsidiary. Commonly cited disadvantages include increased risk due to the magnification of losses, double taxation, difficulty of analysis, and the high cost of administration. Although U.S. merger practices differ greatly from practices in other countries, during recent years mergers of companies in Western European countries have exploded as they move toward the U.S.-style corporate control and financing model, and both European and Japanese companies have become active acquirers of U.S. companies.

 **Understand the types and major causes of business failure and the use of voluntary settlements to sustain or liquidate the failed firm.** A firm may fail because it has negative or low returns, because it is technically insolvent, or because it is bankrupt. The major causes of business failure are mismanagement, downturns in economic activity, and corporate maturity. Voluntary settlements are initiated by the debtor and can result in sustaining the firm through an extension, a composition, creditor control of the firm, or a combination of these strategies. If creditors do not agree to a plan to sustain a firm, they may recommend voluntary liquidation, which bypasses many of the legal requirements and costs of bankruptcy proceedings.

 **Explain bankruptcy legislation and the procedures involved in reorganizing or liquidating a bankrupt firm.** A failed firm that cannot or does not want to arrange a voluntary settlement can voluntarily or involuntarily file in federal bankruptcy court for reorganization under Chapter 11 or for liquidation under Chapter 7 of the *Bankruptcy Reform Act of 1978*. Under Chapter 11 the judge appoints the debtor in possession (DIP). With court supervision the DIP develops, if feasible, a reorganization plan. A firm that cannot be reorganized under Chapter 11 of the bankruptcy law or does not petition for reorganization is liquidated under Chapter 7. The responsibility for liquidation is placed in the hands of a court-appointed trustee, whose duties include the liquidation of assets, the distribution of the proceeds, and making a final accounting. Liquidation procedures follow a priority of claims for distribution of the proceeds from the sale of assets.

# KEY EQUATION
## Equation[5]

Market price ratio of exchange

[Eq.21.1]

$$MPR = \frac{MP_{acquiring} \times RE}{MP_{target}}$$

---

[5]See page 598 for key variable definitions.

L E A R N I N G    G O A L S

After studying this chapter, you should be able to

 **LG 1** Understand the major factors influencing the financial operations of multinational companies (MNCs).

 **LG 2** Describe the key differences between purely domestic and international financial statements—particularly consolidation, translation of individual accounts, and international profits.

 **LG 3** Review the basics of cash management, credit and inventory management, and the use of the Eurocurrency market in short-term borrowing and investing (lending) in international operations.

 **LG 4** Discuss the two risks—exchange rate and political—requiring special consideration by the multinational company, and explain how MNCs manage them.

 **LG 5** Describe foreign direct investment, investment cash flows and decisions, the factors that influence an MNC's capital structure, and the international debt and equity instruments that are available to MNCs.

**LG 6** Explain the growth of and special factors relating to international mergers and joint ventures.

# 22 International Managerial Finance

It's difficult to find companies today that *aren't* part of the global marketplace. Most firms export, manufacture, or market their goods and services in at least a few non-U.S. markets. Even a "domestic" company may raise or invest funds in international capital markets, import product components, or have overseas competitors.

> ## International treasury operations require a thorough understanding of accounting and taxation as well as finance.

Sara Lee Corporation manufactures and markets high-quality, branded consumer packaged foods, apparel, and household and personal products worldwide. We manufacture in over 30 countries and market our products in over 120. International operations represent about 35 percent of sales, 41 percent of pretax income, and 48 percent of assets. Sara Lee is one of the largest U.S. consumer products companies in Europe.

Companies expand internationally to move into growing markets and take advantage of changing markets. For example, Europe was a growth market 10 years ago and is now restructuring as the European Union lowers trade barriers there. Freer trade, fostered by the recent NAFTA and GATT accords, is bringing the Pacific rim and Latin America closer to the center of the global economy. The rising standard of living in these regions generates greater demand for well-known, brand-name products like ours.

International operations expose companies to many more risks. Political risk can be controlled but not really eliminated. Treasury managers focus on foreign exchange and interest rate risks, which are simply another cost of doing business. Foreign exchange rates are more volatile than any other cost input and can introduce considerable volatility into financial statements. They also affect a company's ability to compete. Purchasing materials in a currency that appreciates against the currency in which you sell raises your total costs. Therefore, you have to reduce margins or raise prices—and perhaps lose market share, if your competitors are either sourcing in a depreciating currency or hedging.

Companies must monitor interest rates locally and in related markets. For example, German rates can affect French rates. The financial manager evaluates alternative strategies to finance working capital and fixed assets, including raising local-currency debt or borrowing elsewhere and swapping into the local currency, which can be cheaper than the direct route.

A multinational corporation like Sara Lee has a central tax and treasury "clearinghouse" for international finance. It considers the whole picture; a firm can't look at Spain today and France tomorrow. For instance, some countries restrict the proportion of debt in your capital structure. The more places you are, the better your chance of creating good financing transactions at favorable rates.

International treasury operations require a thorough understanding of accounting and taxation as well as finance. And you can't ignore nonfinancial variables. It's important to be sensitive to cultural differences, including how people elsewhere think and conduct business. That makes the job more demanding and more interesting. There's little risk of getting bored in this job!

*Stewart Schoder received an A.B. in history from Princeton University. From 1976 to 1981 he was in Citibank's international division, serving as manager and chief dealer in Saudi Arabia and resident vice-president and regional treasurer in Côte d'Ivoire. In 1985 he received an M.A. in business economics from the Wharton School, University of Pennsylvania. After six years in corporate finance at Salomon Brothers, in 1991 he joined Sara Lee as director, international treasury.*

In recent years, as world markets have become significantly more interdependent, international finance has become an increasingly important element in the management of **multinational companies (MNCs).** These firms, being based in the United States, Western Europe, Japan, and many other countries, have international assets and operations in foreign markets and draw part of their total revenues and profits from such markets. The foundations of managerial finance presented in this text are applicable to the management of MNCs. However, certain factors unique to the international setting tend to complicate the financial management of multinational companies. A simple comparison between a domestic U.S. firm (firm A) and a U.S.-based MNC (firm B), as illustrated in Table 22.1, indicates the influence of some of the international factors on MNCs' operations. This chapter highlights the key aspects of the multinational company and its environment, financial statements, short-term financial decisions, risk, long-term investment and financing decisions, and mergers and joint ventures.

**multinational companies (MNCs)**
Firms that have international assets and operations in foreign markets and draw part of their total revenues and profits from such markets.

# The Multinational Company and Its Environment

LG 1

The MNC's operating environment cuts across national boundaries, thereby creating opportunities and challenges for the financial manager. Accompanying an expanded financial marketplace in which to borrow and invest

**TABLE 22.1    International Factors and Their Influence on MNCs' Operations**

| Factor | Firm A (Domestic) | Firm B (MNC) |
|---|---|---|
| Foreign ownership | All assets owned by domestic entities | Portions of equity of foreign investments owned by foreign partners, thus affecting foreign decision making and profits |
| Multinational financial markets | All debt and equity structures based on the domestic financial market | Opportunities and challenges arise from the existence of different financial markets where debt and equity can be issued |
| Multinational accounting | All consolidation of financial statements based on one currency | The existence of different currencies and of specific translation rules influence the consolidation of financial statements into one currency |
| Foreign exchange risks | All operations in one currency | Fluctuations in foreign exchange markets can affect foreign revenues and profits as well as the overall value of the firm |

are a variety of laws, restrictions, and taxes that are significantly different from those affecting a purely domestic firm. Here we take a brief look at the newly emerging trading blocs in North America and Western Europe, legal forms of business, financial markets, and taxes.

## Emerging Trading Blocs: NAFTA and the European Open Market

**North American Free Trade Agreement (NAFTA)**
The treaty establishing free trade and open markets among Canada, Mexico, and the United States.

During the early 1990s, two important trading blocs emerged, centered in North America and Western Europe. Chile, Mexico, and several other Latin American countries began to adopt market-oriented economic policies in the late 1980s, forging very close financial and economic ties to the United States. In 1988, Canada and the United States negotiated essentially unrestricted trade between the countries, and this free trade zone was extended to include Mexico in late 1992 when the **North American Free Trade Agreement (NAFTA)** was signed by the presidents of the United States and Mexico and the prime minister of Canada. Eventually, the agreement may include Chile and other countries. NAFTA was, after much debate, ratified by the U.S. Congress in November of 1993. This trade pact simply mirrors underlying economic reality—Canada is already the United States' largest trading partner, and Mexico is the third largest (after Japan) and fastest growing U.S. export market.

The European Economic Community (EC, also called EEC) has been in existence since 1959. It has a current membership of 12 nations. With a total population estimated at more than 350 million and an overall gross national income paralleling that of the United States, the EC is a significant global economic force. Now, because of a series of major economic, monetary, financial, and legal provisions set forth by the member countries during the 1980s, the countries of Western Europe opened a new era of free trade within the community when tariff barriers fell at the end of 1992. This transformation into a *single* market is commonly called the **European Open Market.** Although the EC has managed to reach agreements on most of these provisions, debates continue on certain other aspects (some key), including those related to automobile production and imports, monetary union, taxes, and workers' rights.

**European Open Market**
The transformation of the European Economic Community (EC) into a *single* market at year-end 1992.

It is generally believed that the EC can expect to enjoy enhanced economic growth rates for much of the 1990s and perhaps beyond. The new community offers both challenges and opportunities to a variety of players, including multinational firms. MNCs, especially those based in the United States, face heightened levels of competition when operating inside the EC. As more of the existing restrictions and regulations are eliminated, for instance, U.S. multinationals must compete with other MNCs. Some, such as the larger and perhaps more efficient firms resulting from mergers, will come from within the community. Others, including the giants from Japan, could challenge the U.S. MNCs in a manner similar to that already done in the U.S. market.

U.S. companies can benefit from a single European market, but only if they are prepared. They must offer the correct mix of products to a collection of varied consumers and be ready to take advantage of a variety of currencies (including the EC's own, the *European currency unit, ECU*) as well as financial markets and instruments (such as the emerging Euro-equities). They must staff their operations with the appropriate combination of local and foreign personnel and, when necessary, enter into joint ventures and strategic alliances.

## Legal Forms of Business

In many countries outside the United States, operating a foreign business as a subsidiary or affiliate can take two forms, both similar to the U.S. corporation. In German-speaking nations the two forms are the *Aktiengesellschaft* (A.G.) or the *Gesellschaft mit beschrankter Haftung* (GmbH). In many other countries the similar forms are a *Société Anonyme* (S.A.) or a *Société à Responsibilité Limitée* (S.A.R.L.). The A.G. or the S.A. is the most common form, but the GmbH or the S.A.R.L. enjoys much greater freedom and requires fewer formalities for formation and operation.

Although establishing a business in a form such as the S.A. can involve most of the provisions that govern a U.S.-based corporation, to operate in many foreign countries, especially in most of the less developed nations, it is often essential to enter into joint-venture business agreements with private investors or with government-based agencies of the host country. A **joint venture** is a partnership under which the participants have contractually agreed to contribute specified amounts of money and expertise in exchange for stated proportions of ownership and profit. The governments of numerous countries, such as Brazil, Colombia, Mexico, and Venezuela in Latin America as well as Indonesia, Malaysia, the Philippines, and Thailand in East Asia, have in recent years instituted new laws and regulations governing MNCs. The basic rule introduced by most of these nations requires that the majority ownership (i.e., at least 51 percent of the total equity) of MNCs' joint-venture projects be held by domestically based investors. In other regions of the world, MNCs, especially those based in the United States and Japan, face new challenges and opportunities, particularly in terms of ownership requirements, and mergers. Two regions providing these challenges and opportunities in the near future are Western Europe as it approaches a truly open trading system and Eastern Europe as it attempts to adopt more market-based economic principles.

The existence of joint-venture laws and restrictions has certain implications for the operation of foreign-based subsidiaries. First of all, majority foreign ownership may result in a substantial degree of management and control by host-country participants; this in turn can influence day-to-day operations to the detriment of the managerial policies and procedures that are normally pursued by MNCs. Next, foreign ownership may result in disagreements among the partners about the exact distribution of profits and the portion to be allocated for reinvestment. Moreover, operating in foreign countries, especially on a joint-venture basis, can entail problems regarding the actual remission of profits. In the past, the governments of Argentina, Brazil, Nigeria, and Thailand, among others, have imposed ceilings not only on the repatriation (return) of capital by MNCs but also on profit remittances by these firms back to the parent companies. These governments usually cite the shortage of foreign exchange as the motivating factor. Finally, from a "positive" point of view, it can be argued that to operate in many of the less developed countries, it is beneficial for MNCs to enter into joint-venture agreements, given the potential risks stemming from political instability in the host countries. This issue is addressed in detail later.

**joint venture**
A partnership under which the participants have contractually agreed to contribute specified amounts of money and expertise in exchange for stated proportions of ownership and profit.

## Financial Markets

**Euromarket**
The international financial market that provides for borrowing and lending currencies outside their country of origin.

During the last two decades the **Euromarket**—which provides for borrowing and lending currencies outside their country of origin—has grown quite rapidly. The Euromarket provides multinational companies with an "external" opportunity to borrow or lend funds with the additional feature of less government regulation.

**Growth of the Euromarket**   The Euromarket has grown so large for several reasons. First, beginning in the early 1960s, the Russians wanted to maintain their dollar earnings outside the legal jurisdiction of the United States, mainly because of the Cold War. Second, the consistently large U.S. balance of payments deficits helped to "scatter" dollars around the world. Third, the existence of specific regulations and controls on dollar deposits in the United States, including interest rate ceilings imposed by the government, helped to send such deposits to places outside the United States.

These and other factors have combined and contributed to the creation of an "external" capital market the size of which cannot be accurately determined, mainly because of its lack of regulation and control. Several sources that periodically estimate its size are the Bank for International Settlements (BIS), Morgan Guaranty Trust, the World Bank, and the Organization for Economic Cooperation and Development (OECD). The latest available estimates (1992) put the overall size of the market at $6.1 trillion gross value of deposits.

**offshore centers**
Certain cities or states (including London, Singapore, Bahrain, Nassau, Hong Kong, and Luxembourg) that have achieved prominence and are considered major centers for Euromarket business.

One aspect of the Euromarket is the so-called **offshore centers.** Certain cities or states around the world—including London, Singapore, Bahrain, Nassau, Hong Kong, and Luxembourg—have achieved prominence and are considered major offshore centers for Euromarket business. The availability of communication and transportation facilities, along with the importance of language, costs, time zones, taxes, and local banking regulations, are among the main reasons for the prominence of these centers.

Another important point is that in recent years a variety of new financial instruments have appeared in the international financial markets. One is interest rate and currency swaps. Another is various combinations of forward and options contracts on different currencies. A third is new types of bonds and notes—along with an international version of U.S. commercial paper— with flexible characteristics in terms of currency, maturity, and interest rate. More details are discussed in subsequent sections.

**Major Participants**   The Euromarket is still dominated by the U.S. dollar. However, activities in other major currencies, including the Deutsche mark, Swiss franc, Japanese yen, British pound sterling, French franc, and European currency unit (ECU), have in recent years grown much faster than those denominated in the U.S. currency. Similarly, although U.S. banks and other financial institutions continue to play a significant role in the global markets, financial giants from Japan and Europe have become major participants in Euromarkets. Today, a majority of the top 10 largest banks in the world as measured in terms of total assets are based in Japan.

Following the oil price increases by the Organization of Petroleum Exporting Countries (OPEC) in 1973–1974 and 1979–1980, massive amounts of dollars were placed in various Euromarket financial centers. International banks, in turn, as part of the so-called *redistribution* of "oil money," began lending to different groups of borrowers. At the end of 1992, for example, a group of Latin American countries had total borrowings outstanding of about $357 billion. Although developing countries have become a major borrowing group in recent years, the industrialized nations continue to borrow actively in international markets. Included in the latter group's borrowings are the funds obtained by multinational companies. The multinationals use the Euromarket to raise additional funds as well as to invest excess cash. Both Eurocurrency and Eurobond markets are extensively used by MNCs. Further details on MNCs' Euromarket activities are presented later.

## Taxes

Multinational companies, unlike domestic firms, have financial obligations—as well as opportunities—in foreign countries. One of their basic responsibilities is international taxation—a complex issue because national governments follow a variety of tax policies. In general, from the point of view of a U.S.-based MNC, several factors must be taken into account.

**Tax Rates and Taxable Income**   First, the *level* of foreign taxes needs to be examined. Among the major industrial countries, corporate tax rates do not vary too widely. For many less industrialized nations, relatively moderate rates are maintained, partly as an incentive for attracting foreign capital inflows. Certain countries, meanwhile, including the Bahamas, Switzerland, Liechtenstein, the Cayman Islands, and Bermuda, are known for their "low" tax levels. These nations typically have no withholding taxes on *intra-MNC dividends*.

Next, the definition of *taxable income* varies. Some countries tax profits as received on a cash basis, whereas others tax profits earned on an accrual basis. Differences can also exist in treatments of noncash charges, such as depreciation, amortization, and depletion. Finally, the existence of tax agreements between the United States and other governments can influence not only the total tax bill of the parent MNC, but also its international operations and financial activities. Effective January 1, 1988, for example, the U.S. Treasury terminated a 1948 tax treaty with the Netherlands Antilles, affecting about $32 billion of debt issued by U.S.-based MNCs. Under this treaty, debt issued in the Netherlands Antilles had been exempt from a 30 percent withholding tax imposed by the United States.

**Tax Rules**   Different parent or home countries apply varying tax rates and rules to the global earnings of their own multinationals. Moreover, tax rules are subject to frequent modifications. In the United States, for instance, the *Tax Reform Act of 1986* resulted in certain changes affecting the taxation of U.S.-based MNCs. Special provisions apply to tax deferrals by MNCs on foreign income; operations set up in U.S. possessions, such as the U.S. Virgin Islands, Guam, and American Samoa; capital gains from the sale of stock in a foreign corporation; and withholding taxes. Furthermore, MNCs (both U.S. and foreign) can be subject to national as well as local taxes. As an example, a number of individual state governments in the United States have in recent years introduced new measures—in the form of special **unitary tax laws**—that tax the multinationals on a percentage of their *total* worldwide income rather than, as is generally accepted elsewhere, on their earnings arising within the jurisdiction of each respective government. (As a part of their response to unitary tax laws, the multinationals

**unitary tax laws**
Laws in some U.S. states that tax multinationals (both U.S. and foreign) on a percentage of their *total* worldwide income rather than the usual taxation of the MNCs' earnings arising within their jurisdiction.

have already pressured a number of state governments into abolishing the laws. In addition, some MNCs have relocated their investments away from those states that continue to apply such laws.) For updated details on various countries' tax laws, consult relevant publications by international accounting firms.

As a general practice, the U.S. government claims jurisdiction over *all* the income of an MNC, wherever earned. (Special rules apply to foreign corporations conducting business in the United States.) However, it may be possible for a multinational company to take foreign income taxes as a direct credit against its U.S. tax liabilities. The following simple example illustrates one way of accomplishing this objective.

## EXAMPLE

American Enterprises, a U.S.-based MNC that manufactures heavy machinery, has a foreign subsidiary that earns $100,000 before local taxes. All of the after-tax funds are available to the parent in the form of dividends. The applicable taxes consist of a 35 percent foreign income tax rate, a foreign dividend withholding tax rate of 10 percent, and a U.S. tax rate of 34 percent.

| | |
|---|---:|
| Subsidiary income before local taxes | $100,000 |
| Foreign income tax at 35% | − 35,000 |
| Dividend available to be declared | $ 65,000 |
| Foreign dividend withholding tax at 10% | − 6,500 |
| MNC's receipt of dividends | $ 58,500 |

# FINANCE IN ACTION

## International

### Can State Tax Differences Start an International Trade War?

Although it's widely known that different federal tax policies across different countries can affect international commercial activity, is it possible for state tax differences to interfere with international trade? That's the question the U.S. Supreme Court faces in mid-1994, as it rules on the recent British challenge to California's controversial unitary tax system. Under California's unitary tax laws, foreign-owned companies are taxed on a percentage of their worldwide income, not just on the income these firms earn in the state of California.

The British government has threatened to retaliate by raising British taxes on U.S. corporations operating in the United Kingdom unless California changes its tax statute. At stake is some $4 billion in tax revenue that California must return to British companies if the state loses before the Supreme Court. How could California compensate for this substantial revenue loss? By increasing taxes on all businesses—foreign and domestic—operating in the state. Either way, it's a lose-lose proposition, as California struggles to discover new ways to fill its state coffers without igniting an international trade war with Britain.

Source: K. Cahill, "Unitary Taxes Take Center Stage," *CFO Magazine*, January 1994, p. 7.

Using the so-called *grossing up procedure,* the MNC adds the full before-tax subsidiary income to its total taxable income. Next, the U.S. tax liability on the grossed-up income is calculated. Finally, the related taxes paid in the foreign country are applied as a credit against the additional U.S. tax liability.

| | | |
|---|---:|---:|
| Additional MNC income | | $100,000 |
| U.S. tax liability at 34% | $34,000 | |
| Total foreign taxes paid to be used as a credit ($35,000 + $6,500) | −41,500 | − 41,500 |
| U.S. taxes due | | 0 |
| Net funds available to the parent MNC | | $ 58,500 |

Because the U.S. tax liability is less than the total taxes paid to the foreign government, *no additional U.S. taxes are due* on the income from the foreign subsidiary. In our example, if tax credits had not been allowed, then "double taxation" by the two authorities, as shown below, would have resulted in a substantial drop in the overall net funds available to the parent MNC.

| | |
|---|---:|
| Subsidiary income before local taxes | $100,000 |
| Foreign income tax at 35% | − 35,000 |
| Dividend available to be declared | $ 65,000 |
| Foreign dividend withholding tax at 10% | − 6,500 |
| MNC's receipt of dividends | $ 58,500 |
| U.S. tax liability at 34% | − 19,890 |
| Net funds available to the parent MNC | $ 38,610 |

The preceding example clearly demonstrates that the existence of bilateral tax treaties and the subsequent application of tax credits can significantly enhance the overall net funds available to MNCs from their worldwide earnings. Consequently, in an increasingly complex and competitive international financial environment, international taxation is one of the variables that multinational corporations should fully utilize to their advantage.

# Progress Review Questions

**22-1.** What are *NAFTA* and the *European Open Market?* What challenges and opportunities do they offer to MNCs, especially those based in the United States?

**22-2.** What is a *joint venture?* Why is it often essential to use this arrangement? What effect do joint-venture laws and restrictions have on the operation of foreign-based subsidiaries?

**22-3.** Discuss the major reasons for the growth of the Euromarket. What is an *offshore center?* Name the major participants in the Euromarket.

**22-4.** From the point of view of a U.S.-based MNC, what key tax factors need to be considered? What are *unitary tax laws?*

LG 2

# Financial Statements

Several features distinguish domestically oriented financial statements and internationally based reports. Among these are the issues of consolidation, translation of individual accounts within the financial statements, and overall reporting of international profits.

## Consolidation

At present, U.S. rules require the consolidation of financial statements of subsidiaries according to the percentage of ownership by the parent of the subsidiary. Table 22.2 illustrates this point. As indicated, the regulations range from requiring a one-line income-item reporting of dividends to a pro rata inclusion of profits and losses to a full disclosure in the balance sheet and income statement. (When ownership is less than 50 percent, because the balance sheet and thus the subsidiary's financing do not get reported, it is possible for the parent MNC to have off-balance-sheet financing.)

## Translation of Individual Accounts

**FASB No. 52**
Statement issued by the FASB requiring U.S. multinationals first to convert the financial statement accounts of foreign subsidiaries into their *functional currency* and then to translate the accounts into the parent firm's currency using the *all-current-rate method.*

**functional currency**
The currency of the host country in which a business entity primarily generates and expends cash and in which its accounts are maintained.

Unlike domestic items in financial statements, international items require translation back into U.S. dollars. Since December 1982, all financial statements of U.S. multinationals have to conform to Statement No. 52 issued by the Financial Accounting Standards Board (FASB). The basic rules of FASB No. 52 are given in Figure 22.1.

Under **FASB No. 52,** the *current rate method* is implemented in a two-step process. First, each subsidiary's balance sheet and income statement are *measured* in terms of their functional currency by using generally accepted accounting principles (GAAP). That is, foreign currency elements are translated by each subsidiary into the **functional currency**—the currency of the host

---

**TABLE 22.2   United States Rules for Consolidation of Financial Statements**

| Percentage of Beneficial Ownership by Parent in Subsidiary | Consolidation for Financial Reporting Purposes |
| --- | --- |
| 0–19% | Dividends as received |
| 20–49% | Pro rata inclusions of profits and losses |
| 50–100% | Full consolidation[a] |

[a]Consolidation may be avoided in the case of some majority-owned foreign operations if the parent can convince its auditors that it does not have control of the subsidiaries or if there are substantial restrictions on the repatriation of cash.

Source: Rita M. Rodriguez and E. Eugene Carter, *International Financial Management,* 3rd ed. Englewood Cliffs, NJ: Prentice-Hall, 1984, p. 492.

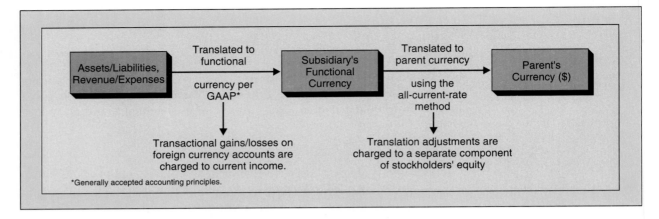

**FIGURE 22.1   DETAILS OF FASB No. 52**
Under FASB No. 52, financial statement accounts of a foreign subsidiary are first translated using GAAP into the host country's functional currency, which is then translated using the all-current-rate method into the parent firm's currency. The first translation can result in transaction (cash) gains or losses, and the second can result in translation (accounting) adjustments.

country in which an entity primarily generates and expends cash and in which its accounts are maintained before financial statements are submitted to the parent for consolidation.

Through the second step, as shown in Figure 22.1, by using the **all-current-rate method** (which requires the translation of all balance sheet items at the closing rate and all income statement items at average rates), the functional-currency-denominated financial statements are translated into the parent's currency.

Each of these steps can result in certain gains or losses. The first step can lead to transaction (cash) gains or losses, which, whether realized or not, are charged directly to net income. The completion of the second step can result in translation (accounting) adjustments, which are excluded from current income. Instead, they are disclosed and charged to a separate component of stockholders' equity.

**all-current-rate method**
The method by which the *functional-currency*-denominated financial statements of an MNC's subsidiary are translated into the parent company's currency.

## International Profits

Before January 1976 the practice for most U.S. multinationals was to utilize a special account called the *reserve account* to show "smooth" international profits. Excess international profits due to favorable currency fluctuations were deposited in this account. Withdrawals were made during periods of high losses stemming from unfavorable currency movements. The overall result was to display a smooth pattern in an MNC's international profits.

Between 1976 and 1982, however, the existence of *FASB No. 8* required that both transaction gains or losses and translation adjustments be included in net income, with the separate disclosure of only the aggregate foreign exchange gain or loss. This requirement caused highly visible swings in the reported net earnings of U.S. multinationals. Under FASB No. 52, only certain transactional gains or losses are reflected in the income statement. Overall, assuming a positive income flow for a subsidiary, the income statement risk is positive and is similarly enhanced or reduced by an appreciation or depreciation of the functional currency.

## Progress Review Question

**22-5.** State the rules for consolidation of foreign subsidiaries. Under *FASB No. 52*, what are the translation rules for financial statement accounts?

---

LG 3

## Short-Term Financial Decisions

Short-term financial management of an MNC offers a number of unique opportunities and challenges for the financial manager. Specific areas of decision-making include cash management, credit and inventory management, and short-term financing, which makes available to the firm a number of foreign sources of short-term funds.

### Cash Management

Because the revenues and costs of a multinational company are based on different foreign currencies, it must protect itself against changing relationships between them. In its international cash management, the firm can protect against changing relationships between currencies either by hedging them or by making certain adjustments in its operations. Each of these two approaches is examined here.

**hedging strategies**
Techniques used to offset or protect against risk; in the international context these include borrowing or lending in different currencies; undertaking contracts in the forward, futures, or options markets; and swapping assets or liabilities with other parties.

**Hedging Strategies**   **Hedging strategies** are techniques used to offset or protect against risk. In international cash management these strategies include borrowing or lending in different currencies; undertaking contracts in the forward, futures, or options markets; and swapping assets or liabilities with other parties. Table 22.3 provides a brief summary of some of the major exchange rate risk-hedging tools available to MNCs.

**Adjustments in Operations**   In responding to exchange rate fluctuations, MNCs can give some protection to international cash flows through appropriate adjustments in assets and liabilities. Two routes are available to a multinational company. The first centers on the operating relationships that a subsidiary of an MNC maintains with *other* firms—*third parties*. Depending on management's expectation of a local currency's position, adjustments in operations involve the reduction of liabilities if the currency is appreciating or the reduction of financial assets if it is depreciating. For example, if a U.S.-based MNC with a subsidiary in Mexico expects the Mexican currency to *appreciate* in value relative to the U.S. dollar, local customers' accounts receivable are *increased* and accounts payable are reduced if at all possible. Because the dollar is the currency in which the MNC parent must prepare consolidated financial statements, the net result in this case is to increase favorably the Mexican subsidiary's resources in local currency. If the Mexican currency is, instead, expected to *depreciate,* the local customers' accounts receivable are *reduced* and accounts payable are increased, thereby reducing the Mexican subsidiary's resources in the local currency.

**TABLE 22.3   Exchange Rate Risk-Hedging Tools**

| Tool | Description | Impact on Risk |
|---|---|---|
| Borrowing or lending | Borrowing or lending in different currencies to take advantage of interest rate differentials and foreign exchange appreciation or depreciation; can be either on a certainty basis with "up-front" costs or speculative. | Can be used to offset exposures in existing assets or liabilities and in expected revenues or expenses. |
| Forward contract | "Tailor-made" contracts representing an *obligation* to buy or sell, with the amount, rate, and maturity agreed on between the two parties; has little up-front cost. | Can eliminate downside risk but locks out any upside potential. |
| Futures contract | Standardized contracts offered on organized exchanges; same basic tool as a forward contract, but less flexible because of standardization; more flexibility because of secondary market access; has some up-front cost or fee. | Can also eliminate downside risk, plus position can be nullified, creating possible upside potential. |
| Options | Tailor-made or standardized contracts providing the *right* to buy or to sell an amount of the currency, at a particular price, during a specified period; has up-front cost (premium). | Can eliminate downside risk and retain unlimited upside potential. |
| Interest rate swap | Allows the trading of one interest rate stream (e.g., on a fixed-rate U.S. dollar instrument) for another (e.g., on a floating-rate U.S. dollar instrument); fee is paid to the intermediary. | Permits firms to change the interest rate structure of their assets or liabilities and achieves cost savings due to broader market access. |
| Currency swap | Two parties exchange principal amounts of two different currencies initially; they pay each other's interest payments, then reverse principal amounts at a preagreed exchange rate at maturity; more complex than interest rate swaps. | All the features of interest rate swaps, plus it allows firms to change the currency structure of their assets or liabilities. |
| Hybrids | A variety of combinations of some of the above tools; may be quite costly or speculative. | Can create, with the right combination, a perfect hedge against certain foreign exchange exposures. |

*Note:* The participants in the above activities include MNCs, financial institutions, and brokers. The organized exchanges include Amsterdam, Chicago, London, New York, Philadelphia, and Zurich, among others. It should be emphasized that whereas most of these tools can be utilized for short-term exposure management, some, such as swaps, are more appropriate for long-term hedging strategies.

The second route focuses on the operating relationship a subsidiary has with its parent or with other subsidiaries within the same MNC. In dealing with exchange rate risks, a subsidiary can rely on *intra-MNC accounts*. Specifically, undesirable exposures from foreign exchange can be corrected to the extent that the subsidiary can take the following steps:

1. In appreciation-prone countries, intra-MNC accounts receivable are collected as soon as possible, and payment of intra-MNC accounts payable is delayed as long as possible.
2. In devaluation-prone countries, intra-MNC accounts receivable are collected as late as possible, and intra-MNC accounts payable are paid as soon as possible.

Again using the example of a Mexican subsidiary, the net result of step 1 or step 2 is the potential increase or decrease of that subsidiary's resources in the Mexican currency, depending on whether that currency is appreciating or depreciating relative to the parent MNC's main currency, the U.S. dollar.

From a *global* point of view and as far as an MNC's consolidated intra-company accounts are concerned, the manipulation of such accounts by one subsidiary can produce the opposite results for another subsidiary or the parent firm. For example, if an MNC's subsidiaries in Brazil and Mexico are dealing with each other, the Brazilian subsidiary's manipulations of intra-MNC accounts, along the lines just discussed, in anticipation of an appreciation of that country's currency relative to that of Mexico can mean exchange gains for the Brazilian subsidiary but losses for the Mexican one. The exact degree and direction of the actual manipulations, however, may depend on the tax status of each country. The MNC obviously wants the exchange losses to occur in the country with the higher tax rate. Finally, changes in intra-MNC accounts can also be subject to restrictions and regulations put forward by the respective host countries of various subsidiaries.

## Credit and Inventory Management

Multinational firms based in different countries compete for the same global export markets. Therefore it is essential that they offer attractive credit terms to potential customers. Increasingly, however, the maturity and saturation of developed markets is forcing MNCs to maintain and increase revenues by exporting and selling a higher percentage of their output to developing countries. Given the risks associated with the latter group of buyers, as partly evidenced by their lack of a major (hard) currency, the MNC must use a variety of tools to protect such revenues. In addition to the use of hedging and various asset and liability adjustments (described earlier), MNCs should seek the backing of their respective governments in both identifying target markets and extending credit. Multinationals based in a number of Western European nations and those based in Japan currently benefit from extensive involvement of government agencies that provide them with the needed service and financial support suggested here. For U.S.-based MNCs the international positions of government agencies such as the Export-Import Bank currently do not provide a comparable level of support.

In terms of inventory management, MNCs must consider a number of factors related to both economics and politics. In the former category, in addition to maintaining the appropriate level of inventory in various locations around the world, a multinational firm is compelled to deal with exchange rate fluctuations, tariffs, nontariff barriers, integration schemes such as the EC, and other rules and regulations. Politically, inventories can be subject to wars, expropriations, blockages, and other forms of government intervention.

## Short-Term Financing

In international operations the usual domestic sources of short-term financing, along with other sources, are available to MNCs. Included are accounts payable as well as accruals, bank and nonbank sources in each subsidiary's local environment, and the Euromarket discussed earlier. Our emphasis here is on the "foreign" sources.

For a subsidiary of a multinational company its local economic market is a basic source of both short- and long-term financing. Moreover, the subsidiary's borrowing and lending status can be superior relative to a local firm in the same economy, because the subsidiary can rely on the potential backing and guarantee of its parent MNC. One drawback, however, is that most local markets and local currencies are regulated by local authorities. Thus a subsidiary may ultimately choose to turn to the Euromarket and take advantage of borrowing and investing in an unregulated financial forum.

The Euromarket offers nondomestic financing opportunities for both the short term (Eurocurrency) and the long term (Eurobonds). (Eurobonds are discussed later.) In the case of short-term financing, the forces of supply and demand are among the main factors determining exchange rates in **Eurocurrency markets.** Each currency's normal interest rate is influenced by economic policies pursued by the respective "home" government. In other words, the interest rates offered in the Euromarket on, for example, the U.S. dollar are greatly affected by the prime rate inside the United States, and the dollar's exchange rates with other major currencies are influenced by the supply and demand forces acting in such markets (and in response to interest rates).

Unlike borrowing in the domestic markets, where only one currency and a **nominal interest rate** is involved, financing activities in the Euromarket can involve several currencies and both nominal and effective interest rates. **Effective interest rates** are equal to nominal rates plus (or minus) any forecast appreciation (or depreciation) of a foreign currency relative to the currency of the MNC parent—say, the U.S. dollar. An example illustrates the issues involved.

**Eurocurrency markets**
The portion of the Euromarket that provides short-term foreign-currency financing to subsidiaries of MNCs.

**nominal interest rate**
In the international context, the stated interest rate charged on financing when only the MNC parent's currency is involved.

**effective interest rate**
In the international context, the rate equal to the nominal rate plus (or minus) any forecast appreciation (or depreciation) of a foreign currency relative to the currency of the MNC parent.

▶ **E X A M P L E**

A multinational plastics company, J. Cannon Molding, has subsidiaries in Switzerland (local currency, Swiss franc, Sf) and Belgium (local currency, Belgian franc, Bf). Based on each subsidiary's forecast operations, the short-term financial needs (in equivalent U.S. dollars) are as follows:

Switzerland: $80 million excess cash to be invested (lent)
Belgium: $60 million funds to be raised (borrowed)

On the basis of all the available information, the parent firm has provided each subsidiary with the figures, given in the following table, regarding exchange rates and interest rates. (The figures for the effective rates shown are derived by adding the forecast percentage changes to the nominal rates.)

| | Currency | | |
|---|---|---|---|
| Item | US$ | Sf | Bf |
| Spot exchange rates | | Sf 1.42/US$ | Bf 32.85/US$ |
| Forecast % change | | +1.0% | −2.5% |
| Interest rates | | | |
| Nominal | | | |
|   Euromarket | 4.6% | 6.2% | 8.5% |
|   Domestic | 4.0 | 5.5 | 9.0 |
| Effective | | | |
|   Euromarket | 4.6% | 7.2% | 6.0% |
|   Domestic | 4.0 | 6.5 | 6.5 |

From the point of view of a multinational, the effective rates of interest, which take into account each currency's forecast percentage change (appreciation or depreciation) relative to the U.S. dollar, are the main items to be considered for investment and borrowing decisions. (It is assumed here that because of local regulations, a subsidiary is *not* permitted to use the domestic market of *any other* subsidiary.) The relevant question is, where should funds be invested and borrowed?

For investment purposes the highest available rate of interest is the effective rate for the Swiss franc in the Euromarket. Therefore the Swiss subsidiary should invest the $80 million in Swiss francs in the Euromarket. In the case of raising funds the cheapest source *open* to the Belgian subsidiary is the 4.6 percent in the US$ Euromarket. The subsidiary should therefore raise the $60 million in U.S. dollars. These two transactions result in the most revenues and least costs, respectively.

Several points should be made with respect to the preceding example. First, this is a simplified case of the actual workings of the Eurocurrency markets. The example ignores taxes, intersubsidiary investing and borrowing, and periods longer or shorter than a year. Nevertheless, it shows how the existence of many currencies can provide both challenges and opportunities for MNCs. Next, the focus has been solely on accounting values; of greater importance is the effect of these actions on market value. Finally, it is important to note the following details about the figures presented. The forecast percentage change (appreciation or depreciation) data are regarded as those normally supplied by the MNC's international financial managers. The management may have a *range of forecasts,* from the most likely to the least likely. In addition, the company's management is likely to take a specific position in terms of its response to any remaining foreign exchange exposures. If any action is to be taken, certain amounts of one or more currencies are borrowed and then invested in other currencies in the hope of realizing potential gains to offset potential losses associated with the exposures.

## Progress Review Questions

**22-6.** Discuss the steps to be followed in adjusting a subsidiary's accounts relative to *third parties* when that subsidiary's local currency is expected to appreciate in value in relation to the currency of the parent MNC.

**22-7.** Outline the changes to be undertaken in *intra-MNC accounts* if a subsidiary's currency is expected to depreciate in value relative to the currency of the parent MNC.

**22-8.** What is the *Eurocurrency market?* What are the main factors determining exchange rates in that market? Define and differentiate between the *nominal interest rate* and *effective interest rate* in this market.

LG 4

## Risk

The concept of risk clearly applies to international investments as well as to purely domestic ones. However, MNCs must take into account additional factors including both exchange rate and political risks.

## Exchange Rate Risks

Because multinational companies operate in many different foreign markets, portions of these firms' revenues and costs are based on foreign currencies. To understand the **exchange rate risk** caused by varying exchange rates between two currencies, we examine both the relationships that exist among various currencies and the effect of currency fluctuations.

**Relationships Among Currencies**   Since the mid-1970s, the major currencies of the world have had a *floating*—as opposed to *fixed*—relationship with respect to the U.S. dollar and to one another. Among the currencies regarded as being major (or "hard") are the British pound sterling (£), the Swiss franc (Sf), the Deutsche mark (DM), the French franc (Ff), the Japanese yen (¥), the Canadian dollar (C$), and, of course, the U.S. dollar (US$). The value of two currencies with respect to each other, or their **foreign exchange rate,** is expressed as follows:

$$US\$ \ 1.00 = Sf \ 1.42$$

$$Sf \ 1.00 = US\$ \ .704$$

The usual exchange rate quotation in international markets is given as Sf 1.42/US$, in which the unit of account is the Swiss franc and the unit of currency being priced is one U.S. dollar.

For the major currencies the existence of a **floating relationship** means that the value of any two currencies with respect to each other is allowed to fluctuate on a daily basis. On the other hand, many of the nonmajor currencies of the world try to maintain a **fixed (or semifixed) relationship** with respect to one of the major currencies, a combination (basket) of major currencies, or some type of international foreign exchange standard.

On any given day the relationship between any two of the major currencies contains two sets of figures, one reflecting the **spot exchange rate** (the rate on that day) and the other indicating the **forward exchange rate** (the rate at some specified future date). The foreign exchange rates given in Figure 22.2 can be used to illustrate these concepts. For instance, the figure shows that on Wednesday, June 2, 1993, the spot rate for the Swiss franc was Sf 1.4242/US$, and the forward (future) rate was Sf 1.4268/US$ for 30-day delivery. In other words, on June 2, 1993, one could take a contract on Swiss francs for 30 days hence at an exchange rate of Sf 1.4268/US$. *Forward delivery rates* are also available for 90-day and 180-day contracts. For all such contracts, the agreements and signatures are completed on, say, June 2, 1993, whereas the actual exchange of dollars and Swiss francs between buyers and sellers takes place on the future date, say, 30 days later.

Figure 22.2 can also be used to illustrate the differences between floating and fixed currencies. All the major currencies previously mentioned have spot and forward rates with respect to the U.S. dollar. Moreover, a comparison of the exchange rates prevailing on Wednesday, June 2, 1993, *versus* those on Tuesday, June 1, 1993, indicates that the floating major currencies (or other currencies that also float in relation to the U.S. dollar, such as the Austrian schilling and the Belgian franc) experienced changes in rates. Other currencies, however, such as the United Arab dirham, do not exhibit relatively large fluctuations on a daily basis with respect to either the U.S. dollar

**exchange rate risk**
The risk caused by varying exchange rates between two currencies.

**foreign exchange rate**
The value of two currencies with respect to each other.

**floating relationship**
The fluctuating relationship of the values of two currencies with respect to each other.

**fixed (or semifixed) relationship**
The constant (or relatively constant) relationship of a currency to one of the major currencies, a combination (basket) of major currencies, or some type of international foreign exchange standard.

**spot exchange rate**
The rate of exchange between two currencies on any given day.

**forward exchange rate**
The rate of exchange between two currencies at some specified future date.

## EXCHANGE RATES
### Wednesday, June 2, 1993

The New York foreign exchange selling rates below apply to trading among banks in amounts of $1 million and more, as quoted at 3 p.m. Eastern time by Bankers Trust Co., Telerate and other sources. Retail transactions provide fewer units of foreign currency per dollar.

| Country | U.S. $ equiv. Wed. | U.S. $ equiv. Tues. | Currency per U.S. $ Wed. | Currency per U.S. $ Tues. |
|---|---|---|---|---|
| Argentina (Peso) | 1.01 | 1.01 | .99 | .99 |
| Australia (Dollar) | .6782 | .6788 | 1.4745 | 1.4732 |
| Austria (Schilling) | .08887 | .08940 | 11.25 | 11.19 |
| Bahrain (Dinar) | 2.6522 | 2.6522 | .3771 | .3771 |
| Belgium (Franc) | .03044 | .03060 | 32.85 | 32.68 |
| Brazil (Cruzeiro) | .0000244 | .0000247 | 40972.02 | 40447.00 |
| Britain (Pound) | 1.5405 | 1.5485 | .6491 | .6458 |
| 30-Day Forward | 1.5368 | 1.5448 | .6507 | .6473 |
| 90-Day Forward | 1.5302 | 1.5388 | .6535 | .6499 |
| 180-Day Forward | 1.5223 | 1.5304 | .6569 | .6534 |
| Canada (Dollar) | .7867 | .7862 | 1.2712 | 1.2719 |
| 30-Day Forward | .7857 | .7852 | 1.2728 | 1.2735 |
| 90-Day Forward | .7837 | .7833 | 1.2760 | 1.2767 |
| 180-Day Forward | .7797 | .7793 | 1.2825 | 1.2832 |
| Czech. Rep. (Koruna) | | | | |
| Commercial rate | .0358809 | .0358809 | 27.8700 | 27.8700 |
| Chile (Peso) | .002544 | .002544 | 393.12 | 393.11 |
| China (Renminbi) | .174856 | .174856 | 5.7190 | 5.7190 |
| Colombia (Peso) | .001514 | .001501 | 660.54 | 666.40 |
| Denmark (Krone) | .1632 | .1641 | 6.1258 | 6.0953 |
| Ecuador (Sucre) | | | | |
| Floating rate | .000535 | .000535 | 1870.03 | 1870.03 |
| Finland (Markka) | .18375 | .18498 | 5.4422 | 5.4061 |
| France (Franc) | .18563 | .18613 | 5.3870 | 5.3725 |
| 30-Day Forward | .18484 | .18530 | 5.4101 | 5.3967 |
| 90-Day Forward | .18352 | .18404 | 5.4491 | 5.4335 |
| 180-Day Forward | .18192 | .18238 | 5.4970 | 5.4830 |
| Germany (Mark) | .6254 | .6287 | 1.5990 | 1.5905 |
| 30-Day Forward | .6228 | .6260 | 1.6057 | 1.5975 |
| 90-Day Forward | .6183 | .6217 | 1.6173 | 1.6084 |
| 180-Day Forward | .6133 | .6166 | 1.6306 | 1.6217 |
| Greece (Drachma) | .004609 | .004624 | 216.95 | 216.25 |
| Hong Kong (Dollar) | .12947 | .12947 | 7.7237 | 7.7235 |
| Hungary (Forint) | .0115500 | .0116050 | 86.5800 | 86.1700 |
| India (Rupee) | .03211 | .03211 | 31.14 | 31.14 |
| Indonesia (Rupiah) | .0004811 | .0004811 | 2078.53 | 2078.53 |
| Ireland (Punt) | 1.5243 | 1.5319 | .6560 | .6528 |
| Israel (Shekel) | .3763 | .3681 | 2.6575 | 2.7170 |
| Italy (Lira) | .0006842 | .0006804 | 1461.50 | 1469.64 |
| Japan (Yen) | .009320 | .009337 | 107.30 | 107.10 |
| 30-Day Forward | .009319 | .009337 | 107.30 | 107.10 |
| 90-Day Forward | .009320 | .009337 | 107.30 | 107.10 |
| 180-Day Forward | .009326 | .009344 | 107.23 | 107.02 |
| Jordan (Dinar) | 1.4984 | 1.4984 | .6674 | .6674 |
| Kuwait (Dinar) | 3.3267 | 3.3267 | .3006 | .3006 |
| Lebanon (Pound) | .000577 | .000577 | 1733.00 | 1733.00 |
| Malaysia (Ringgit) | .3914 | .3915 | 2.5550 | 2.5542 |
| Malta (Lira) | 2.7248 | 2.7248 | .3670 | .3670 |
| Mexico (Peso) | | | | |
| Floating rate | .3197953 | .3197953 | 3.1270 | 3.1270 |
| Netherland (Guilder) | .5574 | .5604 | 1.7939 | 1.7845 |
| New Zealand (Dollar) | .5425 | .5407 | 1.8433 | 1.8495 |
| Norway (Krone) | .1474 | .1480 | 6.7862 | 6.7584 |
| Pakistan (Rupee) | .0373 | .0373 | 26.81 | 26.81 |
| Peru (New Sol) | .5219 | .5233 | 1.92 | 1.91 |
| Philippines (Peso) | .03752 | .03752 | 26.65 | 26.65 |
| Poland (Zloty) | .00006202 | .00006196 | 16125.13 | 16140.00 |
| Portugal (Escudo) | .006508 | .006522 | 153.66 | 153.32 |
| Saudi Arabia (Riyal) | .26702 | .26702 | 3.7450 | 3.7450 |
| Singapore (Dollar) | .6218 | .6243 | 1.6005 | 1.6018 |
| Slovak Rep. (Koruna) | .0358809 | .0358809 | 27.87000 | 27.8700 |
| South Africa (Rand) | | | | |
| Commercial rate | .3141 | .3144 | 3.1838 | 3.1811 |
| Financial rate | .2162 | .2165 | 4.6250 | 4.6200 |
| South Korea (Won) | .0012449 | .0012466 | 803.30 | 802.20 |
| Spain (Peseta) | .007984 | .007964 | 125.25 | 125.57 |
| Sweden (Krona) | .1388 | .1391 | 7.2059 | 7.1914 |
| Switzerland (Franc) | .7021 | .7030 | 1.4242 | 1.4225 |
| 30-Day Forward | .7009 | .7017 | 1.4268 | 1.4252 |
| 90-Day Forward | .6987 | .6996 | 1.4312 | 1.4294 |
| 180-Day Forward | .6965 | .6973 | 1.4358 | 1.4342 |
| Taiwan (Dollar) | .038685 | .038256 | 25.85 | 26.14 |
| Thailand (Baht) | .03981 | .03981 | 25.12 | 25.12 |
| Turkey (Lira) | .0001004 | .0001004 | 9956.00 | 9956.00 |
| United Arab (Dirham) | .2723 | .2723 | 3.6725 | 3.6725 |
| Uruguay (New Peso) | | | | |
| Financial | .251256 | .251256 | 3.98 | 3.98 |
| Venezuela (Bolivar) | | | | |
| Floating rate | .01155 | .01162 | 86.58 | 86.07 |
| SDR | 1.42658 | 1.43064 | .70098 | .6899 |
| ECU | 1.21940 | 1.22460 | | |

Special Drawing Rights (SDR) are based on exchange rates for the U.S., German, British, French and Japanese currencies. Source: International Monetary Fund.

European Currency Unit (ECU) is based on a basket of community currencies.

**FIGURE 22.2   Spot and Forward Exchange Rate Quotations**
On each business day the exchange rate between the U.S. dollar and other currencies is reported as a spot rate on either a floating or fixed-rate basis, depending on the currency. For major currencies, forward exchange rates are also reported. Source: *The Wall Street Journal*, June 3, 1993, p. C14.

or the currency to which they are pegged (i.e., they have very limited movements with respect to either the U.S. dollar or other currencies).

Finally, note the concept of changes in the value of a currency with respect to the U.S. dollar or another currency. For the floating currencies, changes in the value of foreign exchange rates are called *appreciation* or *depreciation*. For example, referring to Figure 22.2, it can be seen that the value of the French franc has depreciated from Ff 5.3725/US$ on Tuesday to Ff 5.3870/US$ on Wednesday. In other words, it takes more francs to buy one dollar. For the fixed currencies, changes in values are called official *revaluation* or *devaluation,* but these terms have the same meanings as *appreciation* and *depreciation,* respectively.

### Effect of Currency Fluctuations

Multinational companies face foreign exchange risks under both floating and fixed arrangements. The case of floating currencies can be used to illustrate these risks. Returning to the U.S. dollar-Swiss franc relationship, we note that the forces of international supply and demand as well as internal and external economic and political elements help to shape both the spot and forward rates between these two currencies. Because the MNC cannot control much (or most) of these "outside" elements, the company faces potential changes in exchange rates in the form of appreciation or depreciation. These changes can in turn affect the MNC's revenues, costs, and profits as measured in U.S. dollars. For currencies that are fixed in relation to each other, the risks come from the same set of elements indicated above. Again, these official changes, like the ones brought about by the market in the case of floating currencies, can affect the MNC's operations and its dollar-based financial position.

The risks stemming from changes in exchange rates can be illustrated by examining the balance sheet and income statement of MNC, Inc. We focus on its subsidiary in Switzerland.

▶ E X A M P L E

MNC, Inc., a multinational manufacturer of dental drills, has a subsidiary in Switzerland that at the end of 1995 had the financial statements shown in Table 22.4. The figures for the balance sheet and income statement are given in the local currency, Swiss franc (Sf). Using the foreign exchange rate of Sf 1.50/US$ for December 31, 1995, MNC has translated the statements into U.S. dollars. For simplicity it is assumed that all the local figures are expected to remain the same during 1996. As a result, as of January 1, 1996, the subsidiary expects to show the same Swiss franc figures on 12/31/96 as on 12/31/95. However, because of the change in the value of the Swiss franc relative to the dollar, from Sf 1.50/US$ to Sf 1.30/US$, the translated dollar values of the items on the balance sheet, along with the dollar profit value on 12/31/96, are higher than those of the previous year, the changes being due only to fluctuations in foreign exchange.

Additional complexities are attached to each individual account in the financial statements. For instance, it is important whether a subsidiary's debt is all in the local currency, in U.S. dollars, or in several currencies. Moreover, it is important which currency (or currencies) the revenues and costs are denominated in. The risks shown so far relate to what is called the **accounting exposure.** In other words, foreign exchange fluctuations affect individual accounts in the financial statements. A different, and perhaps more important, risk element concerns **economic exposure,** which is the potential effect of exchange rate fluctuations on the firm's value. Given that all future revenues and thus net profits can be subject to exchange rate changes, it is obvious that the *present value* of the net profits derived from foreign operations has, as a part of its total diversifiable risk, an element reflecting appreciation (revaluation) or depreciation (devaluation) of various currencies with respect to the U.S. dollar.

What can the management of MNCs do about these risks? The actions depend on the attitude of the management toward risk. This attitude, in turn, translates into how aggressively management wants to hedge (i.e., protect against) the company's undesirable positions and exposures. The money markets, the forward (futures) markets, and the foreign currency options markets can be used—either individually or in conjunction with one another—to hedge foreign exchange exposures. Further details on certain hedging strategies are described later.

**accounting exposure**
The risk resulting from the effects of changes in foreign exchange rates on the translated value of a firm's financial statement accounts denominated in a given foreign currency.

**economic exposure**
The risk resulting from the effects of changes in foreign exchange rates on the firm's value.

**TABLE 22.4   Financial Statements for MNC, Inc.'s, Swiss Subsidiary**

### Translation of Balance Sheet

| | 12/31/95 | | 12/31/96 |
|---|---|---|---|
| **Assets** | Sf | US$ | US$ |
| Cash | 8.00 | 5.33 | 6.15 |
| Inventory | 60.00 | 40.00 | 46.15 |
| Plant and equipment (net) | 32.00 | 21.33 | 24.61 |
| Total | 100.00 | 66.66 | 76.91 |

| **Liabilities and Stockholders' Equity** | | | |
|---|---|---|---|
| Debt | 48.00 | 32.00 | 36.92 |
| Paid-in capital | 40.00 | 26.66 | 30.76 |
| Retained earnings | 12.00 | 8.00 | 9.23 |
| Total | 100.00 | 66.66 | 76.91 |

### Translation of Income Statement

| | | | |
|---|---|---|---|
| Sales | 600.00 | 400.00 | 461.53 |
| Cost of goods sold | 550.00 | 366.66 | 423.07 |
| Operating profits | 50.00 | 33.34 | 38.46 |

*Note:* This example is simplified to show how the balance sheet and income statement are subject to exchange rate fluctuations. For the applicable rules on the translation of foreign accounts, review the discussion of international financial statements presented earlier.

**political risk**
The potential discontinuity or seizure of an MNC's operations in a host country due to the host's implementation of specific rules and regulations (such as nationalization, expropriation, or confiscation).

**macro political risk**
The subjection of *all* foreign firms to political risk (takeover) by a host country because of political change, revolution, or the adoption of new policies.

## Political Risks

Another important risk facing MNCs is political risk. **Political risk** refers to the implementation by a host government of specific rules and regulations that can result in the discontinuity or seizure of the operations of a foreign company in that country. Political risk is usually manifested in the form of nationalization, expropriation, or confiscation. In general, the assets and operations of a foreign firm are taken over by the host government, usually without proper (or any) compensation.

Political risk has two basic paths: *macro* and *micro*. **Macro political risk** means that because of political change, revolution, or the adoption of new policies by a host government, *all* foreign firms in the country are subjected to political risk. In other words, no individual country or firm is treated differently; all assets and operations of foreign firms are taken over wholesale. An example of macro political risk is China in 1949 or Cuba in 1959–1960. **Micro political risk,** on the other hand, refers to the case in which an individual firm, a specific industry, or companies from a particular foreign country are subjected to takeover. Examples include the nationalization by a majority of the oil-exporting countries of the assets of the international oil companies in their territories.

Although political risk can take place in any country—even in the United States—political instability in developing nations generally makes the positions of multinational companies most vulnerable there. At the same time, some of the countries in this group have the most promising markets for the goods and services being offered by MNCs. The main question, therefore, is how to engage in operations and foreign investment in such countries and yet avoid or minimize the potential political risk.

Table 22.5 shows some of the approaches that MNCs may be able to adopt to cope with political risk. The negative approaches are generally used by firms in extractive industries. The external approaches are also of limited use. The best policies MNCs can follow are the positive approaches, which have both economic and political aspects.

In recent years, MNCs have been relying on a variety of complex forecasting techniques whereby "international experts," using available historical data, predict the chances for political instability in a host country and the po-

**micro political risk**
The subjection of an individual firm, a specific industry, or companies from a particular foreign country to political risk (takeover) by a host country.

### TABLE 22.5   Approaches for Coping with Political Risks

| Positive Approaches | | Negative Approaches |
|---|---|---|
| Prior negotiation of controls and operating contracts | | License or patent restrictions under international agreements |
| Prior agreement for sale | Direct | |
| Joint venture with government or local private sector | | Control of external raw materials |
| Use of locals in management | | Control of transportation to (external) markets |
| Joint venture with local banks | | Control of downstream processing |
| Equity participation by middle class | Indirect | |
| Local sourcing | | Control of external markets |
| Local retail outlets | | |

**External Approaches to Minimize Loss**

International insurance or investment guarantees
Thinly capitalized firms:
   Local financing
   External financing secured only by the local operation

Source: Rita M. Rodriguez and E. Eugene Carter, *International Financial Management,* 3rd ed. Englewood Cliffs, NJ: Prentice-Hall, 1984, p. 512.

tential effects on MNC operations. Events in Iraq and the former Yugoslavia, among others, however, point to the limited use of such techniques and tend to reinforce the usefulness of the positive approaches.

A final point relates to the introduction by most "host" governments in the last two decades of comprehensive sets of rules, regulations, and incentives. Known as **national entry control systems,** they are aimed at regulating inflows of *foreign direct investments* involving MNCs. They are designed to extract more benefits from MNCs' presence by regulating such flows in terms of a variety of factors—local ownership, level of exportation, use of local inputs, number of local managers, internal geographic location, level of local borrowing, and the respective percentages of profits to be remitted and of capital to be repatriated back to parent firms. Host countries expect that as MNCs comply with these regulations, the potential for acts of political risk will decline, thus benefiting MNCs as well.

**national entry control systems**
Comprehensive rules, regulations, and incentives introduced by most "host" governments, and aimed at regulating inflows of *foreign direct investments* involving MNCs and at the same time extracting more benefits from their presence.

▼▼▼▼▼▼▼▼▼▼▼▼▼▼▼▼▼▼▼▼▼▼▼▼▼▼▼▼▼▼

## Progress Review Questions

**22-9.** Define *spot* and *forward exchange rates.* Define and compare *accounting exposures* and *economic exposures* to exchange rate fluctuations.

**22-10.** Discuss *macro* and *micro political risk.* Describe some techniques for dealing with political risk.

▲▲▲▲▲▲▲▲▲▲▲▲▲▲▲▲▲▲▲▲▲▲▲▲▲▲▲▲▲▲

LG  5

# Long-Term Investment and Financing Decisions

Important long-term aspects of international managerial finance include foreign direct investment, investment cash flows and decisions, capital structure, long-term debt, and equity capital. Here we briefly consider the international dimensions of each of these topics.

## Foreign Direct Investment

**foreign direct investment (FDI)**
The transfer, by a multinational firm, of capital, managerial, and technical assets from its home country to a host country.

**Foreign direct investment (FDI)** is the transfer by a multinational firm of capital, managerial, and technical assets from its home country to a host country. The equity participation on the part of an MNC can be 100 percent (resulting in a wholly owned foreign subsidiary) or less (leading to a joint-venture project with foreign participants). In contrast to short-term, foreign portfolio investments undertaken by individuals and companies (e.g., internationally diversified mutual funds), FDI involves equity participation, managerial control, and day-to-day operational activities on the part of MNCs. Therefore FDI projects are subject not only to business, financial, inflation, and foreign exchange risks (as are foreign portfolio investments) but also to the additional element of political risk.

For a number of decades, U.S.-based MNCs had dominated the international scene in terms of both the *flow* and *stock* of FDI. The total FDI stock of

U.S.-based MNCs, for instance, increased from $7.7 billion in 1929 to over $450.2 billion at the end of 1991. Since the 1970s, though, their global presence is being challenged by MNCs based in Western Europe, Japan, and other developed and developing nations. In fact, even the "home" market of U.S. multinationals is being challenged by foreign firms. For instance, in 1960, FDI into the United States amounted to only 11.5 percent of U.S. investment overseas. By the end of 1991, the *book value* of FDI into the Untied States, at US $407.6 billion, was almost as large as the comparable figure of US$450.2 billion, for U.S. FDI abroad. However, the *market value* of U.S. FDI, at US$802 billion, still exceeded that of FDI into the United States at US$654, by a substantial margin at year-end 1991.

## Investment Cash Flows and Decisions

Measuring the amount invested in a foreign project, its resulting cash flows, and the associated risk is difficult. The returns and net present values (NPVs) of such investments can vary significantly from the subsidiary's and parent's point of view. Therefore several factors unique to the international setting need to be examined in making long-term investment decisions.

First, elements relating to a parent company's *investment* in a subsidiary and the concept of taxes must be considered. For example, in the case of manufacturing investments, questions may arise about the value of the equipment a parent may contribute to the subsidiary. Is the value based on the market conditions in the parent country or the local host economy? In general, the market value in the host country is the relevant "price."

The existence of different taxes—as was pointed out earlier—can complicate measurement of the *cash flows* to be received by the parent, because different definitions of taxable income can arise. Other complications still arise when measuring the actual cash flows. From a parent firm's viewpoint the cash flows are those that are repatriated from the subsidiary. In some countries, however, such cash flows may be totally or partially blocked. Obviously, depending on the life of the project in the host country, the returns and NPVs associated with such projects can vary significantly from the subsidiary's and the parent's point of view. For instance, for a project of only five years' duration, if all yearly cash flows are blocked by the host government, the subsidiary may show a "normal" or even superior return and NPV, although the parent may show no return at all. On the other hand, for a project of longer life, even if cash flows are blocked for the first few years, the remaining years' cash flows can contribute toward the parent's returns and NPV.

Finally, the issue of *risk* attached to international cash flows arises. The three basic types of risk categories are (1) business and financial risks, (2) inflation and exchange rate risks, and (3) political risks. The first category relates to the type of industry the subsidiary is in as well as its financial structure (more details on financial risks are presented later). As for the other two categories, we have already discussed both the risks of having investments, profits, and assets and liabilities in different currencies and the potential effects of political risks and how MNCs can combat them.

Here it is important to note that the presence of such risks influences the discount rate (or the cost of capital) to be used in evaluating international cash flows. The basic rule, however, is that the *local cost of equity capital* (applicable to the local business and financial environments within which a subsidiary operates) is the starting discount rate to which risks stemming from exchange rate and political factors can be added and from which benefits reflecting the parent's lower capital costs may be subtracted.

## Capital Structure

Both theory and empirical evidence indicate that the capital structures of multinational companies differ from those of purely domestic firms. Furthermore, differences are also observed among the capital structures of MNCs domiciled in various countries. Several factors tend to influence the capital structures of MNCs. Each is briefly discussed here.

**International Capital Markets**   MNCs, unlike smaller size domestic firms, have access to the Euromarket (discussed earlier) and the variety of financial instruments available there (to be described later). Because of their access to the international bond and equity markets, MNCs may have lower costs of various sources of long-term financing, thus resulting in differences between the capital structures of these firms and those of purely domestic companies. Similarly, MNCs based in different countries and regions, such as those domiciled in the United States, Western Europe, and Japan, may have access to different currencies and markets, resulting in variances in capital structures for these multinationals.

**International Diversification**   It is well established that MNCs, in contrast to domestic firms, can achieve further risk reduction in their cash flows by diversifying internationally. International diversification, in turn, may lead to varying degrees of debt versus equity. Empirically, the evidence on debt ratios is mixed. Some studies have found MNCs' debt proportions to be higher than those of domestic firms. Other studies have concluded the opposite, citing imperfections in certain foreign markets, political risk factors, and complexities in the international financial environment that cause higher costs of debt for MNCs.

**Country Factors**   A number of studies have concluded that certain factors unique to each host country, including legal, tax, political, social, and financial aspects, as well as the overall relationship between the public and private sectors can cause differences in capital structures. Due to these factors, differences have been found not only among MNCs based in various countries but among the foreign affiliates of an MNC as well. However, because no one capital structure is ideal for all MNCs, each multinational has to consider a set of global and domestic factors in deciding on the appropriate capital structure for both the overall corporation and its subsidiaries.

## Long-Term Debt

As noted earlier, multinational companies, in conducting their global operations, have access to a variety of international financial instruments. International bonds are among the most widely used, so we begin by focusing on them. Next, we discuss the role of international financial institutions in underwriting such instruments. Finally, we consider the use of various techniques (such as swaps) by MNCs to change the structure of their long-term debt.

# FINANCE IN ACTION

International

## The Contemporary Polish Stock Market Is No Joke

In 1993, novice investor Lukasz Zuk placed $10,000 into stocks traded on the local Warsaw exchange, and one year later his investment was worth $150,000. In the last year, Warsaw's 22-share stock market index has risen nearly 800 percent in U.S. dollar terms, beating emergent equities markets in Brazil, Thailand, and Turkey.

Rapidly developing economies throughout Eastern Europe are fueling significant gains within the continent's fledgling stock markets. Equities exchanges in the Czech Republic, Hungary, and Poland are reaching critical mass as local businesses unable to obtain debt financing from local banks turn to new equity issues. As share prices in these new publicly traded companies rise along with profits and cash flows, more money flows into the local economy, accelerating privatization and prompting even greater investment in local stocks.

And foreign money managers are starting to take notice, too. Boston's Pioneer Group, Inc., recently established a $400 million open-end mutual fund, First Polish Trust, invested in Polish equities. Encouraged by the success of this fund, Pioneer has added Polish stocks to two of its U.S.-based mutual funds, and the firm has plans for a $75 million Polish venture-capital fund in 1994. The growth in Poland's economy is expected to continue for several years, as gross domestic product is forecast to advance by 4 to 7 percent annually for the next five years. When it comes to international investment opportunities, contemporary Poland is very serious business.

Source: G. Schares, "Go East, Young Man—and Buy Stocks," *Business Week*, January 17, 1994, p. 44.

**International Bonds**   In general, an **international bond** is one that is initially sold outside the country of the borrower and often distributed in several countries. When a bond is sold primarily in the country of the currency of the issue, it is called a **foreign bond.** For example, an MNC based in West Germany might float a bond issue in the French capital market underwritten by a French syndicate and denominated in French francs. When an international bond is sold primarily in countries other than the country of the currency in which the issue is denominated, it is called a **Eurobond.** Thus an MNC based in the United States might float a Eurobond in several European capital markets, underwritten by an international syndicate and denominated in U.S. dollars.

The U.S. dollar continues to dominate the Eurobond issues, with the Japanese yen gaining popularity. The importance of the U.S. currency in all aspects of international transactions, and thus its importance to MNCs, can explain this continued dominance. In the foreign bond category the Swiss franc continues to be the major choice. Low interest rates, the general stability of the currency, and the overall efficiency of the Swiss capital markets are among the primary reasons for the ongoing popularity of the Swiss franc. However, Eurobonds are much more widely used than foreign bonds. These

**international bond**
A bond that is initially sold outside the country of the borrower and often distributed in several countries.

**foreign bond**
An international bond that is sold primarily in the country of the currency of the issue.

**Eurobond**
An international bond that is sold primarily in countries other than the country of the currency in which the issue is denominated.

instruments are heavily used, especially in relation to Eurocurrency loans in recent years, by major market participants, including U.S. corporations. These so-called equity-linked Eurobonds (i.e., convertible to equity), especially those offered by a number of U.S. firms, have found strong demand among Euromarket participants. It is expected that more of these innovative types of instruments will emerge on the international scene in the coming years.

A final point concerns the levels of interest rates in international markets. In the case of foreign bonds, interest rates are usually directly correlated with the domestic rates prevailing in the respective countries. For Eurobonds several interest rates may be influential. For instance, for a Eurodollar bond, the interest rate reflects several different rates, most notably the U.S. long-term rate, the Eurodollar rate, and long-term rates in other countries.

### The Role of International Financial Institutions

For *foreign bonds* the underwriting institutions are those that handle bond issues in the respective countries in which such bonds are issued. For *Eurobonds* a number of financial institutions in the United States, Western Europe, and Japan form international underwriting syndicates. The underwriting costs for Eurobonds are comparable to those for bond flotation in the U.S. domestic market. Although U.S. institutions used to dominate the Eurobond scene, recent economic and financial strengths exhibited by some Western European (especially German) and Japanese financial firms have led to a change in that dominance. Since 1986 a number of European and Japanese firms have held the top positions in terms of acting as lead underwriters of Eurobond issues. However, U.S. investment banks continue to dominate most other international security issuance markets—such as international equity, medium-term note, syndicated loan, and commercial paper markets—and U.S. corporations accounted for almost two-thirds of the $1.5 trillion in worldwide securities issues in 1993.

To raise funds through international bond issues, many MNCs establish their own financial subsidiaries. Many U.S.-based MNCs, for example, have created subsidiaries in the United States and Western Europe, especially in Luxembourg. Such subsidiaries can be used to raise large amounts of funds in "one move," the funds being redistributed wherever MNCs need them. (Special tax rules applicable to such subsidiaries also make them desirable to MNCs.)

### Changing the Structure of Debt

As noted in a subsequent discussion, MNCs can use *hedging strategies* to change the structure or characteristics of their long-term assets and liabilities. For instance, multinationals can utilize *interest rate swaps* to obtain a desired stream of interest payments (e.g., fixed-rate) in exchange for another (e.g., floating-rate) and use *currency swaps* to exchange an asset or liability denominated in one currency (e.g., U.S. dollar) for another (e.g., Swiss franc). The use of these tools allows MNCs to gain access to a broader set of markets, currencies, and maturities, thus leading to both cost savings and a means of restructuring their existing assets or liabilities. Such use has experienced significant growth during the last few years, and this trend is expected to continue.

## Equity Capital

Here we look at how multinational companies can raise equity capital abroad. First, they can sell their shares in international capital markets. Second, they can use join ventures, which are sometimes required by the host country. We also consider the role of equity (versus debt) in the MNCs' foreign direct investment in international joint ventures.

**Equity Issues and Markets**   One means of raising equity funds for MNCs is to have the parent's stock distributed internationally and owned by stockholders of different nationalities. In the 1980s the world's equity markets became more "internationalized" (i.e., becoming more standardized and thus closer in character to the Eurobond market discussed earlier). In other words, although distinct *national* stock markets (such as New York, London, and Tokyo) continue to exist and grow, an *international* stock market has also emerged on the global financial scene.

In recent years the terms **Euroequity market** and "Euroequities" have become widely known. Although a number of capital markets—including New York, Tokyo, Frankfurt, Zurich, and Paris—play major roles by being hosts to international equity issues, London has become *the* center of Euroequity activity. For the year 1993, for instance, the *new issue* volume was close to $28 billion and included 388 offerings. As in most recent years, a large part of this issue volume represented government sales of state-owned firms to private investors, referred to as *share-issue privatizations*.

As the time for the full financial integration of the EC approaches, some European stock exchanges continue to compete with each other. Others have called for more cooperation in forming a single market capable of competing with New York and Tokyo. From the multinationals' perspective the most desirable outcome would be to have uniform international rules and regulations with respect to all the major national stock exchanges. Such uniformity would allow MNCs to have unrestricted access to an international equity market paralleling that of the international currency and bond markets.

**Euroequity market**
The capital market around the world that deals in international equity issues; London has become the center of Euroequity activity.

**Joint Ventures**   The basic aspects of foreign ownership of international operations were discussed earlier. Worth emphasizing here is that certain laws and regulations enacted during the 1960s and 1970s by a number of host countries required MNCs to maintain less than 50 percent ownership in their subsidiaries in most of those countries. For a U.S.-based MNC, for example, establishing foreign subsidiaries in the form of joint ventures means that a certain portion of the firm's total international equity stock is (indirectly) held by foreign owners.

Some of the advantages and disadvantages of joint ventures were previously highlighted. In establishing a foreign subsidiary an MNC may wish to have as little equity and as much debt as possible, the debt coming from local sources in the host country or the MNC itself. Each of these actions can be supported. The host country may allow *more local debt* for a subsidiary; this is a good protective measure in terms of lessening the potential effects of political risk. In other words, because local sources are involved in the capital structure of a subsidiary, fewer threats may arise from local authorities in the event of changes in government or the enactment of new regulations on foreign business.

In support of the other action—having *more MNC-based debt* in a subsidiary's capital structure—it is true that many host governments are less restrictive, in terms of taxation and actual repatriation, toward intra-MNC interest payments than toward intra-MNC dividend remittances. The parent firm may therefore be in a better position if it has more MNC-based debt than equity in the capital structure of its subsidiaries.

▼▼▼▼▼▼▼▼▼▼▼▼▼▼▼▼▼▼▼▼▼▼▼▼▼▼▼▼

# Progress Review Questions

**22-11.** Indicate how net present value (NPV) can differ if measured from the parent MNC's point of view or from that of the foreign subsidiary when cash flows may be blocked by local authorities.

**22-12.** Briefly discuss some of the international factors that cause the capital structures of MNCs to differ from those of purely domestic firms.

**22-13.** Describe the difference between *foreign bonds* and *Eurobonds*. Explain how each is sold, and discuss the determinant(s) of their interest rates.

**22-14.** What are the long-run advantages of having more *local* debt and less MNC-based equity in the capital structure of a foreign subsidiary?

▲▲▲▲▲▲▲▲▲▲▲▲▲▲▲▲▲▲▲▲▲▲▲▲▲▲▲▲

LG 6

# Mergers and Joint Ventures

The motives for domestic mergers—growth or diversification, synergy, fund raising, increased managerial skill or technology, tax considerations, increased ownership liquidity, and defense against takeover—are all applicable to MNCs' international mergers and joint ventures. Several points, nevertheless, need attention.

First, international mergers and joint ventures, especially those involving European firms acquiring assets in the United States, increased significantly beginning in the 1980s. MNCs based in Western Europe, Japan, and North America have made substantial contributions to this increase. Moreover, a fast-growing group of MNCs has emerged in the past two decades, based in the so-called newly industrializing countries (which include, among others, Brazil, Argentina, Mexico, Hong Kong, Singapore, South Korea, Taiwan, India, and Pakistan). This growth has added further to the number and value of international mergers.

Foreign direct investments (i.e., *new* investments or *mergers* or both, on the basis of either wholly owned or joint ventures) in the United States have gained popularity in the past few years. Most of the foreign direct investors in the United States come from seven countries: Britain, Canada, France, the Netherlands, Japan, Switzerland, and Germany. The heaviest investments are concentrated in manufacturing, followed by the petroleum, and trade and service sectors. Another interesting trend is the current rise in the number of joint ventures between companies based in Japan and firms domiciled elsewhere in the industrialized world, especially U.S.-based MNCs. While Japanese authorities continue their discussions and debates with other governments regarding Japan's international trade surpluses as well as perceived trade barriers, mergers and joint ventures continue to take place. In the eyes of some U.S. corporate executives, such business ventures are viewed as a "ticket into the Japanese market" as well as a way to curb a potentially tough competitor.

Developing countries, too, have been attracting foreign direct investments in both horizontal and vertical industries. Meanwhile, during the last two decades a number of these nations have adopted specific policies and regulations aimed at controlling the inflows of foreign investments, a major provision being the 49 percent ownership limitation applied to MNCs. Of course, international competition among differently based MNCs has been of benefit to some developing countries in their attempts to extract concessions from the multinationals. However, an increasing number of such nations have shown greater flexibility in their recent dealings with MNCs as the latter group has become more reluctant to form joint ventures under the stated conditions. Furthermore, given the present, as well as the expected, international economic and trade status, it is likely that as more developing countries recognize the need for foreign capital and technology, they will show even greater flexibility in their agreements with MNCs.

A final point relates to the existence of international *holding companies*. Places such as Liechtenstein and Bermuda have long been considered favorable spots for forming holding companies because of their conducive legal, corporate, and tax environments. International holding companies control many business entities in the form of subsidiaries, branches, joint ventures, and other agreements. For international legal (especially tax-related) reasons, as well as anonymity, such holding companies have become increasingly popular in recent years.

## Progress Review Question

**22-15.** What are some of the major reasons for the rapid expansion in international business mergers and joint ventures of firms?

# SUMMARY OF LEARNING GOALS

**Understand the major factors influencing the financial operations of multinational companies (MNCs).** The emergence of new trading blocs, especially in North America and Western Europe, will result in new challenges and opportunities for MNCs. Setting up operations in foreign countries can entail special problems due to, among other things, the legal form of business organization chosen, the degree of ownership allowed by the host country, and possible restrictions and regulations on the return of capital and profits. The existence and expansion of dollars held outside the United States have contributed in recent years to the development of a major international financial market, the Euromarket. The large international banks, developing and industrialized nations, and multinational companies participate as borrowers and lenders in this market. Taxation of multinational companies is a complex issue because of the existence of varying tax rates, differing definitions of taxable income, measurement differences, and tax treaties. For U.S. MNCs it may be possible to take foreign taxes as a direct credit against U.S. tax liabilities.

LG 1

LG **2**
**Describe the key differences between purely domestic and international financial statements—particularly consolidation, translation of individual accounts, and international profits.** Certain regulations that apply to international operations tend to complicate the preparation of foreign-based financial statements. Rules in the United States require the consolidation of financial statements of subsidiaries according to the percentage of ownership by the parent in the subsidiary. Individual accounts of subsidiaries must be translated back into U.S. dollars by using the procedures outlined in FASB No. 52. This standard also requires that only certain transactional gains or losses from international operations be included in the U.S. parent's income statement.

LG **3**
**Review the basics of cash management, credit and inventory management, and the use of the Eurocurrency market in short-term borrowing and investing (lending) in international operations.** In international cash management, multinational companies can respond to foreign exchange risks by hedging (protecting) their undesirable exposures of cash and marketable securities or by making certain adjustments in their operations—specifically assets and liabilities. MNCs must offer competitive credit terms and maintain adequate inventories to provide timely delivery to foreign buyers. Obtaining the backing of foreign governments is helpful to the MNC in effectively managing credit and inventory. Eurocurrency markets allow multinationals to take advantage of unregulated financial markets to invest (lend) and raise (borrow) short-term funds in a variety of currencies and to protect themselves against foreign exchange risk exposures. The effective rates of interest, which take into account each country's forecasted percentage change relative to the MNC parent's currency, are the main items considered by an MNC in making investment and borrowing decisions. The MNC invests in the currency with the highest effective rate and borrows in the currency with the lowest effective rate.

LG **4**
**Discuss the two risks—exchange rate and political—requiring special consideration by the multinational company, and explain how MNCs manage them.** Operating in international markets involves certain factors that can influence the risk and return characteristics of an MNC. Economic exposure from exchange rate risk results from the existence of different currencies and the potential effect they can have on the value of foreign operations. The money markets, the forward (futures) markets, and the foreign currency options markets can be used to hedge (i.e., protect against) foreign exchange exposure. Political risks stem mainly from political instability in a number of countries and from the associated implications for the assets and operations of MNCs with subsidiaries located in such countries. MNCs can employ negative, external, and positive approaches to cope with political risk.

LG **5**
**Describe foreign direct investment, investment cash flows and decisions, the factors that influence an MNC's capital structure, and the international debt and equity instruments that are available to MNCs.** Foreign direct investment (FDI) involves an MNC's transfer of capital, managerial, and technical assets from its home country to the host country. The investment cash flows of FDIs are subject to a variety of factors, including local taxes in host countries, host-country regulations that may block the return (repatriation) of MNCs' cash flow, the usual business and financial risks, risks stemming

from inflation and different currency and political actions by host governments, and the application of a local cost of capital. The capital structures
of MNCs differ from those of purely domestic firms because of the MNCs'
access to the Euromarket and the variety of financial instruments it offers;
the ability to reduce risk in their cash flows through international diversification; and the effect of legal, tax, political, social, and financial factors
unique to each host country. International capital markets provide MNCs
with an opportunity to raise long-term debt through the issuance of international bonds in various currencies. Foreign bonds are sold primarily in
the country of the currency of issue; Eurobonds are sold primarily in countries other than the country of the currency in which the issue is denominated. MNCs can raise equity through the sale of their shares in the international capital markets or through joint ventures. In establishing foreign
subsidiaries it may be more advantageous to issue debt (either local or
MNC-based) than MNC-owned equity.

**Explain the growth of and special factors relating to international mergers
and joint ventures.** International mergers and joint ventures, including international holding companies, increased significantly beginning in the
1980s. Special factors affecting these mergers relate to various regulations
imposed on MNCs by host countries and economic and trade conditions.

LG    6

# Appendix A

# Financial Tables

**Table A.1**  Future-Value Interest Factors for One Dollar Compounded at $k$ Percent for $n$ Periods:

$$FVIF_{k,n} = (1 + k)^n$$

**Table A.2**  Future-Value Interest Factors for a One-Dollar Annuity Compounded at $k$ Percent for $n$ Periods:

$$FVIFA_{k,n} = \sum_{t=1}^{n} (1 + k)^{t-1}$$

**Table A.3**  Present-Value Interest Factors for One Dollar Discounted at $k$ Percent for $n$ Periods:

$$PVIF_{k,n} = \frac{1}{(1 + k)^n}$$

**Table A.4**  Present-Value Interest Factors for a One-Dollar Annuity Discounted at $k$ Percent for $n$ Periods:

$$PVIFA_{k,n} = \sum_{t=1}^{n} \frac{1}{(1 + k)^t}$$

**TABLE A.1    Future-Value Interest Factors for One Dollar Compounded at $k$ Percent for $n$ Periods: $FVIF_{k,n} = (1 + k)^n$**

| Period | 1% | 2% | 3% | 4% | 5% | 6% | 7% | 8% | 9% | 10% | 11% | 12% | 13% | 14% | 15% | 16% | 17% | 18% | 19% | 20% |
|---|---|---|---|---|---|---|---|---|---|---|---|---|---|---|---|---|---|---|---|---|
| 1 | 1.010 | 1.020 | 1.030 | 1.040 | 1.050 | 1.060 | 1.070 | 1.080 | 1.090 | 1.100 | 1.110 | 1.120 | 1.130 | 1.140 | 1.150 | 1.160 | 1.170 | 1.180 | 1.190 | 1.200 |
| 2 | 1.020 | 1.040 | 1.061 | 1.082 | 1.102 | 1.124 | 1.145 | 1.166 | 1.188 | 1.210 | 1.232 | 1.254 | 1.277 | 1.300 | 1.322 | 1.346 | 1.369 | 1.392 | 1.416 | 1.440 |
| 3 | 1.030 | 1.061 | 1.093 | 1.125 | 1.158 | 1.191 | 1.225 | 1.260 | 1.295 | 1.331 | 1.368 | 1.405 | 1.443 | 1.482 | 1.521 | 1.561 | 1.602 | 1.643 | 1.685 | 1.728 |
| 4 | 1.041 | 1.082 | 1.126 | 1.170 | 1.216 | 1.262 | 1.311 | 1.360 | 1.412 | 1.464 | 1.518 | 1.574 | 1.630 | 1.689 | 1.749 | 1.811 | 1.874 | 1.939 | 2.005 | 2.074 |
| 5 | 1.051 | 1.104 | 1.159 | 1.217 | 1.276 | 1.338 | 1.403 | 1.469 | 1.539 | 1.611 | 1.685 | 1.762 | 1.842 | 1.925 | 2.011 | 2.100 | 2.192 | 2.288 | 2.386 | 2.488 |
| 6 | 1.062 | 1.126 | 1.194 | 1.265 | 1.340 | 1.419 | 1.501 | 1.587 | 1.677 | 1.772 | 1.870 | 1.974 | 2.082 | 2.195 | 2.313 | 2.436 | 2.565 | 2.700 | 2.840 | 2.986 |
| 7 | 1.072 | 1.149 | 1.230 | 1.316 | 1.407 | 1.504 | 1.606 | 1.714 | 1.828 | 1.949 | 2.076 | 2.211 | 2.353 | 2.502 | 2.660 | 2.826 | 3.001 | 3.185 | 3.379 | 3.583 |
| 8 | 1.083 | 1.172 | 1.267 | 1.369 | 1.477 | 1.594 | 1.718 | 1.851 | 1.993 | 2.144 | 2.305 | 2.476 | 2.658 | 2.853 | 3.059 | 3.278 | 3.511 | 3.759 | 4.021 | 4.300 |
| 9 | 1.094 | 1.195 | 1.305 | 1.423 | 1.551 | 1.689 | 1.838 | 1.999 | 2.172 | 2.358 | 2.558 | 2.773 | 3.004 | 3.252 | 3.518 | 3.803 | 4.108 | 4.435 | 4.785 | 5.160 |
| 10 | 1.105 | 1.219 | 1.344 | 1.480 | 1.629 | 1.791 | 1.967 | 2.159 | 2.367 | 2.594 | 2.839 | 3.106 | 3.395 | 3.707 | 4.046 | 4.411 | 4.807 | 5.234 | 5.695 | 6.192 |
| 11 | 1.116 | 1.243 | 1.384 | 1.539 | 1.710 | 1.898 | 2.105 | 2.332 | 2.580 | 2.853 | 3.152 | 3.479 | 3.836 | 4.226 | 4.652 | 5.117 | 5.624 | 6.176 | 6.777 | 7.430 |
| 12 | 1.127 | 1.268 | 1.426 | 1.601 | 1.796 | 2.012 | 2.252 | 2.518 | 2.813 | 3.138 | 3.498 | 3.896 | 4.334 | 4.818 | 5.350 | 5.936 | 6.580 | 7.288 | 8.064 | 8.916 |
| 13 | 1.138 | 1.294 | 1.469 | 1.665 | 1.886 | 2.133 | 2.410 | 2.720 | 3.066 | 3.452 | 3.883 | 4.363 | 4.898 | 5.492 | 6.153 | 6.886 | 7.699 | 8.599 | 9.596 | 10.699 |
| 14 | 1.149 | 1.319 | 1.513 | 1.732 | 1.980 | 2.261 | 2.579 | 2.937 | 3.342 | 3.797 | 4.310 | 4.887 | 5.535 | 6.261 | 7.076 | 7.987 | 9.007 | 10.147 | 11.420 | 12.839 |
| 15 | 1.161 | 1.346 | 1.558 | 1.801 | 2.079 | 2.397 | 2.759 | 3.172 | 3.642 | 4.177 | 4.785 | 5.474 | 6.254 | 7.138 | 8.137 | 9.265 | 10.539 | 11.974 | 13.589 | 15.407 |
| 16 | 1.173 | 1.373 | 1.605 | 1.873 | 2.183 | 2.540 | 2.952 | 3.426 | 3.970 | 4.595 | 5.311 | 6.130 | 7.067 | 8.137 | 9.358 | 10.748 | 12.330 | 14.129 | 16.171 | 18.488 |
| 17 | 1.184 | 1.400 | 1.653 | 1.948 | 2.292 | 2.693 | 3.159 | 3.700 | 4.328 | 5.054 | 5.895 | 6.866 | 7.986 | 9.276 | 10.761 | 12.468 | 14.426 | 16.672 | 19.244 | 22.186 |
| 18 | 1.196 | 1.428 | 1.702 | 2.026 | 2.407 | 2.854 | 3.380 | 3.996 | 4.717 | 5.560 | 6.543 | 7.690 | 9.024 | 10.575 | 12.375 | 14.462 | 16.879 | 19.673 | 22.900 | 26.623 |
| 19 | 1.208 | 1.457 | 1.753 | 2.107 | 2.527 | 3.026 | 3.616 | 4.316 | 5.142 | 6.116 | 7.263 | 8.613 | 10.197 | 12.055 | 14.232 | 16.776 | 19.748 | 23.214 | 27.251 | 31.948 |
| 20 | 1.220 | 1.486 | 1.806 | 2.191 | 2.653 | 3.207 | 3.870 | 4.661 | 5.604 | 6.727 | 8.062 | 9.646 | 11.523 | 13.743 | 16.366 | 19.461 | 23.105 | 27.393 | 32.429 | 38.337 |
| 21 | 1.232 | 1.516 | 1.860 | 2.279 | 2.786 | 3.399 | 4.140 | 5.034 | 6.109 | 7.400 | 8.949 | 10.804 | 13.021 | 15.667 | 18.821 | 22.574 | 27.033 | 32.323 | 38.591 | 46.005 |
| 22 | 1.245 | 1.546 | 1.916 | 2.370 | 2.925 | 3.603 | 4.430 | 5.436 | 6.658 | 8.140 | 9.933 | 12.100 | 14.713 | 17.861 | 21.644 | 26.186 | 31.629 | 38.141 | 45.923 | 55.205 |
| 23 | 1.257 | 1.577 | 1.974 | 2.465 | 3.071 | 3.820 | 4.740 | 5.871 | 7.258 | 8.954 | 11.026 | 13.552 | 16.626 | 20.361 | 24.891 | 30.376 | 37.005 | 45.007 | 54.648 | 66.247 |
| 24 | 1.270 | 1.608 | 2.033 | 2.563 | 3.225 | 4.049 | 5.072 | 6.341 | 7.911 | 9.850 | 12.239 | 15.178 | 18.788 | 23.212 | 28.625 | 35.236 | 43.296 | 53.108 | 65.031 | 79.496 |
| 25 | 1.282 | 1.641 | 2.094 | 2.666 | 3.386 | 4.292 | 5.427 | 6.848 | 8.623 | 10.834 | 13.585 | 17.000 | 21.230 | 26.461 | 32.918 | 40.874 | 50.656 | 62.667 | 77.387 | 95.395 |
| 30 | 1.348 | 1.811 | 2.427 | 3.243 | 4.322 | 5.743 | 7.612 | 10.062 | 13.267 | 17.449 | 22.892 | 29.960 | 39.115 | 50.949 | 66.210 | 85.849 | 111.061 | 143.367 | 184.672 | 237.373 |
| 35 | 1.417 | 2.000 | 2.814 | 3.946 | 5.516 | 7.686 | 10.676 | 14.785 | 20.413 | 28.102 | 38.574 | 52.799 | 72.066 | 98.097 | 133.172 | 180.311 | 243.495 | 327.988 | 440.691 | 590.657 |
| 40 | 1.489 | 2.208 | 3.262 | 4.801 | 7.040 | 10.285 | 14.974 | 21.724 | 31.408 | 45.258 | 64.999 | 93.049 | 132.776 | 188.876 | 267.856 | 378.715 | 533.846 | 750.353 | 1051.642 | 1469.740 |
| 45 | 1.565 | 2.438 | 3.781 | 5.841 | 8.985 | 13.764 | 21.002 | 31.920 | 48.325 | 72.888 | 109.527 | 163.985 | 244.629 | 363.662 | 538.752 | 795.429 | 1170.425 | 1716.619 | 2509.583 | 3657.176 |
| 50 | 1.645 | 2.691 | 4.384 | 7.106 | 11.467 | 18.419 | 29.456 | 46.900 | 74.354 | 117.386 | 184.559 | 288.996 | 450.711 | 700.197 | 1083.619 | 1670.669 | 2566.080 | 3927.189 | 5988.730 | 9100.191 |

# Using the Calculator to Compute the Future Value of a Single Amount

**Before you begin,** make sure to clear the memory, ensure that you are in the correct mode, and set the number of decimal places you want (usually two for dollar-related accuracy).

## SAMPLE PROBLEM

You place $800 in a savings account at 6 percent interest compounded annually. What is your account balance at the end of five years?

### Hewlett-Packard HP 12C, 17 BII, and 19 BII[1]

**Inputs:**    800        5    6

**Functions:**    CHS    PV    n    i    FV

**Outputs:**    1070.58

---

[1]For the 17 BII and 19 BII use the +/− key instead of the CHS key, the N key instead of the n key, and the I% YR key instead of the i key.

| Period | 21% | 22% | 23% | 24% | 25% | 26% | 27% | 28% | 29% | 30% | 31% | 32% | 33% | 34% | 35% | 40% | 45% | 50% |
|---|---|---|---|---|---|---|---|---|---|---|---|---|---|---|---|---|---|---|
| 1 | 1.210 | 1.220 | 1.230 | 1.240 | 1.250 | 1.260 | 1.270 | 1.280 | 1.290 | 1.300 | 1.310 | 1.320 | 1.330 | 1.340 | 1.350 | 1.400 | 1.450 | 1.500 |
| 2 | 1.464 | 1.488 | 1.513 | 1.538 | 1.562 | 1.588 | 1.613 | 1.638 | 1.664 | 1.690 | 1.716 | 1.742 | 1.769 | 1.796 | 1.822 | 1.960 | 2.102 | 2.250 |
| 3 | 1.772 | 1.816 | 1.861 | 1.907 | 1.953 | 2.000 | 2.048 | 2.097 | 2.147 | 2.197 | 2.248 | 2.300 | 2.353 | 2.406 | 2.460 | 2.744 | 3.049 | 3.375 |
| 4 | 2.144 | 2.215 | 2.289 | 2.364 | 2.441 | 2.520 | 2.601 | 2.684 | 2.769 | 2.856 | 2.945 | 3.036 | 3.129 | 3.224 | 3.321 | 3.842 | 4.421 | 5.063 |
| 5 | 2.594 | 2.703 | 2.815 | 2.932 | 3.052 | 3.176 | 3.304 | 3.436 | 3.572 | 3.713 | 3.858 | 4.007 | 4.162 | 4.320 | 4.484 | 5.378 | 6.410 | 7.594 |
| 6 | 3.138 | 3.297 | 3.463 | 3.635 | 3.815 | 4.001 | 4.196 | 4.398 | 4.608 | 4.827 | 5.054 | 5.290 | 5.535 | 5.789 | 6.053 | 7.530 | 9.294 | 11.391 |
| 7 | 3.797 | 4.023 | 4.259 | 4.508 | 4.768 | 5.042 | 5.329 | 5.629 | 5.945 | 6.275 | 6.621 | 6.983 | 7.361 | 7.758 | 8.172 | 10.541 | 13.476 | 17.086 |
| 8 | 4.595 | 4.908 | 5.239 | 5.589 | 5.960 | 6.353 | 6.767 | 7.206 | 7.669 | 8.157 | 8.673 | 9.217 | 9.791 | 10.395 | 11.032 | 14.758 | 19.541 | 25.629 |
| 9 | 5.560 | 5.987 | 6.444 | 6.931 | 7.451 | 8.004 | 8.595 | 9.223 | 9.893 | 10.604 | 11.362 | 12.166 | 13.022 | 13.930 | 14.894 | 20.661 | 28.334 | 38.443 |
| 10 | 6.727 | 7.305 | 7.926 | 8.594 | 9.313 | 10.086 | 10.915 | 11.806 | 12.761 | 13.786 | 14.884 | 16.060 | 17.319 | 18.666 | 20.106 | 28.925 | 41.085 | 57.665 |
| 11 | 8.140 | 8.912 | 9.749 | 10.657 | 11.642 | 12.708 | 13.862 | 15.112 | 16.462 | 17.921 | 19.498 | 21.199 | 23.034 | 25.012 | 27.144 | 40.495 | 59.573 | 86.498 |
| 12 | 9.850 | 10.872 | 11.991 | 13.215 | 14.552 | 16.012 | 17.605 | 19.343 | 21.236 | 23.298 | 25.542 | 27.982 | 30.635 | 33.516 | 36.644 | 56.694 | 86.380 | 129.746 |
| 13 | 11.918 | 13.264 | 14.749 | 16.386 | 18.190 | 20.175 | 22.359 | 24.759 | 27.395 | 30.287 | 33.460 | 36.937 | 40.745 | 44.912 | 49.469 | 79.371 | 125.251 | 194.620 |
| 14 | 14.421 | 16.182 | 18.141 | 20.319 | 22.737 | 25.420 | 28.395 | 31.691 | 35.339 | 39.373 | 43.832 | 48.756 | 54.190 | 60.181 | 66.784 | 111.119 | 181.614 | 291.929 |
| 15 | 17.449 | 19.742 | 22.314 | 25.195 | 28.422 | 32.030 | 36.062 | 40.565 | 45.587 | 51.185 | 57.420 | 64.358 | 72.073 | 80.643 | 90.158 | 155.567 | 263.341 | 437.894 |
| 16 | 21.113 | 24.085 | 27.446 | 31.242 | 35.527 | 40.357 | 45.799 | 51.923 | 58.808 | 66.541 | 75.220 | 84.953 | 95.857 | 108.061 | 121.713 | 217.793 | 381.844 | 656.841 |
| 17 | 25.547 | 29.384 | 33.758 | 38.740 | 44.409 | 50.850 | 58.165 | 66.461 | 75.862 | 86.503 | 98.539 | 112.138 | 127.490 | 144.802 | 164.312 | 304.911 | 553.674 | 985.261 |
| 18 | 30.912 | 35.848 | 41.523 | 48.038 | 55.511 | 64.071 | 73.869 | 85.070 | 97.862 | 112.454 | 129.086 | 148.022 | 169.561 | 194.035 | 221.822 | 426.875 | 802.826 | 1477.892 |
| 19 | 37.404 | 43.735 | 51.073 | 59.567 | 69.389 | 80.730 | 93.813 | 108.890 | 126.242 | 146.190 | 169.102 | 195.389 | 225.517 | 260.006 | 299.459 | 597.625 | 1164.098 | 2216.838 |
| 20 | 45.258 | 53.357 | 62.820 | 73.863 | 86.736 | 101.720 | 119.143 | 139.379 | 162.852 | 190.047 | 221.523 | 257.913 | 299.937 | 348.408 | 404.270 | 836.674 | 1687.942 | 3325.257 |
| 21 | 54.762 | 65.095 | 77.268 | 91.591 | 108.420 | 128.167 | 151.312 | 178.405 | 210.079 | 247.061 | 290.196 | 340.446 | 398.916 | 466.867 | 545.764 | 1171.343 | 2447.515 | 4987.883 |
| 22 | 66.262 | 79.416 | 95.040 | 113.572 | 135.525 | 161.490 | 192.165 | 228.358 | 271.002 | 321.178 | 380.156 | 449.388 | 530.558 | 625.601 | 736.781 | 1639.878 | 3548.896 | 7481.824 |
| 23 | 80.178 | 96.887 | 116.899 | 140.829 | 169.407 | 203.477 | 244.050 | 292.298 | 349.592 | 417.531 | 498.004 | 593.192 | 705.642 | 838.305 | 994.653 | 2295.829 | 5145.898 | 11222.738 |
| 24 | 97.015 | 118.203 | 143.786 | 174.628 | 211.758 | 256.381 | 309.943 | 374.141 | 450.974 | 542.791 | 652.385 | 783.013 | 938.504 | 1123.328 | 1342.781 | 3214.158 | 7461.547 | 16834.109 |
| 25 | 117.388 | 144.207 | 176.857 | 216.539 | 264.698 | 323.040 | 393.628 | 478.901 | 581.756 | 705.627 | 854.623 | 1033.577 | 1248.210 | 1505.258 | 1812.754 | 4499.816 | 10819.242 | 25251.164 |
| 30 | 304.471 | 389.748 | 497.904 | 634.810 | 807.793 | 1025.904 | 1300.477 | 1645.488 | 2078.208 | 2619.936 | 3297.081 | 4142.008 | 5194.516 | 6503.285 | 8128.426 | 24201.043 | 69348.375 | 191751.000 |
| 35 | 789.716 | 1053.370 | 1401.749 | 1861.020 | 2465.189 | 3258.053 | 4296.547 | 5653.840 | 7423.988 | 9727.598 | 12719.918 | 16598.906 | 21617.363 | 28096.695 | 36448.051 | 130158.687 | * | * |
| 40 | 2048.309 | 2846.941 | 3946.340 | 5455.797 | 7523.156 | 10346.879 | 14195.051 | 19426.418 | 26520.723 | 36117.754 | 49072.621 | 66519.313 | 89962.188 | 121388.437 | 163433.875 | 700022.688 | * | * |
| 45 | 5312.758 | 7694.418 | 11110.121 | 15994.316 | 22958.844 | 32859.457 | 46897.973 | 66748.500 | 94739.937 | 134102.187 | * | * | * | * | * | * | * | * |
| 50 | 13779.844 | 20795.680 | 31278.301 | 46889.207 | 70064.812 | 104354.562 | 154942.687 | 229345.875 | 338440.000 | 497910.125 | * | * | * | * | * | * | * | * |

*Not shown due to space limitations.

## Texas Instruments BA-35, BAII, BAII Plus[2]

**Inputs:**   ( 800 )   ( 5 )   ( 6 )

**Functions:**   ( +/− )   ( PV )   ( N )   ( %i )   ( CPT )   ( FV )

**Outputs:**   ( 1070.58 )

[2]For the Texas Instruments BAII use the ( 2nd ) key instead of the ( CPT ) key; for the Texas Instruments BAII Plus you use the ( I/Y ) key instead of the ( %i ) key. When using the Texas Instruments BAII Plus, make sure that your calculator is set to *1 payment per year* ( I/Y ) *key* to work with annual compounding.

**TABLE A.2**   Future-Value Interest Factors for a One-Dollar Annuity Compounded at $k$ Percent for $n$ Periods: $FVIFA_{k,n} = \sum_{t=1}^{n} (1 + k)^{t-1}$

| Period | 1% | 2% | 3% | 4% | 5% | 6% | 7% | 8% | 9% | 10% | 11% | 12% | 13% | 14% | 15% | 16% | 17% | 18% | 19% | 20% |
|---|---|---|---|---|---|---|---|---|---|---|---|---|---|---|---|---|---|---|---|---|
| 1 | 1.000 | 1.000 | 1.000 | 1.000 | 1.000 | 1.000 | 1.000 | 1.000 | 1.000 | 1.000 | 1.000 | 1.000 | 1.000 | 1.000 | 1.000 | 1.000 | 1.000 | 1.000 | 1.000 | 1.000 |
| 2 | 2.010 | 2.020 | 2.030 | 2.040 | 2.050 | 2.060 | 2.070 | 2.080 | 2.090 | 2.100 | 2.110 | 2.120 | 2.130 | 2.140 | 2.150 | 2.160 | 2.170 | 2.180 | 2.190 | 2.200 |
| 3 | 3.030 | 3.060 | 3.091 | 3.122 | 3.152 | 3.184 | 3.215 | 3.246 | 3.278 | 3.310 | 3.342 | 3.374 | 3.407 | 3.440 | 3.472 | 3.506 | 3.539 | 3.572 | 3.606 | 3.640 |
| 4 | 4.060 | 4.122 | 4.184 | 4.246 | 4.310 | 4.375 | 4.440 | 4.506 | 4.573 | 4.641 | 4.710 | 4.779 | 4.850 | 4.921 | 4.993 | 5.066 | 5.141 | 5.215 | 5.291 | 5.368 |
| 5 | 5.101 | 5.204 | 5.309 | 5.416 | 5.526 | 5.637 | 5.751 | 5.867 | 5.985 | 6.105 | 6.228 | 6.353 | 6.480 | 6.610 | 6.742 | 6.877 | 7.014 | 7.154 | 7.297 | 7.442 |
| 6 | 6.152 | 6.308 | 6.468 | 6.633 | 6.802 | 6.975 | 7.153 | 7.336 | 7.523 | 7.716 | 7.913 | 8.115 | 8.323 | 8.535 | 8.754 | 8.977 | 9.207 | 9.442 | 9.683 | 9.930 |
| 7 | 7.214 | 7.434 | 7.662 | 7.898 | 8.142 | 8.394 | 8.654 | 8.923 | 9.200 | 9.487 | 9.783 | 10.089 | 10.405 | 10.730 | 11.067 | 11.414 | 11.772 | 12.141 | 12.523 | 12.916 |
| 8 | 8.286 | 8.583 | 8.892 | 9.214 | 9.549 | 9.897 | 10.260 | 10.637 | 11.028 | 11.436 | 11.859 | 12.300 | 12.757 | 13.233 | 13.727 | 14.240 | 14.773 | 15.327 | 15.902 | 16.499 |
| 9 | 9.368 | 9.755 | 10.159 | 10.583 | 11.027 | 11.491 | 11.978 | 12.488 | 13.021 | 13.579 | 14.164 | 14.776 | 15.416 | 16.085 | 16.786 | 17.518 | 18.285 | 19.086 | 19.923 | 20.799 |
| 10 | 10.462 | 10.950 | 11.464 | 12.006 | 12.578 | 13.181 | 13.816 | 14.487 | 15.193 | 15.937 | 16.722 | 17.549 | 18.420 | 19.337 | 20.304 | 21.321 | 22.393 | 23.521 | 24.709 | 25.959 |
| 11 | 11.567 | 12.169 | 12.808 | 13.486 | 14.207 | 14.972 | 15.784 | 16.645 | 17.560 | 18.531 | 19.561 | 20.655 | 21.814 | 23.044 | 24.349 | 25.733 | 27.200 | 28.755 | 30.403 | 32.150 |
| 12 | 12.682 | 13.412 | 14.192 | 15.026 | 15.917 | 16.870 | 17.888 | 18.977 | 20.141 | 21.384 | 22.713 | 24.133 | 25.650 | 27.271 | 29.001 | 30.850 | 32.824 | 34.931 | 37.180 | 39.580 |
| 13 | 13.809 | 14.680 | 15.618 | 16.627 | 17.713 | 18.882 | 20.141 | 21.495 | 22.953 | 24.523 | 26.211 | 28.029 | 29.984 | 32.088 | 34.352 | 36.786 | 39.404 | 42.218 | 45.244 | 48.496 |
| 14 | 14.947 | 15.974 | 17.086 | 18.292 | 19.598 | 21.015 | 22.550 | 24.215 | 26.019 | 27.975 | 30.095 | 32.392 | 34.882 | 37.581 | 40.504 | 43.672 | 47.102 | 50.818 | 54.841 | 59.196 |
| 15 | 16.097 | 17.293 | 18.599 | 20.023 | 21.578 | 23.276 | 25.129 | 27.152 | 29.361 | 31.772 | 34.405 | 37.280 | 40.417 | 43.842 | 47.580 | 51.659 | 56.109 | 60.965 | 66.260 | 72.035 |
| 16 | 17.258 | 18.639 | 20.157 | 21.824 | 23.657 | 25.672 | 27.888 | 30.324 | 33.003 | 35.949 | 39.190 | 42.753 | 46.671 | 50.980 | 55.717 | 60.925 | 66.648 | 72.938 | 79.850 | 87.442 |
| 17 | 18.430 | 20.012 | 21.761 | 23.697 | 25.840 | 28.213 | 30.840 | 33.750 | 36.973 | 40.544 | 44.500 | 48.883 | 53.738 | 59.117 | 65.075 | 71.673 | 78.978 | 87.067 | 96.021 | 105.930 |
| 18 | 19.614 | 21.412 | 23.414 | 25.645 | 28.132 | 30.905 | 33.999 | 37.450 | 41.301 | 45.599 | 50.396 | 55.749 | 61.724 | 68.393 | 75.836 | 84.140 | 93.404 | 103.739 | 115.265 | 128.116 |
| 19 | 20.811 | 22.840 | 25.117 | 27.671 | 30.539 | 33.760 | 37.379 | 41.446 | 46.018 | 51.158 | 56.939 | 63.439 | 70.748 | 78.968 | 88.211 | 98.603 | 110.283 | 123.412 | 138.165 | 154.739 |
| 20 | 22.019 | 24.297 | 26.870 | 29.778 | 33.066 | 36.785 | 40.995 | 45.762 | 51.159 | 57.274 | 64.202 | 72.052 | 80.946 | 91.024 | 102.443 | 115.379 | 130.031 | 146.626 | 165.417 | 186.687 |
| 21 | 23.239 | 25.783 | 28.676 | 31.969 | 35.719 | 39.992 | 44.865 | 50.422 | 56.764 | 64.002 | 72.264 | 81.698 | 92.468 | 104.767 | 118.809 | 134.840 | 153.136 | 174.019 | 197.846 | 225.024 |
| 22 | 24.471 | 27.299 | 30.536 | 34.248 | 38.505 | 43.392 | 49.005 | 55.456 | 62.872 | 71.402 | 81.213 | 92.502 | 105.489 | 120.434 | 137.630 | 157.414 | 180.169 | 206.342 | 236.436 | 271.028 |
| 23 | 25.716 | 28.845 | 32.452 | 36.618 | 41.430 | 46.995 | 53.435 | 60.893 | 69.531 | 79.542 | 91.147 | 104.602 | 120.203 | 138.295 | 159.274 | 183.600 | 211.798 | 244.483 | 282.359 | 326.234 |
| 24 | 26.973 | 30.421 | 34.426 | 39.082 | 44.501 | 50.815 | 58.176 | 66.764 | 76.789 | 88.496 | 102.173 | 118.154 | 136.829 | 158.656 | 184.166 | 213.976 | 248.803 | 289.490 | 337.007 | 392.480 |
| 25 | 28.243 | 32.030 | 36.459 | 41.645 | 47.726 | 54.864 | 63.248 | 73.105 | 84.699 | 98.346 | 114.412 | 133.333 | 155.616 | 181.867 | 212.790 | 249.212 | 292.099 | 342.598 | 402.038 | 471.976 |
| 30 | 34.784 | 40.567 | 47.575 | 56.084 | 66.438 | 79.057 | 94.459 | 113.282 | 136.305 | 164.491 | 199.018 | 241.330 | 293.192 | 356.778 | 434.738 | 530.306 | 647.423 | 790.932 | 966.698 | 1181.865 |
| 35 | 41.659 | 49.994 | 60.461 | 73.651 | 90.318 | 111.432 | 138.234 | 172.314 | 215.705 | 271.018 | 341.583 | 431.658 | 546.663 | 693.552 | 881.152 | 1120.699 | 1426.448 | 1816.607 | 2314.173 | 2948.294 |
| 40 | 48.885 | 60.401 | 75.400 | 95.024 | 120.797 | 154.758 | 199.630 | 259.052 | 337.872 | 442.580 | 581.812 | 767.080 | 1013.667 | 1341.979 | 1779.048 | 2360.724 | 3134.412 | 4163.094 | 5529.711 | 7343.715 |
| 45 | 56.479 | 71.891 | 92.718 | 121.027 | 159.695 | 212.737 | 285.741 | 386.497 | 525.840 | 718.881 | 986.613 | 1358.208 | 1874.086 | 2590.464 | 3585.031 | 4965.191 | 6879.008 | 9531.258 | 13203.105 | 18280.914 |
| 50 | 64.461 | 84.577 | 112.794 | 152.664 | 209.341 | 290.325 | 406.516 | 573.756 | 815.051 | 1163.865 | 1668.723 | 2399.975 | 3459.344 | 4994.301 | 7217.488 | 10435.449 | 15088.805 | 21812.273 | 31514.492 | 45496.094 |

# Using the Calculator to Compute Future Value of an Annuity

**Before you begin,** make sure to clear the memory, ensure that you are in the correct mode, and set the number of decimal places you want (usually two for dollar-related accuracy).

## S A M P L E   P R O B L E M

You want to know what the future value will be at the end of five years if you place five end-of-year deposits of $1,000 in an account paying 7 percent annually. What is your account balance at the end of five years?

### Hewlett-Packard HP 12C, 17 BII, and 19 BII[1]

**Inputs:**   1000         5      7

**Functions:**   CHS    PMT    n    i    FV

**Outputs:**   5750.74

---

[1]For the 17 BII and 19 BII use the +/− key instead of the CHS key, the N key instead of the n key, and the I% YR key instead of the i key.

| Period | 21% | 22% | 23% | 24% | 25% | 26% | 27% | 28% | 29% | 30% | 31% | 32% | 33% | 34% | 35% | 40% | 45% | 50% |
|---|---|---|---|---|---|---|---|---|---|---|---|---|---|---|---|---|---|---|
| 1 | 1.000 | 1.000 | 1.000 | 1.000 | 1.000 | 1.000 | 1.000 | 1.000 | 1.000 | 1.000 | 1.000 | 1.000 | 1.000 | 1.000 | 1.000 | 1.000 | 1.000 | 1.000 |
| 2 | 2.210 | 2.220 | 2.230 | 2.240 | 2.250 | 2.260 | 2.270 | 2.280 | 2.290 | 2.300 | 2.310 | 2.320 | 2.330 | 2.340 | 2.350 | 2.400 | 2.450 | 2.500 |
| 3 | 3.674 | 3.708 | 3.743 | 3.778 | 3.813 | 3.848 | 3.883 | 3.918 | 3.954 | 3.990 | 4.026 | 4.062 | 4.099 | 4.136 | 4.172 | 4.360 | 4.552 | 4.750 |
| 4 | 5.446 | 5.524 | 5.604 | 5.684 | 5.766 | 5.848 | 5.931 | 6.016 | 6.101 | 6.187 | 6.274 | 6.362 | 6.452 | 6.542 | 6.633 | 7.104 | 7.601 | 8.125 |
| 5 | 7.589 | 7.740 | 7.893 | 8.048 | 8.207 | 8.368 | 8.533 | 8.700 | 8.870 | 9.043 | 9.219 | 9.398 | 9.581 | 9.766 | 9.954 | 10.946 | 12.022 | 13.188 |
| 6 | 10.183 | 10.442 | 10.708 | 10.980 | 11.259 | 11.544 | 11.837 | 12.136 | 12.442 | 12.756 | 13.077 | 13.406 | 13.742 | 14.086 | 14.438 | 16.324 | 18.431 | 20.781 |
| 7 | 13.321 | 13.740 | 14.171 | 14.615 | 15.073 | 15.546 | 16.032 | 16.534 | 17.051 | 17.583 | 18.131 | 18.696 | 19.277 | 19.876 | 20.492 | 23.853 | 27.725 | 32.172 |
| 8 | 17.119 | 17.762 | 18.430 | 19.123 | 19.842 | 20.588 | 21.361 | 22.163 | 22.995 | 23.858 | 24.752 | 25.678 | 26.638 | 27.633 | 28.664 | 34.395 | 41.202 | 49.258 |
| 9 | 21.714 | 22.670 | 23.669 | 24.712 | 25.802 | 26.940 | 28.129 | 29.369 | 30.664 | 32.015 | 33.425 | 34.895 | 36.429 | 38.028 | 39.696 | 49.152 | 60.743 | 74.887 |
| 10 | 27.274 | 28.657 | 30.113 | 31.643 | 33.253 | 34.945 | 36.723 | 38.592 | 40.556 | 42.619 | 44.786 | 47.062 | 49.451 | 51.958 | 54.590 | 69.813 | 89.077 | 113.330 |
| 11 | 34.001 | 35.962 | 38.039 | 40.238 | 42.566 | 45.030 | 47.639 | 50.398 | 53.318 | 56.405 | 59.670 | 63.121 | 66.769 | 70.624 | 74.696 | 98.739 | 130.161 | 170.995 |
| 12 | 42.141 | 44.873 | 47.787 | 50.895 | 54.208 | 57.738 | 61.501 | 65.510 | 69.780 | 74.326 | 79.167 | 84.320 | 89.803 | 95.636 | 101.840 | 139.234 | 189.734 | 257.493 |
| 13 | 51.991 | 55.745 | 59.778 | 64.109 | 68.760 | 73.750 | 79.106 | 84.853 | 91.016 | 97.624 | 104.709 | 112.302 | 120.438 | 129.152 | 138.484 | 195.928 | 276.114 | 387.239 |
| 14 | 63.909 | 69.009 | 74.528 | 80.496 | 86.949 | 93.925 | 101.465 | 109.611 | 118.411 | 127.912 | 138.169 | 149.239 | 161.183 | 174.063 | 187.953 | 275.299 | 401.365 | 581.858 |
| 15 | 78.330 | 85.191 | 92.669 | 100.815 | 109.687 | 119.346 | 129.860 | 141.302 | 153.750 | 167.285 | 182.001 | 197.996 | 215.373 | 234.245 | 254.737 | 386.418 | 582.980 | 873.788 |
| 16 | 95.779 | 104.933 | 114.983 | 126.010 | 138.109 | 151.375 | 165.922 | 181.867 | 199.337 | 218.470 | 239.421 | 262.354 | 287.446 | 314.888 | 344.895 | 541.985 | 846.321 | 1311.681 |
| 17 | 116.892 | 129.019 | 142.428 | 157.252 | 173.636 | 191.733 | 211.721 | 233.790 | 258.145 | 285.011 | 314.642 | 347.307 | 383.303 | 422.949 | 466.608 | 759.778 | 1228.165 | 1968.522 |
| 18 | 142.439 | 158.403 | 176.187 | 195.993 | 218.045 | 242.583 | 269.885 | 300.250 | 334.006 | 371.514 | 413.180 | 459.445 | 510.792 | 567.751 | 630.920 | 1064.689 | 1781.838 | 2953.783 |
| 19 | 173.351 | 194.251 | 217.710 | 244.031 | 273.556 | 306.654 | 343.754 | 385.321 | 431.868 | 483.968 | 542.266 | 607.467 | 680.354 | 761.786 | 852.741 | 1491.563 | 2584.665 | 4431.672 |
| 20 | 210.755 | 237.986 | 268.783 | 303.598 | 342.945 | 387.384 | 437.568 | 494.210 | 558.110 | 630.157 | 711.368 | 802.856 | 905.870 | 1021.792 | 1152.200 | 2089.188 | 3748.763 | 6648.508 |
| 21 | 256.013 | 291.343 | 331.603 | 377.461 | 429.681 | 489.104 | 556.710 | 633.589 | 720.962 | 820.204 | 932.891 | 1060.769 | 1205.807 | 1370.201 | 1556.470 | 2925.862 | 5436.703 | 9973.762 |
| 22 | 310.775 | 356.438 | 408.871 | 469.052 | 538.101 | 617.270 | 708.022 | 811.993 | 931.040 | 1067.265 | 1223.087 | 1401.215 | 1604.724 | 1837.068 | 2102.234 | 4097.203 | 7884.215 | 14961.645 |
| 23 | 377.038 | 435.854 | 503.911 | 582.624 | 673.626 | 778.760 | 900.187 | 1040.351 | 1202.042 | 1388.443 | 1603.243 | 1850.603 | 2135.282 | 2462.669 | 2839.014 | 5737.078 | 11433.109 | 22443.469 |
| 24 | 457.215 | 532.741 | 620.810 | 723.453 | 843.032 | 982.237 | 1144.237 | 1332.649 | 1551.634 | 1805.975 | 2101.247 | 2443.795 | 2840.924 | 3300.974 | 3833.667 | 8032.906 | 16579.008 | 33666.207 |
| 25 | 554.230 | 650.944 | 764.596 | 898.082 | 1054.791 | 1238.617 | 1454.180 | 1706.790 | 2002.608 | 2348.765 | 2753.631 | 3226.808 | 3779.428 | 4424.301 | 5176.445 | 11247.062 | 24040.555 | 50500.316 |
| 30 | 1445.111 | 1767.044 | 2160.459 | 2640.881 | 3227.172 | 3941.953 | 4812.891 | 5873.172 | 7162.785 | 8729.805 | 10632.543 | 12940.672 | 15737.945 | 19124.434 | 23221.258 | 60500.207 | 154105.313 | 383500.000 |
| 35 | 3755.814 | 4783.520 | 6090.227 | 7750.094 | 9856.746 | 12527.160 | 15909.480 | 20188.742 | 25596.512 | 32422.090 | 41028.887 | 51868.563 | 65504.199 | 82634.625 | 104134.500 | 325394.688 | * | * |
| 40 | 9749.141 | 12936.141 | 17153.691 | 22728.367 | 30088.621 | 39791.957 | 52570.707 | 69376.562 | 91447.375 | 120389.375 | * | * | * | * | * | * | * | * |
| 45 | 25294.223 | 34970.230 | 48300.660 | 66638.937 | 91831.312 | 126378.937 | 173692.875 | 238384.312 | 326686.375 | 447005.062 | * | * | * | * | * | * | * | * |

*Not shown due to space limitations.

## Texas Instruments BA-35, BAII, BAII Plus[2]

Inputs:      [ 1000 ]              [ 5 ]   [ 7 ]

Functions:   [ +/− ]   [ PMT ]   [ N ]   [ %i ]   [ CPT ]   [ FV ]

Outputs:                                                [ 5750.74 ]

---

[2]For the Texas Instruments BAII use the [2nd] key instead of the [CPT] key; for the Texas Instruments BAII Plus use the [I/Y] key instead of the [%i] key. When using the Texas Instruments BAII Plus, make sure that your calculator is set to *1 payment per year* [I/Y] *key* to work with annual compounding.

**TABLE A.3**   Present-Value Interest Factors for One Dollar Discounted at $k$ Percent for $n$ Periods: $PVIF_{k,n} = \dfrac{1}{(1 + k)^n}$

| Period | 1% | 2% | 3% | 4% | 5% | 6% | 7% | 8% | 9% | 10% | 11% | 12% | 13% | 14% | 15% | 16% | 17% | 18% | 19% | 20% |
|---|---|---|---|---|---|---|---|---|---|---|---|---|---|---|---|---|---|---|---|---|
| 1 | .990 | .980 | .971 | .962 | .952 | .943 | .935 | .926 | .917 | .909 | .901 | .893 | .885 | .877 | .870 | .862 | .855 | .847 | .840 | .833 |
| 2 | .980 | .961 | .943 | .925 | .907 | .890 | .873 | .857 | .842 | .826 | .812 | .797 | .783 | .769 | .756 | .743 | .731 | .718 | .706 | .694 |
| 3 | .971 | .942 | .915 | .889 | .864 | .840 | .816 | .794 | .772 | .751 | .731 | .712 | .693 | .675 | .658 | .641 | .624 | .609 | .593 | .579 |
| 4 | .961 | .924 | .888 | .855 | .823 | .792 | .763 | .735 | .708 | .683 | .659 | .636 | .613 | .592 | .572 | .552 | .534 | .516 | .499 | .482 |
| 5 | .951 | .906 | .863 | .822 | .784 | .747 | .713 | .681 | .650 | .621 | .593 | .567 | .543 | .519 | .497 | .476 | .456 | .437 | .419 | .402 |
| 6 | .942 | .888 | .837 | .790 | .746 | .705 | .666 | .630 | .596 | .564 | .535 | .507 | .480 | .456 | .432 | .410 | .390 | .370 | .352 | .335 |
| 7 | .933 | .871 | .813 | .760 | .711 | .665 | .623 | .583 | .547 | .513 | .482 | .452 | .425 | .400 | .376 | .354 | .333 | .314 | .296 | .279 |
| 8 | .923 | .853 | .789 | .731 | .677 | .627 | .582 | .540 | .502 | .467 | .434 | .404 | .376 | .351 | .327 | .305 | .285 | .266 | .249 | .233 |
| 9 | .914 | .837 | .766 | .703 | .645 | .592 | .544 | .500 | .460 | .424 | .391 | .361 | .333 | .308 | .284 | .263 | .243 | .225 | .209 | .194 |
| 10 | .905 | .820 | .744 | .676 | .614 | .558 | .508 | .463 | .422 | .386 | .352 | .322 | .295 | .270 | .247 | .227 | .208 | .191 | .176 | .162 |
| 11 | .896 | .804 | .722 | .650 | .585 | .527 | .475 | .429 | .388 | .350 | .317 | .287 | .261 | .237 | .215 | .195 | .178 | .162 | .148 | .135 |
| 12 | .887 | .789 | .701 | .625 | .557 | .497 | .444 | .397 | .356 | .319 | .286 | .257 | .231 | .208 | .187 | .168 | .152 | .137 | .124 | .112 |
| 13 | .879 | .773 | .681 | .601 | .530 | .469 | .415 | .368 | .326 | .290 | .258 | .229 | .204 | .182 | .163 | .145 | .130 | .116 | .104 | .093 |
| 14 | .870 | .758 | .661 | .577 | .505 | .442 | .388 | .340 | .299 | .263 | .232 | .205 | .181 | .160 | .141 | .125 | .111 | .099 | .088 | .078 |
| 15 | .861 | .743 | .642 | .555 | .481 | .417 | .362 | .315 | .275 | .239 | .209 | .183 | .160 | .140 | .123 | .108 | .095 | .084 | .074 | .065 |
| 16 | .853 | .728 | .623 | .534 | .458 | .394 | .339 | .292 | .252 | .218 | .188 | .163 | .141 | .123 | .107 | .093 | .081 | .071 | .062 | .054 |
| 17 | .844 | .714 | .605 | .513 | .436 | .371 | .317 | .270 | .231 | .198 | .170 | .146 | .125 | .108 | .093 | .080 | .069 | .060 | .052 | .045 |
| 18 | .836 | .700 | .587 | .494 | .416 | .350 | .296 | .250 | .212 | .180 | .153 | .130 | .111 | .095 | .081 | .069 | .059 | .051 | .044 | .038 |
| 19 | .828 | .686 | .570 | .475 | .396 | .331 | .277 | .232 | .194 | .164 | .138 | .116 | .098 | .083 | .070 | .060 | .051 | .043 | .037 | .031 |
| 20 | .820 | .673 | .554 | .456 | .377 | .312 | .258 | .215 | .178 | .149 | .124 | .104 | .087 | .073 | .061 | .051 | .043 | .037 | .031 | .026 |
| 21 | .811 | .660 | .538 | .439 | .359 | .294 | .242 | .199 | .164 | .135 | .112 | .093 | .077 | .064 | .053 | .044 | .037 | .031 | .026 | .022 |
| 22 | .803 | .647 | .522 | .422 | .342 | .278 | .226 | .184 | .150 | .123 | .101 | .083 | .068 | .056 | .046 | .038 | .032 | .026 | .022 | .018 |
| 23 | .795 | .634 | .507 | .406 | .326 | .262 | .211 | .170 | .138 | .112 | .091 | .074 | .060 | .049 | .040 | .033 | .027 | .022 | .018 | .015 |
| 24 | .788 | .622 | .492 | .390 | .310 | .247 | .197 | .158 | .126 | .102 | .082 | .066 | .053 | .043 | .035 | .028 | .023 | .019 | .015 | .013 |
| 25 | .780 | .610 | .478 | .375 | .295 | .233 | .184 | .146 | .116 | .092 | .074 | .059 | .047 | .038 | .030 | .024 | .020 | .016 | .013 | .010 |
| 30 | .742 | .552 | .412 | .308 | .231 | .174 | .131 | .099 | .075 | .057 | .044 | .033 | .026 | .020 | .015 | .012 | .009 | .007 | .005 | .004 |
| 35 | .706 | .500 | .355 | .253 | .181 | .130 | .094 | .068 | .049 | .036 | .026 | .019 | .014 | .010 | .008 | .006 | .004 | .003 | .002 | .002 |
| 40 | .672 | .453 | .307 | .208 | .142 | .097 | .067 | .046 | .032 | .022 | .015 | .011 | .008 | .005 | .004 | .003 | .002 | .001 | .001 | .001 |
| 45 | .639 | .410 | .264 | .171 | .111 | .073 | .048 | .031 | .021 | .014 | .009 | .006 | .004 | .003 | .002 | .001 | .001 | .001 | * | * |
| 50 | .608 | .372 | .228 | .141 | .087 | .054 | .034 | .021 | .013 | .009 | .005 | .003 | .002 | .001 | .001 | .001 | * | * | * | * |

*$PVIF$ is zero to three decimal places.

# Using the Calculator to Compute the Present Value of a Single Amount

**Before you begin,** make sure to clear the memory, ensure that you are in the correct mode, and set the number of decimal places you want (usually two for dollar-related accuracy).

## SAMPLE PROBLEM

Calculate the present value of $1,700 to be received in eight years, assuming an 8 percent opportunity cost.

### Hewlett-Packard HP 12C, 17 BII, and 19 BII[1]

Inputs:      1700            8     8

Functions:   CHS    FV    n    i    PV

Outputs:                              918.46

| Period | 21% | 22% | 23% | 24% | 25% | 26% | 27% | 28% | 29% | 30% | 31% | 32% | 33% | 34% | 35% | 40% | 45% | 50% |
|---|---|---|---|---|---|---|---|---|---|---|---|---|---|---|---|---|---|---|
| 1 | .826 | .820 | .813 | .806 | .800 | .794 | .787 | .781 | .775 | .769 | .763 | .758 | .752 | .746 | .741 | .714 | .690 | .667 |
| 2 | .683 | .672 | .661 | .650 | .640 | .630 | .620 | .610 | .601 | .592 | .583 | .574 | .565 | .557 | .549 | .510 | .476 | .444 |
| 3 | .564 | .551 | .537 | .524 | .512 | .500 | .488 | .477 | .466 | .455 | .445 | .435 | .425 | .416 | .406 | .364 | .328 | .296 |
| 4 | .467 | .451 | .437 | .423 | .410 | .397 | .384 | .373 | .361 | .350 | .340 | .329 | .320 | .310 | .301 | .260 | .226 | .198 |
| 5 | .386 | .370 | .355 | .341 | .328 | .315 | .303 | .291 | .280 | .269 | .259 | .250 | .240 | .231 | .223 | .186 | .156 | .132 |
| 6 | .319 | .303 | .289 | .275 | .262 | .250 | .238 | .227 | .217 | .207 | .198 | .189 | .181 | .173 | .165 | .133 | .108 | .088 |
| 7 | .263 | .249 | .235 | .222 | .210 | .198 | .188 | .178 | .168 | .159 | .151 | .143 | .136 | .129 | .122 | .095 | .074 | .059 |
| 8 | .218 | .204 | .191 | .179 | .168 | .157 | .148 | .139 | .130 | .123 | .115 | .108 | .102 | .096 | .091 | .068 | .051 | .039 |
| 9 | .180 | .167 | .155 | .144 | .134 | .125 | .116 | .108 | .101 | .094 | .088 | .082 | .077 | .072 | .067 | .048 | .035 | .026 |
| 10 | .149 | .137 | .126 | .116 | .107 | .099 | .092 | .085 | .078 | .073 | .067 | .062 | .058 | .054 | .050 | .035 | .024 | .017 |
| 11 | .123 | .112 | .103 | .094 | .086 | .079 | .072 | .066 | .061 | .056 | .051 | .047 | .043 | .040 | .037 | .025 | .017 | .012 |
| 12 | .102 | .092 | .083 | .076 | .069 | .062 | .057 | .052 | .047 | .043 | .039 | .036 | .033 | .030 | .027 | .018 | .012 | .008 |
| 13 | .084 | .075 | .068 | .061 | .055 | .050 | .045 | .040 | .037 | .033 | .030 | .027 | .025 | .022 | .020 | .013 | .008 | .005 |
| 14 | .069 | .062 | .055 | .049 | .044 | .039 | .035 | .032 | .028 | .025 | .023 | .021 | .018 | .017 | .015 | .009 | .006 | .003 |
| 15 | .057 | .051 | .045 | .040 | .035 | .031 | .028 | .025 | .022 | .020 | .017 | .016 | .014 | .012 | .011 | .006 | .004 | .002 |
| 16 | .047 | .042 | .036 | .032 | .028 | .025 | .022 | .019 | .017 | .015 | .013 | .012 | .010 | .009 | .008 | .005 | .003 | .002 |
| 17 | .039 | .034 | .030 | .026 | .023 | .020 | .017 | .015 | .013 | .012 | .010 | .009 | .008 | .007 | .006 | .003 | .002 | .001 |
| 18 | .032 | .028 | .024 | .021 | .018 | .016 | .014 | .012 | .010 | .009 | .008 | .007 | .006 | .005 | .005 | .002 | .001 | .001 |
| 19 | .027 | .023 | .020 | .017 | .014 | .012 | .011 | .009 | .008 | .007 | .006 | .005 | .004 | .004 | .003 | .002 | .001 | * |
| 20 | .022 | .019 | .016 | .014 | .012 | .010 | .008 | .007 | .006 | .005 | .005 | .004 | .003 | .003 | .002 | .001 | .001 | * |
| 21 | .018 | .015 | .013 | .011 | .009 | .008 | .007 | .006 | .005 | .004 | .003 | .003 | .003 | .002 | .002 | .001 | * | * |
| 22 | .015 | .013 | .011 | .009 | .007 | .006 | .005 | .004 | .004 | .003 | .003 | .002 | .002 | .002 | .001 | .001 | * | * |
| 23 | .012 | .010 | .009 | .007 | .006 | .005 | .004 | .003 | .003 | .002 | .002 | .002 | .001 | .001 | .001 | * | * | * |
| 24 | .010 | .008 | .007 | .006 | .005 | .004 | .003 | .003 | .002 | .002 | .002 | .001 | .001 | .001 | .001 | * | * | * |
| 25 | .009 | .007 | .006 | .005 | .004 | .003 | .003 | .002 | .002 | .001 | .001 | .001. | .001 | .001 | .001 | * | * | * |
| 30 | .003 | .003 | .002 | .002 | .001 | .001 | .001 | .001 | * | * | * | * | * | * | * | * | * | * |
| 35 | .001 | .001 | .001 | .001 | * | * | * | * | * | * | * | * | * | * | * | * | * | * |
| 40 | * | * | * | * | * | * | * | * | * | * | * | * | * | * | * | * | * | * |
| 45 | * | * | * | * | * | * | * | * | * | * | * | * | * | * | * | * | * | * |
| 50 | * | * | * | * | * | * | * | * | * | * | * | * | * | * | * | * | * | * |

*PVIF is zero to three decimal places.

### Texas Instruments BA-35, BAII, BAII Plus[2]

**Inputs:** 1700    8   8

**Functions:** +/−   FV   N   %i   CPT   PV

**Outputs:** 918.46

[1]For the 17 BII and 19 BII use the +/− key instead of the CHS key, the N key instead of the n key, and the I% YR key instead of the i key.

[2]For the Texas Instruments BAII use the 2nd key instead of the CPT key; for the Texas Instruments BAII Plus use the I/Y key instead of the %i key. When using the Texas Instruments BAII Plus, make sure that your calculator is set to *1 payment per year* I/Y *key* to work with annual compounding.

**TABLE A.4**   Present-Value Interest Factors for a One-Dollar Annuity Discounted at $k$ Percent for $n$ Periods: $PVIFA_{k,n} = \sum_{t=1}^{n} \dfrac{1}{(1+k)^t}$

| Period | 1% | 2% | 3% | 4% | 5% | 6% | 7% | 8% | 9% | 10% | 11% | 12% | 13% | 14% | 15% | 16% | 17% | 18% | 19% | 20% |
|---|---|---|---|---|---|---|---|---|---|---|---|---|---|---|---|---|---|---|---|---|
| 1 | .990 | .980 | .971 | .962 | .952 | .943 | .935 | .926 | .917 | .909 | .901 | .893 | .885 | .877 | .870 | .862 | .855 | .847 | .840 | .833 |
| 2 | 1.970 | 1.942 | 1.913 | 1.886 | 1.859 | 1.833 | 1.808 | 1.783 | 1.759 | 1.736 | 1.713 | 1.690 | 1.668 | 1.647 | 1.626 | 1.605 | 1.585 | 1.566 | 1.547 | 1.528 |
| 3 | 2.941 | 2.884 | 2.829 | 2.775 | 2.723 | 2.673 | 2.624 | 2.577 | 2.531 | 2.487 | 2.444 | 2.402 | 2.361 | 2.322 | 2.283 | 2.246 | 2.210 | 2.174 | 2.140 | 2.106 |
| 4 | 3.902 | 3.808 | 3.717 | 3.630 | 3.546 | 3.465 | 3.387 | 3.312 | 3.240 | 3.170 | 3.102 | 3.037 | 2.974 | 2.914 | 2.855 | 2.798 | 2.743 | 2.690 | 2.639 | 2.589 |
| 5 | 4.853 | 4.713 | 4.580 | 4.452 | 4.329 | 4.212 | 4.100 | 3.993 | 3.890 | 3.791 | 3.696 | 3.605 | 3.517 | 3.433 | 3.352 | 3.274 | 3.199 | 3.127 | 3.058 | 2.991 |
| 6 | 5.795 | 5.601 | 5.417 | 5.242 | 5.076 | 4.917 | 4.767 | 4.623 | 4.486 | 4.355 | 4.231 | 4.111 | 3.998 | 3.889 | 3.784 | 3.685 | 3.589 | 3.498 | 3.410 | 3.326 |
| 7 | 6.728 | 6.472 | 6.230 | 6.002 | 5.786 | 5.582 | 5.389 | 5.206 | 5.033 | 4.868 | 4.712 | 4.564 | 4.423 | 4.288 | 4.160 | 4.039 | 3.922 | 3.812 | 3.706 | 3.605 |
| 8 | 7.652 | 7.326 | 7.020 | 6.733 | 6.463 | 6.210 | 5.971 | 5.747 | 5.535 | 5.335 | 5.146 | 4.968 | 4.799 | 4.639 | 4.487 | 4.344 | 4.207 | 4.078 | 3.954 | 3.837 |
| 9 | 8.566 | 8.162 | 7.786 | 7.435 | 7.108 | 6.802 | 6.515 | 6.247 | 5.995 | 5.759 | 5.537 | 5.328 | 5.132 | 4.946 | 4.772 | 4.607 | 4.451 | 4.303 | 4.163 | 4.031 |
| 10 | 9.471 | 8.983 | 8.530 | 8.111 | 7.722 | 7.360 | 7.024 | 6.710 | 6.418 | 6.145 | 5.889 | 5.650 | 5.426 | 5.216 | 5.019 | 4.833 | 4.659 | 4.494 | 4.339 | 4.192 |
| 11 | 10.368 | 9.787 | 9.253 | 8.760 | 8.306 | 7.887 | 7.499 | 7.139 | 6.805 | 6.495 | 6.207 | 5.938 | 5.687 | 5.453 | 5.234 | 5.029 | 4.836 | 4.656 | 4.486 | 4.327 |
| 12 | 11.255 | 10.575 | 9.954 | 9.385 | 8.863 | 8.384 | 7.943 | 7.536 | 7.161 | 6.814 | 6.492 | 6.194 | 5.918 | 5.660 | 5.421 | 5.197 | 4.988 | 4.793 | 4.611 | 4.439 |
| 13 | 12.134 | 11.348 | 10.635 | 9.986 | 9.394 | 8.853 | 8.358 | 7.904 | 7.487 | 7.013 | 6.750 | 6.424 | 6.122 | 5.842 | 5.583 | 5.342 | 5.118 | 4.910 | 4.715 | 4.533 |
| 14 | 13.004 | 12.106 | 11.296 | 10.563 | 9.899 | 9.295 | 8.745 | 8.244 | 7.786 | 7.367 | 6.982 | 6.628 | 6.302 | 6.002 | 5.724 | 5.468 | 5.229 | 5.008 | 4.802 | 4.611 |
| 15 | 13.865 | 12.849 | 11.938 | 11.118 | 10.380 | 9.712 | 9.108 | 8.560 | 8.061 | 7.606 | 7.191 | 6.811 | 6.462 | 6.142 | 5.847 | 5.575 | 5.324 | 5.092 | 4.876 | 4.675 |
| 16 | 14.718 | 13.578 | 12.561 | 11.652 | 10.838 | 10.106 | 9.447 | 8.851 | 8.313 | 7.824 | 7.379 | 6.974 | 6.604 | 6.265 | 5.954 | 5.668 | 5.405 | 5.162 | 4.938 | 4.730 |
| 17 | 15.562 | 14.292 | 13.166 | 12.166 | 11.274 | 10.477 | 9.763 | 9.122 | 8.544 | 8.022 | 7.549 | 7.120 | 6.729 | 6.373 | 6.047 | 5.749 | 5.475 | 5.222 | 4.990 | 4.775 |
| 18 | 16.398 | 14.992 | 13.754 | 12.659 | 11.690 | 10.828 | 10.059 | 9.372 | 8.756 | 8.201 | 7.702 | 7.250 | 6.840 | 6.467 | 6.128 | 5.818 | 5.534 | 5.273 | 5.033 | 4.812 |
| 19 | 17.226 | 15.679 | 14.324 | 13.134 | 12.085 | 11.158 | 10.336 | 9.604 | 8.950 | 8.365 | 7.839 | 7.366 | 6.938 | 6.550 | 6.198 | 5.877 | 5.584 | 5.316 | 5.070 | 4.843 |
| 20 | 18.046 | 16.352 | 14.878 | 13.590 | 12.462 | 11.470 | 10.594 | 9.818 | 9.129 | 8.514 | 7.963 | 7.469 | 7.025 | 6.623 | 6.259 | 5.929 | 5.628 | 5.353 | 5.101 | 4.870 |
| 21 | 18.857 | 17.011 | 15.415 | 14.029 | 12.821 | 11.764 | 10.836 | 10.017 | 9.292 | 8.649 | 8.075 | 7.562 | 7.102 | 6.687 | 6.312 | 5.973 | 5.665 | 5.384 | 5.127 | 4.891 |
| 22 | 19.661 | 17.658 | 15.937 | 14.451 | 13.163 | 12.042 | 11.061 | 10.201 | 9.442 | 8.772 | 8.176 | 7.645 | 7.170 | 6.743 | 6.359 | 6.011 | 5.696 | 5.410 | 5.149 | 4.909 |
| 23 | 20.456 | 18.292 | 16.444 | 14.857 | 13.489 | 12.303 | 11.272 | 10.371 | 9.580 | 8.883 | 8.266 | 7.718 | 7.230 | 6.792 | 6.399 | 6.044 | 5.723 | 5.432 | 5.167 | 4.925 |
| 24 | 21.244 | 18.914 | 16.936 | 15.247 | 13.799 | 12.550 | 11.469 | 10.529 | 9.707 | 8.985 | 8.348 | 7.784 | 7.283 | 6.835 | 6.434 | 6.073 | 5.746 | 5.451 | 5.182 | 4.937 |
| 25 | 22.023 | 19.524 | 17.413 | 15.622 | 14.094 | 12.783 | 11.654 | 10.675 | 9.823 | 9.077 | 8.422 | 7.843 | 7.330 | 6.873 | 6.464 | 6.097 | 5.766 | 5.467 | 5.195 | 4.948 |
| 30 | 25.808 | 22.396 | 19.601 | 17.292 | 15.373 | 13.765 | 12.409 | 11.258 | 10.274 | 9.427 | 8.694 | 8.055 | 7.496 | 7.003 | 6.566 | 6.177 | 5.829 | 5.517 | 5.235 | 4.979 |
| 35 | 29.409 | 24.999 | 21.487 | 18.665 | 16.374 | 14.498 | 12.948 | 11.655 | 10.567 | 9.644 | 8.855 | 8.176 | 7.586 | 7.070 | 6.617 | 6.215 | 5.858 | 5.539 | 5.251 | 4.992 |
| 40 | 32.835 | 27.356 | 23.115 | 19.793 | 17.159 | 15.046 | 13.332 | 11.925 | 10.757 | 9.779 | 8.951 | 8.244 | 7.634 | 7.105 | 6.642 | 6.233 | 5.871 | 5.548 | 5.258 | 4.997 |
| 45 | 36.095 | 29.490 | 24.519 | 20.720 | 17.774 | 15.456 | 13.606 | 12.108 | 10.881 | 9.863 | 9.008 | 8.283 | 7.661 | 7.123 | 6.654 | 6.242 | 5.877 | 5.552 | 5.261 | 4.999 |
| 50 | 39.196 | 31.424 | 25.730 | 21.482 | 18.256 | 15.762 | 13.801 | 12.233 | 10.962 | 9.915 | 9.042 | 8.304 | 7.675 | 7.133 | 6.661 | 6.246 | 5.880 | 5.554 | 5.262 | 4.999 |

# Using the Calculator to Compute the Present Value of an Annuity

**Before you begin,** make sure to clear the memory, ensure that you are in the correct mode, and set the number of decimal places you want (usually two for dollar-related accuracy).

## S A M P L E    P R O B L E M

You want to know what the present value will be of an annuity of $700 per year at the end of each year for five years, given a required return of 8 percent.

**Hewlett-Packard HP 12C, 17 BII, and 19 BII[1]**

Inputs:  [ 700 ]          [ 5 ]  [ 8 ]

Functions:  ( CHS )  ( PMT )  ( n )  ( i )  ( PV )

Outputs:                                   [ 2794.90 ]

---

[1]For the 17 BII and 19 BII use the ⌊+/−⌋ key instead of the ⌊CHS⌋ key, the ⌊N⌋ key instead of the ⌊n⌋ key, and the ⌊I% YR⌋ key instead of the ⌊i⌋ key.

| Period | 21% | 22% | 23% | 24% | 25% | 26% | 27% | 28% | 29% | 30% | 31% | 32% | 33% | 34% | 35% | 40% | 45% | 50% |
|---|---|---|---|---|---|---|---|---|---|---|---|---|---|---|---|---|---|---|
| 1 | .826 | .820 | .813 | .806 | .800 | .794 | .787 | .781 | .775 | .769 | .763 | .758 | .752 | .746 | .741 | .714 | .690 | .667 |
| 2 | 1.509 | 1.492 | 1.474 | 1.457 | 1.440 | 1.424 | 1.407 | 1.392 | 1.376 | 1.361 | 1.346 | 1.331 | 1.317 | 1.303 | 1.289 | 1.224 | 1.165 | 1.111 |
| 3 | 2.074 | 2.042 | 2.011 | 1.981 | 1.952 | 1.923 | 1.896 | 1.868 | 1.842 | 1.816 | 1.791 | 1.766 | 1.742 | 1.719 | 1.696 | 1.589 | 1.493 | 1.407 |
| 4 | 2.540 | 2.494 | 2.448 | 2.404 | 2.362 | 2.320 | 2.280 | 2.241 | 2.203 | 2.166 | 2.130 | 2.096 | 2.062 | 2.029 | 1.997 | 1.849 | 1.720 | 1.605 |
| 5 | 2.926 | 2.864 | 2.803 | 2.745 | 2.689 | 2.635 | 2.583 | 2.532 | 2.483 | 2.436 | 2.390 | 2.345 | 2.302 | 2.260 | 2.220 | 2.035 | 1.876 | 1.737 |
| 6 | 3.245 | 3.167 | 3.092 | 3.020 | 2.951 | 2.885 | 2.821 | 2.759 | 2.700 | 2.643 | 2.588 | 2.534 | 2.483 | 2.433 | 2.385 | 2.168 | 1.983 | 1.824 |
| 7 | 3.508 | 3.416 | 3.327 | 3.242 | 3.161 | 3.083 | 3.009 | 2.937 | 2.868 | 2.802 | 2.739 | 2.677 | 2.619 | 2.562 | 2.508 | 2.263 | 2.057 | 1.883 |
| 8 | 3.726 | 3.619 | 3.518 | 3.421 | 3.329 | 3.241 | 3.156 | 3.076 | 2.999 | 2.925 | 2.854 | 2.786 | 2.721 | 2.658 | 2.598 | 2.331 | 2.109 | 1.922 |
| 9 | 3.905 | 3.786 | 3.673 | 3.566 | 3.463 | 3.366 | 3.273 | 3.184 | 3.100 | 3.019 | 2.942 | 2.868 | 2.798 | 2.730 | 2.665 | 2.379 | 2.144 | 1.948 |
| 10 | 4.054 | 3.923 | 3.799 | 3.682 | 3.570 | 3.465 | 3.364 | 3.269 | 3.178 | 3.092 | 3.009 | 2.930 | 2.855 | 2.784 | 2.715 | 2.414 | 2.168 | 1.965 |
| 11 | 4.177 | 4.035 | 3.902 | 3.776 | 3.656 | 3.544 | 3.437 | 3.335 | 3.239 | 3.147 | 3.060 | 2.978 | 2.899 | 2.824 | 2.752 | 2.438 | 2.185 | 1.977 |
| 12 | 4.278 | 4.127 | 3.985 | 3.851 | 3.725 | 3.606 | 3.493 | 3.387 | 3.286 | 3.190 | 3.100 | 3.013 | 2.931 | 2.853 | 2.779 | 2.456 | 2.196 | 1.985 |
| 13 | 4.362 | 4.203 | 4.053 | 3.912 | 3.780 | 3.656 | 3.538 | 3.427 | 3.322 | 3.223 | 3.129 | 3.040 | 2.956 | 2.876 | 2.799 | 2.469 | 2.204 | 1.990 |
| 14 | 4.432 | 4.265 | 4.108 | 3.962 | 3.824 | 3.695 | 3.573 | 3.459 | 3.351 | 3.249 | 3.152 | 3.061 | 2.974 | 2.892 | 2.814 | 2.478 | 2.210 | 1.993 |
| 15 | 4.489 | 4.315 | 4.153 | 4.001 | 3.859 | 3.726 | 3.601 | 3.483 | 3.373 | 3.268 | 3.170 | 3.076 | 2.988 | 2.905 | 2.825 | 2.484 | 2.214 | 1.995 |
| 16 | 4.536 | 4.357 | 4.189 | 4.033 | 3.887 | 3.751 | 3.623 | 3.503 | 3.390 | 3.283 | 3.183 | 3.088 | 2.999 | 2.914 | 2.834 | 2.489 | 2.216 | 1.997 |
| 17 | 4.576 | 4.391 | 4.219 | 4.059 | 3.910 | 3.771 | 3.640 | 3.518 | 3.403 | 3.295 | 3.193 | 3.097 | 3.007 | 2.921 | 2.840 | 2.492 | 2.218 | 1.998 |
| 18 | 4.608 | 4.419 | 4.243 | 4.080 | 3.928 | 3.786 | 3.654 | 3.529 | 3.413 | 3.304 | 3.201 | 3.104 | 3.012 | 2.926 | 2.844 | 2.494 | 2.219 | 1.999 |
| 19 | 4.635 | 4.442 | 4.263 | 4.097 | 3.942 | 3.799 | 3.664 | 3.539 | 3.421 | 3.311 | 3.207 | 3.109 | 3.017 | 2.930 | 2.848 | 2.496 | 2.220 | 1.999 |
| 20 | 4.657 | 4.460 | 4.279 | 4.110 | 3.954 | 3.808 | 3.673 | 3.546 | 3.427 | 3.316 | 3.211 | 3.113 | 3.020 | 2.933 | 2.850 | 2.497 | 2.221 | 1.999 |
| 21 | 4.675 | 4.476 | 4.292 | 4.121 | 3.963 | 3.816 | 3.679 | 3.551 | 3.432 | 3.320 | 3.215 | 3.116 | 3.023 | 2.935 | 2.852 | 2.498 | 2.221 | 2.000 |
| 22 | 4.690 | 4.488 | 4.302 | 4.130 | 3.970 | 3.822 | 3.684 | 3.556 | 3.436 | 3.323 | 3.217 | 3.118 | 3.025 | 2.936 | 2.853 | 2.498 | 2.222 | 2.000 |
| 23 | 4.703 | 4.499 | 4.311 | 4.137 | 3.976 | 3.827 | 3.689 | 3.559 | 3.438 | 3.325 | 3.219 | 3.120 | 3.026 | 2.938 | 2.854 | 2.499 | 2.222 | 2.000 |
| 24 | 4.713 | 4.507 | 4.318 | 4.143 | 3.981 | 3.831 | 3.692 | 3.562 | 3.441 | 3.327 | 3.221 | 3.121 | 3.027 | 2.939 | 2.855 | 2.499 | 2.222 | 2.000 |
| 25 | 4.721 | 4.514 | 4.323 | 4.147 | 3.985 | 3.834 | 3.694 | 3.564 | 3.442 | 3.329 | 3.222 | 3.122 | 3.028 | 2.939 | 2.856 | 2.499 | 2.222 | 2.000 |
| 30 | 4.746 | 4.534 | 4.339 | 4.160 | 3.995 | 3.842 | 3.701 | 3.569 | 3.447 | 3.332 | 3.225 | 3.124 | 3.030 | 2.941 | 2.857 | 2.500 | 2.222 | 2.000 |
| 35 | 4.756 | 4.541 | 4.345 | 4.164 | 3.998 | 3.845 | 3.703 | 3.571 | 3.448 | 3.333 | 3.226 | 3.125 | 3.030 | 2.941 | 2.857 | 2.500 | 2.222 | 2.000 |
| 40 | 4.760 | 4.544 | 4.347 | 4.166 | 3.999 | 3.846 | 3.703 | 3.571 | 3.448 | 3.333 | 3.226 | 3.125 | 3.030 | 2.941 | 2.857 | 2.500 | 2.222 | 2.000 |
| 45 | 4.761 | 4.545 | 4.347 | 4.166 | 4.000 | 3.846 | 3.704 | 3.571 | 3.448 | 3.333 | 3.226 | 3.125 | 3.030 | 2.941 | 2.857 | 2.500 | 2.222 | 2.000 |
| 50 | 4.762 | 4.545 | 4.348 | 4.167 | 4.000 | 3.846 | 3.704 | 3.571 | 3.448 | 3.333 | 3.226 | 3.125 | 3.030 | 2.941 | 2.857 | 2.500 | 2.222 | 2.000 |

### Texas Instruments BA-35, BAII, BAII Plus[2]

**Inputs:** [ 700 ]   [ 5 ] [ 8 ]

**Functions:** [ +/− ] [ PMT ] [ N ] [ %i ] [ CPT ] [ FV ]

**Outputs:** [ 2794.90 ]

[2]For the Texas Instruments BAII use the [2nd] key instead of the [CPT] key; for the Texas Instruments BAII Plus use the [I/Y] key instead of the [%i] key. When using the Texas Instruments BAII Plus, make sure that your calculator is set to *1 payment per year* [I/Y] *key* to work with annual compounding.

# Appendix B

# Using Computers and Spreadsheets in Managerial Finance

Harnessing massive amounts of information is the challenge of every manager today. Fortunately, many tools are available for gathering, storing, analyzing, and processing mounds of data. Here we briefly discuss the two key components of a computer system—hardware and software—and some of the key features of electronic spreadsheets—an extremely popular type of software that is widely used by financial managers.

## Hardware

*Hardware* refers to the physical components of a computer system. The basic components of a personal computer are a microprocessor (the "brain"), an input device (keyboard and/or mouse), a video display terminal, an output device (printer), and one or more storage devices (disk, tape, or CD-ROM drives). Critical to the decision of which type of computer is appropriate for the application software is the amount of memory available. Most general management applications programs (word processor, database management, and spreadsheets) require at least 1 MB (megabyte) of memory. Systems based on the Intel 80286, 80386, and 80486 microprocessors and the corresponding Macintosh series are able to run the most popular management applications software available.

# Software

*Software* are the programs that instruct the computer about the functions it is to perform. Without adequate software the computer is useless. With the increased ownership of personal computers (PCs) has come a growing proliferation of software programs that cater to the financial manager. Moreover, PCs have become more "user-friendly" (the user can communicate more easily with the computer and thus utilize it more fully), enabling managers to design programs to meet their objectives. The three basic tools of information management for use on the personal computer are word processing, database management, and spreadsheet software. In addition, integrated software packages are available.

## Word Processing Software

*Word processing software* is rapidly making the conventional typewriter obsolete. It allows text to be keyed into a computer and saved. While viewing the document on the display terminal, the user may easily edit, delete, or add more text. A variety of formats, type styles, and other features are available in most word processing programs to ease document preparation. (For a listing of popular word processing software, see Table B.1.)

## Database Management Software

*Database management software* stores information in discrete "parcels." These parcels may then be sorted in a variety of ways. Needed information can be easily extracted from the database by user-specified criteria. The parcel may contain only a single piece of data or hundreds of pieces. For example, some common applications of a database management program are storage of customer data (name, address, and city), inventory records, personnel data, and accounts receivable information. (For a listing of popular database management software, see Table B.1.)

## Spreadsheet Software

*Spreadsheet software* facilitates extensive calculations based on models developed by the user. A spreadsheet appears on the screen divided into cells of rows and columns. Spreadsheet rows are generally numbered 1, 2, 3, etc., and columns are lettered A, B, C, etc. Some programs have as many as 16,000 rows and columns available. The user may enter text or numeric data or program a formula into each cell. Most programs also allow data to be shown graphically. (For a listing of popular spreadsheet software, see Table B.1.)

## TABLE B.1   Popular Word Processing, Database Management, Spreadsheet, and Integrated Software Packages[a]

| Title | Hardware family | Company |
|---|---|---|
| **Word Processing** | | |
| Microsoft Word | Available for both IBM PC compatibles and Macintosh | Microsoft Corp.<br>One Microsoft Way<br>Redmond, WA 98073 |
| WordPerfect | Available for both IBM PC compatibles and Macintosh | WordPerfect Corp.<br>1555 N. Technology Way<br>Oren, UT 84057 |
| MacWrite II | Macintosh | Claris Corporation<br>440 Clyde Ave.<br>Mountain View, CA 94043 |
| **Database Management** | | |
| dBase IV | IBM PC compatibles | Ashton-Tate<br>20101 Hamilton Ave.<br>Torrance, CA 90502 |
| FileMaker II | Macintosh | Claris Corporation<br>440 Clyde Ave.<br>Mountain View, CA 94043 |
| Paradox | IBM PC compatibles | Borland International<br>4585 Scotts Valley Drive<br>Scotts Valley, CA 95066 |
| Access | IBM PC compatibles | Microsoft Corp.<br>One Microsoft Way<br>Redmond, WA 98073 |
| **Spreadsheet** | | |
| Lotus 1-2-3 | Available for both IBM PC compatibles and Macintosh | Lotus Development Corp.<br>55 Cambridge Parkway<br>Cambridge, MA 92142 |
| Excel | Available for both IBM PC compatibles and Macintosh | Microsoft Corp.<br>One Microsoft Way<br>Redmond, WA 98073 |
| Quattro Pro | IBM PC compatibles | Borland International<br>4585 Scotts Valley Drive<br>Scotts Valley, CA 95066 |
| SuperCalc5 | IBM PC compatibles | Computer Associates<br>International Inc.<br>Micro Products Division<br>1240 McKay Drive<br>San Jose, CA 95131 |
| Wingz | Macintosh | Informix Software<br>16011 College Blvd.<br>Lenexa, KS 66219 |
| **Integrated** | | |
| Microsoft Works | Available for both IBM PC compatibles and Macintosh | Microsoft Corp.<br>One Microsoft Way<br>Redmond, WA 98073 |
| First Choice | IBM PC compatibles | Software Publishing Corp.<br>1901 Landings Drive<br>Mountain View, CA 94039 |

[a]It is important to check the specific system requirements (such as amount of memory) of a software package to ensure that the program is compatible with your hardware.

## Integrated Software

*Integrated software* combines more than one function into a single program. For example, an integrated software package might include a word processor, database, graphics, and spreadsheet. With this type of software the same information can be used in the different modules of the program. Integrated software packages have become quite popular and can be an economical alternative to purchasing separate programs. The individual modules generally have fewer features, however, than single-purpose programs, so it is important to review the package carefully to see what compromises were made when the component programs were combined. (For a listing of popular integrated software, see Table B.1.)

# Electronic Spreadsheets

A strength of electronic spreadsheets is the ability to customize formulas to make automatic calculations using the desired model. Because the automatic calculation feature takes the drudgery out of the financial analysis of large amounts of data, the analyst may spend more time asking "what if." The data or the formulas may be easily changed, often by a mere keystroke, to simulate various business conditions. (Table B.2 illustrates a spreadsheet with data and formulas.)

## Additional Features

The most powerful spreadsheet software has several additional features beyond the basic calculating power: linking worksheets, using predefined functions, auditing of design logic, and the ability to use macros. These features are necessary for the serious "number cruncher" or "power user." *Worksheet linking* allows the user to maintain multiple spreadsheets to support a final spreadsheet. For example, in developing a pro forma income statement, multiple supporting spreadsheets like sales, cost of goods sold, and general and administrative expense forecasts, among others, may be linked to produce the final summary pro forma spreadsheet. A *predefined function* is one that need not be programmed by the user. Some programs have predefined functions like depreciation calculation using the sum-of-the-years'-digits method or net present value and internal rate of return calculations. The *auditing feature* is a simple check of the programmer's logic to ensure the model's feasibility. It does not, however, make the program design foolproof. *Macros* allow the user to program a sequence of operations to be used to manipulate data. For complicated manipulation, using a macro to record a frequently used sequence of operations reduces tedious duplication of effort.

## Spreadsheet Applications

For the financial manager the electronic spreadsheet can be customized to fit a range of financial tasks, from a simple calculation of return on invest-

**TABLE B.2   Illustration of a Spreadsheet with Data and Formulas**

| | A | B | C | D | E | F |
|---|---|---|---|---|---|---|
| | | INPUT SECTION | | | | |
| 7 | | | Sun Valley Prune Company | | | |
| 8 | | | Income Statement | | | |
| 9 | | | For the Year Ended December 31 | | | |
| 10 | | | | | | 1995 |
| 11 | | SALES | | | | $4,300,000 |
| 12 | | COST OF GOODS SOLD | | | | |
| 13 | | | FIXED | | | $300,000 |
| 14 | | | VARIABLE | | | $2,250,000 |
| 15 | | | GROSS PROFIT | | | $1,750,000 |
| 16 | | GENERAL AND ADMIN EXPENSES | | | | |
| 17 | | | FIXED | | | $100,000 |
| 18 | | | VARIABLE | | | $333,000 |
| 19 | | | EARNINGS BEFORE INT AND TAX | | | $1,317,000 |
| 20 | | INTEREST EXPENSE (ALL FIXED) | | | | $150,000 |
| 21 | | | EARNINGS BEFORE TAXES | | | $1,167,000 |
| 22 | | TAXES (40%) | | | | $466,800 |
| 23 | | | NET INCOME | | | $700,200 |
| 24 | | RESULTS SECTION | | | | |
| 25 | | | Sun Valley Prune Company | | | |
| 26 | | | Pro Forma Income Statement | | | |
| 27 | | | Percent-of-Sales Method | | | |
| 28 | | | For the Year Ended December 31 | | | |
| 29 | | | | | | 1996 |
| 30 | | SALES | | | | $4,750,000 |
| 31 | | COST OF GOODS SOLD | | | | FORMULA A |
| 32 | | | GROSS PROFIT | | | FORMULA B |
| 33 | | GENERAL AND ADMIN EXPENSES | | | | FORMULA C |
| 34 | | | EARNINGS BEFORE INT AND TAX | | | FORMULA D |
| 35 | | INTEREST EXPENSE (ALL FIXED) | | | | FORMULA E |
| 36 | | | EARNINGS BEFORE TAXES | | | FORMULA F |
| 37 | | TAXES (40%) | | | | FORMULA G |
| 38 | | | NET INCOME | | | FORMULA H |

| | |
|---|---|
| FORMULA A:   +(F13+F14)/F11*F30 | FORMULA B: +F30-F31 |
| FORMULA C:   +(F17+F18)/F11*F30 | FORMULA D: +F32-F33 |
| FORMULA E:        +F20/F11*F30 | FORMULA F: +F34-F35 |
| FORMULA G:           +F36*0.4 | FORMULA H: +F36-F37 |

ment to a sophisticated merger analysis. The most common applications are forecasting models for preparation of cash budgets and pro forma income statements and balance sheets.

**Pro Forma Balance Sheet Illustration**   In the case of the pro forma balance sheet, the final spreadsheet may be supported by multiple spreadsheets that calculate various asset and liability values. For instance, the depreciation schedule for the existing fixed assets plus the projected purchases and sales of fixed assets might support the calculation of the net fixed asset account. Likewise, a supporting spreadsheet for the amortization of debt might take into account all existing loans, lines of credit, and their payment terms and interest rates and project the pro forma balance with no new borrowings. All other asset and liability account spreadsheets may then be linked to the final spreadsheet, which has user-defined mathematical relationships common to balance sheets. The user may impose any type of restriction, such as a minimum cash balance or a desired current ratio.

**Other Applications**   A wide variety of financial analysis applications are available to the user who is willing to spend the time to develop the model. Accounts receivable and inventory can be managed through the use of database software (for large amounts of data stored) and spreadsheets to analyze the data stored in the database. Capital-budgeting analysis is made easier by many of the spreadsheet programs having predefined functions, such as net present value and the internal rate of return formulas. The WMCC and IOS analysis and breakeven analysis may be brought to life through the graphic abilities of an integrated spreadsheet program that translates the numerical data into a chart or graph. Other financial applications include cost of capital, lease-versus-purchase decisions, economic order quantity for inventory, and merger analysis, among many others.

## Spreadsheet Design

Designing a spreadsheet is as basic as the preparation of blueprints before building a house. Spreadsheets may contain four basic sections: the assumptions, the input data, the calculations, and the results summary. The *assumptions* are often grouped together at the top of the spreadsheet and are used as references to drive the calculations section. If the user decides that an assumption is not reasonable, it may be changed and the entire spreadsheet immediately recalculated. Stating the assumptions up front also aids the reader of the report. The *input data* section is the area where the data are to be manipulated and stored. For large sets of data, multiple spreadsheets are recommended. The data may then be imported from various other worksheets for manipulation. The *calculation* section sets forth the mathematical relationships among the data. The *results summary* section ends the spreadsheet and capsulizes the results. A spreadsheet that is divided into the four sections may more clearly communicate the what, how, and why of the report to its reader and allows for easy verification. Planning the layout of a spreadsheet is essential to its success.

## Spreadsheet Errors

The ease with which a spreadsheet may be programmed and calculations performed may disguise the fact that errors are easy to make. Two independent

"Silicon Valley" consulting firms, Input and Palo Alto Research, estimated that approximately one out of three business spreadsheets has some kind of error! The error to which these consulting firms refer is not a bug in the computer program; it is a programmer error—an illogical command or misplaced data. It is essential to test the program with simplified data and to verify the expected results with a hand-held, business/financial calculator on the first pass. The results are only as good as the program.

## Conclusion

Financial management applications for the computer are plentiful, but first, many decisions need to be made. The selection of hardware and software is one that must be investigated thoroughly to determine whether the capabilities of each meet the manager's needs. Actually using a computer at a dealer location and requesting "demo" disks to "test drive" the software are recommended. Talk with other professionals about the products that they use, and keep current on new products through computer periodicals. Once the hardware and software selection is made and the program has been mastered, the manager is one step closer to conquering the massive amount of information that complicates most business decisions.

# I N D E X